SIX RESTORATION AND
FRENCH NEOCLASSIC PLAYS

Also edited by David Thomas and published by Macmillan

FOUR GEORGIAN AND
PRE-REVOLUTIONARY PLAYS
THE RIVALS, SHE STOOPS TO CONQUER,
THE MARRIAGE OF FIGARO, EMILIA GALOTTI

Six Restoration and French Neoclassic Plays

Phedra
The Miser
Tartuffe
All for Love
The Country Wife
Love for Love

Introduced and Edited by

DAVID THOMAS

Professor of Theatre Studies, University of Warwick

First published 1998 by
MACMILLAN PRESS LTD
Houndmills, Basingstoke, Hampshire RG21 6XS
and London
Companies and representatives
throughout the world

ISBN 0–333–63674–0 hardcover
ISBN 0–333–63675–9 paperback

A catalogue record for this book is available
from the British Library.

This book is printed on paper suitable for recycling and
made from fully managed and sustained forest sources.

10 9 8 7 6 5 4 3 2 1
07 06 05 04 03 02 01 00 99 98

Typeset by Forewords, Oxford/Longworth Editorial Services
Longworth, Oxfordshire.

Printed in Malaysia

 Published in the United States of America 1998 by
ST. MARTIN'S PRESS, INC.,
Scholarly and Reference Division,
175 Fifth Avenue, New York, N.Y. 10010

ISBN 0–312–21400–6 cloth
ISBN 0–312–21401–4 paperback

Contents

List of Illustrations

(Reproduced from the author's collection)

Acknowledgements

In preparing this volume, I have had invaluable help from staff in the Reading Room of the British Library, and the University Libraries of Warwick and Bristol. I should also like to record my thanks to the University of Warwick for generous research leave and for making a grant to cover some of the costs involved in preparing this volume for publication. My thanks are also due to Dr Edward Forman of the Department of French, University of Bristol, for his helpful comments on my introductions to the plays of Molière and Racine. As ever, the staff at Macmillan Press have given their unstinting help and support in bringing this volume to publication. I am particularly indebted to my commissioning editors, Margaret Bartley and Belinda Holdsworth. I would also like to thank Valery Rose and Nick Allen for their attention to detail in copy-editing and setting the text. On a more personal note, I would like to thank Coucou Lyall for her warm and untiring support.

General Introduction

France: The Cultural and Political Context

During the course of the seventeenth century, both France and England experienced far-reaching cultural and political upheavals, which had a profound effect on the drama and theatre of the period. In France, there was a sustained attempt to impose cultural unity and political centralisation on a nation that had been riven by religious and regional conflicts. The instigator of this drive for centralisation was Cardinal Richelieu, chief counsellor to the weak and ineffective King Louis XIII and his Queen, Anne of Austria. During the 1620s Richelieu successfully broke the power of the Protestant free cities in France, commencing with the siege of La Rochelle in 1628. Simultaneously he began to pick off those feudal nobles who had sided with the Protestants. In 1634 he founded the Académie française in order to impose the same degree of centralised control over language and literature as he was gradually imposing on society. Richelieu was arguably the first great states-man to recognise the importance of language as a crucial building block in the creation of cultural and political identity.

In 1637, a public squabble over the merits of Corneille's play *Le Cid* gave Richelieu an ideal opportunity to set out guidelines for playwriting. Corneille's play had enjoyed enormous public success, but was attacked by fellow writers, notably Scudéry. Richelieu invited the newly founded Académie française to examine the play and pronounce its judgement on it. He himself greatly disliked the work, which seemed to him to glorify the values of those free-booting, feudal noblemen whom he had for years been fighting. He therefore made sure that the evaluation of the play, written for the Académie by Jean Chapelain, would amount to a powerful condemnation of the piece. *Les Sentiments de l'Académie française sur le Cid*, published in 1637, amounted to a swingeing official critique of the whole play, which in turn implied a set of principles to be followed by authors in future. Possibly the key statement in this document is the assertion that, 'not all truths are good for the theatre';[1] authors should therefore be prepared to alter even the facts of history rather than risk offending the universal and ideal values implied in propriety, decorum and verisimilitude. Plays should offer a pattern of moral instruction rather than reflect the imperfections of history and everyday life.

Richelieu was only partially successful in building a centralised state in France: in politics, as in literature, he met with continuous opposition. Even after his death, there was another brief period of feudal civil war during the 1650s (known as la Fronde), when disaffected noblemen made a last attempt to preserve their feudal privileges. The latter half of the seventeenth century in France saw the final creation of the absolutist state by Louis XIV who came to the throne in 1661. Louis was a remarkable man who achieved what Richelieu had only dreamt of. He tamed the nobility and imposed the strictest of limitations on contemporary literature, and all of this was achieved with single-minded determination. Versailles was the key to it all. By extending his father's hunting chateau at Versailles, miles from the capital, and by transferring the centre of government to his court there, Louis ensured that he became the centre of attention and that any nobleman who wanted to further his own interests would be in constant attendance. At Versailles, Louis used ritual, dress codes and conventions as primary weapons in controlling people and their ideas. The expensive rituals and dress codes helped to impoverish the nobility and made them totally dependent on the king,[2] and the generous grants and subventions given to artists and writers ensured that they became the king's creatures. In this context, neoclassicism became an essential tool for ensuring unquestioning adherence to literary principles favoured by the state.

The battle over *Le Cid* had established the undisputed importance of neoclassic precepts for contemporary authors. By the age of Louis XIV, the whole canon of neoclassic expectations could be taken for granted. These included the pursuit of an ideal truth; a cautious approach to history; characters whose behaviour would always be socially and philosophically appropriate and acceptable; tightly structured plots obeying the unities of time, place and action; stylised language used within an overall didactic framework. The problem confronting the critics and authors of Louis XIV's day was to determine how best to operate within the known limitations imposed by accepted laws and conventions. How much imaginative freedom was left to an author working within the neoclassic tradition? How far could an author safely permit himself to go in pursuit of a particular theme or approach to character? These issues were brought to a head in the lives of both Racine and Molière.

England: The Cultural and Political Context

In contrast to France, England at the beginning of the seventeenth century was seemingly a prosperous united kingdom. The various regional, religious and feudal conflicts which had almost destroyed the fabric of ordered society in France were unknown in Elizabethan and Jacobean England. But the apparent stability of English society was misleading. Both James I and his son Charles I, who came to the throne in 1628, were obsessed by the notion of divinely sanctioned kingship. Their single-minded pursuit of absolute authority inevitably brought them into conflict with the Puritan merchant classes and minor gentry who were equally determined in their commitment to parliamentary rule. While the king enjoyed the trappings of power, it was the merchant classes who controlled the real wealth of the nation. During the reign of Charles I, neither side was willing to compromise; civil discord was therefore inevitable.

The mistake made by Charles I was to believe his own rhetoric rather than acknowledge the realities of political life which confronted him. Architects, painters and playwrights were all enlisted to illustrate the mythology of divinely approved kingship to which he was so fervently committed. The focus for this activity was the magnificent Banqueting House in Whitehall, constructed by Inigo Jones for James I in the early 1620s. Jones's imposing design, based on the example of Palladio in Renaissance Italy, was London's first neoclassic state building. Towering above the rambling Tudor Palace of Whitehall, it was a self-confident assertion of James I's vision of himself as a powerful Renaissance ruler. His son Charles I embellished this vision by commissioning Rubens to decorate the Banqueting House in 1635 with a number of splendid ceiling panels depicting *The Union of England and Scotland*, *The Benefits of the Government of James I* and finally *The Apotheosis of James I*. Throughout the 1630s sumptuous masques were performed in the Banqueting House (or in a masquing house constructed alongside it) which showed Charles I as the true inheritor of his father's wise vision of kingship. Even in 1640, at the very point in time when the country was sliding inexorably into Civil War, Charles I took part in a masque entitled *Salmacida Spolia,* which was designed to show him as a wise and just ruler, the bringer of peace and concord to a troubled realm. Reality and mythology were now diametrically opposed.

By 1642, instead of bringing peace and concord, Charles I found himself raising his battle standards to fight a full-scale civil war against his own subjects. After six weary years of conflict, the royalist forces were decisively beaten by Oliver Cromwell's New Model Army at Preston in 1648. The king found himself arraigned before a Rump Parliament purged of all dissenting voices; he was tried, found guilty and sentenced to death. In a deliberate attempt to destroy the myth of divinely sanctioned kingship that Charles I had so carefully constructed, Cromwell ordered that the king should be led to his execution in Whitehall through the Banqueting House which the Stuart monarchs had built, decorated and used to celebrate their myth.

During the reign of Charles I, the king's personal enthusiasm for all the arts and his profound distaste for Puritan views guaranteed that writers and actors could pursue their craft relatively unhindered. As a result, London in the 1630s was a thriving cultural centre with a significant number of large outdoor and smaller indoor playhouses, catering for a wide variety of tastes. In Puritan eyes, however, playhouses were not only intrinsically sinful, they were also viewed as politically undesirable disseminators of royalist propaganda. It was therefore not surprising that, after the outbreak of Civil War in 1642, Parliament enacted legislation to suppress the theatres, effectively silencing playwrights and actors for the next two decades.

Cromwell's death in 1658 brought a rapid deterioration in ordered government. This prompted General Monck to march on London from Scotland, setting in train a process that led to Parliament inviting Charles II to return from exile. Restored to the throne in 1660, Charles II had the supremely difficult task of reconciling the hierarchical view of kingship and society he had inherited from his father with the more egalitarian, Puritan sensibilities of a significant section of the population. He trod a cautious path through this political minefield. Although the process began with a deliberate symbolic reversal of his father's last journey – both Houses of Parliament were summoned to greet him at the Banqueting House on 29 May 1660 and testify their 'Vows of Affection and Fidelity to the utmost Degree of Loyalty'[3] – Charles II avoided giving unnecessary offence to the Puritan classes who had so effectively rebelled against his late father's authority.

Following the Restoration, Puritan objections to playwrights and playhouses were no longer an immediate threat. One of Charles II's earliest pieces of legislation was the granting of a warrant in August 1660 to Sir William Davenant and Thomas Killigrew to set up two theatre companies in London. However, the stated excuse for granting this warrant, namely the king's desire to suppress any plays containing 'much matter of profanation and scurrility',[4] was clearly designed to placate Puritan sensibilities. The real problem confronting a new generation of playwrights at the Restoration was knowing where to begin. The links with the traditions of the Elizabethan and Jacobean age had been broken by the civil war, although the plays of this period were still a powerful influence to be reckoned with. On the other hand, a new and equally powerful literary tradition, based on strict neoclassic ideas, had been developed in France. Which way should writers turn? Dryden, Wycherley and Congreve found their own individual responses to this dilemma.

The Plays

The plays chosen for inclusion in this volume represent some of the finest achievements of French and English theatre in the late seventeenth century. All of them explore the theme of sex, marriage and society. In each case, the treatment of the theme reflects the profoundly divergent values and beliefs underpinning French and English society in the late seventeenth century. In the France of Louis XIV, the iron grip of the king over political life was matched by the steely grip of the Catholic church over the spiritual and moral welfare of the nation. In contrast, England in the reign of Charles II, and even more during the brief reign of James II, was a nation divided both spiritually and politically. This meant that in France there were generally accepted moral and political codes of behaviour which dramatists ignored at their peril. In England, however, there was a spiritual and intellectual vacuum at the Restoration which gave dramatists unprecedented scope to challenge and question accepted patterns of behaviour.

Both *Phèdre/Phedra* and *All for Love* explore the consequences of an adulterous passion, but the treatment could not be more divergent.

The very notion of unlawful passion, as experienced by Phèdre, is treated with utter revulsion by Racine. Phèdre's destructive and irrational passion, over which she has no control at all, threatens and ultimately overwhelms the ordered fabric of society. As Racine shows it in his play, marriage is a far from perfect institution but it brings order and stability to a world that might otherwise fragment. Adulterous passion leads to chaos, disorder, poison and death. In complete contrast, the adulterous love affair of Antony and Cleopatra in Dryden's *All for Love* is treated with sympathetic warmth. Although the adulterous passion of Antony and Cleopatra threatens the ordered stability of the contemporary world, the subtitle of Dryden's play, 'the World well lost', makes it clear that the values of the world are so flawed that they are not worth preserving. The love of Antony and Cleopatra is therefore shown as something pure and innocent, rather than something disordered and discreditable. A hostile world inevitably destroys their love, but the whole thrust of the play suggests that it is the world that is at fault and not their love.

In his comedies, Molière tends to satirise the conduct of characters who threaten or flout a generally accepted set of moral values. Tartuffe can be shown to be a dangerous impostor because he uses the cloak of religious hypocrisy to disguise his real, and far more earthy intentions. His real aims are distinctly menacing, namely to procure Orgon's daughter as a subservient wife and to acquire Orgon's wife as an equally submissive mistress. Masquerading as a saint, his aggressive behaviour is a very real threat to the normal ordered stability of family life. Orgon is satirised for too readily believing Tartuffe's lies. His completely absurd infatuation with Tartuffe's saintliness puts his own marriage at risk and threatens the future happiness of his children. For Molière, marriage and family life are tangible realities that can be put at risk through irrational folly. In complete contrast, Wycherley shows characters struggling to make sense of a world where there are no meaningful norms against which conduct can be measured. Contemporary society is shown by Wycherley to be so completely corrupt and hypocritical that Horner, who is at least refreshingly honest, seems by comparison with the others to be an attractive character. Like Tartuffe, he is an impostor who uses a strategy of deliberate deception to obtain the sexual gratification he desires, but in contrast to Tartuffe there is no suggestion of any hidden threat or menace in his behaviour. His various sexual partners are more than willing accomplices. Marriage has become an empty shell, a form of financially based entrapment, which offers its female victims no real social or sexual satisfaction. The only thing that prevents open rebellion by the bored and frustrated wives of contemporary London is the threat of scandal and the consequent loss of reputation. Horner is astute enough to realise this and offers his partners a way of preserving their 'reputation' intact, while together they gleefully subvert the normal laws and conventions governing patriarchal society.

It is not until Congreve writes his comedies in the reign of William and Mary that English society begins to acquire a generally shared set of social and political values. This enables Congreve to satirise the behaviour of characters who deviate from this newly accepted norm. Because of this, his comedies are closer in approach to those of Molière than is the case with earlier Restoration comedies, but the tone is still significantly different. In *L'Avare* Molière never questions Harpagon's right to exercise his authority as a father; what is questioned is the way he exercises that authority. His attempt to marry his son's beloved is satirised as a clear abuse of his authority. He is a foolish older man attempting to purchase a young bride who is already in love with his son. Instead of contemplating a deed of such crass folly, his clear duty as a father is to think of his son's future happiness. Harpagon is satirised because he is too self-absorbed to think of anyone else at all. This makes him useless as a father, in contrast to Anselme. In Congreve's *Love for Love*, the political base has shifted from an acceptance of absolute authority to the acknowledgement of consent as the underlying basis of personal and political life. This means that Sir Sampson Legend's attempt to marry his son's beloved is not satirised as an abuse of his rightful authority as a father. What is satirised is his attempt to exercise absolute authority in the first place. As Congreve sees it, Sir Sampson has no right to demand total obedience from his son without offering real affection in return. Having tried to bring Valentine to heel by crushing him financially, Sir Sampson now attempts to humiliate his son sexually by marrying Angelica. Such behaviour is not simply foolish, it is pernicious. That is why he is dismissed with such cutting disdain at the end of the play. All relationships – personal, sexual and political – must be based on consent. That will be the foundation of Valentine's and Angelica's marriage, which ensures that it will be a genuine relationship and not just an empty shell.

Given the firm political and moral constraints facing them, there is an understandably greater caution in the approach of both Racine and Molière than in the work of their English contemporaries. Even so, both Racine and Molière managed to offend powerful factions in society. Racine offended many at court with his ruthless, amoral dissection of human passion, while Molière offended many in the church with his frank exposure of religious hypocrisy in contemporary society. The challenge facing English writers was quite different: it was to gain the attention and esteem of a sceptical and demanding audience who wished to see their own views and behaviour patterns reflected on stage. Playwrights were expected to probe the paradoxes and uncertainties of contemporary life with honesty and wit, but without boring or alienating a fickle and capricious audience. The taste of the town demanded a greater honesty and earthy realism than would have been tolerated in France. But the taste of contemporary audiences could also change rapidly, as Congreve discovered to his cost. The constraints facing English playwrights were therefore more overtly commercial than was the case in France.

By the end of the seventeenth century, Louis XIV's grip on political and cultural life in France was undiminished. The theatre was under firm royal control, with the remains of Molière's troupe instructed to amalgamate with the actors from the Hôtel de Bourgogne to form La Comédie-Française in 1680. One further troupe of players was tolerated, the Italian players, who had previously shared the Palais-Royal with Molière. However, they were unceremoniously ordered out of France in 1697 for satirising the King's mistress, Mme de Maintenon, in a satirical piece called *La fausse prude*. They were not allowed to return for the remainder of Louis XIV's reign.[5] In England, the situation was very different. The Lord Chamberlain exercised direct control over the theatre, but there were frequent challenges to his authority. There was also a far stronger commercial base for the theatre in London than was the case in Paris. By the turn of the century, there were two rival theatre companies operating in London. Soon the pressure would increase for a proliferation in theatre companies to cater for a growth in audiences with widely divergent tastes. Two divergent theatre traditions had been established by 1700 in France and England – the one state controlled, the other commercially based. Both traditions were to come under pressure in the eighteenth century, but that is another story for another volume.

Playhouses in Paris and London in the Seventeenth Century

At the beginning of the seventeenth century there was only one playhouse in Paris, the Hôtel de Bourgogne, built in 1548 by the Confrérerie de la Passion. The confraternity was a loose association of merchants, tradesmen and representatives of the professions, formed in the late fourteenth century with the express intention of presenting Passion plays to audiences in Paris. Ironically, in the very decade when they acquired their theatre, they were forbidden to perform religious plays.[6] Instead they were given permission to perform secular plays or to rent out their playhouse to visiting troupes. Designed to suit the demands of medieval theatre practice, the Hôtel de Bourgogne had a large standing pit, a single tier of raised side boxes, a raked amphitheatre at one end of the building and, at the other end, a cramped raised stage approximately at head height of those standing in the pit. There was no provision for changeable scenery; any locations were indicated by static mansions.[7] The function of this interior layout was to bring a large number of standing spectators into immediate contact with players performing increasingly earthy and robust farces, while allowing a smaller number of well-to-do spectators to remain aloof from the rest.

A similar interior layout was copied from the Hôtel de Bourgogne when Paris acquired its second indoor playhouse, the Théâtre du Marais in 1634. Like the Hôtel de Bourgogne, it was converted from one of the many real tennis courts in the city, this time in the fashionable Marais district. Once again a standing pit was flanked by raised side boxes, although here there was also a single tier of front boxes with a stepped amphitheatre above. The stage was at head height of those standing in the pit, and initially had no provision for changeable scenery. This was the theatre in which Corneille's tragedies and tragi-comedies were performed throughout the 1630s. In the 1660s, Racine's tragedies were performed at the Hôtel de Bourgogne, which had been significantly refurbished in 1647, but which still retained its original configuration of raised stage, standing pit and tiers of raised boxes.[8] It could be argued that this auditorium lay-out, inspired by the earthy traditions of medieval theatre, was no longer appropriate for the subtlety and complexity of French neoclassic theatre with its appeal to a more sophisticated audience. Nevertheless, it continued to inspire French playhouse design throughout the seventeenth century. For instance, the Théâtre du Palais-Royal, refurbished for use by Molière, still had a standing pit flanked by raised side and front boxes (in a flattened V-shape, rather than the rectangular shape of the Marais). However, the amphitheatre which, in the Hôtel de Bourgogne, had been a tiered structure on the far end wall opposite the stage, now began to encroach into the standing pit and took on the appearance of a seated pit area immediately behind the standing pit.[9] Essentially this same lay-out was utilised by d'Orbey when he designed the new Comédie-Française in 1689.[10]

In complete contrast to Paris, London had a widespread and thriving theatre culture prior to the Civil War. By the 1630s there were some ten so-called public and private playhouses in the capital. The public playhouses, such as the Globe, the Swan, the Hope, the Fortune, and the Red Bull, were substantial structures (most were circular or octagonal), with a large, open-air pit surrounded by tiers of seating in covered galleries for the well-to-do. The raised stages in these structures were covered by a canopied roof, supported in most buildings by pillars; there was no provision for changeable scenery. Many of these buildings were used for animal-baiting as well as theatrical performances, which suggests that the stages may have been easy to dismantle. The basic layout of these playhouses grew organically from the robust traditions of medieval theatre practice.[11] The private playhouses, such as the Cockpit (or Phoenix) in Drury Lane, Salisbury Court and the Blackfriars, were smaller, indoor structures, some of which were converted from existing buildings. Higher ticket prices were charged than in the public playhouses, which in turn meant that seating was provided in both pit and galleries for a more discerning audience. A section and ground-plan by Inigo Jones for a roofed private playhouse, which may have been used for the Phoenix or the Salisbury Court, shows an intimate theatre structure with a curved auditorium divided into a seated pit and galleries, and a small stage backed by a permanent *scenæ frons* of neoclassic design.[12]

During the civil war, London's playhouses were closed by Parliament and many were subsequently destroyed by Cromwell's soldiers. At the Restoration, Charles II granted only two patents to Thomas Killigrew and Sir William Davenant to set up theatre companies and provide suitable buildings for their companies. For the first few months they made use of the two remaining roofed playhouses in London, the Phoenix in Drury Lane and the Salisbury

Court Theatre. But both were too small for the audience capacity that would be needed for commercially profitable theatrical enterprises. Some other model had to be found for the indoor playhouses needed by both companies.

Killigrew and Davenant had stayed in Paris at various points during the troubled times of the 1640s and 1650s. While there, they had the opportunity of seeing the French solution to the problem of creating commercially viable indoor playhouses by converting real tennis courts into theatres. Both of them were sufficiently impressed by the Parisian tennis court theatre, the Théâtre du Marais, to realise that converting real tennis courts in London could provide an immediate and practical solution to their needs. Even though they were probably rather less impressed by the internal layout of the theatre, notably the standing pit, both of them resolved to adapt real tennis courts for their respective theatre companies in London. Killigrew opened his conversion of Gibbons's Tennis Court in Vere Street, Clare Market in November 1660. Although he had intended to make provision for changeable scenery, there is no evidence that he did so. Davenant took greater pains over his conversion and finally opened his scenic theatre at Lisle's Tennis Court in Lincoln's Inn Fields in June 1661.

Brief contemporary descriptions suggest that the auditorium of the playhouse in Lincoln's Inn Fields was divided into a seated pit, flanked by two tiers of side and front boxes. Lighting was provided by hooped chandeliers over the stage area, a trough of oil lamps to serve as footlights at the front of the stage, and wall-mounted sconces in the auditorium. The stage area was divided into two sections; a downstage acting area in the auditorium, approached through one or possibly even two pairs of stage or proscenium doors with balconies above them; and an upstage scenic area, separated from the acting area by the proscenium arch. The advantage of intimate actor–audience contact was preserved by extending the side boxes up to the edge of the non-scenic stage area. Finally, the practical doors that were an essential feature of Elizabethan and Jacobean theatres, mounted in the *scenæ frons* of the non-scenic stage, were pushed to the side in order to open up the stage for scenic display. The scenic stage, located beyond the proscenium arch, was essentially a background for the actors, not a surround. This meant that stage settings could be illustrative rather than detailed. The side wings, for instance, normally remained unchanged throughout the performance. Important changes of location were indicated by painted shutters drawn across the stage to meet in the centre.

In arriving at this pragmatic solution, Davenant established the basic shape and structure of most theatres built in London and the provinces for the next 150 years. In doing so, he achieved a typical English compromise between the traditions of an Elizabethan actors' theatre and the demands of the scenic stage. His theatre in Lincoln's Inn Fields seems designed to break down the barriers between stage and auditorium by deliberating extending a working space for the actors right into the middle of the auditorium.

By the mid-1670s, Davenant's pragmatic adaptation of Lisle's Tennis Court in Lincoln's Inn Fields inspired the design of the most successful purpose-built theatre in Restoration London. This was Sir Christopher Wren's Theatre Royal in Drury Lane, which was completed for Thomas Killigrew's company in 1674. Wren's new playhouse was not much longer but was significantly wider than the early tennis court theatres. The benches in the pit followed the same gently curving line as the front of the stage, while tiers of front and side boxes provided elegant accommodation for wealthy patrons, who were nevertheless close enough to those seated in the pit to be able to talk to them.[13] Even the more ornate Dorset Garden Theatre, built in 1671 after the death of Sir William Davenant, still followed essentially the same basic disposition of stage and auditorium, albeit on a larger scale, that was established at Lincoln's Inn Fields.[14] The enduring success of Davenant's original tennis court adaptation was underscored yet again in 1695 when the leading actors at Drury Lane rebelled against their manager, Christopher Rich. The building they chose for their actors' company was Lisle's Tennis Court, Lincoln's Inn Fields, hastily reconverted from tennis court to playhouse, using Davenant's tried and tested conversion scheme. It was to provide them with a secure base until 1705, when they moved to Vanbrugh's new playhouse, the Queen's Theatre in the Haymarket.

Note on the Texts

The texts of the plays by Dryden, Wycherley and Congreve correspond as far as possible to the first editions. I have retained the original spelling and punctuation of the first editions, though a number of silent editorial changes have been made. Obvious typographical errors have been corrected on the basis of later editions; the modern spelling of the letter 's' has been used throughout; all

characters' names have been fully spelled out, as have abbreviations
in stage directions. All stage directions have been placed between
square brackets. Conventions of punctuation and syntax within the
brackets have been silently standardised. I have made no attempt to
list variant readings in later editions in footnotes. Generally,
footnotes have been kept to a minimum so that the text may be read
without constant editorial interruption.

The same general editorial principles have been applied to the
translations of plays by Racine and Molière. However, these texts
have required far greater editorial intervention. In the case of
Racine, there were a number of adaptations of his plays in the late
seventeenth century, but no accurate translations. (John Crowne
published an adaptation of *Andromache* in 1675 and Ambrose
Phillips published his version of the same play called *The Distrest
Mother*, in 1712. Edmund Smith's *Phædra and Hippolytus*, published
in 1707, drew extensively on Racine's *Phèdre*.)[15] The translation of
Phèdre chosen for this volume is the first listed in the catalogue of the
British Library. It was published anonymously in 1776. Although in
many respects it offers a lively and spirited version of the original,
the translator has omitted and occasionally mistranslated a number
of key passages. I have supplied my own versions of the missing or
incorrect sections, some of which are based loosely on a nineteenth-
century version of the play published by Robert Bruce Boswell in
1890; I have indicated in the footnotes where this happens.

The translation of Molière's *The Miser* is by John Ozell, published
in 1732. This is an updated and corrected version of a translation
Ozell first published in 1714. (Prior to this date, Shadwell had
published an adaptation of *The Miser* in 1672; Fielding was to
publish a further adaptation of *The Miser* in 1733.) A further
translation of *The Miser* was also published in 1732 by Martin Clare,
in the first volume of a set entitled *Select Comedies of M. de Molière*.
Generally, Ozell's translation is a superior rendering of Molière's
text. However, a few passages are translated more accurately by
Clare; where this happens, they have been incorporated in this
volume and Ozell's version is given in a footnote. (Clare's version of
the play was subsequently published by Baker and Miller in the
second volume of their 1739 edition of *The Works of Molière*.)

An adaptation of *Tartuffe*, called *Tartuffe, or the French Puritan*, was
published by the actor Matthew Medbourne in 1670. There were
further extensive borrowings from *Tartuffe* by John Crowne in his
play *The English Friar* in 1690 and by Colley Cibber in his play *The*

Nonjuror in 1717. The first full translation of Molière's *Tartuffe* was undertaken by Martin Clare. It was first published in 1732 as an individual volume and in the fifth volume of *Select Comedies of M. de Molière*. Subsequently it was used by Baker and Miller (with a few corrections and alterations) in the fifth volume of their 1739 edition of Molière's plays, entitled *The Works of Molière* (10 vols). The version used for this volume is from the 1739 edition. It is usually ascribed to Baker and Miller, but as the greater part is by Martin Clare, it seems only just that he should be given credit for it. Neither edition includes a translation of Molière's Preface and his three petitions addressed to the king. The translation of these items is taken from Henri van Laun's edition, *The Dramatic Works of Molière*, vol. 4, published in Edinburgh in 1876.

The editions of the plays consulted may be found at the following locations in the British Library:

Text	*British Library Press Mark*
John Dryden, *All for Love*	
First edition (London: Henry Herringman, 1678)	[644.g.68]
Second edition (London: Henry Herringman, 1692)	[11774.g.19]
William Wycherley, *The Country Wife*	
First edition (London: Thomas Dring, 1675)	[C.34.l.26]
Second edition (London: Thomas Dring, 1683)	[11778.g.36]
Third edition (London: Thomas Dring, 1688)	[644.i.81]
William Congreve, *Love for Love*	
First edition (London: Jacob Tonson, 1695)	[Ashley 2913]
Second edition (London: Jacob Tonson, 1695)	[841.c.20]
Third edition (London: Jacob Tonson, 1697)	[11783.ff.32]
Jean Racine, *Phedra*, unknown translator	
(London: T. Bell, 1776)	[11735.e.36]
The Dramatic Works of Jean Racine, a metrical English version by Robert Bruce Boswell, 2 vols	
(London: George Bell & Sons, 1889–90)	[2504.k.10]
Molière, *The Miser*, trans. John Ozell	
(London: B. Lintot, 1732)	[164.g.62]
Select Comedies of M. de Molière, 8 vols, trans. Martin Clare	
(London: John Watts, 1732)	[241.l.28-35]
Tartuffe, trans. Martin Clare	
(London: John Watts, 1732)	[11736.aa.33.(1)]
The Works of Molière, 10 vols, trans. H. Baker and J. Miller	

xxii General Introduction

(London: John Watts, 1739)   [11736.aaa.33]
The Dramatic Works of Molière, 6 vols,
trans. Henri van Laun
(Edinburgh: William Paterson, 1876)   [2298.e.9]

A number of modern scholarly editions of the plays by Dryden, Wycherley and Congreve have been consulted. These include:

The Works of John Dryden, vol. 13, ed. Maximillian E. Novak (Berkeley: University of California Press, 1984).
The Plays of William Wycherley, ed. Arthur Friedman (Oxford: Clarendon Press, 1979).
The Complete Plays of William Congreve, ed. Herbert Davis (Chicago and London: University of Chicago Press, 1967).

A number of modern translations of Racine and Molière are in print, but at present there are no scholarly editions of these plays in translation.

Notes to the Introduction

1. Pierre Corneille, *Writings on the Theatre*, ed. H. T. Barnwell (Oxford: Blackwell, 1965) p. 203.
2. This process was convincingly illustrated in Roberto Rossellini's film *The Rise to Power of Louis XIV* (1967).
3. John Charlton, *The Banqueting House in Whitehall* (HMSO, 1964) p. 11.
4. Quoted from D. Thomas (ed.), *Theatre in Europe: A Documentary History. Restoration and Georgian England, 1660–1788* (Cambridge: Cambridge University Press, 1989) pp. 11–12.
5. See G. Mongrédien, *Daily Life in the French Theatre at the Time of Molière* (London: George Allen & Unwin, 1969) pp. 110–11.
6. See Peter D. Arnott, *An Introduction to the French Theatre* (London: Macmillan, 1977) pp. 5–16.
7. For a conjectural reconstruction of the interior, see Richard Leacroft and Helen Leacroft, *Theatre and Playhouse* (London: Methuen, 1984) p. 50.
8. See ibid., p. 50.
9. See Donald C. Mullin, *The Development of the Playhouse* (Berkeley and Los Angeles: University of California Press, 1970) p. 51.
10. Illustrated in Leacroft and Leacroft, *Theatre and Playhouse*, p. 69.
11. For a more detailed account of Elizabethan playhouses, see Mullin, *The Development of the Playhouse*, pp. 32–9.
12. See Thomas, *Theatre in Europe*, pp. 55–7.
13. For a detailed account of the design of Wren's Theatre Royal, Drury Lane, see ibid., pp. 69–72.
14. For a conjectural reconstruction of Dorset Garden by Edward Langhans, see Mullin, *The Development of the Playhouse*, p. 69.
15. See Katherine Wheatley, *Racine and English Classicism* (Austin: University of Texas Press, 1956).

Phedra

RACINE

INTRODUCTION

Orphaned at the age of four in 1643, Racine was brought up by various relatives who were adherents of the strict Jansenist movement within the Catholic church. For Racine, this was a mixed blessing. It gave him access to a sound education at the outstanding school of Port-Royal, run by committed Jansenist teachers, and enabled him to make contact there with children from aristocratic families who were to prove useful in his later life. But it also confronted him, at a formative period in his development, with a dark and pessimistic view of existence which was to haunt him for the remainder of his life. Jansenists saw the world as utterly fallen and human beings as depraved victims of their own wayward desires, from which they could be saved only by God's grace. But God's grace could never be merited. Some were chosen by God to be recipients of His grace, but others were damned in all eternity. This belief in predestination (which brought the Jansenists paradoxically very close to extreme Protestant Calvinists) left precious little scope for free will, even if believers were expected to lead a life of blameless virtue. As a young man, Racine initially rebelled against this pessimistic view of existence, but he never entirely escaped from its grip.

The first opportunity for rebellion came in 1658 when he left Port-Royal to study logic at the Collège d'Harcourt in Paris. After completing a year of study, Racine began to embrace the life of a man of letters. He made a number of important friendships with other writers, including La Fontaine, and published an ode on the marriage of Louis XIV called 'La Nymphe de la Seine'. He also wrote two early tragedies that were never performed. This initial attempt to break with his severe training came to an end in 1661, when he decided to travel to Uzès in Languedoc and to ask his uncle Antoine Sconin, who was vicar-general of the diocese, to help him find a clerical living in the area. Despite his uncle's friendly support and encouragement, a clerical appointment failed to materialise. Increasingly bored with his provincial exile, Racine finally returned to Paris in 1663, filled with renewed determination to make a success of a literary career.

His sycophantic 'Ode sur la convalescence du roi' (Louis had just suffered an attack of measles) brought him the promise of a royal gift of 600 livres; an 'Ode de la renommée aux muses' (further praise of Louis, written in the hope of turning the promise of patronage into reality) brought him the friendship of Boileau. His new tragedy *La Thébaïde ou les frères ennemis* caught Molière's eye, and in June 1664 it was given a moderately successful first performance by Molière's troupe at the Théâtre du Palais-Royal. A year later in December 1665, Molière mounted a successful production of Racine's next tragedy *Alexandre le Grand* at the Palais-Royal. At this point, Racine showed the first clear signs of the calculating ruthlessness that was to characterise his later career as a courtier. After only six performances, Racine withdrew his play from Molière's troupe and gave it to the rival troupe at the Hôtel de Bourgogne. Whether he was merely dissatisfied with Molière's actors, as his son was later to claim in his *Mémoires sur la vie de Jean Racine* (1747),[1] or whether he felt there was more prestige attaching to the work of the troupe at the Hôtel de Bourgogne, Racine did not hesitate to abandon Molière, his erstwhile friend and supporter, when he felt it was to his advantage to do so.

In the following year, 1666, Racine made an equally ruthless and public break with his Jansenist past. The immediate cause was the irritation he felt at the publication of an essay by the Jansenist writer Pierre Nicole in which writers were described as 'poisoners, not of the body, but of the souls of the faithful'. Racine's reply, a public letter addressed to Nicole, amounted to a swingeing critique of the Jansenist position.[2] This was a wise career move on Racine's part. In the same year, Louis decided to enforce a papal bull which had

---

1. Louis Racine, 'Mémoires sur la vie et les ouvrages de Jean Racine', in Racine, *Œuvres complètes* (Paris: aux éditions du seuil, 1962) p. 25.
2. Reproduced in *Œuvres complètes*, pp. 308–11.

branded a number of Jansenist beliefs as heretical. Racine was already beginning to find acceptance in court circles, and his burgeoning career as a courtier might well have been compromised by his Jansenist past. A public break with Jansenism was therefore distinctly to his advantage.

Racine's success at court can be charted in the dedications of his plays. The process began with Louis agreeing to have the published text of *Alexandre le Grand* dedicated to him in January 1666. That same year Racine joined the entourage of Henrietta of England, the wife of Louis's only brother, Philippe de France, Duc d'Orléans. His next play *Andromaque* (1667) was appropriately dedicated to her. *Britannicus* (1669) was dedicated to the Duc de Chevreuse, son of the Duc de Luynes who had been one of Racine's earliest supporters at court. *Bérénice* (1670) was dedicated to Colbert, Louis's powerful minister of finance and superintendent of all state building projects. Two years later, in 1672, Racine was elected a member of the Académie française; his name was proposed by Colbert. Following his election to the Académie, Racine's pre-eminence in the world of letters was now so well established that he did not feel the need to dedicate any of his remaining plays to named patrons. *Bajazet* (1672), *Mithridate* (1673), *Iphigénie* (1675) and *Phèdre* (*Phedra*, 1677) were all published without dedications but with introductory prefaces.

Racine's position at court was built on secure foundations. Apart from enjoying the support of the king himself, he increasingly found favour with the king's current mistress, Mme de Montespan, and her glittering circle of admirers. However, with the untimely death of Henrietta of England in June 1670, he lost a key friend and patron. He had also made a number of enemies during the triumphant progress of his career. Some of these were literary rivals, including well-known men of letters such as Pierre and Thomas Corneille, and lesser writers such as Le Clerc and Pradon. Others were courtiers who heartily disliked his main supporter at court, Mme de Montespan. These included the Comtesse de Soissons, the Duc de Nevers and the Duchesse de Bouillon. Finally, there were personal enemies: in particular Molière's widow and the relatives of the actress Thérèse Du Parc. Du Parc had been Racine's mistress between 1666 and 1668, but she had died in mysterious circumstances in December 1668. From the outset, Du Parc's mother had claimed that Racine had poisoned her daughter out of jealousy. Later the same charge was repeated by the famous poisoner la Voisin when she was interrogated in 1679; Racine was fortunate to escape arrest.

This group of enemies and plotters was to cause Racine enormous embarrassment in January 1677 when his masterpiece *Phèdre* was given its première at the Hôtel de Bourgogne. The dramatist Pradon was commissioned by the Duchesse de Bouillon to write a rival play *Phèdre et Hippolyte* for the Théâtre Guénégaud, controlled by Molière's widow. In his account of Racine's life, the dramatist's son claims that the Duchesse de Bouillon bought up all the boxes in both theatres for the first six nights to ensure that Racine's tragedy would play to empty houses.[1] There is no evidence to confirm this suggestion, but the cabal organised against Racine's *Phèdre* was sufficiently effective to deny the play the initial public success it merited.

Worse was to follow. An exchange of sonnets by opponents and supporters of Racine led to threats of violence against the writer. For a while he even had to take refuge at the Hôtel de Condé, having sought the protection of the Duc d'Enghien. These events must have played a large part in the decision he now took to withdraw from the world of the theatre, and to reconcile himself with his mentors at Port-Royal. He discarded his mistress, the actress Marie Desmares (known as la Champmeslé), whom he had trained to play the leading roles in his tragedies from *Bérénice* to *Phèdre* and with whom he had endured yet another jealous and tempestuous relationship. In June he married the wealthy and pious Catherine de Romanet: even his own son called this 'un mariage de raison' in his account of his father's life.[2] In October, the King solved any further social or financial problems facing Racine by promoting him, along with his friend Boileau, to the rank and role of Historiographer Royal.

These are the bare facts surrounding the momentous events of 1677, but hidden behind these events is a complex web of interlaced personal and political issues. Obviously Racine's work had begun to offend important members of court society. It was seen as ruthless and amoral, provocative and destructive. The cabal mounted against him and the scandal that broke out following the war of the sonnets was sufficient to endanger Racine's status at court. That alone was sufficient grounds to make Racine pause and consider his position. In addition, however, he was beginning to regret his earlier decision to break with Port-Royal. The final paragraph of his Preface to

1. See *Œuvres complètes*, p. 33.
2. Ibid., p. 37.

Phèdre suggests that he was already contemplating a reconciliation with Port-Royal when he wrote his tragedy:

> It is to be wished that our modern productions were as instructive and useful as those of the ancients. It might possibly be a means of reconciling many persons who are justly celebrated for their virtue and piety to dramatic writing, who have in these latter times condemned it. They, no doubt, would judge more favourably of it, if authors would study as much to instruct as to divert, and if they closely followed the real intention of Tragedy.

Viewed from a Jansenist perspective, his life hitherto must have seemed an offence. Having turned away from even the possibility of God's grace, Racine was only too painfully aware of the various physical and spiritual temptations to which he had succumbed. He had had two lengthy affairs with the leading actresses of the day, and there were rumours of one or more illegitimate children resulting from these liaisons; both relationships had been characterised by jealousy and bitter recriminations. In the case of the first, with Thérèse Du Parc, he had even been accused of poisoning her out of jealousy. In his career as a courtier, he had operated with unrelenting efficiency, calculating his every move with a cool rational pragmatism that would brook no opposition. If Racine was intending a reconciliation with Jansenism, he must have experienced a considerable degree of self-loathing and disgust at his past life.[1] It is precisely this feeling that spills over into each page of *Phèdre*, a play filled with a sense of loathing and nausea at the effects of sensual passion.

Phèdre/Phedra

The play is written with a technical minimalism that is quite astonishing. Racine's use of language is sparse and tightly controlled, with a highly compressed vocabulary and a series of formal, stylised images. There is no sign of the striking imagery and wide-ranging vocabulary one finds in Elizabethan theatre. Even the rhyming couplets of the French Alexandrine verse form help to reinforce the

---

1. He continued to experience this feeling up to his dying day. In his last will and testament, dated 10 October 1698, he asked to be buried at Port-Royal, despite the scandals of his past life: 'Because I have greatly offended God, I have great need of the prayers of a holy community to draw down His mercy upon me' (*Œuvres complètes*, p. 62).

impression of an action held together by an exceptionally tight control of language. The setting is a vaulted palace, as indicated in the records of the Hôtel de Bourgogne[1] and as is clearly suggested by Phèdre's speech in Act 3, where she says,

> I know my passion; and these walls, this arched
> Roof, seem ready to accuse me . . .

The physical environment is, however, far less important than the inner spiritual landscape inhabited by the characters.

Viewed superficially, the play appears to follow all the main demands of neoclassicism; its tight analytic structure permits the work effortlessly to obey the unities of time, place and action. The language used by the characters is elegantly heightened and purified of the defects of everyday speech. The various characters have a strong sense of decorum and seemingly behave with a dignity befitting their elevated status. However, the tightly controlled exterior forms of language and behaviour hold together emotional states that are fragmenting and disordered. A seemingly perfect demonstration of neoclassic control and artistry, the play in fact embodies a neoclassicism that begins to crack open under the pressure of the emotional forces it holds in check. Phèdre's death on stage marks the culmination of this process. Normally, in neoclassic tragedies, any deaths occur off stage and are described in reported speech. Here Phèdre's death throes are shown on stage as the havoc she has created destroys the whole ordered fabric of society.

In his Preface to the play Racine claimed that:

> I have not yet written any one [tragedy], where virtue is stronger held forth to view. The smallest faults are therein severely punished: the sole idea of a crime is looked upon with as much horror as the crime itself. Love is painted in its true colours: the passions are represented only to show the disorders and evils they occasion, and vice is every where so strongly depicted, that its deformity is easily perceived and detected.

This is perhaps how he wished to defend the play to his contemporaries. Phèdre is indeed punished with a violent death and

---

1. Henry Carrington Lancaster, *Le mémoire de Mahelot, Laurent et d'autres décorateurs de l'Hôtel de Bourgogne et de la Comédie-Française* (Paris: Librairie Ancienne Honoré Champion, 1920) p. 114.

faces the prospect of eternal damnation at the hands of her father Minos, who exercises judgement over the dead in Hades. But the play also shows passion sweeping all aside in its fury. There is no restraint, no decorum, no ideal virtue here. Phèdre is totally obsessed by her incestuous passion for her stepson Hippolyte: a destructive and all-consuming stream of feeling which none of the normal constraints of society can stop. Even Hippolyte, who is viewed as a paragon of chaste virtue, finds himself swept away in his turn by his passionate feelings for Aricie, whom he is prepared to wed in open defiance of his father's wishes. As for Thésée, the king, the very opening of the play makes it clear that much of his past behaviour has been determined by a succession of love affairs. Indeed Théramène even speculates that his current absence from the court may be due to the fact that, 'some new amour detains the hero'. When he eventually appears, his behaviour is impulsive and threatening, as he succumbs to a series of violent emotional responses. This was hardly a flattering image of kingship.

The only person who attempts to use rational strategies to deal with the lethal mixture of powerful emotions unleashed in the play is Phèdre's confidante Œnone. However, her two interventions – the first when she persuades Phèdre to confront Hippolyte face to face and 'meet his sight with guiltless eye', following the reported death of Thésée; and the second when she falsely suggests to Thésée that Hippolyte had attempted to rape Phèdre – produce disastrous consequences. Confronted by naked passion, there is nothing that rationality can achieve.

At the end of the play, the world is in tatters. Hippolyte is pointlessly and absurdly destroyed by an undeserved curse, called down upon him by his rash and unthinking father. Aricie faces a life of bitter mourning. Phèdre, a helpless victim of passions engendered by Venus, dies from poison she has administered to herself but will find no peace in death, only the prospect of eternal damnation (a damnation in which images of Hades merge imperceptibly with the hell fires of Jansenist Christian theology). Thésée is surrounded by the corpses of those he has loved and now faces a life of utter desolation. There is no reconciliation here, no restoration of a moral order, merely suffering and emptiness. An almost mechanical process has taken its course (as in one of Samuel Beckett's plays) and the audience is sent away feeling drained and spent by a play in which themes of emotional devastation are treated within a framework of extraordinary poetic beauty.

It is no wonder that high-ranking members of Louis's court campaigned against the play. It was obviously viewed as a highly subversive piece that had overstepped the limits of what was acceptable to contemporary sensibilities. Quite apart from the unflattering image of kingship shown in the play, *Phèdre* represented an unacceptable challenge to the rationally ordered basis of contemporary society. With its uncompromising portrayal of the reality of violent and destructive passion, *Phèdre* shattered the whole framework of neoclassic decorum and verisimilitude and showed it, almost contemptuously, to be no more than an empty poetic fiction. In *Phèdre* Racine had clearly gone too far. It is even conceivable that Racine the calculating courtier was horrified at what Racine the intuitive poet had actually written. It is therefore not surprising to find him agreeing with his mentors at Port-Royal by the end of 1677 that writers were indeed poisoners of the mind and that he perhaps was the most dangerous of these poisoners.[1]

This left the king the problem of what to do with Racine. It must have been clear to him after the scandal and fuss surrounding the first performance of *Phèdre*, and the ensuing war of the sonnets, that it would not be wise to encourage Racine to continue writing, even if he wished to. Louis's mistress, Mme de Maintenon, suggested the perfect solution. Racine and Boileau had already begun to plan, at the suggestion of Mme de Montespan, a flattering history of Louis's reign. Why not give them both an official position of Historio-grapher Royal? The courtier in Racine would feel honoured; he would also be delighted to work with his close friend Boileau; and he would doubtless himself be relieved that he would have no more time for playwriting.[2] Much to the chagrin of Racine's enemies at court, notably Mme de Sévigné, he was duly confirmed in his new office in October 1677 with a generous payment of 6000 livres. Louis XIV had once again shown himself to be an astute and pragmatic ruler. In silencing a potentially subversive writer by promoting him, Louis ensured that Racine would remain a devoted and compliant admirer for the future.

Racine never reverted to his former ways. For the remainder of his life he was a totally committed courtier, and a loyal husband and father. He wrote two further plays, *Esther* (1688) and *Athalie* (1689), but these treated biblical subjects and were written at the specific

1. See Louis Racine's account of his father's life in *Œuvres complètes*, p. 37.
2. Louis Racine confirms that his father welcomed the King's decision as a means of distancing himself from the world of creative writing (ibid., p. 39).

request of Mme de Maintenon for the young ladies of the boarding school at Saint-Cyr. The history of France he was supposed to be writing was never completed: only fragments remain. Having once looked into the abyss, Racine drew back and settled for a life of calm contentment as a courtier. However, even that was not entirely without its perils. Shortly before he died in 1699, his son describes how he lost the favour of the king because of an essay on poverty he had written at the request of Mme de Maintenon.[1] He therefore faced his final hours without the comfort of basking in Louis's favour. His last wishes were respected and he was buried in the cemetery of Port-Royal. When both the abbey and the cemetery at Port-Royal were destroyed in 1709, on the orders of the king, his remains were exhumed and taken to the church of Saint-Etienne-du-Mont in Paris and placed behind the chancel, near those of Pascal.[2]

1. Ibid., pp. 58–60.
2. This small but attractive church, completed during Richelieu's term of office, is situated just behind the Panthéon and has recently been beautifully restored.

Phedra

A
Tragedy

translated from the French
of
M. de Racine

LONDON

Printed for and Sold by T. BELL, No. 26, BELL YARD, TEMPLE BAR, and
G. BURNET, STRAND

MDCCLXXVI

Preface of the Author

The subject of the Tragedy of PHEDRA is taken from EURIPEDES; and, although I have struck into a different road from that Author, yet I have not omitted to enrich my piece with all that appeared striking and beautiful in his. If all I had taken from him was the idea for the character of Phedra, I might yet claim that I owed to him the most truthful work I have ever written for the theatre.[1] I am not astonished that PHEDRA met with such great applause in the time of EURIPEDES, and that it has been so well received in mine, since it has all the qualities ARISTOTLE requires in the hero of a Tragedy, proper to excite compassion and terror. In fact, PHEDRA is neither entirely guilty, nor entirely innocent; fate and the wrath of the Gods have engaged her in an illegitimate passion, for which she feels the utmost horror. She uses every effort to surmount it, and prefers rather a voluntary death, than to declare her feelings to any one: and even when she is compelled to discover it, she speaks with confusion, which plainly shows that her crime is rather a punishment of the Gods, than the impulse of her own will.

I have also been careful to render her not so disagreeable as she appears in the tragedies of the ancients, where she accuses HIPPOLYTUS herself. I thought that such calumny was somewhat too low and too black to proceed from the mouth of a queen, who in other respects has such noble and virtuous sentiments. This meanness appeared to me more suitable to her servant, who, may be supposed to have more servile inclinations, and who nevertheless undertakes this false accusation only to save the life and honour of her mistress. PHEDRA only consents, because her agitation of mind makes her desperate; but, in a short time after she returns with a design of justifying the innocence and declaring the virtue of the prince.

In EURIPEDES and SENECA, HIPPOLYTUS is accused of having violated his father's bed: *Vim Corpus tulit*. But here he is supposed only to have had the intention. I would spare THESEUS a confusion which would make him appear less agreeable to the audience.[2]

I have remarked that the ancients reproached EURIPEDES with having represented HIPPOLYTUS as a philosopher entirely exempt from imperfection, which causes the death of this young prince to be received with more indignation than pity.[3] I have thought it necessary not to make him so wholly perfect, that he might appear a little guilty to his father, without depriving him of that nobleness of soul with which he saves PHEDRA's honour, and suffers himself to be oppressed without accusing her. When I

---

1. This sentence is omitted in the 1776 edition.
2. This paragraph is mistranslated in the 1776 edition. In the final sentence of the paragraph, Racine implies that a contemporary audience would find a cuckold a figure of ridicule.
3. The opening of this sentence is mistranslated in the 1776 edition.

speak of his weakness, I would be understood to mean his passion for ARICIA, who is the daughter and sister of his father's mortal enemies.

This ARICIA is not a person of my own invention. VIRGIL speaks of the marriage of HIPPOLYTUS, and of his having a son by her after ÆSCULAPIUS had restored him to life. I have also read in some authors, that HIPPOLYTUS married and brought a young Athenian lady of noble birth into Italy, who was called ARICIA, and who had given her name to a little town in that country.

I speak of the above authorities, because I have scrupulously followed the fable, and even the history of THESEUS as represented in PLUTARCH.

It is from this historian I gathered that the origin of the fable of THESEUS'S descent into Hell to bring away PROSERPINE was a voyage that prince made into Epirus towards the source of Acheron, to assist PIRITHOUS in the rape of the queen, but PIRITHOUS was killed and THESEUS detained as a prisoner.

Thus have I endeavoured to preserve the probability of the History, without losing any of the ornaments of the fable; and the report of the death of THESEUS founded on this fabulous voyage, gives room for PHEDRA to make a declaration of her love, which becomes one of the principal causes of her misfortunes, and which she never would have done had she known the king had been alive.

On the whole, I dare not assert that this is the best of my Tragedies: I shall leave the decision of its value to judges and time; all that I can assert is, that I have not yet written any one, where virtue is stronger held forth to view. The smallest faults are therein severely punished: the sole idea of a crime is looked upon with as much horror as the crime itself. Love is painted in its true colours: the passions are represented only to show the disorders and evils they occasion, and vice is every where so strongly depicted, that its deformity is easily perceived and detected. This is properly the aim which every person who labours for the public should have in view; and this is what our first tragic writers studied on every subject: their Theatre was a school where virtue was not less taught than in the schools of the philosophers. – Thus ARISTOTLE has laid down the rules for dramatic writing: and SOCRATES, the wisest among philosophers, did not disdain to assist EURIPIDES in his Tragedies. It is to be wished that our modern productions were as instructive and useful as those of the ancients. It might possibly be a means of reconciling many persons who are justly celebrated for their virtue and piety to dramatic writing, who have in these latter times condemned it. They, no doubt, would judge more favourably of it, if authors would study as much to instruct as to divert, and if they closely followed the real intention of Tragedy.

Dramatis Personae

THESEUS, Son of EGEUS King of ATHENS.
PHEDRA, Wife of THESEUS, Daughter of MINOS and PASIPHAE.
HIPPOLYTUS, Son of THESEUS and ANTIOPE, Queen of the Amazons.
ARICIA, Princess of the Blood royal of ATHENS.
OENONE, Nurse and Confident of PHEDRA.
THERAMENES, Governor of HIPPOLYTUS.
ISMENIA, Confident of ARICIA.
PANOPE, Attendant on PHEDRA.
GUARDS.

SCENE: Trezenium, a City of PELEPONESUS

Act I, Scene I

[SCENE, *Trezenium, a City of* PELEPONESUS.
HIPPOLYTUS *and* THERAMENES.]

HIPPOLYTUS: My resolution's fixed, Theramenes. I quit Trezenium;
  Torn by doubt, I grow ashamed of my long idleness.
  Six months and more my father has been gone,[1]
  His long and silent absence
  Leaves me ignorant of his fate.
THERAMENES: And where, my lord, dost thou hope to find him?
  To appease your fears, already have I crossed the seas
  To seek the king at Corinth, and on the coasts of Acheron;
  Visited Elidus, and quitting Tenarus, bent my enquiring
  Steps towards the seas, where Icarus met his fate.
  On what new hope then build you your success:
  In what happy clime thinkst thou to trace his footsteps?
  Who even knows whether your royal father
  Conceals his situation through a private motive?
  And while we here, in vain, lament his absence,
  Some new amour detains the hero.
HIPPOLYTUS: Stop, Theramenes, and speak of Theseus with a due respect.
  Reclaimed from juvenile errors, no ignoble obstacle detains him:
  Phedra has fix'd his heart, nor longer dreads a rival.
  In seeking then a parent, I only obey the call of duty,
  And quit a spot I no longer view with pleasure.
THERAMENES: Ah! my lord, how long then have these peaceful walls
  Been irksome to you, which from your infancy you have admired

---

1. These two lines are omitted in the 1776 edition.

And preferred to the pompous tumult of Athens and the court:
What peril, or what anguish, drives you hence?[1]

HIPPOLYTUS: Those happy days are over. Since the daughter of Minos and
Pasiphae visited our court, the sight of objects are reversed.[2]

THERAMENES: I understand you. Phedra, your dangerous step-mother
Causes this affliction; but her hate, formerly so strong against you,
Is now totally effaced, or much abated: besides, my lord,
What canst thou dread from a dying woman? Phedra daily consumes
With some secret ill; and weary of her life, impatient
Wishes for the stroke of death. Is it therefore possible she can form
Designs against you?

HIPPOLYTUS: 'Tis not the enmity of Phedra that disturbs me. No, Hippolytus
Flies from a more dangerous foe, the young Aricia, the sole remains
Of the fatal blood which conspired against our family.

THERAMENES: How! my lord, dost thou persecute thyself?
The lovely sister of the cruel Pallantides,
Never assisted in the plots of her perfidious brothers.
Why then this aversion to her innocence?

HIPPOLYTUS: If I hated her, I would not fly from her presence.

THERAMENS: Your mysterious discourse makes me think
Your nature is changed. What then is become of this haughty
Hippolytus
– This implacable enemy to amorous laws, and the yoke which
So often has subjected Theseus? Venus whose power
You disown'd, seems to justify your parent by punishing your pride.
And by evincing you are not superior to the rest of mortals
Compels you to offer incense at her shrin? You feel then my lord,
The power of beauty?

HIPPOLYTUS: And canst thou, my friend, who so long hast known
The real sentiments of this proud, this stubborn heart, ask me
To own such a shameful weakness?
Born of an Amazon, the pride that awes thee
I sucked with my mother's milk:
When to a riper age I came,
My mind approved what from nature I had learnt.[3]
Attached to me by a sincere zeal, thou
Hast often recounted me the exploits of my father, and when you
depicted
The intrepid Hero, comforting mortals for the loss of Alcides,[4]

---

1. This line is omitted in the 1776 edition.
2. Phedra's father was Minos, son of Zeus, who became King of Crete. After his death
he was a Judge in Hades. Pasiphae, Phedra's mother, was a daughter of the Sun.
3. The reference to his Amazon mother is omitted in the 1776 edition.
4. Hercules.

The Centaurs worsted, Procrusta, Cercyon, Sciron and Sinnis punished,
The bones of the Epidaurus giants scattered o'er the plain, and
Crete reeking with the foaming blood of the destructive Minotaur,[1]
Thou knowst how my attentive soul has hung upon thy voice,
And glowed at the recital. But when thou toldst me of
His less glorious feats, his proffered faith, Helen
Ravished from her parents, the lamentation
Of Peribeus, Ariadne breathing her complaints to the obdurate rocks
And Phedra stole away, thou must remember with what regret I heard
The tale and pressed thee to go no farther. Happy, could I obliterate
From my mind, that ignoble part which sullies a father's fame,
And shall I then in turn suffer myself to be thus fettered?
Shall I be thus humiliated? so much the more despicable by my
    effeminate sighs,
As a long train of honours renders Theseus's failings excusable.
What single monster have I subdu'd, to give me e'en a shadow of erring
Like my father? Could I, even if this stubborn heart gave way,
Chuse Aricia for my conqueror? No, an obstacle eternally divides us.
My father by severe and rigorous laws
Forbids the nuptial tye, and with the sister would extinguish the name
Of those hated brothers who conspired against him.
Shall I, then shew a weak example of temerity,
And, on a foolish passion, embark my youth?
THERAMENES: If once our hour is come, my lord,
    The gods care little for our views.
    Eager to close your eyes, Theseus unseals them;
    His hatred only serves to fan the flame of love
    And lends his enemy new charms.
    In vain, my lord, you strive to conceal the flame and oppose
    The soft impressions of a guiltless love.
    Why fear you to stray where Hercules has wandered?
    What mighty heroes has not Venus
    Overcome, and think'st thou to withstand her power? Away then with
    This stubborn, this haughty boasting, and generously own, what thy
    Actions render but too apparent.
    Seldom now you drive with furious ardour the splendid car,[2] or,
    Skilful in the art that Neptune taught, bend the stubborn steed;
    The forests now no longer re-echo back your cries, but loaded with
    A secret fire, you only breathe the soft amorous sigh. No doubt, then
    Can remain. You love, my lord, and consume with a disorder
    You strive in vain to conceal. The charming Aricia – [3]

---

1. For a concise account of Theseus's various exploits, see H.A. Guerber, *The Myths of Greece and Rome* [1907] (London: Harrap, 1991) pp. 146–55.
2. Chariot.
3. A number of lines are omitted from this speech in the 1776 edition.

HIPPOLYTUS: No more, Theramenes, I fly immediately in quest of Theseus.
THERAMENES: But e'er you depart, will you not take leave of Phedra?
HIPPOLYTUS: It is my intention, you may inform her of it! – But what
New misfortune troubles her faithful Oenone?

Act I, Scene II

[Enter OENONE.]

OENONE: Alas! my lord, what trouble can equal mine.
The Queen is close to her life's end;
Vainly I watch by day and night.
In my arms, she still consumes with a secret grief,
Sleep ne'er closes her watery eyes, and her silent sorrows forbid
The approach of any one but me – but see she comes.[1]
HIPPOLYTUS: It is sufficient, I quit Terzenium
Nor let this hateful person appear before her.   [*Exit.*]

Act I, Scene III

[PHEDRA *and* OENONE.]

PHEDRA: Stop, dear Oenone. My strength forsakes me,
My eyes grow dim and my trembling knees totter under
Their wretched burden. Alas! [*sits down.*]
OENONE: All powerful Gods! let our tears appease you.
PHEDRA: How these vain and gaudy ornaments encumber me,
What officious hand has tied these knots
And gathered o'er my brow these coils of hair?
All disturbs and hurts me, and all conspires to wound me.
OENONE: In vain, madam, we strive to please;
Your wishes wavering destroy each other:
Only now you bid us dress you,
And, with your former energy revived,
Desired to go abroad and see the light of day.
Scarce have you seen it,
And then unsatisfied long for the return of night.
PHEDRA: Thou glorious author of a hapless race,
Thou whose daughter my mother could boast to be,
Who well may'st blush to see me in such plight,

1. This speech is more compressed in the 1776 edition

For the last time I come to look on thee,
O Sun![1]

OENONE: Will you not forego these cruel accents of despair?
Must I see you, for ever tired of life,
Prepare yourself thus mournfully for death?

PHEDRA: Would I were seated in the forests' shade:
There might I follow, through the glorious dust,
A car in full career –

OENONE: Madam?

PHEDRA: Where am I? I know how far my senses wander. The gods
Have deprived me of them: oh! Oenone, blushes cover this
Face for the shameful grief which now afflicts me.[2]

OENONE: If then, madam, you must blush, blush for silence
Of your grief, which only aids its destructive fury;
Deaf to all our prayers and rebellious to our cares
Would you with furious rage,
Hastily and unpitied end your days?
Thrice have the shades of night spread o'er the heavens,
Without thy wonted rest: and thrice the sun has
Took his diurnal course, yet thou takest no
Nutriment to preserve thy precious life.
What right have you to offend the gods who gave you breath,
And grieve the king to whom you are bound in wedlock,
Or, by such fatal means to precipitate misfortunes on
Your wretched children. Think that the moment you are
Robbed of life, that moment re-establishes the haughty enemy of you
And your blood; that son of an Amazon, that Hippolytus.

PHEDRA: Oh! gracious powers.

OENONE: My reproach affects you.

PHEDRA: Oh! that accursed name.

OENONE: Your anger's just; I love to see you shudder at the hateful name.
Live then: let love, let duty excite you. Live, and suffer not
A Scythian's offspring, to command o'er the richest blood of
Greece, and o'er the descendants of the gods. Do not then delay
A moment to resolve; quickly repair your abated strength, and shine
Again with renewed power.

PHEDRA: I have too long prolonged a guilty life.

OENONE: How! with what remorse art thou torn?
What crime can have produced this great affliction?
Thy hands have never bathed in innocent blood.

PHEDRA: Thank heavens! my hands are untainted of any crime.

---

1. The Sun was Pasiphae's father, and hence Phedra's grandfather.
2. The opening speeches of this scene have been greatly compressed in the 1776 edition.

Would to God, my heart was as innocent as those.
OENONE: What hideous project then hast thou conceived,
    To stain thy heart?
PHEDRA: I have said enough: spare me the rest;
    And let me die, to avoid the black confession.
OENONE: Die then, a victim to inhuman silence,
    But seek another friend to close those eyes.
    Altho' thy days appear but short,
    Yet first shall Oenone seek the grave;
    A thousand paths lead to the gates of death,
    My grief will choose the shortest!
    Cruel queen!
    Remember, first at thy birth these arms received you,
    Since when I never have deserted you: but left my country,
    My children, and all that was dear in nature to follow you.
    And will you not now trust me with this fatal secret
    Which torments you?
PHEDRA: Why, will thou press me farther?
    Thy generous soul would shudder with horror
    If I informed you.
OENONE: What horror can equal that
    Of seeing you expire?
PHEDRA: When you are acquainted with my crime, and the fate which
    Awaits me, I shall die still more guilty.
OENONE [*kneeling.*]
    Madam, if e'er Oenone was dear to you, by those tears,
    Which now fall from these aged eyes; by all that's precious to thy sight,
    Deliver my soul from this anxiety.
PHEDRA: Since then thou wilt hear my guilt, rise.
OENONE: I hear you. Speak.
PHEDRA: But heavens! how shall I speak it,
    Or where shall I begin.[1]
OENONE: Wound me no longer with your vain fear.
PHEDRA: O Venus! into what errors did not thy
    Hate and fatal rage plunge my mother![2]
OENONE: Forget them, madam, and henceforth bury them in eternal silence.
PHEDRA: Ariadne,[3] my sister too, struck by her cruel hand,
    Fell a victim to her power.
OENONE: What mortal distraction animates you?

---

1. These brief speeches have been cut in the 1776 edition.
2. Venus had inspired Pasiphae with a grotesque love of a bull: their unnatural union
   led to the birth of the minotaur.
3. Venus made Ariadne, Phedra's elder sister, fall in love with Theseus. She had
   eloped with him, only to be cruelly abandoned on the island of Naxos.

PHEDRA: Since Venus ordains, that I shall perish the last and most miserable
    Victim of my race, I consent.[1]
OENONE: Art thou in love, then?
PHEDRA: I feel its utmost power.
OENONE: For whom?
PHEDRA: Prepare thyself to hear the crowning horror. I love –
    I tremble at the fatal name – I love –
OENONE: Who?
PHEDRA: Thou know'st the son of the Amazon,
    The prince I so long have oppressed.
OENONE: Hippolytus! gracious powers!
PHEDRA: Thou hast named him.
OENONE: Just heaven! my blood freezes in my veins!
    O despair! O deplorable race! O unfortunate coast,
    Why did we ever approach thee?
PHEDRA: My misfortunes are more distant. Scarcely was I
    Engaged by the laws of Hymen to Egeus's son,[2]
    When Athens presented me my
    Haughty enemy. I saw him, blushed and felt a sudden flame
    Rise in my soul: my sight forsook me, my faltering tongue forgot
    Its duty, and my trembling frame felt the sudden shock.
    The power of Venus and the inevitable torments with which she
    Pursues our race, rushed quickly to my mind, and by assiduous vows
    I hoped to o'erturn them. For this intent I rais'd a temple to the goddess,
    Adorned it with the richest gifts, and offered victims at her shrine.
    In vain, I sought a remedy for my incurable love:
    In vain, the altars smoked with my daily incense offered
    When I implored the protection of the goddess;
    I adored Hippolytus; while he was continually in my sight,
    Even at the foot of the altar,
    I offered all my adoration to that God I dare not name.
    My misery still encreased! if I flew from him, the
    Son again presented himself before me, in
    The features of the father. At length, I resolved to subdue
    The fatal flame, I rouz'd up all my courage to persecute the
    Youth I loved. To accomplish this point
    I affected all the chagrin of a cruel stepmother,
    Pressed his exile, and by my eternal prayers, tore him from the paternal
      breast.
    My days then calmly flowed with innocence;
    Concealing my disquiets, I only obeyed the dictates

---

1. Venus had an implacable hatred for all the offspring of the sun god Apollo, because
   he had revealed her love for Mars.
2. Theseus.

Of my duty: but my cruel destiny still pursued me.
Conducted hither by my royal consort,
I again discovered the enemy to my rest:
Immediately my wounds began to bleed
Afresh; and the subtle flame almost smothered
By long absence, blazed once more with redoubled fury:
Venus, in all her might, seized her prey.[1]
I blushed in secret for my shameful passion;
Despised my life, and only wished to save my honour
By a hasty death. – Thus Oenone have I
Declared my shameful passion to thee, nor do I
Regret it; if thou in future cease from
Thy generous attempts, to keep alight a vital spark
Of fire, ready to extinguish.

Act I, Scene IV

[*Enter* PANOPE.]

PANOPE: The news I bring you, madam, I would fain conceal,
    Did not my duty enforce the dismal tidings.
    Death has robbed my royal master of that life
    His foes in vain essayed.
OENONE: How! what say'st thou, Panope?
PANOPE: That in vain to heaven, our queen offers up her prayers
    For Theseus's return: since by vessels just arrived,
    Hippolytus has learnt his father's death.
OENONE: Good heavens!
PANOPE: For another master, Athens already seems divided in its
    Choice. Some loudly give their suffrages
    For Phedra's son, while others forgetting the laws
    Which bind the state, speak strongly for Hippolytus,
    – Nay, public report spread by an insolent faction,
    Calls Aricia to the throne – pardon, then madam,
    This abrupt intrusion; my duty urged me to
    Warn you of your danger. Hippolytus already
    Is eager to depart, and 'tis feared will meet with
    Too great success, among a wavering people.
OENONE: Enough, Panope, thy important counsel our
    Queen will not neglect.   [*Exit* PANOPE.]

---

1. This crucial line is omitted in the 1776 edition.

Act I, Scene V

[PHEDRA *and* OENONE.]

OENONE: No longer, madam, would I have pressed thee to drag on
    A weary life; nay, would have followed thee to the
    Silent tomb, where every sorrow's hushed.
    But this sudden change, this new calamity
    Prescribes you other laws. The king's no more;
    You, madam, must supply his place:
    The child he has left, now claims all your care,
    And demands your life; to whom, if thy rash hand
    Had giv'n the fatal stroke, could he apply for shelter:
    No longer would the maternal hand be ready to assuage his grief:
    His innocent cries, borne aloft to the gods,
    Would call down on you his forbears' wrath.[1]
    Live then, for now
    No longer can reproach affect you with a treach'rous
    Flame, since Theseus's death has left you free.
    Hippolytus now no longer bears that formidable
    Appearance, which so lately disturbed your mind;
    Now you may meet his sight with
    Guiltless eye – Perhaps already struck with your
    Feigned aversion, he is become the seditious
    Chief, and heads the revolt. Exercise then all
    A woman's art, and bend him to your will.
    Trezenium is his, but the law ordains your son
    Master of Minerva's favourite city.[2]
    Join therefore your united forces, against Aricia's claim.
PHEDRA: True, Oenone; it shall be done – thy counsel
    Has relieved me. I will live then, if a mother's[3]
    Love will re-animate this feeble frame.

Act II, Scene I

[ARICIA *and* ISMENIA.]

ARICIA: What say'st thou, Ismenia? does Hippolytus
    Request to see me; surely thou'rt mistaken?
ISMENIA: Madam, this is the first effect of Theseus's

---

1. These two lines are omitted in the 1776 edition.
2. Athens was Minerva's favourite city.
3. Mistakenly translated as Hippolytus's Love in the 1776 edition.

Death, therefore prepare thyself, to find every heart
By him perverted, turn'd towards you, and Aricia
Mistress of the fate of Greece.
ARICIA: This report of Theseus's death has some
Foundation then? My enemy is no more?
ISMENIA: The Gods no longer frown on you;
And Theseus has gone to join your brothers' shades.
ARICIA: But how was it occasioned?
ISMENIA: Rumours incredible are spread,
Some say that, eloping with a new love,
The waters closed over his faithless head.
Others tell, and this report prevails,
That with Pirithous he descended to the world below,
Beheld the sombre shores of Cocytus,[1]
And showed himself alive to the infernal shades.
But that he could not, from this sad abode of death,
Recross the river whence there is no return.
ARICIA: Shall I believe that a mortal man, before his destined hour,
May descend into the kingdom of the dead?
What spell lured him to that dreaded shore?[2]
ISMENIA: No doubt remains in any breast but thine:
Athens mourns its loss, and Trezenium
Appriz'd of the news, already acknowledges
Hippolytus for its king, while Phedra
Trembling for the fate of her son, seeks counsel
Of her friends.
ARICIA: And think'st thou, Ismenia, that Hippolytus,
Blest with more humanity than his parent, will relieve
My slavery? canst thou imagine that my misfortune
Touches him?
ISMENIA: Indeed, I think so.
ARICIA: Sure thou dost not know this insensible Hippolytus?
On what frivolous hope canst thou have raised a thought,
That he should pity Aricia's fate, and respect in me
A sex he utterly contemns? Ah! Ismenia, hast thou
Not observed, with what studious care he avoids our presence,
And shuns the spot where we resort?
ISMENIA: The slights he pays our sex, I'm well convinced of:
But I have seen this haughty youth, in spite of all
His pride, struck at the sight of Aricia; – have seen
His eyes, with pleasure wandering o'er your charms,

---

1. One of four rivers in Hades, the river of wailing.
2. A number of speeches are omitted from the beginning of the scene, and the detailed rumours of Theseus's death are also missing in the 1776 edition.

Refuse the dictates of his stubborn nature, which bid
Him shun thee. Yes, I have seen Hippolytus; have read
His mind; and though the name of lover, may offend
His haughty spirit, yet his eyes have declared his
Thoughts, and spoke a milder language.

ARICIA: With what avidity, my heart attends to thy discourse,
Perhaps unfounded. O, Ismenia, thou
Partner of my hopes and fears, thinkst thou it
Credible, that this heart, the wretched sport of cruel fate,
Can be impressed by Love? I, the sole remains of
Royal blood, who alone, saved from the rage of war,
Have seen my brothers lost in the flower of
Their youth, and the earth moistened with
The blood of Erecteus's offspring. Thou also know'st
The law severe Theseus has enacted since their death,
Which prescribes it death for any Greek to wed me,
Fearing lest the sister should re-animate the
Ashes of her brothers. Thou know'st with what disdain
I regarded this jealous attention to my fate,
How, ever averse to love, I thanked the unjust
And cruel Theseus for his proscription. –
But then, my eyes had not seen Hippolytus
Nor taught me love. – Not that alone
Allured by his person, his beauty, and
Other gifts which Nature gave him, I was
Captivated. No, I loved him for much nobler
Qualities, and praised in him, the virtues of his
Father, unstained with any of his crimes.
I loved, I own Ismenia, I loved him for his noble pride,
Which disdained to bend beneath the amorous yoke.
Phedra reaps little glory from Theseus' lavish sighs:[1]
I have more pride and despise an easy conquest,
The heart which ever open, is assailed at
Every point successfully. But to bend the
Inflexible hero, to strike an obdurate heart,
And enchain the captive, who wonders at his fetters,
And vainly mutinies against a yoke which pleases him,
That Ismenia is my desire, my chief wish
Which prompts me on. To disarm Hercules, is
An inferior conquest to Hippolytus, and gives less
Glory to her who subdued him. – But,
My dear Ismenia, alas! how great is my
Imprudence! too many obstacles oppose my

---

1. This line is missing from the 1776 edition.

Desire. Thou, perhaps will see my wishes
Humbled, and I deploring that pride I now
So much admire. – Should Hippolytus
Love? But by what extremity of fortune
Could I have softened –
ISMENIA: He'll answer you in person, madam,
Hippolytus approaches.

Act II, Scene II

[HIPPOLYTUS, ARICIA, ISMENIA.]

HIPPOLYTUS: Madam, e'er I quite Trezenium,
I come to acquaint you of your fate.
My father is no more. My fears divined
The reasons for his lengthy absence.
Death alone, ending his mighty toils,
Could so long keep him from the world.[1]
The Gods have taken
The friend, companion and successor of Alcides.[2]
Abating your hatred for him, I perceive
You hear without rancour[3]
Titles which are his due. But one hope remains
To calm my grief, since 'tis in my power
To free you from your slavery. Therefore I
Revoke those laws, I long have mourned
The rigour of; you, madam, now are free
And have liberty to dispose of your heart,
And person, as your will directs.
In this Trezenium, now my heritage,
Where once my grandsire Pittheus reigned,
And where I am now acknowledged king,
I leave you free, free as myself, – and more.
ARICIA: This goodness, generous prince embarrasses
And confounds me, and lends more force than you can think
To those harsh laws from which you would release me.[4]
HIPPOLYTUS: Athens, madam, divided in the choice of a successor,
Speaks of Aricia, Hippolytus and Phedra's son.
ARICIA: Of me, my lord!
HIPPOLYTUS: I know the law which rejects me from the throne,

1. These four lines are missing in the 1776 edition.
2. Hercules.
3. This line is mistranslated in the 1776 edition.
4. These two speeches are compressed in the 1776 edition.

And willingly submit to the justice of it. Greece reproaches
Me with a foreign mother. But, if I had only
My brother for competitor, I should not
Hesitate a moment how to act. But now
A more legitimate rein curbs my audacity.
And I cede, or rather return what is your right,
A scepter, which in a former age, your ancestors
Received from that famous mortal, the earth conceiv'd.[1]
Egeus after sway'd it and Athens protected and
Increased by Theseus, with joy acknowledged
So generous a monarch, and in oblivion sunk
Your unfortunate brothers. – Athens now
Loudly calls for you within its walls, and enough
Has mourn'd this long dispute, while her plains
Have reeked with blood.
Trezenium is my province. Crete offers
A rich retreat to Phedra's son. Athens
Belongs to you alone, and requires your
Presence; I go, therefore, madam, to accomplish
This end and render you mistress of a faithful people.
ARICIA: All I hear, astonishes and confounds me;
    I almost fear, a dream deceives me.
    Am I awake? Can this be true?
    What God, my lord, what God reigns
    Within your breast? Your glory already spread
    Abroad, loudly proclaims your fame.
    Would you for me prove traitor to yourself?[2]
    Is it not enough, my lord, that you do not
    Hate Aricia? and that you so long
    Have fenced your heart against any
    Enmity towards me?
HIPPOLYTUS: I hate you, madam?
    However savage my nature may have been painted
    Do you suppose some monster bore me?
    What savage manners, what obdurate hate
    Would not be assuaged in your presence?
    And could I resist those powerful charms –
ARICIA: How, my lord?
HIPPOLYTUS: I find that reason must give way to the violence
    Of my passion. Since then, madam, I have broke silence
    I must go on, and inform you, of a secret

---

1. A reference to Erectheus, the legendary King of Athens, whose mother was Gæa,
   the earth goddess.
2. This line is missing in the 1776 edition.

My heart no longer can conceal.
You see before you, madam, an unfortunate prince,
A memorable example of an inconsiderate pride.
I who so strongly revolted against the power of love
And have long insulted the fetters of its captives,
At present bend under the common law.
One single moment conquered my imprudent boldness,
This proud, obdurate heart is at length enchained.
For six months past, desperate I have struggled
With this passion; but in vain. Your image
Is perpetually before me. Where e'er I go
You are ever in my sight. The light of the day and
The darkness of the night, all place before my eyes
The charms I would avoid. Hippolytus no longer is himself,
My bow, my spear, my car, all now disturb me,
The lessons Neptune taught me are unheeded.[1]
The forests now but echo back my sighs
And my inactive steeds forget my voice.
But this recital of so wild a flame,
May only raise a blush, at so rude a conquest:
But the offer of this stubborn, this untractable heart,
Ought to receive a greater value. Think that I
Now speak a language, hitherto I was a stranger of.
Do not then reject my vows, though rude exprest,
Which ne'er would have been framed by Hippolytus,
Had not Aricia's charms compelled them.

Act II, Scene III

[HIPPOLYTUS, ARICIA, THERAMENES, ISMENIA.]

THERAMENES: My lord, the queen approaches, and requests an audience.
HIPPOLYTUS: With me?
THERAMENES: What she intends, I know not.
    A servant came to ask for you;
    Before you leave, Phedra would speak with you.[2]
HIPPOLYTUS: Phedra desires to see me? What shall I say to her?
    What business can call her hither?
ARICIA: My lord, you cannot refuse the queen's request,
    Tho' no doubt, your mind still bears the impression

1. This line is missing in the 1776 edition. Neptune was the god of horsemanship as well as god of the sea.
2. These lines are missing in the 1776 edition.

Of her enmity. Yet to her tears some compassion
Is due.
HIPPOLYTUS: And must I leave you, then Aricia, ignorant
Of my fate and fearful lest this tongue, unused
To the soft expressions of love, has offended
Those charms my heart adores.
ARICIA: Go, prince, pursue your generous designs,
Render Athens tributary to my power.
I thankfully accept this gift you offer me,
But this mighty empire, so great,
So glorious as it is, believe me, is not the
Richest offer you have made me, nor that
On which I set the greatest value.   [*Exit* ARICIA.]

Act II, Scene IV

[HIPPOLYTUS *and* THERAMENES.]

HIPPOLYTUS: My friend, are all things ready? But see, the queen,
Fly then, prepare in haste for our departure;
And return with utmost speed to rescue me
From a tedious interview.

Act II, Scene V

[PHEDRA, HIPPOLYTUS *and* OENONE.]

PHEDRA: [*to* Oenone] Oh! Oenone, his sight deprives my words an utterance
And makes my blood recede.
OENONE: Remember, thy son, think, that his fate rests on you alone.
PHEDRA: My lord, we hear you soon will leave us,
Yet, e'er you quit Trezenium; permit a mother
To utter her complaints. My son is now deprived
Of a father's succouring hand, and the day is not
Far distant when he'll be robbed of mine.
Already, numerous enemies attack
His infant years. To you, my lord, alone he can
Look up for succour, to support his cause;
But my mind troubled by a secret remorse,
Presages that your ears are shut to
My complaints, and I tremble lest your anger, justly
Merited against a hateful mother, should pursue

Her son.

HIPPOLYTUS: Madam, such mean sentiments never entered the
      Breast of Hippolytus.

PHEDRA: Yet should you despise me, I should not complain.
      In appearance cruel, you thought me bent
      On your destruction; but you could not penetrate
      The bottom of this heart. I exerted every art to raise
      Your enmity; I railed against you,
      In public and in private, used every means to force
      You from my sight; I even prohibited by an express law
      The mention of your name before me. Yet, for all this
      The offence was measured by the pain I felt.
      Never woman, my lord, deserved your pity more than Phedra,
      Nor is less deserving of your enmity.

HIPPOLYTUS: I know, a mother is ever jealous of her children's
      Rights before another's. Importunate suspicions are
      The too common fruit of a second marriage,
      Another Stepmother might have taken more
      Umbrage at me, and excited still greater cruelties
      Against me.

PHEDRA: Ah! my lord! I here declare, that the Gods
      Have excepted Phedra from this general law:
      A different anxiety troubles and afflicts me.

HIPPOLYTUS: Madam, calm your afflictions. The king
      May still be living. The Gods in pity to our prayers,
      May grant his return. Neptune will not in
      Vain be implored for my father's safety but will
      Protect him.

PHEDRA: Oh! my lord, in vain we hope the Gods will
      Return Theseus to us; greedy Acheron[1] never
      Quits his prey, nor suffers a mortal twice
      To see the bounds of death. But, what am I saying?
      He is not dead, while Hippolytus lives.
      Whene'er you are before my eyes, I see,
      I talk to my royal husband and my throbbing heart –
      How strangely do I wander – my lord,
      Excuse my folly.

HIPPOLYTUS: I see the prodigious effect of your love for Theseus;
      Though dead, his image still is present to your eyes
      And your mind is ever employed on the thoughts of him.

PHEDRA: True, prince, I languish, burn for Theseus,
      I love him, not such as he was
      Seen when rioting in his dishonourable acts of love. But

---

1. Another of the rivers of Hades, the river of woe.

Faithful, haughty, wild, young and charming,
Attracting every heart towards him, such as our Gods are painted;
Or, such as you now appear;
That air, those eyes, that speech, and that
Noble modesty which crimsons o'er your face. Such Theseus was
When he crossed the seas to Crete,[1]
The object of Phedra's wishes.
Where then was Hippolytus? Why did not the
Grecian heroes fix their choice on you?
Why then, did not your years permit
Your presence on our coasts? Then, by you,
The Cretan monster would have perished,
In spite of every obstacle that opposed.
My sister[2] then would have armed your hand
With the fatal thread. My sister, did I say,
No, I myself, Phedra, would have stept forth
In that attempt. Love would then have formed
The thought, and I would have led you thro' the
Dangerous labyrinth; with what care
Would I have conducted you along,
Nor trusted your safety to a single thread. Companion
Of the danger I would have led the way,
Phedra herself would have trod the labyrinth
And either lived, or died with her Hippolytus.
HIPPOLYTUS: Gracious Gods! What do I hear? Madam,
Have you forgotten, Theseus, is my father.
PHEDRA: And why prince, do you think my memory
Has forsook me? Should I –
HIPPOLYTUS: Pardon me, madam, I blush to own
That I wrongly accused your innocence,
Shame will no longer suffer me in your presence.
And I go –
PHEDRA: Stop, cruel prince, thou hast too well observed
My meaning. Know then I love; I own it, am tormented with an
Ardent flame. But think not in the moment that
I felt it, I weakly fed the poison. No,
I abhored myself more than thou canst detest me,
Wretched object of celestial vengeance.
The Gods are witnesses, the Gods, who in my breast
Have lighted up this fatal flame, those Gods
Who cruelly delight to seduce the heart
Of a feeble mortal. Recall then in thy mind

1. To slay the minotaur.
2. Ariadne.

What lately has passed; to fly from thee was not all
I tried, I wanted to appear odious and inhuman to thy sight,
And to resist the flame, I strove to gain thy hate.
But what avails all my ineffectual cares,
You hated me the more, as my love
Increased. Thy misfortunes lent thee new charms,
I languish'd and consumed in secret with my passion:
Thine eyes would see it,
If, for a moment, thou woulds't deign to view me.[1]
But, what do I say? This declaration,
This shameful declaration is not voluntary.
Trembling for my son, I came in his behalf.
But, alas, I could only speak to thee of my own
Hateful passion. Revenge thyself then,
Punish the wretch before thee. Thou worthy son
Of Theseus, deliver the universe from this abandoned monster.
Alas! Theseus's widow
Loves Hippolytus! Believe me, prince, the
Hideous Wretch must not escape thee.
Here is this treacherous heart. Strike then,
And let thy hand expiate its offence.
Strike then. Or if thou think'st it unworthy
Of thy rage; if thy hate denies me
So mild a punishment: or, if thy hand fears to be
Polluted by this infamous blood –
Give me thy sword, and let me thus –　　　　　*[snatches his sword.]*
OENONE: *[seizing her hand]*
What mean you, madam! Just powers!
But see, Theramenes is nigh. Fly then,
And let none be witness of thy shameful weakness.

Act II, Scene VI

[HIPPOLYTUS, THERAMENES.]

THERAMENES: Was that Phedra who fled, who was hurried hence?
How, my lord, what mean these signs of grief!
I find thee speechless, pale, and without thy sword.[2]
HIPPOLYTUS: Theramenes, let us quit this place immediately.
Astonishment and horror confound me.[3]

1. These two lines are missing in the 1776 edition.
2. Part of this speech is missing in the 1776 edition.
3. This line is missing in the 1776 edition.

Phedra – But stop, let this horrible secret
Ever be buried in an eternal oblivion.
THERAMENES: The sails, my lord, are ready bent, and
    Wait your presence. But Athens, has
    Already declared her choice. Her chiefs
    Have had the voice of all her tribunes,
    Your brother and Phedra have gained the day.
HIPPOLYTUS: Phedra!
THERAMENES: A herald charged with the will of Athens
    Is come to present her with the reins of government,
    Her son is elected king.
HIPPOLYTUS: Ye Gods, who know her heart,
    Is it then her virtue that you thus reward?
THERAMENES: Besides a murmur runs, that the king is
    Still alive, and has been seen in Epirus.
    But I who have sought him there, know
    Full well –
HIPPOLYTUS: It does not matter, let us learn all we can
    And leave no step neglected. Let us examine
    This murmur, trace it to its source.
    And whatever it may cost,[1]
    Let us place the sceptre in hands worthy
    To sway it.

Act III, Scene I

[PHEDRA, OENONE.]

PHEDRA: Ah! what avail these proffered honours;
    They suit not me, but should be given
    To one that more deserves them. And, oh! Oenone,
    How can'st thou, thus importunate, strive to flatter my
    Disorder'd mind? No, rather conceal me from
    The sight of all the world, and bury me in
    Eternal oblivion. My raging passions have
    Divulged, what should never have escaped this
    Tortured breast. - Heavens! with what surprize
    He heard me, and by how many forced evasions
    Strove to elude my plaints, as if he only
    Wished a quick retreat. – How his blushes also
    Redoubled my disgrace. – Why, Oenone, why
    Didst thou, with officious care, prevent

---

1. Hippolytus is prepared to contemplate armed rebellion.

My desperate attempt? – Alas! with what
Silent scorn he saw my rage; nor when his
Sword was ready to pierce my heart,
Did he with the least attempt strive to save me.
I had but to touch his sword
To render it odious in his sight,
As if the blade itself would defile his hand.[1]

OENONE: Thus, madam, your afflicted mind,
Ever intent on your unhappy fate, only
Keeps alive a flame you should extinguish.
Would it not better suit the blood of Minos,
To seek repose in nobler pursuits;
And, by accepting of this proffered crown,
Forget Hippolytus in the care of Athens.

PHEDRA: How can'st thou vainly think that I, who cannot
Rule this erring mind, can ever rule a kingdom;
Or now, my senses have forsook their seat,
And I am sinking under a disgraceful yoke,
How can I with prudence govern?

OENONE: Fly, then, madam.

PHEDRA: Would I had power.

OENONE: You had power to enforce his banishment, and
Yet dare not avoid his sight.

PHEDRA: It is now too late. He knows my distracted mind.
The bounds of modesty are now passed over.
I have declared my shame to this haughty conqueror,
And a hope, in spite of this disgrace,
Still remains to flatter me. Thou, thyself, Oenone,
Recalled my drooping spirits; and when my soul
Was ready to depart, thou re-animated me with
Thy flattering advice
And persuaded me that I might yet love him.[2]

OENONE: Alas! what would I not do to save my royal
Mistress? But if ever offence has hurt thy mind,
Or raised thy anger, think of Hippolytus's scorn.
Can you forget the disdain with which he treated you?
Or with what cruelty the haughty prince
Saw you prostrate at his feet? Would that
Phedra saw him with Oenone's eyes! she'd contemn
This stubborn pride, and think him odious.

PHEDRA: That pride which thou dislik'st, he may wear off;
Bred in the forests, he is rude and unpolished;

---

1. These three lines are missing in the 1776 edition.
2. This line is missing in the 1776 edition.

Wild and hardened by savage laws,
Has never hear the word of love before.
Perhaps his wonder caused his silence,
And our complaints were too rashly urged.
OENONE: Some Barbarian bore him.
PHEDRA: Scythian and Barbarian, yet she loved.
OENONE: But Hippolytus with a mortal hate
  Disdains the sex.
PHEDRA: Then need I fear no rival.[1]
  Thy counsel, Oenone, is no longer seasonable;
  And instead of calming, only aids my passion.
  His heart is to love impenetrable; in vain we seek to wound it.
  Let us then find some part, in which he is accessible;
  The charms of empire dazzle him: Athens
  Is his aim. Already his sails are bent for
  His departure. – Fly then, Oenone, fly and stop this
  Ambitious youth: place the crown of Athens
  'Fore his eyes: tell him, that I, that Phedra will place the sacred
  Diadem on his head. My son, instructed
  By him, will learn the art to rule. Hippolytus
  Will be to him a second father, and Phedra and her son
  Wholly in his power. Go, then, Oenone, tempt
  Him by every method: thy words will
  Meet with more success than mine. Use every
  Art; nor let prayers, intreaties,
  Sighs, nor tears, be wanting. Depict thy royal
  Mistress languishing in death; nor hesitate
  To take the suppliant form to gain thy purpose. Away then, my only
  Hope's in thee, and on thy success depends my future
  Bliss or misery.   [*Exit* OENONE.]

Act III, Scene II

PHEDRA: [*Solus.*]
  O, implacable Venus! thou who seest the disgrace
  Of Phedra, am I sufficiently humbled?
  Farther thy cruelty cannot extend; thy
  Triumph's perfect. Cruel goddess, if you seek
  A still greater glory, attack an enemy who is
  More rebellious than thy present victim.
  Hippolytus braves thy anger, nor ever
  Humbly bent at thy altars. Thy name
  Offends him. O goddess, then,

1. This line is missing in the 1776 edition.

Revenge thyself, and make this youth,
This proud Hippolytus, feel thy power:
Let him love. But see, Oenone, quick returns.
Ah! I see he detests, not accepts my offer.

Act III, Scene III

[PHEDRA, OENONE.]

OENONE: Now, madam, you must stifle every thought of love,
    And recall your former virtue. The king, whom
    We thought dead, will soon appear.
    Theseus is arrived, and the people press
    With eager haste in crouds to see their
    King. For while I sought Hippolytus
    At your request, loud acclamations
    Pierced the skies, for Theseus's return.
PHEDRA: My husband lives! 'tis enough, Oenone,
    I have made a disgraceful avowal
    Of my love – He lives – I would know no farther.
OENONE: How, madam?
PHEDRA: I before informed you, but thou would'st
    Not permit me: thy tears prevailed o'er my
    Just remorse. This morning I had died
    Lamented: but now, thy advice pursued, I die
    Dishonoured.
OENONE: You mean to die?
PHEDRA: Just heavens! what have I
    This day done. My husband soon appears,
    And with him Hippolytus. With what face can
    I see Theseus, with the witness of my adulterous flame before me;
    My heart still throbbing with sighs that he scorned,
    My eyes still moistened with tears he disdained.[1]
    Can'st thou form a thought that Hippolytus will conceal from
    His father the flame with which I burn?
    Will he, whose honour is so strictly nice, suffer
    His father and his king to be betrayed?
    Or contain his horror for my weakness?
    Or if he should be secret – I know my perfidy, Oenone,
    And am not of those hardened of my sex,
    Who can in tranquility and peace enjoy their crime,
    Nor suffer a blush to paint it on their face.

1. These two lines are mistranslated in the 1776 edition.

I know my passion; and these walls, this arched
Roof, seem ready to accuse me, and expect
My consort, to acquaint him with my crime.
Die then, and let one fault deliver me from
Horrors innumerable. Is it so painful then
To quit this life? – Death strikes no terror to
The wretched mind; but the disgrace I leave
Behind me is my only dread. – Heavens, what an
Hideous portion for my children! The burthen
Must oppress the offspring of mighty Jove,[1]
Who, branded with my infamy, must detest
The name of Phedra.
I tremble, lest crushed beneath this odious burthen,
They will never dare lift up their heads.[2]

OENONE: Your fears are just. But why will Phedra
    Suffer her offspring to meet with such insult?
    Why expose them to the scoffings of a censorious
    World? Phedra, the world will say, fled in guilt
    From the the consort she betrayed.[3]
    Hippolytus, happy at your expence,
    Views with pleasure your approaching end:
    And, when thou art passed the shades of death,
    What can Oenone answer your accuser;
    Confounded and disgraced at his reproaches, must
    I see him tamely enjoy his triumph?
    No, first let the flames consume me, e'er
    I live to see the day. – But say, my royal
    Mistress, say, is this haughty prince still
    Esteemed? Dost thou still love him? or
    In what light does he now appear?

PHEDRA: Not as the lovely youth, I once did love;
    But as the hateful monster my revenge
    Would crush.

OENONE: Why then, madam, tamely yield the victory
    To this stubborn prince? Rather boldly resolve,
    And with firm audacity accuse him first, and
    Render him guilty of the crime which you
    Are threatened with. – Who can contradict you?
    All, all conspires against him. His sword,
    Which so late afflicted you, is fortunately in
    Your possession; and his father, long prejudiced

1. Jove, or Zeus, was father to Minos and hence grandfather to Phedra.
2. These two lines are omitted in the 1776 edition.
3. These two lines are omitted in the 1776 edition.

Against him, thro' your complaints, will hear
Your accusation, ease your fear, and restore
Your tottering honour.
PHEDRA: Ha! what, shall I oppress innocence, and
    With malignant cruelty, stab the virtuous mind!
OENONE: My zeal demands your silence only;
        Like you, my trembling soul feels some remorse
        And shudders at the deed; nay, would brave a
        Thousand deaths, rather than commit this act.
        But, when thy life's in danger – the mistress
        Whom I love, when her fate depends on this
        Remedy alone, I must not hesitate,
        But boldly speak. Theseus, by my
        Suspicions waked, will revenge thy cause;
        And as a father never can obliterate,
        A father's feelings, will only exile the
        Stubborn prince. But, if so decreed,
        And innocent blood must be shed,
        Let it – What does your menaced
        Honour not require? 'tis a treasure, so precious
        In its nature, you must not hazard:
        And, however the law of Conscience urges,
        You must submit; sacrifice all then,
        Even virtue for that gem. – But see, the king.
PHEDRA: And Hippolytus with him. – Oh! I read
    My ruin in his eyes. Act then, Oenone, as
    Thy will directs; to thy advice I yield
    My troubled mind, incapable of itself to guide.

Act III, Scene IV

[THESEUS, HIPPOLYTUS, PHEDRA, OENONE *and* THERAMENES.]

THESEUS: Thanks to th' almighty powers, my
    Wishes are compleat: since to these
    Arms my Phedra –
PHEDRA: Stop, Theseus
    Do not profane thy fervent transports –
    I no longer merit those endearments;
    You are wronged, basely wronged, and
    In your absence, while fortune sported
    With your fate; she has not forgotten
    Your wretched Phedra. – Unworthy

Thy embraces: I can only in
Future shun that injured presence.   [*Exit.*]

Act III, Scene V

[THESEUS, HIPPOLYTUS *and* THERAMENES.]

THESEUS: What means this strange reception? this
    Sudden damp to all my ardor? speak,
    Hippolytus, know'st thou the cause?
HIPPOLYTUS: This mystery, my lord, Phedra can
    Best explain. – But if my strenuous prayers
    E'er met reception in thy breast, permit
    Me ne'er again to meet the queen; but let
    Me unhappy quit the spot where she
    Resides.
THESEUS: How, Hippolytus, would you already
    Quit your father?
HIPPOLYTUS: Pardon me, my lord, 'tis not
    My father that I willingly quit. But
    Remember sir, you left your consort
    And Aricia under my protection:
    The trust I've executed with fidelity.
    But, now, my father, my presence here is
    No longer needful; and my inactive
    Youth passed 'midst the forests, has only
    Tried its efforts on abject beasts. – Indulge
    Me then, my lord, and let my spear be dyed
    With richer blood. – Before my age,
    You had, with victorious arm, slain
    The mighty tyrant, and cleared the coasts
    From infesting pyrates. The traveller
    No longer feared their ravages, and
    Hercules, relying on your exploits
    Rested with pleasure from his weary toils.
    And shall I then, the offspring of so
    Glorious a sire; shall I, suffer my life
    To glide in indolence, unknown to fame,
    Eclipsed even by my mother's deeds.[1]
    No, my lord, indulge my prayer, and
    If some monster has escaped thy sword,
    Let me exert my power, and lay the spoils

1. This line is mistranslated in the 1776 edition.

Respectfully before you. – Or by a noble
Death, Hippolytus may prove to[1]
Future ages, that he was the son of Theseus.
THESEUS: What do I hear? what horror spreads
    Around me. Just heavens! why didst
    Thou take me from my dreary prison?
    I had but one friend;[2] and his imprudent passion
    Aimed at Epirus's Queen, while I regretfully
    Served his amorous designs. But fate
    Opposed our wishes: the tyrant surpriz'd
    Me, defenceless and unarmed: Pirithous
    Too, I saw him thrown by this
    Barbarian, to those cruel monsters, that
    Glutted on human blood: while I,
    Imprisoned in the dark and dreary cavern,
    Could only mourn his fate. The Gods
    At length took pity on my sufferings
    And I deceived my keeper: then with
    What pleasure I purged the world of
    The perfidious tyrant, and left him to
    His monsters, a greedy prey. – And now
    When I thought to have embraced all
    That the Gods have left me dear,
    I only meet with cold receptions;
    All fly me, and refuse my ardors,
    While, struck with the terror
    These thoughts inspire, I wish myself
    Once more a prisoner at Epirus.
    Tell me then, my Son. Phedra complains
    Of some outrage. Who has deceived me?
    Why am I not revenged? Greece to
    Whom my arm so long was useful,
    Has she given refuge to some base
    Villain? – You answer not – speak.
    Is then my darling son, my Hippolytus,
    Is he conspired against me with my enemies?
    – But, let us farther search this hidden cause;
    Phedra, no doubt, will ease my troubled
    Soul, and point out the culprit and the crime.   *[Exit.]*

1. This line is mistranslated in the 1776 edition.
2. Pirithous.

Act III, Scene VI

[HIPPOLYTUS *and* THERAMENES.]

HIPPOLYTUS: What mean Phedra's mysterious words,
    They freeze my soul with horror: what,
    Will she accuse herself? Gods,
    How great will be my father's rage?
    What fatal poison, Love has shed o'er
    This royal mansion. – Myself, terrified
    With dark presages, know not which
    Which way to turn. – But innocence has nought
    To fear. – Let me then haste, and in some
    Happy moment, move my father's pity;
    Open to him my love for Aricia, and with
    Intreaties gain his favour for what
    His power never can extinguish.

Act IV, Scene I

[THESEUS *with a sword in his hand and* OENONE.]

THESEUS: Ah! What's this I hear,
    And does the traitor strive to abuse
    The honour of his father? O fate!
    How ingloriously thou pursuest me!
    I know not where I go, nor where I am.
    – Traiterous rebel! – audacious villain!
    Oh, detestable thought! – and would the wretch
    To gain his infernal purpose, would he make
    Use of force, and basely arm his hand against
    A woman. – Ah! I know this sword too well,
    This sword with which I arm'd him for a
    Nobler end, he made the instrument of his incestuous love.
    Could not then the ties of blood constrain him!
    Why did Phedra, too, too merciful, neglect to
    Punish the temerarious monster, and by her silence
    Save him?
OENONE: Phedra would not afflict the mind of Theseus:
    And blushing for the horrid intent of so mad
    A lover, Phedra would have no longer lived,
    And her murderous hand had nigh robbed her of life.
    I saw her arm extended to give the fatal stroke
    And ran in haste to save her, and preserv'd

Her for your love.
In pity for her anguish and your fears,
I come, against my will, to give her tears a voice.[1]
THESEUS: Perfidious villain,
  I saw his colour change at my approach;
  I was surpriz'd at his cold, unwelcome
  Salute, and perceived his crime written in his looks.
  But say, Oenone, had this guilty passion that devours him
  Aready declared itself in Athens?[2]
OENONE: Think my lord, of the queen's complaints;
  This infamous passion provoked her hatred.[3]
THESEUS: But tell me, Oenone, did this flame
  Break out again in Trezenium?
OENONE: I have told you all, nor can no longer stay;
  The queen with mortal grief oppressed,
  Too long has been alone. – Permit
  Then my return to calm her sorrows.   [*Exit.*]

Act IV, Scene II

[THESEUS *and* HIPPOLYTUS.]

THESEUS: Ah! here he comes. Gracious gods,
  Who would not be deceived at those
  Noble looks? Why on the adulterer's face
  Does Virtue's sacred character reside?
  Why are there not certain marks stampt
  On the human visage, to denote the treacherous
  Heart?
HIPPOLYTUS: What fatal cloud hangs o'er my
  Royal father's brow? Let me request
  His confidence and –
THESEUS: Wretch! monster! perfidious villain!
  Why is the thunder hush'd, why the wrath of Jove not
  Sent with vengeance at thee!
  Foul survivor of the brigands I swept away.[4]
  Darest thou then appear before me,
  And expect my confidence, after thy
  Incestuous love threatened to

1. These two lines are missing in the 1776 edition.
2. These two lines are mistranslated in the 1776 edition.
3. These two lines are mistranslated in the 1776 edition.
4. This line is omitted in the 1776 edition.

Stain thy father's bed!
  – Matchless assurance! – consummate villain!
Here to remain, here in this very spot,
The witness of thy infamy, and not direct
Thy baneful steps to some unknown clime,
Some undiscovered land, where thy father's name
Has ne'er been known! – Hence then, traitor,
Fly, nor longer brave my anger.
'Tis enough for me, to endure the
Opprobrious thought of having such a son,
Without sullying the glory of my days,
With staining these hands in thy incestuous
Blood. Hence, then, I say, if thou would'st
Avoid a sudden death. – But, be cautious
Ne'er in future you are seen in my dominions.
  And thou, O Neptune, thou   [*kneels.*]
Hear my earnest pray'r; if e'er I cleared thy
Shores from infamous assassins, remember
That thou promised, as a reward for all
My labours, to grant the first request I
Should ask thee. – In the long torments
Of a rigorous prison, I ne'er implored
Thy immortal aid: now, then, I invoke thee, and let thy vengeance quick
Be sent to rid the world of this traiterous
Boy. Let his blood be shed to wash away
His villainous desires, his incestuous flame.
HIPPOLYTUS: Ha! does Phedra then
  Accuse Hippolytus of base desires?
  Such unforeseen misfortunes, such excess
  Of horror, which crouds on my astonished soul,
  Denies my words their utterance.
THESEUS: Traitor,
  Did'st thou imagine, that Phedra,
  In a shameful silence, would bury
  Thy brutal insolence? Thy sword,
  Thy sword, which in her hands you left,
  Is sufficient to condemn thee.
  You should have crowned your perfidy
  And robbed her of speech and life.[1]
HIPPOLYTUS: Justly irritated by such a cruel
  Falsity, my duty requires me to explain
  The truth. My lord – But I will suppress
  A recital which must affect you:

1. These two lines are omitted in the 1776 edition.

Therefore, condemn not the respect
Which enjoins me silence; for your
Repose and quiet, and without farther
Increasing your despair, examine
All my conduct, all my actions thro'
The small course of life I've run.
Think, my lord, some smaller crimes
Precede those of a blacker dye. – Who
E'er infringes a lawful boundary
Will in future violate the most sacred
Laws. Vice as well as virtue has its
Degrees; nor hast thou ever seen
Innocence suddenly plunge to extreme
Licentiousness. One day alone is not
Sufficient to turn the virtuous mortal
To the perfidious assassin, or incestuous
Villain. Reared by a virtuous mother,
I have not sullied the blood from which
I sprang: Pitheus too, esteemed the wisest
Of human race, next taught me virtue.
But I will not place myself in
Too great a light; yet, if any merit fell
To my lot, let that disperse the hateful
Thought, that Hippolytus could wrong thee.
By virtue Hippolytus is known in Greece:
And the sun, which illumines this glorious
Sphere, is not more pure, than is this
Heart. No incestuous flame e'er –

THESEUS: Yes, Coward,
  'Tis that pride you boast of, which
  Condemns thee. I see the odious
  Principle of all thy actions.
  Phedra alone charmed thy lascivious
  Eyes; and for every other object, thy
  Haughty soul disdain'd to feel an
  Innocent and glorious passion.

HIPPOLYTUS: No, my lord, this heart has not
  Disdained to burn with a pure and
  Real flame. Here at your feet
  I confess my true offence.
  I love, 'tis true, I love Aricia, her
  Whom you forbid to wed. Yes, my lord,
  The daughter of Pallantus has conquered
  Your son, and my wounded soul, rebellious
  To your orders, only sighs and burns for her.

THESEUS: Thou lovest Aricia, heavens! – but stop – it
    Cannot be, the artifice is too gross.
    To justify thyself, you feign another crime.
HIPPOLYTUS: For six months have I loved her, and yet
    Strove to shun this attractive beauty.
    – But, I see that nought can turn aside
    Your anger, or relieve your error. –
    By what sacred oath then shall I confirm
    The truth of my assertions, and my innocence? –
    May heaven, earth and all nature –
THESEUS: The wicked ever have recourse to perjury;
    Cease, then, no longer trouble me with
    Thy importunate tale, if thy pretended
    Virtue has no other prop.
HIPPOLYTUS: It may appear pretended, and full of
    Artifice, but Phedra in her heart must
    Justify me from such crimes.
THESEUS: How thy impudence excites my anger.
HIPPOLYTUS: Since, then, thou wilt not hear me, I
    Obey; but whither shall I go in exile?
THESEUS: Even were't thou beyond Alcides' pillars,[1]
    Thy perfidious villainy would yet be too close.[2]
HIPPOLYTUS: Branded with a false and ignominious
    Crime. What friend will pity me, when
    Thou forsakest me?
THESEUS: Go, seek for friends
    Among those, whose wretched mind
    Honours adultery, and applauds the
    Incestuous villain. Traitors; who
    Without law or honour, will deign
    To protect such a wretch as thou.
HIPPOLYTUS: Still, my lord, you speak to me of
    Incest and adultery. I am silent. But
    Remember, Phedra sprang from a
    Blood, more replete with crimes
    Than mine.
THESEUS: How! dost thou then lose the
    Respect that is due before me. Hence,
    I say, fly traitor, nor wait the
    Fatal effects of an enraged father.   [*Exit* HIPPOLYTUS.]

1. The pillars of Hercules, or Gibraltar.
2. This speech is omitted in the 1776 edition.

Act IV, Scene III

THESEUS: [*Solus.*]
>   Wretched youth, thou goest to thy fate!
>   By Styx, an oath feared by the gods themselves,
>   Neptune has sworn to execute his promises to me. [1]
>   A revengeful god pursues thee; thou
>   Can'st not avoid him. I once did
>   Love thee, and now I feel, in spite of
>   All thy crimes, my heart is weeping for thee.
>   But 'twas too much; and never parent
>   Was so abused. Just gods, who see
>   The grief which now surrounds me,
>   Why had I a son so guilty as Hippolytus!

Act IV, Scene IV

[PHEDRA, THESEUS.]

PHEDRA: My lord, your anger reached my ears,
>   And by terror urged I come, lest your
>   Sudden rage, might commit a deed,
>   Hereafter you might mourn. – Yet, Theseus
>   Yet, if the fatal moment is not passed,
>   Spare, oh, spare Hippolytus; 'tis
>   Phedra kneels, implores you to have
>   Mercy; oh, let not an eternal
>   Grief o'erwhelm my soul with
>   The accursed thought, of having been
>   The cause of the paternal hand,
>   Shedding its offspring's blood.
THESEUS: No, madam, as yet my hands were
>   Never imbrued in my children's blood;
>   But the audacious rebel will not
>   Escape from justice, an immortal
>   Hand will strongly punish his atrocious
>   Crime. Neptune will avenge the
>   Wrongs of Theseus.
PHEDRA: Neptune, will avenge, – Oh heavens!
>   Has then your exasperated rage –
THESEUS: Fears't thou then, my prayers will

---

1. These two lines are mistranslated in the 1776 edition.

Not be heard! join thy supplications
Unto mine; paint his malignant
Crime in the blackest colours:
Raise up all my rage, now too calm,
And shower down vengeance on th'incestuous
Villain. – But, yet you know not all
His crimes; for, struck with the
Thought of his attempt being known,
The faithless villain burst into reproaches
Against my Phedra, and with hardened
Front, accuses you of uttering
Nought but falsities. Aricia, too, the
Daughter of my mortal enemy, he declares,
Has sole possession of his treach'rous heart.

PHEDRA: How! my lord?

THESEUS: This he but now declared,
And with consummate art, braved it
To my face; but his artifice is frivolous,
I heed it not: once more
I go, and at Neptune's altars offer up
My reiterated prayers for his destruction.   [*Exit.*]

Act IV, Scene V

[PHEDRA *alone.*]

PHEDRA: He's gone; what do I hear?
The smothered flame rekindles in
My breast, and burns with greater fury.
Oh, heavens! to save the innocent
Victim, from Oenone's arms I flew,
But whither had my fury nearly
Drove me, had not my voice died in my throat.[1]
I might have divulged the truth,
And accused myself, to save Hippolytus.
– But, why, this haughty youth feels
Not for me; but plights his vows
To Aricia. Oh! gracious powers,
When this inexorable Hippolytus
Armed his haughty looks against
My proffered love, I thought his heart
Ne'er had felt its shafts,

1. This line is mistranslated in the 1776 edition.

But was proof 'against all my sex.
But, alas! Aricia has bent this
Stubborn hero, and I, unhappy Phedra,
Remain the only object of his scorn.

Act IV, Scene VI

[PHEDRA, OENONE.]

PHEDRA: Oh, Oenone, what have I heard?
OENONE: Trembling, madam, I hither come,
    And shrink with fear, lest your
    Fatal intent has revealed the secret.
PHEDRA: Oenone, could'st thou e'er have thought
    I had a rival?
OENONE: A rival, madam?
PHEDRA: Yes, yes, he loves, Hippolytus,
    My haughty foe, whom all my prayers,
    My tears, and wailings, could not conquer, –
    This monster, whom I ne'er approached
    But with awe and dread, and tamely owned
    Him as my conqueror; adores Aricia.
OENONE: Aricia?
PHEDRA: Ah, Aricia! Heavens! whither will
    My sorrows drive me? – To what new
    Torments am I yet reserved? – All my
    Former fears, my love, my rage,
    Remorse, and the unsupportable thought of
    A refusal of my proffered bed, was
    Only a feeble essay of what I now endure.
    They love! Say, then, thou flatterer of my flame,
    How have they escaped my sight?
    Where, when, and how, did first their passion rise?
    – You knew it all, yet let me be deceived;
    Nor warned me of their stolen loves.
    Hast thou not seen them speak, and breathe
    Their amorous sighs together. Say, what
    Shady groves, what gloomy woods, concealed
    Their hidden loves. Alas! they had the utmost liberty,[1]
    The well pleased sun approv'd their guiltless flame:
    Each unclouded day rose

1. This line is mistranslated in the 1776 edition.

Clear and serene to bless their amorous wishes,
While I, the shame of nature, fly the all chearing
Light, and hide myself in darkness, imploring
Death to ease my anguish'd soul.
I waited for the grave's release,
Nourished with gall and watered with tears,
Even in my grief I was too closely watched
To weep without restraint.
In mortal dread, that melancholy pleasure I enjoyed,
I hid my woes beneath a tranquil brow
And often had to check my tears.[1]
OENONE: Ne'er heed their amorous flame,
   – They never more will meet.
PHEDRA: Yet, they will ever love:
Now, even now, ah! accursed thought,
They brave my scorn, and in spite
Of separation, offer up their vows to heaven,
Ne'er to forget each other. I can no longer
Bear the distressful thought. Hear me, Oenone,
And pity my jealous fury. – Aricia dies,
Her bleeding wounds shall appease my vengeance,
Fly then, Oenone, rouse my husband's utmost rage,
Against this odious fair, let not his
Punishment be light, but joined with every
Pang thy fury can inspire. I e'en Phedra,
Will join thy prayers and implore the king,
To extinguish the brother's crimes in their Sister's blood.
But whither does my reason stray?
My jealousy drives me beyond its bounds!
Theseus, whom I'd implore for vengeance,
Is my husband faithful to my bed, while I
Burn with an incestuous flame; - for whom?
Alas, each thought only adds more horror.
My crimes already too enormous, not
Content with an hideous incest would
Imbrue my hands in guiltless blood:
   – And yet, wretch that I am, I bear the sight
of that glorious sun from which I am descended.
My grandsire is Lord of all the gods,
And my forebears fill the sky and universe.[2]
Where can I fly to hide myself from my
God-like ancestors? If to the infernal shades I go,

---

1. The last few lines of this speech are omitted in the 1776 edition.
2. These two lines are omitted in the 1776 edition.

There my father holds the fatal urn.
How would his trembling shade freeze
With horror, at his daughter's sight, and
Hear me relate crimes, unknown to
Hell itself. – What would'st thou say, my
Father, at this horrid tale? I think, I see thee
Now, motionless with surprize; the urn
Falling from thy hand, and every nerve shuddering
With horror at my crime. Oh, now I see thee
Seeking some unknown, unheard of
Punishment. Forgive, forgive thy child;
'Twas not her will, but the impulsion of
A powerful God, destroyed thy injur'd race:
Alas! my wretched heart has never reap'd
Its criminal desires; and I drag on a painful
Life, with reiterated sighs and insupportable torments.

OENONE: Throw off, madam, thy unjust fear,
And with a more favourable eye look on your error.
You love indeed; who can o'ercome their fate?
Has the powerful God triumphed o'er you alone?
No; mortals must submit to human weakness;
And while you lament your too painful yoke,
Remember that the Gods, who punish mortal crimes
Have sometimes burnt with an incestuous flame.

PHEDRA: Stop Oenone, to what new crime would'st thou advise me?
Thou, who first led me on, would still conduct
Me wretched to the end. Thou, who by
Thy prayers, when duty bid me fly Hippolytus;
Recalled me to my ruin, and
Made me see him. Thou, who with impious
Voice dare blacken his unspotted life?
By some new scheme would add redoubled
Torments to my affliction. Already, perhaps he
Dies, and the sacrilegious prayer of an incensed
Parent is heard. – I'll no longer hear thy
Baneful counsels. – Hence, execrable monster,
Hence and leave me to my deplorable and unhappy fate:
May heaven with vengeance punish
Thy atrocious deeds, and grant that thy
Expected fate, may warn
Those deceitful fiends, who with base
And wicked counsels cause the ruin of unhappy princes,
Urging them to yield to their desires,
Daring to smooth for them the path of crime:
Foul flatterers, the deadliest of gifts

The angry gods can make to kings.[1]   [*Exit.*]
OENONE: Oh, gracious powers! this the reward
    For leaving all – this the price
    Of all my anxious cares to serve her.
    This is all I merit.[2]   [*Exit.*]

Act V, Scene I

[HIPPOLYTUS, ARICIA.]

ARICIA: Nay, my lord, when on the brink of
    Danger thus you stand exposed, would you
    Restrain your speech and leave your father
    In a treacherous error? O cruel youth,
    My streaming eyes have lost
    Their power o'er your heart, – yet return to Theseus
    And reveal the crime of Phedra. – Quit Aricia
    And leave her to her sorrows; but e'er you go
    Defend your honour, and force your parent
    To revoke his oaths, and save thy precious life.
    – 'Tis not yet too late; why stand you
    Thus with downcast look, and leave the
    Cruel Phedra free to accuse you in your absence?
HIPPOLYTUS: Alas, Aricia!
    Can I then expose the violator of my father's bed,
    And by a sincere recital of Phedra's shame,
    Spread an ignoble blush o'er a parent's
    Face! forbid it heaven. To you and the Gods alone
    This odious mystery is divulged; from you my
    Love would not conceal the crime; why then
    Suspect thou art no longer dear to Hippolytus?
    Forget then what thou hast heard, nor let
    The horrible tale e'er again be told, but
    With firm reliance let us rest on the goodness
    Of the immortal power, whose equity will
    Justify my wrongs. Phedra cannot avoid
    The ignominy that hereafter waits her.
    Mean while, if e'er Hippolytus was dear
    To Aricia, let her quit this hateful bondage
    And fly with him from this impious spot,
    Where virtue breathes an envenomed air,

1. The last few lines are omitted in the 1776 edition.
2. The 1776 edition includes further lines, not found in the original.

And dare not shew her face in safety.
Come, be the kind companion of my flight;
Come haste with me to leave this fatal shore.
Argos stretches out its arms, and Sparta calls us
To seek for shelter in their peaceful coasts;
To our friends, let us take our just complaints;
Let not Phedra profit from our fall,
And drive us from my father's throne,
To give the spoils of our estates to her son.[1]
Haste then, while our friends expectant wait,
And all is ready for our quick departure.
  – Why does my fair one hesitate, when e'en
Her interest should inspire her with courage.
  – Fear'st thou to take Hippolytus for thy guide?
ARICIA: Alas! how blest would such an exile make me;
United with Hippolytus, I could live
Forgotten by the rest of mortals. Full well I know the
Most rigid laws of honour would not blame
My escaping from your father's hands. Flight
Is permitted those who would escape the tyrant's yoke.
  – But, my lord, my own honour, Aricia's fame must
Not be sullied with the reproach, of escaping with
Hippolytus e'er hymen's torch –
HIPPOLYTUS: Believe me, my Aricia, your honour is too
Precious to Hippolytus, e'er to suffer reproach to
Wound it. By a nobler motive
Urged, I hither came. Quit then this hateful spot
And fly with Hippolytus. The nuptial bonds of hymen
Shall make Aricia mine, the priest expectant waits.
  – Near to Trezenium's gates, and midst the tombs
Those ancient sepulchres of my godlike ancestors,
There stands a sacred temple, formidable to perjured
Villains, where mortals dare not swear in vain.
There the perfidious wretch receives a sudden check
And meets inevitable death. – The lyar there must not
Profane the sacred edifice with his treacherous tongue.
  – Thither, will Hippolytus lead his lovely fair,
And by a solemn vow confirm his plighted faith.
The temple's godhead shall witness all my vows
And we shall pray for his paternal care.
The most sacred gods shall be invoked:
Chaste Diana, majestic Juno,
And all the gods shall bear witness to my love

_____

1. These lines are omitted from the 1776 edition.

And lend their strength to my holy vows.[1]
ARICIA: See, the king approaches, fly then, my lord; a moment
    Will I remain behind, to conceal thy flight.
    Fly then, but leave me some faithful guide
    Who shall conduct me to the sacred temple.   [*Exit* HIPPOLYTUS.]

Act V, Scene II

[THESEUS, ARICIA.]

THESEUS: Ye righteous powers, restore my troubled mind
    And reveal this mystery which so sore disturbs me.
ARICIA: See all's prepared, Ismene, and made ready for our flight.
THESEUS: Your colour changes and you seem perplexed.
    Was not Hippolytus this moment with you?[2]
ARICIA: He was, my lord, and came to take a last farewell.
THESEUS: Ah! thy beauty has subdued that proud rebellious heart
    And found the means to wound Hippolytus.[3]
ARICIA: My lord, I scorn a falsity, and boldly own 'tis true,
    Your honour'd son, inheriting nought of his father's
    Hate towards me, has never used me like a slave.
THESEUS: I understand you, madam, he has sworn an
    Eternal love, and plighted his perjured vows.
    But, Aricia, think not his inconstant heart
    Is fixed, to others he has sworn as much.
ARICIA: He, Sire?
THESEUS: You know his crime, and can permit his baneful
    Words to sink into your heart.
ARICIA: And, how can you, my lord, permit such
    Cruel malaspersions to blacken o'er a life so spotless?
    Know you so little of his untainted soul?
    Can you so weakly distinguish between vice and innocence?
    From your eye alone, the hateful cloud of slander
    Prevents the sight of his brilliant virtues.
    Oh! too credulous monarch, repent e'er 'tis too late,
    Repent your murderous prayers. Tremble, my lord,
    Tremble, lest you have not merited the hate of
    Heaven yet so greatly, but it will grant your wishes.
    The wrath of the Almighty Gods, sometimes
    Receives the victims that we offer them,

---

1. These lines are omitted in the 1776 edition.
2. These two lines are mistranslated in the 1776 edition.
3. These two lines are mistranslated in the 1776 edition.

And their gifts often prove the rigorous
Punishment of our mortal crimes.
THESEUS: In vain you varnish o'er his incestuous aim,
    Your love, too strong for such an ungrateful villain,
    Only serves to blind you from the truth.
    But, madam, I do not rashly judge, I have
    Credible, irreproachable proofs; have not
    I seen the heartfelt tears stream from the eyes
    Of the chaste, the innocent –
ARICIA: Take care, my lord. Your invincible hands
    have freed mankind from innumerable monsters:
    But not all are yet destroyed. One you still
    permit to live – But your son forbids me speak.
    Mindful of his regard for you,
    I should too much distress him if I said more.
    In deference to his wishes, I withdraw,
    Before I break my silence.[1]   [*Exit* ARICIA.]

Act V, Scene III

[THESEUS.]

THESEUS: What can she mean? And what is hidden behind her speech
    So oft begun and then broke off again?[2]
    But no wonder my mortal foe should join to set me on the rack.
    Hippolytus and she would disguise the crime.
    It must be so. But yet, in spite of all my prayers,
    Some plaintive voice pleads for him at my heart,
    A secret compassion for his fate afflicts and wounds me.
    – Let us again interrogate Oenone.
    This mysterious crime must be better cleared.
    Guards, bring Oenone here, and see she is alone.[3]

Act V, Scene IV

[THESEUS, PANOPE.]

PANOPE: My lord, the queen, agitated by some

---

1. The last part of the speech is mistranslated in the 1776 edition.
2. This line is mistranslated in the 1776 edition.
3. This line is mistranslated in the 1776 edition.

Inward grief, appears to meditate a rash design.
Despair strongly painted on her face,
The hand of death is already on her.
Oenone too, whom late the queen discharged,
Has plunged into the sea.
None knows what drove her to this frantic deed;
And now the waves hide her for ever from our sight.[1]
THESEUS: What do I hear?
PANOPE: Her rashness has not calmed the mind of Phedra,
Trouble and despair increase on her. Sometimes
To asswage her secret grief, she clasps her children
To her breast, while the tears in torrents flow.
Then again, she drives them from her, with
The utmost horror, and wild with despair
No longer knows her attendants. Thrice has
She written, then sudden changing her mind,
Thrice has she torn the unfinished letter.
Deign to see her, and to help her, we beg you.[2]
THESEUS: Heavens! what can all this mean?
Oenone dead, and Phedra ready to expire?
Ah! I fear I have been too hasty.
Fly! call back my son, e'er my prayers are granted.
Let him defend himself against his accusers;
And thou, O Neptune! do not too hastily accomplish,
Thy fatal favours: I perhaps, have given too
Easy faith to Oenone's words, and rashly
Lifted my murdering hands, against my son.
Oh Hippolytus! what torture wrings thy
Father's breast.

Act V, Scene V

[THESEUS, THERAMENES.]

THESEUS: Theramenes, where is my son? where hast
Thou left Hippolytus? to thy virtuous care,
I entrusted him in his earliest years:
And – but what – speak – why flow those tears?
– I dread thy answer, – yet speak,
Thou good old man, where is Hippolytus?
THERAMENES: O tardy, idle concern.

1. These lines are omitted in the 1776 edition.
2. These lines are omitted in the 1776 edition.

Futile affection. Alas! he is no more
THESEUS: Ye Gods.
THERAMENES: These eyes, these streaming
    Eyes saw Hippolytus perish,
    The best and most innocent of mortals.
THESEUS: My son, no more?
    Yet why, ye powerful Gods, why so quick
    To grant my prayers, when I was about to embrace him?
    – But tell me, Theramenes,
    What sudden bolt destroyed him.[1]
THERAMENES: Scarce had we left Trezenium's gates,
    He, mounted in his car, while his silent
    Attendants around him ranged,
    Imitated his silence and were dumb with grief.
    Pensive he bent his course towards Mycenes,
    His coursers' reins neglected lay,
    While his folded arms clasped his sorrowful breast;
    His proud, his stately steeds, who before were
    Full of vigour and chearfully obeyed their master's voice,
    With heavy look and heads bent down to earth
    Seemed to feel their master's woe.
    In this solemnity proceeding, a horrid
    Cry issued from the waves, the air was troubled,
    And from the bosom of the earth, another voice returned
    The formidable sound. Struck with amaze,
    Our blood congealed within our veins,
    And the attentive steeds bristled up their hairs,
    Affrighted at the uncommon noise;
    Presently, from the waves with hideous
    Bubblings reared a humid mountain,
    Which approached towards us.
    Bursting in our sight; a furious monster
    Issued from the foaming surge,
    Half wild bull, half fierce dragon, large
    Branching horns sprang from his hideous front;
    His body covered o'er with jaundiced scales,
    While the earth trembled with his
    Hideous roaring. Heaven, with horror saw
    The monster, the earth was moved, the air infected
    At its sight, and the wave which brought it to the
    Shore returned affrighted back. All except
    Hippolytus flew to a neighbouring temple. But
    Your son stopt his affrighted steeds, and seizing

---

1. Some lines are omitted from the beginning of the scene in the 1776 edition.

His unerring spear, darted it at the monster.
Raging with the wound, he roaring fell before
The horses feet, opened its fiery mouth and
Enveloped them in smoke, in
Fire and in blood. Enraged, affrighted at this scene,
And deaf to Hippolytus's cries, they no longer obeyed
The bridle's check, but stained the bit with their bloody foam.
In all the tumult, some say, they saw
A god pricking their dusty flanks with pointed darts.
They hurried impetuous on,
O'er rocks where their terror carried them.
The car, no longer able to support the shock,
Broke in shivers, and Hippolytus fell, entangled
In the reins. – I saw him, excuse my grief
My lord, – I saw your unfortunate son
Dragged by his steeds, his hands so long had fed;
His voice that called them only added to their fright.
Along the craggy precipe they flew, his body all
O'er blood, exhibited to our view, a terrible appearance;
The plains echoed with our cries of woe.
At length they stopt, near the ancient tombs
Where the cold relics of his royal forbears are kept.
I and the guards hastened
To the fatal spot; the rocks were tinctured with
His blood, his hair, and all his body dropping
With the gore, – he heard my voice, and reaching
Out his hand, his eyes half closed by death,
He faintly said:
"Heaven! Theramenes has taken away a life,
Thou knowst was guiltless,
Let Aricia be your future care, guard her from ev'ry ill;
And oh! my friend, if e'er my father should be undeceived,
Tell him the misfortune of his wronged son,
That's all I ask, with this dying breath, to appease
My plaintive shade, he treats his captive not severe,
And restores her." – He could say no more.
And of the expiring hero, only a mangled corpse remained,
A sad victim of the anger of the gods,
So changed, his own father would not know him.[1]
THESEUS: O, my son; thou dearest hope of my aged years!
    O, inexorable gods! Ye have indeed too punctually
    Heard an enraged parent.
THERAMENES: No sooner was Hippolytus expired, e'er

---

1. A number of lines are omitted from this speech in the 1776 edition.

Aricia came, fled from your anger, to
Accept your son as a faithful spouse;
But, as she nearer came, the red and smoking grass
Struck her with surprize; but when she saw
(Good Heavens! what an object for a bride:)
Hippolytus extended, pale and breathless,
Who can paint her looks? Awhile she
Doubted it was the hero she adored;
Called for Hippolytus, with anxious voice,
'Till at length, too certain of his death,
She accused the gods, and throwing herself
On the mangled body, clasp'd it to her breast,
till at last o'ercome, and her spirits sunk, she fell
A lifeless corps by Hippolytus's side.
Ismene, all in tears, kneels down beside her
And calls her back to life, a life of endless pain.
And I have come, cursing the very daylight,
To tell you of a hero's last wish
And to discharge the bitter embassy
He entrusted to me as he died.
This, Sir, is the fatal catastrophe – but see
His mortal enemy approaches.[1]

Scene the Last

[THESEUS, PHEDRA, THERAMENES, PANOPE *and* GUARDS.]

THESEUS: Now, Madam, your victory is compleat, my son
    Is dead. Oh! how my soul's alarmed with doubt, and suspicion,
    Pleads his excuse within my heart. Accept your victim,
    Phedra, and whether his death was just or criminal,
    Never! Oh never! let me be undeceived, since
    You accused him of the guilt; his crime alone
    Will furnish me with cause sufficient for my tears,
    Without more enquiries which might
    Only heap greater sorrows on my head;
    Leave me to deplore his fate, and avoid his
    Bleeding image, far from these hateful shores.
    – But whither shall I fly? – persecuted with the
    Dreadful thought, no place can obliterate him
    From my mind. – Besides all nature seems

1. A number of lines are omitted from this speech in the 1776 edition.

In arms against my cruelty. – My fame, the
Honours I have gained, conspire to punish me.
Had I been less known, I might have concealed
My disgrace the better.
The favours the Gods have granted, I view with hatred,
And bewail their murderous gifts;
Nor will I further importune them with my useless prayers.
Give me what they may,
What they have taken all else outweighs.[1]

PHEDRA: No Theseus, 'tis time to clear this horrid mystery,
    Your son was innocent, and has been basely wrong'd.

THESEUS: Ah! say'st thou so,
    Then am I compleatly wretched. – Think'st thou
    Monster! thou, on whose virtue I relied, and for thee
    Prayed the gods to hurt their vengeance on him,
    Think'st thou to avoid, –

PHEDRA: My time is precious, – hear me, Theseus,
    'Twas me, your Phedra, whom you deem'd so virtuous,
    That with profane, and incestuous eye, looked on Hippolytus;
    Heaven in my breast raised this fatal flame,
    The detestable Oenone was the cause of the rest.
    She, fearing lest Hippolytus should declare to thee,
    My shame, which he detested: abused my confidence
    And flattered a woman's weakness. She
    Accused him of the crime, and raised your indignation.
    – But Oenone has been punished; fleeing my anger,
    She has found beneath the waves too gentle a fate.
    E'er now mine would have ended by the sword;
    Had not my remorse urged me,
    To explain this horrid secret.
    I resolved to choose a lingering path to death,
    Confessing first my penitence to you.
    A poison brought to Athens by Medea
    I have instilled into my burning veins.
    – Ah! I feel the wish'd
    For moment is at hand – the baneful poison
    Trickles thro' my veins, and spreads an unknown
    Coldness o'er my heart – before my eyes a cloud
    With dimness hangs, and gives back to the Sun and to my consort
    That purity which they sullied.   *[Dies.]*

PANOPE: She expires!

THESEUS: And let the remembrance of so dark a crime
    Expire with her. Alas! Crimes too late revealed.

---

1. A number of lines are omitted from this speech in the 1776 edition.

But let us hence, and with the blood of my
Unfortunate son, mingle my flowing tears:
Let us endeavour to expiate my horrid vow,
By rendering his corpse the honours which it merits.
And to appease the anger of his shade
May his beloved, despite her brothers' crimes,
Be as a daughter to me from this day.[1]

Finis.

---

1. A number of lines have been changed in the 1776 edition.

The Miser

MOLIÈRE

INTRODUCTION

Molière's life is shrouded in almost as much mystery as Shakespeare's. In an age when people had begun to place some value on collections of books, manuscripts and letters, it is strange that not one single manuscript of Molière's, or even a letter of any significance, remains. It is as if someone had deliberately resolved to eradicate all trace of his private and professional life. The story of Molière's life can therefore only be pieced together from a few fragments of documentary evidence;[1] for the most part it is dependent upon the anecdotal evidence of his contemporaries.

The bare facts, such as we know them, are these. Molière was born in Paris in 1622: his father, Jean Poquelin, was a wealthy merchant upholsterer. Molière was baptised with the same name as his father on 15 January 1622; two years later, after the birth of another son, Molière's name was changed to Jean-Baptiste Poquelin. Between 1633 and 1639 Jean-Baptiste was educated at the Jesuit Collège de Clermont, one of the leading schools in Paris at the time, which also catered for the sons of the nobility. (These were separated from the other pupils by a barrier of gilded wood.) Molière's father purchased an office at court in 1631 as a Groom Upholsterer of the Royal Bedchamber: in 1637 he obtained the reversion of this office for his son, and in 1642 ceded the office to Jean-Baptiste. At this point, Jean-Baptiste was studying law at university and was

---

1. The existing documentary evidence has been gathered together in G. Mongrédien, *Recueil des textes et documents du XVIIe siècle relatifs à Molière*, 2 vols (Paris: CNRS, 1966).

probably showing early signs of excessive interest in the theatre. His
father may have hoped to counteract this interest by giving his son
the privilege of an office at court. If that was the intention, then the
plan failed.

On 16 June 1643, having resigned his office at court, and obtained
his share of his deceased mother's estate, Molière signed articles of
association with members of the Béjart family (Joseph, Geneviève
and Madeleine) to found a theatre company called l'Illustre Théâtre,
to be directed by Madeleine Béjart. What exactly made this well-
educated and well-to-do son of a wealthy merchant family give up
all hopes of social advancement and embrace the uncertainties of life
in the contemporary theatre is simply not known. What is clear is
that the decision was not taken lightly. Having chosen the path of a
theatrical career, Molière never deviated from it for one instant for
the remainder of his life.

The newly formed company decided to challenge the two
established theatres in Paris at the Hôtel de Bourgogne and the
Marais. They set about renting a 'real' tennis court, Les Mestayers, in
the rue Mazarine, located on the left bank of the Seine. The rent was
high, 1900 livres, payable monthly in advance.[1] The adaptation and
refurbishment of the tennis court was not completed until January
1644. Even when the theatre eventually opened, the running costs
were high and were never matched by the takings. This meant that
the theatre company had soon accumulated significant debts.

In July 1644 Jean-Baptiste took the professional name of Molière
(this was common practice in the contemporary French theatre
where actors often chose a variety of exotic or pastoral names such
as Bellerose, Floridor, Montdory) and was made director of L'Illustre
Théâtre. Under his leadership, the company decided to vacate their
original tennis court theatre and to move across the Seine to a more
fashionable location, near the Marais district. They took out a lease
on the Croix Noire tennis court on the Quai des Célestins, opposite
l'Île St Louis: here the rent was even higher, 2400 livres, and there
were further costs of adaptation and refurbishment.[2] All too soon,
the budget of the enterprise had spiralled out of control and Molière
briefly found himself imprisoned for debt. The company was
wound up and all their remaining belongings, including their
theatre wardrobe, were pawned. Molière left Paris in October 1645,

1. See G. Mongrédien, *Daily Life in the French Theatre at the Time of Molière* (London:
   George Allen & Unwin, 1969) p. 84.
2. Ibid., p. 85.

accompanied by Madeleine Béjart who was to be his companion, mistress and colleague for the next thirteen years of life in provincial France.

They began their new careers as wandering players in the troupe of the Duc d'Epernon, which was at the time directed by Charles Dufresne. The Duc d'Epernon was Governor of Guyenne (the ancient province of Aquitaine). Typically, a troupe protected by a nobleman like this would be expected to give a number of command performances each year for their patron and would then be free to tour in and around the area over which their patron had jurisdiction. This meant, in Molière's case, that command performances for the duke were given at his castle in Cadillac (south-east of Bordeaux) or for his court at Agen (further south-east along the river Garonne). These were then supplemented by tours to a range of towns and cities in and often beyond the province of Aquitaine: Toulouse, Albi and Carcassonne in 1647; Nantes, Fontenay-le-Comte and Poitiers in 1648; Toulouse, Montpellier and Carcasonne 1649; Narbonne and Agen in 1650.[1]

In July 1650, this relatively stable, if arduous pattern of work was broken when the actors lost the protection of their patron. Because of the troubles of the Fronde in Bordeaux, the Duc d'Epernon was ousted from his role as Governor of Guyenne. At this point, Molière, with the support of Madeleine Béjart, was made director of the troupe and the decision was taken to seek the support of the Estates of Languedoc. This ancient assembly of the three estates (the church, the barons and the towns) met for lengthy deliberations each year with the king's commissioners to determine the fiscal dues and contributions to be levied within the area of Languedoc. The Estates' meetings revolved between major centres: Montpellier, Béziers, Narbonne, Carcassonne and Pézenas. The Illustre Théâtre had already performed for members of the Estates, in Montpellier in 1649. In October 1650, the troupe spent three months in the delightful town of Pézenas entertaining the Estates for which they received the generous sum of 4000 livres.[2] The following year, they were present at the opening of the Estates in Carcassonne.

However, the early 1650s were times of unrest. The Fronde had brought bloodshed and upheaval to Aquitaine and Provence, with less dramatic acts of rebellion in the Languedoc. Molière and his

1. For a more detailed account of Molière's tours in the provinces, see Claude Alberge, *Le voyage de Molière en Languedoc* (Presses du Languedoc, 1988) and Jessie Mahoudeau, *Molière au Pays d'Oc* (Montpellier, 1973).
2. See Mahoudeau, *Molière au Pays d'Oc*, pp. 12–13.

theatre troupe decided to travel to less troubled areas for the next few seasons. They are known to have visited Poitiers, Grenoble and Lyon in 1652 and to have spent a whole season in Lyon in the following year 1653. Towards the end of 1653 they returned to the Languedoc where calm had been restored. At this point their fortunes took a distinct turn for the better.

Armand de Bourbon, Prince de Conti (a prince of the royal blood), had been persuaded to lead the anti-royalist Fronde in Bordeaux (ousting Molière's former patron as Governor of Guyenne). Having been defeated by royalist forces and briefly imprisoned, he was given permission to take up residence in a château (la Grange des Prés) owned by his family on the outskirts of Pézenas in the summer of 1653. Soon he was to be pardoned and made Governor of Languedoc. He had already installed his mistress, Mme de Calvimont, in the château, and she wanted a troupe of players to divert her. The prince instructed his adviser the abbé (and Marquis) Daniel de Cosnac to send for a suitable troupe. Cosnac duly obeyed the prince's instructions and commanded Molière to travel to la Grange des Prés, only to find himself thwarted by Mme de Calvimont's own initiative in inviting a rival troupe. After further intrigue, Molière's troupe were finally invited to perform for the prince. Cosnac continues the narrative in his memoirs:

> In the opinion of Mme de Calvimont, and therefore of course in the opinion of the Prince de Conti, this troupe was not a success at its first performance, even though in the opinion of all the other spectators it was far superior to Cormier's troupe both in the quality of the actors and the magnificence of their costumes. Some days later they gave another performance, and Sarrasin [the Prince's secretary], singing their praises, managed to persuade the Prince de Conti to engage Molière's troupe rather than that of Cormier. Initially he had followed and supported them because of me; but then, having fallen in love with Mlle Du Parc, he thought to pursue his own advantage. He even won over Mme de Calvimont, and not only engineered the dismissal of Cormier's troupe, but also obtained a subvention for Molière's troupe.[1]

Thus it was that Molière's troupe acquired their new patron and came to enjoy several years of prosperity at the château of la Grange

1. Daniel de Cosnac, *Mémoires*, vol. I (Paris: Jules Renouard, 1852) p. 127. Quoted in Alberge, *Le voyage de Molière en Languedoc*, pp. 150–1.

des Prés and in the town of Pézenas. Cosnac's vivid account, doubly important because of the dearth of other contemporary documentary evidence, indicates the precarious dividing line between success and failure for a provincial touring company seeking aristocratic patronage. Molière's troupe finally prevailed because an important figure in the Prince de Conti's entourage fell in love with one of Molière's actresses, Thérèse Du Parc (who was later to become Racine's mistress). Cosnac's account also makes it clear that Molière's troupe included outstanding actors whose costumes were magnificent. The rigours of touring made it difficult to transport scenic effects, but to compensate for this Molière had obviously built up a splendid wardrobe of costumes over the years. Finally, Cosnac's reference to a subvention underlines the importance of aristocratic patronage; it not only brought social acceptance but also the possibility of financial security.[1]

Molière's performances for the Prince de Conti at la Grange des Prés and at subsequent meetings of the Estates in Montpellier and Pézenas gave him the opportunity of regular contact with a man of the highest social rank, which was later to stand him in good stead in his various dealings with Louis XIV. The prince and his entourage also provided him with useful role models for his later work as a playwright. Echoes of the rivalry of men such as Cosnac and Sarrasin can be found in *Le Misanthrope,* while traces of the opinionated vacuousness of Mme de Calvimont can be detected in *Les Précieuses ridicules.* The conversion of the Prince de Conti in 1657 from a pleasure-loving libertine to an austere religious fanatic provided Molière with the raw material for two major figures, Don Juan in the play of the same title and Orgon in *Tartuffe.* Tartuffe himself was in part modelled on another figure from the prince's close circle of advisers: the oily Guilleragues who became the prince's secretary after the sudden death of Sarrasin in 1654. Molière made good use of this period of prosperity, writing a number of one-act farces which could be presented as entertaining afterpieces, following the performance of a tragedy or tragi-comedy. Many of these, based on *commedia dell'arte* scenarios, have been lost but some were kept in the troupe's repertoire and provided the starting point for Molière's subsequent career as a playwright.

The years of fun, feasting and high-spirited performance for the

1. Cosnac's account also makes it clear that Molière played in the 'theatre' at Pézenas, probably the town's real tennis court, which makes this semi-derelict building in Pézenas the one remaining tennis court structure where Molière may have presented plays to a fee-paying public.

Prince de Conti between 1653 and 1657 were followed, after the
Prince's spectacular conversion, by a renewed period of uncertainty.
The search for a new patron took Molière from Lyon to Rouen
in Normandy where his troupe won the support of the Governor of
Normandy. However, by the summer of 1658, friends were advising
Molière to return to Paris. In July 1658, in preparation for this move,
Madeleine Béjart took out a lease for the Marais tennis court in Paris.
Meanwhile, however, Molière had succeeded in negotiating an even
more impressive return to the capital city he had left in such
disarray in 1645. In Paris he made renewed contact with Cosnac,
who had left the service of the Prince de Conti and had become the
almoner for Monsieur, the king's brother. Cosnac clearly remained a
firm admirer of Molière's work and was quite willing to persuade
Monsieur to become Molière's new patron. On 24 October 1658,
Molière's troupe gave their first performance for their new patron in
the Hall of the Gardes du Louvre. For this glittering occasion,
the king was also present. After presenting Corneille's tragedy
Nicomède, Molière humbly requested permission to perform one of
the short farces he had written in the provinces, *Le Docteur amoureux*.
The king, his brother and his court were enchanted: Paris had not
seen such exuberant farce for over twenty years. Molière's return
was a triumphant one.

Permission was given for Molière's troupe to share, with the
Italian players, the Théâtre du Petit Bourbon (built alongside the
Louvre). On 2 November, Molière opened there with two further
comedies he had written in the provinces, *L'Étourdi* and *Le Dépit
amoureux*. Later that month, having worked at a furious pace, he
presented his first comedy written specifically for Paris, *Les
Précieuses ridicules*, which was enthusiastically received by the city.
Molière's success stirred up jealousy among the two rival troupes in
Paris, who made attempts to poach some of his best actors. But
Molière enjoyed the unqualified loyalty and support of his
colleagues. The only player subsequently to leave his troupe was the
actress Thérèse Du Parc, whose affair with Racine meant that she felt
obliged to leave when Racine withdrew his work and gave it to the
Hôtel de Bourgogne. Molière also enjoyed the favour of the king.
Not only was he invited to perform at court, but he was given help
of a more tangible kind when the Théâtre du Petit Bourbon had to
be demolished in 1659 to enlarge the Louvre. Louis ordered the
Superintendent of the royal buildings to refurbish Richelieu's
former theatre in the Palais-Royal, in order to provide a new

permanent home for Molière's troupe, which was subsequently installed there on a rent-free basis.

For the remaining twelve years of his life, Molière continued his role as actor-manager of his company which, from 1665, acquired Louis as its patron and became known as La Troupe du Roi. He also embarked on an intensive programme of playwriting, completing some thirty-three plays at breakneck speed. Racine's desertion to the Hôtel de Bourgogne in 1665 meant that thereafter Molière's main rivals enjoyed the privilege of performing Racine's new work as well as the majority of Corneille's new plays. The dearth of other writers of quality meant that Molière himself had to shoulder the burden of providing a steady stream of new plays for the Palais-Royal. In addition, Molière was regularly called upon to write and direct a whole variety of entertainments and ballet-comedies for Louis's court at Versailles, St Germain, Fontainebleau and Chambord. The prestige and financial rewards associated with this activity were considerable. But it all involved a crippling amount of work which undermined and eventually wrecked Molière's health.

In 1662 the outstanding success of *L'École des femmes* roused the jealousy of the rival actors at the Hôtel de Bourgogne who openly began to intrigue against Molière and to accuse him of impiety. That same year Molière married Armande Béjart, who was twenty years younger than him: to this day it is still not known whether she was the sister or daughter of Madeleine Béjart. However, his enemies in Paris at the time were swift to accuse him of incest.

In May 1664 Molière performed an early version of *Tartuffe* in three acts for the king at Versailles. Louis greatly enjoyed the play but immediately forbad any public presentation. Astute and pragmatic as ever, Louis realised that the play would give grave offence to the powerful religious zealots of the period, and in particular to the influential Company of the Blessed Sacrament. Molière's former patron, the Prince de Conti, had become Secretary and hence effectively the head of this powerful organisation in 1660 and had already conducted a series of witch-hunts against individuals in the Languedoc.[1] The influence of this powerful cabal extended from the church into the army, the magistrature and the court. Louis was not prepared at this stage of his reign to risk antagonising influential figures in the church and at court. Molière

---

1. Racine describes these in a letter to his cousin Nicolas Vitart from Uzès on 25 July 1662. See *Œuvres complètes*, p. 493.

wrote the first of his humble *placets* (petitions) to the king requesting permission to perform the play in public, but to no avail. Louis continued to support him (he even agreed to act as godfather to Molière's first child) and did not object to private performances of the play in the houses and châteaux of the great and the good, but he would not permit a public performance of the play.

However, the damage had already been done. The Company of the Blessed Sacrament were outraged by a play that they saw as a direct attack on themselves: the Prince de Conti may even have recognised a refracted image of his own 'conversion' in the play. From this point, the Company waged an unceasing and vitriolic campaign against Molière. His response was to write another play, *Dom Juan,* in 1665 which included further diatribes against religious hypocrites and fraudulent zealots. The furious response of the Prince de Conti and the cabal meant that this play too was forbidden after only a few performances.

In August 1667, Molière made a second unsuccessful attempt to perform *Tartuffe* in Paris under the title of *The Impostor.* This time the play was forbidden by Lamoignon, President of the Parliament of Paris, acting on behalf of the king who was absent at the siege of Lille. Lamoignon was a member of the Company of the Blessed Sacrament: his opposition was therefore only to be expected. Molière wrote a second *placet* to the King, but to no avail. The play was forbidden under pain of excommunication. This was a low ebb in Molière's professional life. His difficulties were compounded by problems in his personal life. He had already suffered long periods of illness; now, growing marital discord led to the decision to live apart from his young and frivolous wife.

L'Avare/The Miser

For some time Molière had been working on a new play, *L'Avare,* which was finally ready for performance in September 1668. Although the play revolved around the issue of Harpagon's miserliness, another central theme must be seen as something of a self-critique, namely Harpagon's folly in attempting to marry a much younger woman, Mariane, who is already attracted to his son, Cléante. Each act adds its own twist to these parallel lines of interest until the action is brought to an impasse in the fifth act which is only resolved by the arrival of a benevolent newcomer, Anselme.

For Molière, as for the painter Goya, the sleep of reason produces monsters. Harpagon has become a monster because he has relinquished all trace of rationality in his lust for money. There is no longer any part of his life that is responsive to rational judgement. He has become a self-obsessed monomaniac. His two children still deeply regret the death of their mother, which suggests that she at least had had a tempering effect on Harpagon's behaviour. Without her restraining influence, Harpagon's passion for money assumes grotesque proportions. In addition, his lack of judgement extends into every sphere of family life. He attempts to rule his household with absolute authority but with none of the responsibility that comes with authority. This means that his treatment of his children is harsh and unfeeling, while his treatment of his servants and his horses (whom he has almost starved to death) is appalling. His most striking lack of judgement comes when he decides to marry a girl of the same age as his daughter. Here Molière's satire takes on a personal and savage note. The thought that a young girl, in the bloom of her youth, would find anything vaguely attractive in a short-sighted miser in his sixties, with a chesty cough, is plainly ridiculous. It is only economic pressure that forces Mariane to consider such a match in the first place. Its outcome would be a disaster for both parties, as Molière to his cost had discovered. He had succumbed to the very same temptation he depicts in the character of Harpagon and had paid a very dear price for his own lack of judgement. It is perhaps this personal involvement in Harpagon's folly that enables him to show Harpagon as at times poignant in his stupidity, with something almost touching in his total humiliation at the end of the play. Molière knew only too well what it felt like to be humiliated because of one's own folly.

Harpagon's son Cléante is no paragon of virtue. His love of fine clothes, gaming and good living have brought him to a sorry financial state at the beginning of the play. Here too there are perhaps echoes of Molière's own life when, as a young man, his financially ruinous decision to embark on a theatrical career must have brought him into conflict with a cautious father. Otherwise, the young people in the play are surprisingly dutiful, given Harpagon's uncaring and provocative actions towards them. They are not prepared to step beyond the bounds of accepted patterns of behaviour, which means that their primary concern is to obtain Harpagon's consent. Viewed as a whole, this is a play in which the duties and obligations of family life are taken very seriously indeed; what is satirised is Harpagon's failure to observe the responsibilities of family life that are freely accepted by his children and their chosen partners.

As so often in Molière's plays, there is one figure whose views are balanced and rational and whose responses provide a yardstick of sound behaviour against which the conduct of the other characters may be measured. Here that figure is Anselme. Interestingly he too was willing to contemplate marrying a much younger woman, but only on the basis of freely given consent. When he discovers the identity of his long-lost children, he at once behaves with a proper fatherly concern for their well-being and places their happiness first. Unlike Harpagon, Anselme has a natural authority which is grounded on a full and proper acceptance of his responsibilities as a father and a husband.

The remaining characters in the play are delightfully depicted variants of classical stereotypes, such as the go-between (Frosine), the quick-witted servant (La Flèche) and the foolish servant (Maître Jacques). They are deftly drawn and offer considerable scope to comic actors. All the parts in the play require comic, and at times farcical acting of great precision. But this was something at which Molière's troupe excelled. Harpagon, who is on stage for most of the action, is a part requiring virtuoso acting skills which Molière possessed in abundance. It was therefore a natural choice for him to play the part. Furthermore, by playing the part of Harpagon himself, Molière would have established the dominant rhythm and tone of the piece for the other actors. In a stroke of irony that would not have been lost on his contemporaries, Harpagon's daughter Élise was played by Molière's wife, who was indeed young enough to be his own daughter.

The whole action of the play revolves around Harpagon in an almost circular pattern, as the consequences of his folly are traced out in a series of concentric variations. No significant development or change takes place in Harpagon's behaviour, which remains utterly predictable throughout the play. This makes for an episodic rather than a linear structural pattern, whose cumulative effect is a gradual build towards an impasse that can only be resolved by the arrival of a stranger (Anselme) acting as a *deus ex machina*. The setting for the play is simply a house in Paris. The stage needs very little scenery, though the action requires a few props and some items of furniture. The minimal effects required suggest that Molière had not forgotten the lessons of visual economy learnt during his long years of touring in the provinces.

L'Avare was a probing and disconcerting piece that touched on difficult and even painful issues relating to family life. Its satire was both general and personal. The general satire showed the way that obsessive behaviour can undermine the very fabric of family life, turning a widowed father into the enemy of his children. There was also a political edge to the general satire which suggested that any demand for absolute loyalty brought with it clear obligations and responsibilities If these were neglected, the ordered stability of family and social life could be threatened. This was not a message that would endear itself to those who believed in absolute political authority. The personal satire directed at older men lusting after younger women and attempting to use their financial status to buy sexual compliance was an equally uncomfortable topic for a society dominated by patriarchal assumptions. Even the ending of the play, in which Harpagon is left totally isolated because of his obsessive folly, is both uncomfortable and disconcerting. It is therefore perhaps not surprising that *L'Avare*, despite the brilliant qualities of Molière's writing and acting, achieved no more than a modest success when first performed in Paris in September 1668.

The Miser

A
Comedy

New done into ENGLISH from the
FRENCH of MOLIERE.
By Mr. OZELL.

With the Original *French* opposite to the
English; and Both more correctly Printed
than any that have yet appear'd.
Highly Useful and Entertaining for the LEARNERS
of either LANGUAGE.

LONDON
Printed for B. Lintot: And Sold by H.Lintot,
at the *Cross-Keys*, against St *Dunstan's* Church in
Fleet-Street. M.DCC.XXXII.
(Price One Shilling)

Dramatis Personae

HARPAGON, the Miser, Father to CLEANTHES and ELIZA, and in Love with
  MARIANA.
CLEANTHES, his Son, MARIANA's Lover.
ELIZA, HARPAGON's Daughter, in love with VALERIO.
VALERIO, Son to ANSELMO; in Love with ELIZA.
MARIANA, in Love with CLEANTHES, and beloved by HARPAGON.
ANSELMO, Father to VALERIO and MARIANA.
FROSINA, a Woman of Intrigue.
Mr SIMON, a Broker.
Mr JAMES, Cook and Coachman to HARPAGON.
LA FLECHE, CLEANTHES's Servant.
CLAUDIA, HARPAGON's Servant.
BRINDAVOIN, LA MERLUCHE, HARPAGON's Lacqueys.
A Commissary and his Clerk.

SCENE at PARIS.

Act I, Scene I

[VALERIO, ELIZA.]

VALERIO: How! my Charming *Eliza*, turn melancholy just after the obliging
    Assurances you have so kindly given me of your Faith? In the very
    midst of my Joy I hear you sigh! Tell me; is it for grief that you have
    made me happy? Do you repent of that Engagement which the Ardor
    of my Flames has extorted from you?
ELIZA: No, *Valerio*, I can never repent of any thing I do for you: Too soft a
    Power hurries me on to do it, nor am I ev'n able to wish that things were
    undone. But, to tell you the truth, the Consequences give me some
    Uneasiness, and I'm afraid I love you a little more than I ought.
VALERIO: What Apprehensions, *Eliza*, can you have from your Kindness to
    me? What can ye fear?
ELIZA: Alas! A Hundred things at once; The Anger of a Father; the
    Reproaches of a Family; the Censures of the World; but most of
    all, *Valerio*, the Change of your Heart, and that criminal Coldness
    with which those of your Sex most commonly repay the too warm
    Testimonies of an innocent Love.
VALERIO: Do me not so much wrong as to judge of me by others. Suspect me
    in any thing, *Eliza*, rather than of failing in my Respects to you. My Love
    is too great for that, and shall be as durable as my Life.
ELIZA: Ah, *Valerio*, every one talks the same Language. All Men are alike in
    Words, and only Actions can distinguish them.

VALERIO: Since only Actions can shew what we are, suspend at least your judgment of my Heart till it has been prov'd by them alone, and do not look for Accusations against me, in the groundless Fears of an uneasy Foresight. Kill me not, I beseech ye, with the cruel Blows of an unreasonable Suspicion, but give me time to convince you, by a thousand and a thousand Proofs, of the pureness of my Flame.

ELIZA: Alas! With how much ease we suffer ourselves to be persuaded by those we love! Yes, *Valerio*, I think your Heart incapable of abusing me. I believe you love me with a real Love, and that you will be faithful to me; I will not make the least doubt of it; and I am only disturb'd at the Apprehensions of the blame that I may incur.

VALERIO: But why this uneasiness?

ELIZA: I shou'd have nothing to fear, if every body beheld you with the same Eyes that I do; I find in your Person wherewith to excuse the things I have done for you. My Heart, for its Defence, has all your Merit to plead, supported by an Acknowledgment whereto Heaven has engag'd me towards you. I every Moment represent to myself that amazing Danger, which first gave occasion to our seeing one another; that suprizing Generosity which made you risk your Life to snatch mine from the Fury of the Waves; that extreme Tenderness which you could not help shewing, when you had drag'd me out of the Water; and the assiduous Homages of that ardent Love which neither Time nor Difficulties have abated, and which, causing you to neglect both your Parents and your Country, detains you here, keeps you disguis'd, and has reduc'd you, for my sake, to become one of my Father's Servants. All this has undoubtedly a wonderful effect upon me, and is sufficient in my Opinion, to justify the Engagements I have consented to; but perhaps not sufficient to justify me to others, who may not enter into my Sentiments.

VALERIO: Of all that you have been recounting, 'tis only by my Love that I pretend to have deserv'd any thing from you; and as for your Scruples, your Father himself takes but too much care to justify you to the World; the Excess of his Avarice, and the austere Manner wherein he lives with his Children, may authorize much stranger Things. Pardon me, charming *Eliza*, that I speak so of him before You. You know that upon that Head one cannot say any good. But if I can (as I hope I shall) find my Relations again, we shall not have much trouble to render him favourable to us. I impatiently expect News of them, and if I receive none quickly, I'll go in search of them myself.

ELIZA: Ah! *Valerio*, do not go from hence, I beg you; think only how to get into my Father's favour.

VALERIO: You see how I go about it, and what dextrous Complaisance I was forced to use to introduce myself into his Service; under what a Mask of Sympathy and Congruity of Sentiments I disguise myself to please him, and what a Part I every day act with him to acquire his Good-will. I make great progress in it, and find that to work upon Men, there is no better way than seeming to be of their Inclinations, giving into their Maxims, praising their Faults, and commending whatever they do. One need not be afraid of being too complaisant; and the manner in which they are play'd upon, may be as visible as you will, your cunning'st People are always the greatest Bubbles[1] on the side of Flattery, and there is nothing so impertinent or ridiculous but what will go down, provided it be season'd with Praise. Sincerity indeed suffers a little in the Part I act; but when one has need of People, one must adjust one's self to them; and if they cannot be gain'd but by that means, 'tis not the fault of the Flatterer, but of those who will be Flattered.

ELIZA: But why don't you try to gain my Brother's help, in case the Maid should reveal our Secret?

VALERIO: One cannot manage both of them; the Temper of the Father and that of the Son are so opposite, that 'tis hard to make the Confidence of the One fadge with that of the Other.[2] But do you, on your side, deal with your Brother, and make use of the Friendship that is between you two, to bring him into our Interest. Here he comes. I'll leave you. Take this time to speak to him, and discover no more to him than needs must.

ELIZA: I know not whether or no I shall have Power to make him my Confident in this Affair.

Act I, Scene II

[CLEANTHES, ELIZA.]

CLEANTHES: I am glad to find you alone, Sister; and I was impatient to speak with you, to unfold a Secret to you.

ELIZA: I'm ready to hear you, Brother; what have you to say to me?

CLEANTHES: A great many Things included in one Word; *I'm in love.*

ELIZA: You in love?

CLEANTHES: Yes, in love. But before I proceed any further, I know I depend upon a Father, and that the name of Son makes me subject to his Will; that we ought not to engage our Faith, without the Consent of those who gave us Birth; that Heaven has made them the Masters of our Vows, and that we are enjoin'd not to dispose of them otherwise than as they wou'd have us; that not being byass'd with any extravagant Folly, they are much less liable to be deceived than we, and more capable of seeing what is fit for us; that we ought rather to trust to Their clear-sighted Prudence, than Our blind Passion; and that the Heat of Youth often hurries us on to dreadful Precipices. I say all this to you,

1. Most easily duped.
2. It is hard to gain the confidence of both at the same time.

Sister, that you may not give yourself the trouble to say it to me; for, in short, my Love will hear nothing, and I desire you would make me no Remonstrances.

ELIZA: Are you engaged, Brother, to her you love?

CLEANTHES: No, but I'm resolv'd to be so, and conjure you once more to use no Reasons to dissuade me from it.

ELIZA: Am I such a strange Person, then, Brother?

CLEANTHES: No, Sister; but you are not in love. You are ignorant of the gentle Violence which a tender Passion exercises over our Hearts, and I'm afraid of your Wisdom.

ELIZA: No more of my Wisdom, I beseech you, Brother. There are none but what are sometimes without it, at least once in their Lives; and shou'd I open my Heart to you, perhaps I might appear much less wise than you.

CLEANTHES: Wou'd to Heaven your Heart, like mine –

ELIZA: First make an end of your Affair, and tell me who is she you love?

CLEANTHES: A young Person who of late has lodg'd not far from hence, and who seems to be form'd to strike all that see her with Love. Nature, Sister, has made nothing more amiable, and I was transported the very moment I saw her. She is called *Mariana*, and is under the Government of a good Mother, who is almost continually sick, and for whom that amiable Creature has Sentiments of Friendship, that are not to be imagined. She tends her, bemoans her, comforts her with a dutifulness that wou'd touch your very Soul. She goes about all she does with the most charming Air in the World, and a thousand Graces shine in all her Actions; a softness full of attractions, a perfectly engaging Goodness, an adorable Virtue, a – Ah, Sister, wou'd you had seen her!

ELIZA: I see her sufficiently, Brother, in the things you tell me of her, and your loving her is enough to inform me what she is.

CLEANTHES: I have secretly discovered that they are but in indifferent Circumstances, and that their discreet Conduct has enough to do to make what little income they have, serve all their Necessities. Imagine, Sister, what pleasure it must be to raise the Fortune of a Person one loves; dextrously to convey some little Relief to the modest Necessities of a virtuous Family; and conceive what a Torment 'tis to me, that by the Avarice of a Father I am made unable to taste that Pleasure, and to shew to that Fair-one the least Testimony of my Passion.

ELIZA: Yes, Brother, I sufficiently conceive what your Grief must be.

CLEANTHES: Ah, Sister, 'tis greater than can be believed. For can any thing be more cruel than that excessive Niggardness, that's exercised upon us? that strange Want, that Destitution in which we are forced to languish? What good will it do us to have Riches, if they don't come till we shall not be able to enjoy them with pleasure? If even to maintain myself, I'm obliged to run in every body's debt; and if I'm reduced, together with you, to be beholden every day to the Tradesmen for but bare necessary Apparel? In short, my Design in speaking to you, is to help me to sound my Father upon my Sentiments; and if I find him against them, I am resolved to go somewhere else with that lovely Person, and enjoy what Fortune Heaven shall afford us. I am seeking on all sides to borrow Money for the execution of this Design, and if your Affairs, Sister, are agreeable to mine, and our Father opposes our Desires, we will both leave him, and free ourselves from the Slavery his insupportable Covetousness has so long kept us in.

ELIZA: 'Tis true, he daily gives us more and more occasion to deplore the Loss of our Mother, and –

CLEANTHES: I hear his Voice. Let us go aside a little, to finish the communicating of our Thoughts, and we will afterwards join our Forces to attack the obduracy of his Humour.

Act I, Scene III

[HARPAGON *and* LA FLECHE.]

HARPAGON: Be gone this Minute; make me no Answer. Out of my House, thou sworn Master-Cutpurse, true Newgate-bird.[1]

LA FLECHE: I never knew any body so cross as this damn'd old Fellow. I think (under correction)[2] the Devil possesses him.

HARPAGON: What's that you mutter?

LA FLECHE: Why do you turn me out?

HARPAGON: Rascal, is't for you to ask me Questions? Be gone quickly, or I'll brain you.

LA FLECHE: What have I done to you?

HARPAGON: Thus much, that I'll have you be gone.

LA FLECHE: Your Son, my Master, bade me wait for him.

HARPAGON: Go and wait for him in the Street, and don't stand in my House planted just like a Post to observe all that passes, that you may make your advantage of it. I won't always have a Spy over what I do, a Rogue whose cursed Eyes besiege all my Actions, who devours my Goods, and ferrets on all sides to see if there's nothing to steal.

LA FLECHE: How the deuce can any body steal from You? Are You one that can be robb'd, when you lock up every thing, and keep watch Night and Day?

HARPAGON: I'll lock up what I have a mind to, and keep watch as I please. This is one of your Tell-tale Rascals that is set to spy all my Actions. [*Aside.*] I tremble for fear he has some suspicion of my hoard. You are

1. Jailbird.
2. Taken from John Clare's translation of 1732. Instead of 'under correction', Ozell uses the phrase, 'under the Rose'.

one that will go about, I warrant ye, and spread a Report that I have Money hid in my House.

LA FLECHE: Have you Money hid in your House?

HARPAGON: No Rascal, I don't say so. [*Aside.*] I shall grow mad. [*Aloud.*] I ask you whether out of malice, you won't go and report that I have?

LA FLECHE: 'Oons, What business is't of ours, whether you have or have not, since 'tis all one to us?

HARPAGON: What; do you argue? I'll ring your ears an Argument. [*Holds his hand up at him to box his ears.*] Out of my House once more.

LA FLECHE: Well I'll go.

HARPAGON: Stay. Do you carry nothing of mine away with you?

LA FLECHE: What should I carry away with me?

HARPAGON: Come hither, that I may see. Shew me your Hands.

LA FLECHE: There.

HARPAGON: The t'other.

LA FLECHE: The t'other?

HARPAGON: Yes.

LA FLECHE: There.

HARPAGON: Have you put nothing in here?

LA FLECHE: Look and see.

HARPAGON: [*He feels the Knees of his Breeches.*] These Trowser Breeches are fit to conceal stol'n goods; I wish the Inventor were hang'd for them.

LA FLECHE: Ah, how well does such a Man as this deserve what he fears! How glad shou'd I be to rob him!

HARPAGON: Ha?

LA FLECHE: What!

HARPAGON: What's that you say of robbing?

LA FLECHE: I say you make a very narrow search to see if I han't robb'd you.

HARPAGON: [*Searches in his Pockets.*] That's what I mean to do.

LA FLECHE: Pox on Stinginess and Misers. [*Aside.*]

HARPAGON: What's that you say?

LA FLECHE: What do I say?

HARPAGON: Yes. What was that you said of Stinginess and Misers?

LA FLECHE: I say, Pox on Stinginess and Misers.

HARPAGON: Who do you mean?

LA FLECHE: Misers.

HARPAGON: Who are those Misers?

LA FLECHE: Sneaking, sordid, base Fellows.

HARPAGON: But who do you mean by that?

LA FLECHE: What are you concerned at?

HARPAGON: I am concerned at what I ought to be.

LA FLECHE: Do you think I mean you?

HARPAGON: I think what I think; but I'll make you tell me who you speak to, when you say so.

LA FLECHE: I speak – I speak to my Cap.

HARPAGON: And I have a good mind to cuff your Cap.

LA FLECHE: Won't you let me curse the Covetous?

HARPAGON: Yes, but I won't let you chatter and be insolent. Hold your peace.

LA FLECHE: I name no body.

HARPAGON: I'll thresh you if you speak.

LA FLECHE: If any body's Nose wants wiping, let him wipe it.

HARPAGON: Will you be silent?

LA FLECHE: Yes, against my will.

HARPAGON: Ha, ha.

LA FLECHE: [*Shewing him one of his waistcoat Pockets.*] Here's another Pocket. Are you satisfied yet?

HARPAGON: Come; restore it to me without searching you.

LA FLECHE: What?

HARPAGON: What thou hast taken from me.

LA FLECHE: I have taken nothing at all from you.

HARPAGON: Sincerely?

LA FLECHE: Sincerely.

HARPAGON: Adieu then, and to Hell.

LA FLECHE: A blessed Discharge, this!

HARPAGON: I leave it to your own Conscience, however.[1] [*Exit* LA FLECHE.] 'Tis a vile Rascal that was very troublesome to me; I don't love the sight of such Vermin.

Act I, Scene IV

[ELIZA *and* CLEANTHES *at the further part of the Stage.*
HARPAGON.]

HARPAGON: Verily 'tis no small trouble to keep a great Sum of Money at home. And happy is he, who has all his Concerns well placed out, and reserves just enough to live on! One's not a little at a loss to find out in a whole House a secure place for a Hoard; for in my opinion strong Boxes are very unsafe, and I'll never trust them. I think 'em nothing but a bait for Thieves; and they are always the first things that are attack'd. However, I don't know whether I've been in the right in burying in my Garden the ten thousand Crowns I received yesterday. Ten thousand Crowns of Gold in one's house is a Sum pretty – [*Seeing the Brother and Sister discoursing privately.*] Oh Heavens! I have betray'd my self. My Heat hurry'd me away, and I believe I have spoken aloud in talking to my self. What do you want?

CLEANTHES: Nothing, Father.

HARPAGON: Have you been there long?

1. Taken from John Clare's translation of 1732. Instead of 'however', Ozell uses the phrase, 'after all'.

ELIZA: We were but just come.

HARPAGON: Did not you hear –

CLEANTHES: What? Father.

HARPAGON: The –

CLEANTHES: What?

HARPAGON: What I just now said?

CLEANTHES: No.

HARPAGON: You did, you did.

ELIZA: Indeed, Sir, we did not.

HARPAGON: I know you heard some Words. I was discoursing to my self about the difficulty of coming at Money in these times; and I said that he who can have ten thousand Crowns in his House was very happy.

CLEANTHES: We did not care to speak to you, for fear of interrupting you.

HARPAGON: I willingly tell you what I said, that you may not take things wrong, and imagine that I said 'twas I who had ten thousand Crowns.

CLEANTHES: We don't meddle with your Affairs.

HARPAGON: Wou'd I had the ten thousand Crowns!

CLEANTHES: I don't think –

HARPAGON: 'Twould be well for me!

ELIZA: These are things –

HARPAGON: I should know what to do with 'em.

CLEANTHES: I believe –

HARPAGON: They'd be of great use to me.

ELIZA: You are –

HARPAGON: I should not complain, as I do, of the Hardness of the Times.

CLEANTHES: Lord, Father, you have no need to complain. 'Tis well known you are rich enough.

HARPAGON: How! I rich enough! Those that say so, lye. Nothing can be falser; and those are Knaves that spread such Reports.

ELIZA: Don't put yourself in a passion.

HARPAGON: 'Tis strange that my own Children should betray me, and become my Enemies!

CLEANTHES: Is't the part of an Enemy to say you are rich?

HARPAGON: Yes, such talk, and your extravagant Living, will some time or other cause somebody to cut my throat, imagining I am lined with Gold.

CLEANTHES: What extravagant Living?

HARPAGON: What? Is any thing more scandalous, than the sumptuous Equipage you go with thro' the town? Yesterday I was angry with your Sister; but this is ten times worse. It cries out for Vengeance to Heaven; and if you were taken from head to foot, there's enough to purchase an Estate for life. I have said to you twenty times, Son, all your ways displease me very much; you affect the Marquiss, furiously;[1] you must certainly rob me to go so fine.

1. Pretend to be a marquis.

CLEANTHES: How rob you?

HARPAGON: How should I know? How else can you get the wherewithall to maintain yourself at this rate?

CLEANTHES: I, Father? I game, and being very lucky, I lay out all I win in Clothes.

HARPAGON: 'Tis very ill done of you: If you are lucky at play, you ought to improve it, and to put out to honest Interest the Money you win, that it may be your own another day. I'd fain know, without mentioning any thing else, what need there is of all these Ribbons you are bedizon'd with from Head to Foot, and if half a dozen Points would not do as well to tie the Knees of your Breeches? What need is there for laying out Money in Perrukes, when one may wear the Hair of one's own Growth which costs nothing? I'd lay a Wager that in Perrukes and Ribbons there's at least twelve Pound, and twelve Pound in a Year will produce fourteen Shillings and four Pence three Farthings, at but six *per Cent.*

CLEANTHES: You are in the right.

HARPAGON: But enough of this; let's talk of something else. Hah! I believe they make signs to one another to pick my Pocket. What do you mean by those Motions?

ELIZA: My Brother and I are disputing who shall speak first; both of us have something to say to you.

HARPAGON: And I have something to say to both of you.

CLEANTHES: 'Tis of Marriage, Father, we want to speak to you.

HARPAGON: And 'tis of Marriage I want to speak to you.

ELIZA: Ah! Father.

HARPAGON: Why that Cry? Is that Word, Daughter, so terrible to you? or is it the Thing frightens you?

CLEANTHES: Marriage may be terrible to us both, as you design it perhaps; and we are afraid our Sentiments may not be agreeable to your Choice.

HARPAGON: Have a little patience; don't alarm your selves. I know what's fit for both of you, nor shall either of you have cause to complain of any thing I intend to do. And to begin at the right end; pray tell me, have you seen a young Person call'd *Mariana*, who lives not far from hence?

CLEANTHES: Yes, Father.

HARPAGON: And have you, Daughter?

ELIZA: I have heard speak of her.

HARPAGON: Son, how do you like her?

CLEANTHES: I think her a very charming Person.

HARPAGON: Her Countenance?

CLEANTHES: Very ingenuous and sprightly.

HARPAGON: Her Air and Manner?

CLEANTHES: Admirable.

HARPAGON: Do you not think such a Girl deserves one's Attention?

CLEANTHES: Yes, Father.

HARPAGON: Would not she be a desirable Match?

CLEANTHES: Very desirable.

HARPAGON: Has not she the Air of a good Housewife?

CLEANTHES: Yes.

HARPAGON: Might not a Man be happy with her?

CLEANTHES: Certainly.

HARPAGON: There's still one small Difficulty; I'm afraid she han't so great a Portion[1] as might be wish'd for.

CLEANTHES: Ah! Father, no matter for Money, when one's upon marrying a virtuous Person.

HARPAGON: I beg your pardon for that: But this may be said for it, if that's the case, we must try to make up what's wanting in Portion with something else.

CLEANTHES: That's to be supposed.

HARPAGON: Well, I'm glad to see you agree in my Opinion; for her virtuous Carriage and Mildness have gained my Heart, and I'm resolv'd to marry her if she has any Portion.

CLEANTHES: Ah, Heavens!

HARPAGON: What now?

CLEANTHES: You are resolv'd, you say –

HARPAGON: To marry *Mariana*.

CLEANTHES: Who, you, you?

HARPAGON: Yes, I, I, I. What can this mean?

CLEANTHES: A certain Dizziness has suddenly taken me; I must leave you.

HARPAGON: 'Twill be soon over. Go quickly into the Kitchen and drink a large Glass of fair Water. These are your Milksops, your wishy-washy Fellows, that have no more Vigour than a Chicken. This, Daughter, is what I have resolv'd upon, as to myself. And as for your Brother, I design him a certain Widow that I was spoken to about, this Morning; and as for you, I'll give you to Signior *Anselmo*.

ELIZA: To Signior *Anselmo*!

HARPAGON: Yes. A grave, prudent, wise Man, not above fifty Years old, and is said to be very rich.

ELIZA: [*Curt'sying.*] I won't marry, Father, if you please.

HARPAGON: [*Curt'sying again.*] But, dear Daughter, you shall marry, if you please.

ELIZA: I beg your pardon, Father.

HARPAGON: I beg yours, Daughter.

ELIZA: I am Signior *Anselmo's* very humble Servant; but, with your leave, won't marry him.

HARPAGON: I am Your very humble Slave; but, with your leave, you shall marry him, and to-night too.

ELIZA: To-night!

HARPAGON: Yes, to-night.

1. Dowry

ELIZA: It can't be, Father.

HARPAGON: It shall be, Daughter.

ELIZA: No.

HARPAGON: Yes.

ELIZA: No, I say.

HARPAGON: Yes, I say.

ELIZA: 'Tis a thing you shall never force me to.

HARPAGON: 'Tis a thing which I shall force you to.

ELIZA: I'll sooner kill myself than marry such a Man.

HARPAGON: You shan't kill yourself, and yet you shall marry him! What Audaciousness is this? Was a Child ever heard to talk thus to a Father before?

ELIZA: Was a Father ever heard to propose such a Match to his Child before?

HARPAGON: 'Tis a Match that can have nothing said against it, and I'll lay a Wager that every body will approve my Choice.

ELIZA: And I'll lay that no reasonable body can approve of it.

HARPAGON: Here comes *Valerio*; will you let him be Judge between us?

ELIZA: With all my heart.

HARPAGON: Will you yield to his Judgment?

ELIZA: Yes; I'll abide by whatever he says.

HARPAGON: 'Tis done.

Act I, Scene V

[HARPAGON, ELIZA *and* VALERIO.]

HARPAGON: Come hither, *Valerio*. We have chosen you to tell us which has Reason on their side, my Daughter or I?

VALERIO: You, Sir, without contradiction.

HARPAGON: Why? do you know what we are talking of?

VALERIO: No; but you cannot be in the wrong; you are all Reason.

HARPAGON: This very Night I mean to marry her to a Man who is as rich as he is prudent, and the Slut tells me to my face, she won't have him. What do you say to it?

VALERIO: What do I say to it?

HARPAGON: Yes.

VALERIO: Ah, ah!

HARPAGON: What?

VALERIO: I say, that in the main I am of your opinion, and you can't but be in the right. But yet she mayn't be quite in the wrong; and –

HARPAGON: Why, Signior *Anselmo* is a considerable Match; he's a Gentleman that's noble, mild, sedate, wise and very well to pass, and who has no Child left of his first Wife. Can she be better fitted?

VALERIO: That's true; but yet she may tell you you're a little too hasty, and that you ought at least to give her time that she may suit her Inclinations with –

HARPAGON: Such an Opportunity ought to be taken by the Forelock. I have an advantage in this which I mayn't find elsewhere, for he offers to take her without a Portion.

VALERIO: Without a Portion?

HARPAGON: Yes.

VALERIO: Oh! I have done, then. This Reason, do you see, is so convincing, that you ought certainly to yield to't.

HARPAGON: I shall save considerably by it.

VALERIO: This, doubtless, is unanswerable. 'Tis true, your Daughter may represent to you, that Marriage is a thing of greater moment than some may think; that it makes People happy or unhappy all their Life-time, and that an Engagement which is to endure till death, ought never to be made without great Precaution.

HARPAGON: Without a Portion!

VALERIO: That's true again. That decides all, to be sure. Some indeed may tell you, that on such occasions the Inclination of a Child is a thing which ought to have some regard shewn it; and that such a great Inequality of Age, Humour and Sentiments, render a Match subject to very ill Accidents.

HARPAGON: Without a Portion!

VALERIO: Ah! That cannot be answer'd, we are very sensible of it. The deuce is in't, if any thing can weigh down That. Not but that there are a great many Fathers, who wou'd prefer their Childrens Happiness before the hoarding up of Money; who wou'd not sacrifice them to Interest, but wou'd chiefly endeavour to procure in a Match that sweet Unity which continually keeps up the Honour, Tranquility, and Joy of it; and –

HARPAGON: Without a Portion!

VALERIO: 'Tis true. That stops all Mouths. WITHOUT A PORTION! How can any one resist so powerful an Argument!

HARPAGON: [*Looking towards the Garden.*] What now? I thought I heard a Dog bark. Sure nobody's going to steal my Money? Don't stir; I'll be here immediately. [*Exit.*]

ELIZA: Are you in earnest, *Valerio*, in speaking to him as you do?

VALERIO: I do it that I mayn't enrage him, and in order to bring things about the better. To run directly counter to his opinion wou'd spoil all; there are some People that must be taken only the round-about way; Tempers that hate all resistance; restive Natures, who kick against Truth; who always stiffen their Necks against the Paths of right Reason, and must be led by turnings and windings to the point you wou'd bring 'em to. Seem to consent to what he has a mind to, and you'll the better effect your Designs, and –

ELIZA: But this Marriage, *Valerio*?

VALERIO: Some way must be found out to break it off.

ELIZA: But what way, if 'tis to be concluded tonight?

VALERIO: You must desire it may be defer'd, and pretend you're sick.

ELIZA: But that Pretence will soon be discover'd, if the Physicians are call'd.

VALERIO: You joke, sure? Do you think They know any thing of the matter? No, no; you may pretend to be as ill as you will with them; they'll find out Reasons to tell you from whence it proceeds.

HARPAGON: [*Returning.*] 'Tis nothing, thank God.

VALERIO: In short, our last Remedy is Flight, which will secure us from every thing; and if your Love, Fair *Eliza*, is capable of a Firmness – [*Seeing* HARPAGON.] – Yes, a Daughter, ought to obey her Father, and not look on the outside of a Husband. And when the prevailing Argument, WITHOUT A PORTION, presents itself, she ought to be contented with any thing that's offer'd her.

HARPAGON: Good. That was very well said.

VALERIO: Sir, I beg your Pardon, if I'm a little angry with her, and take the liberty to speak to her as I do.

HARPAGON: Why I'm glad you do so, and I will give you an absolute Power over her. [*Exit* ELIZA.] Yes, you may run away as much as you please, Mistress. I give him the Authority which Heaven has given me over you, and intend you shall do whatever he commands you –

VALERIO: After this, resist my Arguments if you dare. Sir, I will follow her, to continue the Lessons I gave her.

HARPAGON: You'll oblige me. In troth –

VALERIO: 'Tis good to keep a high hand over her.

HARPAGON: 'Tis true. We must –

VALERIO: Don't trouble yourself, I believe I shall bring it about.

HARPAGON: Do so. I'll go and take a little walk in the City, and return presently.

VALERIO: Yes, Money is more precious than any thing in the world; and you ought to thank Heaven for the good Father it has given you. He knows what 'tis to live. When any one offers to take a Daughter without a Portion, there's no need of looking any further: That includes all Things, and WITHOUT A PORTION stands for Beauty, Youth, Birth, Honour, Wisdom and Equity.

HARPAGON: Brave Boy! he talks like an Oracle. How happy is he who has such a Servant!

Act II, Scene I

[CLEANTHES, LA FLECHE.]

CLEANTHES: Ah! Rogue as you are; where have you been interloping? Did not I order you –

LA FLECHE: Yes, Sir, and I came hither to wait for you, resolutely and without budging; but your most discourteous Mortal of a Father drove me out in spite of me,[1] and I'd like to have been beaten into the bargain.

CLEANTHES: Well, and how goes our Business on? Things press more than ever; and since I left you, I have discover'd that my Father is my Rival.

LA FLECHE: Your Father in love!

CLEANTHES: Yes; and I had much ado to hide from him the Disturbance the News of it gave me.

LA FLECHE: He pretend to be in love! How the devil came he to take that in his head! Is he in jest or earnest! Was Love made for such as he!

CLEANTHES: Sure it was for the Punishment of my Sins that he was struck with this Passion.

LA FLECHE: But why do you conceal your Love from him?

CLEANTHES: To give him the less Suspicion, and that I may have the better Opportunity to break off this Match. What Answer did you receive?

LA FLECHE: Faith, Sir, those that go a Borrowing go a Sorrowing; and when any one, like you, is obliged to pass thro' the Hands of Usurers and Extortioners, he must endure strange things.

CLEANTHES: Can't it be done then?

LA FLECHE: I don't say That. Our Mr. *Simon*, the Broker we were recommended to, a bustling zealous Man, says he has left no stone unturn'd to serve you; and assures me that your Physiognomy alone has gain'd his Heart.

CLEANTHES: I shall have the fifteen thousand Livres I desir'd then?

LA FLECHE: Yes; but on some small Conditions, which you must accept of, if you have a mind to have things done.

CLEANTHES: Did he bring you to him that was to lend the Money?

LA FLECHE: No, no. Things must not be carry'd on so. He's more careful to conceal himself than you are; these are greater Mysteries than you imagine. His Name must not be discover'd, and he will be brought to confer with you today, not in his own House, but some other, where you're to have an Interview with him, and give him an account by your own Mouth of your Estate and Family; I don't doubt but the sole Name of your Father will satisfy all Scruples.

CLEANTHES: And especially my Mother being dead, whose Estate cannot be given away from me.

LA FLECHE: Here are some Articles which he gave our Go-between, to shew 'em you before any thing is done.

The Lender must be suppos'd to see all his Securities; the Borrower must be of age, and of a Family whose Estate is ample, solid, secure, clear and free from all Incumbrances; a good and safe Bond must be given before a Notary, who must be the honestest Man that can be found, and who for that end must be chosen

---

1. Clare and Ozell both use the phrase 'in spite of my teeth' in this passage. At a later point in the play, Clare translates the same French phrase as 'in spite of me'.

by the Lender, to whom 'tis of most importance that the Instrument be duly drawn up.

CLEANTHES: There's nothing to be said against this.

LA FLECHE: *The Lender, not being willing to load his Conscience with the least Scruple, intends to take but about five* per Cent. *for his Money.*

CLEANTHES: Five *per Cent!* O' my Conscience a very honest Man. Here's no cause of Complaint.

LA FLECHE: 'Tis true.

But as the said Lender has not the requisite Sum by him, and as to serve the Borrower he is obliged himself to borrow it of another at twenty per Cent. *it will be incumbent on the said Borrower to pay that Interest, besides the other; seeing he borrows it only to oblige him.*

CLEANTHES: The Devil! What a *Jew!* What a *Saracen* is this! Why 'tis above five and twenty *per Cent.*

LA FLECHE: 'Tis true, and so I told him myself. You had best think of it.

CLEANTHES: What wou'd you have me think? I want Money, and must consent to every thing.

LA FLECHE: So I told him.

CLEANTHES: Is there any thing else?

LA FLECHE: Another little Article.

Of the fifteen thousand Livres required, the Lender can lay down in Money but twelve thousand; and for the other thousand Crowns, the Borrower must take Houshold-Goods, Clothes, Trinkets, and other things, of which an Inventory follows, and on which the said Lender has conscientiously set the most moderate Prices he can afford them at.

CLEANTHES: What's the meaning of that?

LA FLECHE: Hear the Inventory.

Imprimis, A four-footed Bed, with Point *of* Hungary, *very neatly stitch'd on an olive-colour'd Cloth, with six Chairs, and the Counterpain of the same; all well conditioned, and lined with a changeable Taffeta of a Red and Blue.*

Item, A Tent-Bed of a good dry Rose-colour Serge d'Aumale, with Silken Fringes.

CLEANTHES: What wou'd he have me do with this?

LA FLECHE: Attend.

Item, A suit of Tapistry Hangings, of the Loves of Gombaud *and* Macæa.

Item, A great Table made of Wallnut-Tree, with twelve twisted Legs, drawing out at each end, with half a dozen Stools thereunto belonging.

CLEANTHES: What the devil have I to do with –

LA FLECHE: Have patience.

Item, Three great Muskets, adorn'd with Mother of Pearl, with Rests suitable to them.

Item, A Brick Furnace, with two Retorts and three Recipients, very useful to those that love distilling.

CLEANTHES: 'Sblood!

LA FLECHE: Be calm.

Item, *A Bologna Lute, with all its Strings, at least very few wanting.*
Item, *A Nine-hole Board, and a Draught-Board, with a Box to play at the Goose, which Play was revived from the Greeks; all which things are very fit to pass away the time, when one has nothing else to do.*
Item, *An Alligator's Skin, of three foot and an half, stuff'd with Hay; an agreeable Curiosity to hang up to the Ceiling in a Room.*
All which things above-mention'd, which are very well worth more than four thousand five hundred Livres, the said Lender, in moderation, reckons but at a thousand Crowns.

CLEANTHES: Plague take him with his Moderation for a cut-throat Rascal. Was ever such Extortion heard of? Is he not content with the cursed Interest he exacts, without obliging me to take at the rate of the three thousand Livres, the old Lumber he has pick'd up? I shan't have two hundred Crowns of all this; and yet I must consent to it, for he can make me accept what he pleases; I lie at the Villain's mercy.

LA FLECHE: I see, Sir, without Offence,[1] you're in the same high Road to Ruin as *Panurgus*, taking up Money beforehand, buying dear, selling cheap, and eating your Corn in the Ear.[2]

CLEANTHES: What wou'd ye have me to do in this Case? This is what young Men are reduced to thro' their Father's execrable Avarice; and is it any wonder, after this, that their Children wish 'em dead?

LA FLECHE: It must be confess'd, yours wou'd inrage the most sedate Man in the world against his Sordidness. Thank God, I have no very *Tyburnish* Inclinations;[3] and among my Brother Skips, whom I see daily exercising the Nimbleness of their Fingers, I know how to slip my Neck out of the Collar, and prudently disengage myself from all manner of Gallantries that smell ever so little of the Ladder; but to tell you the truth, this Man, by his Proceedings, gives me great Temptations to rob him, and I shou'd think it a meritorious Action to do so.

CLEANTHES: Give me that Inventory a little, that I may peruse it once more.

Act II, Scene II

[MR. SIMON, HARPAGON, CLEANTHES, LA FLECHE.]

MR. SIMON: Yes, Sir, 'tis a young Man that wants Money. His Affairs press him for it, and he'll consent to whatever you demand.

HARPAGON: But do you think, Mr. *Simon*, I shall run no risk? Do you know the Name, the Estate, and Family of the Party?

1. Taken from John Clare's translation of 1732. Instead of 'without Offence', Ozell uses the phrase 'under favour'.
2. A reference to Rabelais's character, Panurge, in his *Third Book* (1546).
3. Inclinations to be hanged. Tyburn was the site of the gallows.

MR. SIMON: No, I can't give you a clear Insight into that; 'tis only by chance I was recommended to him; but he himself will satisfy you in every thing; and his Man assures me you'll be contented when you are acquainted with him. All I know is, that his Family is very rich, that his Mother is already dead, and that if you have a mind to't, he'll engage that his Father will die in less than eight Months.

HARPAGON: That's something indeed.[1] Charity, Mr. *Simon*, obliges us to do good to those we are able.

MR. SIMON: It does so.

LA FLECHE: What's the meaning of this? Our Mr. *Simon* talking to your Father?

CLEANTHES: Have you told him who I am? Are you the first that betrays me?

MR. SIMON: [*To* LA FLECHE.] Hah, you're very hasty! Who told you 'twas here? [*Then turning to* HARPAGON.] 'Twas not I, Sir, however, that discover'd to them your Name, and where you liv'd: But, in my opinion, there's no great harm in't. They are discreet People, and you may talk together here as well as elsewhere.

HARPAGON: How!

MR. SIMON: This Gentleman's he that's to borrow the fifteen thousand Livres I spoke to you about.

HARPAGON: What, Sirrah, is't thou that abandon'st thyself to these culpable Extremities?

CLEANTHES: How! Father, is't you that commit these shameful Actions? [MR. SIMON *runs away and* LA FLECHE *hides.*]

HARPAGON: Is't thou that wou'dst ruin thyself by such damnable Borrowings?

CLEANTHES: Is't you that seek to enrich yourself by such exorbitant Usuries?

HARPAGON: Darest thou, after this, look me in the face?

CLEANTHES: Dare you, after this, shew your Head in the world?

HARPAGON: Tell me, art thou not asham'd to be thus debauch'd? To lash out into such Expences? And to dissipate in this manner what thy Ancestors have heap'd up for thee by the Sweat of their Brows?

CLEANTHES: Do you not blush to dishonour your Condition by these doings? To sacrifice Fame and Reputation to the insatiable Desire of heaping Crown upon Crown? And in point of Interest, to refine upon the most infamous Tricks that the most notorious Usurers ever invented?

HARPAGON: Out of my sight, Knave; out of my sight.

CLEANTHES: Pray who is most faulty, he that borrows Money thro' need, or he that extorts Money he has no need of?

HARPAGON: Be gone, I say, and don't provoke me. [*Alone.*] I am not at all sorry for this Accident; 'twill make me have a stricter eye than ever upon all his Actions.

1. Taken from John Clare's translation of 1732. Instead of 'That's something indeed', Ozell uses the phrase 'There's something in that'.

Act II, Scene III

[FROSINA, HARPAGON.]

FROSINA: Sir –

HARPAGON: Stay but a moment, and I'll come and talk with you. I must go make a small Visit to my Money. [*Aside.*]

Act II, Scene IV

[LA FLECHE, FROSINA.]

LA FLECHE: This is a quite comical Accident. He must needs have a large Magazine of Goods somewhere or other; for we knew nothing before of this Inventory.

FROSINA: Hah, what is it you, honest *La Fleche*! How come we to meet thus?

LA FLECHE: Hah, what is't you, *Frosina*! What do you do here?

FROSINA: What I do every where else; play the *Go-Between*, be officious and serviceable to People, and improve, as well as I can, what few Talents I am mistress of. You know, that in this world we must live by our Wits, and that to such as I, Heaven has given no other Estate than Intrigue and Industry.

LA FLECHE: Have you any business with the Master of this House?

FROSINA: Yes; I manage a small matter for him, which I hope to be rewarded for.

LA FLECHE: By Him? Faith, you'll be cunning indeed, if you get any thing from Him; I give you notice, the Money in this House is very precious.

FROSINA: Some sort of Services are wonderfully affecting.

LA FLECHE: I'm your Servant: I find you don't thoroughly know Signor *Harpagon*. Signor *Harpagon* is of all Humans the Human that's least humane; the Mortal of all Mortals, the most hard and close-fisted. No Service can induce him to open his Hand. As much Praise, Esteem, Good-will in Words, and Friendship as you please; but if you come to Money, there he'll drop you. Nothing can be more dry, more adust, than his Favour and Caresses; and he has so much aversion for the word give, that he never says, *I give you a Good-morrow*, but, *I lend you a Good-morrow*.

FROSINA: Oh, never fear; I know how to milk Men. I have the Art of opening a passage to their Affections, of tickling their Hearts, and find out the Places in which they are most sensible.

LA FLECHE: 'Twon't do here. I defy you to mollify Him we are speaking of, on the Money-side. He's a *Turk* upon that point, and can never be converted. You may kill him, but not cure him; break him, but not bend him. In short, he loves Money more than Reputation, Honour and Virtue, and the sight of a Dunner gives him Convulsions. Taking Money from him, is wounding him in his most mortal Place, piercing his Heart, tearing out his Entrails; and if – but here he comes; I'll be gone.

[*Exit* LA FLECHE.]

Act II, Scene V

[HARPAGON, FROSINA.]

HARPAGON: Every thing is as it shou'd be. Well, *Frosina*, what want You?

FROSINA: Good God, how well you look! You have the very Countenance of Health itself.

HARPAGON: Who, I!

FROSINA: I never saw you look so fresh and jolly.

HARPAGON: Indeed!

FROSINA: Why, you never in your life were so young as you are now; there are some Men of five and twenty that are older than you.

HARPAGON: Yet, *Frosina*, I am full threescore.

FROSINA: What's threescore? Is that such a matter! You're now in the Flower of your Age, and just coming into the pleasantest Part of Life.

HARPAGON: I am so; but yet I think if I were twenty Years younger, 'twou'd be no great harm.

FROSINA: Pshaw, you have no need on't; you're of a Dough that will last a hundred Years.

HARPAGON: Do you think so?

FROSINA: Yes. Shew me your Hand. Bless me! What a Line of Life is here!

HARPAGON: How!

FROSINA: Don't you see how far this Line goes?

HARPAGON: Well; and what does that signify?

FROSINA: I said indeed a hundred Years; but you'll exceed sixscore.

HARPAGON: Is't possible?

FROSINA: You'll live so long, I tell you, that you must be knock'd on the head at last; and you'll bury your Children, and your Children's Children.

HARPAGON: So much the better. But how goes our Business on?

FROSINA: Is that a Question? Do I undertake any thing but what I effect? I have a wonderful Talent in bringing things about, Matches especially. There's nobody but what in a little time I can bring together; and if I had a mind to't, I believe I cou'd marry the Great *Turk* with the Republick of *Venice*. But there's no such difficulty in this Business. Being acquainted with the Parties, I thoroughly discours'd them both concerning you, and told the Mother the Design you had about *Mariana*, having seen her pass thro' the Street, and taking the Air at the Window.

HARPAGON: What Answer did she make you?

FROSINA: She receiv'd the Proposal with joy; and when I told her that you'd fain have her Daughter be present tonight at your Daughter's Contract of Marriage, she readily consented to it, and will entrust me with her.

HARPAGON: 'Tis because I'm to give a Supper to Signor *Anselmo, Frosina*, and shou'd be glad to have her partake of it.

FROSINA: You are in the right. In the Afternoon she'll come and pay a Visit to your Daughter, from whence she means to go and take a turn in the Fair, and afterwards come to Supper.

HARPAGON: Well, I'll lend 'em my Coach, and they shall go together.

FROSINA: That's what she wanted.

HARPAGON: But, *Frosina*, have you talk'd to the Mother about what Portion she's able to give her Daughter? Have you told her she must contribute something, strive a little, and bleed what she can, upon such an Occasion? For, in short, nobody will marry a Wife without she brings something.

FROSINA: Why she'll bring you six hundred a Year.

HARPAGON: Six Hundred a Year!

FROSINA: Yes. *First*, She was nursed and brought up very sparingly as to Food. She's used to live upon Salad, Milk, Cheese and Apples, and consequently she won't want a full Table, nor nice Jelly-Broths, nor peel'd Barley perpetually, nor any of the Delicacies that another Woman must have; and this is not so inconsiderable, but that 'twill amount every Year to at least two hundred Pounds. *Secondly*, Tho' she loves to go neat, yet she is not fond of fine Clothes, nor rich Jewels, nor sumptuous Furniture, which such as she commonly are mighty desirous of; and this Article is at least an hundred and fifty Pounds per Annum. *Thirdly*, She has a huge Aversion to Gaming, and That Women seldom have now-a-days. I know one in our Neighbourhood, who has lost a thousand Pounds this Year: but let's only take a quarter of it. Two hundred and fifty Pounds in Gaming, one hundred and fifty in Clothes and Jewels, That makes four hundred: and two hundred we set down for Eating: is not it just six hundred a Year!

HARPAGON: Why, ay, ay, all that is not amiss; but there's nothing substantial in this Calculation.

FROSINA: Pardon me. Is there nothing substantial in bringing you, in Marriage, great Sobriety, together with the Inheritance of a great Love for Plain-dressing, and a large Fund of Hatred for Play?

HARPAGON: 'Tis a Jest to make up her Portion of what she won't lay out. I'd never give an Acquittance for what I do not receive; I must *touch* something.

FROSINA: Ads my Heart, you shall *touch* enough. I have heard them talk of a certain Country where they have an Estate, which you shall be Master of.

HARPAGON: I must see that. But, *Frosina*, there's another thing that disturbs me. The Girl is young, you know, and young People seldom love any but their Equals in Age, and are fond of Their Company only. I'm afraid she won't like a Man of my Years, which may cause some small Disorders in my Family, that may make me uneasy.

FROSINA: How little you know her Humour! I wanted to acquaint you with this very Particular. She has a mortal Aversion to all young People, and loves none but what are old.

HARPAGON: She?

FROSINA: Yes, She. I wish you had but heard her talk about it. She cannot bear the sight of a young Man; but I'm never more pleas'd, says she, than when I see a fine old Gentleman with a majestick Beard. She thinks the older People are, they're the more charming. Therefore I'd advise you never to go to make yourself younger than you are. She'd have a Man of sixty at least; and 'tis not four Months ago since, being upon the brink of Matrimony, she suddenly broke off the Match, because the Lover discover'd that he was but fifty six, and because he sign'd the Contract without Spectacles.

HARPAGON: For that only?

FROSINA: Yes. She says fifty six Years won't satisfy her; and of all Noses she's for a Nose that wears Spectacles.

HARPAGON: Why, this is a very extraordinary Thing!

FROSINA: It goes further than I can describe to you. In her Chamber she has some Pictures and Cuts; but what do you think they are? Your *Adonis's? Cephalus's? Paris's? Apollo's?* No, no, no such matter; they are fine Pictures of *Saturn*, King *Priam*, old *Nestor*, and good Father *Anchises* upon his Son's Shoulders.

HARPAGON: This is admirable! I cou'd never ha' thought it; and am very glad to hear that she's of such a Humour. And indeed, if I had been a Woman myself, I shou'd never have loved young Men.

FROSINA: I believe you wou'd not. They're fine Stuff indeed to be beloved! Snotty-nos'd Boys, pale-fac'd Fops, to be coveted for their Skin: I'd fain know what they're good for, what pleasure one can take with 'em.

HARPAGON: For my part, I can't imagine; and I wonder there are Women so fond of them.

FROSINA: They must be mad sure. To think Youth amiable! Is it a sign of Common Sense? Are those young goldy-lock'd Striplings Men? Can such Animals charm?

HARPAGON: 'Tis what I say every day, with their Quail-pipe Voices, their three little bits of a Beard turn'd up like a Cat's Whiskers, their Goats-hair Perrukes, their Breeches as if they were falling off, and their Breasts wide open.

FROSINA: They're fine things indeed to such a one as you! You look like a Man. There's what will please the Eye; so ought Men to be form'd and dress'd, to smite the Ladies.

HARPAGON: You think me handsome, do you?

FROSINA: Do I? You are ravishing, and your Picture really deserves to be drawn. Pray turn a little: Nobody can look better. Let me see you walk. There's a well-shap'd Body! free and easy as it ought to be, and shews no Indispositions.

HARPAGON: I have no great ones, thank Heav'n: There's only my Catarrh that seizes me from time to time.[1]

FROSINA: That's nothing. Your Catarrh is not at all unbecoming; you cough with a Grace.

HARPAGON: Pray tell me; has *Mariana* seen me yet? Has not she observ'd me as I pass'd by?

FROSINA: No. But we talk'd very much of you. I described your Person to her, and did not fail to cry up your Merit, and the advantage 'twou'd be to her to have such a Husband.

HARPAGON: You did well; I'm oblig'd to you for it.

FROSINA: Sir, I've a small Request to make to you. I have a Law-Suit which I'm in danger of losing for want of a little Money. [*He looks grave.*] And 'tis in your power, with ease, to gain me my Suit, if you had any Kindness for me. You can't imagine how glad *Mariana* will be to see you. [*He resumes his gay Air.*] Ah! how you'll please her! and how your ancient Ruff will work upon her! But particularly she'll be charmed with your Breeches, ty'd up to your Doublet with Points. You'll make her run mad for you. A Tag-and-Point Lover will give her a wonderful delight.

HARPAGON: In troth, I'm overjoy'd to hear this.

FROSINA: Indeed, Sir, this Suit is of very great consequence to me. [*He resumes his grave Air.*] I am ruin'd if I'm cast, and some small Assistance wou'd settle my Affairs. I wish you had seen the Joy she shew'd when I spoke to her of you. [*He resumes his gay Air.*] Her Eyes sparkled with pleasure at hearing your good Qualities: And in short, I made her quite impatient to have the Marriage entirely concluded.

HARPAGON: You give me a great deal of Pleasure, *Frosina*, and I confess I'm oblig'd to you extremely.

FROSINA: I beg, Sir, you'd grant me the small Request I make to you. [*He looks serious again.*] 'Twou'd set me up again, and I shu'd be eternally oblig'd to you for it.

HARPAGON: Farewell, I must go and finish my Dispatches.

FROSINA: I'll assure you, Sir, you can never assist me in a better time than now.

HARPAGON: I'll order my Coach to be ready to carry you to the Fair.

FROSINA: I shu'd not importune you, if I wasn't forc'd to't by Necessity.

HARPAGON: And I'll take care to have Supper ready betimes, that you may not be sick after it.[2]

1. Taken from John Clare's translation of 1732. Ozell's version reads, 'Only my Ptyssic takes me now and then.'
2. 'After it' is taken from John Clare's translation of 1732. Ozell omits this phrase.

FROSINA: Don't refuse me the Favour I sollicit you for. You can't think, Sir, the pleasure that –

HARPAGON: I must go; I'm call'd. Farewell, till by and by. [*Exit.*]

FROSINA: Ague shake thee; Devil take thee for a miserly Dog. The Blood-hound was deaf to all I said; but I must not quit the Business, however; and on t'other side, let what will come, I'm sure of a good Reward.

Act III, Scene I

[HARPAGON, CLEANTHES, ELIZA, VALERIO, CLAUDIA, MR. JAMES, BRINDAVOINE, LA MERLUCHE.]

HARPAGON: So ho! come hither all of you, that I may give you the necessary Orders for the Evening, and assign to each their respective Employments. Come hither *Claudia*; first for you. [*She has a Broom in her Hand.*] Right, your Arms in your hand. To you I commit the Care of cleaning every thing; but pray take care you don't rub the Moveables too hard, for fear of wearing them out. Besides this, to you I give the Government of the Bottles during Supper, and if any one of 'em is missing, or any thing broke, I'll come upon you for it, and deduct it out of your Wages.

MR. JAMES: A politick Punishment.

HARPAGON: Go. [*Exit* CLAUDIA.] You, *Brindavoine*, and you, *Merluche*, the Office I constitute you in, is, to rince the Glasses, and serve the Drink; but only when the Guests are thirsty, and not like some impertinent Foot-boys, who provoke People to drink, and make 'em guzzle it down, when they think nothing of the matter. Let 'em call for it more than once, and pray remember always to mix the Wine with a good deal of Water.

MR. JAMES: Yes, for neat Wine gets into the Head.

LA MERLUCHE: Must we throw off our Aprons, Sir?

HARPAGON: Yes, when you see the Guests coming, and take care you don't spoil your Liveries.

BRINDAVOINE: You know, Sir, that one of the Fore-lappets of my Doublet has a great Spot of Lamp-Oil upon't.

LA MERLUCHE: And, Sir, my Breeches have a great Hole behind, and you may see my – with reverence be it spoken.

HARPAGON: Silence; turn that side artfully towards the Wall, and always present your Fore-part to People. [HARPAGON *puts his Hat before his Doublet, to shew* BRINDAVOINE *how to hide the Spot.*] And do you always hold your Hat thus when you serve at table. As for you, Daughter, you must have an eye upon what's taken away, and take care that nothing's wasted. This Business becomes young Women well. But, in the mean time, you must be ready to give my Mistress, who designs to pay you a

Visit, a handsome Reception, and go with her to the Fair. Do you hear what I say?

ELIZA: [*Speaking disorder'd.*] Yes, Father.

HARPAGON: [*Mimicking her.*] Yes, Noddy. And you, my sparkish Son, whom I'm so good as to pardon for your last fine Action, don't you pretend, any more than she, to make sour faces, and put on your Vinegar Looks at her.

CLEANTHES: I, Father, make sour faces! For what reason?

HARPAGON: I know the manner of Children when their Father marries again, and what a Look they are used to give what they call a Mother-in-law. But if you'd have me forget your last Prank, pray entertain her with a good Countenance, and give her the best Reception you are able.

CLEANTHES: To tell you the truth, Father, I can't promise you that I shall be very glad to have her for a Mother-in-law: I shou'd tell you a Lye, if I said so; but as to giving her a good Reception, I promise to obey you punctually in that particular.

HARPAGON: See you do.

CLEANTHES: You shall have no cause of Complaint.

HARPAGON: You will do wisely. *Valerio*, help me in this Business. So ho, Mr. *James*, come hither, I kept you till the last.

MR. JAMES: Is't your Coachman or Cook you'd speak to? For I am Both.

HARPAGON: To Both.

MR. JAMES: But which first?

HARPAGON: To the Cook.

MR. JAMES: Stay a little then, if you please. [*Pulls off his Coachman's Long-Coat, and appears dress'd as a Cook.*]

HARPAGON: What a deuce of a Ceremony is this!

MR. JAMES: Now you may speak.

HARPAGON: I'm engag'd, Mr. *James*, to give a Supper tonight.

MR. JAMES: Bless me! Is't possible?

HARPAGON: Tell me a little: will you give us good Cheer?

MR. JAMES: Ay, if you give me a good deal of Money.

HARPAGON: What the devil! always Money! one wou'd think they cou'd say nothing but Money, Money, Money. They have nothing but that word in their mouth, Money: Always Money. The beginning and ending of all their Discourse is Money. *'Tis their Sword at their Bed's-head*, as the saying is; always at hand.

VALERIO: I never heard a more impertinent Answer than that. Where's the wonder of providing good Cheer with a good deal of Money. 'Tis the easiest thing in the world; and every Fool might do as much: but if you'd do like an artful Man, you'd make good Cheer with little Money.

MR. JAMES: Good Cheer with little Money?

VALERIO: Yes.

MR. JAMES: Faith, Mr. Steward, you'd oblige me if you'd let me into that

Secret, and take my Place of Cook; since you pretend to be the *Dominus Factotum* here.

MR. JAMES: Hold your tongue. What must we have?

MR. JAMES: There's Mr. Steward will give you good Cheer for a little Money.

HARPAGON: Hey. I command you to answer me?

MR. JAMES: How many will there be of you at table?

HARPAGON: We shall be eight or ten; but you must imagine but eight. For when there's enough for eight, 'twill serve ten.

VALERIO: Certainly.

MR. JAMES: Well then, there must be four large Dishes of Soop well garnish'd, and five Courses besides; a Bisque-Soop: Partridge-Soop, with young green Sprouts; *Potage de Santé*;[1] Duck-Soop, with Turnips; Fricassee of Chickens, Pigeon-Pye, Veal-Sweetbreads, White Pudding, and Morillos.

HARPAGON: What the deuce; here's enough to treat the whole Town.

MR. JAMES: Roast-Meat in a Mazarine Dish pyramid-wise, a large Loin of Veal *de Rivière*, three Pheasants, three fat Capons, a dozen of tame Pidgeons, a dozen of Barn-door Fowls, six Warren-Rabbits, a dozen of Partridges, two dozen of Quails, three dozen of Ortolans –

HARPAGON: [*Putting his Hand on his Mouth.*] Ah, Traytor! Thou art devouring my whole Estate.

MR. JAMES: Ragoo's –

HARPAGON: Again? [*Putting his Hand on his Mouth again.*]

VALERIO: Have you a mind to burst every body? Has my Master invited Guests to kill them with gutling?[2] Go and read a little the Rules for Health, and ask the Physicians if any thing's more prejudicial to Man, than Excess in Eating.

HARPAGON: Very true.

VALERIO: Know, Mr. *James*, you and your Mates, that a Table overloaded with Victuals is a Cut-throat; that the best way of shewing one self the Friend of those we invite, is to let our Frugality predominate in what we give them to eat; for according to the saying of one of the Ancients, *We must eat to live, and not live to eat.*

HARPAGON: What a fine Sentence that is! Let me embrace you for that Expression. 'Tis the finest Saying I ever heard in my life. *We must live to eat, and not eat to li* – No, 'tis not so. How is it?

VALERIO: *We must eat to live, and not live to eat.*

HARPAGON: Ay, do you hear? Who was the great Man that said that?

VALERIO: I don't remember his Name at present.

HARPAGON: Write me down those Words. I'll have 'em writ in Letters of Gold over my Hall Chimney.

VALERIO: I won't fail to do it. Let me alone for your Supper. I'll order every thing as it ought to be.

1. A vegetable soup.
2. Guzzling.

HARPAGON: Do so.

MR. JAMES: So much the better, I shall have the less trouble with it.

HARPAGON: There must be something that People don't eat a great deal of, and which fills 'em up immediately: Some good Pease-Soop that's very fat, with a Pasty in a Pan, well garnish'd with your large Male-Chestnuts; a – let there be abundance of That.

VALERIO: Let me alone.

HARPAGON: Now, Mr. *James*: you must clean my Coach.

MR. JAMES: Stay a little; this belongs to the Coachman. [*Puts on his Coachman's Long-Coat again.*] Now speak on –

HARPAGON: You must clean my Coach, and get my Horses ready to go to the Fair with –

MR. JAMES: Your Horses, Sir? They're in no manner of case for moving: I won't say they're in the Litter, the poor Beasts have none under 'em, therefore 'twou'd be a very improper Expression: But you make 'em keep such austere Fasts, that they are now no more than Phantomes; perfect Shadows of Horses.

HARPAGON: Why they're mighty sick, and yet they do nothing!

MR. JAMES: And because they do nothing, Sir, must they eat nothing? The poor Animals had better work much and eat accordingly. It pierces me to the heart to see 'em grow so lank; for, in short, I've such a Tenderness for my Horses, that when I see 'em suffer, methinks 'tis mine own self. I every day spare it out of my own Belly for 'em; and to shew no pity to our Neighbour, is a most barbarous Temper, Sir.

HARPAGON: 'Twill be no such great Labour for them to go but to the Fair.

MR. JAMES: No, Sir, I han't the heart to drive 'em, and can't answer it to myself to lash 'em in the case they are now in. How wou'd you have 'em drag a Coach, when they can hardly drag themselves?

VALERIO: Sir, I'll get the *Picardy*-man that lives hard by to drive them; besides we shall have need of him to help dress the Supper.

MR. JAMES: With all my heart; I'd rather they shou'd die under the hands of another than under mine.

VALERIO: Mr. *James* acts the considerate part mainly.

MR. JAMES: Mr. Steward acts like a Busy-body.

HARPAGON: Silence.

MR. JAMES: Sir, I can't endure Flatterers; I see that every thing he does, his perpetual comptrolling the Bread, Wine, Wood, Salt, and Candles, is only to wheedle in with you, and make his court to you. I can't bear this, and am every day griev'd at the Character I hear of you; for, in spite of me,[1] I have a Tenderness for You; and, next my Horses, you are the Person I love most.

---

1. Taken from John Clare's translation of 1732. Ozell uses the phrase, 'in spite of my teeth'.

HARPAGON: Wou'd you be so kind as to tell me, Mr. *James*, what 'tis People say of me?

MR. JAMES: Yes, Sir, if I thought 'twou'd not make you angry.

HARPAGON: No, not at all.

MR. JAMES: I beg your pardon, Sir; I know very well I shou'd put you in a passion.

HARPAGON: Not in the least; on the contrary, 'twou'd please me, and I shou'd be very glad to hear how I'm spoke of in the world.

MR. JAMES: Sir, since you will have it so, I shall tell you freely that you're the common Laughing-Stock; that wherever we go, we have a hundred Gibes and Jokes flung at us on your account; and that People are never better pleas'd, than when they have you upon the hip, and are roasting you, and incessantly telling Tales of your pinch-penny Tricks. One says you get particular Almanacks printed, wherein you double the Ember-weeks and Vigils, that you may save the more by making your Family fast. Another, that you always quarrel with your Footmen when you're to give 'em a New-Year's Gift, or at their going away, that you may have a reason for paying them nothing. This Man says, that once you went to law with one of your Neighbour's Cats, for eating part of a Leg of Mutton[1] you had set by. That Man says, that one Night you were caught stealing away your own Horses Oats; and that your Coachman, who was before me, gave you in the dark I don't know how many Bastinadoes, which you wou'd never mention one word of. In short, wou'd you have me speak all? We can go no where but we're sure to hear you paid off. Your are the standing Jest, the May-game of every body, and you are never spoken of, but with the honourable Surnames of Miser, Niggard,[2] Flay-flint, and Usurer.

HARPAGON: [*Beating him.*] You are a Fool, a Scoundrel, a Knave, and an impertinent Jackanapes.

MR. JAMES: Very well. Did not I guess what wou'd happen? You wou'd not believe me; I told you that I shou'd but anger you by telling you the Truth.

HARPAGON: Learn how to speak another time.

Act III, Scene II

[MR. JAMES, VALERIO.]

VALERIO: As far as I see, Mr. *James*, you have but ill returns made you for your Frankness.

MR. JAMES: 'Zblood, Mr. *Novice*, who take such state upon you, 'tis none of

1. Taken from John Clare's translation of 1732. Instead of 'Leg' Ozell uses 'Giggot'.
2. Taken from John Clare's translation of 1732. Instead of 'Niggard', Ozell uses 'Hunks'.

your business. Laugh when yourself's beaten, but pray don't laugh
when I am.

VALERIO: Good Mr. *James*, don't be angry.

MR. JAMES: [*To himself.*] He's tame. I'll pretend to be valiant, and, if he's Fool
enough to believe me, bastinado him a little. [*Aloud.*] Do you know, Mr.
Sneerer, that I'm not merrily dispos'd; and that if you provoke me, I'll
make you laugh on the wrong side o' your mouth. [MR. JAMES *drives*
VALERIO *to the further end of the Stage, threatning him.*]

VALERIO: Good now, be quiet.

MR. JAMES: What if I han't a mind to't?

VALERIO: Pray now.

MR. JAMES: You're an impertinent Fellow.

VALERIO: Monsieur, Monsieur *James*.

MR. JAMES: There's no such Person as Monsieur Monsieur *James*, with a
repetition, as I know of. If I take a Stick, I shall rib-roast you to some
tune.

VALERIO: How! a Stick?

[VALERIO *drives him back again, as far as the other had driven him.*]

MR. JAMES: No, no; I did not say so.

VALERIO: Do you know, Mr. Dunderpate, I am one that will thresh you?

MR. JAMES: I don't at all doubt it.

VALERIO: That, in short, you're but a poor Devil of a Cook.

MR. JAMES: I know it.

VALERIO: And that you don't yet know me?

MR. JAMES: Well, I beg your pardon.

VALERIO: You'll rib-roast me, ha?

MR. JAMES: I only said it in jest.

VALERIO: I don't love such jesting. [*Canes him.*] Know that you're but a sorry
Jester.

MR. JAMES: Pox take Sincerity, 'tis an ill Trade; henceforth I renounce it, and
will not speak Truth any more. As for my Master, well and good, he has
some right to beat me; but as for this Mr. Steward, I'll be revenged on
him, if I can.

Act III, Scene III

[FROSINA, MARIANA *and* MR. JAMES.]

FROSINA: Do you know, Mr. *James*, if your Master's at home?

MR. JAMES: Yes, to my cost I know it.

FROSINA: Pray tell him that we are here.

MR. JAMES: Hah! 'Twou'd do us no harm to –

Act III, Scene IV

[MARIANA, FROSINA.]

MARIANA: Ah, what a strange condition I am in, *Frosina*! and, if I must speak what I feel, how I dread this meeting!

FROSINA: And pray what's your Uneasiness?

MARIANA: Alas! Do you ask that? Can't you fancy to yourself the Disorder of a Person just ready to behold the Gallows she's to be ty'd up to?

FROSINA: I see, in order to die agreeably, *Harpagon* is not the Gallows you'd willingly be ty'd to; I know the young Gentleman you spoke to me of, is still in your thoughts.

MARIANA: Yes, 'tis a thing, *Frosina*, that I won't try to dissemble; and the respectful Visits he paid us at our House, have, I confess, work'd some effect upon me.

FROSINA: But do you know who he is?

MARIANA: No, but I know he's an agreeable Man; that if I was left to my choice, I shou'd take him sooner than any body; and that he contributes not a little to make me dread the Husband you wou'd give me.

FROSINA: Lord! all these young Beaux are agreeable enough, that's true, and make the best of their Shapes, but they're most of them as poor as Church-Mice; and 'twou'd be better for you to take an old Man that will settle a good Jointure on you. I confess the Senses mayn't be so well gratify'd by it, and one must endure some Uneasiness with such a Husband; but that is not lasting, and his Death will soon set you at liberty to take one that is more amiable, who will make it up to you, never fear.

MARIANA: Ah, 'tis an odd Life, *Frosina*, when, to be happy, one must wish for or expect another's Decease, and Death don't always answer our Projects neither.

FROSINA: All a mere jest. Why, you don't marry him, but on condition he'll soon leave you a Widow, which is to be one of the Articles of the Contract. He'll be very impertinent, if he don't die in three Months. Here he comes in his proper Person.

MARIANA: Ah, *Frosina*, what a Figure he is!

Act III, Scene V

[HARPAGON, FROSINA *and* MARIANA.]

HARPAGON: [*With Spectacles on.*] Be not offended, Fair-One, if I come to you with my Spectacles on. I know that your Charms strike the Eye sufficiently, and are visible enough of themselves, and that there's no need of Glasses to perceive them; but yet 'tis with Glasses Men observe the Stars, and I do maintain and aver, that You are a Star; but a Star, the fairest Star that is in the whole Country of Stars. *Frosina*, she don't answer a word, nor, as I think, shew the least Joy at the sight of me.

FROSINA: 'Tis because she's under a surprize; besides, Maids are always asham'd at first to unbosom their Thoughts.

HARPAGON: You say true. Here comes my Daughter, pretty Creature, to wait on you.

Act III, Scene VI

[ELIZA, HARPAGON, MARIANA *and* FROSINA.]

MARIANA: Madam, I have very long deferr'd paying you this Visit.

ELIZA: You have done what I ought to have done, Madam; 'twas my Part to have prevented you.

HARPAGON: She's a great tall Girl, you see; but ill Weeds grow apace.

MARIANA: [*Aside to* FROSINA.] What a disagreeable Man 'tis!

HARPAGON: What says the Fair-One?

FROSINA: That she thinks you admirable.

HARPAGON: You do me too much Honour, adorable Lady.

MARIANA: What an Animal 'tis! [*Aside.*]

HARPAGON: I'm too much oblig'd to you for these Sentiments.

MARIANA: [*Aside.*] I can hold no longer.

HARPAGON: Here comes my Son too, to pay you his Respects.

MARIANA: [*Aside to* FROSINA.] Ah, Frosina, what an Accident! 'tis the very Person I mention'd to you.

FROSINA: [*Aside to* MARIANA.] The Accident is wonderful.

HARPAGON: I see you're amaz'd that I should have such strapping Children, but I shall soon be rid of both of them.

Act III, Scene VII

[CLEANTHES, HARPAGON, ELIZA, MARIANA, FROSINA.]

CLEANTHES: Madam, this indeed is an Accident I did not in the least expect, and my Father did not a little surprize me, when he just now told me the Design he had form'd.

MARIANA: I may say the same. 'Tis a thing that has surpriz'd me as much as you; nor was I prepared for such an Adventure.

CLEANTHES: 'Tis true, Madam, my Father could not have made a more beautiful Choice, and the Honour of seeing you is a sensible Pleasure to me; but yet I can't say that I am pleased with the Design you may have of becoming my Mother-in-Law.[1] That Compliment, I must confess, is too difficult for me to make; and 'tis a Title I don't at all wish you. What I am going to say may appear brutish to some, but I'm assur'd you are one that will take it right. 'Tis a Match, Madam, which you may well imagine is not very pleasing to me; you are not ignorant, as knowing who I am, how much 'tis against my Interest; and permit me to tell you, with my Father's leave, that if things depended on me, it shou'd be broke off.

HARPAGON: This is a very impertinent Compliment. A very fine Confession to make to her truly!

MARIANA: And for my part, in answer, I must tell you that things are very equal; and that if You're unwilling to have me for a Mother-in-Law, I am no less so to have you for a Son-in-Law. Pray don't think that 'tis my fault you are made thus uneasy. I should be very sorry to create you any Disquiet; and if I am not forced to it by an absolute Power, I give you my Word I will never consent to a Marriage that may give you the least Disturbance.

HARPAGON: Well said. To an extravagant Compliment ought to be return'd an extravagant Answer. I hope you'll pardon my Son's Impertinence, Pretty one. 'Tis a giddy-brain'd young Fool, that as yet don't know the Consequence of what he says.

MARIANA: I promise you, that what he said has not at all offended me; on the contrary, he has pleased me by thus declaring his true Opinion. I love such a Confession from him; and if he had spoken otherwise, I should have had much less Esteem for him.

HARPAGON: It shews a great deal of Goodness in you thus to excuse his Faults. In time he'll be wiser, and you shall see he'll change his Mind.

CLEANTHES: No, no, Father, I am not capable of changing; I earnestly beg the Lady to believe as much.

HARPAGON: Do you see this Extravagance! He goes on the more.

CLEANTHES: Wou'd you have me belye my Heart?

HARPAGON: Again! Will you not change the Discourse?

CLEANTHES: Well then, since you'll have me speak in another Strain;[2] Suffer me, Madam, to stand in my Father's place, and confess to you, that I never saw any thing in the World so charming as you are; that I think nothing equal to the Happiness of pleasing you: and that the Title of Your Husband is a Glory, a Felicity I'd prefer to the condition of the greatest Princes of the Earth. Yes, Madam, the Happiness of possessing You is in my Opinion the greatest Good-Fortune, and wou'd be the highest of my Ambition. There's nothing but what I'd do for so precious a Conquest; and the most powerful Obstacles –

1. Stepmother.
2. Taken from John Clare's translation of 1732. Instead of 'another Strain' Ozell's version reads 'another-guise Fashion'.

HARPAGON: Soft, Son, if you please.

CLEANTHES: 'Tis a Compliment I make in your behalf to the Lady.

HARPAGON: Oh, I've a Tongue to speak for myself, and have no need of such an Interpreter as you. Come, bring Chairs here.

FROSINA: No, we had better go away to the Fair, that we may be the sooner back, and have the more time for Discourse afterwards.

HARPAGON: Put the Horses to the Coach then. Pray pardon me, Fair-One, for not thinking to give you some little Collation before you go.

CLEANTHES: I have provided That, Father, and have sent for some Basins of *China*-Oranges, Pomecitrons, and Sweetmeats, which I have order'd hither in your name.

HARPAGON: [*Aside to* VALERIO.] *Valerio!*

VALERIO: [*To* HARPAGON.] He's mad, sure.

CLEANTHES: Don't you think That enough, Father? The Lady will have the goodness to excuse it, I hope.

MARIANA: There was no manner of need of it.

CLEANTHES: Madam, did you ever see a more lively Diamond than that which is on my Father's Finger?

MARIANA: 'Tis indeed very sparkling.

CLEANTHES: [*Takes it from off his Father's Finger, and gives it* MARIANA.] You must look upon it nearer.

MARIANA: 'Tis indeed very fine, and casts a great Lustre.

CLEANTHES: [*Putting himself before* MARIANA, *who would return it.*] No, Madam, 'tis in too good Hands already. 'Tis a Present my Father makes you.

HARPAGON: I!

CLEANTHES: Is not it true, Father, that you'd have the Lady keep it for your sake?

HARPAGON: How? [*Aside to his Son.*]

CLEANTHES: Nay, indeed, 'twas a silly Question. He bids me by signs prevail on you to accept of it.

MARIANA: I wou'd by no means –

CLEANTHES: You're deceiv'd: He won't take it again.

HARPAGON: [*Aside.*] I can't bear This!

MARIANA: 'Twou'd be –

CLEANTHES: [*Still hind'ring her from returning the Ring.*] No, I tell you; you'll affront him.

MARIANA: Pray –

CLEANTHES: Not at all.

HARPAGON: [*Aside.*] Plague –

CLEANTHES: He is highly offended at your Refusal.

HARPAGON: [*Aside to his Son.*] Ah, Traitor!

CLEANTHES: You see, he's down-right angry.

HARPAGON: [*Aside, threatning his Son.*] Hang-dog as thou art!

CLEANTHES: Father, 'tis not my fault. I do what I can to oblige her to keep it, but she's obstinate.

HARPAGON: Rascal! [*Aside to his Son, in a rage.*]

CLEANTHES: You make my Father angry with me, Madam.

HARPAGON: Villain! [*Aside to his Son, with the same crabbed Looks.*]

CLEANTHES: You'll make him fall into Fits; pray, Madam, refuse it no longer.

FROSINA: Bless me, what Scruples are here! Keep the Ring, since the Gentleman will have it so.

MARIANA: I'll keep it then at present, that I mayn't disoblige you; and shall take another opportunity to restore it.

Act III, Scene VIII

[HARPAGON, MARIANA, FROSINA, CLEANTHES, BRINDAVOINE *and* ELIZA.]

BRINDAVOINE: Sir, here's a Man wants to speak with you.

HARPAGON: Tell him I'm busy, and bid him come again another time.

BRINDAVOINE: He says he brings you Money.

HARPAGON: I beg your pardon; I'll be here again in a moment.

Act III, Scene IX

[HARPAGON, MARIANA, CLEANTHES, ELIZA, FROSINA *and* LA MERLUCHE.]

LA MERLUCHE: [*Hastily running against* HARPAGON, *throws him down.*] Sir –

HARPAGON: Ah! I'm dead.

CLEANTHES: What's the matter, Father? Have you hurt yourself?

HARPAGON: The Rogue is certainly bribed by my Debtors to break my Neck.

VALERIO: There's no hurt done.

LA MERLUCHE: Sir, I beg your pardon; I thought I did well to make haste.

HARPAGON: What do you want, Rascal?

LA MERLUCHE: I come to tell you that your two Horses are unshod.

HARPAGON: Let 'em be carry'd quickly to the Farrier's.

CLEANTHES: While they're shooing, Sir, I'll perform the Honours of the House in your stead, to the Lady, and conduct her into the Garden, whither I'll send the Collation.

HARPAGON: *Valerio*, have an eye a little to all this; and pray take care to save me as much as you can, that I may send it back to the Confectioner's.

VALERIO: It shall be done.

HARPAGON: O Rogue of a Son! Have you a mind to ruin me?

Act IV, Scene I

[CLEANTHES, MARIANA, ELIZA, FROSINA.]

CLEANTHES: Let us retire hither; here we shall be much better. There's no suspicious body about us now, and we may speak freely.

ELIZA: Yes, Madam, my Brother has confided to me the Passion he has for you. I know the Uneasiness and Vexation which such cross Accidents are capable of causing; and I interest myself in your Adventure with an extreme Tenderness.

MARIANA: 'Tis a pleasing Consolation to see in one's Interest such a Person as you; and I conjure you, Madam, always to preserve to me that generous Friendship which is so capable of sweetning the Cruelties of Fortune.

FROSINA: In good truth, you're both unfortunate People, in not having acquainted me with your Affair before all this. I should certainly have prevented this Uneasiness, and not let things have come to this pass.

CLEANTHES: What wou'd you have me do? My evil Destiny will have it so. But, fair *Mariana*, what are Your Resolutions?

MARIANA: Alas! Am I capable of making Resolutions! Can I form any thing but Wishes, in the Dependance I am in?

CLEANTHES: Is there no other Support for me in your Heart but bare wishes? no officious Pity? no relieving Goodness? no active Affection?

MARIANA: What can I say to you? Imagine yourself in my place, and think what I can do. Advise, order things yourself; I refer myself to you; and believe you too reasonable to exact from me any thing, but what the Rules of Honour and Decency will permit.

CLEANTHES: Alas! how narrowly you confine me, when you refer me to the Rules of rigorous Honour and a scrupulous Decency.

MARIANA: But what wou'd you have me do? Even though I could resolve to forego several Ceremonies our Sex is obliged to, yet I've a respect for my Mother. She always bred me up with an extreme Tenderness, and I can't prevail on myself to do any thing to displease her. But use your interest with her; strain all your Power to gain her over; I give you leave to say, and do all you please; and if it only depends upon my declaring in your favour, I'll consent to make a full confession to her myself, of the opinion I have of you.

CLEANTHES: *Frosina*, good dear *Frosina*! will you not assist us?

FROSINA: Adsheartlikins! Is that a Question? I am entirely willing. You know that I am by Nature sufficiently Humane. Heaven has not made my Heart of Brass; and I am but too fond of serving those whom I perceive love each other heartily and honourably. What cou'd we do in this case?

CLEANTHES: Prithee, consider a little.

MARIANA: Strike us out some little Light.

ELIZA: Find out some Invention to unravel what you have done.

FROSINA: This is a difficult Point. As for your Mother, she is not unreasonable, and perhaps may be gained to bestow on the Son, the Gift she promised to the Father. But the deuce on't is, your Father is your Father.

CLEANTHES: That we know.

FROSINA: I mean he'll for ever resent it if he's openly refused; he will never afterwards be in a humour to consent to your marriage. To go rightly to work, we must try to get *Him* to be off first, and endeavour by some means to give him a disgust to your Person.

CLEANTHES: You're in the right.

FROSINA: Yes, I know I'm in the right. This is what we must do; but how to do it, that's the Devil! Stay, suppose we had some Woman, a little super-annuated, of much such a Talent as myself, that might act a Woman of Quality, by means of a Train Hastily made up, and a whimsical Name of Marchioness or a Vicountess, whom we'll imagine of *Lower-Britany*; I dare say I should be cunning enough to make your Father believe she's a very rich Lady, who besides Houses had a hundred thousand Crowns in hard Mony, that she was in love with him to Distraction, and would fain be his Wife, even tho' she made over to him all her Estate by the Contract; I don't doubt but he'd hearken to this Proposal: for in short, though he loves you well, yet he loves Money much better; and when he is dazled with that Lure, and has once consented to what concerns you, 'twou'd be no great matter afterwards if he's disabused, when he comes to look more narrowly into our Marchioness's Wealth.

CLEANTHES: This is a very good Thought.

FROSINA: Let me alone. Now I remember one of my Acquaintance that will serve our Turn.

CLEANTHES: Depend, *Frosina*, upon my Gratitude if you bring it about; but charming *Mariana*, let us begin I beseech you, by gaining your Mother. A great part of our Business is to break off this Match. I beg you'd do whatever you possibly can towards it. Use all the Power which her Fondness of you gives you over her. Display without Reserve the eloquent Graces, the all-potent Charms which Heaven has placed in your Eyes and Mouth; and, if you please, omit none of that endearing Language, those gentle Prayers, and those tender Caresses, which I'm persuaded would obtain any thing.

MARIANA: I'll do all I am able, and will omit nothing.

Act IV, Scene II

[HARPAGON, CLEANTHES, MARIANA, ELIZA, FROSINA.]

HARPAGON: How now! My Son kiss the Hand of his intended Mother-in-Law, and she not seem to be angry at it! There's some Mystery in this.

ELIZA: Here's my Father.

HARPAGON: The Coach is ready, and you may go when you please.

CLEANTHES: Since You don't go, Father, I will wait upon 'em.

HARPAGON: No, stay. They'll go as well by themselves; and I want You here.

Act IV, Scene III

[HARPAGON, CLEANTHES.]

HARPAGON: Well; without considering her as your Mother-in-Law, what do you think of this Lady?

CLEANTHES: What do I think of her?

HARPAGON: Yes, of her Air, her Shape, her Beauty, her Wit?

CLEANTHES: So so.

HARPAGON: But tell me.

CLEANTHES: To speak my Mind freely, I do not find her now what I thought she had been. Her Air is downright Coquette; her Shape but untoward; her Beauty very mean, and her Wit vulgar. Don't think, Sir, I say this to give you a Disgust of her; for, if it must be so, I would as soon chuse her for a Mother-in-Law as another.

HARPAGON: Yet just now you said to her –

CLEANTHES: I made her some Compliments, indeed, in your Name, but 'twas to please You.

HARPAGON: So, then, You cou'd not like her at all?

CLEANTHES: I? Not at all.

HARPAGON: I'm sorry for it, because it breaks a Design which came into my Head. Upon seeing her here, I reflected upon my Age, and consider'd that I might be blamed for marrying so young a Person. This Consideration made me quit my Design; and having asked her in Marriage, and being engaged to her by Promise, I'd have given her to you, had you not shewn this Aversion.

CLEANTHES: To me!

HARPAGON: To You.

CLEANTHES: In Marriage?

HARPAGON: In Marriage.

CLEANTHES: Why, ay, 'tis true, I have no great liking to her; but to please you, Father, I'll resolve to marry her, if you will.

HARPAGON: No, I am not so unreasonable as you imagine. I won't force your inclinations.

CLEANTHES: Pardon me; I'll strain myself in this Case for your sake.

HARPAGON: No, no; Marriage can never be happy where there is not love.

CLEANTHES: That will perhaps come afterwards; and I've heard say, that Love's often the Fruit of Marriage.

HARPAGON: No: on the Man's Side the Affair ought never to be ventured, and such things have often so unhappy Consequences, that I'll not expose you to them. If you had had any Inclination to her, You should have had her with all my Heart, instead of myself; but it not being so, I'll proceed with my former Design, and marry her myself.

CLEANTHES: Well, Father, since things stand upon this Foot, I must open my heart and reveal the Secret to you. The Truth is, I have lov'd her ever since I met her in the publick Walks; 'twas my Design soon to have ask'd her of you for a Wife, and nothing has hindered me from so doing but the Declaration of your Sentiments, and the fear of disobliging you.

HARPAGON: Have you visited her?

CLEANTHES: Yes, Sir.

HARPAGON: Very often?

CLEANTHES: Pretty often, for the time I've known her.

HARPAGON: Was you well receiv'd?

CLEANTHES: Very well, but without knowing who I was; and 'twas that which caus'd *Mariana's* Surprize just now.

HARPAGON: Have you declar'd your Passion to her, and your Design of marrying her?

CLEANTHES: I have; and made some Proposals to the Mother herself upon it.

HARPAGON: Did she hearken to your Proposal about her Daughter?

CLEANTHES: Yes, very civilly.

HARPAGON: And does the Daughter make strong Returns to your Love.

CLEANTHES: If I may believe Appearances, I am persuaded she has some Respect for me.

HARPAGON: I am mighty glad I know this Secret; 'tis the very thing I wanted. Hark'e[1] me, Son, Do ye know what I'm going to say? No other but that you must, if you please, lay aside this Love, give over your Pursuits after a Person I intend for myself, and prepare very soon to marry the Person I design for you.

CLEANTHES: Ay, Father, do you serve me thus! Well, since 'tis come to this, I declare, that I won't give over the Passion I have for *Mariana,* and that there's no Extremity but what I'll undergo to dispute the Conquest of her with you, and that if you have the Consent of the Mother, I shall have other Auxiliaries perhaps that will fight on my Side.

HARPAGON: Sirrah, have you the boldness to tread on my Heels?

CLEANTHES: You tread upon mine; I have an elder title.

HARPAGON: Am not I your Father? Ought you not to respect me?

CLEANTHES: In these things Children are not obliged to pay deference to their Fathers; and Love knows no body.

HARPAGON: I shall make you know me with a good Cudgelling.

CLEANTHES: All your Threats will do no good.

HARPAGON: Won't you renounce *Mariana*?

CLEANTHES: No, Positively, no.

HARPAGON: Give me a Cane here presently.

1. Taken from John Clare's translation of 1732. Instead of 'Hark'e me', Ozell uses the phrase 'Mind ye me'.

Act IV, Scene IV

[MR. JAMES, HARPAGON, CLEANTHES.]

MR. JAMES: What now, Gentlemen? What's here to do!

CLEANTHES: I fear not that.

MR. JAMES: Good Sir, be quiet.

HARPAGON: Talk to Me with that Impudence!

MR. JAMES: Pray, Sir.

CLEANTHES: I'll not eat my Words, Sir.

MR. JAMES: What, to your Father?

HARPAGON: Let me alone.

MR. JAMES: What, to your Son? Give over for my sake.

HARPAGON: Mr. *James*. I'll make you Judge in this Business, to shew how much I'm in the right.

MR. JAMES: I consent. [*To* CLEANTHES.] Fall back a little.

HARPAGON: I love a young Gentlewoman, and wou'd marry her, and this Rascal has the Insolence to love her too, and to pretend to her, notwithstanding my orders to the contrary.

MR. JAMES: Ah! He's in the wrong.

HARPAGON: Is it not a lamentable thing, that a Son shou'd put himself in competition with his Father? Ought he not, out of respect, to forbear interfering with my Inclinations?

MR. JAMES: Ay, certainly. Let me speak to him, and stay you there. [*Goes to* CLEANTHES *at t'other end of the Stage.*]

CLEANTHES: Well, since he has chosen thee for a Judge, I shan't except against it; it don't signify much who 'tis; and I am very willing to let you decide our Difference, Mr.*James*.

MR. JAMES: Sir, You do me a great deal of Honour.

CLEANTHES: I am enamour'd of a young Person, who sympathizes with my Love, and receives with tenderness the Offers of my Faith. My Father takes it in his head to disturb our Love, by asking her of her Mother in Marriage.

MR. JAMES: He's certainly in the wrong.

CLEANTHES: Shou'd he not at his Age be asham'd to think of Marriage? Does it sit well upon him to be again in Love? And ought he not to leave that Affair to young Men?

MR. JAMES: You are in the right; he forgets himself. Let me speak two Words to him. [*Returns to* HARPAGON.] Well, your Son is not so strange a Man as you say he is; he submits to reason. He says he knows the Respect he owes you; that he was hurry'd on by his first Heat, and that he won't refuse to agree to whatever you please, provided you use him better than you do, and give him a Wife that he may be contented with.

HARPAGON: Tell him, Mr. *James*, upon that consideration, he may expect any thing from me; and, except *Mariana,* I give him the liberty to chuse whom he pleases.

MR. JAMES: Let me alone. [*Goes to the Son.*] Well, your Father is not so unreasonable as you make him; he assures me that 'twas your excessive Heat put him in a passion; and that your Manner of proceeding was the only thing that offended him; and that he shou'd be very inclinable to satisfy all your Desires, in case you proceed with Mildness, and pay him the Honour, Respect, and Submission that are due from a Son to his Father.

CLEANTHES: Ah, Mr. *James,* you may assure him that if he grants me *Mariana,* he shall always find me the most obedient of Men; and that I'll never do any thing but what shall please him.

MR. JAMES: [*Returning to the Father.*] 'Tis done; he consents to what you say.

HARPAGON: Why now 'tis as it ought to be.

MR. JAMES: All's concluded; he's content with your Promises.

CLEANTHES: Heaven be prais'd for it.

MR. JAMES: Gentlemen, you need only confer notes together a little. You are Now agreed; whereas you were just going to cut each other's Throat, only for want of understanding one another.

CLEANTHES: Honest Mr. *James,* I shall be eternally obliged to you.

MR. JAMES: There is no occasion, Sir.

HARPAGON: You have done me a Service, Mr. *James,* that deserves a Recompence. Go, I'll assure you I'll remember it. [*Pulls his Handkerchief out of his Pocket, which makes* MR. JAMES *think he's going to give him something.*]

MR. JAMES: Sir, I kiss your Hand.

Act IV, Scene V

[CLEANTHES, HARPAGON.]

CLEANTHES: I beg your pardon, Father, for the Heat I shewed.

HARPAGON: Oh, 'tis nothing.

CLEANTHES: I assure you I'm extremely sorry for it.

HARPAGON: And it rejoices me the most of any thing in the world, to see you submit to Reason.

CLEANTHES: What Goodness 'tis in you to forget my Fault so soon!

HARPAGON: We soon forget the Faults of our Children, when they return to their Duty.

CLEANTHES: What, not to retain the least Resentment of all my Extravagancies!

HARPAGON: 'Tis what your present Submission and Respect oblige me to.

CLEANTHES: Ah, Father! I have nothing more to ask; you have given me enough in bestowing *Mariana* on me.

HARPAGON: How?

CLEANTHES: I say, Father, that I'm abundantly satisfy'd already, and that all things are included in your granting me *Mariana*.

HARPAGON: Who talk'd of granting you *Mariana*?

CLEANTHES: You, Father.

HARPAGON: I?

CLEANTHES: Certainly.

HARPAGON: How? Why, did not you promise to renounce her?

CLEANTHES: I promise to renounce her?

HARPAGON: Yes.

CLEANTHES: Not at all.

HARPAGON: Did not you quit your Pretensions to her?

CLEANTHES: On the contrary, I am more firm than before.

HARPAGON: How! Rascal, what again?

CLEANTHES: Nothing can change me.

HARPAGON: Let me come to you, Sirrah.

CLEANTHES: Do what you please.

HARPAGON: I forbid you the sight of me.

CLEANTHES: With all my heart.

HARPAGON: I abandon you.

CLEANTHES: Do so.

HARPAGON: I disown you for my Son.

CLEANTHES: Be it so.

HARPAGON: I disinherit you.

CLEANTHES: As you think fit.

HARPAGON: And I give you my Curse.

CLEANTHES: I don't want your Gifts.

Act IV, Scene VI

[LA FLECHE, CLEANTHES.]

LA FLECHE: [*coming out of the Garden, with a Casket.*] Well met, Sir. Follow me quickly.

CLEANTHES: What's the matter?

LA FLECHE: Follow me, I tell you, we're all right.[1]

CLEANTHES: What now?

LA FLECHE: Here's what you wanted.

CLEANTHES: What is't?

LA FLECHE: What I've been ogling all day.

CLEANTHES: Prithee what is't?

1. Taken from John Clare's translation of 1732. Instead of 'we're all right', Ozell's version reads, 'I say: Omnia bene'.

LA FLECHE: Your Father's Treasure, which I've caught.
CLEANTHES: How did you get it?
LA FLECHE: You shall know all. Let's be gone, I hear him crying out.

Act IV, Scene VII

[HARPAGON.]

HARPAGON: [*from the Garden, without his Hat, cries Thieves.*] Thieves, Thieves!
Murder, Murder! Justice, just Heaven! I'm ruin'd, I'm murder'd, my
Throat's cut, My Money's stolen. Who can it be? Where can he be?
What's become of him? Where is he? What shall I do to find him? Where
shall I run? Where shall I not run? Is he not there? Is it not here? Who's
that? Stand. Restore me my Money, Knave – [*Takes hold of his own Arm.*]
Ah, 'tis myself, my Mind's disturbed, and I know not where I am, who
I am, or what I do. Alas, my poor Money, my poor Money, my dear
Friend, they have depriv'd me of thee; and now thou art gone, I have
lost my Support, my Comfort, my Joy; every thing's at an end with me;
and I've nothing further to do in the world. Without thee 'tis impossible
for me to live. 'Tis done, I am no more; I'm dying' I'm dead; I'm bury'd.
Will nobody restore me to Life, by giving me my dear Money again, or
by telling me who has got it? Ha! What say you? Alas! 'tis nobody.
Whoever it be, he watch'd his Opportunity very carefully; and just
pitch'd on the time I was talking to my Knave of a Son. Let's away. I'll
go to a Justice, and have all my Family, Servants male and female, Son,
Daughter and even myself put on the Rack. What a Multitude is here! I
look on nobody, but I suspect 'em, and every one seems to me to be my
Thief. Hey, what are they talking of there? of him that robb'd me? What
Noise is that they make above there? is it my Thief that's there? If you
know any tidings of my Thief, for God's sake tell me. Is not he hid there
among you? They all look at me, and set up a Laugh. I'll engage they go
shares in the Theft. Come quickly, Notaries, Provosts, Marshals-men,
Judges, Racks, Gibbets, and Hang-men. I'll hang the whole World; and,
if I don't get my Money again, I'll hang myself afterwards.

Act V, Scene I

[HARPAGON, A COMMISSARY *and his* CLERK.]

COMMISSARY: Let me alone. I understand my Trade, thank Heav'n: This is not
the first day I've been concern'd in discovering Thefts; and I wish I had
as many Thousand-Pound Bags, as I have hang'd Thieves.
HARPAGON: 'Tis the Interest of the whole Magistracy to take this Business in

hand; and if my Money ben't restored to me, I'll demand justice upon Justice itself.

COMMISSARY: We must make all requisite Pursuit. You say there was in the Casket –

HARPAGON: Full ten thousand Crowns.

COMMISSARY: Ten thousand Crowns!

HARPAGON: [*Weeping.*] Ten thousand Crowns.

COMMISSARY: The Robbery is considerable.

HARPAGON: No Punishment can be great enough for the Enormity of the Crime; and if it goes unpunish'd, the most sacred things are no longer in safety.

CLEANTHES: In what Species of Money was this Sum?

HARPAGON: In good *Louis d'Or*, and *Pistoles* down-weight.

COMMISSARY: Who do you suspect of this Robbery?

HARPAGON: Every body; and therefore I'll have you arrest the whole City and Suburbs.

COMMISSARY: If you'll take my Advice, I wou'd not have you frighten any body, but try with mildness to catch hold of some Proofs, and then proceed, by the rigour of the Law, to the recovery of the Money you've been robb'd of.

Act V, Scene II

[MR. JAMES, HARPAGON, THE COMMISSARY *and his* CLERK.]

MR. JAMES: [*at the end of the Stage, turning back towards the Place he came from.*] I shall return presently. Cut me his Throat immediately, let his Feet be sindged, let him be put into scalding water, and then hung up at the Ceiling.

HARPAGON: Who? He that has robb'd me?

MR. JAMES: I speak of a sucking Pig which your Steward has just sent me in, and I am resolv'd to dress it for you after my own way.

HARPAGON: That is not the Business; you must talk of some thing else to Mr. Commissary there.

COMMISSARY: [*To* MR. JAMES.] Don't be frighten'd. I ben't one that will expose you; things shall be carry'd on gently.

MR. JAMES: [To HARPAGON.] Is this Gentleman to be at Supper then?

COMMISSARY: You must hide nothing from your Master, Friend, in the Case before us.

MR. JAMES: Indeed, Sir, I'll Shew him the utmost I can do; and will treat you the best I am able.

HARPAGON: That is not the Business.

MR. JAMES: If I don't give you as good a Supper as I wou'd do, 'tis your

Steward's fault, who has clip'd my Wings with the Cizzars of his
Oeconomy.

HARPAGON: Rascal, we don't talk of Supper; I command you, tell me news of
the Money that's stol'n from me.

MR. JAMES: Has any body robb'd you of your Money?

HARPAGON: Yes, Knave, and I'll have you hang'd if you don't restore it me.

COMMISSARY: Nay, don't use him ill. I see by his Countenance he's an honest
Fellow; and that he'll discover to you what you want to know, without
being sent to Prison. If you confess the Fact, Friend, no harm shall come
to you, and you'll be rewarded by your Master, as you ought to be. He
has been robb'd of some Money to-day, and 'tis impossible but you
must know something of it.

MR. JAMES: [*Aside.*] This is just what I wanted, to be reveng'd on our Steward:
Ever since he came, he has been the Favourite, and the only one
whose Advice cou'd be heard; besides, I can't digest his caning me just
now.

HARPAGON: What are you puzzling[1] about?

MR. JAMES: Sir, since I must tell you, I believe 'tis your dear Mr. Steward has
serv'd you this Trick.

HARPAGON: *Valerio?*

MR. JAMES: Yes.

HARPAGON: What, he that seems so faithful to me?

MR. JAMES: He himself. I believe 'tis he has robb'd you.

HARPAGON: Why do you believe so?

MR. JAMES: Why?

HARPAGON: Yes.

MR. JAMES: I believe so – Because I believe so.

COMMISSARY: But it is necessary you tell us what induces you to believe so.

HARPAGON: Did you see him sauntring about the Place where I put my
Money?

MR. JAMES: Yes. Where did you put your Money?

HARPAGON: In the Garden.

MR. JAMES: Right. I saw him sauntring in the Garden. What was the Money
in?

HARPAGON: In a Casket.

MR. JAMES: Even so. I saw him with a Casket.

HARPAGON: How was the Casket made? I shall soon see whether or no 'tis
mine.

MR. JAMES: How was it made?

HARPAGON: Yes.

MR. JAMES: 'Twas made – 'Twas made like a Casket.

COMMISSARY: We know that. But describe it a little.

1. Taken from John Clare's translation of 1732. Instead of 'puzzling', Ozell uses the
word 'hammering'.

MR. JAMES: 'Tis a great Casket.

HARPAGON: Mine was a little one.

MR. JAMES: Oh, yes, yes, 'twas a little one, if you mean so; but I call it great for what it contains.

COMMISSARY: What Colour was it of?

MR. JAMES: What Colour?

COMMISSARY: Yes.

MR. JAMES: 'Twas of a Colour – A certain sort of – Can't you help one a little?

HARPAGON: Ha!

MR. JAMES: Was it not red?

HARPAGON: No, grey.

MR. JAMES: Oh, ay, ay, grey-red; that's what I meant.

HARPAGON: 'Tis a plain Case. 'Tis certainly the same. Write, Sir, write down his Deposition. Heavens! Whom shall we trust for the future! One must never more swear for any body's Fidelity, and I believe in a little while I shall rob myself.

MR. JAMES: Here he comes, Sir; pray don't tell him that 'twas I discovered it to you.

Act V, Scene III

[VALERIO, HARPAGON, THE COMMISSARY, *his* CLERK, MR. JAMES.]

HARPAGON: Come hither, come and confess the blackest Action, the most horrible Deed that was ever committed.

VALERIO: What wou'd you have, Sir?

HARPAGON: What, Traytor, don't you blush at your Crime?

VALERIO: What Crime do you mean?

HARPAGON: What Crime do I mean, Rascal, as if you did not know what I mean? 'Tis in vain to pretend to disguise it. The Business is discovered, and I have just now heard All. How cou'd you abuse my Goodness thus, and get into my House on purpose to betray me? to serve me a Trick of such a nature!

VALERIO: Sir, since you are told All, I won't go about to prevaricate, nor deny the Thing.

MR. JAMES: Ho, ho; have I hit it, and never knew any thing of the Matter?

VALERIO: 'Twas my Design to speak to you of it, and only wanted a favourable Opportunity; but since 'tis thus, I conjure you not to be in a passion, but hear my Reasons.

HARPAGON: And what fine Reasons can you give me, infamous Thief?

VALERIO: Sir, I don't deserve that Name. 'Tis true, I have committed an Offence against you; but after all, my Fault is pardonable.

HARPAGON: How! Pardonable! A premeditated[1] Crime! An Assassination of this sort, pardonable!

VALERIO: Pray don't put yourself in a Passion. When you have heard me, you'll see the harm is not so great as you make it.

HARPAGON: The Harm not so great as I make it? What, my Blood, my Bowels, Sirrah?

VALERIO: Your Blood, Sir, is not fallen into ill Hands. I am of a Family not to do yours any wrong; and there is nothing in all this but what I can well repair.

HARPAGON: I intend you shall do so, and restore me what you've ravished from me.

VALERIO: Your Honour, Sir, shall be fully satisfy'd.

HARPAGON: What do you talk of Honour for? Tell me, who induced you to this Action?

VALERIO: Alas! do you ask me That?

HARPAGON: Yes, I ask you That.

VALERIO: A God that carries with him his Excuse for whatever he moves us to do! Love.

HARPAGON: Love?

VALERIO: Yes.

HARPAGON: Fine Love indeed! The Love of my *Louis d'Ors.*

VALERIO: No, Sir, 'tis not your Riches that tempted me; I was not dazzled with them; and I protest, that if you'll leave me in the quiet possession of what I have already, I'll never pretend to any thing else you possess.

HARPAGON: The Devil take me if I do. But how insolent he is, to pretend to keep what he has robb'd me of!

VALERIO: Do you call that a Robbery!

HARPAGON: Yes, marry do I. Such a Treasure as That.

VALERIO: 'Tis true, 'tis a Treasure, and the most precious that you have, without doubt; but 'twill not be lost to you, if you let me keep it. I ask of you, on my Knees, this Treasure, this most valuable Treasure, and, by good right, you cannot but grant it me.

HARPAGON: Grant it you, with a Horse-pox: What the devil does all this mean!

VALERIO: We have mutually promised Fidelity, and have sworn never to part.

HARPAGON: The Oath is admirable, and the Promise merry!

VALERIO: Yes, we are engag'd to be each other's for ever.

HARPAGON: I shall hinder you, I'll assure you.

VALERIO: Nothing but Death can part us.

HARPAGON: He's devilishly bewitch'd to my Money.

VALERIO: I have already told you, that 'twas not Interest induced me to do

---

1. Taken from John Clare's translation of 1732. Instead of 'premeditated', Ozell uses the word 'prepense'.

what I have done. My Heart did not act by the Springs you imagine it did, and a more noble Motive inspired me with this Resolution.

HARPAGON: I'll warrant you he'll tell you he lusts after my Money thro' Christian Charity; but I shall know how to deal with you, and Justice shall right me, you impudent Varlet.

VALERIO: You may do as you please. I am ready to suffer whatever Violence you have a mind to inflict; but however I beg you to believe, that if there be any harm in't, I only am in fault, and that your Daughter is not at all to blame.

HARPAGON: There, I believe you. 'Twou'd be strange indeed if my Daughter should be concerned in such a Crime. But I'm resolv'd to have what belongs to me again, and do expect you'll confess whither you have carry'd it.

VALERIO: Not out of your House, I'll assure you. It is still there.

HARPAGON: O my dear Treasure! O my precious Casket! Not gone out of my House!

VALERIO: No, Sir.

HARPAGON: But tell me a little: Have you not had *to do* with my precious Treasure?

VALERIO: Have *to do* with her! You wrong her as well as me; I burn for her with an Ardor that's wholly pure and respectful.

HARPAGON: Burn for my Treasure!

VALERIO: I'd rather die than discover to her the least offensive Thought. She's too discreet and virtuous for any thing like That.

HARPAGON: My Casket too virtuous!

VALERIO: All my Desires reach no further than to enjoy the sight of her, and nothing criminal has prophaned the Passion her fair Eyes have given me.

HARPAGON: The fair Eyes of my Casket! He speaks of it as a Lover wou'd do of his Mistress.

VALERIO: *Claudia*, Sir, knows the truth of this Adventure, and she can bear witness that –

HARPAGON: What! is my Maid an Accomplice in this Affair?

VALERIO: Yes, Sir, she was witness of our Engagement; and after she knew my Flame was honourable, she help'd to persuade your Daughter to give me her Word, and accept mine.

HARPAGON: Hay! Does the fear of Justice make him rave? Why do'st thou puzzle us here about my Daughter?

VALERIO: I say, Sir, I had all the trouble in the world to prevail on her Modesty to consent to what my Love required.

HARPAGON: Whose Modesty?

VALERIO: Your Daughter's; nor cou'd I till Yesterday make her resolve to sign me a Promise of Marriage.

HARPAGON: Why, has my Daughter sign'd You a Promise of Marriage!

VALERIO: Yes, Sir, as I on my part have sign'd her one.

HARPAGON: O Heavens! another Misfortune!

MR. JAMES: Write, Sir. Write.

HARPAGON: Addition of Evil! Encrease of Despair! Come, Sir, do the Duty of your Place, and draw me up a Process against him, as a Thief and Suborner.

MR. JAMES: As a Thief and Suborner.

VALERIO: These are Names not at all due to me; and when 'tis known who I am –

Act V, Scene IV

[ELIZA, MARIANA, FROSINA, HARPAGON, VALERIO, MR. JAMES, THE COMMISSARY *and his* CLERK.]

HARPAGON: Ah! thou wicked Girl! unworthy of such a Father as me! Is't thus you put in practice the Admonitions I have given you? Do you suffer yourself to be enamour'd of an infamous Thief, and give him your Faith without My Consent? But you shall be Both deceived. Four good Walls [*speaking to* ELIZA] shall secure Your Conduct, and a stout Gallows, Sirrah, shall avenge me for your Audaciousness.

VALERIO: I am not to be try'd by your Passion, and shall be heard at least, before I am condemn'd.

HARPAGON: I was in the wrong to say only a Gallows; for thou shalt be broke upon the Wheel alive.

ELIZA: [*Kneeling.*] Ah! Father, pray assume more humane Sentiments, and do not drive things with the utmost Violence of a paternal Power. Do not suffer yourself to be hurry'd away by the first Heat of your Passion, but give yourself time to consider what to do. Take the pains to acquaint yourself better with him you're offended with: He's quite a different Person from what he now seems to you to be; and you'll think it less strange that I have given myself to him, when you are inform'd that but for him you had long since lost me for ever. Yes, Father, 'twas he who saved me from the imminent Danger you know I was in upon the Water, and to whom you owe the Life of that very Daughter, who –

HARPAGON: All this is nothing; and it had been much better for me if he had let you drown, than to do what he has done.

ELIZA: Father, I conjure you by paternal Love to –

HARPAGON: No, no, I'll hear nothing; Justice must take its Course.

MR. JAMES: You shall pay dearly for the Blows you gave me.

FROSINA: Here's a strange Confusion!

Act V, Scene V

[ANSELMO, HARPAGON, ELIZA, MARIANA, FROSINA, VALERIO, MR. JAMES, THE
COMMISSARY *and his* CLERK.]

ANSELMO: What now, Signor *Harpagon*! I see you are in a Passion.

HARPAGON: Ah! Signor *Anselmo*, you behold the most Unfortunate of Men.
You'll find a world of Trouble and Disorder in the Contract you're come
to sign. I am assassinated in my Estate, in my Honour; and there stands
a Traytor, a Rascal, that has violated the most sacred Rights; that
wriggl'd himself into my House under the title of a Servant, to steal my
Money, and seduce my Daughter.

VALERIO: Who troubles themselves with your Money, which you make such
a nonsensical racket about?

HARPAGON: Yes, they have given each other a Promise of Marriage. This
Affront affects you, Signor *Anselmo*; You ought to become a Party
against him, and prosecute him at your own Charges, to revenge his
Insolence.

ANSELMO: 'Tis not my Design to get me a Wife by force, or to pretend to any
share in a Heart that's already disposed of; but as for your Interests, I
am as ready to embrace them as if they were my own.

HARPAGON: That honest Gentleman here, is a Commissary, who says he'll
omit nothing of the Duty of his Office. Charge him as he deserves, Sir,
and make things very criminal.

VALERIO: I can't see what Crime can be made of the Passion I have for your
Daughter, nor what punishment I can be condemn'd to for our
Engagement, when 'tis made appear that I am –

HARPAGON: Away with these Stories; the World now is full of these
Gentlemen Thieves, these Impostors, who take advantage of their
Obscurity, and insolently clothe themselves with the first Illustrious
Name that comes into their head.

VALERIO: Know that I have too much Honour to adorn my self with any
thing that does not belong to me, and that all *Naples* can give Testimony
to my Birth.

ANSELMO: Hold, take care what you say; You run a greater risque here than
you imagine and you speak before a Man to whom all *Naples* is known,
and who can easily judge the Truth of the Story you are about to tell.

VALERIO: [*Putting on his Hat proudly*] I am not a Man that's soon frighted; and
if you are acquainted with *Naples*, you must needs know who Don
Thomas d'Alburci was.

ANSELMO: Without doubt I do so, and few know him better.

HARPAGON: What do I care for Don *Thomas*, or Don *Martin* either? [*Seeing two
Candles lighted, and thinking it waste, blows out one.*]

ANSELMO: Pray let's hear what he will say of him.

VALERIO: I say, 'twas He that gave me Birth.

ANSELMO: He?

VALERIO: Yes.

ANSELMO: Go, You're deceiv'd. Find out some other Story that may fit your purpose better, and don't pretend to save yourself by this Imposture.

VALERIO: Use better Language, Sir. 'Tis not an Imposture, and I advance nothing here, but what I can easily justify.

ANSELMO: What! dare you intitle yourself Son of Don *Thomas d'Alburci*?

VALERIO: Yes, I dare, and am ready to maintain it against any Man alive.

ANSELMO: You're wondrous bold. Know, to your Confusion, that at least sixteen Years ago, the Man you mention perish'd at Sea, with his Children and his Wife, in their flight from the cruel Persecution which accompany'd the Disorders of *Naples*, and which obliged several noble Families to go into Exile.

VALERIO: Yes: but know, to your Confusion, that his Son, aged seven Years, with a Servant, was saved from that Shipwreck by a *Spanish* Ship, and that that Son so saved is he who speaks to you. Know, that the Captain of this Ship, compassionating to my Ill-Fortune, conceiv'd a Kindness for me, brought me up as his own Son, and Arms were my Employ-ment, so soon as I was capable of them. I have since heard that my Father is not dead, as I had always imagined. Going thro' this City, in search of him, an Accident, ordain'd by Heaven, occasion'd my seeing the charming *Eliza*, and render'd me a Slave to her Beauty; the Violence of my Love, and the Severity of Her Father, made me resolve to introduce myself into his House, and, to send another in quest of my Parents.

ANSELMO: But what Testimonies, besides your own Mouth, have you to assure us that this is not a Fable founded upon some little Truth?

VALERIO: The *Spanish* Captain; a Ruby Seal, which was my Father's; a Bracelet of Agat, which my Mother put on my Arm; and old *Pedro*, the Servant, that was saved with me from the Shipwreck.

MARIANA: Alas! by your Words, I myself can answer for't, you do not impose upon us; and all you have said, plainly discovers to me that You are my Brother.

VALERIO: Hah! my Sister?

MARIANA: Yes: my Heart was moved the very moment you open'd your Mouth; and our Mother, who will be transported to see you, has a thousand times related to me the Misfortunes of our Family. Heaven too saved us from that dreadful Shipwreck; but tho' it saved our Lives, yet it threw us into Slavery, and those who took up my Mother and Me, on the Fragments of the Ship, were Pirates. After ten Years Slavery, a happy Accident restored us our Liberty, and we return'd to *Naples*, where we found all our Estate sold, but cou'd get no news of our Father. We then went to *Genoa*, where my Mother pick'd up some poor Remains of a shatter'd Estate; and from thence, flying from the barbarous Injustice of her Kindred, she came hither, where she has lived in an almost continual Sickness and Uneasiness.

ANSELMO: O Heav'n! How great are the Effects of thy Power! How well dost thou shew that it belongs to thee alone to work Miracles! Embrace, my Children, and mix your Joy with that of your Father?

VALERIO: Are you our Father?

MARIANA: Are you the Man whom my Mother has so much bemoaned?

ANSELMO: Yes, Daughter; yes, Son, I am Don *Thomas d'Alburci*, whom Heav'n saved from the Waves, with all the Money he had with him; and who, thinking you had been all dead for above these sixteen Years, was preparing after long Travels, to seek the Consolation of some new Family, by marrying a prudent and sweet-temper'd Person. The little Security my Life was in, if I return'd to *Naples*, made me renounce it for ever; and having found a way to sell all I had there, I settled here; where, under the Name of *Anselmo*, I was willing to wipe away the Grief of that other Name, which had created me so many Troubles and Misfortunes.

HARPAGON: Is that your Son?

ANSELMO: Yes.

HARPAGON: Then you are the Man for the ten thousand Crowns he has robb'd me of.

ANSELMO: He robb'd you?

HARPAGON: He himself.

VALERIO: Who told you this?

HARPAGON: Mr. *James*.

VALERIO: Was't you told him so?

MR. JAMES: You see I say nothing.

HARPAGON: Yes, There's Mr. Commissary, that has taken his Deposition.

VALERIO: Can you think me capable of so base an Action?

HARPAGON: Capable, or not capable, I'll have my Money again.

Act V, Scene VI

[CLEANTHES, VALERIO, MARIANA, ELIZA, FROSINA, HARPAGON, ANSELMO, MR. JAMES, LA FLECHE, THE COMMISSARY *and his* CLERK.]

CLEANTHES: Don't torment yourself, Father: accuse nobody. I have discover'd news of your Affair, and come to tell you, that if you'll let me marry *Mariana*, your Money shall be restored to you.

HARPAGON: Where is it?

CLEANTHES: Don't trouble yourself about that. 'Tis in a place I'm answerable for, and it all depends upon me alone. You must declare what you resolve upon, and either give me *Mariana*, or lose your Casket.

HARPAGON: Has nothing been taken out of it?

CLEANTHES: Nothing at all. Consider whether you'd best subscribe to this Marriage, and join your Consent to that of her Mother, who gives her liberty to chuse which of us two she will.

MARIANA: But you don't yet know, that 'tis not her Consent alone will now be sufficient, and that Heaven, together with a Brother, who you see, has just now restored me a Father, of whom you are to obtain me.

ANSELMO: Heav'n, my Children, does not restore me to you to oppose your Desires. Signor *Harpagon*, you know, that if a young Person were to chuse, she'd rather take the Son than the Father. Come, Don't force 'em to say what is unnecessary for us to hear; but consent, as well as I, to this double Marriage.

HARPAGON: I must see my Casket, that I may take Counsel of it.

CLEANTHES: You shall see it safe and sound.

HARPAGON: I have no Money to give my Children in Marriage.

ANSELMO: Well, I have enough for them, don't let that disturb you.

HARPAGON: Will you oblige yourself to defray the Charges of these two Weddings?

ANSELMO: Yes, I will. Are you satisfy'd?

HARPAGON: Yes, provided you send me in a Suit of Clothes for the Nuptials.

ANSELMO: Agreed, Come, let us enjoy the Pleasure this happy Day has offer'd us.

COMMISSARY: So ho, Gentlemen! soft and fair, if you please. Who pays me for my Writings?

HARPAGON: We have nothing to do with your Writings.

COMMISSARY: Really! But yet I design to be paid for them.

HARPAGON: Take that Fellow there, and hang him for your Payment.

MR. JAMES: Alas! How must one act! I am cudgell'd for speaking Truth, and to be hang'd for Lying.

ANSELMO: Signor *Harpagon*, you must pardon him this piece of Imposture.

HARPAGON: Then You shall pay the Commissary.

ANSELMO: With all my heart. Come, Now let's hasten to give your Mother a share in our Joy.

HARPAGON: And I, to see my dear Casket.

Finis

Tartuffe

MOLIÈRE

INTRODUCTION

1668 was a year when things began to improve for Molière. Louis XIV's power base within France had increased substantially following a series of victories he had won during the course of 1668; these were crowned by the Peace of Aix-la-Chapelle. Louis signalled his new willingness to assert his authority by dissolving the Company of the Blessed Sacrament later that year. (The Company of the Blessed Sacrament had already begun to lose some of its vigour following the deaths in 1666 of the Prince de Conti and Louis's mother who was a staunch supporter of the movement.) This in turn opened the way for the ban on *Tartuffe* to be lifted. In February 1669, Molière was at last able to perform his final version of the play to packed houses and wrote his grateful third *placet* to the King.

Tartuffe

In his Preface to *Tartuffe*, Molière dwelt at some length on the way his play had been vilified and 'persecuted' by the cabal of pious zealots who had felt threatened by his satire. He was at pains to stress that his play should not be seen as an attack on true piety or genuinely held religious beliefs: it was intended as an attack on hypocrites and impostors who exploited religion as a cloak for more venal desires. Molière commented that other groups, including noblemen, pretentious women, cuckolds and doctors, had submitted gracefully to his satire. The religious zealots had not. What he does not mention, however, is the unusually savage quality of his satire in this play. There seems to be an almost personal animosity behind his depiction of Tartuffe's exploitation of Orgon: an animosity that can be explained by Molière's own first-hand experience of the Prince de Conti's dramatic conversion, following a career of libertine excess. Manipulated by members of his own entourage and by religious fanatics within the church, the Prince de Conti had spent the last decade of his life persecuting those he considered to be ungodly, including Molière. In view of Molière's long-running feud with the Prince de Conti and the Company of the Blessed Sacrament, it is not surprising that a strong sense of personal outrage informs the whole play.

The setting of *Tartuffe* is as sparse as that of *L'Avare*: yet another house in Paris, with only a few pieces of furniture required on stage. *Tartuffe* also pursues a number of similar themes to those explored in *L'Avare*. Orgon, like Harpagon, is a father who abuses his own authority, demanding absolute obedience from his children even though he is totally indifferent to their well-being. As if to stress the link, Molière reutilises the names of some of the characters from *L'Avare*. In *L'Avare*, the young lady who has caught the eye of both Harpagon and his son Cléante is called Mariane; in *Tartuffe* it is Orgon's daughter who is called Mariane. In both plays, the young man in love with the daughter of the household is called Valère. Orgon's brother-in-law, Cléante, has the same name as Harpagon's son. Orgon's second wife is called Elmire, which recalls the name of Harpagon's daughter, Élise. These various characters from *Tartuffe*, whose names are either the same as, or reminiscent of the names of the characters in *L'Avare*, are locked in a similar struggle with an unreasonable father. The main difference between the two father figures is that Harpagon is a totally self-obsessed monomaniac whose conduct never changes, while Orgon has turned temporarily into a religious fanatic under the spell of a ruthless con man. Unlike Harpagon, Orgon is reclaimed from his folly at the end of the play, but not before he has almost lost everything: his children, his wife and his property. Once again, Molière shows how the sleep of reason produces monsters.

Orgon is supported in his irrational folly by his mother, Mme Pernelle, a naïve but genuinely devout old lady who sees herself surrounded by wickedness and sin in a fallen world. Brought up by such a mother, it is perhaps not surprising that Orgon should so easily fall a prey to the religious hypocrisy of a con man like Tartuffe. Tartuffe has wormed his way into Orgon's household, having targeted Orgon at church, and now enjoys the life of a rich parasite, feasting and drinking to his heart's content, casting lecherous eyes at Orgon's young second wife Elmire, while persuading Orgon to give him his daughter's hand in marriage. Although Tartuffe does not appear on stage until Act III, his presence is felt as an ominous threat to the well-being of the family from the very opening of the action. Orgon has become strangely infatuated with this smooth-talking sycophant and seems oblivious of the danger facing him and his family.

Ranged against the forces of unreason and hypocrisy are Orgon's brother-in-law, Cléante, and the serving woman Dorine. Cléante, the balanced rationalist, is a typical *raisonneur*. He is inclined to be pompous and to indulge in over-lengthy speeches while giving his good advice. But his responses are sound, his analysis of Orgon's folly is witheringly accurate, and his counsel at times of crisis is balanced and sensible. In contrast to Cléante's world of rational discourse, Dorine inhabits a world of earthy common sense. Quick witted and streetwise, she sees through cant and hypocrisy with effortless ease; she is also prepared to resort to downright cheek and rudeness to help bring her wealthy employer to his senses. Whether confronted by Valère and Mariane, indulging themselves in the folly of a pointless argument, or Orgon surrendering to his latest foolish caprice, Dorine is quick to use her mocking tongue to good effect.

The action in the play is brought to a head with Tartuffe's attempt to seduce Orgon's wife Elmire. When this event is reported to Orgon by his son Damis, he flatly refuses to believe it. Instead he turns on Damis, banishing him from his house and, in a gesture of spite, decides to make over all his property to Tartuffe. Angered by her husband's refusal to believe her story, Elmire engineers another meeting with Tartuffe, but this time she insists that Orgon be present, hidden under the table. As Tartuffe moves swiftly from verbal to physical seduction, Orgon is so slow to emerge from under the table, that his wife's virtue is in real danger of being lost right on top of him. Orgon now has all the proof he has demanded, but it is too late. Tartuffe, having accepted Orgon's earlier gift of his property, has the upper hand and simply orders everyone to leave what is now his property. Worse still, he has even denounced Orgon to the authorities as a traitor.

At this point, as happened in *L'Avare*, the action has arrived at a complete impasse. Valère even offers to help Orgon flee from Paris. But before any flight can be entertained, the king's Officer appears, ostensibly to arrest Orgon. However, as is the case with Anselme in *L'Avare*, the king's Officer turns out to be a *deus ex machina*, a benign character who has come to rescue Orgon from his distress. He reveals that the king, the all-wise, all-seeing ruler has for some time been observing Tartuffe's behaviour and has now decided that the time is right to arrest him for a whole string of crimes. Orgon, who has already recovered his sanity, now has his wealth and property restored. The play closes with him resolving to thank the king in person and to reward the faithful Valère with the hand of his daughter.

By rights, this is a play that should have ended in chaos and confusion. The whole structural logic of the piece points in this direction, and it may well be that one of the two earlier versions of the play that Molière had written did indeed finish on a note of unresolved black comedy. Here, however, in this final version of *Tartuffe*, Molière conjures up a happy ending out of thin air, and in the process pays an ostensibly handsome compliment to a ruler who had continued to offer him firm support during all the attacks made on him by the cabal of zealots. The happy ending is a paper-thin contrivance to avoid the logical conclusions to which the whole action of the play is leading. The message is clear. To give in to the forces of unreason and irrationality, as Orgon did, is to risk the stability of family and state. There are predators abroad who will use even what is most sacred to wrest authority from those who properly enjoy positions of power. As in *L'Avare*, power is shown to bring with it clear responsibilities. Orgon abdicates from his responsibilities and, as a result, almost loses all he possesses. In contrast, the king, as a wise ruler, exercises his power with a proper regard for his responsibilities. But the all-seeing, all-knowing extent of his power is truly awesome. There was perhaps more than a hint of ambivalence in this final piece of flattery addressed to the king, which sits uneasily with the remainder of the play. What happens should Orgon or Molière lose the support of this all-powerful ruler? For Molière this soon became a painfully apposite question.

Tartuffe in many ways marked the high point of his career as a playwright and actor manager. The remaining four years of his life brought a series of personal and professional calamities which contributed to his untimely death in 1673. In 1672, his life-long friend and companion, Madeleine Béjart, died after a long illness. That same year, the king began to withdraw his patronage and support from Molière, as he showed a growing interest in the operatic experiments of the unscrupulous composer Lully. Lully collaborated with Molière on various comedy-ballets, but did not hesitate for a moment to advance his own career at the expense of Molière's. He even attempted to obtain an exclusive right to perform all music theatre in Paris, which would have drastically curtailed Molière's repertoire. As a sign of Louis's waning interest in Molière, the prologue to *Le Malade imaginaire*, written in 1673, makes it clear that the play was intended for performance at court. Instead it was performed only in Paris. It was during the fourth performance of this play, on 17 February 1673, that Molière was taken seriously ill. He died later that night. The local priests refused to offer him the last rites, thus denying him the possibility of renouncing his profession in order to obtain a full Christian burial. Only the intervention of the king with the Archbishop of Paris enabled Molière to be buried at night in consecrated ground. The Company of the Blessed Sacrament may have been dissolved, but its members had their final revenge on a man who had dared to stand up to them.

A scene from *Le Tartuffe*, drawn by J. M. Moreau, reproduced from *Œuvres de Molière* (Paris, 1773)

Tartuffe,

or

The Impostor

A
Comedy

Molière's Petitions and Preface

Molière's First Placet (Petition) to the King, July 1664[1]

SIRE, – The aim of comedy being to correct men by amusing them, I thought that, in the situation which I occupy, I could not do better than attack by pictures full of ridicule the vices of my age; and hypocrisy being no doubt not only one of the most usual among them, but also one of the most annoying as well as most dangerous, I had the idea, Sire, that I would be rendering not a small service to the honest people of your kingdom, if I wrote a comedy that should decry the hypocrites, expose plainly the studied grimaces of those ultra-godly people, all the covert scoundrelism of these false coiners of devotion, who try to inveigle people with their counterfeit zeal, and their sophistic charity.

I have constructed this comedy, Sire, with all the care, and, as I believe, with all the circumspection demanded by the delicacy of the material; and the better to preserve the esteem and respect due to the truly pious, I have distinguished as much as I could the character which I had to sketch. I have left no room for equivocal interpretation, I have left out everything that could confound the good with the bad, and have employed in this picture only those express colours and essential traits which would serve to reveal, at the first glance, the veritable and downright hypocrite. Nevertheless, all my precautions have been useless. People have taken advantage, Sire, of the delicacy of your feelings on the subject of religion, and have succeeded in probing you in your only vulnerable spot, I mean your respect for sacred things. The Tartuffes on the sly, have been artful enough to find grace in your Majesty's sight; in short, the originals have caused the copy to be suppressed, no matter how innocent and startlingly like it may have been.

Great as was the blow caused by the suppression of this work, my misfortune has been mitigated by the manner in which your Majesty explained yourself on this subject; and I have seen, Sire, that all cause of complaint was taken away from me, when you declared kindly that you found nothing objectionable in this comedy, which you nevertheless forbade me to produce in public.

But notwithstanding this glorious declaration of the greatest and most enlightened monarch in the universe, even notwithstanding the approbation of Monsignor the Nuncio, and the majority of our prelates, who, when I privately read my work to them, have all fully concurred in the sentiments of your Majesty, – notwithstanding all this, I say, a book has been published which openly contradicts all those august testimonies.[2] Your Majesty may say what he pleases, the Nuncio and the prelates may proclaim

---

1. The translation of the petitions and the preface is from the edition published by Henri van Laun in 1876.
2. A pamphlet published by Fr Pierre Roullé in August 1664 which suggested that Molière should be burnt in public.

their judgement as much as they like, my comedy, without having even been seen, is diabolical, and as diabolical is my brain; I am a demon incarnate, and dressed like a man, an unbeliever, an impious wretch, deserving of exemplary punishment. It is not enough that the flames expiate my offence in public, I should be quit of it at too cheap a rate; the charitable zeal of this gallant and good man hardly cares to stop there, he requires that I shall find no mercy at the hands of God, he insists absolutely that I must be damned, that is a settled affair.

This book, Sire, has been presented to your Majesty, and you can yourself doubtless judge how annoying it is to me to see myself daily exposed to the insults of these gentlemen; the harm these slanders do me in the eyes of the world, whether they are to be meekly borne, and the interest I have to rid myself of its imposture, and to show the public that my comedy is nothing less than what it is said to be. I shall not say anything, Sire, about the claims due to my reputation, or to the justification of the innocence of my work in the eyes of the world; enlightened kings, like you, have no need to have people's wishes pointed out to them; they perceive, like God, our wants, and know better than we do, what they ought to grant us. It is sufficient for me to place my interests in your Majesty's hands, and to await respectfully from him whatever he may be pleased to ordain on the subject.

Molière's Second Placet to the King, August 1667[1]

SIRE, – It is a very bold step on my part to come and trouble a great monarch in the midst of his glorious conquests; but in the position in which I am, Sire, where am I to find protection except in the place where I have come to seek for it? And what am I to invoke against the authority of the power that overwhelms me, unless it be the source of that power and authority, the just dispenser of the absolute commands, the sovereign judge, and the master of all things.

Until now, Sire, my comedy has not met with your Majesty's favour. In vain have I produced it under the title of The Impostor, and disguised the personage beneath the garb of a man of the world; vainly have I given him a small hat, long hair, a great collar, a sword, and lace over the whole of his dress; in vain have I modified it in several places and carefully cut out everything that I deemed could furnish the shadow of a pretext to the celebrated originals of the portrait I wanted to paint, all has been of no use. The cabal has re-awoke at the simple conjectures which they may have had about the matter. They have found means to surprise minds, who, on any other subject, profess never to allow themselves to be surprised. No sooner did my comedy appear than it has found itself struck down by the blow of a power which is entitled to respect; and all I have been able to do in this struggle, in order to save myself from the burst of this tempest, was to say

1. This petition was taken to Louis, at the time besieging Lille, by the actors La Grange and La Torillière.

that your Majesty had had the kindness to allow me the representation, and that I did not think there was any need to ask this permission from others, seeing that it was your decree only which had prohibited it.

I doubt not, Sire, that the people whom I depict in my comedy will employ many artifices with your Majesty, and will try to enlist among their party many truly pious, who are the more susceptible of being deceived, because they judge others by themselves. They have the knack of investing their intentions with most beautiful colours. Whatever face they may put upon them, it is not really God's interest that causes them to move in this; they have shown this sufficiently well in the comedies which they have allowed so often to be played in public without saying a word about them. Those only attacked piety and religion for which they care very little; but this one attacks and shows them up personally, and that is what they cannot tolerate. They cannot forgive me for having unmasked their impostures to the eyes of the whole world; and, doubtlessly, they will not fail to tell your Majesty that everybody has been scandalised at my comedy. But the real truth, Sire, is that all Paris has only been scandalised at the prohibition of it; that the most scrupulous have found the representation of it most salutary; and that people have been astonished that persons of such well known probity should show such great deference for those whom the whole world ought to hold in horror, and should be so opposed to that true piety which they profess. I await respectfully the verdict which your Majesty will deign to pronounce upon this subject; but certain is it, Sire, that I must no longer think of writing comedies, if the Tartuffes should gain the day, because they will, through this, assume the right to persecute me more than ever, and find something to cavil at in the most innocent things that will fall from my pen.

May your kindness, Sire, vouchsafe to protect me against their venomous hatred and permit me to hope that at your return from so glorious a campaign, I may be able to divert your Majesty after the fatigues of your conquests, to provide you with some innocent pleasures after such noble works, and to make the monarch smile who causes all Europe to tremble.

Molière's Third Placet to the King, February 1669[1]

SIRE, – A most respectable physician whose patient I have the honour to be, promises me, and will bind himself by a legal act, executed before a notary, to make me live thirty years longer if I can procure him a favour of your Majesty. In answer to his promise, I have told him that I do not want as much, and that I would be satisfied if he would only promise me not to kill me. This favour, Sire, is a canonry in your royal chapel of Vincennes, vacant through the death of . . .

1. Molière uses the excuse of a formal petition on behalf of the son of his doctor friend Mauvillain to thank the king for supporting *Tartuffe*. The light-hearted tone of the petition not only shows Molière's relief that his play could at last be performed but also indicates his closeness to the king at this point in time.

May I still venture to ask this favour of your Majesty, the very day of the great resurrection of Tartuffe resuscitated by your kindness? I am, through this first favour, reconciled with the devotees; and through the second, I shall be reconciled with the doctors. For me it is, no doubt, too many favours at one time, but perhaps it is not too many for your Majesty; and I await, with a little respectful expectation, the answer to my petition.

Preface[1]
This is a comedy about which there has been a great deal of noise, which has been for a long time persecuted, and the people whom it holds up have well shown that they are the most powerful in France of all those whom I have hitherto portrayed. The marquises, the blue stockings, the cuckolds and the doctors, have quietly suffered themselves to be represented, and have pretended to be amused, in common with all the world, at the sketches which I have made of them; but the hypocrites have not taken the joke. At first they were somewhat amazed, and found it strange that I should have had the presumption to make free with their grimaces, and wish to decry a trade much indulged in by honest people. It is a crime which they could not pardon me, and they have all risen up in arms against my comedy with a terrible fury. They took particular care not to attack it from the point of view where it wounded them – they have too much policy for that, and are too knowing to lay bare the bottoms of their hearts. In accordance with their laudable customs, they have concealed their interest beneath the cloak of God's cause; and to listen to them, *The Tartuffe* is a piece that offends piety. It is, from beginning to end, full of abominations, and nothing is found in it but what deserves the fire. Every syllable in it is impious; the gesticulations themselves are criminal; and the least glance of the eye, the slightest shake of the head, the smallest step to the right or left, conceal mysteries which they find means to explain to my disadvantage.

Of little avail was it to submit it to the criticism of my friends, and to the censorship of the public; the corrections which I have made, the judgement of the king and the queen, who have seen it;[2] the approbation of the great princes[3] and the great ministers, who honoured the performance with their presence; the testimony of people of worth, who found it instructing – all this was of no use. They will not abate one jot and they still continue, every day to set their indiscreet zealots on to me in public who piously load me with insults, and charitably consign me to perdition.

I would care very little for what they could say, were it not for their artfulness in bringing people whom I respect to be at enmity with me, and in enlisting among their ranks the truly good, whose good faith they take

1. Written for the first published edition of the play in March 1669.
2. The first version of the play was performed for the king and queen at Versailles in May 1664.
3. These included Monsieur, the king's brother, and the Prince de Condé.

advantage of, and who, by the warmth of their interest in the cause of Heaven, are apt to receive the impressions which they wish to give them. It is this which compels me to defend myself. It is with the truly pious that I everywhere wish to justify myself as to the arrangement of my comedy; and I implore them, with all my heart, not to condemn things before they have seen them, to divest themselves of all bias and not to be the tool of the passions of those whose grimaces are a disgrace to them.

If they will take the trouble to examine my comedy in good faith, they will perceive doubtless, the honesty of my intentions everywhere, and that it is not intended to hold sacred things up to ridicule; that I have treated it with every precaution which the delicacy of the subject required; and that I have employed every possible art and care plainly to show the difference between the character of the hypocrite and that of the truly devout. For this purpose I have devoted two entire acts to prepare my audience for the advent of my scoundrel. He does not make the spectator waver for an instant; he is known immediately by the marks which I have given him; and, from first to last, he does not utter a word, nor make a movement but what depicts to the beholder the character of a wicked man, in violent contrast to the really good one whom I have placed in opposition to him. I am well aware that, in reply, those gentlemen have endeavoured to insinuate that the stage is not fit for the discussion of these subjects: but, by their leave, I ask them upon what they base this beautiful maxim. It is a theory which they only advance, and which they do not prove by any means; and it would doubtless, not be difficult to show them that, with the ancients comedy derived its origin from religion, and was a part of their mysteries; that the Spaniards, our neighbours, never celebrate a feast in which comedy is not mixed up; and that, even amongst us it owes its birth to the cares of a brotherhood to which the hôtel de Bourgogne still belongs;[1] that it was a place given to them to represent in it the most important mysteries of our faith; that comedies printed in Gothic characters, under the name of a doctor of the Sorbonne,[2] may still be seen there; and, without carrying the matter so far, that, in our days, sacred pieces of M. de Corneille[3] have been performed, which were the admiration of the whole of France. If it be the aim of comedy to correct man's vices, then I do not see for what reason there should be a privileged class. Such a one is, in the State, decidedly more dangerous in its consequences than any other; and we have seen that the stage possesses a great virtue as a corrective medium. The most beautiful passages in a serious moral are most frequently less powerful than those of a satire; and nothing admonishes the majority of people better than the portrayal of their faults. To expose vices to the ridicule of all the

1. The Confraternity of the Passion, founded in 1402, had built the Hôtel de Bourgogne in 1548.
2. Jean Michel, author of two passion plays.
3. *Polyeucte, martyr* (1643) and *Théodore, virgin and martyr* (1645).

world is a severe blow to them. Reprehensions are easily suffered, but not so ridicule. People do not mind being wicked; but they object to being made ridiculous.

The reproach against me is that I have put pious terms in the mouth of my impostor. How could I avoid it, wishing to represent the character of a hypocrite accurately? It is sufficient, I think, that I show the criminal motives which make him say these things, and that I have eliminated from them the sacred terms, the bad use of which might have caused pain. 'But in the fourth act he gives vent to a pernicious moral.' But has not this moral been dinned into everybody's ears? Does it say aught that is new in my comedy? And is there any fear that things so universally detested shall leave any impression on men's minds? that I can make them dangerous by introducing them on the stage; that they are likely to receive any authority from the lips of a scoundrel? There is not the least indication of that; and one ought to approve the comedy of *Tartuffe*, or condemn all comedies wholesale.

It is that which people have attacked furiously of late; and never has the stage been so fiercely tilted at. I cannot deny that there have been Fathers of the Church who have condemned comedy; but neither can it be denied to me that there have been some who have treated it more leniently. Thus the authority upon which people seek to found their censorship is destroyed by this division; and all that can be deduced from this diversity of opinions in equally enlightened minds, is that they have regarded comedy from a different point of view, and that while some have looked at it in its purifying influence, others have considered it in its corrupting tendency, and confounded it with those vile spectacles, rightly named exhibitions of turpitude.[1]

And in fact since we have to argue upon things, and not upon words; and that the majority of contradictions cannot well be reconciled, and that the same word often envelops two opposite meanings, we have but to lift the veil of the equivocal, and to look what comedy is in itself, to see whether it is to be condemned. It is, doubtless, well known that, being nothing else but an ingenious poem, which, by its agreeable teaching, seeks to point out the faults of mankind, it does not deserve to be so unjustly censured; and if we may listen on that point to the testimony of antiquity, it will tell us that her most famous philosophers have eulogised comedy; they who professed such austere wisdom, and who were incessantly decrying the vices of their age. It will show us that Aristotle devoted many of his vigils to the theatre, and took the trouble to reduce to precept the art of constructing comedies. It will teach us that her greatest men, foremost in dignity, have gloried in composing some themselves; that there were others who did not disdain to recite in public those which they had composed; that Greece proclaimed her

---

1. A reference to St Augustin's condemnation of the Roman games and obscene farces.

appreciation of that art by the glorious prizes she awarded to, and the magnificent theatres she built in honour of it; and lastly that in Rome this same art was crowned with extraordinary honours. I do not say in debauched Rome, under the licentious emperors, but in disciplined Rome, under the wisdom of her consuls, and at the most vigorous period of Roman virtue.

I admit that there have been times in which comedy became corrupt. And what is there in this world that does not become corrupt every day? There is nothing so pure but what mankind can bring crime to bear upon it; no art so salutary but what they can reverse its intentions; nothing so good in itself but what they can turn to a bad use. Medicine is a profitable art, and every one esteems it as one of the most excellent things in existence; and yet there have been periods in which it has made itself odious, and has often been used to poison people. Philosophy is a gift of Heaven; it was given to us to lend our minds to the knowledge of God by the contemplation of nature's wonders; still we are not unaware that it has often been diverted from its use, and employed openly to support impiety. Even the most sacred things are not safe from men's corruption; and we see the greatest scoundrels daily abusing piety, and wickedly making it the tool for the most abominable crimes. But for all that, we do not fail to make those distinctions which it is right we should make. We do not envelop in the same warp of a false deduction the good of the thing corrupted with the malice of the corrupter. We always separate the bad use from the honest intention of art, and no more than we would dream of defending the banishment of medicine from Rome, or the public condemnation of philosophy at Athens, ought we to put a veto upon comedy for having been censured at certain times. This censuring had its reasons which have no existence here. It confined itself strictly to what it saw; and we ought, therefore, not to drag it beyond the limits which it has adopted, extend it farther than necessary, or make it class the guilty with the innocent. The comedy which it designed to attack is not at all the comedy which we wish to defend. We must take good care not to confound the one with the other, They are two persons whose morals are totally opposed. They bear no relation to each other except the resemblance of the name; and it would be a crying injustice to wish to condemn Olympia who is an honest woman, because there was another Olympia who was a loose character. Such verdicts would, doubtless, produce a great disorder in the world. Everything, would be open to condemnation; and, since this rigour is not carried out with reference to all other things which are daily abused, we ought to extend the same grace to comedy, and approve those plays in which instruction and honesty are made manifest.

I am well aware that there are certain minds whose delicacy can tolerate no comedy whatsoever;[1] who say that the most honest ones are the most dangerous; that the passions which they depict are so much the more

---

1. A reference to the Jansenist writer Pierre Nicole and to the Prince de Conti.

touching because they are full of virtue; and that people are too much affected by this kind of representations. I do not see any great crime in becoming affected at the sight of an honourable passion or that the complete state of insensibility to which they would elevate our feelings would indicate a high standard of virtue. I am inclined to doubt whether such great perfection be in the power of human nature, and whether it would not be better to endeavour to rectify and mollify men's passions, than to eliminate them altogether. I admit that there are places which it would be more salutary to frequent than theatres; and if we take it for granted that all things that do not directly concern God and our salvation are reprehensible, then it becomes certain that comedy should be one of them, and I for one could not object that it should be condemned among the rest. But let us suppose, as it is true, that there must be intervals to pious devotions, and that we have need of amusement during that time, then I maintain that nothing more innocent than comedy could be found. I have digressed too far. Let me wind up with the remark of a great prince[1] on the comedy of *Tartuffe*. A week after it had been forbidden, there was performed before the court a piece entitled *Scaramouch a hermit*,[2] and the king, coming out of the theatre, said to the prince of whom I have just spoken, "I should like to know why the people, who are so very much shocked at the comedy of Molière do not say a word about *Scaramouch*," to which the prince answered, "The reason of that is, that the comedy of *Scaramouch* makes game of Heaven and religion, about which these gentlemen care very little; but Molière's makes game of them: it is that which they cannot tolerate."

1. The Prince de Condé.
2. A licentious farce performed by the Italian players.

Actors

MADAM PERNELLE, Mother to Orgon.
ORGON, Husband to Elmira.
ELMIRA, Wife to Orgon.
DAMIS, Son to Orgon.
MARIANA, Daughter to Orgon.
VALERE, in Love with Mariana.
CLEANTHES, Brother-in-law to Orgon.
TARTUFFE, a Hypocrite.
DORINA, Waiting-Maid to Mariana.
MR. LOYAL, a Sergeant.
AN EXEMPT.[1]
FLIPOTE, Madam Pernell's Maid.

SCENE PARIS, in Orgon's House

Act I, Scene I

[MADAM PERNELLE, ELMIRA, MARIANA, DAMIS, CLEANTHES,
DORINA, FLIPOTE.]

MADAM PERNELLE: Come *Flipote*, let's be gone, that I may get rid of them.
ELMIRA: You walk so fast, that one has much ado to follow you.
MADAM PERNELLE: Stay, Daughter, stay; come no father; this is all needless
    Ceremony.
ELMIRA: We only acquit our selves of our Duty to you: but pray, Mother,
    what makes you in such haste to leave us?
MADAM PERNELLE: Because I can't endure to see such Management, and no
    body takes any Care to please me. I leave your House. I tell you, very
    ill edify'd; my instructions are all contradicted: You shew no respect for
    any thing amongst you, every one talks aloud there, and the House is a
    perfect *Dover-Court*.
DORINA: If –
MADAM PERNELLE: You are, Sweet-heart, a noisy and impertinent *Abigail*, and
    mighty free of your Advice on all Occasions.
DAMIS: But –
MADAM PERNELLE: In short, you are a Fool, Child; 'tis I tell you so, who am
    your Grandmother, and I have told my son your Father, a hundred
    times, that you wou'd become a perfect Rake, and wou'd be nothing but
    a Plague to him.

1. A police officer.

MARIANA: I fancy –

MADAM PERNELLE: Good-lack, Sister of his, you act the Prude, and look as if Butter wou'd not melt in your Mouth: but still Waters, they say, are always deepest; and under your sly Airs, you carry on a Trade I don't at all approve of.

ELMIRA: But Mother –

MADAM PERNELLE: By your leave, Daughter, your conduct is absolutely wrong in every thing: you ought to set them a good Example; and their late Mother manag'd 'em much better. You are a sorry Oeconomist, and what I can't endure, dress like any Princess. She who desires only to please her Husband, Daughter, needs not so much Finery.

CLEANTHES: But Madam, after all –

MADAM PERNELLE: As for you, Sir, her Brother, I esteem you very much, I love and respect you; but yet, were I in my Son's her Husband's Place, I shou'd earnestly intreat you not to come within our Doors. You are always laying down Rules of Life, that good People shou'd never follow. I talk a little freely to you; but 'tis my Humour; I never chew upon what I have at Heart.

DAMIS: Your Mr *Tartuffe* is a blessed Soul, no doubt –

MADAM PERNELLE: He's a good Man, and should be listened to; I can't bear, with Patience, to hear him cavill'd at by such a Fool as you.

DAMIS: What! shall I suffer a censorious Bigot to usurp an absolute Authority in the Family? And shall not we take the least Diversion, if this precious Spark thinks not fit to allow of it?

DORINA: If one were to hearken to him, and give into his Maxims, we could do nothing but what would be made a Crime of: for the critical Zealot controuls every thing.

MADAM PERNELLE: And whatever he controuls is well controul'd. He wou'd fain shew you the way to Heaven: and my Son ought to make you all love him.

DAMIS: No, look you, Madam, neither Father, nor any thing else can oblige me to have any regard for him. I shou'd belie my Heart to tell you otherwise. To me his Actions are perfectly odious; and I foresee, that, one time or other, Matters will come to extremity between that Wretch and me.

DORINA: 'Tis downright scandalous, to see an Upstart take on him at that rate here. A Vagabond, that had not a Pair of Shoes to his Feet when he came hither, and all the Clothes on his Back wou'd not fetch Six-pence, that he shou'd so far forget himself, as to contradict every thing, and to play the Master.

MADAM PERNELLE: Mercy on me! Matters wou'd go much better, were every thing manag'd by his pious Directions.

DORINA: He passes for a Saint in your Imagination; but, believe me, all he does is nothing but Hypocrisy.

MADAM PERNELLE: What a Tongue!

DORINA: I wou'd not trust him without good Security, any more than I would his Man *Laurence*.

MADAM PERNELLE: What the Servant may be at bottom, I can't tell; but I'll answer for the Master, that he is a good Man; you wish him ill, and reject him, only because he tells you the naked Truth. 'Tis Sin that his Heart can't brook, and the Interest of Heav'n is his only Motive.

DORINA: Ay; but why, for some time past, can't he endure that any Body shou'd come near us? How can a civil Visit offend Heav'n, so much that we must have a Din about it, enough to stun one? Among Friends, shall I give you my Opinion of the matter? [*pointing to* ELMIRA.] I take him, in troth; to be jealous of my Lady.

MADAM PERNELLE: Hold your peace, and consider what you say. He is not the only Person who condemns these Visits. The Bustle that attends the People you keep Company with, these Coaches continually planted at the Gate, and the noisy Company of such a parcel of Footmen disturb the whole Neighbourhood; I am willing to believe, there's no Harm done; but then it gives People occasion to talk, and that is not well.

CLEANTHES: Alas, Madam, will you hinder People from prating? It wou'd be a very hard thing in Life, if for any foolish Stories that might be raised about People, they shou'd be forc'd to renounce their best Friends; and suppose we shou'd resolve to do so, do you think it would keep all the World from talking? There's no guarding against Calumny: Let us therefore not mind silly tittle-tattle, and leave the gossiping part of Mankind to say what they please.

DORINA: May not Neighbour *Daphne* and her little Spouse be the Persons who speak ill of us? People, whose own Conduct is the most ridiculous, are always readiest to detract from that of others. They never fail readily to catch at the slightest Appearance of any Affair, to set the News about with Joy, and to give things the very Turn they wou'd have them take. By colouring other People's Actions, like their own, they think to justify their Conduct to the World, and fondly hope, by way of some Resemblance, to give their own Intrigues the Air of Innocence, or to shift part of the Blame elsewhere, which they find falls too hard upon themselves.

MADAM PERNELLE: All these Arguments are nothing to the purpose. *Orante* is known to lead an exemplary Life, her Care is all for Heav'n; and I have heard say that she has but an indifferent Opinion of the Company that frequents your House.

DORINA: An admirable Pattern Indeed! She's a mighty good Lady, and lives strictly, 'tis true, but 'tis Age that has brought this ardent Zeal upon her; and we know that she's a Prude in her own Defence. As long as 'twas in her Power to make Conquests, she did not balk any of her Advantages; but when she found the Lustre of her Eyes abate, she wou'd needs renounce the World that was on the point of leaving her; and under the specious Mask of great Prudence, conceals the Decay of her worn-out Charms. That is the antiquated Coquettes's last Shift. It is hard upon them to see themselves deserted by all their Galants. Thus forsaken, their gloomy Disquiet can find no Relief but in Prudery; and then the Severity of these good Ladies censures all and forgives none: They cry out loud upon every one's way of living, not out of Principle of Charity, but Envy, as not being able to suffer that another shou'd taste those Pleasures which People on the Decline have no Relish for.

MADAM PERNELLE [*To* ELMIRA.] These are the idle Stories that are told to please you, Daughter. There's no getting in a Word at your House, for Madam here engrosses all the Talk to herself: But I shall also be heard in my Turn. I tell you my Son never acted a wiser Part, than when he took this devout Man into his Family; that Heav'n in time of need sent him hither to reclaim your wandering Minds: that 'tis your main Interest to hearken to his Counsels, and that he reproves nothing that is not blameable. These Visits, Balls, and Assemblies are all the Inventions of the wicked Spirit; there's not one Word of Godliness to be heard at any of them, but the idle Stuff, Nonsense, and Tales of the Tub, and the Neighbours often come in for a Share, whip you have 'em as in a fencing bout.[1] In short, the Heads of reasonable People are turn'd by the Confusion of such Meetings: A thousand different Fancies are started about less than nothing; and as a good Doctor said the other Day very well, 'Tis a perfect Tower of *Babel*, for every one here babbles out of all measure. Now to give you an Account what brought it in was this. [*Pointing to* CLEANTHES.] What, is that Spark giggling already? Go look for your Fool to make a jest of, and unless – [*To* ELMIRA.] Good-by t'ye, Daughter, I shall say no more. Depend on't, I have not half the Esteem for your House I had, and it shall be very fine Weather when I set my Foot in your Doors again. [*Giving* FLIPOTE *a Box o'th' Ear*.] Come you, you're dreaming and gaping at the Crows; I'fakins! I'll warm your Ears for you. Let's march, Trollop, let's march.

Act I, Scene II

[CLEANTHES, DORINA.]

CLEANTHES: I won't go, for fear she should fall foul on me again. That this good old Lady –

DORINA: 'Tis pity, truly, she does not hear you call her so; she'd give you to understand how she lik'd you, and that she was not old enough to be call'd so yet.

CLEANTHES: What a Heat has she been in with us about nothing? And how fond does she seem of her *Tartuffe*?

---

1. Molière's reference is very specific; it is 'in *Tierce* and *Quarte*', which are the third and fourth parrying thrusts in a sequence of eight.

DORINA: Oh! truly, all this is nothing compar'd to the Infatuation of her Son, and were you to see him you'd say he was much worse. His Behaviour in our publick Troubles[1] had procur'd him the Character of a Man of Sense, and of Bravery for his Prince; but he's grown quite besotted since he became fond of *Tartuffe*. He calls him Brother, and loves him in his Heart a hundred times better than either Mother, Son, Daughter, or Wife. He's the only Confident of all his Secrets, and the wise Director of all his actions; he caresses, he embraces him, and I think one could not have more Affection for a Mistress. He will have him seated at the Upper-end of the Table, and is delighted to see him guttle[2] as much as half a dozen. He must be help'd to all the Tid-bits, and whenever he but belches, he bids G—d bless him. In short, he dotes upon him, he's his All, his Hero; he admires all he does, quotes him on all Occasions, looks on every trifling Action of his as a Wonder, and every Word an Oracle. At the same time the Fellow, knowing his Blind-side, and willing to make the most on't, has a hundred Tricks to impose upon his Judgement, and get his Mony from him in the way of Bigotry. He now pretends truly to take the whole Family to task; even the aukward Fool his Foot-boy takes upon him to lecture us with his Fanatic Face, and to demolish our Patches, Paint, and Ribbons. The Rascal, the other Day, tore us a fine Handkerchief[3] that lay in the *Pilgrim's-Progress*,[4] and cry'd, That it was a horrid Profanation, to mix hellish Ornaments with sanctify'd things.

Act I, Scene III

[ELMIRA, MARIANA, DAMIS, CLEANTHES, DORINA.]

ELMIRA: [*To* CLEANTHES.] You are very happy in not having come to the Harangue she gave us at the Gate. But I saw my Husband, and as he did not see me, I'll go up to wait his coming.
CLEANTHES: I'll wait for him here by way of a little Amusement, only bid him Good-morrow.

Act I, Scene IV

[CLEANTHES, DAMIS, DORINA.]

DAMIS: Hint something to him about my Sister's Wedding; I suspect that *Tartuffe's* against it, and that he puts my Father upon these tedious

---

1. A reference to the troubled times of the Fronde. Clearly Orgon played a positive role in supporting the prince, later King Louis XIV.
2. Guzzle.
3. Lace kerchiefs were used to decorate the *décolletage* of women's dresses.
4. This is an English equivalent for the book of devotion mentioned by Molière, the *Fleur des Saints*.

Evasions; you are not ignorant how nearly I am concern'd in it. If my Friend *Valere* and my Sister are sincerely fond of one another, his Sister, you know, is no less dear to me, and if it must –

DORINA: Here he is.

Act I, Scene V

[ORGON, CLEANTHES, DORINA.]

ORGON: Hah! Brother, good-morrow.

CLEANTHES: I was just going, and am glad to see you come back. The Country at present is not very pleasant.

ORGON: *Dorina.* [*To* CLEANTHES.] Brother, pray stay; you'll give me leave just to inquire the News of the Family; I can't be easy else. [*To* DORINA.] Have Matters gone well the two Days I have been away? What has happen'd here? How do they all do?

DORINA: My Lady the Day before Yesterday had a Fever all Day, and was sadly out of order with a strange Headach.

ORGON: And *Tartuffe*?

DORINA: *Tartuffe*? Extremely well, fat, fair, and fresh-colour'd.

ORGON: Poor Man!

DORINA: At Night she had no Stomach, and could not touch a bit of Supper, the Pain in her Head continu'd so violent.

ORGON: And *Tartuffe*?

DORINA: He supp'd by himself before her, and very heartily eat a Brace of Partridge, and half a Leg of Mutton hash'd.

ORGON: Poor Man!

DORINA: She never clos'd her Eyes, but burnt so that she could not get a wink of Sleep; and we were forc'd to sit up with her all Night.

ORGON: And *Tartuffe*?

DORINA: Being agreeably sleepy, he went from Table to his Chamber, and so into a warm Bed, and slept comfortably till next Morning.

ORGON: The poor Man!

DORINA: At length my Lady, prevail'd upon by our Persuasions, resolv'd to be let Blood; then she soon grew easier.

ORGON: And *Tartuffe*?

DORINA: He pluck'd up his Spirit, as he should; and fortifying his Mind against all Evils, to make amends for the Blood my Lady lost, drank at Breakfast four swinging Draughts of Wine.

ORGON: The poor Man!

DORINA: At present they both are pretty well, and I shall go before and let my Lady know how glad you are of her Recovery.

Act I, Scene VI

[ORGON, CLEANTHES.]

CLEANTHES: She jokes upon you, Brother, to your Face; and without any Design of making you angry, I must tell you freely, that 'tis not without Reason. Was ever such a Whim heard of? Is't possible, that a Man can be so bewitching at this time of Day, as to make you forget every thing for him? That after having, in your own House, relieved his Indigence, you should be ready to –

ORGON: Hold there, Brother, you don't know the Man you speak of.

CLEANTHES: Well, I don't know him, since you will have it so: But then, in order to know what a Man he is, –

ORGON: Brother, you would be charm'd did you know him, and there would be no end to your Raptures. He's a Man – that – ah – a Man – a Man, in short, a Man. Who always practises as he directs, enjoys a profound Peace, and regards the whole World no more than so much Dung. Ay, I am quite another Man by his Conversation. He teaches me to set my Heart upon Nothing; he disengages my Mind from Friendships or Relations; and I could see my Brother, Children, Mother, Wife, all expire, and not regard it more than this.

CLEANTHES: Humane Sentiments, Brother, I must confess!

ORGON: Ah! had you but seen him as I first met with him, you wou'd have loved him as well as I do. He came every Day to Church with a compos'd Mien, and kneel'd down just against me. He attracted the Eyes of the whole Congregation by the Fervency with which he sent up his Prayers to Heaven; He sigh'd and groan'd very heavily, and every Moment humbly kiss'd the Earth: And when I was going out, he would advance before and offer me Holy Water at the Door. Understanding by his Boy, (who copied him in every thing) his low Condition, and who he was, I made him Presents; but he always modestly would offer to return me part. 'Tis too much, he'd say, too much by half. I am not worth your Pity. And when I refus'd to take it again, he would go and give it among the Poor before my Face. At length Heav'n mov'd me to take him home, since which every thing here seems to prosper. I see he reproves without Distinction; and that even with regard to my Wife, he is extremely cautious of my Honour: He acquaints me who ogles her, and is six times more jealous of her than I am. But you can hardly imagine how very good he is: He calls every Trifle in himself a Sin; he's scandaliz'd at the smallest thing imaginable, so far, that the other Day he told me he had caught a Flea, as he was at his Devotions, and had killed it, he doubted, in rather too much Anger.

CLEANTHES: S'death! you must be mad, Brother, I fancy; or do you intend to banter me by such Stuff? What is it you mean? All this Fooling –

ORGON: Brother, what you say savours of Libertinism; you are a little tainted with it; and, as I have told you more than once, you'll draw down some heavy Judgment on your Head one Day or other.

CLEANTHES: This is the usual Strain of such as you. They would have every body as blind as themselves: To be clear-sighted is Libertinism, and such as don't dote upon empty Grimaces, have neither Faith nor Respect for sacred things. Come, come, all this Discourse of yours frights not me; I know what I say, and Heaven sees my Heart. We are not to be Slaves to your Men of Form. There are Pretenders to Devotion as well as to Courage. And as we never find the truly Brave to be such as make much Noise wheresoever they are led by Honour, so the Good and truly Pious, who are worthy of our Imitation, are never those that deal much in Grimace. Pray, would you make no Distinction between Hypocrisy and true Devotion? Would you term them both alike and pay the same Regard to the Mask as you do to the Face? Would you put Artifice on the level with Sincerity, and confound Appearance with Reality? Is the Phantom of the same esteem with you as the Figure? and is bad Mony of the same Value as good? Men generally are odd Creatures: They never keep up to true Nature. The Bounds of Reason are too narrow for them. In every Character they over-act their Parts, and the noblest Designs very often suffer in their Hands, because they will be running things into Extremes, and always carry things too far. This, Brother, by the by.

ORGON: Yes, yes, you are without doubt, a very reverend Doctor; all the Knowledge in the World lies under your Cap. You are the only wise and discerning Man, the Oracle, the *Cato* of the present Age; all Men, compar'd to you, are downright Fools.

CLEANTHES: No, Brother, I am none of your reverend Sages, nor is the whole Learning of the Universe vested in me; but I must tell you, I have Wit enough to distinguish Truth from Falshood: And as I see no Character in Life more great or valuable than to be truly devout, nor any thing more noble, or more beautiful, than the Fervor of a sincere Piety; so I think nothing more abominable than the outside Daubing of a pretended Zeal; than those Mountebanks, those Devotees in shew, whose sacrilegious and treacherous Grimace deceives with Impunity, and according as they please, make a Jest of what is most venerable and sacred among Men. Those Slaves of Interest, who make a Trade of Godliness, and who would purchase Honours and Reputation with an hypocritical turning up of the Eyes, and affected Transports. Those People, I say, who shew an uncommon Zeal for the next World in order to make their Fortunes in this, who, with great Affectation and Earnestness, daily recommend Solitude, while they live in Courts: Men who know how to make their own Vices consistent with their Zeal; they are passionate, revengeful, faithless, full of Artifice; and to effect a Man's Destruction, they insolently urge their private Resentment as the Cause of Heav'n; being so much the more dangerous in their Wrath, as they point against us those Weapons which Men reverence, and because their Passions prompt them to assassinate us with a consecrated Blade. There are too many of this vile Character; but the sincerely Devout are easily known; our Age, Brother, affords us some of these, who might serve for glorious Patterns to us. Observe, *Aristo, Periander, Orontes, Alcidamas, Polidore, Clitander*;[1] the Title is refus'd to them by no body. These are not Braggadocioes in Virtue. We see none of this insufferable Haughtiness in their Conduct; and their Devotion is humane and gentle. They censure not all we do, they think there's too much Pride in these Corrections, and leaving the Fierceness of Words to others, reprove our Actions by their own. They never build upon the Appearance of a Fault, and are always ready to judge favourably of others. They have no Cabals, no Intrigues to carry on; their chief Aim is to live themselves as they should do. They never worry a poor Sinner; their Quarrel is only with the Offence. Nor do they ever exert a keener Zeal for the Interest of Heav'n, than Heav'n itself does. These are the Men for me; this is the true Practice, and this the Example fit to be follow'd. Your Man is indeed not of this Stamp. You cry up his Zeal out of a good Intention, but, I believe you are impos'd on by a very false Gloss.

ORGON: My dear Brother, have you done?

CLEANTHES: Yes.

ORGON: [*Going.*] Then I'm your humble Servant.

CLEANTHES: Pray one Word more, Brother; let us leave this Discourse. You know you promised to take *Valere* for your Son-in-law.

ORGON: Yes.

CLEANTHES: And have appointed a Day for this agreeable Wedding.

ORGON: True.

CLEANTHES: Why then do you put off the Solemnity?

ORGON: I can't tell.

CLEANTHES: Have you some other Design in your Head?

ORGON: Perhaps so.

CLEANTHES: Will you break your Word then?

ORGON: I don't say that.

CLEANTHES: I think there's no Obstacle can hinder you from performing your Promise.

ORGON: That's as it happens.

CLEANTHES: Does the speaking of a single Word require so much Circumspection then? *Valere* sends me to you about it.

ORGON: Heav'n be praised!

CLEANTHES: What Answer shall I return him?

ORGON: What you will.

---

1. These are all names of the kind of exemplary characters one finds in heroic comedies and pastoral plays.

CLEANTHES: But 'tis necessary I should know your Intentions; pray what are they?

ORGON: To do just what Heav'n pleases.

CLEANTHES: But to the point pray. *Valere* has your Promise, do you stand to't, ay or no?

ORGON: Good be t'ye.

CLEANTHES: [*alone.*] I am afraid he'll meet with some Misfortune in his Love. I ought to inform him how matters go.

Act II, Scene I

[ORGON, MARIANA]

ORGON: *Mariana!*

MARIANA: Sir.

ORGON: Come hither; I have something to say to you in private.

MARIANA: [*to* ORGON, *who is looking into a Closet.*] What are you looking for, Sir?

ORGON: I'm looking if any body's there who might overhear us: This little Place is fit for such a purpose. So, we're all safe. I have always, *Mariana,* found you of a sweet Disposition, and you have always been very dear to me.

MARIANA: I am very much oblig'd to you, Sir, for your fatherly Affection.

ORGON: 'Tis very well said, Daughter, and to deserve it, your chief Care shou'd be to make me easy.

MARIANA: That is the height of my Ambition.

ORGON: Very well. Then what say you of *Tartuffe,* our Guest?

MARIANA: Who I?

ORGON: Yes, you; pray take heed how you answer.

MARIANA: Alas! Sir, I'll say what you will of him.

Act II, Scene II

[ORGON, MARIANA, DORINA *coming in softly, and standing behind* ORGON *without being seen.*]

ORGON: That's discreetly said. Tell me then, my Girl, that he's a very deserving Person; that you like him, and that it wou'd be agreeable if, with my Consent, you might have him for a Husband, ha?

MARIANA: How, Sir?

ORGON: What's the matter?

MARIANA: What said you?

ORGON: What?

MARIANA: Did I mistake you?

ORGON: As how?

MARIANA: Whom wou'd you have me say I lik'd, Sir, and shou'd be glad, with your Approbation, to have for a Husband?

ORGON: *Tartuffe*.

MARIANA: I protest to you, Sir; there's nothing in it. Why wou'd you make me tell you such a Story?

ORGON: But I wou'd have it be no Story; and 'tis enough that I have pitch'd upon him for you.

MARIANA: What, wou'd you, Sir –

ORGON: Ay, Child, I purpose, by your Marriage, to join *Tartuffe* to my Family. I have resolv'd upon't, and as I have a Right to – [*Spying* DORINA.] What Business have you there? Your Curiosity is very great, Sweetheart, to bring you to listen in this manner.

DORINA: In troth, Sir, whether this Report proceeds from Conjecture, or Chance, I don't know; but they have been just telling me the News of this Match, and I have been making a very great Jest on't.

ORGON: Why, is the thing so incredible?

DORINA: So incredible, that were you to tell me so yourself, I shou'd not believe you.

ORGON: I know how to make you believe it, tho'.

DORINA: Ay, ay, Sir, you tell us a comical Story.

ORGON: I tell you just what will prove true in a short time.

DORINA: Stuff!

ORGON: Daughter, I promise you I'm not in jest.

DORINA: Go, go; don't believe your Father, Madam, he does but joke.

ORGON: I tell you –

DORINA: No, 'tis in vain, no body will believe you.

ORGON: My Anger at length –

DORINA: Well, Sir, we will believe you; and so much the worse on your side. What, Sir, is it possible that with that Air of Wisdom, and that spacious Beard[1] on your Face, you shou'd be weak enough but to wish –

ORGON: Hearkye, you have taken certain Liberties of late, that I dislike: I tell you that, Child.

DORINA: Good Sir, let us argue this Affair calmly. You really must banter People by this Scheme. Your Daughter is not cut out for a Bigot; he has other things to think on: And then, what will such an Alliance bring you in? For what Reason would you go, with all your Wealth, to chuse a Beggar for a Son-in-law –

ORGON: Hold your Tongue! If he has nothing, know that we ought to esteem him for it. His Poverty is an honest Poverty, which raises him above all Grandeur, because he has suffer'd himself, in short, to be depriv'd of his

---

1. More likely a moustache in terms of contemporary fashion.

Fortune by his Negligence of things temporal, and his strong Attachment to things eternal. But my Assistance may put him in a way of getting out of Trouble, and of recovering his own. As poor as he is, he's a Gentleman, and the Estate he was born to is not inconsiderable.

DORINA: Yes, he says so; and this Vanity, Sir, does not very well suit with Piety. He that embraces the Simplicity of a holy Life, shou'd not set forth his Name and Family so much. The humble Procedure of Devotion does but ill agree with the Glare of Ambition. To what purpose all this Pride? – But this Talk offends you: Then let us lay aside his Quality, and speak to his Person. Can you have the Heart to fling away such a Girl as this upon such Man as he? Shou'd you not consult Propriety, and look a little forward to the Consequences of such a Union as this? Depend upon't, a young woman's Virtue is in some danger when she isn't married to her mind; that her living virtuously afterwards depends, in a great measure, upon the good Qualities of her Husband; and that those whom People every where point at with the Finger to the Forehead,[1] often make their Wives what we find they are. It is no easy Task to be faithful to some sorts of Husbands; and he that gives his Daughter a Man she hates, is accountable to Heav'n for the Slips she makes. Consider then to what danger your Design exposes you.

ORGON: I tell you, she is to learn from me what to do.

DORINA: You cou'd not do better with her than to follow my Advice.

ORGON: Don't let us amuse ourselves, Daughter, with this silly Stuff. I am your Father, and know what you must do. I had indeed promis'd you to *Valere*, but, besides that 'tis reported he is given to Play, I suspect him of being a little profligate: I don't observe that he frequents the Church.

DORINA: Wou'd you have him run to Church at your precise Hours, as People do who go there only to be taken notice of?

ORGON: I am not consulting you about it. The other, in short, is a Favourite of Heav'n, and that is beyond any other Possessions. This Union will crown your Wishes with every sort of Good; it will be one continued Scene of Pleasure and Delight. You'll live in faithful Love together, really like two Children, like two Turtle-Doves: No unhappy debate will e'er rise between you; and you'll make any thing of him you can well desire.

DORINA: She? She'll ne'er make any thing but a Fool of him, I assure you.

ORGON: Hey! What Language!

DORINA: I say, he has the Look of a Fool; and his Ascendant[2] will overbear all the Virtue your Daughter has.

ORGON: Have done with your Interruptions: Learn to hold your Peace, and don't you put in your Oar where you have nothing to do.

DORINA: Nay, Sir, I only speak for your good.

ORGON: You are too officious: Pray hold your Tongue, if you please.

1. Because they are cuckolded by their wives.
2. His destiny as written in the stars.

DORINA: If one had not a Love for you –

ORGON: I desire none of your Love.

DORINA: But I will love you, Sir, in spite of your self.[1]

ORGON: Ha!

DORINA: I have your Reputation much at Heart, and can't bear to have you made the Subject of every Gossip's Tale.

ORGON: Then you won't have done?

DORINA: It would be a Sin to let you make such an Alliance as this.

ORGON: Will you hold your Tongue, you Serpent, whose Impudence –

DORINA: Oh! What, a Devotee, and fly into such a Rage?

ORGON: Yes; my Choler is mov'd at this Impertinence; and I'm resolv'd you shall hold your Tongue.

DORINA: Be it so. But tho' I don't speak a Word, I don't think the less.

ORGON: Think if you will; but take care not to say a Syllable to me about it, or – Enough – [*To his Daughter.*] I have maturely weigh'd all things as a wise Man shou'd.

DORINA: [*aside.*] It makes me mad that I must not speak now!

ORGON: *Tartuffe*, without Foppery, is a Person so form'd –

DORINA: [*aside.*] Yes, 'tis a pretty Phiz.

ORGON: That shou'd you have no great Relish for his other Qualifications –

DORINA: [*aside.*] She'll have a very fine Bargain of him! [ORGON *turns about towards* DORINA, *and eyes her with his Arms across.*] Were I in her Place, tho' no Man alive should marry me against my Will, with Impunity, I'd let him see, soon after the Ceremony was over, that a Wife has a Revenge always at hand.

ORGON: [*to* DORINA.] Then what I say, stands for nothing with you?

DORINA: What do you complain of? I don't speak to you.

ORGON: What is't you do then?

DORINA: I talk to myself.

ORGON: [*aside.*] Very well! I must give her a Slap o'th' Face to correct her prodigious Insolence. [*He puts himself into a Posture to strike* DORINA, *and at every Word he speaks to his Daughter he casts his Eyes upon* DORINA, *who stands bolt-upright, without speaking.*] Daughter, you must needs approve of my Design – and believe that the Husband – which I have pick'd out for you – [*To* DORINA.] Why dost thou not talk to thy self now?

DORINA: Because I have nothing to say to myself.

ORGON: One little Word more.

DORINA: I've no mind to't.

ORGON: To be sure I watch'd you.

DORINA: A downright Fool, I'faith.

ORGON: In short, Daughter, you must obey, and shew an intire Deference to my Choice.

DORINA: [*as she runs off.*] I shou'd scorn to take such a Husband myself.

---

1. Clare uses the phrase ' in spite of your Teeth'.

ORGON: [*strikes at her, but misses.*] You have a pestilent Hussy with you there, Daughter, that I can't live with any longer, without Sin. I a'n't in a condition to proceed at present; her Insolence has put my Spirits into such a Ferment, that I must go take the Air to recover myself a little.

Act II, Scene III

[MARIANA, DORINA.]

DORINA: Pray tell me, have you lost your Tongue? Must I play your Part for you on this occasion? What, suffer a silly Overture to be made you, without saying the least Word against it!

MARIANA: What shou'd one do against a Father with absolute power?[1]

DORINA: Any thing, to ward off such a Menace.

MARIANA: But what?

DORINA: Why, tell him, that Hearts admit of no Proxies; that you marry for your self, and not for him; that you being the Person, for whom the whole Affair is transacted, your Inclinations for the Man, shou'd be consulted, not his; and that if *Tartuffe* seems so lovely in his Eyes, he may marry him himself without Let or Hindrance.

MARIANA: A Father, I own, has such a Command over one, that I never had Courage to make him a Reply.

DORINA: But let us reason the case. *Valere* has made Advances for you: pray, do you love him, or do you not?

MARIANA: Nay, you do Injustice to my Love, to question my Affections! Ought you, *Dorina*, to ask me that? Have I not open'd my Heart to you a hundred times on the Subject? and are you still a Stranger to the Warmth of my Passion?

DORINA: How do I know whether your Heart and Words keep pace together? or whether you really have any particular Regard to this Lover, or not?

MARIANA: You do me wrong, *Dorina*, to doubt it; and the Sincerity of my Sentiments, in that matter has been but too plain.

DORINA: You really love him then?

MARIANA: Ay, extremely.

DORINA: And according to all Appearance, he loves you as well.

MARIANA: I believe so.

DORINA: And you two have a mutual Desire to marry?

MARIANA: Assuredly.

DORINA: What is then your Expectation from this other Match?

MARIANA: To kill my self, if they force me to it.

DORINA: Very good! That's a Relief I did not think of; you need only to die

---

1. Clare translates this as 'with a positive Father'.

to get rid of this Perplexity. 'Tis a wonderful Remedy, for certain. It makes one mad to hear Folks talk at this rate.

MARIANA: Bless me, *Dorina*! what a Humour are you got into! You have not Compassion upon People's Afflictions.

DORINA: I have no Compassion for People who talk idly, and give way in time of Action as you do.

MARIANA: But what wou'd you have, if one is timorous?

DORINA: But Love requires a Firmness of Mind.

MARIANA: But have I waver'd in my Affections towards *Valere*? And is it not his business to gain me of my Father?

DORINA: But what? if your Father be a downright Humourist, who is entirely bewitch'd with his *Tartuffe*, and wou'd set aside a Match he had agreed on, pray is that your Lover's Fault?

MARIANA: But shou'd I, by a flat and confident refusal, let every body know, that I am violently in Love? Wou'd you have me, for his sake, transgress the Modesty of my Sex, and the Bounds of my Duty? Wou'd you have my Passion become a perfect Town-talk?

DORINA: No, no, I don't want any thing. I see you'd fain have Mr. *Tartuffe*; and now I think on't, I shou'd be in the wrong to dissuade you from so considerable an Alliance. To what purpose shou'd I oppose your Inclinations? The Match is in itself too advantageous. Mr. *Tartuffe*, Oh! is this a trifling Offer? If we take it right, he's no Simpleton. It will be no small Honour to be his Mate. All the World has a prodigious Value for him already; he is well born, handsome in his Person, he has a red Ear, and a very florid Complexion: you'll, in short, be but too happy with such a Husband.

MARIANA: Heav'ns!

DORINA: You can't conceive what a Joy 'twill be to you, to be the Consort of so fine a Man!

MARIANA: Poh! prithee give over this Discourse, and rather assist me against this Match. 'Tis now all over; I yield, and am ready to do whatever you'd have me.

DORINA: No, no, a Daughter shou'd do as she's bid, tho' her Father wou'd have her marry a Monkey. Besides what reason have you to complain? Yours is a *Benefit-Ticket*.[1] You'll be coach'd down to his own Borough-Town, which you'll find abounds in Cousins and Uncles: It will be very diverting to you to entertain them all. Then Madam *Tartuffe* will be directly introduc'd to the Beau Monde: You'll go visit, by way of Welcome, the Bailiff's Lady, and the Assessor's Wife: they'll do you the Honour of the Folding-Chair.[2] At a Good-time you may hope for a Ball,

1. The translator has used a popular phrase to convey the spirit of Molière's original, 'Votre sort est fort beau'. In a benefit performance, players were allowed to keep the profits of their benefit night.
2. The lowliest form of chair offered a visitor.

and a great Consort,[1] to wit, two pair of Bagpipes; and perchance you may see Merry-Andrew, and the Puppet-Shew; if however your Husband –

MARIANA: Oh! you kill me! rather contrive how to help me by your Advice.

DORINA: Your humble Servant for that.

MARIANA: Nay, *Dorina*, for Heav'n's sake –

DORINA: No, it must be a Match, to punish you.

MARIANA: Dear Girl do!

DORINA: No.

MARIANA: If my Professions –

DORINA: No, *Tartuffe's* your Man, and you shall have a Taste of him.

MARIANA: You know how much I always confided in you; be so good –

DORINA: No, in troth; you shall be *Tartuff'd*.

MARIANA: Well, since my Misfortunes can't move you, henceforth leave me intirely to my Despair. That shall lend my Heart Relief, and I know an infallible Remedy for all my Sufferings.

[*Offers to go.*]

DORINA: Here, here, come back; I'm appeas'd. I must take Compassion on you, for all this.

MARIANA: I tell you, d'y'see, *Dorina*, if they do expose me to this Torment, it will certainly cost me my Life.

DORINA: Don't vex yourself, it may easily be prevented – But see; here's you humble Servant *Valere*.

Act II, Scene IV

[VALERE, MARIANA, DORINA.]

VALERE: I was just now told an odd piece of News, Madam, that I knew nothing of, and which to be sure is very pretty.

MARIANA: What's that?

VALERE: That you are to be married to *Tartuffe*.

MARIANA: 'Tis certain my Father has such a Design in his Head.

VALERE: Your Father, Madam –

MARIANA: Has alter'd his Mind, and has been just now making the Proposal to me.

VALERE: What, seriously?

MARIANA: Ay seriously. He has been declaring himself strenuously for the Match.

VALERE: And pray, Madam, what may be your Determination in the Affair?

MARIANA: I don't know.

1. A group of musicians.

VALERE: The Answer is honest! You don't know?

MARIANA: No.

VALERE: No?

MARIANA: What wou'd you advise me to?

VALERE: I advise you to accept him for a Husband.

MARIANA: Is that your Advice?

VALERE: Yes.

MARIANA: In good earnest?

VALERE: No doubt on't. The Choice is good, and well worth attending to.

MARIANA: Well, Sir, I shall take your Counsel.

VALERE: You will have no Difficulty to follow it, I believe.

MARIANA: Hardly more than your Counsel gave you.

VALERE: I gave it, Madam, to please you.

MARIANA: And I shall follow it, to do you a Pleasure.

DORINA: [*retiring to the farther part of the Stage.*] So. Let's see what this will come to.

VALERE: Is this then your Affection? And was it all Deceit, when you –

MARIANA: Pray let's talk no more of that. You told me frankly that I ought to accept of the Offer made me: And I tell you, I shall do so, only because you advise me to it as the best.

VALERE: Don't excuse yourself upon my Intentions: Your Resolution was made before; and you now lay hold of a frivolous Pretence, for the breaking of your Word.

MARIANA: 'Tis true; it's well said.

VALERE: Doubtless; and you never had any true Love for me.

MARIANA: Alas! You may think so if you please.

VALERE: Yes, yes, may think so; but my offended Heart may chance to be beforehand with you in that Affair; and I can tell where to offer both my Addresses and my Hand.

MARIANA: I don't doubt it, Sir. The warmth that Merit raises –

VALERE: Lack-a-day! Let us drop Merit: I have little enough of that, and you think so; but I hope, another will treat me in a kinder manner; and I know a Person whose Heart, open to my Retreat, will not be asham'd to make up my Loss.

MARIANA: The Loss is not great, and you will be comforted, upon this change, easily enough.

VALERE: You may believe I shall do all that lies in my Power. A Heart that forgets us, engages our Glory; we must employ our utmost Cares to forget it too; and if we don't succeed, we must at least pretend we do; for to shew a Regard for those that forsake us, is a Meanness one cannot answer to one's self.

MARIANA: The Sentiment is certainly noble and sublime.

VALERE: Very well, and what every body must approve of. What? wou'd you have me languish for ever for you? See you fly into another's Arms before my Face, and not transfer my slighted Affections somewhere else?

MARIANA: So far from that, 'tis what I wou'd have; and I wish 'twere done already.

VALERE: You wish it done?

MARIANA: Yes.

VALERE: That's insulting me sufficiently, Madam; I am just going to give you that Satisfaction.

[*He offers to go.*]

MARIANA: 'Tis very well.

VALERE: [*returning.*] Be pleas'd to remember at least, that 'tis your self that drive me to this Extremity.

MARIANA: Yes.

VALERE: [*returning again.*] And that the Design I have conceiv'd is only from your Example.

MARIANA: My Example be it.

VALERE: [*going.*] Enough; you shall soon be punctually obey'd.

MARIANA: So much the better.

VALERE: [*returning again.*] 'Tis the last time I shall ever trouble you.

MARIANA: With all my Heart.

VALERE: [*goes toward the Door and returns.*] Hey?

MARIANA: What's the matter?

VALERE: Don't you call me?

MARIANA: Who, I? You dream sure.

VALERE: Well then, I'll be gone; farewel, Madam!

MARIANA: Fare ye well, Sir.

DORINA: [*to* MARIANA.] I think for my part, by this piece of Extravagance, you've both lost your Senses; I have let you alone thus long squabbling, to see what end you'd make on't. Heark ye, Mr. *Valere!*

[*She lays hold of* VALERE'S *Arm.*]

VALERE: [*pretending to resist.*] Heh! what wou'd you have, *Dorina?*

DORINA: Come hither.

VALERE: No, no, my Indignation overpowers me; don't hinder me from doing as she wou'd have me.

DORINA: Stay.

VALERE: No, d'ye see, I'm resolv'd upon it.

DORINA: Ah!

MARIANA: [*aside.*] He's uneasy at the Sight of me: My Presence drives him away; I had much better therefore leave the Place.

DORINA: [*quitting* VALERE, *and running after* MARIANA.] What, t'other? whither do you run?

MARIANA: Let me alone.

DORINA: You must come back.

MARIANA: No, no, *Dorina*; in vain you'd hold me.

VALERE: [*aside.*] I find that my Presence is but a Plague to her. I had certainly better free her from it.

DORINA: [*quitting* MARIANA *and running after* VALERE.] What again? Deuce take you for me. Leave this fooling, and come hither both of you.

[*She takes* VALERE *and* MARIANA *by the Hand, and brings them back.*]

VALERE: But what's your Design?

MARIANA: What would you do?

DORINA: Set you two to rights again, and bring you out of this Scrape. [*to* VALERE.] A'n't you mad, to wrangle at this rate?

VALERE: Didn't you hear how she spoke to me?

DORINA: [*to* MARIANA.] Wasn't you a Simpleton, to be in such a Passion?

MARIANA: Didn't you see the thing, and how he treated me?

DORINA: Folly o' both sides; [*to* VALERE.] she has nothing more at Heart, than that she may be one day yours; I am Witness to it. [*to* MARIANA.] He loves none but your self, and has no other Ambition than to become your Husband, I answer for't upon my Life.

MARIANA: [*to* VALERE.] Why then did you give me such Advice?

VALERE: [*to* MARIANA.] And why was I consulted upon such a Subject?

DORINA: You're a couple of Fools. Come, come, your Hands, both of you; [*to* VALERE.] come you.

VALERE: [*giving his Hand to* DORINA.] What will my Hand do?

DORINA: [*to* MARIANA.] So; come, now yours.

MARIANA: [*giving her hand.*] To what purpose is all this?

DORINA: Come along, come quick: you love one another better than you think of.

VALERE: [*turning towards* MARIANA.] But don't do things with an ill grace, and give a Body a civil Look.

[MARIANA *turns toward* VALERE, *and smiles a little.*]

DORINA: In troth, Lovers are silly Creatures!

VALERE: [*to* MARIANA.] Now, have I not room to complain to you? and, without lying, were not you a wicked Creature, to gratify your self in saying a thing so very shocking to me?

MARIANA: But are not you the ungrateful'st Man in the World –

DORINA: Come let's adjourn this Debate 'til another Time; and think how to ward off this plaguy Wedding.

MARIANA: Say then, what Engines shall we set at work?

DORINA: We'll set them every way to work. [*to* MARIANA.] Your Father's in jest; [*to* VALERE.] it must be nothing but Talk. [*to* MARIANA.] But for your part, your best way will be to carry the Appearance of a gentle Compliance with his Extravagance, that so, in case of an Alarm, you may have it more easily in your power to delay the Marriage propos'd. In gaining time we shall remedy every thing. Sometimes you may fob 'em off with some illness, which is to come all of a sudden, and will require Delay: Sometimes you may fob them off with ill Omens: You unluckily met a Corps, broke a Looking-Glass, or dream'd of dirty Water; and at last, the best on't is, they can't possibly join you to any other but him, unless you please to say, Yes. But, the better to carry on the Design, I think it proper you should not be seen conferring together. [*To* VALERE.] Go you immediately and employ your Friends, that he may be forc'd to keep his Word with you. [*To* MARIANA.] Let us go excite his Brother's Endeavours, and engage the Mother-in-Law[1] in our Party. Adieu.

VALERE: [*to* MARIANA.] Whatever Efforts any of us may be preparing, my greatest Hope, to say the truth, is in you.

MARIANA: [*to* VALERE.] I can't promise for the Inclinations of a Father, but I shall be none but Valere's.

VALERE: How you transport me! And tho' I durst –

DORINA: Ah! These Lovers are never weary of Pratling. Away, I tell you.

VALERE: [*goes a Step or two, and returns.*] Once more –

DORINA: What a Clack is yours? Draw you off this way, and you t'other.

[*Pushing 'em each out by the Shoulders.*]

Act III, Scene I

[DAMIS, DORINA.]

DAMIS: May Thunder, this Moment, strike me dead; let me be every where treated like the greatest Scoundrel alive, if any Respect or Power whatever shall stop me, and if I don't strike some masterly Stroke.

DORINA: Moderate your Passion for Heav'n's sake; your Father did but barely mention it: People don't do all they propose, and the Distance is great from the Project to the Execution.

DAMIS: I must put a Stop to this Fool's Projects, and tell him a Word or two in his Ear.

DORINA: Gently, gently pray; let your Mother-in-law alone with him, as well as with your Father. She has some Credit with *Tartuffe*. He is mighty complaisant to all she says, and perhaps he may have a sneaking kindness for her. I wou'd to Heav'n it were true! That could be charming. In short, your Interest obliges her to send for him; she has a mind to sound his Intentions, with regard to the Wedding that disturbs you; and represent to him the fatal Feuds he will raise in the Family, if

1. The stepmother, i.e. Elmira.

he entertains any Hopes of this Affair. His Man says that he's at Prayers, and I cou'd not see him. But this Servant told me, he wou'd not be long before he came down. Then pray be gone, and let me stay for him.

DAMIS: I may be present at this whole Conference.

DORINA: No, they must be by themselves.

DAMIS: I shall say nothing to him.

DORINA: You're mistaken; we know the usual Impatience of your Temper, and 'tis the ready way to spoil all. Get away.

DAMIS: No, I will see him, without putting my self in a Passion.

DORINA: How troublesome you are! He's coming; retire.

[DAMIS *conceals himself in a Closet.*]

Act III, Scene II

[TARTUFFE, DORINA.]

TARTUFFE: [*upon seeing* DORINA *speaks aloud to his Servant who is in the House.*] *Laurence*, lock up my Hair-cloth and Scourge, and beg of Heav'n ever to enlighten you with Grace. If any body comes to see me, I am gone to the Prisons to distribute my Alms.

DORINA: [*aside.*] What Affection and Roguery!

TARTUFFE: What do you want?

DORINA: To tell you –

TARTUFFE: [*drawing a Handkerchief out of his Pocket.*] Oh! lack-a-day! pray take me this Handkerchief before you speak.

DORINA: What for?

TARTUFFE: Cover that Bosom, which I can't bear to see. Such Objects hurt the Soul, and usher in sinful Thoughts.

DORINA: You mightily melt then at a Temptation, and the Flesh makes great Impression upon your Senses? Truly, I can't tell what Heat may inflame you; but, for my part, I am not so apt to hanker. Now I cou'd see you stark naked from Head to Foot, and that whole Hide of yours not tempt me at all.

TARTUFFE: Pray now speak with a little Modesty, or I shall leave you this Minute.

DORINA: No, no, 'tis I who am going to leave you to yourself; and I have only two Words to say to you: My Lady is coming down into this Parlour, and desires the Favour of a Word with you.

TARTUFFE: Alack! with all my Heart.

DORINA: [*aside.*] How sweet he grows upon't! I'faith I still stand to what I said of him.

TARTUFFE: Will she come presently?

DORINA: I think I hear her. Ay, 'tis she herself; I leave you together.

Act III, Scene III

[ELMIRA, TARTUFFE.]

TARTUFFE: May Heav'n, of its Goodness, ever bestow upon you Health both of Body and of Mind! and bless your Days equal to the Wish of the lowest of its Votaries!

ELMIRA: I am much obliged to you for this pious Wish; but let us take a Seat to be more at ease.

TARTUFFE: [*sitting down.*] Do you find your Indisposition any thing abated?

ELMIRA: [*sitting.*] Very well, my Fever soon left me.

TARTUFFE: My Prayers have not sufficient Merit to have drawn down this Favour from above; but I made no Vows to Heav'n that did not concern your Recovery.

ELMIRA: Your Zeal for me was too solicitous.

TARTUFFE: Your dear Health cannot be overrated; and, to re-establish it, I could have sacrific'd my own.

ELMIRA: That is carrying Christian Charity a great way; and I am highly indebted to you for all this Goodness.

TARTUFFE: I do much less for you than you deserve.

ELMIRA: I had a Desire to speak with you in private on a certain Affair, and am glad that no body observes us here.

TARTUFFE: I am also overjoy'd at it; and, be sure, it can be no ordinary Satisfaction, Madam, to find my self alone with you. 'Tis an Opportunity that I have hitherto petitioned Heav'n for in vain.

ELMIRA: What I want to talk with you upon, is a small Matter, in which your whole Heart must be open, and hide nothing from me.

TARTUFFE: And, for this singular Favour, I certainly will unbosom my self to you, without the least Reserve; and I protest to you, that the Stir I made about the Visits paid here to your Charms, was not out of Hatred to you, but rather out of a passionate Zeal which induc'd me to it, and out of a pure Motive –

ELMIRA: For my part I take it very well, and believe 'tis my Good that gives you this Concern.

TARTUFFE: [*taking* ELMIRA'S *Hand, and squeezing her Fingers.*] Yes, Madam, without doubt, and such is the Fervour of my –

ELMIRA: Oh! You squeeze me too hard.

TARTUFFE: 'Tis out of Excess of Zeal; I never intended to hurt you: I had much rather –

[*Puts his Hand upon her Knee.*]

ELMIRA: What does your Hand do there?

TARTUFFE: I'm only feeling your Clothes, Madam; the Stuff is mighty rich.

ELMIRA: Oh! Pray give over; I am very ticklish.

[*She draws away her Chair, and* TARTUFFE *follows with his.*]

TARTUFFE: Bless me! How wonderful is the Workmanship of this Lace! They work to a Miracle now-a-days: Things of all kinds were never better done.

ELMIRA: 'Tis true; but let us speak to our Affair a little. They say that my Husband has a mind to set aside his Promise, and to give you his Daughter: Is that true? Pray tell me?

TARTUFFE: He did hint something towards it: But, Madam, to tell you the Truth, that is not the Happiness I sigh after: I behold elsewhere the wonderful Attractions of the Felicity that engages every Wish of mine.

ELMIRA: That is, you love no earthly Things.

TARTUFFE: My Breast does not inclose a Heart of Flint.

ELMIRA: I am apt to think that your Sighs tend all to Heav'n, and that nothing here below can detain your Desires.

TARTUFFE: The Love which engages us to eternal Beauties, does not extinguish in us the love of temporal ones. Our Senses may easily be charm'd with the perfect Works Heav'n has form'd. Its reflected Charms shine forth, in such as you: But, in your Person, it displays its choicest Wonders. It has diffus'd such Beauties o'er your Face as surprise the Sight, and transport the Heart; nor could I behold you, perfect Creature, without admiring in you the Author of Nature, and feeling my Heart touch'd with an ardent Love, at sight of the fairest of Pourtraits, wherein he has delineated himself. At first I was under Apprehensions lest this secret Flame might be a dexterous Surprize of the foul Fiend; and my Heart even resolv'd to avoid your Eyes, believing you an Obstacle to my future Happiness. But at length I perceive'd, most lovely Beauty, that my Passion could not be blameable, that I could reconcile it with Modesty, and this made me abandon my Heart to it. It is, I confess, a very great Presumption in me, to make you the Offer of this Heart; but, in my vows, I rely wholly on your Goodness, and not on any thing in my own weak Power. In you center my Hope, my Happiness, my Quiet; on you depend my Torment or my Bliss; and I am on the point of being, by your sole Decision, happy if you will, or miserable if you please.

ELMIRA: The Declaration is extremely galant, but, to say the truth, it is a good deal surprising. Methinks you ought to have fortified your Mind better, and to have reason'd a little upon a Design of this Nature. A Devotee as you are, whom every one speaks of as –

TARTUFFE: Ah! being a Devotee does not make me the less a Man; and when one comes to view your celestial Charms, the Heart surrenders, and reasons no more. I know, that such Language from me, seems somewhat strange; but, Madam, after all, I am not an Angel, and shou'd you condemn the Declaration I make, you must lay the Blame upon your attractive Charms. From the Moment I first set Eyes upon your more than human Splendor, you became the Sovereign of my Soul: The ineffable Sweetness of your Divine Looks broke thro' the Resistance which my Heart obstinately made: It surmounted every thing, Fastings, Prayers, Tears, and turn'd all my Vows on the side of your Charms. My Eyes and my Sighs have told it you a thousand times, and the better to explain myself I here make use of Words. Now if you contemplate with some Benignity of Soul, the Tribulations of your unworthy Slave; if your Goodness will give me Consolation, and deign to debase itself so low as my Nothingness, I shall ever entertain for you, Miracle of Sweetness, a Devotion which nothing can equal. Your Honour, with me, runs no Risque, it need fear no Disgrace on my part. All those courtly Galants the Ladies are so fond of, make a Bustle in what they do, and are vain in what they say. We see they are ever vaunting of their Success; they receive no Favours that they don't divulge, and their indiscreet Tongues, which People confide in, dishonour the Altar on which their Hearts offer sacrifice: But Men of our sort burn with a discreet Flame, with whom a Secret is always sure to remain such. The Care we take of our own Reputation, is an undeniable Security of the Person belov'd: And 'tis with us, when they accept our Hearts, that they enjoy Love without Scandal, and Pleasure without Fear.

ELMIRA: I hear what you say, and your Rhetorick explains itself to me in Terms sufficiently strong. Don't you apprehend that I may take a Fancy now, to acquaint my Husband with this Galantry of yours? and that an early Account of an Amour of this sort, might pretty much alter his present Affections towards you?

TARTUFFE: I know that you are too good, and that you will rather pardon my Temerity; that you will excuse me, upon the Score of human Frailty, the Sallies of a Passion that offends you; and will consider, when you consult your Glass, that a Man is not blind, and is made of Flesh and Blood.

ELMIRA: Some might take it perhaps in another manner; but I shall shew my Discretion, and not tell my Husband of it: But in return, I will have one thing of you, that is honestly and sincerely to forward the Match between *Valere* and *Mariana*, and that you yourself renounce the unjust Power whereby you hope to be inrich'd with what belongs to another. And –

Act III, Scene IV

[ELMIRA, DAMIS, TARTUFFE.]

DAMIS: [*coming out of the Closet where he was hid.*] No, Madam, no, this ought to be made publick; I was in this Place, and overheard it all; and the Goodness of Heav'n seems to have directed me thither to confound the Pride of a Traitor that wrongs me; to open me a way to take Vengeance of his Hypocrisy and Insolence; to undeceive my Father, and shew him, in clear Light, the Soul of a Villain that talks to you of Love.

ELMIRA: No, Damis, 'tis enough that he reforms, and endeavours to deserve the Favour I do him. Since I have promis'd him, don't make me break my word: 'Tis not my Humour to make a Noise; a Wife will make herself merry with such Follies, and never trouble her Husband's Ears with them.

DAMIS: You have your Reasons for using him in that manner, and I have mine too for acting otherwise. To spare him would be ridiculous; the insolent Pride of his Bigottry has triumph'd too much over my just Resentment, and created too many Disorders among us already. The Rascal has, but too long, govern'd my Father, and oppos'd my Passion, as well as *Valere's*. 'Tis fit the perfidious Wretch should be laid open to him, and Heav'n for this purpose offers me an easy way to do it. I am greatly indebted to it for the Opportunity; it is too favourable a one to be neglected, and I shou'd deserve to have it taken from me now I have it, shou'd I not make use on't.

ELMIRA: *Damis* –

DAMIS: No, by your leave, I must take my own Counsel. My Heart overflows with Joy, and all you can say wou'd in vain dissuade me from the Pleasure of avenging myself. Without going any farther, I will make an end of the Affair, and here's just what will give me Satisfaction.

Act III, Scene V

[ORGON, ELMIRA, DAMIS, TARTUFFE.]

DAMIS: We are going to entertain you, Sir, with an Adventure spick and span new, which will very much surprize you. You are well rewarded for all your Caresses; and this Gentleman makes a fine Acknowledgement of your Tenderness. His great Zeal for you is just come to light; it aims at nothing less than the Dishonour of your Bed, and I took him here making an injurious Declaration of a criminal Love to your Wife. She is good-natur'd, and her over great Discretion, by all means, would have kept the Secret; but I can't encourage such Impudence, and think that not to apprize you of it is to do you an Injury.

ELMIRA: Yes, I am of opinion that one ought never to break in upon a Husband's Rest with such idle Stuff, that our Honour can by no means depend upon it; and that 'tis enough we know how to defend ourselves. These are my Thoughts of the matter; and you would have said nothing, *Damis*, if I had had any Credit with you.

Act III, Scene VI

[ORGON, DAMIS, TARTUFFE.]

ORGON: Heav'ns! What have I heard? Is this credible?

TARTUFFE: Yes, Brother, I am a wicked, guilty, wretched Sinner, full of Iniquity, the greatest Villain that ever breath'd. Every Instant of my Life is crowded with Stains; 'tis one continued Series of Crimes and Defilements; and I see that Heav'n, for my Punishment, designs to mortify me on this Occasion. Whatever great Offence they can lay to my Charge, I shall have more Humility than to deny it. Believe what they tell you, arm your Resentment, and like a Criminal, drive me out of your House. I cannot have so great a share of Shame but I have still deserv'd a much larger.

ORGON: [*to his Son.*] Ah, Traitor! Dar'st thou, by this Falshood, attempt to tarnish the Purity of his Virtue?

DAMIS: What! shall the feign'd Meekness of this hypocritical Soul make you give the Lye –

ORGON: Thou curs'd Plague! hold thy Tongue.

TARTUFFE: Ah! let him speak; you chide him wrongfully, you had much better believe what he tells you: why so favourable to me upon such a Fact? Do you know after all what I may be capable of? Can you, my Brother, depend upon my Outside? Do you think me the better for what you see of me? No, no, you suffer yourself to be deceiv'd by Appearances, and I am neither better nor worse, alas! than these People think me. The World indeed takes me for a very good Man, but the Truth is, I am a very worthless Creature. [*Turning to* DAMIS.] Yes, my dear Child, say on, call me Treacherous, Infamous, Reprobate, Thief, and Murderer; load me with Names still more detestable; I don't gainsay you; I have deserv'd them all, and am willing on my Knees to suffer the Ignominy, as a Shame due to the Enormities of my Life.

ORGON: [*to* TARTUFFE.] This is too much, Brother. [*To his Son.*] Does not thy Heart relent, Traitor?

DAMIS: What, shall his Words so far deceive you as to –

ORGON: Hold your Tongue, Rascal! [*Raising* TARTUFFE.] For Heav'n's sake, Brother, rise. [*To his Son.*] Infamous Wretch!

DAMIS: He can –

ORGON: Hold thy Tongue.

DAMIS: Intolerable! What! am I taken for –

ORGON: Say one other Word and I'll break thy Bones.

TARTUFFE: For Heav'n's sake, Brother, don't be angry; I had rather suffer any Hardship, than that he should get the slightest Hurt on my Account.

ORGON: [*to his Son.*] Ungrateful Monster!

TARTUFFE: Let him alone; if I must on my Knees ask Forgiveness for him –

ORGON: [*throwing himself also at* TARTUFFE's *Feet, and embracing him.*] Alas! You
     are in jest, sure? [*To his Son.*] See his Goodness, Sirrah!
DAMIS: Then –
ORGON: Have done.
DAMIS: What! I –
ORGON: Peace, I say. I know what put you upon this Attack well enough; ye
     all hate him, and I now see Wife, Children, Servants, are all let loose
     against him. They impudently try every way to remove this devout
     Person from me: But the more they strive to get him out, the greater care
     will I take to keep him in; and therefore will I hasten his Marriage with
     my Daughter, to confound the Pride of the whole Family.
DAMIS: Do you think to force her to accept of him?
ORGON: Yes, Traitor, and this very Evening, to plague you. Nay, I defy you
     all, and shall make you to know that I am Master, and will be obey'd.
     Come Sirrah, do you recant; immediately throw yourself at his Feet to
     beg his Pardon.
DAMIS: Who, I? of this Rascal, who by his Impostures –
ORGON: What, Scoundrel, do you rebel, and call him Names? A Cudgel there,
     a Cudgel [*To* TARTUFFE.] Don't hold me. [*To his Son.*] Get you out of my
     House this Minute, and never dare to set Foot into it again.
DAMIS: Yes, I shall go, but –
ORGON: Quickly then leave the Place; Sirrah, I disinherit thee, and give thee
     my Curse besides.

Act III, Scene VII

[ORGON, TARTUFFE.]

ORGON: To offend a Holy Person in such a manner!
TARTUFFE: [*aside.*] O Heav'n's pardon him the Anguish he gives me! [*To*
     ORGON.] Could you know what a Grief it is to me that they shou'd try
     to blacken me with my dear Brother –
ORGON: Alack-a-day!
TARTUFFE: The very Thought of this Ingratitude wounds me to the very
     quick! – Lord, what Horror! – My Heart's so full that I can't speak; I
     think I shan't outlive it.
ORGON: [*running all in Tears to the Door out of which he drove his son.*] Villain!
     I'm sorry my Hand spar'd, and did not make an end of thee on the Spot.
     [*To* TARTUFFE.] Compose yourself, Brother, and don't be troubled.
TARTUFFE: Let us by all means put an end to the Course of these unhappy
     Debates; I see what Uneasiness I occasion here, and think there's a
     Necessity, Brother, for my leaving your House.
ORGON: How? You're not in earnest sure?

TARTUFFE: They hate me, and seek, I see, to bring my Integrity into question with you.

ORGON: What signifies that? Do you see me listen to them?

TARTUFFE: They won't stop here, you may be sure; and those very Stories which you now reject, may one Day meet with more Credit.

ORGON: No, Brother, never.

TARTUFFE: Ah! Brother, a Wife may easily deceive a Husband.

ORGON: No, no.

TARTUFFE: Suffer me, by removing hence, immediately to remove from them all occasion of attacking me in this manner.

ORGON: No, you must stay, or it will cost me my Life.

TARTUFFE: Well, then I must mortify myself. If you wou'd, however –

ORGON: Ah!

TARTUFFE: Be it so: Let's talk no more about it. But I know how I must behave on this Occasion. Honour is delicate, and Friendship obliges me to prevent Reports, and not to give any room for Suspicion; I'll shun your Wife, and you shall never see me –

ORGON: No, in spite of every body, you shall frequently be with her. To vex the World is my greatest Joy, and I'll have you seen with her at all Hours. This is not all yet; the better to brave them, I'll have no other Heir but you; and I'm going forthwith to sign you a Deed of Gift for my whole Estate. A true and hearty Friend, that I fix on for a Son-in-law, is far dearer to me than either Son, Wife, or Kindred. You won't refuse what I propose?

TARTUFFE: Heav'n's Will be done in all things.

ORGON: Poor Man! Come, let's get the Writings drawn up, and then let Envy burst itself with Spite.

Act IV, Scene I

[CLEANTHES, TARTUFFE.]

CLEANTHES: Yes, 'tis in every Body's Mouth, and you may believe me. The Noise this Rumour[1] makes is not much to your Credit; and I have met with you, Sir, very opportunely, to tell you plainly, in two Words, my Thoughts of the Matter. I shan't inquire into the Ground of what's reported, I pass that by, and take the Thing at worst. We'll suppose that *Damis* has not us'd you well, and that they have accus'd you wrongfully. Is it not the part of a good Christian to pardon the Offence, and extinguish in his Heart all Desire of Vengeance? Ought you to suffer a Son to be turn'd out of his Father's House, on account of your Differences? I tell you once again, and tell you frankly, there is neither

1. The rumour about Damis being banished from the parental home.

small nor great but are scandaliz'd at it. And if you take my Advice, you'll make all up, and not push Matters to extremity. Sacrifice your Resentment to your Duty, and restore the Son to his Father's Favour.

TARTUFFE: Alas! for my own part, I would do it with all my Heart; I, Sir, bear him not the least Ill-will; I forgive him every thing; I lay nothing to his Charge, and would serve him with all my Soul: But the interests of Heaven cannot admit it: and if he comes in here again, I must go out. After such an unparallel'd Action, it would be scandalous for me to have any thing to do with him. Heaven knows what all the World would immediately think on't? They would impute it to pure Policy in me, and People would every where say, that knowing my self guilty, I pretended a charitable Zeal for my Accuser; that I dreaded him at Heart, and would practise upon him, that I might, underhand, engage him to silence.

CLEANTHES: You put us off here with sham Excuses, and all your Reasons, Sir, are too far fetch'd. Why do you take upon you the Interests of Heaven? has it any occasion for our Assistance in punishing the Guilty? Leave, leave the Care of its own Vengeance to it self, and only think of that Pardon of Offences, which it prescribes; have no regard to the Judgment of Men, when you follow the Sovereign Orders of Heaven! What! shall the paltry Interest of what People may believe, hinder the Glory of a good Action! No, no, let us always do what Heaven has prescrib'd, and perplex our Heads with no other Care.

TARTUFFE: I have told you already that I forgive him from my Heart, and that is doing, Sir, what Heaven ordains; but after the Scandal and Affront of to-day, Heaven does not require me to live with him.

CLEANTHES: And does it require you, Sir, to lend an Ear to what mere Caprice dictates to the Father? And to accept of an Estate where Justice obliges you to make no Pretensions?

TARTUFFE: Those that know me will never have the Thought that this is the Effect of an interested Spirit. All the Riches of this World have few Charms for me; I am not dazzled by their false Glare, and if I shou'd resolve to accept this Present, which the Father has a mind to make me, it is, to tell you the Truth, only because I'm afraid this Means will fall into wicked Hands; lest it shou'd come amongst such, as will make an ill Use on't in the World, and not lay it out as I intend to do, for the Glory of Heaven, and the Good of my Neighbour.

CLEANTHES: Oh, entertain none of these very nice Scruples, which may occasion the Complaints of a Right Heir. Let him, without giving your self any Trouble, keep his Estate at his own Peril, and consider that 'twere better he misus'd it, than that People should accuse you for depriving him of it. I only wonder, that you could receive such a Proposal without Confusion. For, in short, has true Zeal any Maxim, which shews how to strip a lawful Heir of his Right? And if it must be that Heaven has put into your Heart an invincible Obstacle to living with *Damis*, wou'd it not be better, like a Man of Prudence, that you shou'd fairly retire from hence, than thus to suffer the eldest Son, contrary to all reason, to be turn'd out of Doors for you? Believe me, Sir, this wou'd give your Discretion –

TARTUFFE: It is half an Hour past three, Sir. Certain Devotions call me above Stairs, and you'll excuse my leaving you so soon.

CLEANTHES: [*alone.*] Ah!

Act IV, Scene II

[ELMIRA, MARIANA, CLEANTHES, DORINA.]

DORINA: [*to* CLEANTHES.] For Goodness sake, lend her what Assistance you can, as we do. She's in the greatest perplexity, Sir, imaginable; the Articles her Father has concluded for to-night, make her every moment ready to despair. He's just a coming, pray let us set on him in a Body, and try, either by Force or Cunning, to frustrate the unlucky Design, that has put us all into this Consternation.

Act IV, Scene III

[ORGON, ELMIRA, MARIANA, CLEANTHES, DORINA.]

ORGON: Hah! I'm glad to see you all together. [*to* MARIANA.] I bring something in this Contract, that will make you smile; you already know what this means.

MARIANA: [*kneeling to* ORGON.] Oh! Sir, in the Name of Heaven that is a Witness of my Grief, by every thing that can move your Heart, forego a little the Right Nature has given you, and dispense with my Obedience in this particular. Don't compel me, by this hard Law, to complain to Heaven of the Duty I owe you; Do not, my Father, render the Life, which you have given me, unfortunate. If, contrary to the tender Hopes, I might have form'd to my self, you won't suffer me to be the Man's I presum'd to love; at least, out of your Goodness, which upon my Knees I implore, save me from the Torment of being the Man's I abhor; and drive me not to despair by exerting your full Power over me.

ORGON: [*aside.*] Come, stand firm, my Heart; no human Weakness.

MARIANA: Your Tenderness for him gives me no Uneasiness: Shew it in the strongest Manner, give him your Estate; and if that's not enough, add mine to it; I consent with all my Heart, and give it up; but at least go not so far as to my Person, suffer a Convent, with its Austerities, to wear out the mournful Days allotted me by Heaven.

ORGON: Ay, these are exactly your she Devotees, when a Father crosses their wanton Inclinations. Get up, get up; the more it goes against you, the more you'll merit by it. Mortify your Senses by this Marriage, and don't din me in the Head any more about it.

DORINA: But what –

ORGON: Hold you your Tongue; speak to your own Concerns. I absolutely forbid you to open your Lips.

CLEANTHES: If you wou'd indulge me, in Answer, to give one Word of Advice.

ORGON: Brother, your Advice is the best in the World; 'tis very rational, and what I have a great Value for: But you must not take it ill if I don't use it now.

ELMIRA: [*to* ORGON.] Seeing what I see, I don't know what to say; I can but wonder at your Blindness. You must be mightily bewitch'd and prepossess'd in his Favour, to give us the Lye upon the Fact of to-day.

ORGON: I am your humble Servant, and believe Appearances. I know your Complaisance for my Rascal of a Son, and you were afraid to disavow the Trick he wou'd have play'd the poor Man. You were, in a word, too little ruffled to gain Credit; you wou'd have appear'd to have been mov'd after a different manner.

ELMIRA: Is it requisite that our Honour shou'd bluster so vehemently at the simple Declaration of an amorous Transport? Can there be no Reply made to what offends us, without Fury in our Eyes and Invectives in our Mouth? For my part, I only laugh at such Overtures; and the Rout made about them, by no means pleases me. I love that we should shew our Discretion with Good-nature, and cannot like your savage Prudes, whose Honour is arm'd with Teeth and Claw and is for tearing a Man's Eye's out for a Word speaking. Heaven preserve me from such Discretion! I would have Virtue that is not diabolical, and believe that a Denial given with Discreet Coldness, is no less powerful to give the Lover a Rebuff.

ORGON: In short I know the whole Affair, and shall not alter my Scheme.

ELMIRA: I admire, still more, at your unaccountable Weakness: But what Answer could your Incredulity make, should one let you see that they told you the Truth?

ORGON: See?

ELMIRA: Ay.

ORGON: Stuff!

ELMIRA: But how, if I shou'd contrive a way to let you see it in a very clear Light?

ORGON: A likely Story indeed!

ELMIRA: What a strange Man! At least give me an Answer. I don't speak of your giving Credit to us; but suppose a Place cou'd be found, where you might see and overhear all, what wou'd you then say of your good Man?

ORGON: In this case, I shou'd say that – I should say nothing: for the thing can't be.

ELMIRA: You have been too long deluded, and too much have tax'd me with Imposture. 'Tis necessary that by way of diversion, and without going any farther, I should make you a Witness of all they told you.

ORGON: Do so; I take you at your Word. We shall see your Address, and how you'll make good your Promise.

ELMIRA: [*to* DORINA.] Bid him come to me.

DORINA: [*to* ELMIRA.] He has a crafty Soul of his own, and perhaps it would be a difficult matter to surprise him.

ELMIRA: [*to* DORINA.] No, People are easily Dup'd by what they love, and Self-love helps 'em to deceive themselves. [*to* CLEANTHES *and* MARIANA.] Call him down to me, and do you retire.

Act IV, Scene IV

[ELMIRA, ORGON.]

ELMIRA: Now do you come and get under this Table.

ORGON: Why so?

ELMIRA: 'Tis a necessary Point that you should be well conceal'd.

ORGON: But why under this Table?

ELMIRA: Lack-a-day! do as I'd have you, I have my Design in my Head, and you shall be Judge on't. Place your self there, I tell you, and when you are there take care that no one either sees or hears you.

ORGON: I must needs say, I am very complaisant: but I must see you go thro' your Enterprise.

ELMIRA: You will have nothing, I believe, to reply to me. [*to* ORGON *under the Table*.] However, as I am going to touch upon a strange Affair, don't be shock'd by any means. Whatever I may say, must be allow'd me, as it is to convince you, according to my Promise. I am going by coxeing Speeches, since I am reduc'd to it, to make this hypocritical Soul drop the Mask, to flatter the impudent Desires of his Love, and give a full Scope to his Boldness. Since 'tis for your sake alone, and to confound him, that I feign a Compliance with his Desires, I may give over when you appear, and things need go no farther than you wou'd have them. It lies on you to stop his mad Pursuit, when you think that Matters are carry'd far enough, to spare your Wife, and not to expose me any farther than is necessary to disabuse you. This is your Interest, it lies at your Discretion, and – He's coming; keep close, and take care not to appear.

Act IV, Scene V

[TARTUFFE, ELMIRA, ORGON *under the Table.*]

TARTUFFE: I was told you desir'd to speak with me here.

ELMIRA: Yes, I have Secrets to discover to you; but pull to that Door before I tell'em you, and look about, for fear of a Surprise. [TARTUFFE *goes and shuts the Door and returns.*] We must not surely make such a Business on't, as the other was just now. I never was in such a Surprise in my whole Life: *Damis* put me into a terrible Fright for you; and you saw very well that I did my utmost to baffle his Designs, and moderate his Passion. I was under so much Concern, 'tis true, that I had not the Thought of contradicting him; but thanks to Heaven, every thing was the better for that, and things are put upon a surer footing. The Esteem you are in laid that Storm, and my Husband can have no Suspicion of you. The better to set the Rumour of ill Tongues at defiance, he desires we shou'd be always together, and from thence it is, that without Fear of Blame I can be lock'd up with you here alone, and this is what justifies me in laying open to you a Heart, a little perhaps, too forward in admitting of your Passion.

TARTUFFE: This Language, Madam, is difficult enough to comprehend, and you talk'd in another kind of Style but just now.

ELMIRA: Alas! if such a Refusal disobliges you, how little do you know the Heart of a Woman! and how little do you know what it means, when we make so feeble a Defence! Our Modesty will always combat, in these Moments, those tender Sentiments you may inspire us with. Whatever Reason we may find for the Passion that subdues us, we shall always be a little asham'd to own it: We defend our selves at first, but by the Air with which we go about it, we give you sufficiently to know, that our Heart surrenders; that our Words oppose our Wishes for the sake of Honour, and that such Refusals promise every thing. Without doubt this is making a very free Confession to you, and having Regard little enough to the Modesty that belongs to us; but in short, since the Word has slipt me, should I have been bent so much upon restraining *Damis*? Should I, pray, with so much Mildness, have hearken'd to the Offer at large which you made of your Heart? should I have took the things as you saw I did, if the Offer of your Heart had had nothing in it to please me? And when I my self wou'd have forc'd you to refuse the Match which had first been propos'd. What is it this Instance shou'd have given you to understand, but the Interest one was inclin'd to take in you, and the Disquiet it wou'd have given me, that the Knot resolv'd on, should at least divide a Heart which I wanted to have wholly my own?

TARTUFFE: 'Tis no doubt, Madam, an extreme Pleasure to hear these Words from the Lips one loves; their Honey plentifully diffuses thro' every Sense a Sweetness I never before tasted. My supreme Study is the

Happiness of pleasing you, and my Heart counts your Affection its Beatitude; but you must excuse this Heart, Madam, if it presumes to doubt a little of its Felicity. I can fancy these Words to be only a sort of Artifice to make me break off the Match that's upon the Conclusion; and if I may with Freedom explain my self to you, I shall not rely upon this so tender Language, till some of the Favours which I sigh after, assure me of the Sincerity of what may be said, and fix in my Mind a firm belief of the transporting Goodness you intend me.

ELMIRA: [*coughing to give her Husband notice.*] What! proceed so fast? Would you exhaust the Tenderness of one's Heart at once? One does Violence to ones self in making you the most melting Declaration; but at the same time this is not enough for you, and one cannot advance so far as to satisfy you, unless one pushes the Affair to the last Favours.

TARTUFFE: The less one deserves a Blessing, the less one presumes to hope for it; our Love can hardly have a full Reliance upon Discourses; one easily suspects a Condition full fraught with Happiness, and one wou'd enjoy it before one believes it. For my Particular, who know I so little deserve your Favours, I doubt the Success of my Rashness, and I shall believe nothing, Madam, 'til by Realities you have convinc'd my Passion.

ELMIRA: Good lack! how your Love plays the very Tyrant! What a strange Confusion it throws me into? With what a furious Sway does it govern the Heart! and with what Violence it pushes for what it desires! What, is there no getting clear of your Pursuit? Do you allow one no time to take breath? Is it decent to persist with so great Rigour? To insist upon the things you demand without Quarter? To abuse in this manner, by your pressing Efforts, the Foible you see People have for you?

TARTUFFE: But if you regard my Addresses with a favourable Eye, why do you refuse me convincing Proofs of it?

ELMIRA: But how can one comply with your Desires, without offending that Heav'n which you are always talking of?

TARTUFFE: If nothing but Heav'n obstructs my Wishes, 'tis a Trifle with me to remove such an Obstacle, and that need be no Restraint upon your Love.

ELMIRA: But they so terrify us with the Judgments of Heav'n.

TARTUFFE: I can dissipate those ridiculous Terrors for you, Madam; I have the Knack of easing Scruples. Heav'n, 'tis true, forbids certain Gratifications. But then there are ways of compounding those Matters. It is a Science to stretch the Strings of Conscience according to the different Exigences of the Case, and to rectify the Immorality of the Action by the Purity of our Intention. These are Secrets, Madam, I can instruct you in; you have nothing to do, but passively to be conducted. Satisfy my Desire, and fear nothing, I'll answer for you, and will take the Sin upon myself. [ELMIRA *coughs loud.*] You cough very much, Madam.

ELMIRA: Yes, I am on the Rack.

TARTUFFE: [*presenting her with a Paper.*] Will you please to have a bit of this Liquorice?

ELMIRA: 'Tis an obstinate Cold, without doubt, and I am satisfy'd that all the Liquorice in the World will do no good in this Case.

TARTUFFE: It is, to be sure, very troublesome.

ELMIRA: Ay, more than one can express.

TARTUFFE: In short your Scruple, Madam, is easily overcome. You are sure of its being an inviolable Secret here, and the Harm never consists in any thing but the Noise one makes; the Scandal of the World is what makes the Offence; and Sinning in private is no Sinning at all.

ELMIRA: [*after coughing again, and striking upon the Table.*] In short, I see that I must resolve to yield, that I must consent to grant you every thing; and that with less than this I ought not to expect that you should be satisfy'd, or give over. It is indeed very hard to go that length, and I get over it much against my Will: But since you are obstinately bent upon reducing me to it, and since you won't believe any thing that can be said, but still inisist on more convincing Testimony, one must e'en resolve upon it, and satisfy People. And if this Gratification carries any Offence in it, so much the worse for him who forces me to this Violence; the Fault certainly ought not to be laid at my Door.

TARTUFFE: Yes, Madam, I take it upon myself, and the thing in itself –

ELMIRA: Open the Door a little, and pray look if my Husband be not in that Gallery.

TARTUFFE: What need you take so much care about him? Betwixt us two, he's a Man to be led by the Nose. He will take a Pride in all our Conversations, and I have wrought him up to the Point of seeing every thing, without believing any thing.

ELMIRA: That signifies nothing, pray go out a little, and look carefully all about.

Act IV, Scene VI

[ORGON, ELMIRA.]

ORGON: [*coming from under the Table.*] An abominable Fellow, I vow! I can't recover my self; this perfectly stuns me.

ELMIRA: How! do you come out so soon? You make Fools of People; get under the Table again, stay to the very last, to see things sure, and don't trust to bare Conjectures.

ORGON: No, nothing more wicked ever came from Hell.

ELMIRA: Dear Heart, you must not believe too lightly; suffer your self to be fully convinc'd, before you yield, and don't be too hasty for fear of a Mistake.

[ELMIRA *places* ORGON *behind her.*]

Act IV, Scene VII

[TARTUFFE, ELMIRA, ORGON.]

TARTUFFE [*not seeing* ORGON.] Every thing conspires, Madam, to my Satisfaction. I have survey'd this whole Apartment; no-body's there, and my
ravish'd Soul – [TARTUFFE *going with open Arms to embrace* ELMIRA, *she
retires, and* TARTUFFE *sees* ORGON.]

ORGON: [*stopping* TARTUFFE.] Gently, gently; you are too eager in your
Amours; you should not be so furious. Ah, ha, good Man! you intended
me a Crest,[1] I suppose! Good-lack, how you abandon your self to
Temptations! What, you'd marry my Daughter, and had a huge Stomach
to my Wife? I was a long while in doubt whether all was in good
Earnest, and always thought you would change your Tone; but this is
pushing the Proof far enough; I am now satisfy'd, and want, for my
part, no farther Conviction.

ELMIRA: [*to* TARTUFFE.] The Part I have play'd was contrary to my Inclination;
but they reduc'd me to the Necessity of treating you in this manner.

TARTUFFE: [*to* ORGON.] What? Do you believe –

ORGON: Come, pray no Noise; turn out, and without Ceremony.

TARTUFFE: My Design –

ORGON: These Speeches are no longer in Season; you must troop off
forthwith.

TARTUFFE: 'Tis You must troop off, You who speak so magisterially. The
House belongs to me, I'll make you know it, and shall plainly shew you,
that you have recourse in vain to these bare Tricks, to pick a Quarrel
with me; that you don't think where you are when you injure me; that
I have wherewithal to confound and punish Imposture, to avenge
offended Heaven, and make them repent it who talk here of turning me
out o' Doors.

Act IV, Scene VIII

[ELMIRA, ORGON.]

ELMIRA: What Language is this? And what can it mean?

ORGON: In truth I'm all Confusion, and have no room to laugh.

ELMIRA: How so?

ORGON: I see my Fault by what he says, and the Deed of Gift perplexes me.

ELMIRA: The Deed of Gift?

ORGON: Ay, 'tis done; but I have somewhat else that disturbs me too.

1. A cuckold's crest. Molière, in the original, refers simply to Orgon being deceived.

ELMIRA: And what's that?

ORGON: You shall know the whole; but let's go immediately and see if a certain Casket is above Stairs.

Act V, Scene I

[ORGON, CLEANTHES.]

CLEANTHES: Whither wou'd you run?

ORGON: Alas! how can I tell?

CLEANTHES: I think we ought, the first thing we do, to consult together what may be done at this Juncture.

ORGON: This Casket intirely confounds me. It gives me even more Vexation than all the rest.

CLEANTHES: This Casket then is some Mystery of Importance.

ORGON: It is a Deposite that *Argas*, my lamented Friend himself committed as a great Secret to my keeping. When he fled, he pitch'd on me for this purpose; and these are the Papers, as he told me, whereon his Life and Fortune depend.

CLEANTHES: Why then did you trust them in other Hands?

ORGON: Merely out of a Scruple of Conscience. I went straight to impart the Secret to my Traitor, and his Casuistry over-persuaded me rather to give him the Casket to keep; so that to deny it, in case of any Inquiry, I might have the Relief of a Subterfuge ready at hand, whereby my Conscience would have been very secure in taking an Oath contrary to the Truth.

CLEANTHES: You are in a bad Situation, at least, if I may believe Appearances; both the Deed of Gift, and the Trust repos'd, are, to speak my Sentiments to you, Steps which you have taken very inconsiderately. One might carry you great Lengths by such Pledges; and this Fellow having these Advantages over you, it is still a great Imprudence in you to urge him; and you ought to think of some gentler Method.

ORGON: What! under the fair Appearance of such affectionate Zeal, to conceal such a double Heart, and a Soul so wicked? And that I, who took him in poor and indigent – 'Tis over, I renounce all pious Folks. I shall henceforth have an utter Abhorrence of them, and shall become, for their sakes, worse than a Devil.

CLEANTHES: Mighty well; here are some of your Extravagances! You never preserve a moderate Temper in any thing. Right Reason and yours are very different, and you are always throwing your self out of one Extreme into another. You see your Error, and are sensible that you have been impos'd on by a hypocritical Zeal, but in order to reform, what reason is there that you should be guilty of a worse Mistake; and that you should make no difference between the Heart of a perfidious worthless Wretch, and those of all honest People? What! because a Rascal has impudently impos'd upon you under the pompous shew of an austere Grimace, will you needs have it that every Body's like him, and that there are no devout People to be found in the World? Leave these foolish Consequences to Libertines; distinguish between Virtue and the Appearance of it; never hazard your Esteem too suddenly; and, in order to this, keep the Mean you should do; Guard, if possible, against doing Honour to Imposture; but, at the same time, don't injure true Zeal; and, if you must fall into one Extreme, rather offend again on the other side.

Act V, Scene II

[ORGON, CLEANTHES, DAMIS.]

DAMIS: What Sir, is it true that the Rascal threatens you? That he has quite forgot every Favour he has received? And that his bare abominable Pride arms your own Goodness against yourself?

ORGON: Yes, Son, and it gives me inconceivable Vexation.

DAMIS: Let me alone, I'll slice both his Ears off. There's no dallying with such Insolence as his. I'll undertake to rid you of your Fears at once; and to put an end to the Affair, I must do his Business for him.

CLEANTHES: That's spoke exactly like a young Fellow. Pray moderate these violent Transports; we live in an Age, and under a Government, in which Violence is but a bad way to promote our Affairs.

Act V, Scene III

[MADAM PERNELLE, ORGON, ELMIRA, CLEANTHES, MARIANA, DAMIS, DORINA.]

MADAM PERNELLE: What's all this? I hear terrible Mysteries here.

ORGON: They are Novelties that I am an Eye-Witness to; you see how finely I am fitted for my Care. I kindly pick up a Fellow in Misery, entertain and treat him like my own Brother, heap daily Favours on him; I give him my Daughter and my whole Fortune; when at the same time the perfidious, infamous Wretch, forms the black Design of seducing my Wife: And not content with these base Attempts, he dares to menace me with my own Favours, and would make use of those Advantages to my Ruin, which too indiscreet Good-nature put into his Hands; to turn me out of my Estate, which I made over to him, and to reduce me to that Condition from which I rescu'd him.

DORINA: The poor Man!

MADAM PERNELLE: I can never believe, Son, he could commit so black an Action.

ORGON: How?

MADAM PERNELLE: Good People are always envy'd.

ORGON: What would you insinuate, Mother, by this Discourse?

MADAM PERNELLE: Why, that there are strange Doings at your House; and the Ill-will they bear him is but too evident.

ORGON: What has this Ill-will to do with what has been told you?

MADAM PERNELLE: I have told you a hundred times when you were a little one,

> That Virtue here is persecuted ever;
> That envious Men may die, but Envy never.

ORGON: But what is all this to the present Purpose?

MADAM PERNELLE: They have trump'd up to you a hundred idle Stories against him.

ORGON: I have told you already, that I saw it all my own self.

MADAM PERNELLE: The Malice of Scandal-Mongers is very great.

ORGON: You'll make me swear, Mother. I tell you that I saw with my own Eyes a Crime so audacious –

MADAM PERNELLE: Tongues never want for Venom to spit; nothing here below can be Proof against them.

ORGON: This is holding a very senseless Argument! I saw it, I say, saw it; with my own Eyes I saw it. What you call, Saw it. Must I din it a hundred times into your Ears, and bawl as loud as four folks?

MADAM PERNELLE: Dear Heart! Appearances very often deceive us. You must not always judge by what you see.

ORGON: I shall run mad.

MADAM PERNELLE: Nature is liable to false suspicions, and Good is oftentimes misconstru'd Evil.

ORGON: Ought I to construe charitably his Desire of kissing my Wife?

MADAM PERNELLE: You ought never to accuse any body but upon good Grounds; and you should have staid till you had seen the thing certain.

ORGON: What the Devil! How should I be more certain? Then, Mother, I should have stay'd till he had – You'll make me say some foolish thing or other.

MADAM PERNELLE: In short, his Soul burns with too pure a Flame, and I can't let it enter my Thoughts that he could attempt the Things that are laid to his Charge.

ORGON: Go, if you were not my Mother I don't know what I might say to you, my Passion is so great!

DORINA: [*to* ORGON.] The just Return, Sir, of things here below: Time was, you wou'd believe no body, and now you can't be believ'd yourself.

CLEANTHES: We are wasting that time in mere Trifles, which should be spent in taking Measures; we shou'dn't sleep when a Knave threatens.

DAMIS: What, can his Impudence come to this pitch?

ELMIRA: I can scarce think this Instance possible, for my part; his Ingratitude would in this be too visible.

CLEANTHES: [*to* ORGON.] Don't you depend upon that, he will be cunning enough to give the Colour of Reason for what he does against you; and for a less Matter than this, the Weight of a Cabal has involv'd People in Dismal Labyrinths.[1] I tell you once again, that, arm'd with what he has, you shou'd never have urg'd him so far.

ORGON: That's true; but what could I do in the Affair? I was not Master of my Resentments at the Haughtiness of the Traitor.

CLEANTHES: I wish with all my Heart that there cou'd be any Shadow of a Peace patch'd up between you.

ELMIRA: Had I but known how well he had been arm'd, I shou'd never have made such an Alarm about the matter, and my –

ORGON: [*to* DORINA, *seeing* MR. LOYAL *coming*.] What wou'd that Man have? Go quickly and ask. I'm in a fine Condition to have People come to see me.

Act V, Scene IV

[ORGON, MADAM PERNELLE, ELMIRA, MARIANA, CLEANTHES, DAMIS, DORINA, MR. LOYAL.]

MR. LOYAL: [*to* DORINA *at the further part of the Stage.*] Good-morrow, sister;[2] pray let me speak to your Master.

DORINA: He's in Company, and I doubt he can see no body now.

MR. LOYAL: Nay, I am not for being troublesome here. I believe my Coming will have nothing in it that will displease him; I come upon an Affair that he'll be very glad of.

DORINA: Your Name, pray?

MR. LOYAL: Only tell him that I come on the part of Mr. *Tartuffe*, for his good.

DORINA: [*to* ORGON.] 'Tis a Man who comes in a civil way, upon Business from Mr. *Tartuffe*, which he says you won't dislike.

CLEANTHES: [*to* ORGON.] You must see who this Man is, and what he wants.

ORGON: [*to* CLEANTHES.] Perhaps he comes to make us Friends. How shall I behave myself to him?

CLEANTHES: Be sure don't be angry, and if he speaks of an Agreement you must listen to him.

MR. LOYAL: [*to* ORGON.] Save you, Sir! Heav'n blast the Man wou'd wrong you, and may it be as favourable to you as I wish.

1. Here Molière appears to be making a general as well as a personal point. See the introduction.
2. The translation uses 'child', but Mr Loyal is clearly using the pious language of the zealots.

ORGON: [*aside to* CLEANTHES.] This mild Beginning favours my Conjecture, and already forebodes some Accommodation.

MR. LOYAL: I always had a prodigious Value for all your Family, and was Servant to the Gentleman your Father.

ORGON: Sir, I am much asham'd, and ask Pardon that I don't know You, or your Name.

MR. LOYAL: My Name is *Loyal*, Sir, by Birth a *Norman*, and I am Tipstaff to the Court in spite of Envy. I have had the good Fortune for forty Years together to fill that Office, thanks to Heav'n, with great Honour; I come, Sir, with your Leave, to signify to you the Execution of a certain Decree.

ORGON: What, are you here –

MR. LOYAL: Sir, without Passion, 'tis nothing but a Summons, an Order to remove hence, You and Yours, to take out your Goods, and to make way for others without Remission or Delay, so that 'tis necessary –

ORGON: I go from hence?

MR. LOYAL: Yes, Sir, if you please. The House at present, as you know but too well, belongs to good Mr. *Tartuffe*, without dispute. He is henceforward Lord and Master of your Estate, by virtue of a Contract I have in charge. 'Tis in due Form, and not to be contested.

DAMIS: [*to* MR. LOYAL.] Most certainly 'tis prodigious Impudence, and what I can't but admire!

MR. LOYAL: [*to* DAMIS.] Sir, my Business is not with you, [*pointing to* ORGON.] but with this Gentleman, who is mild and reasonable, and knows the Duty of an honest Man too well to oppose Authority.

ORGON: But –

MR. LOYAL: [*to* ORGON.] Yes, Sir, I know you wou'd not rebel for a Million, and that, like a good honest Gentleman, you will suffer me here to execute the Orders I have receiv'd.

DAMIS: You may chance, Mr. Tipstaff, to get your black Jacket well brush'd here.

MR. LOYAL: [*to* ORGON.] Either, Sir, cause your Son to be silent or withdraw. I shou'd be very loth to put Pen to Paper, and see your Names in my Information.

DORINA: [*aside.*] This Mr. *Loyal* has a disloyal sort of Look with him!

MR. LOYAL: I have a great deal of Tenderness for all honest People, and shou'd not, Sir, have charg'd myself with these Writs but to serve and oblige you; and to prevent another's being pitch'd on, who not having the Love for you which I have, might have proceeded in a less gentle manner.

ORGON: And what can be worse than to order People to go out of their House?

MR. LOYAL: Why, you are allow'd Time. And, till to-morrow, I shall suspend, Sir, the Execution of the Warrant. I shall only come and pass the Night here with half a Score of Folks, without Noise or Scandal. For Form's sake, if you please, the keys of the Door must, before you go to Bed, be brought to me. I'll take care your Rest shan't be disturb'd, and suffer nothing that is improper to be done. But tomorrow Morning you must be ready to clear the House of every the least Utensil. My People shall assist you; and I have pick'd out a Set of lusty Fellows, that they may do you the more Service in your Removal. No body can use you better, in my Opinion; and as I treat you with great Indulgence, I conjure you, Sir, to make a good use on't, and to give me no Disturbance in the Execution of my Office.

ORGON: [*aside.*] I'd give just now, a hundred of the best *Louis d'ors* I have left, for the Power and Pleasure of laying one sound Blow on your Ass-ship's Muzzle.

CLEANTHES: [*aside to* ORGON.] Give over; don't let's make things worse.

DAMIS: This Impudence is too great; I can hardly refrain; my Fingers itch to be at him.

DORINA: Faith, Mr. Brauny-back'd *Loyal*, some Thwacks of a Cudgel wou'd by no means sit ill upon you.

MR. LOYAL: Those infamous Words are punishable Sweetheart; there's Law against Women too.

CLEANTHES: [*to* MR. LOYAL.] Let us come to a Conclusion, Sir, with this; 'tis enough; pray give up your Paper of Indulgence, and leave us.

MR. LOYAL: Good b't'ye. Heav'n bless you all together!

ORGON: And confound both thee and him that sent thee!

Act V, Scene V

[ORGON, MADAM PERNELLE, ELMIRA, CLEANTHES, MARIANA, DAMIS, DORINA.]

ORGON: Well Mother, you see whether I am in the right or no; and you may judge of the rest by the Warrant. Do you at length perceive his Treacheries?

MADAM PERNELLE: I am stunn'd and am tumbling from the Clouds.

DORINA: [*to* ORGON.] You complain without a Cause, and blame him wrongfully; this does but confirm his pious Intentions. His Virtue is made perfect in the Love of his Neighbour; he knows, very often, that Riches spoil the Man; and he would only, out of pure Charity, take from you every thing that may obstruct your Salvation.

ORGON: Hold your Tongue. Must I always be repeating that to you?

CLEANTHES: [*to* ORGON.] Come let's consult what's proper for you to do.

ELMIRA: Go and expose the Audaciousness of the ungrateful Wretch. This Proceeding of his invalidates the Contract; and his Perfidiousness must needs appear too black to let him have the Success we are apt to surmise.

Act V, Scene VI

[VALERE, ORGON, MADAM PERNELLE, ELMIRA, CLEANTHES, MARIANA,
DAMIS, DORINA.]

VALERE: 'Tis with Regret, Sir, I come to afflict you; but I am constrain'd to't
by the Imminence of the Danger. A very intimate Friend of mine, who
knows the Interest I ought to take in every thing that may concern you,
has for my sake violated, by a delicate Step, the Secrecy due to the
Affairs of State, and has just sent me Advice, the Consequence of which
reduces you to the Expedient of a sudden Flight. The Rogue who has
long impos'd on you, has thought fit, an Hour ago, to accuse you to
your Prince, and to put into his Hands, among other Darts he shoots at
you, the important Casket of a State-Criminal, of which, says he, in
contempt of the Duty of a Subject, you have kept the guilty Secret. I am
not inform'd of the Detail of the Crime laid to your Charge, but an
Order is issued out against your Person, and to execute it the better, he
himself is appointed to accompany the Person that is to arrest you.
CLEANTHES: Now are his Pretensions arm'd, and this is the way that the
Traitor seeks to make himself Master of your Estate.
ORGON: The Man, I must own, is a vile Animal!
VALERE: The least Delay may be fatal to you; I have my Coach at the Door to
carry you off, with a thousand *Louis d'ors* that here I bring you. Let's lose
no time, the Shaft is thrown, and these Blows are only parried by Flight.
I offer my self to conduct you to a Place of Safety, and to accompany you
in your Escape even to the last.
ORGON: Alas, what do I not owe to your obliging Care! I must take another
Time to thank you, and I beseech Heaven to be so propitious to me, that
I may one Day acknowledge this generous Service. Farewel, take care
the rest of you –
CLEANTHES: Go quickly; we shall take care, Brother, to do what is proper.

Act V, Scene VII

[TARTUFFE, AN EXEMPT,[1] MADAM PERNELLE, ORGON, ELMIRA, CLEANTHES,
MARIANA, VALERE, DAMIS, DORINA.]

TARTUFFE: [*stopping* ORGON.] Softly, Sir, softly, don't run so fast, you shan't go
far to find you a Lodging; we take you Prisoner in the King's Name.
ORGON: Traitor, thou hast reserv'd this Shaft for the last: 'Tis the Stroke by

1. An officer of the Paris police.

which thou art to dispatch me, and this crowns all the rest of they Perfidies.

TARTUFFE: Your Abuses have nothing in them that can incense me; I'm instructed to suffer every thing for the sake of Heav'n.

CLEANTHES: The Moderation is great, I must confess.

DAMIS: How impudently the Varlet sports with Heav'n?

TARTUFFE: All your Raving can't move me; I think of nothing but doing my Duty.

MARIANA: You have much Glory to expect from hence; this Employ is a mighty honourable one for you.

TARTUFFE: The Employ can't be other than glorious, when it proceeds from the Power that sent me hither.

ORGON: But do you remember, ungrateful Wretch, that my charitable Hand rais'd you from a miserable Condition?

TARTUFFE: Yes, I know what Succours I might receive from thence, but the Interest of my Prince is my highest Duty: The just Obligation whereof stifles in my Heart all other Acknowledgments; and I could sacrifice to so powerful a Tye, Friend, Wife, Kindred, and my self to boot.

ELMIRA: The Hypocrite!

DORINA: How artfully he can make a Cloke of what is Sacred!

CLEANTHES: But if the Zeal that puts you on, and with which you trick your self out, is so perfect as you say it is, how came it not to shew it self 'till he found means of surprising you soliciting his Wife? How came you not to think of informing against him, 'till his Honour oblig'd him to drive you out of his House? I don't say, that the making over his whole Estate to you lately shou'd draw you from your Duty; but intending to treat him, as now you do, like a Criminal, why did you consent to take any thing from him?

TARTUFFE: [*to the Exempt.*] I beg you, Sir, to free me from this Clamour, and be pleas'd to do as you are order'd.

EXEMPT: Yes, 'tis certainly delaying the Execution too long; you invite me to't *à propos*; and to execute my Order, follow me immediately to the Prison, which we are to allot you for your Habitation.

TARTUFFE: Who? I, Sir?

EXEMPT: Yes, you.

TARTUFFE: Why to Prison, pray?

EXEMPT: You are not the Person I shall give an Account to. [*to* ORGON.] Do you, Sir, compose your self after so warm a Surprise. We live under a Prince who is an Enemy to Fraud, a Prince whose Eyes penetrate into the Heart, and whom all the Art of Impostors can't deceive.[1] His great Soul is furnish'd with a fine Discernment, and always takes things in a

1. Molière's audience would have been well aware that Louis XIV had established what was probably the first effective police force in the world, under the control of Gabriel Nicolas de la Reynie. La Reynie made extensive use of a net of spies and informers.

right Light; there's nothing gets too much footing by Surprise, and his solid Reason falls into no Excess. He bestows lasting Glory on Men of worth, but he dispenses his Favours without Blindness, and his Love for the Sincere, does not foreclose his Heart against the Horrour that's due to those that are otherwise. Even this Person was not able to surprise him, and we find he keeps clear of the most subtle Snares. He soon pierc'd thro' all the Baseness contain'd within his Heart. Coming to accuse you, he betray'd himself, and by a just Stroke of Divine Judgment, he discover'd himself to be a notorious Rogue, of whom his Majesty had receiv'd Information under another Name; the whole Detail of whose horrid Crimes is long enough to fill Volumes of Histories. This Monarch, in a word, detesting his Ingratitude and Undutifulness to you, to his other confusions hath added the following, and hath sent me under his Direction, only to see how far his Assurance wou'd carry him, and to oblige him to give you full Satisfaction. He wills moreover that I should strip the Traitor of all your Papers to which he pretends a Right, and give them you. By Dint of Sovereign Power he dissolves the Obligation of the Contract, which gives him your Estate, and he pardons moreover this Secret Offence in which the Retreat of your Friend involv'd you; and this Recompense he bestows for the Zeal he saw you formerly shew'd in maintaining his Rights: To let you see that his Heart knows, even when 'tis least expected, how to recompense a good Action; that Merit with him is never lost, and that he much better remembers Good than Evil.

DORINA: May Heaven be prais'd!

MADAM PERNELLE: Now I begin to revive.

ELMIRA: Favourable Success!

MARIANA: Who could have foretold this?

ORGON: [*to* TARTUFFE *as the Exempt leads him off.*] Well, Traitor, there you are –

Scene the Last

[MADAM PERNELLE, ORGON, ELMIRA, MARIANA, CLEANTHES, VALERE, DAMIS, DORINA.]

CLEANTHES: Nay, Brother, hold, and don't descend to Indignities; leave the Wretch to his evil Destiny, and don't add to the Remorse that oppresses him. Much rather wish that his Heart may now happily become a Convert to Virtue; that he may reform his Life, thro' Detestation of his Crimes, and may soften the Justice of a glorious Prince; while for his Goodness you go and on your Knees make the due Returns for his Lenity to you.

ORGON: Yes, 'tis well said. Let us, with Joy, go throw our selves at his Royal

Feet, to glory in the Goodness which he generously displays to us; then, having acquitted our selves of this first Duty, 'twill be necessary we should apply our selves, with just care, to another:

With *Hymen's* tend'rest Joys to crown *Valere*
The generous Lover, and the Friend sincere.

The End

All for Love

JOHN DRYDEN

INTRODUCTION

In his *Essay of Dramatick Poesie*, written in 1665 but not published until 1668. John Dryden, then an ambitious young poet and playwright, explored the burning issue of whether to follow English or French literary models in his work. Dryden's essay was cast in the form of a dialogue between four men of culture and taste, discoursing together on critical matters while spending an afternoon on the Thames. The four men – Crites, Eugenius, Lisideius and Neander – are all pseudonyms, Dryden claims, for well-known men of letters. The four men agree on a general definition of a play:

> A just and lively Image of Humane Nature, representing its Passions and Humours, and the Changes of Fortune to which it is subject; for the Delight and Instruction of Mankind[1]

after which they proceed to examine which writers have come closest in their work to fulfilling the demands of this definition: the Ancients, the Moderns, the French or the English.

Although Dryden gives all the best arguments to Neander, who has little difficulty in proving that English plays fulfil the terms of the definition far better than the plays of classical writers (the Ancients) and modern French writers, the importance of classical and French example is not denied. The essay was a subtle examination of the contradictory pressures facing Restoration dramatists

1. John Dryden, *The Works of John Dryden*, vol. 17, ed. S. H. Monk (Berkeley: University of California Press, 1971) p. 15.

185

and was clearly intended to prepare the way for Dryden's own approach to playwriting in which he attempted to reconcile neo-classic order and precision with what he saw as English liveliness and imagination.

John Dryden was destined to become England's most famous man of letters in the late seventeenth century, but the difficulties facing writers in Cromwell's England made for a slow start. Dryden came from a family of minor gentry (his father was the third son of a country baronet) who were committed supporters of the parliamentary cause. Dryden was born in Northamptonshire in August 1631. During the 'distracted times' of the civil war period he was educated at Westminster and in 1650 was elected to a scholarship at Trinity College, Cambridge. After graduating in January 1654, there is evidence to suggest that Dryden went to London to work as a clerk for Sir Gilbert Pickering, who was Dryden's first cousin, and chamberlain to Cromwell.[1] Dryden's only literary output during this period were some 'Heroic Stanzas' written in 1658 upon the death of Cromwell. It was at the Restoration that Dryden's literary career really began to blossom.

He first made his mark, in much the same way as Racine, by writing adulatory poems addressed to the monarch, namely: 'Astræa Redux. A Poem on the Happy Restoration and Return of His Sacred Majesty Charles II' (1660) and 'To His Sacred Majesty, A Panegyrick on His Coronation' (1661). Further occasional poems, addressed to other notable figures, were written during the 1660s, including one 'To my Honoured Friend, Sir Robert Howard' (1660). Sir Robert Howard was a younger son of the Earl of Berkshire who, like Dryden, wished to pursue a literary career, but for fame rather than fortune. Dryden collaborated with him in the writing of a heroic tragedy called *The Indian Queen*, which was performed with great success in January 1664. During this period of shared endeavour, Dryden married Sir Robert's sister, Lady Elizabeth Howard, in December 1663. Contemporary sources suggest that Sir Robert and his brothers persuaded Dryden into marrying Lady Elizabeth, whose reputation was not of the best.[2] Dryden may not have needed much persuading. He was ambitious and determined to make his mark in society. Marrying into the aristocracy could bring both financial and social advantages. In the short term, there

1. See *Dictionary of National Biography*, vol. xvi, p. 65, and David Hopkins, *John Dryden* (Cambridge: Cambridge University Press, 1989) p. 35.
2. See *Dictionary of National Biography*, vol. xvi, p. 65.

were immediate benefits – the gift of a small estate in Wiltshire from his father-in-law and the possibility of prolonged visits to one of the earl's country properties, as when London was ravaged by the plague in 1665/66. (It was during this visit to the earl's seat at Charlton, Wiltshire, that Dryden wrote his *Essay of Dramatick Poesie* and his much admired poem in praise of Charles II, 'Annus Mirabilis'.) In the long term, however, the disadvantages were many. His wife's circle of aristocratic friends never accepted him as a social equal. He also found himself having to work at a furious pace to keep his wife in a style she found appropriate and to pay for his three children to receive a sound education.

Dryden's primary source of income during the 1660s and 1670s came from his work as a playwright. During those two decades, he wrote, adapted or contributed to some twenty different plays for the London stage. For ten years, between 1668 and 1678, he was granted the unique privilege of becoming a shareholder in Killigrew's company, in return for which he was supposed to write three new plays every year. (Normally playwrights were paid the takings of the third night's performance, which could mean no payment at all if a play failed to please.) Dryden experimented with almost every conceivable form of play, including: farce and low comedy (*The Wild Gallant* in 1663, *Sir Martin Mar-all* in 1667 and *An Evening's Love* in 1668); high comedy (*Secret Love* in 1667, and *Marriage A-la-Mode* and *The Assignation*, both performed in 1672); tragi-comedy (*The Rival Ladies* in 1664); adaptations of Shakespeare (*The Tempest* [with Davenant] in 1670 and *Troilus and Cressida* in 1679); heroic tragedy in rhyming verse (*The Indian Queen* [with Sir Robert Howard] in 1664, and its sequel *The Indian Emperour* in 1665, *Tyrannick Love* in 1669, *The Conquest of Granada*, parts 1 and 2 in 1670–1 and *Aureng-Zebe* in 1675); blank-verse tragedy (*All for Love* in 1677), political comedy (*The Spanish Fryar* in 1680); and politically inspired opera (*Albion and Albanius* in 1685). Although this is not a comprehensive list of Dryden's dramatic output, it does indicate the range and vigour of his work as a playwright.

In 1670 Dryden's literary pre-eminence was acknowledged when he was appointed Poet Laureate. (The office was formerly held by Sir William Davenant who had died in 1668.) Inevitably, his public success also made him enemies. Some writers were swift to condemn his toadying dedications to powerful patrons; others accused him of pandering too readily to popular taste, particularly in his more outrageously far-fetched heroic tragedies. These criticisms

came to a head in a burlesque play called *The Rehearsal*, written by
the Duke of Buckingham and various collaborators in 1671. In the
figure of Mr Bayes, Dryden was pilloried as a writer with precious
little wit and even less integrity. Lacy, the actor playing Bayes, was
instructed by Buckingham to impersonate Dryden's mannerisms of
speech and gesture. The play shows a town wit, Mr Johnson, and a
country wit, Mr Smith, invited by Mr Bayes to watch a rehearsal of
his latest heroic play. As Bayes comments with pedantic seriousness
on even the most ridiculous of scenes shown in rehearsal, Johnson
and Smith mock him behind his back and eventually grow so tired
of his antics that they leave him in mid-rehearsal to find themselves
a meal. In the various extracts shown in rehearsal, scenes from
Dryden's plays are burlesqued, and individual lines of verse are
parodied. The cumulative effect is to suggest that Dryden's stylistic
devices were void of sense and meaning and that his overall
approach in his heroic plays lacked any genuine artistic integrity.

Given Buckingham's exalted aristocratic status, there was
nothing Dryden could say or do by way of an immediate response.
Eventually he had his revenge when Buckingham, some years later,
had fallen from grace because of his Whig sympathies. In his
magnificent satiric poem 'Absalom and Achitophel' (1681) Dryden
took particular delight in castigating Buckingham in the figure of
Zimri.[1] The more immediate effect of Buckingham's burlesque play
was to make Dryden rethink his approach to playwriting.

Dryden's heroic tragedies were extravagant pieces, revolving
around titanic clashes of love and honour, invariably located in the
most exotic of settings and expressed in torrid, declamatory verse.
At times, under the excessively flamboyant exterior, serious issues
were addressed. Notably the two-part heroic play *The Conquest of*

---

1. *In the first Rank of these did* Zimri *stand:*
   A man so various that he seem'd to be
   Not one, but all Mankinds Epitome.
   Stiff in Opinions, always in the wrong;
   Was every thing by starts, and nothing long:
   But, in the course of one revolving Moon,
   Was Chymist, Fidler, States-Man and Buffoon;
   Then all for Women, Painting, Rhiming, Drinking;
   Besides ten thousand Freaks that dy'd in thinking. [. . .]
   Begger'd by Fools, whom still he found too late,
   He had his Jest, and they had his Estate.
   He laught himself from Court, then sought Releif
   By forming Parties, but coud ne're be Chief. [. . .]
   The Works of John Dryden, vol. 2, ed. H. T. Swedenberg, Jr
   (Berkeley: University of California Press, 1972) pp. 21–2.

Granada seems full of polemic argument against the ideas of the political philosopher Thomas Hobbes whose key work, *Leviathan* (1651), had described a mechanistic universe in which human beings were no more than matter and hence appetite in motion. Throughout the play the instinctive appetites of the hero Almanzor are countered by Queen Almahide (played by Nell Gwyn) who is determined to show him the civilising power of self-control and restraint.[1] The overall approach taken in these plays was cool and calculating rather than committed: it ensured a stylistically engineered distance from real experience, which tended to produce laughter rather than emotional involvement. Although emotionally brittle and devoid of real human substance, Dryden's heroic plays had a technical flamboyance that was specifically designed to appeal to contemporary audiences. Following Buckingham's critique of his plays in *The Rehearsal*, Dryden turned away from the extravagant, superficial technique he had perfected in his heroic plays and began to explore a world of real feelings. The process began with his next heroic play *Aureng-Zebe* (1675), but it reached its culmination in his blank-verse tragedy *All for Love, or the World well Lost* (1677).

All for Love

In his Preface to *All for Love*, Dryden confessed that he had attempted to imitate 'the divine Shakespeare' in writing his play; in fact there is little obvious trace of Shakespearean influence in the piece. A far stronger influence is the work of Racine with its unique fusion of strict form and powerful feeling. There are few direct borrowings, apart from the end of Act IV, which is reminiscent of the ending of Racine's *Bérénice*, but the retrospective structure of the play, along with the restraint and decorum shown in the handling of character and language, are far more reminiscent of Racine's approach to playwriting than that of Shakespeare. With charac-teristic disingenuousness, Dryden goes out of his way, in his Preface, to mask any debt to Racine by openly mocking *Phèdre* and the nicety of manners depicted in the action, which, he claims, has the effect of transforming 'the Hippolytus of Euripides into Monsieur Hippolyte'. Elsewhere in his Preface, Dryden makes a lengthy attack on his aristocratic detractors, but his refusal to acknowledge his very real debt to Racine lays him open to a charge of intellectual dishonesty of the very kind that his critics (notably Buckingham)

1. See David Thomas, *William Congreve* (London: Macmillan, 1992) pp. 28–31.

had already made against him. One claim, however, in Dryden's Preface does seem entirely justified, namely that in *All for Love* he had excelled himself. This play was Dryden's masterpiece, and he knew it.

Within a tightly controlled and symmetrically patterned structure (each act examines a specific set of relationships), Dryden explores a landscape of decline, decay and poignantly felt loss: loss of innocence, loss of purpose, loss of faith, loss of love. In a world in which the whole ordered fabric of society has disintegrated, individuals are thrown back on themselves to create their own personal framework of meaning, commitment and purpose. When this is threatened, then all is lost. There is nothing else that can any longer validate life and experience. The moral and metaphysical framework that still encompasses Shakespeare's world has disappeared. This makes *All for Love* a distinctly modern, and arguably even a postmodern tragedy: the whole discourse of ideology (or metanarrative) has been discarded, leaving Antony and Cleopatra to face the harsh reality of a randomly experienced universe. The one still centre at the heart of their existence is their love for each other, but this is threatened and finally destroyed by the world that surrounds them. All that then remains is the poignancy of loss.

At a surface level, *All for Love* revolves around a traditional heroic conflict between love and honour. Because of his love for Cleopatra, Antony has deserted his lawful wife Octavia, who is Cæsar's sister. This has incensed Cæsar, who has waged a long and destructive war against both Antony and Cleopatra. When the action of the play opens, the war has reached its final stages. Antony and Cleopatra are besieged by Cæsar's forces in Alexandria and are completely surrounded by land and sea. A succession of characters confront Antony, bringing with them the demands of honour to be set against his love for Cleopatra. The first is Ventidius, his loyal general, who would be equally glad to see Antony lead his remaining soldiers against Cæsar or to see Antony make his peace with Cæsar: the one thing he cannot stand is to see Antony languish in Cleopatra's sensual embrace. The next is Dolabella, Antony's once dear friend, who now serves Cæsar but wishes to achieve a reconciliation between Antony and Cæsar by reuniting Antony with his wife. To this end, he smuggles Octavia into Cleopatra's camp. Octavia then confronts Antony with their two daughters, forcing him to face the physical reality of duty and obligation.

These different characters, who bring with them the demands of honour, all intervene in Antony's life with disastrous consequences. In the process, the notions of honour that they embody are shown to be tainted. Ventidius is loyal but the ultimate limit of his horizon is his obsession with an honourable death. Dolabella brings with him the obligations of friendship and dutiful marriage, but as soon as Antony is persuaded to leave Cleopatra, he finds his own passion for Cleopatra is rekindled. Octavia has the rightful expectations of a high-born wife, but her arrogant responses make it obvious that she wishes to see Antony fulfil his social obligations rather than offer her the kind of warmth and affection he has lavished on Cleopatra. She represents the demands of political expediency and corrupting compromise; hers is a world in which duty is more important than emotion.

Juxtaposed with these tainted representations of the world of honour is the love of Antony and Cleopatra. In one sense their love is a cancer that has eaten away at reputation, obligation and worldly success. As Antony reminds Cleopatra, in her arms the world fell mouldering from his hands each hour. But their love also involves an attempt to wrest something tangible and fulfilling from the flux of time, a vision of richly potent giving that knows no bounds. As Antony expresses it to Cleopatra at the beginning of Act III:

> There's no satiety of Love, in thee;
> Enjoy'd, thou still art new; perpetual Spring
> Is in thy armes; the ripen'd fruit but falls,
> And blossoms rise to fill its empty place.
> And I grow rich by giving.

This vision of lovers who have already been together for ten years and yet who still enjoy perpetual spring in each other's arms, whose love-making is continuous and untiring, is a striking affirmation of the warmth and reality of their relationship. And it is precisely this precious warmth and passion that is destroyed by the political intrigue of the world surrounding them. Whether it be the demands of honour represented by Ventidius, Dolabella and Octavia, or the devious schemes designed by Cleopatra's eunuch Alexas to ward off these Roman interlopers, the effect is the same. The relationship between Antony and Cleopatra is shattered, their trust in each other undermined, their love broken by the demands of political expediency and courtly intrigue.

At the end of the play, all that remains is the poignancy of loss.

The lovers commit suicide, as Cæsar batters down the gates of the city. But Cleopatra ensures that she is dressed in her finest robes and that Antony is crowned with a victor's laurel. When the priest Serapion enters their chamber at the end of the play, he finds the two of them seated, as if 'giving Laws to half Mankind' and concludes that 'No lovers lived so great, or died so well'. Their love may have been destroyed by the world of duty, obligation and honour, but the manner of their death makes it plain, as the subtitle of the play suggests, that the world is 'well lost'. By comparison with the warmth and substance of their relationship, the world of political compromise seems tawdry and superficial. Dryden has deliberately heightened the purity of the love of Antony and Cleopatra, in order to show, by contrast, the emptiness of the world surrounding them: a gew-gaw world of hollow political rhetoric and warlike posturing.[1]

All for Love amounted to a powerful critique of post-Restoration society and its brittle and cynical values. As Dryden depicted it, this was a world that had lost touch with the traditional belief-structures that gave meaning to concepts such as duty and obligation. There was no place in such a world for genuine emotion and commitment. Despite his technical debt to Racine, Dryden had arrived at diametrically opposed conclusions. For Racine, the world of passion was dark and destructive, a threat to the ordered fabric of society. For Dryden, the world of love was the only reality in a universe out of joint. The destructive force was not passion but the engine of social and political coercion, running smoothly and efficiently but without any over-arching purpose or justification.

In marked contrast to the pessimism of these conclusions, Dryden continued to offer loyal service to his monarch. Arguably too much of his income was dependent upon royal bounty and favour for him to do otherwise. As the Whig opposition to Charles II's reign grew in virulence, Dryden demonstrated his loyalty by writing a series of muscular satires attacking Whig grandees and writers: *Absalom and Achitophel* (1681), *The Medal* (1682) and *Mac Flecknoe* (1682). Despite the darkening political climate, Dryden was persuaded to write an opera in praise of Charles II. Called *Albion and Albanius* (1685), this masque-like paean to the god-like rule of Charles II seems as much

---

1. This may well have been a coded reference to the love of Charles II for his French, Catholic mistress, the Duchess of Portsmouth, at a time when he had been forced to imprison a number of Whig grandees, including Shaftesbury and Buckingham, because of their growing public opposition to his rule.

out of tune with the harsh realities of contemporary politics as the masques written for Charles I. Although Charles II saw the work in rehearsal, he died in February 1685 before the opera could be presented in public. Rapid alterations were made so that the opera could be presented following James II's accession to the throne. Once again, fate intervened: after only a few performances political events led to the cancellation of the production. Charles II's illegitimate son, the Duke of Monmouth, who was a staunch Protestant, returned from exile in June 1685 with an invasionary force to dispute the succession of the Catholic James II. The political hysteria generated by his rebellion (eventually put down with considerable violence) meant that Dryden's opera had to be withdrawn.

Dryden continued to offer the same support to the Catholic James II as he had offered to Charles II. Much to the surprise and consternation of his contemporaries, he even converted to Catholicism himself. For many, this was seen as a sign of complete venality. Dryden paid a heavy price for his loyalty. James II's rule was a mercifully brief, but blundering disaster. His attempts to impose Catholicism upon an unwilling population, linked with his passionate and blinkered commitment to the Stuart myth of the divine right of kings, led to open rebellion by 1688. The Glorious Revolution of 1688 saw James II driven from England by his Protestant son-in-law, William of Orange, and his eldest daughter, Mary, whose popular invasion was actively encouraged and supported by an alliance of Whig and Tory politicians. After the accession of William and Mary, Dryden found himself stripped of his office of Poet Laureate and deprived of all his royal pensions. He was still a formidable figure in London's literary scene, publishing a steady stream of poems and translations from the classics and holding court in Will's Coffee House, but he no longer enjoyed any royal favour or patronage. Despite the charges of venality that were earlier levelled against him, he remained a committed Catholic and accepted his fall from grace without complaint.

J.Roberts del.   Publish'd for Bells British Theatre August 12 1776.   Page Sculp.

Mrs HARTLEY in the Character of CLEOPATRA.
I'll die I will not bear it.

Mrs Hartley as Cleopatra in *All for Love*, reproduced from *Bell's British Theatre*, vol. 5 (London: John Bell, 1780)

All for Love:
or,
The World Well Lost

A
Tragedy

As it is Acted at the
THEATRE-ROYAL;
And Written in Imitation of Shakespeare's Stile.

By John Dryden, Servant to His Majesty

Facile est verbum aliquod ardens (ut ita dicam) notare:
idque restinctis animorum incendiis irridere.[1]
Cicero.

In the SAVOY:
Printed by *Tho Newcomb*, for *Henry Herringman*,
at the Blew Anchor in the Lower Walk of the
New-Exchange. 1678

---

1. It is easy, indeed, to criticise some flaming word, if I may use this expression, and to laugh at it when the passion of the moment has cooled.

To the Right Honourable
THOMAS Earl of *Danby*, Viscount Latimer,
and Baron OSBORNE of *Kiveton* in Yorkshire,
Lord High Treasurer of *England*, One of
His Majesties most Honourable Privy-Council,
and Knight of the Most Noble Order of the Garter, &c.[1]

My LORD,
The Gratitude of Poets is so troublesome a Virtue to Great Men, that you are often in danger of your own Benefits: for you are threaten'd with some Epistle, and not suffer'd to do good in quiet, or to compound for their silence whom you have oblig'd. Yet, I confess, I neither am nor ought to be surpriz'd at this Indulgence: for your Lordship has the same right to favour Poetry which the Great and Noble have ever had.

Carmen amat, quisquis carmine digna gerit.[2]

There is somewhat of a tye in Nature betwixt those who are born for Worthy Actions, and those who can transmit them to Posterity: And though ours be much the inferiour part, it comes at least within the Verge of Alliance; nor are we unprofitable Members of the Commonwealth, when we animate others to those Virtues, which we copy and describe from you.

'Tis indeed their Interest, who endeavour the Subversion of Governments, to discourage Poets and Historians; for the best which can happen to them is to be forgotten: But such who, under Kings, are the Fathers of their Country, and by a just and prudent ordering of affairs preserve it, have the same reason to cherish the Chroniclers of their Actions, as they have to lay up in safety the Deeds and Evidences of their Estates: For such Records are their undoubted Titles to the love and reverence of After-Ages. Your Lordships Administration has already taken up a considerable part of the English Annals; and many of its most happy years are owing to it. His Majesty, the most knowing Judge of Men, and the best Master, has acknowledg'd the Ease and Benefit he receives in the Incomes of His Treasury, which You found not only disorder'd, but exhausted. All things were in the confusion of a Chaos, without Form or Method, if not reduc'd beyond it, even to Annihilation: so that you had not only to separate the Jarring Elements, but (if that boldness of expression might be allow'd me) to Create them. Your Enemies had so embroyl'd the management of your Office, that they look'd on your Advancement as the Instrument of your Ruine. And as if the clogging of the Revenue, and the Confusion of Accounts, which you found in your entrance, were not sufficient, they added their

1. Danby was one of the most powerful men in politics at the time. This dedication is a good example of Dryden's consummate skill in the art of flattery. It also demonstrates his firm commitment to the Stuart monarchy and opposition to those Whigs who 'endeavour the Subversion of Governments'.
2. 'He loves song whose exploits deserve the meed of song.' A quotation from Claudian, Book III.

own weight of malice to the Publick Calamity, by forestalling the Credit which shou'd cure it: your Friends on the other side were only capable of pitying, but not of aiding you: No farther help or counsel was remaining to you, but what was founded on your Self: and that indeed was your Security: For your Diligence, your Constancy, and your Prudence, wrought more surely within, when they were not disturb'd by any outward Motion. The highest Virtue is best to be trusted with it Self, for Assistance only can be given by a Genius Superiour to that which it assists. And 'tis the Noblest kind of Debt, when we are only obligd to God and Nature. This then, My Lord, is your just Commendation, That you have wrought out your Self a way to Glory, by those very Means that were design'd for your Destruction: You have not only restor'd, but advanc'd the Revenues of your Master without grievance to the Subject: and as if that were little yet, the Debts of the Exchequer, which lay heaviest both on the Crown, and on Private Persons, have by your Conduct been establish'd in a certainty of satisfaction; an Action so much the more Great and Honourable, because the case was without the ordinary relief of Laws, above the Hopes of the Afflicted, and beyond the Narrowness of the Treasury to redress, had it been manag'd by a less able Hand. 'Tis certainly the happiest, and most unenvy'd part of all your Fortune, to do good to many, while you do injury to none: to receive at once the Prayers of the Subject, and the Praises of the Prince: and by the care of your Conduct, to give Him Means of exerting the chiefest, (if any be the chiefest) of His Royal Virtues, His Distributive Justice to the Deserving, and his Bounty and Compassion to the Wanting. The Disposition of Princes towards their People, cannot better be discover'd than in the choice of their Ministers: who, like the Animal Spirits betwixt the Soul and Body, participate somewhat of both Natures, and make the Communication which is betwixt them. A King, who is just and moderate in his Nature, who Rules according to the Laws, whom God made happy by forming the Temper of his Soul to the Constitution of his Government, and who makes us happy, by assuming over us no other Soveraignty than that wherein our Welfare and Liberty consists; a Prince, I say, of so excellent a Character, and so suitable to the Wishes of all Good Men, could not better have convey'd Him to his Peoples Apprehensions than in your Lordships Person: who so lively express the same Virtues, that you seem not so much a Copy, as an Emanation of Him. Moderation is doubtless an Establishment of Greatness; but there is a steadiness of temper which is likewise requisite in a Minister of State: so equal a mixture of both Virtues that he may stand like an Isthmus betwixt the two encroaching Seas of Arbitrary Power, and Lawless Anarchy. The Undertaking would be difficult to any but an extraordinary Genius, to stand at the Line, and to divide the Limits; to pay what is due to the Great Representative of the Nation, and neither to inhance, nor to yeild up the undoubted Prerogatives of the Crown. These, My Lord, are the proper Virtues of a Noble Englishman, *as indeed they are properly* English *Virtues: No People in the World being capable of using them, but we who have the happiness to be born under so equal, and so well-pois'd a Government; a Government which has all the Advantages of Liberty beyond a Commonwealth, and all the Marks of Kingly Soveraignty without the danger of a Tyranny. Both my Nature, as I am an* Englishman, *and my Reason, as I am a Man, have bred in me a loathing to that specious Name of a Republick: that mock-appearance of a Liberty, where all who have not part in the Government, are Slaves: and Slaves they are of a viler note than such as are Subjects to an absolute Dominion. For no Christian Monarchy is so absolute, but 'tis circumscrib'd with Laws: But when the Executive Power is in the Law-makers, there is no farther check upon them; and the People must suffer without a remedy, because they are oppress'd by their Representatives. If I must serve, the number of my Masters, who were born my Equals, would but add to the ignominy of my Bondage. The Nature of our Government above all others, is exactly suited both to the Situation of our Country, and the Temper of the Natives: An Island being more proper for Commerce and for Defence, than for extending its Dominions on the Continent: for what the Valour of its Inhabitants might gain, by reason of its remoteness, and the casualties of the Seas, it cou'd not so easily preserve: and therefore, neither the Arbitrary Power of one in a Monarchy, nor of many in a Commonwealth, could make us greater than we are. 'Tis true, that vaster and more frequent Taxes might be gather'd, when the consent of the People was not ask'd or needed, but this were only by Conquering abroad to be poor at home: And the Examples of our Neighbours teach us, that they are not always the happiest Subjects whose Kings extend their Dominions farthest. Since therefore we cannot win by an Offensive War, at least a Land-War, the Model of our Government seems naturally contriv'd for the Defensive part: and the consent of a People is easily obtain'd to contribute to that Power which must protect it.* Felices nimium bona si sua norint, Angligenae![1] *And yet there are not wanting Malecontents amongst us, who surfeiting themselves on too much happiness, wou'd perswade the People that they might be happier by a change. 'Twas indeed the policy of their old Forefather, when himself was fallen from the station of Glory, to seduce Mankind into the same Rebellion with him, by telling him he might yet be freer than he was: that is, more free than his Nature wou'd allow, or (if I may so say) than God cou'd make him. We have already all the Liberty which Free-born Subjects can enjoy; and all beyond it is but License. But if it be Liberty of Conscience which they pretend, the Moderation of our Church is such, that its practice extends not to the severity of Persecution, and its Discipline is withal so easie, that it allows more freedom to Dissenters than any of the Sects wou'd allow to it. In the mean time, what right can be pretended by these Men to attempt Innovations in Church or State? Who made them the Trustees, or (to speak a little nearer their own Language) the Keepers of the Liberty of England? If their Call be extraordinary, let them convince us by working Miracles; for ordinary Vocation they can have none to disturb the Government under which they were born, and which protects them. He who has often chang'd his Party, and always has made his Interest the Rule of it, gives little evidence of his sincerity for the Publick Good: 'Tis manifest he changes but for himself, and takes the People for Tools to work his Fortune. Yet the experience of all Ages might let him know, that they who trouble the Waters first, have seldom the benefit of the Fishing: As they who began the late Rebellion, enjoy'd not the fruit of their undertaking, but*

---

1. A reworking of a line from Virgil's *Georgics* II: 'O happy Englishmen, too happy, should they come to know their blessings.'

were crush'd themselves by the Usurpation of their own Instrument. Neither is it enough for them to answer that they only intend a Reformation of the Government, but not the Subversion of it: On such pretences all Insurrections have been founded: 'Tis striking at the Root of Power, which is Obedience. Every Remonstrance of private Men, has the seed of Treason in it; and Discourses which are couch'd in ambiguous Terms, are therefore the more dangerous, because they do all the Mischief of open sedition, yet are safe from the punishment of the Laws. These, My Lord, are Considerations which I should not pass so lightly over, had I room to manage them as they deserve: for no Man can be so inconsiderable in a Nation, as not to have a share in the welfare of it; and if he be a true Englishman, he must at the same time be fir'd with Indignation, and revenge himself as he can on the Disturbers of his Country. And to whom could I more fitly apply my self, than to your Lordship, who have not only an inborn, but an hereditary Loyalty? The memorable constancy and sufferings of your Father, almost to the ruine of his Estate for the Royal Cause, were an earnest of that, which such a Parent and such an Institution wou'd produce in the Person of a Son. But so unhappy an occasion of manifesting your own Zeal in suffering for his present Majesty, the Providence of God, and the Prudence of your Administration, will, I hope, prevent. That as your Fathers Fortune waited on the unhappiness of his Sovereign, so your own may participate of the better Fate which attends his Son. The Relation which you have by Alliance to the Noble Family of your Lady, serves to confirm to you both this happy Augury. For what can deserve a greater place in the English Chronicle, than the Loyalty and Courage, the Actions and Death of the General of an Army Fighting for His Prince and Country? The Honour and Gallantry of the Earl of Lindsey, is so illustrious a Subject, that 'tis fit to adorn an Heroique Poem; for He was the Proto-Martyr of the Cause, and the Type of his unfortunate Royal Master.

Yet, after all, My Lord, if I may speak my thoughts, you are happy rather to us than to your self: for the Multiplicity, the Cares, and the Vexations of your Imployment, have betray'd you from your self, and given you up into the Possession of the Publick. You are Robb'd of your Privacy and Friends, and scarce any hour of your Life you can call your own. Those who envy your Fortune, if they wanted not good Nature, might more justly pity it; and when they see you watch'd by a Croud of Suitors, whose importunity 'tis impossible to avoid, would conclude with Reason, that you have lost much more in true content, than you have gain'd by Dignity; and that a private Gentleman is better attended by a single Servant, than your Lordship with so clamorous a Train. Pardon me, My Lord, If I speak like a Philosopher on this Subject; the Fortune which makes a Man uneasie, cannot make him happy: and a Wise Man must think himself uneasie, when few of his Actions are in his choice.

This last Consideration has brought me to another, and a very seasonable one for your relief; which is, That while I pity your want of leisure, I have impertinently Detain'd you so long a time. I have put off my own Business, which was my Dedication, till 'tis so late, that I am now asham'd to begin it: And therefore I will say nothing of the Poem, which I Present to you, because I know not if you are like to have an Hour, which, with a good Conscience, you may throw away in perusing

it: And for the Author, I have only to beg the continuance of your Protection to him,
who is,

MY LORD,
Your Lordships, most Oblig'd,
most Humble, and most
Obedient Servant,
JOHN DRYDEN.

Preface[1]

The death of *Antony* and *Cleopatra*, is a Subject which has been treated by
the greatest Wits of our Nation, after *Shakespeare*; and by all so variously, that
their example has given me the confidence to try my self in this Bowe of
Ulysses amongst the Crowd of Sutors; and, withal, to take my own
measures, in aiming at the Mark. I doubt not but the same Motive has
prevailed with all of us in this attempt; I mean the excellency of the Moral:
for the chief persons represented, were famous patterns of unlawful love;
and their end accordingly was unfortunate. All reasonable men have long
since concluded, That the Heroe of the Poem, ought not to be a character of
perfect Virtue, for, then, he could not, without injustice, be made unhappy
nor yet altogether wicked, because he could not then be pitied: I have
therefore steer'd the middle course and have drawn the character of *Antony*
as favourably as *Plutarch*, *Appian*, and *Dion Cassius* wou'd give me leave: the
like I have observ'd in *Cleopatra*. That which is wanting to work up the pity
to a greater height, was not afforded me by the story: for the crimes of love
which they both committed, were not occasion'd by any necessity, or fatal
ignorance, but were wholly voluntary; since our passions are, or ought to
be, within our power. The Fabrick of the Play is regular enough, as to the
inferior parts of it; and the Unities of Time, Place and Action, more exactly
observ'd, than, perhaps, the *English* Theater requires. Particularly, the Action
is so much one, that it is the only of the kind without Episode, or Underplot;
every Scene in the Tragedy conducing to the main design, and every Act
concluding with a turn of it. The greatest errour in the contrivance seems to
be in the person of *Octavia*: For, though I might use the priviledge of a Poet,
to introduce her into *Alexandria*, yet I had not enough consider'd, that the
compassion she mov'd to her self and children, was destructive to that
which I reserv'd for *Antony* and *Cleopatra*; whose mutual love being
founded upon vice, must lessen the favour of the Audience to them, when

---

1. This preface gives Dryden the opportunity to attack those aristocrats like
   Buckingham and Rochester who had publicly criticised his work. It also enables
   him to stress the importance of English traditions in playwriting as his preferred
   model.

Virtue and Innocence were oppress'd by it. And, though I justified *Antony* in some measure, by making *Octavia's* departure, to proceed wholly from her self; yet the force of the first Machine still remain'd; and the dividing of pity, like the cutting of a River into many Channels, abated the strength of the natural stream. But this is an Objection which none of my Critiques have urg'd against me; and therefore I might have let it pass, if I could have resolv'd to have been partial to my self. The faults my Enemies have found, are rather cavils concerning little, and not essential Decencies; which a Master of the Ceremonies may decide betwixt us. The French Poets, I confess, are strict Observers of these Punctilio's: They would not, for example, have suffer'd *Cleopatra* and *Octavia* to have met; or if they had met, there must only have pass'd betwixt them some cold civilities, but no eagerness of repartee, for fear of offending against the greatness of their Characters, and the modesty of their Sex. This Objection I foresaw, and at the same time contemn'd: for I judg'd it both natural and probable, that *Octavia*, proud of her new-gain'd Conquest, would search out *Cleopatra* to triumph over her; and that *Cleopatra*, thus attacqu'd, was not of a spirit to shun the encounter: and 'tis not unlikely, that two exasperated Rivals should use such Satyre as I have put into their mouths; for after all, though the one were a *Roman*, and the other a Queen, they were both Women. 'Tis true, some actions, though natural, are not fit to be represented; and broad obscenities in words, ought in good manners to be avoided: expressions therefore are a modest cloathing of our thoughts, as Breeches and Petticoats are of our bodies. If I have kept my self within the bounds of modesty, all beyond it is but nicety and affectation; which is no more but modesty deprav'd into a vice: they betray themselves who are too quick of apprehension in such cases, and leave all reasonable men to imagine worse of them, than of the Poet.

Honest Montaigne goes yet farther: *Nous ne sommes que ceremonie; la ceremonie nous emporte, & laissons la substance des choses: Nous nous tenons aux branches, & abandonnons le tronc & le corps. Nous avons appris aux Dames de rougir, oyans seulement nommer ce qu'elles ne craignent aucunement a faire: Nous n'osons appeller a droict nos membres, & ne craignons pas de les employer a toute sorte de debauche. La ceremonie nous defend d'exprimer par paroles les choses licites & naturelles, & nous l'en croyons; la raison nous defend de n'en faire point d'illicites & mauvaises, & personne ne l'en croid.* My comfort is, that by this opinion my Enemies are but sucking Critiques, who wou'd fain be nibbling ere their teeth are come.

Yet, in this nicety of manners does the excellency of French Poetry consist: their Heroes are the most civil people breathing; but their good breeding seldom extends to a word of sense: All their Wit is in their Ceremony; they want the Genius which animates our Stage; and therefore 'tis but necessary when they cannot please, that they should take care not to offend. But, as the civilest man in the company is commonly the dullest, so these Authors, while they are afraid to make you laugh or cry, out of pure good manners, make you sleep. They are so careful not to exasperate a Critique, that they never leave him any work: so busie with the Broom, and make so clean a riddance, that there is little left either for censure or for praise: for no part of a Poem is worth our discommending, where the whole is insipid; as when we have once tasted of pall'd Wine, we stay not to examine it Glass by Glass. But while they affect to shine in trifles, they are often careless in essentials. Thus their *Hippolitus* is so scrupulous in point of decency, that he will rather expose himself to death, than accuse his Stepmother to his Father; and my Critiques I am sure will commend him for it: but we of grosser apprehensions, are apt to think that this excess of generosity, is not practicable but with Fools and Madmen. This was good manners with a vengeance; and the Audience is like to be much concern'd at the misfortunes of this admirable Heroe: but take *Hippolitus* out of his Poetique Fit, and I suppose he would think it a wiser part, to set the Saddle on the right Horse, and chuse rather to live with the reputation of a plain-spoken honest man, than to die with the infamy of an incestuous Villain. In the mean time we may take notice, that where the Poet ought to have preserv'd the character as it was deliver'd to us by Antiquity, when he should have given us the picture of a rough young man, of the Amazonian strain, a jolly Huntsman, and both by his profession and his early rising a Mortal Enemy to love, he has chosen to give him the turn of Gallantry, sent him to travel from *Athens* to *Paris*, taught him to make love, and transform'd the *Hippolitus* of *Euripides* into Monsieur *Hippolite*. I should not have troubled my self thus far with *French* Poets, but that I find our *Chedreux* Critiques wholly form their judgments by them. But for my part, I desire to be try'd by the Laws of my own Country; for it seems unjust to me, that the *French* should prescribe here, till they have conquer'd. Our little Sonnettiers who follow them, have too narrow Souls to judge of Poetry. Poets themselves are the most proper, though I conclude not the only Critiques. But till some Genius as Universal, as *Aristotle*, shall arise, one who can penetrate into all Arts and Sciences, without the practice of them, I shall think it reasonable, that the Judgment of an Artificer in his own Art should be preferable to the opinion of another man; at least where he is not brib'd by interest, or prejudic'd by malice: and this, I suppose, is manifest by plain induction: For, first, the Crowd cannot be presum'd to have more than a gross instinct, of what pleases or displeases them: every man will grant me this; but then, by a particular kindness to himself, he draws his own stake first, and will be distinguish'd from the multitude, of which other men may think him one. But, if I come closer to those who are allow'd for witty men, either by the advantage of their quality, or by common fame, and affirm that neither are they qualified to decide Sovereignly, concerning Poetry, I shall yet have a strong party of my opinion for most of them severally will exclude the rest, either from the number of witty men, or at least of able Judges. But here again they are all indulgent to themselves: and every one who believes himself a Wit, that is, every man, will pretend at the same time to a right of judging. But to press it yet farther, there are many witty men, but few Poets; neither have all Poets a taste of Tragedy. And this is the Rock on which they are daily splitting. Poetry, which is a Picture of Nature, must generally please: but 'tis not to be understood that all parts of it must please every man; therefore is not Tragedy to be judg'd by a witty man, whose taste is only confin'd to Comedy. Nor is every man who loves Tragedy a sufficient Judge of it: he must understand the excellencies of it too, or he will only prove a blind Admirer, not a Critique. From hence it comes that so many Satyrs on Poets, and censures of their Writings, fly abroad. Men of pleasant Conversation, (at least esteem'd so) and indu'd with a trifling kind of Fancy, perhaps help'd out with some smattering of *Latine*, are ambitious to distinguish themselves from the Herd of Gentlemen, by their Poetry;

> Rarus enim fermè sensus communis in illâ
> Fortunâ.[1]

And is not this a wretched affectation, not to be contented with what Fortune has done for them, and sit down quietly with their Estates, but they must call their Wits in question, and needlesly expose their nakedness to publick view? Not considering that they are not to expect the same approbation from sober men, which they have found from their flatterers after the third Bottle? If a little glittering in discourse has pass'd them on us for witty men, where was the necessity of undeceiving the World? would a man who has an ill Title to an Estate, but yet is in possession of it, would he bring it of his own accord, to be try'd at *Westminster*? We who write, if we want the Talent, yet have the excuse that we do it for a poor subsistence; but what can be urg'd in their defence, who not having the Vocation of Poverty to scribble, out of meer wantonness take pains to make themselves ridiculous? *Horace* was certainly in the right, where he said, That *no man is satisfied with his own condition.* A Poet is not pleas'd because he is not rich; and the Rich are discontented, because the Poets will not admit them of their number. Thus the case is hard with Writers: if they succeed not, they must starve; and if they do, some malicious Satyr is prepar'd to level them for daring to please without their leave. But while they are so eager to destroy the fame of others, their ambition is manifest in their concernment: some Poem of their own is to be produc'd, and the Slaves are to be laid flat with their faces on the ground, that the Monarch may appear in the greater Majesty. [. . .]

It remains that I acquaint the Reader, that I have endeavoured in this Play to follow the practise of the Ancients, who, as Mr. *Rymer* has judiciously observ'd, are and ought to be our Masters. *Horace* likewise gives it for a Rule in his Art of Poetry,

---

1. Juvenal, *Satires* VIII: 'For in those high places regard for others is rarely to be found.'

– Vos exemplaria Græca
Nocturnâ versate manu, versate diurnâ.[1]

Yet, though their Models are regular, they are too little for *English* Tragedy; which requires to be built in a larger compass. I could give an instance in the *Oedipus Tyrannus*, which was the Masterpiece of *Sophocles*; but I reserve it for a more fit occasion, which I hope to have hereafter. In my Stile I have profess'd to imitate the Divine *Shakespeare*; which that I might perform more freely, I have dis-incumber'd my self from Rhyme. Not that I condemn my former way, but that this is more proper to my present purpose. I hope I need not to explain my self, that I have not Copy'd my Author servilely: Words and Phrases must of necessity receive a change in succeeding Ages: but 'tis almost a Miracle that much of his Language remains so pure; and that he who began Dramatique Poetry amongst us, untaught by any, and, as *Ben Johnson* tells us,[2] without Learning, should by the force of his own Genius perform so much, that in a manner he has left no praise for any who come after him. The occasion is fair, and the subject would be pleasant to handle the difference of Stiles betwixt him and *Fletcher*, and wherein, and how far they are both to be imitated. But since I must not be over-confident of my own performance after him, it will be prudence in me to be silent Yet I hope I may affirm, and without vanity, that by imitating him, I have excell'd my self throughout the Play; and particularly, that I prefer the Scene betwixt *Antony* and *Ventidius* in the first Act, to any thing which I have written in this kind.

1. For yourselves, handle Greek models by night, handle them by day.
2. A reference to Jonson's comment that Shakespeare had 'small Latin and less Greek'.

Prologue to *Antony and Cleopatra*

What Flocks of Critiques hover here to day,
As Vultures wait on Armies for their Prey,
All gaping for the Carcass of a Play!
With Croaking Notes they bode some dire event;
And follow dying Poets by the scent.
Ours gives himself for gone; y'have watch'd your time!
He fights this day unarm'd; without his Rhyme;
And brings a Tale which often has been told;
As sad as Dido's; and almost as old.
His Heroe, whom you Wits his Bully call,
Bates of his mettle; and scarce rants at all:
He's somewhat lewd; but a well-meaning mind;
Weeps much; fights little; but is wond'rous kind:
In short, a Pattern, and Companion fit,
For all the keeping Tonyes of the Pit.
I cou'd name more; A Wife, and Mistress too;
Both (to be plain) too good for most of you:
The Wife well-natur'd, and the Mistress true.
    Now, Poets, if your fame has been his care;
Allow him all the candour you can spare.
A brave Man scorns to quarrel once a day;
Like Hectors, in at every petty fray.
Let those find fault whose Wit's so very small,
They've need to show that they can think at all:
Errours like Straws upon the surface flow;
He who would search for Pearls must dive below.
Fops may have leave to level all they can;
As Pigmies wou'd be glad to lopp a Man.
Half-Wits are Fleas; so little and so light;
We scarce cou'd know they live, but that they bite.
But, as the Rich, when tir'd with daily Feasts,
For change, become their next poor Tenants Ghests;[1]
Drink hearty Draughts of Ale, from plain brown Bowls,
And snatch the homely Rasher from the Coals:
So you, retiring from much better Cheer,
For once, may venture to do penance here.
And since that plenteous Autumn now is past,
Whose Grapes and Peaches have Indulg'd your taste,
Take in good part from our poor Poets boord,
Such rivell'd Fruits as Winter can afford.

1. Guests.

Persons Represented

By

MARC ANTONY,   Mr. *Hart.*
VENTIDIUS, his General,   Mr. *Mohun.*
DOLLABELLA, his Friend,   Mr. *Clarke.*
ALEXAS, the Queens Eunuch,   Mr. *Goodman.*
SERAPION, Priest of *Isis,*   Mr. *Griffin.*
Another Priest,   Mr. *Coysh.*
Servants to *Antony.*

CLEOPATRA, Queen of *Ægypt,*   Mrs. *Boutell.*
OCTAVIA, *Antony*'s Wife,   Mrs. *Corey.*
CHARMION, *Iras, Cleopatra*'s Maids
ANTONY'S two little Daughters.

SCENE ALEXANDRIA.

Act I, Scene I

[Scene, the Temple of Isis.
Enter SERAPION, MYRIS, *Priests of* ISIS.]

SERAPION: Portents, and Prodigies, are grown so frequent,
　　That they have lost their Name. Our fruitful *Nile*
　　Flow'd ere the wonted Season, with a Torrent
　　So unexpected, and so wondrous fierce,
　　That the wild Deluge overtook the haste
　　Ev'n of the Hinds that watch'd it: Men and Beasts
　　Were born above the tops of Trees, that grew
　　On th' utmost Margin of the Water-mark.
　　Then, with so swift an Ebb, the Floud drove backward,
　　It slipt from underneath the Scaly Herd:
　　Here monstrous *Phocae*[1] panted on the Shore;
　　Forsaken *Dolphins* there, with their broad tails,
　　Lay lashing the departing Waves: Hard by 'em,
　　Sea-Horses[2] floundring in the slimy mud,
　　Toss'd up their heads, and dash'd the ooze about 'em.

[Enter ALEXAS *behind them.*]

1. Seals.
2. Hippopotamuses.

MYRIS: Avert these Omens, Heav'n.

SERAPION: Last night, between the hours of Twelve and One
In a lone Isle o'th' Temple while I walk'd,
A Whirl-wind rose, that, with a violent blast,
Shook all the *Dome*: the Doors around me clapt,
The Iron Wicket, that defends the Vault,
Where the long Race of *Ptolemies* is lay'd,
Burst open, and disclos'd the mighty dead.
From out each Monument, in order plac'd,
An Armed Ghost start up: the Boy-King last
Rear'd his inglorious head. A peal of groans
Then follow'd, and a lamentable voice
Cry'd, *Ægypt* is no more. My blood ran back,
My shaking knees against each other knock'd;
On the cold pavement down I fell intranc'd,
And so unfinish'd left the horrid Scene.

ALEXAS: [*showing himself.*] And, Dream'd you this? or,
Did invent the Story
To frighten our *Ægypt*ian Boys withal,
And train 'em up betimes in fear of Priesthood?

SERAPION: My Lord, I saw you not,
Nor meant my words should reach your ears; but what
I utter'd was most true.

ALEXAS: A foolish Dream,
Bred from the fumes of indigested Feasts,
And holy Luxury.

SERAPION: I know my duty:
This goes no farther.

ALEXAS: 'Tis not fit it should.
Nor would the times now bear it, were it true.
All Southern, from yon hills, the *Roman* Camp
Hangs o'er us black and threatning, like a Storm
Just breaking on our heads.

SERAPION: Our faint *Ægyptians* pray for *Antony*;
But in their Servile hearts they own *Octavius*.

MYRIS: Why then does *Antony* dream out his hours,
And tempts not Fortune for a noble Day,
Which might redeem, what *Actium* lost?

ALEXAS: He thinks 'tis past recovery.

SERAPION: Yet the Foe
Seems not to press the Siege.

ALEXAS: O, there's the wonder.
Mæcenas and *Agrippa*, who can most
With *Cæsar*, are his Foes. His Wife *Octavia*,
Driv'n from his House, solicits her revenge;

All for Love

And *Dollabella*, who was once his Friend,
Upon some private grudge, now seeks his ruine:
Yet still War seems on either side to sleep.
SERAPION: 'Tis strange that *Antony*, for some dayes past,
Has not beheld the face of *Cleopatra*;
But here, in *Isis* Temple, lives retir'd,
And makes his heart a prey to black despair.
ALEXAS: 'Tis true; and we much fear he hopes by absence
To cure his mind of Love.
SERAPION: If he be vanquish'd,
Or make his peace, *Ægypt* is doom'd to be
A *Roman* Province; and our plenteous Harvests
Must then redeem the scarceness of their Soil.
 While *Antony* stood firm, our *Alexandria*
Rival'd proud *Rome* (Dominions other Seat)
And Fortune striding, like a vast *Colossus*,
Cou'd fix an equal foot of Empire here.
ALEXAS: Had I my wish, these Tyrants of all Nature
Who Lord it o'er Mankind, should perish, perish,
Each by the others Sword; but, since our will
Is lamely follow'd by our pow'r, we must
Depend on one; with him to rise or fall.
SERAPION: How stands the Queen affected?
ALEXAS: O, she dotes,
She dotes, *Serapion*, on this vanquish'd Man,
And winds her self about his mighty ruins;
Whom would she yet forsake, yet yield him up,
This hunted prey, to his pursuers hands,
She might preserve us all; but 'tis in vain –
This changes my designs, this blasts my Counsels,
And makes me use all means to keep him here,
Whom I could wish divided from her Arms
Far as the Earth's deep Center. Well, you know
The state of things; no more of your ill Omens,
And black Prognosticks; labour to confirm
The peoples hearts.

        [*Enter* VENTIDIUS, *talking aside with a Gentleman of* ANTONY'*s.*]

SERAPION: These *Roman*s will o'rehear us.
But, Who's that Stranger? By his Warlike port,
His fierce demeanor, and erected look,
He's of no vulgar note.
ALEXAS: O 'tis *Ventidius*,
Our Emp'rors great Lieutenant in the East,
Who first show'd Rome that *Parthia* could be conquer'd.

When *Antony* return'd from *Syria* last,
He left this Man to guard the *Roman* Frontiers.
SERAPION: You seem to know him well.
ALEXAS: Too well. I saw him in *Cilicia* first,
  When *Cleopatra* there met *Antony*:
  A mortal foe he was to us, and *Ægypt*.
  But, let me witness to the worth I hate,
  A braver *Roman* never drew a Sword:
  Firm to his Prince; but, as a friend, not slave.
  He ne'r was of his pleasures; but presides
  O're all his cooler hours and morning counsels:
  In short, the plainness, fierceness, rugged virtue
  Of an old true-stampt *Roman* lives in him.
  His coming bodes I know not what of ill
  To our affairs. Withdraw, to mark him better;
  And I'll acquaint you why I sought you here,
  And what's our present work.

[*They withdraw to a corner of the Stage; and* VENTIDIUS, *with the other, comes
forwards to the front.*]

VENTIDIUS: Not see him, say you?
  I say, I must, and will.
GENTLEMAN: He has commanded,
  On pain of death, none should approach his presence.
VENTIDIUS: I bring him news will raise his drooping Spirits,
  Give him new life.
GENTLEMAN: He sees not *Cleopatra*.
VENTIDIUS: Would he had never seen her.
GENTLEMAN: He eats not, drinks not, sleeps not, has no use
  Of any thing, but thought; or, if he talks,
  'Tis to himself, and then 'tis perfect raving:
   Then he defies the World, and bids it pass;
   Sometimes he gnawes his Lip, and Curses loud
   The Boy *Octavius*; then he draws his mouth
   Into a scornful smile, and cries, Take all,
  The World's not worth my care.
VENTIDIUS: Just, just his nature.
  Virtues his path; but sometimes 'tis too narrow
  For his vast Soul; and then he starts out wide,
  And bounds into a Vice that bears him far
  From his first course, and plunges him in ills:
  But, when his danger makes him find his fault,
  Quick to observe, and full of sharp remorse,
  He censures eagerly his own misdeeds,

Judging himself with malice to himself,
And not forgiving what as Man he did,
Because his other parts are more than Man.
He must not thus be lost.

[ALEXAS *and the* PRIESTS *come forward.*]

ALEXAS: You have your full Instructions, now advance;
    Proclaim your Orders loudly.
SERAPION: *Romans, Ægyptians*, hear the Queen's Command.
    Thus *Cleopatra* bids, Let Labor cease,
    To Pomp and Triumphs give this happy day,
    That gave the World a Lord: 'tis *Antony's*.
    Live, *Antony*; and *Cleopatra* live.
    Be this the general voice sent up to Heav'n,
    And every publick place repeat this eccho.
VENTIDIUS: [*aside.*] Fine Pageantry!
SERAPION: Set out before your doors
    The Images of all your sleeping Fathers,
    With Laurels crown'd; with Laurels wreath your posts,
    And strow with Flow'rs the Pavement; Let the Priests
    Do present Sacrifice; pour out the Wine,
    And call the Gods to joyn with you in gladness.
VENTIDIUS: Curse on the tongue that bids this general joy.
    Can they be friends of *Antony*, who Revel
    When *Antony's* in danger? Hide, for shame,
    You *Romans*, your Great grandsires Images,
    For fear their Souls should animate their Marbles,
    To blush at their degenerate Progeny.
ALEXAS: A love which knows no bounds to *Antony*,
    Would mark the Day with honors; when all Heaven
    Labor'd for him, when each propitious Star
    Stood wakeful in his Orb, to watch that hour,
    And shed his better influence. Her own Birth-day
    Our Queen neglected, like a vulgar Fate,
    That pass'd obscurely by.
VENTIDIUS: Would it had slept,
    Divided far from his; till some remote
    And future Age had call'd it out, to ruin
    Some other Prince, not him.
ALEXAS: Your Emperor,
    Tho grown unkind, would be more gentle, than
    T' upbraid my Queen, for loving him too well.
VENTIDIUS: Does the mute Sacrifice upbraid the Priest?
    He knows him not his Executioner.

O, she has deck'd his ruin with her love,
Led him in golden bands to gaudy slaughter,
And made perdition pleasing: She has left him
The blank of what he was;
I tell thee, Eunuch, she has quite unman'd him:
Can any *Roman* see, and know him now,
Thus alter'd from the Lord of half Mankind,
Unbent, unsinew'd, made a Womans Toy,
Shrunk from the vast extent of all his honors,
And crampt within a corner of the World?
O, *Antony*!
Thou bravest Soldier, and thou best of Friends!
Bounteous as Nature; next to Nature's God!
Could'st thou but make new Worlds, so wouldst thou give 'em,
As bounty were thy being. Rough in Battel,
As the first *Romans*, when they went to War;
Yet, after Victory, more pitiful,
Than all their Praying Virgins left at home!
ALEXAS: Would you could add to those more shining Virtues,
His truth to her who loves him.
VENTIDIUS: Would I could not.
But, Wherefore waste I precious hours with thee?
Thou art her darling mischief, her chief Engin,
Antony's other Fate. Go, tell thy Queen,
Ventidius is arriv'd, to end her Charms.
Let your *Ægyptian* Timbrels play alone;
Nor mix Effeminate Sounds with *Roman* Trumpets.
You dare not fight for *Antony*; go Pray,
And keep your Cowards-Holy-day in Temples.

[*Exeunt* ALEXAS, SERAPION.]

[*Enter the second Gentleman of* M. ANTONY.]

2. GENTLEMAN: The Emperor approaches, and commands,
On pain of Death, that none presume to stay.
I. GENTLEMAN: I dare not disobey him.

[*Going out with the other.*]

VENTIDIUS: Well, I dare.
But, I'll observe him first unseen, and find
Which way his humour drives: the rest I'll venture.   [*Withdraws.*]

[*Enter* ANTONY, *walking with a disturb'd Motion, before he speaks.*]

All for Love

ANTONY: They tell me, 'tis my Birthday, and I'll keep it
  With double pomp of sadness.
  'Tis what the day deserves, which gave me breath.
  Why was I rais'd the Meteor of the World,
  Hung in the Skies, and blazing as I travel'd,
  Till all my fires were spent; and then cast downward
  To be trod out by *Cæsar*?
VENTIDIUS: [*aside.*]   On my Soul,
  'Tis mournful, wondrous mournful!
ANTONY: Count thy gains.
  Now, *Antony*, Wouldst thou be born for this?
  Glutton of Fortune, thy devouring youth
  Has starv'd thy wanting Age.
VENTIDIUS: [*aside.*]   How sorrow shakes him!
  So, now the Tempest tears him up by th' Roots,
  And on the ground extends the noble ruin.
ANTONY: [*having thrown himself down.*] Lye there, thou shadow of an Emperor;
  The place thou pressest on thy Mother Earth
  Is all thy Empire now: now it contains thee;
  Some few dayes hence, and then twill be too large,
  When thou'rt contracted in thy narrow Urn,
  Shrunk to a few cold Ashes; then *Octavia*,
  (For *Cleopatra* will not live to see it)
  Octavia then will have thee all her own,
  And bear thee in her Widow'd hand to *Cæsar*;
  Cæsar will weep, the Crocodile will weep,
  To see his Rival of the Universe
  Lye still and peaceful there. I'll think no more on't.
  Give me some Musick; look that it be sad:
  I'll sooth my Melancholy, till I swell,
  And burst my self with sighing –   [*Soft Musick.*]
  'Tis somewhat to my humor. Stay, I fancy
  I'm now turn'd wild, a Commoner of Nature;
  Of all forsaken, and forsaking all;
  Live in a shady Forrest's *Sylvan* Scene,
  Stretch'd at my length beneath some blasted Oke;
  I lean my head upon the Mossy Bark,
  And look just of a piece, as I grew from it:
  My uncomb'd Locks, matted like *Misletoe*,
  Hang o're my hoary Face; a murm'ring Brook
  Runs at my foot.
VENTIDIUS: Methinks I fancy
  My self there too.
ANTONY: The Herd come jumping by me,
  And fearless, quench their thirst, while I look on,

And take me for their fellow-Citizen.

More of this Image, more; it lulls my thoughts.   [*Soft Musick again.*]

VENTIDIUS: I must disturb him; I can hold no longer.   [*Stands before him.*]

ANTONY: [*starting up.*] Art thou *Ventidius*?

VENTIDIUS: Are you *Antony*?

    I'm liker what I was, than you to him

    I left you last.

ANTONY: I'm angry.

VENTIDIUS: So am I.

ANTONY: I would be private: leave me.

VENTIDIUS: Sir, I love you,

    And therefore will not leave you.

ANTONY: Will not leave me?

    Where have you learnt that Answer? Who am I?

VENTIDIUS: My Emperor; the Man I love next Heav'n:

    If I said more, I think 'twere scarce a Sin;

    Y'are all that's good, and god-like.

ANTONY: All that's wretched.

    You will not leave me then?

VENTIDIUS: 'Twas too presuming

    To say I would not; but I dare not leave you:

    And, 'tis unkind in you to chide me hence

    So soon, when I so far have come to see you.

ANTONY: Now thou hast seen me, art thou satisfy'd?

    For, if a Friend, thou hast beheld enough;

    And, if a Foe, too much.

VENTIDIUS: [*weeping.*] Look, Emperor, this is no common Deaw,

    I have not wept this Forty year; but now

    My Mother comes afresh into my eyes;

    I cannot help her softness.

ANTONY: By Heav'n, he weeps, poor good old Man, he weeps!

    The big round drops course one another down

    The furrows of his cheeks. Stop 'em, *Ventidius*,

    Or I shall blush to death: they set my shame,

    That caus'd 'em, full before me.

VENTIDIUS: I'll do my best.

ANTONY: Sure there's contagion in the tears of Friends:

    See, I have caught it too. Believe me, 'tis not

    For my own griefs, but thine – Nay, Father.

VENTIDIUS: Emperor.

ANTONY: Emperor! Why, that's the stile of Victory,

    The Conqu'ring Soldier, red with unfelt wounds,

    Salutes his General so: but never more

    Shall that sound reach my ears.

VENTIDIUS: I warrant you.

ANTONY: *Actium, Actium!* Oh –
VENTIDIUS: It sits too near you.
ANTONY: Here, here it lies; a lump of Lead by day,
     And, in my short distracted nightly slumbers,
     The Hag that rides my Dreams
VENTIDIUS: Out with it; give it vent.
ANTONY: Urge not my shame.
     I lost a Battel.
VENTIDIUS: So has *Julius* done.
ANTONY: Thou favour'st me, and speak'st not half thou think'st;
     For *Julius* fought it out, and lost it fairly:
     But *Antony* –
VENTIDIUS: Nay, stop not.
ANTONY: *Antony,*
     (Well, thou wilt have it) like a coward, fled,
     Fled while his Soldiers fought; fled first, *Ventidius.*
     Thou long'st to curse me, and I give thee leave.
     I know thou cam'st prepar'd to rail.
VENTIDIUS: I did.
ANTONY: I'll help thee. – I have been a Man, *Ventidius.*
VENTIDIUS: Yes, and a brave one; but –
ANTONY: I know thy meaning.
     But, I have lost my Reason, have disgrac'd
     The name of Soldier, with inglorious ease.
     In the full vintage of my flowing honors,
     Sate still, and saw it prest by other hands.
     Fortune came smiling to my youth, and woo'd it,
     And purple greatness met my ripen'd years.
     When first I came to Empire, I was born
     On Tides of People, crouding to my Triumphs;
     The wish of Nations; and the willing World
     Receiv'd me as its pledge of future peace;
     I was so great, so happy, so belov'd,
     Fate could not ruine me; till I took pains
     And work'd against my Fortune, chid her from me,
     And turn'd her loose; yet still she came again.
     My careless dayes, and my luxurious nights,
     At length have weary'd her, and now she's gone,
     Gone, gone, divorc'd for ever. Help me, Soldier,
     To curse this Mad-man, this industrious Fool,
     Who labour'd to be wretched: pr'ythee curse me.
VENTIDIUS: No.
ANTONY: Why?
VENTIDIUS: You are too sensible already
     Of what y'have done, too conscious of your failings,

And like a Scorpion, whipt by others first
To fury, sting your self in mad revenge.
I would bring Balm, and pour it in your wounds,
  Cure your distemper'd mind, and heal your fortunes.

ANTONY: I know thou would'st.

VENTIDIUS: I will.

ANTONY: Ha, ha, ha, ha.

VENTIDIUS: You laugh.

ANTONY: I do, to see officious love
  Give Cordials to the dead.

VENTIDIUS: You would be lost then?

ANTONY: I am.

VENTIDIUS: I say, you are not. Try your fortune.

ANTONY: I have, to th' utmost. Dost thou think me desperate,
  Without just cause? No, when I found all lost
  Beyond repair, I hid me from the World,
  And learnt to scorn it here; which now I do
  So heartily, I think it is not worth
  The cost of keeping.

VENTIDIUS: *Cæsar* thinks not so:
  He'l thank you for the gift he could not take.
  You would be kill'd, like *Tully*,[1] would you? do,
  Hold out your Throat to *Cæsar,* and dye tamely.

ANTONY: No, I can kill my self; and so resolve.

VENTIDIUS: I can dy with you too, when time shall serve;
  But Fortune calls upon us now to live,
  To fight, to Conquer.

ANTONY: Sure thou Dream'st, *Ventidius.*

VENTIDIUS: No; 'tis you Dream; you sleep away your hours
  In desperate sloth, miscall'd *Phylosophy.*
  Up, up, for Honor's sake; twelve Legions wait you,
  And long to call you Chief: by painful journeys,
  I led 'em, patient, both of heat and hunger,
  Down from the *Parthian* Marches, to the *Nile.*
  'Twill do you good to see their Sun-burnt faces,
  Their skar'd cheeks, and chopt[2] hands; there's virtue in 'em,
  They'l sell those mangled limbs at dearer rates
  Than yon trim Bands[3] can buy.

ANTONY: Where left you them?

VENTIDIUS: I said, in lower *Syria.*

ANTONY: Bring 'em hither;

1. A reference to Cicero, who faced his execution with stoic resolve.
2. Chapped.
3. Octavius's well-equipped forces.

There may be life in these.

VENTIDIUS: They will not come.

ANTONY: Why did'st thou mock my hopes with promis'd aids
　　To double my despair? They'r mutinous.

VENTIDIUS: Most firm and loyal.

ANTONY: Yet they will not march
　　To succor me. Oh trifler!

VENTIDIUS: They petition
　　You would make hast to head 'em.

ANTONY: I'm besieg'd.

VENTIDIUS: There's but one way shut up: How came I hither?

ANTONY: I will not stir.

VENTIDIUS: They would perhaps desire
　　A better reason.

ANTONY: I have never us'd
　　My Soldiers to demand a reason of
　　My actions. Why did they refuse to March?

VENTIDIUS: They said they would not fight for *Cleopatra*.

ANTONY: What was't they said?

VENTIDIUS: They said, they would not fight for *Cleopatra*.
　　Why should they fight indeed, to make her Conquer,
　　And make you more a Slave? to gain you Kingdoms,
　　Which, for a kiss, at your next midnight Feast,
　　You'l sell to her? then she new names her Jewels,
　　And calls this Diamond such or such a Tax,
　　Each Pendant in her ear shall be a Province.

ANTONY: *Ventidius*, I allow your Tongue free licence
　　On all my other faults; but, on your life,
　　No word of *Cleopatra*: She deserves
　　More World's than I can lose.

VENTIDIUS: Behold, you Pow'rs,
　　To whom you have intrusted Humankind;
　　See *Europe*, *Africk*, *Asia* put in ballance,
　　And all weigh'd down by one light worthless Woman!
　　I think the gods are *Antony*'s, and give,
　　Like Prodigals, this neather World away,
　　To none but wastful hands.

ANTONY: You grow presumptuous.

VENTIDIUS: I take the priviledge of plain love to speak.

ANTONY: Plain love! plain arrogance, plain insolence.
　　Thy Men are Cowards; thou, an envious Traitor;
　　Who, under seeming honesty, hast vented
　　The burden of thy rank o'reflowing Gall.
　　O that thou wert my equal; great in Arms
　　As the first *Cæsar* was, that I might kill thee

Without a Stain to Honor!
VENTIDIUS: You may kill me;
    You have done more already, call'd me Traitor.
ANTONY: Art thou not one?
VENTIDIUS: For showing you your self,
    Which none else durst have done; but had I been
    That name, which I disdain to speak again,
    I needed not have sought your abject fortunes,
    Come to partake your fate, to dye with you.
    What hindred me t' have led my Conqu'ring Eagles
    To fill *Octavius*'s Bands? I could have been
    A Traitor then, a glorious happy Traitor,
    And not have been so call'd.
ANTONY: Forgive me, Soldier:
    I've been too passionate.
VENTIDIUS: You thought me false;
    Thought my old age betray'd you: kill me, Sir;
    Pray kill me; yet you need not, your unkindness
    Has left your Sword no work.
ANTONY: I did not think so;
    I said it in my rage: pr'ythee forgive me:
    Why did'st thou tempt my anger, by discovery
    Of what I would not hear?
VENTIDIUS: No Prince but you,
    Could merit that sincerity I us'd,
    Nor durst another Man have ventur'd it;
    But you, ere Love misled your wandring eyes,
    Were sure the chief and best of Human Race,
    Fram'd in the very pride and boast of Nature,
    So perfect, that the gods who form'd you wonder'd
    At their own skill, and cry'd, A lucky hit
    Has mended our design. Their envy hindred,
    Else you had been immortal, and a pattern,
    When Heav'n would work for ostentation sake,
    To copy out again.
ANTONY: But *Cleopatra* –
    Go on; for I can bear it now.
VENTIDIUS: No more.
ANTONY: Thou dar'st not trust my Passion; but thou may'st:
    Thou only lov'st; the rest have flatter'd me.
VENTIDIUS: Heav'n's blessing on your heart, for that kind word.
    May I believe you love me? speak again.
ANTONY: Indeed I do. Speak this, and this, and this. [*Hugging him.*]
    Thy praises were unjust; but, I'll deserve 'em,
    And yet mend all. Do with me what thou wilt;

    Lead me to victory, thou know'st the way.
VENTIDIUS: And, Will you leave this –
ANTONY: Pr'ythee do not curse her,
    And I will leave her; though, Heav'n knows, I love
    Beyond Life, Conquest, Empire; all, but Honor:
    But I will leave her.
VENTIDIUS: That's my Royal Master.
    And, Shall we fight?
ANTONY: I warrant thee, old Soldier,
    Thou shalt behold me once again in Iron,
    And at the head of our old Troops, that beat
    The *Parthians*, cry alloud, Come follow me.
VENTIDIUS: O now I hear my Emperor! in that word
    Octavius fell. Gods, let me see that day,
    And, if I have ten years behind, take all;
    I'll thank you for th' exchange.
ANTONY: Oh *Cleopatra*!
VENTIDIUS: Again?
ANTONY: I've done: in that last sigh, she went.
    Cæsar shall know what 'tis to force a Lover,
    From all he holds most dear.
VENTIDIUS: Methinks you breath
    Another Soul: Your looks are more Divine;
    You speak a Heroe, and you move a God.
ANTONY: O, thou hast fir'd me; my Soul's up in Arms,   ·
    And Mans each part about me: once again,
    That noble eagerness of fight has seiz'd me;
    That eagerness, with which I darted upward
    To *Cassius's* Camp: In vain the steepy Hill,
    Oppos'd my way; in vain a War of Speares
    Sung round my head; and planted all my shield:
    I won the Trenches, while my formost Men
    Lag'd on the Plain below.
VENTIDIUS: Ye Gods, ye Gods,
    For such another hour.
ANTONY: Come on, My Soldier!
    Our hearts and armes are still the same: I long
    Once more to meet our foes; that Thou and I,
    Like Time and Death, marching before our Troops,
    May taste fate to 'em; Mowe 'em out a passage,
    And, entring where the foremost Squadrons yield,
    Begin the noble Harvest of the Field.   [*Exeunt.*]

Act II, Scene I

[CLEOPATRA, IRAS, *and* ALEXAS.]

CLEOPATRA: What shall I do, or whither shall I turn?
    Ventidius has o'rcome, and he will go.
ALEXAS: He goes to fight for you.
CLEOPATRA: Then he wou'd see me, ere he went to fight:
    Flatter me not: if once he goes, he's lost:
    And all my hopes destroy'd.
ALEXAS: Does this weak passion
    Become a Mighty Queen?
CLEOPATRA: I am no Queen;
    Is this to be a Queen, to be besieg'd
    By yon insulting *Roman*; and to wait
    Each hour the Victor's Chain? These ills are small;
    For *Antony* is lost, and I can mourn
    For nothing else but him. Now come, *Octavius*,
    I have no more to lose; prepare thy Bands;
    I'm fit to be a Captive: *Antony*
    Has taught my mind the fortune of a Slave.
IRAS: Call Reason to assist you.
CLEOPATRA: I have none,
    And none would have: my Love's a noble madness,
    Which shows the cause deserv'd it. Moderate sorrow
    Fits vulgar Love; and for a vulgar Man:
    But I have lov'd with such transcendent passion,
    I soard, at first, quite out of Reasons view,
    And now am lost above it – No, I'm proud
    'Tis thus: would *Antony* could see me now;
    Think you he would not sigh? though he must leave me,
    Sure he would sigh; for he is noble-natur'd,
    And bears a tender heart: I know him well.
    Ah, no, I know him not; I knew him once,
    But now 'tis past.
IRAS: Let it be past with you:
    Forget him, Madam.
CLEOPATRA: Never, never, *Iras*.
    He once was mine; and once, though now 'tis gone,
    Leaves a faint Image of possession still.
ALEXAS: Think him unconstant, cruel, and ungrateful.
CLEOPATRA: I cannot: if I could, those thoughts were vain;
    Faithless, ungrateful, cruel, though he be,
    I still must love him.

[*Enter* CHARMION.]

Now, What news my *Charmion*?
Will he be kind? and, Will he not forsake me?
Am I to live, or dye? nay, Do I live?
Or am I dead? for, when he gave his answer,
Fate took the word, and then I liv'd, or dy'd.

CHARMION: I found him, Madam –

CLEOPATRA: A long Speech preparing?
    If thou bring'st comfort, hast, and give it me;
    For never was more need.

IRAS: I know he loves you.

CLEOPATRA: Had he been kind, her eyes had told me so,
    Before her tongue could speak it: now she studies,
    To soften what he said; but give me death,
    Just as he sent it, *Charmion*, undisguis'd,
    And in the words he spoke.

CHARMION: I found him then
    Incompass'd round, I think, with Iron Statues;
    So mute, so motionless his Soldiers stood,
    While awfully he cast his eyes about,
    And ev'ry Leaders hopes or fears survey'd:
    Methought he look'd resolv'd, and yet not pleas'd.
    When he beheld me strugling in the croud,
    He blush'd, and bade, make way.

ALEXAS: There's comfort yet.

CHARMION: *Ventidius* fixt his eyes upon my passage,
    Severely, as he meant to frown me back,
    And sullenly gave place: I told my message,
    Just as you gave it, broken and disorder'd;
    I numbred in it all your sighs and tears:
    And while I mov'd your pitiful request,
    That you but only beg'd a last farewel,
    He fetch'd an inward groan, and ev'ry time
    I nam'd you, sigh'd, as if his heart were breaking,
    But shun'd my eyes, and guiltily look'd down;
    He seem'd not now that awful *Antony*
    Who shook an Arm'd Assembly with his Nod,
    But making show as he would rub his eyes,
    Disguis'd and blotted out a falling tear.

CLEOPATRA: Did he then weep? and, Was I worth a tear?
    If what thou hast to say be not as pleasing,
    Tell me no more, but let me dye contented.

CHARMION: He bid me say, He knew himself so well,
    He could deny you nothing, if he saw you;

And therefore –
CLEOPATRA: Thou would'st say, he wou'd not see me?
CHARMION: And therefore beg'd you not to use a power,
Which he could ill resist; yet he should ever
Respect you as he ought.
CLEOPATRA: Is that a word
For *Antony* to use to *Cleopatra*?
Oh that faint word, Respect! how I disdain it!
Disdain my self, for loving after it!
He should have kept that word for cold *Octavia*.
Respect is for a Wife: Am I that thing,
That dull insipid lump, without desires,
And without pow'r to give 'em.
ALEXAS: You misjudge;
You see through Love, and that deludes your sight;
As, what is strait, seems crooked through the Water;
But I, who bear my reason undisturb'd,
Can see this *Antony*, this dreaded Man,
A fearful slave, who fain would run away,
And shuns his Master's eyes: if you pursue him,
My life on't, he still drags a chain along,
That needs must clog his flight.
CLEOPATRA: Could I believe thee! –
ALEXAS: By ev'ry circumstance I know he Loves.
True, he's hard prest, by Intrest and by Honor;
Yet he but doubts, and parlyes, and casts out
Many a long look for succor.
CLEOPATRA: He sends word,
He fears to see my face.
ALEXAS: And would you more?
He shows his weakness who declines the Combat;
And you must urge your fortune. Could he speak
More plainly? To my ears, the Message sounds
Come to my rescue, *Cleopatra*, come;
Come, free me from *Ventidius*; from my Tyrant:
See me, and give me a pretence to leave him.
I hear his Trumpets. This way he must pass.
Please you, retire a while; I'll work him first,
That he may bend more easie.
CLEOPATRA: You shall rule me;
But all, I fear, in vain. [*Exit with* CHARMION *and* IRAS.]
ALEXAS: I fear so too;
Though I conceal'd my thoughts, to make her bold:
But, 'tis our utmost means, and Fate befriend it. [*Withdraws.*]

[*Enter* LICTORS *with Fasces; one bearing the Eagle: then enter* ANTONY *with* VENTIDIUS, *follow'd by other Commanders.*]

ANTONY: *Octavius* is the Minion of blind Chance,
    But holds from Virtue nothing.
VENTIDIUS: Has he courage?
ANTONY: But just enough to season him from Coward.
    O, 'tis the coldest youth upon a Charge,
    The most deliberate fighter! if he ventures
    (As in *Illyria* once they say he did
    To storm a Town) 'tis when he cannot chuse,
    When all the World have fixt their eyes upon him;
    And then he lives on that for seven years after.
    But, at a close revenge he never fails.
VENTIDIUS: I heard, you challeng'd him.
ANTONY: I did, *Ventidius.*
    What think'st thou was his answer? 'twas so tame, –
    He said he had more wayes than one to dye;
    I had not.
VENTIDIUS: Poor!
ANTONY: He has more wayes than one;
    But he would chuse 'em all before that one.
VENTIDIUS: He first would chuse an Ague, or a Fever.
ANTONY: No: it must be an Ague, not a Fever;
    He has not warmth enough to dye by that.
VENTIDIUS: Or old Age, and a Bed.
ANTONY: I, there's his choice.
    He would live, like a Lamp, to the last wink,
    And crawl upon the utmost verge of life:
    O *Hercules*! Why should a Man like this,
    Who dares not trust his fate for one great action,
    Be all the care of Heav'n? Why should he Lord it
    O're Fourscore thousand Men, of whom, each one
    Is braver than himself?
VENTIDIUS: You conquer'd for him:
    Philippi knows it; there you shar'd with him
    That Empire, which your Sword made all your own.
ANTONY: Fool that I was, upon my Eagles Wings
    I bore this Wren, till I was tir'd with soaring,
    And now he mounts above me.
    Good Heav'ns, Is this, is this the Man who braves me?
    Who bids my age make way: drives me before him,
    To the World's ridge, and sweeps me off like rubbish?
VENTIDIUS: Sir, we lose time; the Troops are mounted all.
ANTONY: Then give the word to March:

I long to leave this Prison of a Town,
To joyn thy Legions; and, in open Field,
Once more to show my face. Lead, my Deliverer.

[*Enter* ALEXAS.]

ALEXAS: Great Emperor,
 In mighty Arms renown'd above Mankind,
 But, in soft pity to th' opprest, a God:
 This message sends the mournful *Cleopatra*
 To her departing Lord.
VENTIDIUS: Smooth Sycophant!
ALEXAS: A thousand wishes, and ten thousand Prayers,
 Millions of blessings wait you to the Wars,
 Millions of sighs and tears she sends you too,
 And would have sent
 As many dear embraces to your Arms,
 As many parting kisses to your Lips;
 But those, she fears, have weary'd you already.
VENTIDIUS: [*aside.*] False Crocodyle!
ALEXAS: And yet she begs not now, you would not leave her,
 That were a wish too mighty for her hopes,
 Too presuming for her low Fortune, and your ebbing love,
 That were a wish for her more prosp'rous dayes,
 Her blooming beauty, and your growing kindness.
ANTONY: [*aside.*] Well, I must Man it out; What would the Queen?
ALEXAS: First, to these noble Warriors, who attend
 Your daring courage in the Chase of Fame,
 (Too daring, and too dang'rous for her quiet)
 She humbly recommends all she holds dear,
 All her own cares and fears, the care of you.
VENTIDIUS: Yes, witness *Actium*.
ANTONY: Let him speak, *Ventidius*.
ALEXAS: You, when his matchless valor bears him forward,
 With ardor too Heroick, on his foes,
 Fall down, as she would do, before his feet;
 Lye in his way, and stop the paths of Death;
 Tell him, this God is not invulnerable,
 That absent *Cleopatra* bleeds in him;
 And, that you may remember her Petition,
 She begs you wear these Trifles, as a pawn,
 Which, at your wisht return, she will redeem

[*Gives Jewels to the Commanders.*]

With all the Wealth of *Ægypt*.
This, to the great *Ventidius* she presents,

Whom she can never count her Enemy,
  Because he loves her Lord.
VENTIDIUS: Tell her I'll none on't;
  I'm not asham'd of honest Poverty:
  Not all the Diamonds of the East can bribe
  Ventidius from his faith. I hope to see
  These, and the rest of all her sparkling store,
  Where they shall more deservingly be plac'd.
ANTONY: And who must wear 'em then?
VENTIDIUS: The wrong'd *Octavia.*
ANTONY: You might have spar'd that word.
VENTIDIUS: And he that Bribe.
ANTONY: But have I no remembrance?
ALEXAS: Yes, a dear one:
  Your slave, the Queen –
ANTONY: My Mistress.
ALEXAS: Then your Mistress,
  Your Mistress would, she sayes, have sent her Soul,
  But that you had long since; she humbly begs
  This Ruby bracelet, set with bleeding hearts,
  (The emblems of her own) may bind your Arme. [*Presenting a Bracelet.*]
VENTIDIUS: Now, my best Lord, in Honor's name, I ask you,
  For Manhood's sake, and for your own dear safety,
  Touch not these poyson'd gifts,
  Infected by the sender, touch 'em not,
  Miriads of blewest Plagues lye underneath 'em,
  And more than Aconite[1] has dipt the Silk.
ANTONY: Nay, now you grow too Cynical, *Ventidius.*
  A Lady's favors may be worn with honor.
  What, to refuse her Bracelet! On my Soul,
  When I lye pensive in my Tent alone,
  'Twill pass the wakeful hours of Winter nights,
  To tell these pretty Beads upon my arm,
  To count for every one a soft embrace,
  A melting kiss at such and such a time;
  And now and then the fury of her love.
  When – And what harm's in this?
ALEXAS: None, none my Lord,
  But what's to her, that now 'tis past for ever.
ANTONY: [*going to tye it.*] We Soldiers are so aukward – help me tye it.
ALEXAS: In faith, my Lord, we Courtiers too are aukward
  In these affairs: so are all Men indeed;
  Ev'n I, who am not one. But shall I speak?

1. A lethal poison, also known as wolfsbane.

ANTONY: Yes, freely.

ALEXAS: Then, my Lord, fair hands alone
 Are fit to tye it; she, who sent it, can.

VENTIDIUS: Hell, Death; this Eunuch Pandar ruins you.
 You will not see her?

[ALEXAS *whispers an Attendant, who goes out.*]

ANTONY: But to take my leave.

VENTIDIUS: Then I have wash'd an *Æthiope.* Y'are undone;
 Y'are in the Toils; y'are taken; y'are destroy'd:
 Her eyes do *Cæsar's* work.

ANTONY: You fear too soon.
 I'm constant to my self: I know my strength;
 And yet she shall not think me Barbarous, neither;
 Born in the depths of *Africk*: I'm a *Roman*,
 Bred to the Rules of soft humanity.
 A guest, and kindly us'd, should bid farewel.

VENTIDIUS: You do not know
 How weak you are to her, how much an Infant;
 You are not proof against a smile, or glance;
 A sigh will quite disarm you.

ANTONY: See, she comes!
 Now you shall find your error. Gods, I thank you:
 I form'd the danger greater than it was,
 And, now 'tis near, 'tis lessen'd.

VENTIDIUS: Mark the end yet.

[*Enter* CLEOPATRA, CHARMION *and* IRAS.]

ANTONY: Well, Madam, we are met.

CLEOPATRA: Is this a Meeting?
 Then, we must part?

ANTONY: We must.

CLEOPATRA: Who sayes we must?

ANTONY: Our own hard fates.

CLEOPATRA: We make those Fates our selves.

ANTONY: Yes, we have made 'em; we have lov'd each other
 Into our mutual ruin.

CLEOPATRA: The Gods have seen my Joys with envious eyes;
 I have no friends in Heav'n; and all the World,
 (As 'twere the bus'ness of Mankind to part us)
 Is arm'd against my Love: ev'n you your self
 Joyn with the rest; you, you are arm'd against me.

ANTONY: I will be justify'd in all I do

To late Posterity, and therefore hear me.
If I mix a lye
With any truth, reproach me freely with it;
Else, favor me with silence.
CLEOPATRA: You command me,
   And I am dumb.
VENTIDIUS: [*aside.*] I like this well: he shows Authority.
ANTONY: That I derive my ruin
   From you alone –
CLEOPATRA: O Heav'ns! I ruin you!
ANTONY: You promis'd me your silence, and you break it
   Ere I have scarce begun.
CLEOPATRA: Well, I obey you.
ANTONY: When I beheld you first, it was in *Ægypt*,
   Ere *Cæsar* saw your Eyes; you gave me love,
   And were too young to know it; that I setled
   Your Father in his Throne, was for your sake:
   I left th' acknowledgment for time to ripen.
   Cæsar stept in, and with a greedy hand
   Pluck'd the green fruit, ere the first blush of red,
   Yet cleaving to the bough. He was my Lord,
   And was, beside, too great for me to rival,
   But, I deserv'd you first, though he enjoy'd you.
   When, after, I beheld you in *Cilicia*,
   An Enemy to *Rome*, I pardon'd you.
CLEOPATRA: I clear'd my self –
ANTONY: Again you break your Promise.
   I lov'd you still, and took your weak excuses,
   Took you into my bosome, stain'd by *Cæsar*,
   And not half mine: I went to *Ægypt* with you
   And hid me from the bus'ness of the World,
   Shut out enquiring Nations from my sight,
   To give whole years to you.
VENTIDIUS: Yes, to your shame be't spoken. [*Aside.*]
ANTONY: How I lov'd
   Witness ye Dayes and Nights, and all your hours,
   That Danc'd away with Down upon your Feet,
   As all your bus'ness were to count my passion.
   One day past by, and nothing saw but Love;
    Another came, and still 'twas only Love:
   The Suns were weary'd out with looking on,
   And I untyr'd with loving.
   I saw you ev'ry day, and all the day;
   And ev'ry day was still but as the first:
   So eager was I still to see you more.

VENTIDIUS: 'Tis all too true.

ANTONY: *Fulvia*, my Wife, grew jealous,
    As she indeed had reason; rais'd a War
    In *Italy*, to call me back.

VENTIDIUS: But yet
    You went not.

ANTONY: While within your arms I lay,
    The World fell mouldring from my hands each hour,
    And left me scarce a grasp (I thank your love for't.)

VENTIDIUS: Well push'd: that last was home.

CLEOPATRA: Yet may I speak?

ANTONY: If I have urg'd a falshood, yes; else, not.
    Your silence says I have not. *Fulvia* dy'd;
    (Pardon, you gods, with my unkindness dy'd)
    To set the World at Peace, I took *Octavia*,
    This *Cæsar's* Sister; in her pride of youth
    And flow'r of Beauty did I wed that Lady,
    Whom blushing I must praise, because I left her.
    You call'd; my Love obey'd the fatal summons:
    This rais'd the *Roman* Arms; the Cause was yours.
    I would have fought by Land, where I was stronger;
    You hindred it: yet, when I fought at Sea,
    Forsook me fighting; and (Oh stain to Honor!
    Oh lasting shame!) I knew not that I fled;
    But fled to follow you.

VENTIDIUS: What haste she made to hoist her purple Sails!
    And, to appear magnificent in flight,
    Drew half our strength away.

ANTONY: All this you caus'd.
    And, Would you multiply more ruins on me?
    This honest Man, my best, my only friend,
    Has gather'd up the Shipwrack of my Fortunes;
    Twelve Legions I have left, my last recruits,
    And you have watch'd the news, and bring your eyes
    To seize them too. If you have ought to answer,
    Now speak, you have free leave.

ALEXAS: [*aside.*]   She stands confounded:
    Despair is in her eyes.

VENTIDIUS: Now lay a Sigh i'th' way, to stop his passage:
    Prepare a Tear, and bid it for his Legions;
    'Tis like they shall be sold.

CLEOPATRA: How shall I plead my cause, when you, my Judge
    Already have condemn'd me? Shall I bring
    The Love you bore me for my Advocate?
    That now is turn'd against me, that destroys me;

For, love once past, is, at the best, forgotten;
But oftner sours to hate: 'twill please my Lord
To ruine me, and therefore I'll be guilty.
But, could I once have thought it would have pleas'd you,
That you would pry, with narrow searching eyes
Into my faults, severe to my destruction,
And watching all advantages with care,
That serve to make me wretched? Speak, my Lord,
For I end here. Though I deserve this usage,
Was it like you to give it?
ANTONY: O you wrong me,
    To think I sought this parting, or desir'd
    To accuse you more than what will clear my self,
    And justifie this breach.
CLEOPATRA: Thus low I thank you.
    And, since my innocence will not offend,
    I shall not blush to own it.
VENTIDIUS: After this I think she'll blush at nothing.
CLEOPATRA: You seem griev'd,
    (And therein you are kind) that *Cæsar* first
    Enjoy'd my love, though you deserv'd it better:
    I grieve for that, my Lord, much more than you;
    For, had I first been yours, it would have sav'd
    My second choice: I never had been his,
    And ne'r had been but yours. But *Cæsar* first,
    You say, possess'd my love. Not so, my Lord:
    He first possess'd my Person; you my Love:
    Cæsar lov'd me; but I lov'd *Antony*.
    If I endur'd him after, 'twas because
    I judg'd it due to the first name of Men;
    And, half constrain'd, I gave, as to a Tyrant,
    What he would take by force.
VENTIDIUS: O Syren! Syren!
    Yet grant that all the love she boasts were true,
    Has she not ruin'd you? I still urge that,
    The fatal consequence.
CLEOPATRA: The consequence indeed,
    For I dare challenge him, my greatest foe,
    To say it was design'd: 'tis true, I lov'd you,
    And kept you far from an uneasie Wife,
    (Such *Fulvia* was.)
    Yes, but he'll say, you left *Octavia* for me; –
    And, Can you blame me to receive that love,
    Which quitted such desert, for worthless me?
    How often have I wish'd some other *Cæsar*,

Great as the first, and as the second young,
Would court my Love to be refus'd for you!

VENTIDIUS: Words, words; but *Actium*, Sir, remember *Actium*.

CLEOPATRA: Ev'n there, I dare his malice. True, I Counsel'd
To fight at Sea; but, I betray'd you not.
I fled; but not to th' Enemy. 'Twas fear;
Would I had been a Man, not to have fear'd,
For none would then have envy'd me your friendship,
Who envy me your Love.

ANTONY: We're both unhappy:
If nothing else, yet our ill fortune parts us.
Speak; Would you have me perish, by my stay?

CLEOPATRA: If as a friend you ask my Judgment, go;
If as a Lover, stay. If you must perish:
'Tis a hard word; but stay.

VENTIDIUS: See now th' effects of her so boasted love!
She strives to drag you down to ruine with her:
But, could she scape without you, oh how soon
Would she let go her hold, and haste to shore,
And never look behind!

CLEOPATRA: Then judge my love by this. [*Giving* ANTONY *a Writing.*]
Could I have born
A life or death, a happiness or woe
From yours divided, this had giv'n me means.

ANTONY: By *Hercules*, the Writing of *Octavius*!
I know it well; 'tis that Proscribing hand,
Young as it was, that led the way to mine,
And left me but the second place in Murder. –
See, see, *Ventidius*! here he offers *Ægypt*,
And joyns all *Syria* to it, as a present,
So, in requital, she forsake my fortunes,
And joyn her Arms with his.

CLEOPATRA: And yet you leave me!
You leave me, *Antony*; and, yet I love you.
Indeed I do: I have refus'd a Kingdom,
That's a Trifle:
For I could part with life; with any thing,
But onely you. O let me dye but with you!
Is that a hard request?

ANTONY: Next living with you,
'Tis all that Heav'n can give.

ALEXAS: [*aside.*]   He melts; We conquer.

CLEOPATRA: No: you shall go: your Int'rest calls you hence;
Yes, your dear int'rest pulls too strong, for these
Weak Armes to hold you here. – [*Takes his hand.*]

Go; leave me, Soldier;
(For you're no more a Lover:) leave me dying:
Push me all pale and panting from your bosome,
And, when your March begins, let one run after,
Breathless almost for Joy, and cry, she's dead:
The Souldiers shout; you then perhaps may sigh,
And muster all your *Roman* Gravity:
Ventidius chides; and strait your Brow cleares up,
As I had never been.

ANTONY: Gods, 'tis too much; too much for Man to bear!

CLEOPATRA: What is't for me then,
A weak forsaken Woman? and a Lover? –
Here let me breathe my last: envy me not
This minute in your Armes: I'll dye apace
As fast as ere I can; and end your trouble,

ANTONY: Dye! Rather let me perish: looss'nd Nature
Leap from its hinges, sink the props of Heav'n,
And fall the Skyes to crush the neather World.
My Eyes, my Soul; my all! –   [*Embraces her.*]

VENTIDIUS: And what's this Toy
In ballance with your fortune, Honor, Fame?

ANTONY: What is't, *Ventidius*? it out-weighs 'em all;
Why, we have more than conquer'd *Cæsar* now:
My Queen's not only Innocent, but Loves me.
This, this is she who drags me down to ruin!
But, could she scape without me, with what haste
Would she let slip her hold, and make to shore,
And never look behind!
Down on thy knees, Blasphemer as thou art,
And ask forgiveness of wrong'd Innocence.

VENTIDIUS: I'll rather dye, than take it. Will you go?

ANTONY: Go! Whither? go from all that's excellent!
Faith, Honor, Virtue, all good things forbid,
That I should go from her, who sets my love
Above the price of Kingdoms. Give, you Gods,
Give to your Boy, your *Cæsar*,
This Rattle of a Globe to play withal,
This Gu-gau World, and put him cheaply off:
I'll not be pleas'd with less than *Cleopatra*.

CLEOPATRA: She's wholly yours. My heart's so full of joy,
That I shall do some wild extravagance
Of Love, in publick; and the foolish World,
Which knows not tenderness, will think me Mad.

VENTIDIUS: O Women! Women! Women! all the gods
Have not such pow'r of doing good to Man,

As you of doing harm.   [*Exit.*]
ANTONY: Our Men are Arm'd.
  Unbar the Gate that looks to *Cæsar's* Camp;
  I would revenge the Treachery he meant me:
  And long security makes Conquest easie.
  I'm eager to return before I go;
  For, all the pleasures I have known, beat thick
  On my remembrance: how I long for night!
  That both the sweets of mutual love may try,
  And once Triumph o're *Cæsar* ere we dye.   [*Exeunt.*]

Act III, Scene I

[At one door, Enter CLEOPATRA, CHARMION, IRAS, *and* ALEXAS, *a Train of*
ÆGYPTIANS: *at the other,* ANTONY *and* ROMANS.
The entrance on both sides is prepar'd by Musick; the Trumpet first sounding on
ANTONY'S *part: then answer'd by Timbrels, &c on* CLEOPATRA'S. CHARMION *and*
IRAS *hold a Laurel Wreath betwixt them. A Dance of* ÆGYPTIANS. *After the*
Ceremony, CLEOPATRA *Crowns* ANTONY.]

ANTONY: I thought how those white arms would fold me in,
    And strain me close, and melt me into love;
    So pleas'd with that sweet Image, I sprung forwards,
    And added all my strength to every blow.
CLEOPATRA: Come to me, come, my Soldier, to my Arms,
    You've been too long away from my embraces;
    But, when I have you fast, and all my own,
    With broken murmurs, and with amorous sighs,
    I'll say, you were unkind, and punish you,
    And mark you red with many an eager kiss.
ANTONY: My Brighter *Venus*!
CLEOPATRA: O my greater *Mars*!
ANTONY: Thou joinst us well, my Love!
    Suppose me come from the *Phlegræan* Plains,[1]
    Where gasping Gyants lay, cleft by my Sword:
    And Mountain tops par'd off each other blow,
    To bury those I slew: receive me, goddess:
    Let *Cæsar* spread his subtile Nets, like *Vulcan*,
    In thy embraces I would be beheld
    By Heav'n and Earth at once:
    And make their envy what they meant their sport.

1. A mythical area where the gods, helped by Hercules, had defeated the giants and
   buried each of them under a volcano.

Let those who took us blush; I would love on
With awful State, regardless of their frowns,
As their superior god.
There's no satiety of Love, in thee;
Enjoy'd, thou still art new; perpetual Spring
Is in thy armes; the ripen'd fruit but falls,
And blossoms rise to fill its empty place;
And I grow rich by giving.

[*Enter* VENTIDIUS, *and stands apart.*]

ALEXAS: O, now the danger's past, your General comes.
    He joyns not in your joys, nor minds your Triumphs;
    But, with contracted brows, looks frowning on,
    As envying your Success.
ANTONY: Now, on my Soul, he loves me; truely loves me;
    He never flatter'd me in any vice,
    But awes me with his virtue: ev'n this minute
    Methinks he has a right of chiding me.
    Lead to the Temple: I'll avoid his presence;
    It checks too strong upon me.   [*Exeunt the rest.*]

[*As* ANTONY *is going,* VENTIDIUS *pulls him by the Robe.*]

VENTIDIUS: Emperor.
ANTONY: [*looking back.*] 'Tis the old argument; I pr'ythee spare me.
VENTIDIUS: But this one hearing, Emperor.
ANTONY: Let go
    My Robe; or, by my Father *Hercules* –
VENTIDIUS: By *Hercules* his Father,[1] that's yet greater,
    I bring you somewhat you would wish to know.
ANTONY: Thou see'st we are observ'd; attend me here,
    And I'll return.   [*Exit.*]
VENTIDIUS: I'm waining in his favor, yet I love him;
    I love this Man, who runs to meet his ruine;
    And, sure the gods, like me, are fond of him:
    His Virtues lye so mingled with his Crimes,
    As would confound their choice to punish one,
    And not reward the other.   [*Enter* ANTONY.]
ANTONY: We can conquer, you see, without your aid.
    We have dislodg'd their Troops,
    They look on us at distance, and, like Curs
    Scap'd from the Lions paws, they bay far off,

1. Jupiter.

And lick their wounds, and faintly threaten War.
Five thousand *Roman*s with their faces upward,
Lye breathless on the Plain.

VENTIDIUS: 'Tis well: and he
Who lost 'em, could have spar'd Ten thousand more.
Yet if, by this advantage, you could gain
An easier Peace, while *Cæsar* doubts the Chance
Of Arms! –

ANTONY: O think not on't, *Ventidius*;
The Boy pursues my ruin, he'll no peace:
His malice is considerate in advantage;
O, he's the coolest Murderer, so stanch,
He kills, and keeps his temper.

VENTIDIUS: Have you no friend
In all his Army, who has power to move him?
Mæcenas, or *Agrippa* might do much.

ANTONY: They're both too deep in *Cæsar's* interests.
We'll work it out by dint of Sword, or perish.

VENTIDIUS: Fain I would find some other.

ANTONY: Thank thy love.
Some four or five such Victories as this,
Will save thy farther pains.

VENTIDIUS: Expect no more; *Cæsar* is on his Guard:
I know, Sir, you have conquer'd against ods;
But still you draw Supplies from one poor Town,
And of *Ægyptians*: he has all the World,
And, at his back, Nations come pouring in,
To fill the gaps you make. Pray think again.

ANTONY: Why dost thou drive me from my self, to search
For Forreign aids? to hunt my memory,
And range all o're a waste and barren place
To find a Friend? The wretched have no Friends –
Yet I had one, the bravest youth of *Rome*,
Whom *Cæsar* loves beyond the love of Women;
He could resolve his mind, as Fire does Wax,
From that hard rugged Image, melt him down,
And mould him in what softer form he pleas'd.

VENTIDIUS: Him would I see; that man of all the world:
Just such a one we want.

ANTONY: He lov'd me too,
I was his Soul; he liv'd not but in me:
We were so clos'd within each others brests,
The rivets were not found that join'd us first.
That does not reach us yet: we were so mixt,
As meeting streams, both to our selves were lost;

We were one mass; we could not give or take,
But from the same; for he was I, I he.
VENTIDIUS: [*aside.*] He moves as I would wish him.
ANTONY: After this,
   I need not tell his name: 'twas *Dollabella*.
VENTIDIUS: He's now in *Cæsar's* Camp.
ANTONY: No matter where,
   Since he's no longer mine. He took unkindly
   That I forbade him *Cleopatra's* sight;
   Because I fear'd he lov'd her: he confest
   He had a warmth, which, for my sake, he stifled;
   For 'twere impossible that two, so one,
   Should not have lov'd the same. When he departed,
   He took no leave; and that confirm'd my thoughts.
VENTIDIUS: It argues that he lov'd you more than her,
    Else he had staid; but he perceiv'd you jealous,
    And would not grieve his friend: I know he loves you.
ANTONY: I should have seen him then ere now.
VENTIDIUS: Perhaps
   He has thus long been lab'ring for your peace.
ANTONY: Would he were here.
VENTIDIUS: Would you believe he lov'd you?
   I read your answer in your eyes; you would.
   Not to conceal it longer, he has sent
   A Messenger from *Cæsar's* Camp, with Letters.
ANTONY: Let him appear.
VENTIDIUS: I'll bring him instantly.

   [*Exit* VENTIDIUS, *and re-enters immediately with* DOLLABELLA.]

ANTONY: 'Tis he himself, himself, by holy Friendship! [*Runs to embrace him.*]
   Art thou return'd at last, my better half?
   Come, give me all my self.
   Let me not live,
   If the young Bridegroom, longing for his night,
   Was ever half so fond.
DOLLABELLA: I must be silent; for my Soul is busie
   About a nobler work: she's new come home,
   Like a long-absent man, and wanders o'er
   Each room, a stranger to her own, to look
   If all be safe.
ANTONY: Thou hast what's left of me.
   For I am now so sunk from what I was,
   Thou find'st me at my lowest water-mark.
   The Rivers that ran in, and rais'd my fortunes,

Are all dry'd up, or take another course:
What I have left is from my native Spring;
I've still a heart that swells, in scorn of fate,
And lifts me to my banks.
DOLLABELLA: Still you are Lord of all the World to me.
ANTONY: Why, then I yet am so; for thou art all.
If I had any joy when thou wert absent,
I grudg'd it to my self; methought I robb'd
Thee of thy part. But, Oh my *Dollabella*!
Thou hast beheld me other than I am.
Hast thou not seen my morning Chambers fill'd
With Scepter'd Slaves, who waited to salute me:
With Eastern Monarchs, who forgot the Sun,
To worship my uprising? Menial Kings
Ran coursing up and down my Palace-yard,
Stood silent in my presence, watch'd my eyes,
And, at my least command, all started out
Like Racers to the Goal.
DOLLABELLA: Slaves to your fortune.
ANTONY: Fortune is *Cæsar's* now; and what am I?
VENTIDIUS: What you have made your self; I will not flatter.
ANTONY: Is this friendly done?
DOLLABELLA: Yes, when his end is so, I must join with him;
Indeed I must, and yet you must not chide:
Why am I else your friend?
ANTONY: Take heed, young man,
How thou upbraid'st my love: the Queen has eyes,
And thou too hast a Soul. Canst thou remember
When, swell'd with hatred, thou beheld'st her first
As accessary to thy Brothers death?
DOLLABELLA: Spare my remembrance; 'twas a guilty day,
And still the blush hangs here.
ANTONY: To clear her self,
For sending him no aid, she came from *Ægypt*.
Her Gally down the Silver *Cydnos* row'd,
The Tackling Silk, the Streamers wav'd with Gold,
The gentle Winds were lodg'd in Purple sails:
Her Nymphs, like *Nereids*, round her Couch, were plac'd;
Where she, another Sea-born *Venus*, lay.
DOLLABELLA: No more: I would not hear it.
ANTONY: O, you must!
She lay, and leant her cheek upon her hand,
And cast a look so languishingly sweet,
As if, secure of all beholders hearts,
Neglecting she could take 'em: Boys, like *Cupids*,

Stood fanning, with their painted wings, the winds
That plaid about her face: but if she smil'd,
A darting glory seem'd to blaze abroad:
That mens desiring eyes were never weary'd;
But hung upon the object: to soft Flutes
The Silver Oars kept time; and while they plaid,
The hearing gave new pleasure to the sight;
And both to thought: 'twas Heav'n, or somewhat more;
For she so charm'd all hearts, that gazing crowds
Stood panting on the shore, and wanted breath
To give their welcome voice.
Then, *Dollabella*, where was then thy Soul?
Was not thy fury quite disarm'd with wonder?
Didst thou not shrink behind me from those eyes,
And whisper in my ear, Oh tell her not
That I accus'd her of my Brothers death?
DOLLABELLA: And should my weakness be a plea for yours?
Mine was an age when love might be excus'd,
When kindly warmth, and when my springing youth
Made it a debt to Nature. Yours –
VENTIDIUS: 　　　　　　　　　　Speak boldly.
Yours, he would say, in your declining age,
When no more heat was left but what you forc'd,
When all the sap was needful for the Trunk,
When it went down, then you constrain'd the course,
And robb'd from Nature, to supply desire;
In you (I would not use so harsh a word)
But 'tis plain dotage.
ANTONY: 　　　　　　　Ha!
DOLLABELLA: 　　　　　　　　　'Twas urg'd too home.
But yet the loss was private that I made;
'Twas but my self I lost: I lost no Legions;
I had no World to lose, no peoples love.
ANTONY: This from a friend?
DOLLABELLA: 　　　　　　　　Yes, *Antony*, a true one;
A friend so tender, that each word I speak
Stabs my own heart, before it reach your ear.
O, judge me not less kind because I chide:
To *Cæsar* I excuse you.
ANTONY: 　　　　　　　O ye Gods!
Have I then liv'd to be excus'd to *Cæsar*?
DOLLABELLA: As to your equal.
ANTONY: 　　　　　　　　　Well, he's but my equal:
While I wear this, he never shall be more.
DOLLABELLA: I bring Conditions from him.

ANTONY: Are they Noble?
   Methinks thou shouldst not bring 'em else; yet he
   Is full of deep dissembling; knows no Honour,
   Divided from his Int'rest. Fate mistook him;
   For Nature meant him for an Usurer:
   He's fit indeed to buy, not conquer Kingdoms.
VENTIDIUS: Then, granting this,
   What pow'r was theirs who wrought so hard a temper
   To honourable Terms!
ANTONY: It was my *Dollabella*, or some God.
DOLLABELLA: Nor I; nor yet *Mæcenas*, nor *Agrippa*:
   They were your Enemies; and I a Friend
   Too weak alone; yet 'twas a *Roman*'s deed.
ANTONY: 'Twas like a *Roman* done: show me that man
   Who has preserv'd my life, my love, my honour;
   Let me but see his face.
VENTIDIUS: That task is mine,
   And, Heav'n thou know'st how pleasing.   [*Exit* VENTIDIUS.]
DOLLABELLA: You'll remember
   To whom you stand oblig'd?
ANTONY: When I forget it,
   Be thou unkind, and that's my greatest curse.
   My Queen shall thank him too.
DOLLABELLA: I fear she will not.
ANTONY: But she shall do't: the Queen, my *Dollabella*!
   Hast thou not still some grudgings of thy Fever?
DOLLABELLA: I would not see her lost.
ANTONY: When I forsake her,
   Leave me, my better Stars; for she has truth
   Beyond her beauty. *Cæsar* tempted her,
   At no less price than Kingdoms, to betray me;
   But she resisted all: and yet thou chid'st me
   For loving her too well. Could I do so?
DOLLABELLA: Yes, there's my reason.

[*Re-enter* VENTIDIUS, *with* OCTAVIA, *leading* ANTONY'S *two little Daughters.*]

ANTONY: Where? – *Octavia* there! [*Starting back.*]
VENTIDIUS: What, is she poyson to you? a Disease?
   Look on her, view her well; and those she brings:
   Are they all strangers to your eyes? has Nature
   No secret call, no whisper they are yours?
DOLLABELLA: For shame, my Lord, if not for love, receive 'em
   With kinder eyes. If you confess a man,
   Meet 'em, embrace 'em, bid 'em welcome to you.

Your arms should open, ev'n without your knowledge,
To clasp 'em in; your feet should turn to wings,
To bear you to 'em; and your eyes dart out,
And aim a kiss ere you could reach the lips.

ANTONY: I stood amaz'd to think how they came hither.

VENTIDIUS: I sent for 'em; I brought 'em in, unknown
　　To *Cleopatra*'s Guards.

DOLLABELLA: 　　　　　　　　Yet are you cold?

OCTAVIA: Thus long I have attended for my welcome;
　　Which, as a stranger, sure I might expect.
　　Who am I?

ANTONY: 　　　*Cæsar's* Sister.

OCTAVIA: 　　　　　　　　　　That's unkind!
　　Had I been nothing more than *Cæsar's* Sister,
　　Know, I had still remain'd in *Cæsar's* Camp;
　　But your *Octavia*, your much injur'd Wife,
　　Tho' banish'd from your Bed, driv'n from your House,
　　In spight of *Cæsar's* Sister, still is yours.
　　'Tis true, I have a heart disdains your coldness,
　　And prompts me not to seek what you should offer;
　　But a Wife's Virtue still surmounts that pride:
　　I come to claim you as my own; to show
　　My duty first, to ask, nay beg, your kindness:
　　Your hand, my Lord; 'tis mine, and I will have it.　　　　[*Taking his hand.*]

VENTIDIUS: Do, take it, thou deserv'st it.

DOLLABELLA: 　　　　　　　　　　On my Soul,
　　And so she does: she's neither too submissive,
　　Nor yet too haughty; but so just a mean,
　　Shows, as it ought, a Wife and *Roman* too.

ANTONY: I fear, *Octavia*, you have begg'd my life.

OCTAVIA: Begg'd it, my Lord?

ANTONY: 　　　　　　　　Yes, begg'd it, my Ambassadress,
　　Poorly and basely begg'd it of your Brother.

OCTAVIA: Poorly and basely I could never beg;
　　Nor could my Brother grant.

ANTONY: Shall I, who, to my kneeling Slave, could say,
　　Rise up, and be a King; shall I fall down
　　And cry, Forgive me, *Cæsar*? shall I set
　　A Man, my Equal, in the place of Jove,
　　As he could give me being? No; that word,
　　Forgive, would choke me up,
　　And die upon my tongue.

DOLLABELLA: 　　　　　　　　You shall not need it.

ANTONY: I will not need it. Come, you've all betray'd me:
　　My Friend too! To receive some vile conditions.

My Wife has bought me, with her prayers and tears;
And now I must become her branded Slave:
In every peevish mood she will upbraid
The life she gave: if I but look awry,
She cries, I'll tell my Brother.
OCTAVIA: My hard fortune
Subjects me still to your unkind mistakes.
But the Conditions I have brought are such
You need not blush to take: I love your Honour,
Because 'tis mine; it never shall be said
Octavia's Husband was her Brothers Slave.
Sir, you are free; free, ev'n from her you loath;
For, tho' my Brother bargains for your love,
Makes me the price and cement of your peace,
I have a Soul like yours; I cannot take
Your love as alms, nor beg what I deserve.
I'll tell my Brother we are reconcil'd;
He shall draw back his Troops, and you shall march
To rule the East: I may be dropt at *Athens*;
No matter where, I never will complain,
But only keep the barren Name of Wife,
And rid you of the trouble.
VENTIDIUS: Was ever such a strife of sullen Honour!
Both scorn to be oblig'd.
DOLLABELLA: O, she has toucht him in the tender'st part;
See how he reddens with despight and shame
To be out-done in Generosity!
VENTIDIUS: See how he winks![1] how he dries up a tear,
That fain would fall!
ANTONY: *Octavia*, I have heard you, and must praise
The greatness of your Soul;
But cannot yield to what you have propos'd:
For I can ne'er be conquer'd but by love;
And you do all for duty. You would free me,
And would be dropt at *Athens*; was't not so?
OCTAVIA: It was, my Lord.
ANTONY: Then I must be oblig'd
To one who loves me not, who, to her self,
May call me thankless and ungrateful Man:
I'll not endure it, no.
VENTIDIUS: [*aside.*]   I'm glad it pinches there.
OCTAVIA: Would you triumph o'er poor *Octavia*'s Virtue?
That pride was all I had to bear me up;

1. Blinks.

That you might think you ow'd me for your life,
And ow'd it to my duty, not my love.
I have been injur'd, and my haughty Soul
Could brook but ill the Man who slights my Bed.
ANTONY: Therefore you love me not.
OCTAVIA: Therefore, my Lord,
I should not love you.
ANTONY: Therefore you wou'd leave me?
OCTAVIA: And therefore I should leave you – if I could.
DOLLABELLA: Her Souls too great, after such injuries,
To say she loves; and yet she lets you see it.
Her modesty and silence plead her cause.
ANTONY: O, *Dollabella*, which way shall I turn?
I find a secret yielding in my Soul;
But *Cleopatra*, who would die with me,
Must she be left? Pity pleads for *Octavia*;
But does it not plead more for *Cleopatra*?
VENTIDIUS: Justice and Pity both plead for *Octavia*;
For *Cleopatra*, neither,
One would be ruin'd with you; but she first
Had ruin'd you: the other, you have ruin'd,
And yet she would preserve you.
In every thing their merits are unequal.
ANTONY: O, my distracted Soul!
OCTAVIA: Sweet Heav'n compose it.
Come, come, my Lord, if I can pardon you,
Methinks you should accept it. Look on these;
Are they not yours? Or stand they thus neglected
As they are mine? Go to him, Children, go;
Kneel to him, take him by the hand, speak to him;
For you may speak, and he may own you too,
Without a blush; and so he cannot all
His Children: go, I say, and pull him to me,
And pull him to your selves, from that bad Woman.
You, *Agrippina*, hang upon his arms;
And you, *Antonia*, clasp about his waste:
If he will shake you off, if he will dash you
Against the Pavement, you must bear it, Children;
For you are mine, and I was born to suffer.

[*Here the Children go to him, &c.*]

VENTIDIUS: Was ever sight so moving! Emperor!
DOLLABELLA: Friend!
OCTAVIA: Husband!

BOTH CHILDREN: Father!
ANTONY:I am vanquish'd: take me,
    Octavia; take me, Children; share me all.   [*Embracing them.*]
    I've been a thriftless Debtor to your loves,
    And run out much, in riot, from your stock;
    But all shall be amended.
OCTAVIA: O blest hour!
DOLLABELLA: O happy change!
VENTIDIUS: My joy stops at my tongue;
    But it has found two chanels here for one,
    And bubbles out above.
ANTONY: [*to* OCTAVIA.] This is thy Triumph; lead me where thou wilt;
    Ev'n to thy Brothers Camp.
OCTAVIA: All there are yours.

[*Enter* ALEXAS *hastily.*]

ALEXAS: The Queen, my Mistress, Sir, and yours –
 ANTONY: 'Tis past.
    Octavia, you shall stay this night; To morrow,
    Cæsar and we are one.

[*Exit leading* OCTAVIA; DOLLABELLA *and the Children follow.*]

VENTIDIUS: There's news for you; run, my officious Eunuch,
    Be sure to be the first; haste foreward:
    Haste, my dear Eunuch, haste.   [*Exit.*]
ALEXAS: This downright fighting Fool, this thick-scull'd Hero,
    This blunt unthinking Instrument of death,
    With plain dull Virtue, has out-gone my Wit:
    Pleasure forsook my early'st Infancy,
    The luxury of others robb'd my Cradle,
    And ravish'd thence the promise of a Man:
    Cast out from Nature, disinherited
    Of what her meanest Children claim by kind;
    Yet, greatness kept me from contempt: that's gone.
    Had *Cleopatra* follow'd my advice,
    Then he had been betray'd, who now forsakes.
    She dies for love; but she has known its joys:
    Gods, is this just, that I, who know no joys,
    Must die, because she loves?

[*Enter* CLEOPATRA, CHARMION, IRAS, *Train.*]

Oh, Madam, I have seen what blasts my eyes!
Octavia's here!

CLEOPATRA: Peace with that Raven's note.
　　I know it too; and now am in
　　The pangs of death.
ALEXAS: You are no more a Queen;
　　Ægypt is lost.
CLEOPATRA: What tell'st thou me of *Ægypt*!
　　My Life, my Soul is lost! *Octavia* has him!
　　O fatal name to *Cleopatra*'s love!
　　My kisses, my embraces now are hers;
　　While I – But thou hast seen my Rival; speak,
　　Does she deserve this blessing? Is she fair,
　　Bright as a Goddess? and is all perfection
　　Confin'd to her? It is. Poor I was made
　　Of that course matter which, when she was finish'd,
　　The Gods threw by, for rubbish.
ALEXAS: She's indeed a very Miracle.
CLEOPATRA: Death to my hopes, a Miracle!
ALEXAS: [*bowing.*]   A Miracle;
　　I mean of Goodness; for in Beauty, Madam,
　　You make all wonders cease.
CLEOPATRA: I was too rash:
　　Take this in part of recompence. But, Oh,   [*Giving a Ring.*]
　　I fear thou flatter'st me.
CHARMION: She comes! she's here!
IRAS: Flie, Madam, *Cæsar's* Sister!
CLEOPATRA: Were she the Sister of the Thund'rer *Jove*,
　　And bore her Brothers Lightning in her eyes,
　　Thus would I face my Rival.

　　　　　[*Meets* OCTAVIA *with* VENTIDIUS. OCTAVIA *bears up to her.*
　　　　　　Their Trains come up on either side.]

OCTAVIA: I need not ask if you are *Cleopatra*,
　　Your haughty carriage –
CLEOPATRA: Shows I am a Queen:
　　Nor need I ask you who you are.
OCTAVIA: A *Roman*:
　　A name that makes, and can unmake a Queen.
CLEOPATRA: Your Lord, the Man who serves me, is a *Roman*.
OCTAVIA: He was a *Roman*, till he lost that name
　　To be a Slave in *Ægypt*; but I come
　　To free him thence.
CLEOPATRA: Peace, peace, my Lover's *Juno*.[1]

1. Juno was the wife of Jupiter, who suffered greatly from her husband's infidelities.

When he grew weary of that Houshold-Clog,
He chose my easier bonds.

OCTAVIA: I wonder not
Your bonds are easie; you have long been practis'd
In that lascivious art: he's not the first
For whom you spread your snares: let *Cæsar* witness.

CLEOPATRA: I lov'd not *Cæsar*; 'twas but gratitude
I paid his love: the worst your malice can,
Is but to say the greatest of Mankind
Has been my Slave. The next, but far above him,
In my esteem, is he whom Law calls yours,
But whom his love made mine.

OCTAVIA: [*coming up close to her.*] I would view nearer
That face, which has so long usurp'd my right,
To find th' inevitable charms, that catch
Mankind so sure, that ruin'd my dear Lord.

CLEOPATRA: O, you do well to search; for had you known
But half these charms, you had not lost his heart.

OCTAVIA: Far be their knowledge from a *Roman* Lady,
Far from a modest Wife. Shame of our Sex,
Dost thou not blush, to own those black endearments
That make sin pleasing?

CLEOPATRA: You may blush, who want 'em.
If bounteous Nature, if indulgent Heav'n
Have giv'n me charms to please the bravest Man;
Should I not thank 'em? should I be asham'd,
And not be proud? I am, that he has lov'd me;
And, when I love not him, Heav'n change this Face
For one like that.

OCTAVIA: Thou lov'st him not so well.

CLEOPATRA: I love him better, and deserve him more.

OCTAVIA: You do not; cannot: you have been his ruine.
Who made him cheap at *Rome*, but *Cleopatra*?
Who made him scorn'd abroad, but *Cleopatra*?
At *Actium*, who betray'd him? *Cleopatra*.
Who made his Children Orphans? and poor me
A wretched Widow? only *Cleopatra*.

CLEOPATRA: Yet she who loves him best is *Cleopatra*.
If you have suffer'd, I have suffer'd more.
You bear the specious Title of a Wife,
To guild your Cause, and draw the pitying World
To favour it: the World contemns poor me;
For I have lost my Honour, lost my Fame,
And stain'd the glory of my Royal House,
And all to bear the branded Name of Mistress.

There wants but life, and that too I would lose
For him I love.

OCTAVIA: Be't so then; take thy wish.   [*Exit cum suis.*]

CLEOPATRA: And 'tis my wish,
Now he is lost for whom alone I liv'd.
My sight grows dim, and every object dances,
And swims before me, in the maze of death.
My spirits, while they were oppos'd, kept up;
They could not sink beneath a Rivals scorn:
But now she's gone they faint.

ALEXAS: Mine have had leisure
To recollect their strength, and furnish counsel,
To ruine her; who else must ruine you.

CLEOPATRA: Vain Promiser!
Lead me, my *Charmion*; nay, your hand too, *Iras*:
My grief has weight enough to sink you both.
Conduct me to some solitary Chamber,
And draw the Curtains round;
Then leave me to my self, to take alone
My fill of grief:
There I till death will his unkindness weep:
As harmless Infants moan themselves asleep.   [*Exeunt.*]

Act IV, Scene I

[*Enter* ANTONY, DOLLABELLA.]

DOLLABELLA: Why would you shift it from your self, on me?
Can you not tell her you must part?

ANTONY: I cannot.
I could pull out an eye, and bid it go,
And t'other should not weep. Oh, *Dollabella*,
How many deaths are in this word *Depart*!
I dare not trust my tongue to tell her so:
One look of hers, would thaw me into tears
And I should melt till I were lost agen.

DOLLABELLA: Then let *Ventidius*;
He's rough by nature.

ANTONY: Oh, he'll speak too harshly;
He'll kill her with the news: Thou, only thou.

DOLLABELLA: Nature has cast me in so soft a mould,
That but to hear a story feign'd for pleasure
Of some sad Lovers death, moistens my eyes,

And robs me of my Manhood. – I should speak
So faintly; with such fear to grieve her heart,
She'd not believe it earnest.
ANTONY: Therefore, therefore
Thou only, thou art fit: think thy self me,
And when thou speak'st (but let it first be long)
Take off the edge from every sharper sound,
And let our parting be as gently made
As other Loves begin: wilt thou do this?
DOLLABELLA: What you have said, so sinks into my Soul,
That, if I must speak, I shall speak just so.
ANTONY: I leave you then to your sad task: Farewel.
I sent her word to meet you.   [*Goes to the door, and comes back.*]
                            I forgot;
Let her be told, I'll make her peace with mine:
Her Crown and Dignity shall be preserv'd,
If I have pow'r with *Cæsar.* – O, be sure
To think on that.
DOLLABELLA: Fear not, I will remember.

[ANTONY *goes again to the door, and comes back.*]

ANTONY: And tell her, too, how much I was constrain'd;
I did not this, but with extreamest force:
Desire her not to hate my memory,
For I still cherish hers; – insist on that.
DOLLABELLA: Trust me, I'll not forget it.
ANTONY: Then that's all.

[*Goes out, and returns again.*]

Wilt thou forgive my fondness this once more?
Tell her, tho' we shall never meet again,
If I should hear she took another Love,
The news would break my heart. – Now I must go;
For every time I have return'd, I feel
My Soul more tender; and my next command
Would be to bid her stay, and ruine both.   [*Exit.*]
DOLLABELLA: Men are but Children of a larger growth,
Our appetites as apt to change as theirs,
And full as craving too, and full as vain;
And yet the Soul, shut up in her dark room,
Viewing so clear abroad, at home sees nothing;
But, like a Mole in Earth, busie and blind,
Works all her folly up, and casts it outward
To the Worlds open view: thus I discover'd,
And blam'd the love of ruin'd *Antony;*

Yet wish that I were he, to be so ruin'd.

[*Enter* VENTIDIUS *above.*]

VENTIDIUS: Alone? and talking to himself? concern'd too?
　　Perhaps my ghess is right; he lov'd her once,
　　And may pursue it still.
DOLLABELLA:　　　　　　　　O Friendship! Friendship!
　　Ill canst thou answer this; and Reason, worse:
　　Unfaithful in th' attempt; hopeless to win;
　　And, if I win, undone: meer madness all.
　　And yet th' occasion's fair. What injury,
　　To him, to wear the Robe which he throws by?
VENTIDIUS: None, none at all. This happens as I wish,
　　To ruine her yet more with *Antony*.

[*Enter* CLEOPATRA, *talking with* ALEXAS; CHARMION, IRAS *on the other side.*]

DOLLABELLA: She comes! What charms have sorrow on that face!
　　Sorrow seems pleas'd to dwell with so much sweetness;
　　Yet, now and then, a melancholy smile
　　Breaks loose, like Lightning, in a Winter's night,
　　And shows a moments day.
VENTIDIUS: If she should love him too! Her Eunuch there!
　　That *Porcpisce*[1] bodes ill weather. Draw, draw nearer,
　　Sweet Devil, that I may hear.
ALEXAS:　　　　　　　　　　Believe me; try

[DOLLABELLA *goes over to* CHARMION *and* IRAS; *seems to talk with them.*]

　　To make him jealous; jealousie is like
　　A polisht Glass held to the lips when life's in doubt:
　　If there be breath, 'twill catch the damp and show it.
CLEOPATRA: I grant you jealousie's a proof of love,
　　But 'tis a weak and unavailing Med'cine;
　　It puts out the disease, and makes it show,
　　But has no pow'r to cure.
ALEXAS: 'Tis your last remedy, and strongest too:
　　And then this *Dollabella*, who so fit
　　To practice on? He's handsom, valiant, young,
　　And looks as he were laid for Nature's bait
　　To catch weak Womens eyes.
　　He stands already more than half suspected
　　Of loving you: the least kind word, or glance,

1. Porpoise.

You give this Youth, will kindle him with love:
Then, like a burning Vessel set adrift,
You'll send him down amain before the wind,
To fire the heart of jealous *Antony*.

CLEOPATRA: Can I do this? Ah no; my love's so true,
That I can neither hide it where it is,
Nor show it where it is not. Nature meant me
A Wife, a silly harmless houshold Dove,
Fond without art; and kind without deceit;
But Fortune, that has made a Mistress of me,
Has thrust me out to the wide World, unfurnish'd
Of falshood to be happy.

ALEXAS: Force your self.
Th' event will be, your Lover will return
Doubly desirous to possess the good
Which once he fear'd to lose.

CLEOPATRA: I must attempt it;
But Oh with what regret!   [*Exit* ALEXAS. *She comes up to* DOLLABELLA.]

VENTIDIUS: So, now the Scene draws near; they're in my reach.

CLEOPATRA: [*to* DOLLABELLA.] Discoursing with my Women! Might not I
Share in your entertainment?

CHARMION: You have been
The Subject of it, Madam.

CLEOPATRA: How; and how?

IRAS: Such praises of your beauty!

CLEOPATRA: Meer Poetry.
Your *Roman* Wits, your *Gallus*[1] and *Tibullus*,[2]
Have taught you this from *Citheris* and *Delia*.

DOLLABELLA: Those *Roman* Wits have never been in *Ægypt*,
Citheris and *Delia* else had been unsung:
I, who have seen – had I been born a Poet,
Should chuse a nobler name.

CLEOPATRA: You flatter me.
But, 'tis your Nation's vice: all of your Country
Are flatterers, and all false. Your Friend's like you.
I'm sure he sent you not to speak these words.

DOLLABELLA: No, Madam; yet he sent me –

CLEOPATRA: Well, he sent you –

DOLLABELLA: Of a less pleasing errand.

CLEOPATRA: How less pleasing?
Less to your self, or me?

DOLLABELLA: Madam, to both;

1. Gallus wrote love poetry to the courtesan Cytheris.
2. Tibullus wrote in his elegies of his faithless mistress Delia.

For you must mourn, and I must grieve to cause it.

CLEOPATRA: You, *Charmion*, and your Fellow, stand at distance.

[*Aside.*] Hold up, my Spirits. – Well, now your mournful matter;

For I'm prepar'd, perhaps can ghess it too.

DOLLABELLA: I wish you would; for 'tis a thankless office

To tell ill news: and I, of all your Sex,

Most fear displeasing you.

CLEOPATRA: Of all your Sex,

I soonest could forgive you, if you should.

VENTIDIUS: Most delicate advances! Woman! Woman!

Dear damn'd, inconstant Sex!

CLEOPATRA: In the first place,

I am to be forsaken; is't not so?

DOLLABELLA: I wish I could not answer to that question.

CLEOPATRA: Then pass it o'er, because it troubles you:

I should have been more griev'd another time.

Next, I'm to lose my Kingdom. – Farewel, *Ægypt*.

Yet, is there any more?

DOLLABELLA: Madam, I fear

Your too deep sense of grief has turn'd your reason.

CLEOPATRA: No, no, I'm not run mad; I can bear Fortune:

And Love may be expell'd by other Love,

As Poysons are by Poysons.

DOLLABELLA: You o'erjoy me, Madam,

To find your griefs so moderately born.

You've heard the worst; all are not false, like him.

CLEOPATRA: No; Heav'n forbid they should.

DOLLABELLA: Some men are constant.

CLEOPATRA: And constancy deserves reward, that's certain.

DOLLABELLA: Deserves it not; but give it leave to hope

VENTIDIUS: I'll swear thou hast my leave. I have enough:

But how to manage this! Well, I'll consider.   [*Exit.*]

DOLLABELLA: I came prepar'd,

To tell you heavy news; news, which I thought,

Would fright the blood from your pale cheeks to hear:

But you have met it with a cheerfulness

That makes my task more easie; and my tongue,

Which on anothers message was employ'd,

Would gladly speak its own.

CLEOPATRA: Hold, *Dollabella*.

First tell me, were you chosen by my Lord?

Or sought you this employment?

DOLLABELLA: He pick'd me out; and, as his bosom-friend,

He charg'd me with his words.

CLEOPATRA: The message then

I know was tender, and each accent smooth,
To mollifie that rugged word *Depart*.
DOLLABELLA: Oh, you mistake: he chose the harshest words,
With fiery eyes, and with contracted brows,
He coyn'd his face in the severest stamp:
And fury, shook his Fabrick like an Earthquake;
He heav'd for vent, and burst like bellowing *Ætna*,
In sounds scarce humane, 'Hence, away for ever:
Let her begone, the blot of my renown,
And bane of all my hopes:

    [*All the time of this speech,* CLEOPATRA *seems more and more concern'd,*
                  till she sinks quite down.]

Let her be driv'n as far as men can think
From Mans commerce: She'll poyson to the Center.'
CLEOPATRA: Oh, I can bear no more!
DOLLABELLA: Help, help! Oh Wretch! Oh cursed, cursed Wretch!
    What have I done!
CHARMION: Help, chafe her Temples, *Iras*.
IRAS: Bend, bend her forward quickly.
CHARMION: Heav'n be prais'd,
    She comes again.
CLEOPATRA: Oh, let him not approach me.
Why have you brought me back to this loath'd Being,
Th' abode of Falshood, violated Vows,
And injur'd Love? For pity, let me go;
For, if there be a place of long repose,
I'm sure I want it. My disdainful Lord
Can never break that quiet; nor awake
The sleeping Soul, with hollowing in my Tomb
Such words as fright her hence. Unkind, unkind.
DOLLABELLA: [*kneeling.*] Believe me, 'tis against my self I speak;
That sure deserves belief; I injur'd him:
My Friend ne'er spoke those words. Oh, had you seen
How often he came back, and every time
With something more obliging and more kind,
To add to what he said; what dear Farewels;
How almost vanquisht by his love he parted,
And lean'd to what unwillingly he left:
I, Traitor as I was, for love of you,
(But what can you not do, who made me false!)
I forg'd that lye; for whose forgiveness kneels
This self-accus'd, self-punish'd Criminal.
CLEOPATRA: With how much ease believe we what we wish!
    Rise, *Dollabella*; if you have been guilty,

I have contributed, and too much love
Has made me guilty too.
Th' advance of kindness which I made, was feign'd,
To call back fleeting love by jealousie;
But 'twould not last. Oh, rather let me lose
Than so ignobly trifle with his heart.

DOLLABELLA: I find your breast fenc'd round from humane reach,
Transparent as a Rock of solid Crystal;
Seen through, but never pierc'd. My Friend, my Friend!
What endless treasure hast thou thrown away,
And scatter'd, like an Infant, in the Ocean,
Vain sums of Wealth which none can gather thence.

CLEOPATRA: Could you not beg
An hours admittance to his private ear?
Like one who wanders through long barren Wilds,
And yet foreknows no hospitable Inn
Is near to succour hunger,
Eats his fill, before his painful march:
So would I feed a while my famish'd eyes
Before we part; for I have far to go,
If death be far, and never must return.

[*Enter* VENTIDIUS, *with* OCTAVIA, *behind.*]

VENTIDIUS: From hence you may discover – Oh, sweet, sweet!
Would you indeed? the pretty hand in earnest?

DOLLABELLA: [*takes her hand.*] I will, for this reward. – Draw it not back,
'Tis all I e'er will beg.

VENTIDIUS: They turn upon us.

OCTAVIA: What quick eyes has guilt!

VENTIDIUS: Seem not to have observ'd 'em, and go on.   [*They come forward.*]

DOLLABELLA: Saw you the Emperor, *Ventidius*?

VENTIDIUS: No.
I sought him; but I heard that he was private,
None with him, but *Hipparchus* his Freedman.

DOLLABELLA: Know you his bus'ness?

VENTIDIUS: Giving him Instructions,
And Letters, to his Brother *Cæsar*.

DOLLABELLA: Well,
He must be found.   [*Exeunt* DOLABELLA *and* CLEOPATRA.]

OCTAVIA: Most glorious impudence!

VENTIDIUS: She look'd methought
As she would say, Take your old man, Octavia;
Thank you, I'm better here. Well, but what use
Make we of this discovery?

OCTAVIA: Let it die.
VENTIDIUS: I pity *Dollabella*; but she's dangerous:
    Her eyes have pow'r beyond *Thessalian* Charms
    To draw the Moon from Heav'n; for Eloquence,
    The Sea-green Syrens taught her voice their flatt'ry;
    And, while she speaks, Night steals upon the Day,
    Unmark'd of those that hear: Then she's so charming,
    Age buds at sight of her, and swells to youth:
    The holy Priests gaze on her when she smiles;
    And with heav'd hands forgetting gravity,
    They bless her wanton eyes: Even I who hate her,
    With a malignant joy behold such beauty;
    And, while I curse, desire it. *Antony*
    Must needs have some remains of passion still,
    Which may ferment into a worse relapse,
    If now not fully cur'd. I know, this minute,
    With *Cæsar* he's endeavouring her peace.
OCTAVIA: You have prevail'd: – but for a farther purpose   *[Walks off.]*
    I'll prove how he will relish this discovery.
    What, make a Strumpet's peace! it swells my heart:
    It must not, sha' not be.
VENTIDIUS: His Guards appear.
    Let me begin, and you shall second me.

[Enter ANTONY.]

ANTONY: *Octavia*, I was looking you, my love:
    What, are your Letters ready? I have giv'n
    My last Instructions.
OCTAVIA: Mine, my Lord, are written.
ANTONY: *Ventidius!*   *[Drawing him aside.]*
VENTIDIUS: My Lord?
ANTONY: A word in private.
    When saw you *Dollabella?*
VENTIDIUS: Now, my Lord,
    He parted hence; and *Cleopatra* with him.
ANTONY: Speak softly. 'Twas by my command he went,
    To bear my last farewel.
VENTIDIUS: *[aloud.]* It look'd indeed
    Like your farewel.
ANTONY: More softly. – My farewel?
    What secret meaning have you in those words
    Of my Farewel? He did it by my Order.
VENTIDIUS: *[aloud.]* Then he obey'd your Order. I suppose
    You bid him do it with all gentleness,

All kindness, and all – love.

ANTONY: How she mourn'd, the poor forsaken Creature!

VENTIDIUS: She took it as she ought; she bore your parting
    As she did *Cæsar's*, as she would anothers,
    Were a new Love to come.

ANTONY: [*aloud.*]   Thou dost belye her;
    Most basely, and maliciously belye her.

VENTIDIUS: I thought not to displease you; I have done.

OCTAVIA: [*coming up.*] You seem disturb'd, my Lord.

ANTONY: A very trifle.
    Retire, my Love.

VENTIDIUS: It was indeed a trifle.
    He sent –

ANTONY: [*angrily.*] No more. Look how thou disobey'st me;
    Thy life shall answer it.

OCTAVIA: Then 'tis no trifle.

VENTIDIUS: [*to* OCTAVIA.] 'Tis less; a very nothing: you too saw it,
    As well as I, and therefore 'tis no secret.

ANTONY: She saw it!

VENTIDIUS: Yes: she saw young *Dollabella* –

ANTONY: Young *Dollabella*!

VENTIDIUS: Young, I think him young,
    And handsom too; and so do others think him.
    But what of that? He went by your command,
    Indeed 'tis probable, with some kind message;
    For she receiv'd it graciously; she smil'd:
    And then he grew familiar with her hand,
    Squeez'd it, and worry'd it with ravenous kisses;
    She blush'd, and sigh'd, and smil'd, and blush'd again;
    At last she took occasion to talk softly,
    And brought her cheek up close, and lean'd on his:
    At which, he whisper'd kisses back on hers;
    And then she cry'd aloud, That constancy
    Should be rewarded.

OCTAVIA: This I saw and heard.

ANTONY: What Woman was it, whom you heard and saw
    So playful with my Friend! Not *Cleopatra*?

VENTIDIUS: Ev'n she, my Lord!

ANTONY: My *Cleopatra*?

VENTIDIUS: Your *Cleopatra*;
    Dollabella's Cleopatra:
    Every Man's *Cleopatra*.

ANTONY: Thou ly'st.

VENTIDIUS: I do not lye, my Lord.
    Is this so strange? Should Mistresses be left,

And not provide against a time of change?
You know she's not much us'd to lonely nights.
ANTONY: I'll think no more on't.
    I know 'tis false, and see the plot betwixt you.
    You needed not have gone this way, *Octavia*.
    What harms it you that *Cleopatra*'s just?
    She's mine no more. I see; and I forgive:
    Urge it no farther, Love.
OCTAVIA: Are you concern'd
    That she's found false?
ANTONY: I should be, were it so;
    For, tho 'tis past, I would not that the World
    Should tax my former choice: That I lov'd one
    Of so light note; but I forgive you both.
VENTIDIUS: What has my age deserv'd, that you should think
    I would abuse your ears with perjury?
    If Heav'n be true, she's false.
ANTONY: Tho Heav'n and Earth
    Should witness it, I'll not believe her tainted.
VENTIDIUS: I'll bring you then a Witness
    From Hell to prove her so. Nay, go not back;

        [*Seeing* ALEXAS *just entring, and starting back.*]

For stay you must and shall.
ALEXAS: What means my Lord?
VENTIDIUS: To make you do what most you hate; speak truth.
    You are of *Cleopatra*'s private
    Counsel, Of her Bed-Counsel, her lascivious hours;
    Are conscious of each nightly change she makes,
    And watch her, as *Chaldeans* do the Moon,
    Can tell what Signs she passes through, what day.
ALEXAS: My Noble Lord.
VENTIDIUS: My most Illustrious Pandar,
    No fine set Speech, no Cadence, no turn'd Periods,
    But a plain home-spun Truth, is what I ask:
    I did, my self, o'erhear your Queen make love
    To *Dollabella*. Speak; for I will know,
    By your confession, what more past betwixt 'em;
    How near the bus'ness draws to your employment;
    And when the happy hour.
ANTONY: Speak truth, *Alexas*, whether it offend
    Or please *Ventidius*, care not: justifie
    Thy injur'd Queen from malice: dare his worst.
OCTAVIA: [*aside.*] See, how he gives him courage! how he fears
    To find her false! and shuts his eyes to truth,

Willing to be misled!

ALEXAS: As far as love may plead for Woman's frailty,
    Urg'd by desert and greatness of the Lover;
    So far (Divine *Octavia!*) may my Queen
    Stand ev'n excus'd to you, for loving him,
    Who is your Lord: so far, from brave *Ventidius*,
    May her past actions hope a fair report.

ANTONY: 'Tis well, and truly spoken: mark, *Ventidius*.

ALEXAS: To you, most Noble Emperor, her strong passion
    Stands not excus'd, but wholly justifi'd.
    Her Beauty's charms alone, without her Crown,
    From *Ind* and *Meroe*[1] drew the distant vows
    Of sighing Kings; and at her feet were laid
    The Scepters of the Earth, expos'd on heaps,
    To choose where she would Reign:
    She thought a *Roman* only could deserve her;
    And, of all *Romans*, only *Antony*.
    And, to be less than Wife to you, disdain'd
    Their lawful passion.

ANTONY: 'Tis but truth.

ALEXAS: And yet, tho love, and your unmatch'd desert,
    Have drawn her from the due regard of Honor,
    At last, Heav'n open'd her unwilling eyes
    To see the wrongs she offer'd fair *Octavia*,
    Whose holy Bed she lawlesly usurpt;
    The sad effects of this improsperous War,
    Confirm'd those pious thoughts.

VENTIDIUS: [*aside.*]   O, wheel you there?
    Observe him now; the Man begins to mend,
    And talk substantial reason. Fear not, Eunuch,
    The Emperor has giv'n thee leave to speak.

ALEXAS: Else had I never dar'd t'offend his ears
    With what the last necessity has urg'd
    On my forsaken Mistress; yet I must not
    Presume to say her heart is wholly alter'd.

ANTONY: No, dare not for thy life, I charge thee dare not,
    Pronounce that fatal word.

OCTAVIA: [*aside.*] Must I bear this? good Heav'n, afford me patience.

VENTIDIUS: On, sweet Eunuch; my dear half man, proceed.

ALEXAS: Yet *Dollabella*
    Has lov'd her long: he, next my God-like Lord,
    Deserves her best; and should she meet his passion,
    Rejected, as she is, by him she lov'd –

1. India and the upper Nile.

ANTONY: Hence, from my sight; for I can bear no more:
    Let Furies drag thee quick to Hell; let all
    The longer damn'd have rest; each torturing hand
    Do thou employ, till *Cleopatra* comes,
    Then joyn thou too, and help to torture her.
                [*Exit* ALEXAS, *thrust out by* ANTONY.]
OCTAVIA: 'Tis not well,
    Indeed, my Lord, 'tis much unkind to me,
    To show this passion, this extream concernment
    For an abandon'd, faithless Prostitute.
ANTONY: *Octavia*, leave me: I am much disorder'd.
    Leave me, I say.
OCTAVIA: My Lord?
ANTONY: I bid you leave me.
VENTIDIUS: Obey him, Madam: best withdraw a while,
    And see how this will work.
OCTAVIA: Wherein have I offended you, my Lord,
    That I am bid to leave you? Am I false,
    Or infamous? Am I a *Cleopatra*?
    Were I she,
    Base as she is, you would not bid me leave you;
    But hang upon my neck, take slight excuses,
    And fawn upon my falshood.
ANTONY: 'Tis too much,
    Too much, *Octavia*; I am prest with sorrows
    Too heavy to be born; and you add more:
    I would retire, and recollect what's left
    Of Man within, to aid me.
OCTAVIA: You would mourn
    In private, for your Love, who has betray'd you;
    You did but half return to me: your kindness
    Linger'd behind with her. I hear, my Lord,
    You make Conditions for her,
    And would include her Treaty. Wondrous proofs
    Of love to me!
ANTONY: Are you my Friend, *Ventidius*?
    Or are you turn'd a *Dollabella* too,
    And let this Fury loose?
VENTIDIUS: Oh, be advis'd,
    Sweet Madam, and retire.
OCTAVIA: Yes, I will go; but never to return.
    You shall no more be haunted with this Fury.
    My Lord, my Lord, love will not always last,
    When urg'd with long unkindness, and disdain;
    Take her again whom you prefer to me;

She stays but to be call'd. Poor cozen'd Man!
Let a feign'd parting give her back your heart,
Which a feign'd love first got; for injur'd me,
Tho' my just sense of wrongs forbid my stay,
My duty shall be yours.
To the dear pledges of our former love,
My tenderness and care shall be transferr'd,
And they shall cheer, by turns, my Widow'd Nights:
So, take my last farewel; for I despair
To have you whole, and scorn to take you half.   [*Exit.*]
VENTIDIUS: I combat Heav'n, which blasts my best designs:
My last attempt must be to win her back;
But Oh, I fear in vain.   [*Exit.*]
ANTONY: Why was I fram'd with this plain honest heart,
Which knows not to disguise its griefs and weakness,
But bears its workings outward to the World?
I should have kept the mighty anguish in,
And forc'd a smile at *Cleopatra*'s falshood:
Octavia had believ'd it, and had staid;
But I am made a shallow-forded Stream,
Seen to the bottom: all my clearness scorn'd,
And all my faults expos'd! – See, where he comes

[*Enter* DOLLABELLA.]

Who has prophan'd the Sacred Name of Friend,
And worn it into vileness!
With how secure a brow, and specious form
He guilds the secret Villain! Sure that face
Was meant for honesty; but Heav'n mis-match'd it,
And furnish'd Treason out with Natures pomp,
To make its work more easie.
DOLLABELLA: O, my Friend!
ANTONY: Well, *Dollabella*, you perform'd my message?
DOLLABELLA: I did, unwillingly.
ANTONY: Unwillingly?
Was it so hard for you to bear our parting?
You should have wisht it.
DOLLABELLA: Why?
ANTONY: Because you love me.
And she receiv'd my message, with as true,
With as unfeign'd a sorrow, as you brought it?
DOLLABELLA: She loves you, ev'n to madness.
ANTONY: Oh, I know it.
You, *Dollabella*, do not better know
How much she loves me. And should I

Forsake this Beauty? This all-perfect Creature?
DOLLABELLA: I could not, were she mine.
ANTONY: And yet you first
    Perswaded me: how come you alter'd since?
DOLLABELLA: I said at first I was not fit to go;
    I could not hear her sighs, and see her tears,
    But pity must prevail: and so, perhaps,
    It may again with you; for I have promis'd
    That she should take her last farewel: and, see,
    She comes to claim my word.

[Enter CLEOPATRA.*]*

ANTONY: False *Dollabella!*
DOLLABELLA: What's false, my Lord?
ANTONY: Why, *Dollabella's* false,
    And *Cleopatra's* false; both false and faithless.
    Draw near, you well-join'd wickedness, you Serpents,
    Whom I have, in my kindly bosom, warm'd
    Till I am stung to death.
DOLLABELLA: My Lord, have I
    Deserv'd to be thus us'd?
CLEOPATRA: Can Heav'n prepare
    A newer Torment? Can it find a Curse
    Beyond our separation?
ANTONY: Yes, if Fate
    Be just, much greater: Heav'n should be ingenious
    In punishing such crimes. The rowling Stone,
    And gnawing Vulture,[1] were slight pains, invented
    When *Jove* was young, and no examples known
    Of mighty ills; but you have ripen'd sin
    To such a monstrous growth, 'twill pose the Gods
    To find an equal Torture. Two, two such,
    Oh there's no farther name, two such – to me,
    To me, who lock'd my Soul within your breasts,
    Had no desires, no joys, no life, but you;
    When half the Globe was mine, I gave it you
    In Dowry with my heart; I had no use,
    No fruit of all, but you: a Friend and Mistress
    Was what the World could give. Oh, *Cleopatra!*
    Oh, *Dollabella!* how could you betray
    This tender heart, which with an Infant-fondness
    Lay lull'd betwixt your bosoms, and there slept

1. A reference to the myth of Sisyphus.

Secure of injur'd Faith?

DOLLABELLA: If she has wrong'd you,
   Heav'n, Hell, and You revenge it.

ANTONY: If she wrong'd me,
   Thou wouldst evade thy part of guilt; but swear
   Thou lov'st not her.

DOLLABELLA: Not so as I love you.

ANTONY: Not so! Swear, swear, I say, thou dost not love her.

DOLLABELLA: No more than Friendship will allow.

ANTONY: No more?
   Friendship allows thee nothing: thou art perjur'd. –
   And yet thou didst not swear thou lov'dst her not;
   But not so much, no more. Oh trifling Hypocrite,
   Who dar'st not own to her thou dost not love,
   Nor own to me thou dost! *Ventidius* heard it;
   Octavia saw it.

CLEOPATRA: They are enemies.

ANTONY: *Alexas* is not so: he, he confest it;
   He, who, next Hell, best knew it, he avow'd it.
   [*To* DOLABELLA.] Why do I seek a proof beyond your self?
   You whom I sent to bear my last Farewel,
   Return'd to plead her stay.

DOLLABELLA: What shall I answer?
   If to have lov'd be guilt, then I have sinn'd;
   But if to have repented of that love
   Can wash away my crime, I have repented.
   Yet, if I have offended past forgiveness,
   Let not her suffer: she is innocent.

CLEOPATRA: Ah, what will not a Woman do who loves!
   What means will she refuse, to keep that heart
   Where all her joys are plac'd! 'Twas I encourag'd,
   'Twas I blew up the fire that scorch'd his Soul,
   To make you jealous; and by that regain you.
   But all in vain; I could not counterfeit:
   In spight of all the damms, my love broke o'er,
   And drown'd my heart again: Fate took th' occasion;
   And thus one minutes feigning has destroy'd
   My whole life's truth.

ANTONY: Thin Cobweb Arts of Falshood;
   Seen, and broke through at first.

DOLLABELLA: Forgive your Mistress.

CLEOPATRA: Forgive your Friend.

ANTONY: You have convinc'd your selves,
   You plead each others Cause: What Witness have you,
   That you but meant to raise my jealousie?

CLEOPATRA: Our selves, and Heav'n.
ANTONY: Guilt witnesses for guilt. Hence, Love and Friendship;
    You have no longer place in humane breasts,
    These two have driv'n you out: avoid my sight;
    I would not kill the Man whom I have lov'd;
    And cannot hurt the Woman; but avoid me,
    I do not know how long I can be tame;
    For, if I stay one minute more to think
    How I am wrong'd, my Justice and Revenge
    Will cry so loud within me, that my pity
    Will not be heard for either.
DOLLABELLA: Heav'n has but
    Our sorrow for our sins; and then delights
    To pardon erring Man: sweet Mercy seems
    Its darling Attribute, which limits Justice;
    As if there were degrees in Infinite;
    And Infinite would rather want perfection
    Than punish to extent.
ANTONY: I can forgive
    A Foe; but not a Mistress, and a Friend:
    Treason is there in its most horrid shape,
    Where trust is greatest: and the Soul resign'd
    Is stabb'd by its own Guards: I'll hear no more;
    Hence from my sight, for ever.
CLEOPATRA: How? for ever!
    I cannot go one moment from your sight,
    And must I go for ever?
    My joys, my only joys are center'd here:
    What place have I to go to? my own Kingdom?
    That I have lost for you. Or to the *Romans*?
    They hate me for your sake. Or must I wander
    The wide World o'er, a helpless, banish'd Woman,
    Banish'd for love of you; banish'd from you?
    I, there's the Banishment! Oh hear me; hear me,
    With strictest Justice: for I beg no favour:
    And if I have offended you, then kill me,
    But do not banish me.
ANTONY: I must not hear you.
    I have a Fool within me takes your part;
    But Honour stops my ears.
CLEOPATRA: For pity hear me!
    Wou'd you cast off a Slave who follow'd you,
    Who crouch'd beneath your Spurn? – He has no pity!
    See, if he gives one tear to my departure;
    One look, one kind farewel. Oh Iron heart!

Let all the Gods look down, and judge betwixt us,
If he did ever love!
ANTONY: No more: *Alexas*!
DOLLABELLA: A perjur'd Villain!
ANTONY: [*to* CLEOPATRA.]   Your *Alexas*; yours.
CLEOPATRA: O 'twas his plot: his ruinous design
    T' ingage you in my love by jealousie.
    Hear him; confront him with me; let him speak.
ANTONY: I have; I have.
CLEOPATRA: And if he clear me not –
ANTONY: Your Creature! one who hangs upon your smiles!
    Watches your eye to say or to unsay
    Whate'er you please! I am not to be mov'd.
CLEOPATRA: Then must we part? Farewel, my cruel Lord,
    Th' appearance is against me; and I go
    Unjustifi'd, for ever from your sight.
    How I have lov'd, you know; how yet I love,
    My only comfort is, I know my self:
    I love you more, ev'n now you are unkind,
    Than when you lov'd me most; so well, so truly,
    I'll never strive against it; but die pleas'd
    To think you once were mine.
ANTONY: Good Heav'n, they weep at parting.
    Must I weep too? that calls 'em innocent.
    I must not weep; and yet I must, to think
    That I must not forgive. –
    Live; but live wretched, 'tis but just you shou'd,
    Who made me so: Live from each others sight:
    Let me not hear you meet: Set all the Earth,
    And all the Seas, betwixt your sunder'd Loves:
    View nothing common but the Sun and Skys:
    Now, all take several ways;
    And each your own sad fate with mine deplore;
    That you were false, and I could trust no more.   [*Exeunt severally.*]

Act V, Scene I

[*Enter* CLEOPATRA, CHARMION, IRAS.]

CHARMION: Be juster, Heav'n: such virtue punish'd thus,
    Will make us think that Chance rules all above,
    And shuffles, with a random hand, the Lots
    Which Man is forc'd to draw.

CLEOPATRA: I cou'd tear out these eyes, that gain'd his heart,
    And had not pow'r to keep it. O the curse
    Of doting on, ev'n when I find it Dotage!
    Bear witness, Gods, you heard him bid me go;
    You whom he mock'd with imprecating Vows
    Of promis'd Faith. – I'll die, I will not bear it.
    You may hold me –   [*She pulls out her Dagger, and they hold her.*]
    But I can keep my breath; I can die inward,
    And choak this Love.

[*Enter* ALEXAS.]

IRAS: Help, O *Alexas*, help!
    The Queen grows desperate, her Soul struggles in her,
    With all the Agonies of Love and Rage,
    And strives to force its passage.
CLEOPATRA: Let me go.
    Art thou there, Traitor! – O,
    O, for a little breath, to vent my rage!
    Give, give me way, and let me loose upon him.
ALEXAS: Yes, I deserve it, for my ill-tim'd truth.
    Was it for me to prop
    The Ruins of a falling Majesty?
    To place my self beneath the mighty flaw,
    Thus to be crush'd, and pounded into Atomes,
    By its o'erwhelming weight? 'Tis too presuming
    For Subjects, to preserve that wilful pow'r
    Which courts its own destruction.
CLEOPATRA: I wou'd reason
    More calmly with you. Did not you o'er-rule,
    And force my plain, direct, and open love
    Into these crooked paths of jealousie?
    Now, what's th' event? *Octavia* is remov'd;
    But *Cleopatra*'s banish'd. Thou, thou, Villain,
    Hast push'd my Boat, to open Sea; to prove,
    At my sad cost, if thou canst steer it back.
    It cannot be; I'm lost too far; I'm ruin'd:
    Hence, thou Impostor, Traitor, Monster, Devil –
    I can no more: thou, and my griefs, have sunk
    Me down so low, that I want voice to curse thee.
ALEXAS: Suppose some shipwrack'd Seaman near the shore,
    Dropping and faint, with climbing up the Cliff,
    If, from above, some charitable hand
    Pull him to safety, hazarding himself
    To draw the others weight; wou'd he look back
    And curse him for his pains? The case is yours;

But one step more, and you have gain'd the height.
CLEOPATRA: Sunk, never more to rise.
ALEXAS: *Octavia*'s gone, and *Dollabella* banish'd.
    Believe me, Madam, *Antony* is yours.
    His heart was never lost; but started off
    To Jealousie, Love's last retreat and covert:
    Where it lies hid in Shades, watchful in silence,
    And list'ning for the sound that calls it back.
    Some other, any man, ('tis so advanc'd)
    May perfect this unfinish'd work, which I
    (Unhappy only to my self) have left
    So easie to his hand.
CLEOPATRA: Look well thou do't; else –
ALEXAS: Else, what your silence threatens. – *Antony*
    Is mounted up the *Pharos*;[1] from whose Turret,
    He stands surveying our *Ægyptian* Gallies,
    Engag'd with *Cæsar's* Fleet: now Death, or Conquest.
    If the first happen, Fate acquits my promise:
    If we o'ercome, the Conqueror is yours.

[*A distant Shout within.*]

CHARMION: Have comfort, Madam: did you mark that Shout?

[*Second Shout nearer.*]

IRAS: Hark; they redouble it.
ALEXAS: 'Tis from the Port.
    The loudness shows it near: good news, kind Heavens.
CLEOPATRA: *Osiris* make it so.

[*Enter* SERAPION.]

SERAPION: Where, where's the Queen?
ALEXAS: How frightfully the holy Coward stares!
    As if not yet recover'd of th' assault,
    When all his Gods, and what's more dear to him,
    His Offerings were at stake.
SERAPION: O horror, horror!
    Ægypt has been; our latest hour is come:
    The Queen of Nations from her ancient seat,
    Is sunk for ever in the dark Abyss:
    Time has unrowl'd her Glories to the last,

1. The lighthouse in the harbour of Alexandria.

And now clos'd up the volume.

CLEOPATRA: Be more plain:
Say, whence thou com'st, (though Fate is in thy face,
Which from thy haggard eyes looks wildly out,
And threatens ere thou speak'st.)

SERAPION: I came from *Pharos*;
From viewing (spare me and imagine it)
Our Lands last hope, your Navy –

CLEOPATRA: Vanquish'd?

SERAPION: No.
They fought not.

CLEOPATRA: Then they fled.

SERAPION: Nor that. I saw,
With *Antony*, your well-appointed Fleet
Row out; and thrice he wav'd his hand on high,
And thrice with cheerful cries they shouted back:
'Twas then, false Fortune, like a fawning Strumpet,
About to leave the Bankrupt Prodigal,
With a dissembled smile wou'd kiss at parting,
And flatter to the last; the well-tim'd Oars
Now dipt from every bank, now smoothly run
To meet the Foe; and soon indeed they met,
But not as Foes. In few,[1] we saw their Caps
On either side thrown up; th' *Ægyptian* Gallies
(Receiv'd like Friends) past through, and fell behind
The *Roman* rear: and now, they all come forward,
And ride within the Port.

CLEOPATRA: Enough, *Serapion*:
I've heard my doom. This needed not, you Gods:
When I lost *Antony*, your work was done;
'Tis but superfluous malice. Where's my Lord?
How bears he this last blow?

SERAPION: His fury cannot be express'd by words:
Thrice he attempted headlong to have faln
Full on his foes, and aim'd at *Cæsar's* Galley:
With-held, he raves on you; cries, He's betray'd.
Should he now find you –

ALEXAS: Shun him, seek your safety,
Till you can clear your innocence.

CLEOPATRA: I'll stay.

ALEXAS: You must not, haste you to your Monument,
While I make speed to *Cæsar*.

CLEOPATRA: *Cæsar*! No,

1. In short.

I have no business with him.

ALEXAS: I can work him

To spare your life, and let this madman perish.

CLEOPATRA: Base fawning Wretch! wouldst thou betray him too?

Hence from my sight, I will not hear a Traytor;

'Twas thy design brought all this ruine on us.

Serapion, thou art honest; counsel me:

But haste, each moment's precious.

SERAPION: Retire; you must not yet see *Antony*.

He who began this mischief,

'Tis just he tempt the danger: let him clear you;

And, since he offer'd you his servile tongue,

To gain a poor precarious life from *Cæsar*,

Let him expose that fawning eloquence,

And speak to *Antony*.

ALEXAS: O Heavens! I dare not,

I meet my certain death.

CLEOPATRA: Slave, thou deserv'st it.

Not that I fear my Lord, will I avoid him;

I know him noble: when he banish'd me,

And thought me false, he scorn'd to take my life;

But I'll be justifi'd, and then die with him.

ALEXAS: O pity me, and let me follow you.

CLEOPATRA: To death, if thou stir hence. Speak, if thou canst,

Now for thy life, which basely thou wou'dst save;

While mine I prize at this. Come, good *Serapion*.

[*Exeunt* CLEOPATRA, SERAPION, CHARMION, IRAS.]

ALEXAS: O that I less cou'd fear to lose this being,

Which, like a Snow-ball, in my coward hand,

The more 'tis grasp'd, the faster melts away.

Poor Reason! what a wretched aid art thou!

For still, in spight of thee,

These two long Lovers, Soul and Body, dread

Their final separation. Let me think:

What can I say, to save my self from death?

No matter what becomes of *Cleopatra*.

ANTONY: [*within.*] Which way? where?

VENTIDIUS: [*within.*]   This leads to the Monument.

ALEXAS: Ah me! I hear him; yet I'm unprepar'd:

My gift of lying's gone;

And this Court-Devil, which I so oft have rais'd,

Forsakes me at my need. I dare not stay;

Yet cannot far go hence.   [*Exit.*]

[*Enter* ANTONY *and* VENTIDIUS.]

ANTONY: O happy *Cæsar*! Thou hast men to lead:
　　Think not 'tis thou hast conquer'd *Antony*;
　　But *Rome* has conquer'd *Ægypt*. I'm betray'd.
VENTIDIUS: Curse on this treach'rous Train!
　　Their Soil and Heav'n infect 'em all with baseness:
　　And their young Souls come tainted to the World
　　With the first breath they draw.
ANTONY: Th' original Villain sure no God created;
　　He was a Bastard of the Sun, by *Nile*,
　　Ap'd into Man; with all his Mother's Mud
　　Crusted about his Soul.
VENTIDIUS:　　　　　　　　The Nation is
　　One Universal Traitor; and their Queen
　　The very Spirit and Extract of 'em all.
ANTONY: Is there yet left
　　A possibility of aid from Valor?
　　Is there one God unsworn to my Destruction?
　　The least unmortgag'd hope? for, if there be,
　　Methinks I cannot fall beneath the Fate
　　Of such a Boy as *Cæsar*.
　　The World's one half is yet in *Antony*;
　　And, from each limb of it that's hew'd away,
　　The Soul comes back to me.
VENTIDIUS:　　　　　　　　There yet remain
　　Three Legions in the Town. The last assault
　　Lopt off the rest: if death be your design,
　　(As I must wish it now) these are sufficient
　　To make a heap about us of dead Foes,
　　An honest Pile for burial.
ANTONY:　　　　　　　　They're enough.
　　We'll not divide our Stars; but side by side
　　Fight emulous: and with malicious eyes
　　Survey each other's acts: so every death
　　Thou giv'st, I'll take on me, as a just debt,
　　And pay thee back a Soul.
VENTIDIUS: Now you shall see I love you. Not a word
　　Of chiding more. By my few hours of life,
　　I am so pleas'd with this brave *Roman* Fate,
　　That I wou'd not be *Cæsar*, to out-live you.
　　When we put off this flesh, and mount together,
　　I shall be shown to all th' Etherial crowd;
　　Lo, this is he who dy'd with *Antony*.
ANTONY: Who knows but we may pierce through all their Troops,

And reach my Veterans yet? 'Tis worth the tempting,
T' o'er-leap this Gulph of Fate,
And leave our wond'ring Destinies behind.

[*Enter* ALEXAS, *trembling.*]

VENTIDIUS: See, see, that Villain;
    See *Cleopatra* stampt upon that face,
    With all her cunning, all her arts of falshood!
    How she looks out through those dissembling eyes!
    How he has set his count'nance for deceit;
    And promises a lye, before he speaks!
    Let me dispatch him first.   [*Drawing.*]
ALEXAS: O, spare me, spare me.
ANTONY: Hold; he's not worth your killing. On thy life,
    (Which thou mayst keep, because I scorn to take it)
    No syllable to justifie thy Queen;
    Save thy base tongue its office.
ALEXAS: Sir, she's gone,
    Where she shall never be molested more
    By Love, or you.
ANTONY: Fled to her *Dollabella!*
    Die, Traitor, I revoke my promise, die.   [*Going to kill him.*]
ALEXAS: O hold, she is not fled.
ANTONY: She is: my eyes
    Are open to her falshood; my whole life
    Has been a golden dream, of Love and Friendship.
    But, now I wake, I'm like a Merchant, rows'd
    From soft repose, to see his Vessel sinking,
    And all his Wealth cast o'er. Ingrateful Woman!
    Who follow'd me, but as the Swallow Summer,
    Hatching her young ones in my kindly Beams,
    Singing her flatt'ries to my morning wake;
    But, now my Winter comes, she spreads her wings,
    And seeks the Spring of *Cæsar.*
ALEXAS: Think not so:
    Her Fortunes have, in all things, mixt with yours.
    Had she betray'd her Naval force to *Rome,*
    How easily might she have gone to *Cæsar,*
    Secure by such a bribe!
VENTIDIUS: She sent it first,
    To be more welcome after.
ANTONY: 'Tis too plain;
    Else wou'd she have appear'd, to clear her self.
ALEXAS: Too fatally she has; she could not bear

To be accus'd by you; but shut her self
Within her Monument: look'd down, and sigh'd;
While, from her unchang'd face, the silent tears
Dropt, as they had not leave, but stole their parting.
Some undistinguish'd words she inly murmur'd;
At last, she rais'd her eyes; and, with such looks
As dying *Lucrece* cast, –

ANTONY: My heart forebodes. –

VENTIDIUS: All for the best: go on.

ALEXAS: She snatch'd her Ponyard,
And, ere we cou'd prevent the fatal blow,
Plung'd it within her breast: then turn'd to me,
Go, bear my Lord (said she) my last Farewel;
And ask him if he yet suspect my Faith.
More she was saying. but death rush'd betwixt.
She half pronounc'd your Name with her last breath,
And bury'd half within her.

VENTIDIUS: Heav'n be prais'd.

ANTONY: Then art thou innocent, my poor dear Love?
And art thou dead?
O those two words! their sound shou'd be divided:
Hadst thou been false, and dy'd; or hadst thou liv'd,
And hadst been true – But Innocence and Death!
This shows not well above. Then what am I,
The Murderer of this Truth, this Innocence!
Thoughts cannot form themselves in words so horrid
As can express my guilt!

VENTIDIUS: Is't come to this? The Gods have been too gracious:
And thus you thank 'em for't.

ANTONY: [*to* ALEXAS.]   Why stay'st thou here?
Is it for thee to spy upon my Soul,
And see its inward mourning? Get thee hence;
Thou art not worthy to behold, what now
Becomes a *Roman* Emperor to perform.

ALEXAS: [*aside.*] He loves her still:
His grief betrays it. Good! The joy to find
She's yet alive, compleats the reconcilement.
I've sav'd my self, and her. But, Oh the *Romans*!
Fate comes too fast upon my Wit,
Hunts me too hard, and meets me at each double.   [*Exit.*]

VENTIDIUS: Wou'd she had dy'd a little sooner tho,
Before *Octavia* went; you might have treated:
Now 'twill look tame, and wou'd not be receiv'd.
Come, rouze your self, and lets die warm together.

ANTONY: I will not fight: there's no more work for War.

The bus'ness of my angry hours is done.
VENTIDIUS: *Cæsar* is at your Gates.
ANTONY: Why, let him enter;
    He's welcom now.
VENTIDIUS: What Lethargy has crept into your Soul?
ANTONY: 'Tis but a scorn of life, and just desire
    To free my self from bondage.
VENTIDIUS: Do it bravely.
ANTONY: I will; but not by fighting. O, *Ventidius*!
    What shou'd I fight for now? My Queen is dead.
    I was but great for her; my Pow'r, my Empire,
    Were but my Merchandise to buy her love;
    And conquer'd Kings, my Factors. Now she's dead,
    Let *Cæsar* take the World, An Empty Circle, since the Jewel's gone
    Which made it worth my strife: my being's nauseous;
    For all the bribes of life are gone away.
VENTIDIUS: Wou'd you be taken?
ANTONY: Yes, I wou'd be taken;
    But, as a *Roman* ought, dead, my *Ventidius*:
    For I'll convey my Soul from *Cæsar's* reach,
    And lay down life my self. 'Tis time the World
    Shou'd have a Lord, and know whom to obey.
    We two have kept its homage in suspence,
    And bent the Globe on whose each side we trod,
    Till it was dinted inwards: Let him walk
    Alone upon't; I'm weary of my part.
    My Torch is out; and the World stands before me
    Like a black Desart, at th' approach of night:
    I'll lay me down, and stray no farther on.
VENTIDIUS: I cou'd be griev'd,
    But that I'll not out-live you: choose your death;
    For, I have seen him in such various shapes.
    I care not which I take: I'm only troubled
    The life I bear, is worn to such a rag,
    'Tis scarce worth giving. I cou'd wish indeed
    We threw it from us with a better grace;
    That, like two Lyons taken in the Toils,
    We might at least thrust out our paws, and wound
    The Hunters that inclose us.
ANTONY: I have thought on't.
    Ventidius, you must live.
VENTIDIUS: I must not, Sir.
ANTONY: Wilt thou not live, to speak some good of me?
    To stand by my fair Fame, and guard th' approaches
    From the ill Tongues of Men?

VENTIDIUS: Who shall guard mine,
    For living after you?
ANTONY: Say, I command it.
VENTIDIUS: If we die well, our deaths will speak themselves,
    And need no living witness.
ANTONY: Thou hast lov'd me,
    And fain I wou'd reward thee: I must die;
    Kill me, and take the merit of my death
    To make thee Friends with *Cæsar*.
VENTIDIUS: Thank your kindness
    You said I lov'd you; and, in recompence,
    You bid me turn a Traitor: did I think
    You wou'd have us'd me thus? that I shou'd die
    With a hard thought of you?
ANTONY: Forgive me, *Roman*.
    Since I have heard of *Cleopatra*'s death,
    My reason bears no rule upon my tongue.
    But lets my thoughts break all at random out:
    I've thought better; do not deny me twice.
VENTIDIUS: By Heav'n, I will not.
    Let it not be t' out-live you.
ANTONY: Kill me first,
    And then die thou: for 'tis but just thou serve
    Thy Friend, before thy self.
VENTIDIUS: Give me your hand.
    We soon shall meet again. Now, Farewel, Emperor.   [*Embrace.*]
    Methinks that word's too cold to be my last:
    Since Death sweeps all distinctions, Farewel, Friend.
    That's all. –
    I will not make a bus'ness of a trifle:
    And yet I cannot look on you, and kill you;
    Pray turn your face.
ANTONY: I do: strike home, be sure.
VENTIDIUS: Home, as my Sword will reach.   [*Kills himself.*]
ANTONY: O, thou mistak'st;
    That wound was none of thine: give it me back:
    Thou robb'st me of my death.
VENTIDIUS: I do indeed;
    But, think 'tis the first time I e'er deceiv'd you;
    If that may plead my pardon. And you, Gods,
    Forgive me, if you will; for I die perjur'd,
    Rather than kill my Friend.   [*Dies.*]
ANTONY: Farewel. Ever my Leader, ev'n in death!
    My Queen and thou have got the start of me,
    And I'm the lag of Honour. – Gone so soon?

Is death no more? He us'd him carelesly,
With a familiar kindness: ere he knock'd,
Ran to the door, and took him in his arms,
As who shou'd say, Y'are welcome at all hours,
A Friend need give no warning. Books had spoil'd him;
For all the Learn'd are Cowards by profession.
'Tis not worth
My farther thought; for death, for ought I know,
Is but to think no more. Here's to be satisfi'd.   [*Falls on his Sword.*]
I've mist my heart. O unperforming hand!
Thou never cou'dst have err'd in a worse time.
My Fortune jades me to the last; and death,
Like a great Man, takes state, and makes me wait
For my admittance. –   [*Trampling within.*]
Some perhaps from *Cæsar*:
If he shou'd find me living, and suspect
That I plaid booty with my life! I'll mend
My work, ere they can reach me.   [*Rises upon his knees.*]

[*Enter* CLEOPATRA, CHARMION, IRAS.]

CLEOPATRA: Where is my Lord? where is he?
CHARMION: There he lies,
    And dead *Ventidius* by him.
CLEOPATRA: My fears were Prophets; I am come too late.
    O that accurs'd *Alexas*!   [*Runs to him.*]
ANTONY: Art thou living?
    Or am I dead before I knew? and thou
    The first kind Ghost that meets me?
CLEOPATRA: Help me seat him.
    Send quickly, send for help.   [*They place him in a Chair.*]
ANTONY: I am answer'd.
    We live both. Sit thee down, my *Cleopatra*:
    I'll make the most I can of life, to stay
    A moment more with thee.
CLEOPATRA: How is it with you?
ANTONY: 'Tis as with a man
    Removing in a hurry; all pack'd up,
    But one dear Jewel that his haste forgot;
    And he, for that, returns upon the spur:
    So I come back, for thee.
CLEOPATRA: Too long, you Heav'ns, you have been cruel to me;
    Now show your mended Faith, and give me back
    His fleeting life.
ANTONY: It will not be, my Love.

I keep my Soul by force.
Say but thou art not false.
CLEOPATRA: 'Tis now too late
  To say I'm true: I'll prove it, and die with you.
  Unknown to me, *Alexas* feign'd my death:
  Which, when I knew, I hasted, to prevent
  This fatal consequence. My Fleet betray'd
  Both you and me.
ANTONY: And *Dollabella* –
CLEOPATRA: Scarce
  Esteem'd before he lov'd; but hated now.
ANTONY: Enough: my life's not long enough for more.
  Thou sayst thou wilt come after: I believe thee;
  For I can now believe whate'er thou sayst,
  That we may part more kindly.
CLEOPATRA: I will come:
  Doubt not, my life, I'll come, and quickly too:
  Cæsar shall triumph o'er no part of thee.
ANTONY: But grieve not, while thou stay'st
  My last disastrous times:
  Think we have had a clear and glorious day;
  And Heav'n did kindly to delay the storm
  Just till our close of ev'ning. Ten years love,
  And not a moment lost, but all improv'd
  To th' utmost joys: What Ages have we liv'd!
  And now to die each others; and, so dying,
  While hand in hand we walk in Groves below,
  Whole Troops of Lovers Ghosts shall flock about us,
  And all the Train be ours.
CLEOPATRA: Your words are like the Notes of dying Swans,
  Too sweet to last. Were there so many hours
  For your unkindness, and not one for love?
ANTONY: No, not a minute. – This one kiss – more worth
  Than all I leave to *Cæsar*.   [*Dies.*]
CLEOPATRA: O, tell me so again,
  And take ten thousand kisses, for that word.
  My Lord, my Lord: speak, if you yet have being;
  Sigh to me, if you cannot speak; or cast
  One look: Do any thing that shows you live.
IRAS: He's gone too far, to hear you;
  And this you see, a lump of sensless Clay,
  The leavings of a Soul.
CHARMION: Remember, Madam,
  He charg'd you not to grieve.
CLEOPATRA: And I'll obey him.

I have not lov'd a *Roman* not to know
What should become his Wife; his Wife, my *Charmion*;
For 'tis to that high Title I aspire,
And now I'll not die less. Let dull *Octavia*
Survive, to mourn him dead: my Nobler Fate
Shall knit our Spousals with a tie too strong
For *Roman* Laws to break.

IRAS: Will you then die?

CLEOPATRA: Why shou'dst thou make that question?

IRAS: *Cæsar* is merciful.

CLEOPATRA: Let him be so
To those that want his mercy: my poor Lord
Made no such Cov'nant with him, to spare me
When he was dead. Yield me to *Cæsar's* pride?
What, to be led in triumph through the Streets,
A spectacle to base *Plebeian* eyes;
While some dejected Friend of *Antony's*,
Close in a corner, shakes his head, and mutters
A secret curse on her who ruin'd him?
I'll none of that.

CHARMION: Whatever you resolve,
I'll follow ev'n to death.

IRAS: I only fear'd
For you; but more shou'd fear to live without you.

CLEOPATRA: Why, now 'tis as it shou'd be. Quick, my Friends,
Dispatch; ere this, the Town's in *Cæsar's* hands:
My Lord looks down concern'd, and fears my stay,
Lest I shou'd be surpriz'd;
Keep him not waiting for his love too long.
You, *Charmion*, bring my Crown and richest Jewels,
With 'em, the Wreath of Victory I made
(Vain Augury!) for him who now lies dead.
You, *Iras*, bring the cure of all our ills.

IRAS: The Aspicks,[1] Madam?

CLEOPATRA: Must I bid you twice?

[*Exeunt* CHARMION *and* IRAS.]

'Tis sweet to die, when they wou'd force life on me,
To rush into the dark aboad of death,
And seize him first; if he be like my Love,
He is not frightful sure.
We're now alone, in secresie and silence;
And is not this like Lovers? I may kiss

1. Asps.

These pale, cold lips; *Octavia* does not see me;
And, Oh! 'tis better far to have him thus,
Than see him in her arms. – O welcome, welcome.

[*Enter* CHARMION, IRAS.]

CHARMION: What must be done?
CLEOPATRA: Short Ceremony, Friends;
But yet it must be decent. First, this Laurel
Shall crown my Hero's Head: he fell not basely,
Nor left his Shield behind him. Only thou
Cou'dst triumph o'er thy self; and thou alone
Wert worthy so to triumph.
CHARMION: To what end
These Ensigns of your Pomp and Royalty?
CLEOPATRA: Dull, that thou art! why, 'tis to meet my Love;
As when I saw him first, on *Cydnos* bank,
All sparkling, like a Goddess; so adorn'd,
I'll find him once again: my second Spousals
Shall match my first, in Glory. Haste, haste, both,
And dress the Bride of *Antony*.
CHARMION: 'Tis done.
CLEOPATRA: Now seat me by my Lord. I claim this place;
For I must conquer *Cæsar* too, like him,
And win my share o'th'World. Hail, you dear Relicks
Of my Immortal Love!
O let no Impious hand remove you hence;
But rest for ever here. Let *Ægypt* give
His death that peace, which it deny'd his life.
Reach me the Casket.
IRAS: Underneath the fruit the Aspick lies.
CLEOPATRA: [*putting aside the leaves.*] Welcom, thou kind Deceiver!
Thou best of Thieves; who, with an easie key,
Dost open life, and, unperceiv'd by us,
Ev'n steal us from our selves: discharging so
Death's dreadful office, better than himself,
Touching our limbs so gently into slumber,
That Death stands by, deceiv'd by his own Image,
And thinks himself but Sleep.
SERAPION: [*within.*]   The Queen, where is she?
The Town is yielded, *Cæsar's* at the Gates.
CLEOPATRA: He comes too late t' invade the Rights of Death.
Haste, bare my Arm, and rouze the Serpent's fury.

[*Holds out her Arm, and draws it back.*]

Coward Flesh –

Wou'dst thou conspire with *Cæsar*, to betray me,
As thou wert none of mine? I'll force thee to't,
And not be sent by him,
But bring my self my Soul to *Antony*.

                    [*Turns aside, and then shows her Arm bloody.*]

Take hence; the work is done.
SERAPION: [*within.*]   Break ope the door,
    And guard the Traitor well.
CHARMION: The next is ours.
IRAS: Now, *Charmion*, to be worthy
    Of our great Queen and Mistress.   [*They apply the Aspicks.*]
CLEOPATRA: Already, Death, I feel thee in my Veins;
    I go with such a will to find my Lord,
    That we shall quickly meet.
    A heavy numness creeps through every limb,
    And now 'tis at my head: my eye-lids fall,
    And my dear Love is vanish'd in a mist.
    Where shall I find him, where? O turn me to him,
    And lay me on his breast. – *Cæsar*, thy worst;
    Now part us, if thou canst.   [*Dies.*]

[IRAS *sinks down at her feet, and dies;* CHARMION *stands behind her Chair,
                    as dressing her head.*]
          [*Enter* SERAPION, *two Priests,* ALEXAS *bound,* ÆGYPTIANS.]

TWO PRIESTS: Behold, *Serapion*, what havock Death has made!
SERAPION: 'Twas what I fear'd.
    Charmion, is this well done?
CHARMION: Yes, 'tis well done, and like a Queen, the last
    Of her great Race: I follow her.   [*Sinks down; Dies.*]
ALEXAS: 'Tis true,
    She has done well: much better thus to die,
    Than live to make a Holy-day in *Rome*.
SERAPION: See, see how the Lovers sit in State together,
    As they were giving Laws to half Mankind.
    Th' impression of a smile left in her face,
    Shows she dy'd pleas'd with him for whom she liv'd,
    And went to charm him in another World.
    Cæsar's just entring; grief has now no leisure.
    Secure that Villain, as our pledge of safety
    To grace th' Imperial Triumph. Sleep, blest Pair,
    Secure from humane chance, long Ages out,
    While all the Storms of Fate fly o'er your Tomb;
    And Fame, to late Posterity, shall tell,
    No Lovers liv'd so great, or dy'd so well.   [*Exeunt.*]

Epilogue

Poets, like Disputants, when Reasons fail,
Have one sure Refuge left; and that's to rail.
Fop, Coxcomb, Fool, *are thunder'd through the* Pit;
And this is all their Equipage of Wit.
We wonder how the Devil this diff'rence grows,
Betwixt our Fools in Verse, and yours in Prose:
For, 'Faith, the quarrel rightly understood,
'Tis Civil War *with their own Flesh and Blood.*
The thread-bare Author hates the gawdy Coat;
And swears at the Guilt Coach, but swears a-foot:
For 'tis observ'd of every Scribling Man,
He grows a Fop as fast as e'er he can;
Prunes up, and asks his Oracle the Glass,
If Pink or Purple best become his face.
For our poor Wretch, he neither rails nor prays;
Nor likes your Wit just as you like his Plays;
He has not yet so much of Mr. Bays.
He does his best; and, if he cannot please,
Wou'd quietly sue out his Writ of Ease.
Yet, if he might his own Grand Jury call,
By the Fair Sex he begs to stand or fall.
Let Cæsar's *Pow'r the Mens ambition move,*
But grace You him who lost the World for Love.
Yet if some antiquated Lady say,
The last Age is not Copy'd in his Play;
Heav'n help the Man who for that face must drudge,
Which only has the wrinkles of a Judge.
Let not the Young and Beauteous join with those;
For shou'd you raise such numerous Hosts of Foes,
Young Wits and Sparks he to his aid must call;
'Tis more than one Man's work to please you all.

Finis

The Country Wife

WILLIAM WYCHERLEY

INTRODUCTION

William Wycherley was born in the hamlet of Clive, Shropshire around 1640. His father, Daniel, was a country gentleman who became steward to the Marquis of Winchester and gradually built up an estate of some substance for himself. In the mid-1650s Daniel sent his son to France to receive a sound education, untainted by the Puritan chill of intellectual life in Cromwellian England. During the five years he lived in western France, William Wycherley was admitted to the company of high-ranking society ladies, including Mme de Montausier, formerly Mlle de Rambouillet, who was regarded as one of the most fashionable ladies of the French court and a leading exponent of *précieux* wit. Under her tutelage at Angoulême, Wycherley not only learnt to admire the *précieux* code, which taught that marriage and wit were incompatible, but also became a Catholic convert.

Shortly before the Restoration of Charles II, Wycherley returned to England. He was sent by his father to board, as a gentleman commoner, with Dr Barlow, Provost of Queen's College, Oxford. One of the objectives of this placement was to effect Wycherley's reconversion to the Protestant faith. This was achieved fairly swiftly. Dr (later Bishop) Barlow was a fine teacher and a staunch debater: intellectually, young William Wycherley was no match for him. After his reconversion, Wycherley left Oxford without matriculating and moved to London, to enter the Middle Temple. His father, who was a tireless litigant, clearly approved of the notion of a legal career for his son. Wycherley's aim, however, was to lead the life of a man of leisure in the fun-loving milieu of Restoration London.

Little is known of his life during the 1660s. He seems to have devoted just enough of his time to his studies to satisfy his father. There is also some evidence to suggest that in 1665 he followed the example of other young gentlemen in London and enlisted with the Duke of York to fight briefly against the Dutch at sea.[1] Most of his time, however, was spent in the pursuit of pleasure in the fashionable meeting places of the town: the restaurants and taverns in and around Covent Garden; the playhouses; the Mall; the Mulberry Garden and St James's Park. The experience of these years of idle pleasure provided him with the raw material for his plays, once he decided to make his mark in society as a playwright.

The decision to try his hand at playwriting may have been prompted by the example of Etherege (another well-to-do young man) whose success as a playwright had brought him into the circle of wits gathered around the Earls of Rochester and Dorset. Wycherley completed his first play *Love in a Wood* in 1671[2] when it was presented at Killigrew's Theatre Royal in Bridges Street. It was an outstanding success, which brought him the fame and attention he desired, including the friendship of the circle of wits gathered around Rochester and an affair with Barbara Villiers, who was at the time the king's favourite mistress and who had been given the title of Duchess of Cleveland by Charles II. It is claimed that she and Wycherley first met by chance as their carriages jostled in the Mall. The duchess, recognising Wycherley as the author of *Love in a Wood*, reportedly stuck her head out of her carriage window and, borrowing a line from the play, shouted out, 'You, Wycherley, you're the son of a whore!'[3]

Barbara Villiers was a passionate and tempestuous woman who had already borne six children for Charles II. Their relationship was a stormy one, with frequent infidelities on both sides. However, when the duchess and Wycherley first met, the king was in a jealous and possessive mood, which meant that their affair, at least to start with, had to be hidden. Within a year, however, Charles's attention had strayed to a young French woman, Louise de Querouaille,

---

1. See Willard Connely, *Brawny Wycherley* [1930] (Port Washington: Kennikat Press, 1969) pp. 50–2.
2. In his later life Wycherley boasted to the young writer Pope that he had written all his plays in the early 1660s. Some biographers have taken this claim seriously (see *Dictionary of National Biography*, vol. lxiii, p. 195), but most have discounted it.
3. See Connely, *Brawny Wycherley*, p. 72.

whom he made Duchess of Portsmouth. Wycherley was then able to dedicate the published text of his play to the Duchess of Cleveland and to proffer in his Dedication his 'humble acknowledgements for the favours I have receiv'd from you'. The duchess in turn was able to present him to the king, who instantly took a liking to the witty and intelligent young man and thereafter often sought his company.

Wycherley was now launched on a glittering career as an admired wit, man of letters and courtier. Even the Duke of Buckingham befriended him (despite his initial jealousy of Wycherley's success with Barbara Villiers) and made him one of his equerries. Within a year, Wycherley had completed his second play, *The Gentleman Dancing Master* (1672). This was a slender piece which was less than enthusiastically received, but the lukewarm reception afforded the play does not appear to have greatly damaged his reputation with the wits. Wycherley took rather more time over his next play, *The Country Wife*, which was not ready for performance until January 1675. Discreet borrowings from Terence's *The Eunuch* and from Molière's *L'École des femmes* and *L'École des maris* were woven into a play that reflected the stuff and substance of life in contemporary London, as Wycherley himself had experienced it. *The Country Wife* was an immediate success and confirmed Wycherley as the leading satiric playwright of the age.

The Country Wife

Horner, as his name suggests, is a phallic gymnast. His primary aim in life is copulation without commitment. Like Molière's Tartuffe, he presents a false image of himself to the world in order to obtain sexual gratification. But there any similarity ceases. In Molière's play, Tartuffe's behaviour is seen as evil and destructive. He is a dangerous hypocrite who uses the cloak of religious zeal to mask his selfish lusts. Molière is writing for a society which accepts a clear scale of moral values against which the behaviour of a hypocritical deviant can be measured. His play also reaffirms traditional family values of loyalty, affection, duty and obligation. Tartuffe is a dangerous outsider who threatens these values and hence the ordered stability of family life, which is why he is both ridiculed and faced with the prospect of severe punishment at the end of the play. In Wycherley's London there are no such moral certainties. In *The Country Wife*, there is no mention of family life at all: this is a world populated by hard-drinking, amoral young bachelors, calculating young women and loveless older couples conjoined in dull marriages of convenience. What we are shown is a society that has completely lost its faith in the received values of the past. All that is left is a hollow shell of social convention and formal decorum; there is no substance and therefore no certainty left. Society itself has become utterly hypocritical.

Confronted by society's universal hypocrisy, Horner deliberately makes himself an outsider in order to enjoy some honestly shared sexual pleasure. By spreading the false rumour that he has been made a harmless eunuch through a French surgeon's mistake, Horner finds a way of subverting the hypocritical barriers of 'honour' and 'reputation' which otherwise prevent society women from following their natural instincts. Once the husbands accept as true the false report of Horner's maimed sexuality, he is given free access to their wives. Horner then discovers, as he expected, that they are lusty and boisterous bedroom partners now that their honour and reputation are secure. The most telling demonstration of this comes when Lady Fidget shouts joyfully through the bedroom door to her unsuspecting husband, 'Let him come and whichever way he likes'. Even after the society women, known as the virtuous gang, discover that they have all been pleasured by Horner, they do not give in to feelings of possessive jealousy but instead experience a sense of relief because they can now drop their masks to each other. Society expects them to be demure, cautious and chaste; with Horner, they can revel in their own sexuality as well as his and let themselves go in drunken, bacchic disorder. There is a sense of moral inversion here. Traditional values of loyalty, fidelity and honourable behaviour are seen as a false and constraining veneer. In contrast, the natural sexual urges felt by all and celebrated by Horner are shown to have a refreshing honesty when set against the empty veneer of socially accepted conduct. There seems to be an irreconcilable clash here between natural instinct and convention, and precious little chance of reconciling sexuality, emotion and marital commitment.

A particularly biting critique of contemporary marital hypocrisy is shown in the figure of Pinchwife, who regards his wife as a piece of property, to be locked up and disposed of according to his sole will. When she rebels, he threatens extreme physical violence, offering to stab out her eyes with his penknife. He even admits at one point that he only married because he could never keep a whore to himself. In the figure of Pinchwife, the former whoremaster turned respectable husband, Wycherley comes perilously close to writing an unacceptably barbed critique of patriarchal values. In contrast to Pinchwife's hypocrisy, his young bride Margery represents in her responses instinctive sexuality in its pure and unadulterated form. There is nothing smutty or evil about it: it is a natural appetite which not even threats of violence can put down. Margery has been forced into a loveless match with Pinchwife. But having been brought to town, and having met with Horner, she is determined to find her way to his bed. It takes her only one day to discover the delights of London and only a few more hours to find a way of deceiving her husband. Her education is completed by the society women who teach her how to lie brazenly in order to find sexual fulfilment.

The only character in the play who at first sight seems able to reconcile sexual and emotional attraction with marital commitment is Harcourt. Harcourt has fallen in love with Alithea and wishes to marry her, despite the fact that she is already promised to Sparkish. His attempts to undo this match are witty and at times farcical. However, Harcourt eventually allows his emotions to get the better of his judgement by declaring himself prepared to marry Alithea at a point in time when her honour is in question. Does this make him a fool or a truly romantic hero? Wycherley leaves the burden of interpretation to the audience. Alithea, for her part, is far more calculating. She originally intended marrying the fop Sparkish because she wanted a nominal husband who would be sufficiently disinterested in her never to be jealous. This is the best guarantee of her future freedom and pleasure. When she meets Harcourt, she is fearful of becoming involved with him precisely because she feels strongly attracted to him and will thus too easily be made vulnerable. In the end, she gratefully accepts him as a husband when her honour and reputation are in question and when she has discovered to her cost that Sparkish can indeed be made jealous. Even in the case of Harcourt and Alithea, who feel a genuine attraction for each other, emotions are seen to be dangerous because they can all too easily override the cool judgement one needs to survive in the jungle of contemporary society.

In complete contrast to Molière, Wycherley does not satirise socially deviant and destructive behaviour but rather the whole accepted base of social convention, which is shown to be a false and hypocritical veneer. Given Molière's interest in a deviant individual, the physical setting is for him relatively unimportant: Tartuffe could operate in any house in Paris. In Wycherley's case, the setting is very important. In addition to Horner's and Pinchwife's lodgings, he shows scenes of contemporary London – the New Exchange and the Piazza of Covent Garden – as if to stress that his aim is to give an accurate reflection of the society he saw around him and the values underpinning contemporary social intercourse.

The Country Wife is a powerful satire, which directs its barbs less at individuals and more at the hypocritical social conventions which fetter and inhibit human behaviour. Wycherley can see no easy solutions to the problems he has addressed, which is why his play deliberately avoids a neatly rounded happy ending. Instead it is structured in such a way as to underline the stalemate left at the end. Each character in turn expresses a view of marriage which shows them, just like the audience watching the play, to be locked in stereotyped roles from which there is no easy escape. In this way the audience is provoked through satire into considering their own solution.

Following his success with *The Country Wife*, Wycherley completed one further play, *The Plain Dealer*, which was published in 1677 and performed at some point in the previous year at Drury Lane.[1] Once again there were discreet borrowings from Molière, but Wycherley's study of misanthropy is altogether darker than Molière's in *Le Misanthrope*. Most of the characters behave like amoral predators in the social wilderness of contemporary London. Captain Manly is the only character with any real moral integrity (apart from the doggedly faithful Fidelia who seems a deliberately ironic throwback to a lost Arcadian world), but his behaviour seems designed to induce a sense of moral vertigo in the audience. Outraged by the way his former mistress Olivia has betrayed his trust in her and secretly married his best friend, Manly contemplates resorting to rape as a means of avenging himself. Wycherley rescues his audience from the moral chasm that begins to open in front of them by giving his play a deliberately contrived happy ending. Once again, Wycherley has directed his satire at the way social conventions offer a veneer of hypocritical respectability to more primitive and this time more destructive impulses. But the satire is so dark that the smile almost freezes on the lips.

Wycherley was now at the height of his popularity. The king showed him marks of esteem that he had never before offered to one who was not of noble birth. When Wycherley was ill in 1678, he

---

1. The only certain record is of a performance in December 1676, but it seems likely that the play was performed before this date.

visited him in his lodgings and subsequently paid for him to recover his health with a journey to Montpellier. In 1679 he even offered him the honour of acting as tutor to one of his many illegitimate children, the six-year-old Duke of Richmond. There would be a generous salary attached to the post and a pension when the office ceased. Wycherley's prospects were glowing: had he followed along this track, in due course he might even have found himself ennobled. At this point, another chance encounter with a woman both changed and ultimately wrecked the glittering life he had so carefully engineered for himself.

While taking the waters in Tunbridge Wells in 1677, he was introduced to a woman in a bookshop on the Parade who had asked for a copy of *The Plain Dealer*. The woman in question was Lætitia Isabella, Countess of Drogheda. As with his previous chance encounter (with the Duchess of Cleveland), Wycherley soon found himself embroiled in a new love affair. This time, however, his new-found partner was neither wealthy nor well connected. Her husband, it is true, was master of a large estate, but kept his wife on a tight rein. She was a beautiful and impetuous redhead who obviously found in Wycherley an emotional and sexual excitement that was lacking in her marriage. When the Earl of Drogheda died in the spring of 1679, the countess made it plain that she expected to marry Wycherley. He discussed the proposal with his father who advised him to go ahead with the marriage, even though at that point the countess's inheritance was already being disputed by the brother of the late earl.[1] Having spent his whole career as a writer casting doubt on the viability of marriage, Wycherley was now faced by the prospect of a marriage that would cause him serious embarrassment with the king (a married man would not be able to act as tutor to the Duke of Richmond) and wreck any chances of further social advancement. Despite his misgivings, Wycherley opted for marriage, only to find his worse fears confirmed.

The marriage was contracted in secret to avoid giving offence to the king. Inevitably the king found out and felt doubly betrayed. Wycherley was now *persona non grata* at court. The countess had hardly a penny to her name and was soon embroiled in a series of costly lawsuits to contest her frozen inheritance. As a marriage partner, she proved to be a female version of Pinchwife, using every form of emotional violence and blackmail to keep Wycherley at home and out of the clutches of his friends and other women. It is

1. See Connely, *Brawny Wycherley* (1969), p. 162.

reported that even when he visited the Cock Tavern in Bow Street, just opposite their lodgings, she insisted that he sit by an open window so that she might observe him with his friends.[1] Nor was she prepared to allow him to present himself at court and make any attempt to heal the breach with Charles II. Wycherley found himself, in his own life, committing the very same errors he had satirised in his plays.

After the sudden death of the countess in January 1682, Wycherley remained completely trapped by the aftermath of his union with her. Following the example of his litigious father, he fought endless legal battles for her estate, only to find himself bankrupted in the process. He was eventually thrown into Newgate for debt and then left to languish in the Fleet prison for years on end. No one, not even his father, was prepared to come to his assistance. Wycherley's release was as sudden as his initial imprisonment. Near the beginning of his reign in December 1685, James II witnessed a performance of *The Plain Dealer* at court, which prompted him to enquire of the author. When told of Wycherley's fate, he ordered that the author's debts should be paid and that he should be given an annual pension of £200. However, that ceased when James II was deposed at the Glorious Revolution.

Wycherley left prison broken in health and spirit. He particularly mourned the loss of his youthful good looks; there were to be no more chance encounters with society ladies. He contented himself with the friendship of writers such as Dryden and the young Pope and enjoyed the convivial gatherings of men of letters in Will's Coffee House. He never recovered any form of financial stability or prosperity; his wily father made sure that he never inherited any hard cash from the family estate. Living as 'a humble hermit' (as the critic John Dennis called him),[2] he managed to eke out a frugal existence in London or in the confines of the family estate in Clive until his death in 1716. It was a sad end to what had once been a life of glittering success and seemingly boundless promise.

1. Ibid., p. 170.
2. See *Dictionary of National Biography*, vol. lxiii, p. 199.

The Country Wife

A
Comedy

Acted at the
<small>THEATRE ROYAL</small>
Written by Mr. *Wycherley*

Indignor quicquam reprehendi, non quia crasse
Compositum illepideve putetur, sed quia nuper:
Nec veniam Antiquis, sed honorem & præmia posei[1]
Horat.

LONDON,
Printed for *Thomas Dring*, at the *Harrow*, at the
Corner of *Chancery-Lane* in *Fleet-Street*, 1675.

---

1. 'I grow impatient when a work is condemned not for being crudely and inelegantly composed but for being modern, while for the ancients not indulgence but honour and rewards are demanded' (Horace, *Epistles II*).

Prologue

spoken by MR. HART

Poets like Cudgel'd Bullys, never do
At first, or second blow, submit to you;
But will provoke you still, and ne're have done,
Till you are weary first, with laying on:
The late so bafled Scribler of this day,[1]
Though he stands trembling, bids me boldly say,
What we, before most Playes are us'd to do,
For Poets out of fear, first draw on you;
In a fierce Prologue, the still Pit defie,
And e're you speak, like Castril, give the lye;[2]
But though our Bayses Batles oft I've fought,[3]
And with bruis'd knuckles, their dear Conquests bought;
Nay, never yet fear'd Odds upon the Stage,
In Prologue dare not Hector with the Age,
But wou'd take Quarter from your saving hands,
Though Bayse within[4] all yielding Countermands,
Says you Confed'rate Wits no Quarter give,
Ther'fore his Play shan't ask your leave to live:
Well, let the vain rash Fop, by huffing so,
Think to obtain the better terms of you;
But we the Actors humbly will submit,
Now, and at any time, to a full Pit;
Nay, often we anticipate your rage,
And murder Poets for you, on our Stage:
We set no Guards upon our Tyring-Room;
But when with flying Colours, there you come,
We patiently you see, give up to you,
Our Poets, Virgins, nay our Matrons too.

---

1. Wycherley's preceding play, *The Gentleman Dancing Master*, had not enjoyed much popularity.
2. A reference to Jonson's play *The Alchemist*.
3. John Dryden was known as Bayes, having been satirised under that name in Buckingham's play *The Rehearsal*. Hart had acted all the major roles in Dryden's plays.
4. This time Bayes is used as a general name for authors.

The Persons

MR. HORNER,
MR. HARCOURT,
MR. DORILANT,
MR. PINCHWIFE,
MR. SPARKISH,
SIR JASPAR FIDGET,
MRS. MARGERY PINCHWIFE,
MRS. ALITHEA,
MY LADY FIDGET,
MRS. DAINTY FIDGET,
MRS. SQUEAMISH,
OLD LADY SQUEAMISH,
Waiters, Servants, and Attendants.
A BOY.
A QUACK,
LUCY, ALITHEA'S MAID,

Mr. *Hart.*
Mr. *Kenaston.*
Mr. *Lydal.*
Mr. *Mohun.*
Mr. *Haynes.*
Mr. *Cartwright.*
Mrs. *Bowtel.*
Mrs. *James.*
Mrs. *Knep.*
Mrs. *Corbet.*
Mrs. *Wyatt.*
Mrs. *Rutter.*

Mr. *Schotterel.*
Mrs. *Cory.*

THE SCENE LONDON.

Act I, Scene I

[*Enter* HORNER, *and* QUACK *following him at a distance.*]

HORNER: A Quack is as fit for a Pimp, as a Midwife for a Bawd; they are still but in their way, both helpers of Nature. – [*Aside.*]
Well, my dear Doctor, hast thou done what I desired.

QUACK: I have undone you for ever with the Women, and reported you throughout the whole Town as bad as an *Eunuch*, with as much trouble as if I had made you one in earnest.

HORNER: But have you told all the Midwives you know, the Orange Wenches at the Playhouses, the City Husbands, and old Fumbling Keepers of this end of the Town, for they'l be the readiest to report it.

QUACK: I have told all the Chamber-maids, Waiting women, Tyre women, and Old women of my acquaintance; nay, and whisper'd it as a secret to'em, and to the Whisperers of *Whitehal*;[1] so that you need not doubt 'twill spread, and you will be as odious to the handsome young Women, as –

HORNER: As the small Pox. – Well –

QUACK: And to the married Women of this end of the Town, as –

1. The royal palace.

HORNER: As the great ones;[1] nay, as their own Husbands.

QUACK: And to the City Dames as Annis-seed *Robin*[2] of filthy and contemptible memory; and they will frighten their Children with your name, especially their Females.

HORNER: And cry *Horner's* coming to carry you away: I am only afraid 'twill not be believ'd; you told'em 'twas by an *English-French* disaster, and an *English-French* Chirurgeon, who has given me at once, not only a Cure, but an Antidote for the future, against that damn'd malady, and that worse distemper, love, and all other Womens evils.

QUACK: Your late journey into *France* has made it the more credible, and your being here a fortnight before you appear'd in publick, looks as if you apprehended the shame, which I wonder you do not: Well I have been hired by young Gallants to bely'em t'other way; but you are the first wou'd be thought a Man unfit for Women.

HORNER: Dear Mr. Doctor, let vain Rogues be contented only to be thought abler Men than they are, generally 'tis all the pleasure they have, but mine lyes another way.

QUACK: You take, methinks, a very preposterous way to it, and as ridiculous as if we Operators in Physick, shou'd put forth Bills to disparage our Medicaments, with hopes to gain Customers.

HORNER: Doctor, there are Quacks in love, as well as Physick, who get but the fewer and worse Patients, for their boasting; a good name is seldom got by giving it ones self, and Women no more than honour are compass'd by bragging: Come, come Doctor, the wisest Lawyer never discovers the merits of his cause till the tryal; the wealthiest Man conceals his riches, and the cunning Gamster his play; Shy Husbands and Keepers like old Rooks are not to be cheated, but by a new unpractis'd trick; false friendship will pass now no more than false dice upon'em, no, not in the City.

[*Enter* BOY.]

BOY: There are two Ladies and a Gentleman coming up.

HORNER: A Pox, some unbelieving Sisters of my former acquaintance, who I am afraid, expect their sense shou'd be satisfy'd of the falsity of the report.

[*Enter Sir* JASPAR FIDGET, *Lady* FIDGET, *and Mrs.* DAINTY FIDGET.]

No – this formal Fool and Women!

QUACK: His Wife and Sister.

SIR JASPAR: My Coach breaking just now before your door Sir, I look upon as an occasional repremand to me Sir, for not kissing your hands Sir, since

1. The great pox or syphilis.
2. A famous hermaphrodite.

your coming out of *France* Sir; and so my disaster Sir, has been my good
fortune Sir; and this is my Wife, and Sister Sir.

HORNER: What then, Sir?

SIR JASPAR: My Lady, and Sister, Sir. – Wife, this is Master *Horner*.

LADY FIDGET: Master *Horner*, Husband!

SIR JASPAR: My Lady, my Lady *Fidget*, Sir.

HORNER: So, Sir.

SIR JASPAR: Won't you be acquainted with her Sir? (So the report is true, I
find by his coldness or aversion to the Sex; but I'll play the wag with
him.)   [*Aside.*]

Pray salute my Wife, my Lady, Sir.

HORNER: I will kiss no Mans Wife, Sir, for him, Sir; I have taken my eternal
leave, Sir, of the Sex already, Sir

SIR JASPAR: Hah, hah, hah; I'll plague him yet.   [*Aside.*]

Not know my Wife, Sir?

HORNER: I do know your Wife, Sir, she's a Woman, Sir, and consequently a
Monster, Sir, a greater Monster than a Husband, Sir.

SIR JASPAR: A Husband; how, Sir?

HORNER: So, Sir; [*makes horns.*] but I make no more Cuckholds, Sir.

SIR JASPAR: Hah, hah, hah, *Mercury, Mercury.*[1]

LADY FIDGET: Pray, Sir *Jaspar*, let us be gone from this rude fellow.

DAINTY: Who, by his breeding, wou'd think, he had ever been in *France*?

LADY FIDGET: Foh, he's but too much a French fellow, such as hate Women of
quality and virtue, for their love to their Husbands, Sr. *Jaspar*; a Woman
is hated by'em as much for loving her Husband, as for loving their
Money: But pray, let's be gone.

HORNER: You do well, Madam, for I have nothing that you came for: I have
brought over not so much as a Bawdy Picture, new Postures, nor the
second Part of the *Escole de Filles;*[2] Nor –

QUACK: Hold for shame, Sir; what d'y mean? you'l ruine your self for ever
with the Sex –   [*Apart to* Horner.]

SIR JASPAR: Hah, hah, hah, he hates Women perfectly I find.

DAINTY: What pitty 'tis he shou'd.

LADY FIDGET: Ay, he's a base rude Fellow for't; but affectation makes not a
Woman more odious to them, than Virtue.

HORNER: Because your Virtue is your greatest affectation, Madam.

LADY FIDGET: How, you sawcy Fellow, wou'd you wrong my honour?

HORNER: If I cou'd.

LADY FIDGET: How d'y mean, Sir?

SIR JASPAR: Hah, hah, hah, no he can't wrong your Ladyships honour, upon
my honour; he poor Man – hark you in your ear – a meer Eunuch.

---

1. Mercury was seen as an emblem of wit.
2. The references are to erotic drawings and books.

LADY FIDGET: O filthy French Beast, foh, foh; why do we stay? let's be gone; I can't endure the sight of him.

SIR JASPAR: Stay, but till the Chairs come, they'l be here presently.

LADY FIDGET: No, no.

SIR JASPAR: Nor can I stay longer; 'tis – let me see, a quarter and a half quarter of a minute past eleven; the Council will be sate, I must away: business must be preferr'd always before Love and Ceremony with the wise Mr. *Horner*.

HORNER: And the Impotent Sir *Jaspar*.

SIR JASPAR: Ay, ay, the impotent Master *Horner*, hah, ha, ha.

LADY FIDGET: What leave us with a filthy Man alone in his lodgings?

SIR JASPAR: He's an innocent Man now, you know; pray stay, I'll hasten the Chaires to you. – Mr. *Horner* your Servant, I shou'd be glad to see you at my house; pray, come and dine with me, and play at Cards with my Wife after dinner, you are fit for Women at that game; yet hah, ha – ('Tis as much a Husbands prudence to provide innocent diversion for a Wife, as to hinder her unlawful pleasures; and he had better employ her, than let her employ her self.)   [*Aside.*]
Farewel.   [*Exit Sir* JASPAR.]

HORNER: Your Servant Sr. *Jaspar*.

LADY FIDGET: I will not stay with him, foh –

HORNER: Nay, Madam, I beseech you stay, if it be but to see, I can be as civil to Ladies yet, as they wou'd desire.

LADY FIDGET: No, no, foh, you cannot be civil to Ladies.

DAINTY: You as civil as Ladies wou'd desire.

LADY FIDGET: No, no, no, foh, foh, foh.   [*Exeunt Ladie* FIDGET *and* DAINTY.]

QUACK: Now I think, I, or you your self rather, have done your business with the Women.

HORNER: Thou art an Ass, don't you see already upon the report and my carriage, this grave Man of business leaves his Wife in my lodgings, invites me to his house and wife, who before wou'd not be acquainted with me out of jealousy.

QUACK: Nay, by this means you may be the more acquainted with the Husbands, but the less with the Wives.

HORNER: Let me alone, if I can but abuse the Husbands, I'll soon disabuse the Wives: Stay – I'll reckon you up the advantages, I am like to have by my Stratagem: First, I shall be rid of all my old Acquaintances, the most insatiable sorts of Duns, that invade our Lodgings in a morning: And next, to the pleasure of making a New Mistriss, is that of being rid of an old One, and of all old Debts; Love when it comes to be so, is paid the most unwillingly.

QUACK: Well, you may be so rid of your old Acquaintances; but how will you get any new Ones?

HORNER: Doctor, thou wilt never make a good Chymist, thou art so incredulous and impatient; ask but all the young Fellows of the Town, if they do not loose more time like Huntsmen, in starting the game, than in running it down; one knows not where to find'em, who will, or will not; Women of Quality are so civil, you can hardly distinguish love from good breeding, and a Man is often mistaken; but now I can be sure, she that shews an aversion to me loves the sport, as those Women that are gone, whom I warrant to be right:[1] And then the next thing, is your Women of Honour, as you call'em, are only chary of their reputations, not their Persons, and 'tis scandal they wou'd avoid, not Men: Now may I have, by the reputation of an Eunuch, the Priviledges of One; and be seen in a Ladies Chamber, in a morning as early as her Husband; kiss Virgins before their Parents, or Lovers; and may be in short the *Pas par tout* of the Town. Now Doctor.

QUACK: Nay, now you shall be the Doctor; and your Process is so new, that we do not know but it may succeed.

HORNER: Not so new neither, *Probatum est* Doctor.[2]

QUACK: Well, I wish you luck and many Patients whil'st I go to mine.

[*Exit* Quack.]

[*Enter* HARCOURT, *and* DORILANT *to* HORNER.]

HARCOURT: Come, your appearance at the Play yesterday, has I hope hardned you for the future against the Womens contempt, and the Mens raillery; and now you'l abroad as you were wont.

HORNER: Did I not bear it bravely?

DORILANT: With a most Theatrical impudence; nay more than the Orange-wenches shew there, or a drunken vizard Mask,[3] or a great belly'd Actress; nay, or the most impudent of Creatures, an ill Poet; or what is yet more impudent, a second-hand Critick.

HORNER: But what say the Ladies, have they no pitty?

HARCOURT: What Ladies? the vizard Masques you know never pitty a Man when all's gone, though in their Service.

DORILANT: And for the Women in the boxes, you'd never pitty them, when 'twas in your power.

HARCOURT: They say 'tis pitty, but all that deal with common Women shou'd be serv'd so.

DORILANT: Nay, I dare swear, they won't admit you to play at Cards with them, go to Plays with'em, or do the little duties which other Shadows of men, are wont to do for'em.

HORNER: Who do you call Shadows of Men?

DORILANT: Half Men

HORNER: What Boyes?

1. Ready and willing.
2. 'It has already been tried', namely in Terence's classical comedy *The Eunuch*.
3. A prostitute, wearing a mask.

DORILANT: Ay your old Boyes, old *beaux Garcons*, who like superannuated Stallions are suffer'd to run, feed, and whinney with the Mares as long as they live, though they can do nothing else.

HORNER: Well a Pox on love and wenching, Women serve but to keep a Man from better Company; though I can't enjoy them, I shall you the more: good fellowship and friendship, are lasting, rational and manly pleasures.

HARCOURT: For all that give me some of those pleasures, you call effeminate too, they help to relish one another.

HORNER: They disturb one another.

HARCOURT: No, Mistresses are like Books; if you pore upon them too much, they doze you, and make you unfit for Company; but if us'd discreetly, you are the fitter for conversation by'em.

DORILANT: A Mistress shou'd be like a little Country retreat near the Town, not to dwell in constantly, but only for a night and away; to tast the Town the better when a Man returns.

HORNER: I tell you, 'tis as hard to be a good Fellow, a good Friend, and a Lover of Women, as 'tis to be a good Fellow, a good Friend, and a Lover of Money: You cannot follow both, then choose your side; Wine gives you liberty, Love takes it away.

DORILANT: Gad, he's in the right on't.

HORNER: Wine gives you joy, Love grief and tortures; besides the Chirurgeon's. Wine makes us witty, Love only Sots: Wine makes us sleep, Love breaks it.

DORILANT: By the World he has reason, *Harcourt*.

HORNER: Wine makes –

DORILANT: Ay, Wine makes us – makes us Princes, Love makes us Beggars, poor Rogues, y gad – and Wine –

HORNER: So, there's one converted. – No, no, Love and Wine, Oil and Vinegar.

HARCOURT: I grant it; Love will still be uppermost.

HORNER: Come, for my part I will have only those glorious, manly pleasures of being very drunk, and very slovenly.

[*Enter* BOY.]

BOY: Mr. *Sparkish* is below, Sir.

HARCOURT: What, my dear Friend! a Rogue that is fond of me, only I think for abusing him.

DORILANT: No, he can no more think the Men laugh at him, than that Women jilt him, his opinion of himself is so good.

HORNER: Well, there's another pleasure by drinking, I thought not of; I shall loose his acquaintance, because he cannot drink; and you know 'tis a very hard thing to be rid of him, for he's one of those nauseous offerers at wit, who like the worst Fidlers run themselves into all Companies.

HARCOURT: One, that by being in the Company of Men of sense wou'd pass for one.

HORNER: And may so to the short-sighted World, as a false Jewel amongst true ones, is not discern'd at a distance; his Company is as troublesome to us, as a Cuckolds, when you have a mind to his Wife's.

HARCOURT: No, the Rogue will not let us enjoy one another, but ravishes our conversation, though he signifies no more to't, than Sir *Martin Mar-all's* gaping, and auker'd[1] thrumming upon the Lute, does to his Man's Voice, and Musick.[2]

DORILANT: And to pass for a wit in Town, shewes himself a fool every night to us, that are guilty of the plot.

HORNER: Such wits as he, are, to a Company of reasonable Men, like Rooks to the Gamesters, who only fill a room at the Table, but are so far from contributing to the play, that they only serve to spoil the fancy of those that do.

DORILANT: Nay, they are us'd like Rooks too, snub'd, check'd, and abus'd; yet the Rogues will hang on.

HORNER: A Pox on'em, and all that force Nature, and wou'd be still what she forbids'em; Affectation is her greatest Monster.

HARCOURT: Most Men are the contraries to that they wou'd seem; your bully you see, is a Coward with a long Sword; the little humbly fawning Physician with his Ebony cane, is he that destroys Men.

DORILANT: The Usurer, a poor Rogue, possess'd of moldy Bonds, and Mortgages; and we they call Spend-thrifts, are only wealthy, who lay out his money upon daily new purchases of pleasure.

HORNER: Ay, your errantest cheat, is your Trustee, or Executor; your jealous Man, the greatest Cuckhold; your Church-man, the greatest Atheist; and your noisy pert Rogue of a wit, the greatest Fop, dullest Ass, and worst Company as you shall see: For here he comes.

[Enter SPARKISH *to them.]*

SPARKISH: How is't, Sparks, how is't? Well Faith, *Harry*, I must railly thee a little, ha, ha, ha, upon the report in Town of thee, ha, ha, ha, I can't hold y Faith; shall I speak?

HORNER: Yes, but you'l be so bitter then.

SPARKISH: Honest *Dick* and *Franck* here shall answer for me, I will not be extream bitter by the Univers.

HARCOURT: We will be bound in ten thousand pound Bond, he shall not be bitter at all.

DORILANT: Nor sharp, nor sweet.

HORNER: What, not down right insipid?

SPARKISH: Nay then, since you are so brisk, and provoke me, take what

1. Awkward.
2. A reference to Dryden's play *Sir Martin Mar-all*.

follows; you must know, I was discoursing and raillying with some
Ladies yesterday, and they hapned to talk of the fine new signes in
Town.

HORNER: Very fine Ladies I believe.

SPARKISH: Said I, I know where the best new sign is. Where, says one of the
Ladies? In *Covent-Garden*, I reply'd. Said another, In what street? In
Russel-street, answer'd I. Lord says another, I'm sure there was ne're a
fine new sign there yesterday. Yes, but there was, said I again, and it
came out of *France*, and has been there a fortnight.

DORILANT: A Pox I can hear no more, prethee.

HORNER: No hear him out; let him tune his crowd[1] a while.

HARCOURT: The worst Musick the greatest preparation.

SPARKISH: Nay faith, I'll make you laugh. It cannot be, says a third Lady. Yes,
yes, quoth I again. Says a fourth Lady,

HORNER: Look to't, we'l have no more Ladies.

SPARKISH: No. – then mark, mark, now, said I to the fourth, did you never see
Mr. *Horner*; he lodges in *Russel-street*, and he's a sign of a Man, you
know, since he came out of *France*, heh, hah, he.

HORNER: But the Divel take me, if thine be the sign of a jest.

SPARKISH: With that they all fell a laughing, till they bepiss'd themselves;
what, but it do's not move you, methinks? well see one had as good go
to Law without a witness, as break a jest without a laugher on ones
side. – Come, come Sparks, but where do we dine, I have left at *Whitehal*
an Earl to dine with you.

DORILANT: Why, I thought thou hadst lov'd a Man with a title better, than a
Suit with a French trimming to't.

HARCOURT: Go, to him again.

SPARKISH: No, Sir, a wit to me is the greatest title in the World.

HORNER: But go dine with your Earl, Sir, he may be exceptious;[2] we are your
Friends, and will not take it ill to be left, I do assure you.

HARCOURT: Nay, faith he shall go to him.

SPARKISH: Nay, pray Gentlemen.

DORILANT: We'l thrust you out, if you wo'not, what disappoint any Body for
us.

SPARKISH: Nay, dear Gentlemen hear me.

HORNER: No, no, Sir, by no means; pray go Sir.

SPARKISH: Why, dear Rogues.   [*They all thrust him out of the room.*]

DORILANT: No, no.

ALL: Ha, ha, Ha.

[SPARKISH *returns.*]

SPARKISH: But, Sparks, pray hear me; what d'ye think I'll eat then with gay

1. A fiddle.
2. Take exception.

shallow Fops, and silent Coxcombs? I think wit as necessary at dinner as a glass of good wine, and that's the reason I never have any stomach when I eat alone. – Come, but where do we dine?

HORNER: Ev'n where you will.

SPARKISH: At *Chateline's.*

DORILANT: Yes, if you will.

SPARKISH: Or at the *Cock.*

DORILANT: Yes, if you please.

SPARKISH: Or at the *Dog* and *Partridg.*[1]

HORNER: Ay, if you have mind to't, for we shall dine at neither.

SPARKISH: Pshaw, with your fooling we shall loose the new Play; and I wou'd no more miss seing a new Play the first day, than I wou'd miss sitting in the wits Row;[2] therefore I'll go fetch my Mistriss and away.

[*Exit* SPARKISH.]

[*Manent* HORNER, HARCOURT, DORILANT; *Enter to them Mr.* PINCHWIFE.]

HORNER: Who have we here, *Pinchwife?*

PINCHWIFE: Gentlemen, your humble Servant.

HORNER: Well, *Jack,* by thy long absence from the Town, the grumness[3] of thy countenance, and the slovenlyness of thy habit; I shou'd give thee joy, shou'd I not, of Marriage?

PINCHWIFE: (Death does he know I'm married too? I thought to have conceal'd it from him at least.) [*Aside.*]
My long stay in the Country will excuse my dress, and I have a suit of Law, that brings me up to Town, that puts me out of humour; besides I must give *Sparkish* to morrow five thousand pound to lye with my Sister.[4]

HORNER: Nay, you Country Gentlemen rather than not purchase, will buy any thing, and he is a crackt title, if we may quibble: Well, but am I to give thee joy, I heard thou wert marry'd.

PINCHWIFE: What then?

HORNER: Why, the next thing that is to be heard, is thou'rt a Cuckold.

PINCHWIFE: Insupportable name. [*Aside.*]

HORNER: But I did not expect Marriage from such a Whoremaster as you, one that knew the Town so much, and Women so well.

PINCHWIFE: Why, I have marry'd no *London* Wife.

HORNER: Pshaw, that's all one, that grave circumspection in marrying a Country Wife, is like refusing a deceitful pamper'd *Smithfield* Jade,[5] to go and be cheated by a Friend in the Country.

1. The three places mentioned were all popular restaurants near Covent Garden.
2. In the playhouse the 'wits' preferred to sit in the pit.
3. Moroseness.
4. The reference is to the dowry he will pay on behalf of his sister.
5. A reference to the horse market in Smithfield with its dubious jades, meaning both horses and women.

PINCHWIFE: A Pox on him and his Simile.   [*Aside.*]
   At least we are a little surer of the breed there, know what her keeping
   has been, whether soyl'd or unsound.
HORNER: Come, come, I have known a clap gotten in *Wales*, and there are
   Cozens, Justices, Clarks, and Chaplains in the Country, I won't say
   Coach-men, but she's handsome and young.
PINCHWIFE: I'll answer as I shou'd do.   [*Aside.*]
   No, no, she has no beauty, but her youth; no attraction, but her modesty,
   wholesome, homely, and huswifely, that's all.
DORILANT: He talks as like a Grasier as he looks.[1]
PINCHWIFE: She's too auker'd, ill favour'd, and silly to bring to Town.
HARCOURT: Then methinks you shou'd bring her, to be taught breeding.
PINCHWIFE: To be taught; no, Sir, I thank you, good Wives, and private
   Souldiers shou'd be ignorant. – (I'll keep her from your instructions, I
   warrant you.)   [*Aside.*]
HARCOURT: The Rogue is as jealous, as if his wife were not ignorant.
HORNER: Why, if she be ill favour'd, there will be less danger here for you,
   than by leaving her in the Country; we have such variety of dainties,
   that we are seldom hungry.
DORILANT: But they have always coarse, constant, swinging stomachs in the
   Country.
HARCOURT: Foul Feeders indeed.
DORILANT: And your Hospitality is great there.
HARCOURT: Open house, every Man's welcome.
PINCHWIFE: So, so, Gentlemen.
HORNER: But prethee, why woud'st thou marry her? if she be ugly, ill-bred,
   and silly, she must be rich then.
PINCHWIFE: As rich as if she brought me twenty thousand pound out of this
   Town; for she'l be as sure not to spend her moderate portion, as a
   London Baggage wou'd be to spend hers, let it be what it wou'd; so 'tis
   all one: then because shes ugly, she's the likelyer to be my own; and
   being ill-bred, she'l hate conversation; and since silly and innocent, will
   not know the difference betwixt a Man of one and twenty, and one of
   forty.
HORNER: Nine – to my knowledge; but if she be silly, she'l expect as much
   from a Man of forty nine, as from him of one and twenty: But methinks
   wit is more necessary than beauty, and I think no young Woman ugly
   that has it, and no handsome Woman agreable without it.
PINCHWIFE: 'Tis my maxime, he's a Fool that marrys, but he's a greater that
   does not marry a Fool; what is wit in a Wife good for, but to make a Man
   a Cuckold?
HORNER: Yes, to keep it from his knowledge.
PINCHWIFE: A Fool cannot contrive to make her husband a Cuckold.

1. A grasier, or grazier fattens cattle for market.

HORNER: No, but she'l club with a Man that can; and what is worse, if she cannot make her Husband a Cuckold, she'l make him jealous, and pass for one, and then 'tis all one.

PINCHWIFE: Well, well, I'll take care for one, my Wife shall make me no Cuckold, though she had your help Mr. *Horner*; I understand the Town, Sir.

DORILANT: His help! [*Aside.*]

HARCOURT: He's come newly to Town it seems, and has not heard how things are with him. [*Aside.*]

HORNER: But tell me, has Marriage cured thee of whoring, which it seldom does.

HARCOURT: 'Tis more than age can do.

HORNER: No, the word is, I'll marry and live honest; but a Marriage vow is like a penitent Gamesters Oath, and entring into Bonds, and penalties to stint himself to such a particular small sum at play for the future, which makes him but the more eager, and not being able to hold out, looses his Money again, and his forfeit to boot.

DORILANT: Ay, ay, a Gamester will be a Gamester, whilst his Money lasts; and a Whoremaster, whilst his vigour.

HARCOURT: Nay, I have known'em, when they are broke and can loose no more, keep a fumbling with the Box in their hands to fool with only, and hinder other Gamesters.

DORILANT: That had wherewithal to make lusty stakes.

PINCHWIFE: Well, Gentlemen, you may laugh at me, but you shall never lye with my Wife, I know the Town.

HORNER: But prethee, was not the way you were in better, is not keeping better than Marriage?

PINCHWIFE: A Pox on't, the Jades wou'd jilt me, I cou'd never keep a Whore to my self.

HORNER: So then you only marry'd to keep a Whore to your self; well, but let me tell you, Women, as you say, are like Souldiers made constant and loyal by good pay, rather than by Oaths and Covenants, therefore I'd advise my Friends to keep rather than marry; since too I find by your example, it does not serve ones turn, for I saw you yesterday in the eighteen penny place[1] with a pretty Country-wench.

PINCHWIFE: How the Divel, did he see my Wife then? I sate there that she might not be seen; but she shall never go to a play again. [*Aside.*]

HORNER: What dost thou blush at nine and forty, for having been seen with a Wench?

DORILANT: No Faith, I warrant 'twas his Wife, which he seated there out of sight, for he's a cunning Rogue, and understands the Town.

HARCOURT: He blushes, then 'twas his Wife; for Men are now more ashamed to be seen with them in publick, than with a Wench.

---

1. The middle gallery: less expensive and less fashionable than pit and boxes.

PINCHWIFE: Hell and damnation, I'm undone, since *Horner* has seen her, and
they know 'twas she.   [*Aside.*]

HORNER: But prethee, was it thy Wife? she was exceedingly pretty; I was in
love with her at that distance.

PINCHWIFE: You are like never to be nearer to her. Your Servant Gentlemen.
[*Offers to go.*]

HORNER: Nay, prethee stay.

PINCHWIFE: I cannot, I will not.

HORNER: Come you shall dine with us.

PINCHWIFE: I have din'd already.

HORNER: Come, I know thou hast not; I'll treat thee dear Rogue, thou sha't
spend none of thy *Hampshire* Money to day.

PINCHWIFE: Treat me; so he uses me already like his Cuckold.   [*Aside.*]

HORNER: Nay, you shall not go.

PINCHWIFE: I must, I have business at home.   [*Exit* PINCHWIFE.]

HARCOURT: To beat his Wife, he's as jealous of her, as a *Cheapside* Husband of
a *Covent-garden* Wife.[1]

HORNER: Why, 'tis as hard to find an old Whoremaster without jealousy and
the gout, as a young one without fear or the Pox.

> As Gout in Age, from Pox in Youth proceeds;
> So Wenching past, then jealousy succeeds:
> The worst disease that Love and Wenching breeds.

Act II, Scene I

[*Mrs.* MARGERY PINCHWIFE, *and* ALITHEA.
Mr. PINCHWIFE *peeping behind at the door.*]

MRS. PINCHWIFE: Pray, Sister, where are the best Fields and Woods, to walk in
in *London*?

ALITHEA: A pretty Question; why, Sister! *Mulberry Garden*, and St. *James's
Park*; and for close walks the *New Exchange*.[2]

MRS. PINCHWIFE: Pray, Sister, tell me why my Husband looks so grum here in
Town? and keeps me up so close, and will not let me go a walking, nor
let me wear my best Gown yesterday?

ALITHEA: O he's jealous, Sister.

MRS. PINCHWIFE: Jealous, what's that?

ALITHEA: He's afraid you shou'd love another Man.

1. A merchant husband of a fashionable wife.
2. The Mulberry Garden was in St James's Park, and the New Exchange was a
   fashionable arcade of shops.

MRS. PINCHWIFE: How shou'd he be afraid of my loving another man, when he will not let me see any but himself.

ALITHEA: Did he not carry you yesterday to a Play?

MRS. PINCHWIFE: Ay, but we sate amongst ugly People, he wou'd not let me come near the Gentry, who sate under us, so that I cou'd not see'em: He told me, none but naughty Women sate there, whom they tous'd and mous'd;[1] but I wou'd have ventur'd for all that.

ALITHEA: But how did you like the Play?

MRS. PINCHWIFE: Indeed I was aweary of the Play, but I lik'd hugeously the Actors; they are the goodlyest proper'st Men, Sister.

ALITHEA: O but you must not like the Actors, Sister.

MRS. PINCHWIFE: Ay, how shou'd I help it, Sister? Pray, Sister, when my Husband comes in, will you ask leave for me to go a walking?

ALITHEA: A walking, hah, ha; Lord, a Country Gentlewomans leasure is the drudgery of a foot-post;[2] and she requires as much airing as her Husbands Horses. *[Aside.]*

[*Enter Mr.* PINCHWIFE *to them.*]

But here comes your Husband; I'll ask, though I'm sure he'l not grant it

MRS. PINCHWIFE: He says he won't let me go abroad, for fear of catching the Pox.

ALITHEA: Fye, the small Pox you shou'd say.

MRS. PINCHWIFE: Oh my dear, dear Bud, welcome home; why dost thou look so fropish,[3] who has nanger'd thee?

PINCHWIFE: Your a Fool.[*Mrs.* PINCHWIFE *goes aside, & cryes.*]

ALITHEA: Faith so she is, for crying for no fault, poor tender Creature!

PINCHWIFE: What you wou'd have her as impudent as your self, as errant a Jilflirt, a gadder, a Magpy, and to say all a meer notorious Town-Woman?

ALITHEA: Brother, you are my only Censurer; and the honour of your Family shall sooner suffer in your Wife there, than in me, though I take the innocent liberty of the Town.

PINCHWIFE: Hark you Mistriss, do not talk so before my Wife, the innocent liberty of the Town!

ALITHEA: Why, pray, who boasts of any intrigue with me? what Lampoon has made my name notorious? what ill Women frequent my Lodgings? I keep no Company with any Women of scandalous reputations.

PINCHWIFE: No, you keep the Men of scandalous reputations Company.

ALITHEA: Where? wou'd you not have me civil? answer'em in a Box at the Plays? in the drawing room at *Whitehal*? in St. *James's Park*? *Mulberry-garden*? or –

1. The modern equivalent would be 'felt up' or 'touched up'.
2. A footman.
3. Grumpy or fed up.

PINCHWIFE: Hold, hold, do not teach my Wife, where the Men are to be found; I believe she's the worse for your Town documents already; I bid you keep her in ignorance as I do.

MRS. PINCHWIFE: Indeed be not angry with her Bud, she will tell me nothing of the Town, though I ask her a thousand times a day.

PINCHWIFE: Then you are very inquisitive to know, I find?

MRS. PINCHWIFE: Not I indeed, Dear, I hate *London*; Our Place-house[1] in the Country is worth a thousand of't, wou'd I were there again.

PINCHWIFE: So you shall I warrant; but were you not talking of Plays, and Players, when I came in? you are her encourager in such discourses.

MRS. PINCHWIFE: No indeed, Dear, she chid me just now for liking the Player Men.

PINCHWIFE: Nay, if she be so innocent as to own to me her liking them, there is no hurt in't –   [*Aside.*]
Come my poor Rogue, but thou lik'st none better than me?

MRS. PINCHWIFE: Yes indeed, but I do, the Player Men are finer Folks.

PINCHWIFE: But you love none better than me?

MRS. PINCHWIFE: You are mine own Dear Bud, and I know you, I hate a Stranger.

PINCHWIFE: Ay, my Dear, you must love me only, and not be like the naughty Town Women, who only hate their Husbands, and love every Man else, love Plays, Visits, fine Coaches, fine Cloaths, Fidles, Balls, Treates, and so lead a wicked Town-life.

MRS. PINCHWIFE: Nay, if to enjoy all these things be a Town-life, *London* is not so bad a place, Dear.

PINCHWIFE: How! if you love me, you must hate *London*.

ALITHEA: The Fool has forbid me discovering to her the pleasures of the Town, and he is now setting her a gog upon them himself.

MRS. PINCHWIFE: But, Husband, do the Town-women love the Player Men too?

PINCHWIFE: Yes, I warrant you.

MRS. PINCHWIFE: Ay, I warrant you.

PINCHWIFE: Why, you do not, I hope?

MRS. PINCHWIFE: No, no, Bud; but why have we no Player-men in the Country?

PINCHWIFE: Ha – Mrs. Minx, ask me no more to go to a Play.

MRS. PINCHWIFE: Nay, why, Love? I did not care for going; but when you forbid me, you make me as't were desire it.

ALITHEA: So 'twill be in other things, I warrant.   [*Aside.*]

MRS. PINCHWIFE: Pray, let me go to a Play, Dear.

PINCHWIFE: Hold your Peace, I wo'not.

MRS. PINCHWIFE: Why, Love?

PINCHWIFE: Why, I'll tell you.

1. Manor-house.

ALITHEA: Nay if he tell her, she'l give him more cause to forbid her that place.
[*Aside.*]

MRS. PINCHWIFE: Pray, why, Dear?

PINCHWIFE: First, you like the Actors, and the Gallants may like you.

MRS. PINCHWIFE: What, a homely Country Girl? no Bud, no body will like me.

PINCHWIFE: I tell you, yes, they may.

MRS. PINCHWIFE: No, no, you jest – I won't believe you, I will go.

PINCHWIFE: I tell you then, that one of the lewdest Fellows in Town, who saw
you there, told me he was in love with you.

MRS. PINCHWIFE: Indeed! who, who, pray who wast?

PINCHWIFE: I've gone too far, and slipt before I was aware; how overjoy'd
she is! [*Aside.*]

MRS. PINCHWIFE: Was it any *Hampshire* Gallant, any of our Neighbours? I
promise you, I am beholding to him.

PINCHWIFE: I promise you, you lye; for he wou'd but ruin you, as he has done
hundreds: he has no other love for Women, but that, such as he, look
upon Women like Basilicks,[1] but to destroy'em.

MRS. PINCHWIFE: Ay, but if he loves me, why shou'd he ruin me? answer me
to that: methinks he shou'd not, I wou'd do him no harm.

ALITHEA: Hah, ha, ha.

PINCHWIFE: 'Tis very well; but I'll keep him from doing you any harm, or me
either.

[*Enter* SPARKISH *and* HARCOURT.]

But here comes Company, get you in, get you in.

MRS. PINCHWIFE: But pray, Husband, is he a pretty Gentleman, that loves me?

PINCHWIFE: In baggage, in. [*Thrusts her in: shuts the door.*]
What all the lewd Libertines of the Town brought to my Lodging, by
this easie Coxcomb! S'death I'll not suffer it.

SPARKISH: Here *Harcourt*, do you approve my choice?
Dear, little Rogue, I told you, I'd bring you acquainted with all my
Friends, the wits, and – [HARCOURT *salutes her.*]

PINCHWIFE: Ay, they shall know her, as well as you your self will, I warrant
you.

SPARKISH: This is one of those, my pretty Rogue, that are to dance at your
Wedding to morrow; and him you must bid welcom ever, to what you
and I have.

PINCHWIFE: Monstrous! – [*Aside.*]

SPARKISH: *Harcourt* how dost thou like her, Faith? Nay, Dear, do not look down;
I should hate to have a Wife of mine out of countenance at any thing.

PINCHWIFE: Wonderful!

SPARKISH: Tell me, I say, *Harcourt*, how dost thou like her? thou hast star'd
upon her enough, to resolve me.

1. A legendary reptile whose eyes supposedly had the power to kill.

HARCOURT: So infinitely well, that I cou'd wish I had a Mistriss too, that might differ from her in nothing, but her love and engagement to you.

ALITHEA: Sir, Master *Sparkish* has often told me, that his Acquaintance were all Wits and Raillieurs, and now I find it.

SPARKISH: No, by the Universe, Madam, he does not railly now; you may believe him: I do assure you, he is the honestest, worthyest, true hearted Gentleman – A man of such perfect honour, he wou'd say nothing to a Lady, he does not mean.

PINCHWIFE: Praising another Man to his Mistriss!

HARCOURT: Sir, you are so beyond expectation obliging, that –

SPARKISH: Nay, I gad, I am sure you do admire her extreamly, I see't in your eyes. – He does admire you Madam. – By the World, don't you?

HARCOURT: Yes, above the World, or, the most glorious part of it, her whole Sex; and till now I never thought I shou'd have envy'd you, or any Man about to marry, but you have the best excuse for Marriage I ever knew.

ALITHEA: Nay, now, Sir, I'm satisfied you are of the Society of the Wits, and Raillieurs, since you cannot spare your Friend, even when he is but too civil to you; but the surest sign is, since you are an Enemy to Marriage, for that I hear you hate as much as business or bad Wine.

HARCOURT: Truly, Madam, I never was an Enemy to Marriage, till now, because Marriage was never an Enemy to me before.

ALITHEA: But why, Sir, is Marriage an Enemy to you now? Because it robs you of your Friend here; for you look upon a Friend married, as one gone into a Monastery, that is dead to the World.

HARCOURT: 'Tis indeed, because you marry him; I see Madam, you can guess my meaning: I do confess heartily and openly, I wish it were in my power to break the Match, by Heavens I wou'd.

SPARKISH: Poor *Franck*!

ALITHEA: Wou'd you be so unkind to me?

HARCOURT: No, no, 'tis not because I wou'd be unkind to you.

SPARKISH: Poor *Franck*, no gad, 'tis only his kindness to me.

PINCHWIFE: Great kindness to you indeed; insensible Fop, let a Man make love to his Wife to his face. [*Aside.*]

SPARKISH: Come dear *Franck*, for all my Wife there that shall be, thou shalt enjoy me sometimes dear Rogue; by my honour, we Men of wit condole for our deceased Brother in Marriage, as much as for one dead in earnest: I think that was prettily said of me, ha *Harcourt*? – But come *Franck*, be not melancholy for me.

HARCOURT: No, I assure you I am not melancholy for you.

SPARKISH: Prethee, *Frank*, dost think my Wife that shall be there a fine Person?

HARCOURT: I cou'd gaze upon her, till I became as blind as you are.

SPARKISH: How, as I am! how!

HARCOURT: Because you are a Lover, and true Lovers are blind, stockblind.[1]

1. Blind as a lifeless thing.

SPARKISH: True, true; but by the World, she has wit too, as well as beauty: go, go with her into a corner, and trye if she has wit, talk to her any thing, she's bashful before me.

HARCOURT: Indeed if a Woman wants wit in a corner, she has it no where.

ALITHEA: Sir, you dispose of me a little before your time. [*Aside to* SPARKISH.]

SPARKISH: Nay, nay, Madam let me have an earnest of your obedience, or – go, go, Madam –

[HARCOURT *courts* ALITHEA *aside.*]

PINCHWIFE: How, Sir, if you are not concern'd for the honour of a Wife, I am for that of a Sister; he shall not debauch her: be a Pander to your own Wife, bring Men to her, let'em make love before your face, thrust'em into a corner together, then leav'em in private! is this your Town wit and conduct?

SPARKISH: Hah, ha, ha, a silly wise Rogue, wou'd make one laugh more than a stark Fool, hah, ha: I shall burst. Nay, you shall not disturb'em; I'll vex thee, by the World.

[*Struggles with* PINCHWIFE *to keep him from* HARCOURT *and* ALITHEA.]

ALITHEA: The writings are drawn, Sir, settlements made; 'tis too late, Sir, and past all revocation,

HARCOURT: Then so is my death.

ALITHEA: I wou'd not be unjust to him.

HARCOURT: Then why to me so?

ALITHEA: I have no obligation to you.

HARCOURT: My love.

ALITHEA: I had his before.

HARCOURT: You never had it; he wants you see jealousie, the only infallible sign of it.

ALITHEA: Love proceeds from esteem; he cannot distrust my virtue, besides he loves me, or he wou'd not marry me.

HARCOURT: Marrying you, is no more sign of his love, than bribing your Woman, that he may marry you, is a sign of his generosity: Marriage is rather a sign of interest, than love; and he that marries a fortune, covets a Mistress, not loves her: But if you take Marriage for a sign of love, take it from me immediately.

ALITHEA: No, now you have put a scruple in my head; but in short, Sir, to end our dispute, I must marry him, my reputation wou'd suffer in the World else.

HARCOURT: No, if you do marry him, with your pardon, Madam, your reputation suffers in the World, and you wou'd be thought in necessity for a cloak.

ALITHEA: Nay, now you are rude, Sir. – Mr. *Sparkish*, pray come hither, your Friend here is very troublesom, and very loving.

HARCOURT: Hold, hold –   [*Aside to* ALITHEA.]

PINCHWIFE: D'ye hear that?

SPARKISH: Why, d'ye think I'll seem to be jealous, like a Country Bumpkin?

PINCHWIFE: No, rather be a Cuckold, like a credulous Cit.[1]

HARCOURT: Madam, you wou'd not have been so little generous as to have told him.

ALITHEA: Yes, since you cou'd be so little generous, as to wrong him.

HARCOURT: Wrong him, no Man can do't, he's beneath an injury; a Bubble,[2] a Coward, a sensless Idiot, a Wretch so contemptible to all the World but you, that –

ALITHEA: Hold, do not rail at him, for since he is like to be my Husband, I am resolv'd to like him: Nay, I think I am oblig'd to tell him, you are not his Friend. – Master *Sparkish*, Master *Sparkish*.

SPARKISH: What, what; now dear Rogue, has not she wit?

HARCOURT: Not so much as I thought, and hoped she had.   [*Speaks surlily.*]

ALITHEA: Mr. *Sparkish*, do you bring People to rail at you?

HARCOURT: Madam –

SPARKISH: How! no, but if he does rail at me, 'tis but in jest I warrant; what we wits do for one another, and never take any notice of it.

ALITHEA: He spoke so scurrilously of you, I had no patience to hear him; besides he has been making love to me.

HARCOURT: True damn'd tell-tale-Woman.   [*Aside.*]

SPARKISH: Pshaw, to shew his parts – we wits rail and make love often, but to shew our parts; as we have no affections, so we have no malice, we –

ALITHEA: He said, you were a Wretch, below an injury.

SPARKISH: Pshaw.

HARCOURT: Damn'd, sensless, impudent, virtuous Jade; well since she won't let me have her, she'1 do as good, she'1 make me hate her.

ALITHEA: A Common Bubble.

SPARKISH: Pshaw.

ALITHEA: A Coward.

SPARKISH: Pshaw, pshaw.

ALITHEA: A sensless driveling Idiot.

SPARKISH: How, did he disparage my parts? Nay, then my honour's concern'd, I can't put up that, Sir; by the World, Brother help me to kill him; (I may draw now, since we have the odds of him: – 'tis a good occasion too before my Mistriss) –   [*Aside.*] [*Offers to draw.*]

ALITHEA: Hold, hold.

SPARKISH: What, what.

ALITHEA: I must not let'em kill the Gentleman neither, for his kindness to me;

1. Citizen.
2. A dupe.

I am so far from hating him, that I wish my Gallant had his person and understanding: –

(Nay if my honour –)   [*Aside.*]

SPARKISH: I'll be thy death.

ALITHEA: Hold, hold, indeed to tell the truth, the Gentleman said after all, that what he spoke, was but out of friendship to you.

SPARKISH: How! Say, I am, I am a Fool, that is no wit, out of friendship to me.

ALITHEA: Yes, to try whether I was concern'd enough for you, and made love to me only to be satisfy'd of my virtue, for your sake.

HARCOURT: Kind however –   [*Aside.*]

SPARKISH: Nay, if it were so, my dear Rogue, I ask thee pardon; but why wou'd not you tell me so, faith.

HARCOURT: Because I did not think on't, faith.

SPARKISH: Come, *Horner* does not come, *Harcourt*, let's be gone to the new Play. – Come Madam.

ALITHEA: I will not go, if you intend to leave me alone in the Box, and run into the pit, as you use to do.

SPARKISH: Pshaw, I'll leave *Harcourt* with you in the Box, to entertain you, and that's as good; if I sate in the Box, I shou'd be thought no Judge, but of trimmings. – Come away *Harcourt*, lead her down.

[*Exeunt* SPARKISH, HARCOURT, *and* ALITHEA.]

PINCHWIFE: Well, go thy wayes, for the flower of the true Town Fops, such as spend their Estates, before they come to'em, and are Cuckolds before they'r married. But let me go look to my own Free-hold – How –

[*Enter my Lady* FIDGET, *Mistriss* DAINTY FIDGET, *and Mistriss* SQUEAMISH.]

LADY FIDGET: Your Servant, Sir, where is your Lady? we are come to wait upon her to the new Play.

PINCHWIFE: New Play!

LADY FIDGET: And my Husband will wait upon you presently.

PINCHWIFE: Damn your civility –   [*Aside.*]

Madam, by no means, I will not see Sir *Jaspar* here, till I have waited upon him at home; nor shall my Wife see you, till she has waited upon your Ladyship at your lodgings.

LADY FIDGET: Now we are here, Sir –

PINCHWIFE: No, Madam.

DAINTY: Pray, let us see her.

SQUEAMISH: We will not stir, till we see her.

PINCHWIFE: A Pox on you all –   [*Aside.*]

she has lock'd the door, and is gone abroad.

[*Goes to the door, and returns.*]

LADY FIDGET: No, you have lock'd the door, and she's within.

DAINTY: They told us below, she was here.

PINCHWIFE: (Will nothing do?) – Well it must out then, to tell you the truth,

Ladies, which I was afraid to let you know before, least it might endanger your lives, my Wife has just now the Small Pox come out upon her, do not be frighten'd; but pray, be gone Ladies, you shall not stay here in danger of your lives; pray get you gone Ladies.

LADY FIDGET: No, no, we have all had'em.

SQUEAMISH: Alack, alack.

DAINTY: Come, come, we must see how it goes with her, I understand the disease.

LADY FIDGET: Come.

PINCHWIFE: Well, there is no being too hard for Women at their own weapon, lying, therefore I'll quit the Field.   [*Aside.*] [*Exit* PINCHWIFE.]

SQUEAMISH: Here's an example of jealousy.

LADY FIDGET: Indeed as the World goes, I wonder there are no more jealous, since Wives are so neglected.

DAINTY: Pshaw, as the World goes, to what end shou'd they be jealous.

LADY FIDGET: Foh, 'tis a nasty world.

SQUEAMISH: That Men of parts, great acquaintance, and quality shou'd take up with, and spend themselves and fortunes, in keeping little Play-house Creatures, foh.

LADY FIDGET: Nay, that Women of understanding, great acquaintance, and good quality, shou'd fall a keeping too of little Creatures, foh.

SQUEAMISH: Why, 'tis the Men of qualities fault, they never visit Women of honour, and reputation, as they us'd to do; and have not so much as common civility, for Ladies of our rank, but use us with the same indifferency, and ill breeding, as if we were all marry'd to'em.

LADY FIDGET: She says true, 'tis an errant shame Women of quality shou'd be so slighted; methinks, birth, birth, shou'd go for something; I have known Men admired, courted, and followed for their titles only.

SQUEAMISH: Ay, one wou'd think Men of honour shou'd not love no more, than marry out of their own rank.

DAINTY: Fye, fye upon'em, they are come to think cross breeding for themselves best, as well as for their Dogs, and Horses.

LADY FIDGET: They are Dogs, and Horses for't.

SQUEAMISH: One wou'd think if not for love, for vanity a little.

DAINTY: Nay, they do satisfy their vanity upon us sometimes; and are kind to us in their report, tell all the World they lye with us.

LADY FIDGET: Damn'd Rascals, that we shou'd be only wrong'd by'em; to report a Man has had a Person, when he has not had a Person, is the greatest wrong in the whole World, that can be done to a person.

SQUEAMISH: Well, 'tis an errant shame, Noble Persons shou'd be so wrong'd, and neglected.

LADY FIDGET: But still 'tis an erranter shame for a Noble Person, to neglect her own honour, and defame her own Noble Person, with little inconsiderable Fellows, foh! –

DAINTY: I suppose the crime against our honour, is the same with a Man of quality as with another.

LADY FIDGET: How! no sure the Man of quality is likest one's Husband, and therefore the fault shou'd be the less.

DAINTY: But then the pleasure shou'd be the less.

LADY FIDGET: Fye, fye, fye, for shame Sister, whither shall we ramble? be continent in your discourse, or I shall hate you.

DAINTY: Besides an intrigue is so much the more notorious for the man's quality.

SQUEAMISH: 'Tis true, no body takes notice of a private Man, and therefore with him, 'tis more secret, and the crime's the less, when 'tis not known.

LADY FIDGET: You say true; y faith I think you are in the right on't: 'tis not an injury to a Husband, till it be an injury to our honours; so that a Woman of honour looses no honour with a private Person; and to say truth –

DAINTY: So the little Fellow is grown a private Person – with her –

                                        [*Apart to* SQUEAMISH.]

LADY FIDGET: But still my dear, dear Honour.

            [*Enter Sir* JASPAR, HORNER, DORILANT.]

SIR JASPAR: Ay, my dear, dear of honour, thou hast still so much honour in thy mouth –

HORNER: That she has none elsewhere –   [*Aside.*]

LADY FIDGET: Oh, what d'ye mean to bring in these upon us?

DAINTY: Foh, these are as bad as Wits.

SQUEAMISH: Foh!

LADY FIDGET: Let us leave the Room.

SIR JASPAR: Stay, stay, faith to tell you the naked truth.

LADY FIDGET: Fye, Sir *Jaspar*, do not use that word naked.

SIR JASPAR: Well, well, in short I have business at *Whitehal*, and cannot go to the play with you, therefore wou'd have you go –

LADY FIDGET: With those two to a Play?

SIR JASPAR: No, not with t'other, but with Mr. *Horner*, there can be no more scandal to go with him, than with Mr. *Tatle*,[1] or Master *Limberham*.

LADY FIDGET: With that nasty Fellow! no – no.

SIR JASPAR: Nay, prethee Dear, hear me.   [*Whispers to Lady* FIDGET.]

HORNER: Ladies.

      [HORNER, DORILANT *drawing near* SQUEAMISH *and* DAINTY.]

DAINTY: Stand off.

SQUEAMISH: Do not approach us.

DAINTY: You heard[2] with the wits, you are obscenity all over.

---

1. Names for the old men whose presence cannot pose a threat to the ladies.
2. Herd.

SQUEAMISH: And I wou'd as soon look upon a Picture of *Adam* and *Eve*, without fig leaves, as any of you, if I cou'd help it, therefore keep off, and do not make us sick.

DORILANT: What a Divel are these?

HORNER: Why, these are pretenders to honour, as criticks to wit, only by censuring others; and as every raw peevish, out-of-humour'd, affected, dull, Tea-drinking, Arithmetical Fop sets up for a wit, by railing at men of sence, so these for honour, by railing at the Court, and Ladies of as great honour, as quality.

SIR JASPAR: Come, Mr. *Horner*, I must desire you to go with these Ladies to the Play, Sir.

HORNER: I! Sir.

SIR JASPAR: Ay, ay, come, Sir.

HORNER: I must beg your pardon, Sir, and theirs, I will not be seen in Womens Company in publick again for the World.

SIR JASPAR: Ha, ha, strange Aversion!

SQUEAMISH: No, he's for Womens company in private.

SIR JASPAR: He – poor Man – he! hah, ha, ha.

DAINTY: 'Tis a greater shame amongst lew'd fellows to be seen in virtuous Womens company, than for the Women to be seen with them.

HORNER: Indeed, Madam, the time was I only hated virtuous Women, but now I hate the other too; I beg your pardon Ladies.

LADY FIDGET: You are very obliging, Sir, because we wou'd not be troubled with you.

SIR JASPAR: In sober sadness he shall go.

DORILANT: Nay, if he wo'not, I am ready to wait upon the Ladies; and I think I am the fitter Man.

SIR JASPAR: You, Sir, no I thank you for that – Master *Horner* is a privileg'd Man amongst the virtuous Ladies, 'twill be a great while before you are so; heh, he, he, he's my Wive's Gallant, heh, he, he; no pray withdraw, Sir, for as I take it, the virtuous Ladies have no business with you.

DORILANT: And I am sure, he can have none with them: 'tis strange a Man can't come amongst virtuous Women now, but upon the same terms, as Men are admitted into the great Turks Seraglio; but Heavens keep me, from being an hombre[1] Player with'em: but where is *Pinchwife* –

[*Exit* DORILANT.]

SIR JASPAR: Come, come, Man; what avoid the sweet society of Woman-kind? that sweet, soft, gentle, tame, noble Creature Woman, made for Man's Companion –

HORNER: So is that soft, gentle, tame, and more noble Creature a Spaniel, and has all their tricks, can fawn, lye down, suffer beating, and fawn the more; barks at your Friends, when they come to see you; makes your bed hard, gives you Fleas, and the mange sometimes: and all the

1. Ombre was a popular card game.

difference is, the Spaniel's the more faithful Animal, and fawns but upon one Master.

SIR JASPAR: Heh, he, he.

SQUEAMISH: O the rude Beast.

DAINTY: Insolent brute.

LADY FIDGET: Brute! stinking mortify'd rotten French Weather,[1] to dare –

SIR JASPAR: Hold, an't please your Ladyship; for shame Master, *Horner* your Mother was a Woman – (Now shall I never reconcile'em)   [*Aside.*] Hark you, Madam, take my advice in your anger; you know you often want one to make up your droling pack of hombre Players; and you may cheat him easily, for he's an ill Gamester, and consequently loves play: Besides you know, you have but two old civil Gentlemen (with stinking breaths too) to wait upon you abroad, take in the third, into your service; the other are but crazy: and a Lady shou'd have a supernumerary Gentleman-Usher,[2] as a supernumerary Coach-horse, least sometimes you shou'd be forc'd to stay at home.

LADY FIDGET: But are you sure he loves play, and has money?

SIR JASPAR: He loves play as much as you, and has money as much as I.

LADY FIDGET: Then I am contented to make him pay for his scurrillity; money makes up in a measure all other wants in Men. – Those whom we cannot make hold for Gallants, we make fine.[3]   [*Aside.*]

SIR JASPAR: So, so; now to mollify, to wheedle him, –   [*Aside.*] Master *Horner* will you never keep civil Company, me-thinks 'tis time now, since you are only fit for them: Come, come, Man you must e'en fall to visiting our Wives, eating at our Tables, drinking Tea with our virtuous Relations after dinner, dealing Cards to'em, reading Plays, and Gazets to'em, picking Fleas out of their shocks for'em, collecting Receipts, New Songs, Women, Pages, and Footmen for'em.

HORNER: I hope they'l afford me better employment, Sir.

SIR JASPAR: Heh, he, he, 'tis fit you know your work before you come into your place; and since you are unprovided of a Lady to flatter, and a good house to eat at, pray frequent mine, and call my Wife Mistriss, and she shall call you Gallant, according to the custom.

HORNER: Who I? –

SIR JASPAR: Faith, thou sha't for my sake, come for my sake only.

HORNER: For your sake –

SIR JASPAR: Come, come, here's a Gamester for you, let him be a little familiar sometimes; nay, what if a little rude; Gamesters may be rude with Ladies, you know.

LADY FIDGET: Yes, losing Gamesters have a privilege with Women.

HORNER: I alwayes thought the contrary, that the winning Gamester had

1. A wether, or castrated ram.
2. A man hired to attend upon a lady.
3. We impose a fine on those we cannot oblige to be gallants.

most privilege with Women, for when you have lost your money to a Man, you'l loose any thing you have, all you have, they say, and he may use you as he pleases.

SIR JASPAR: Heh, he, he, well, win or loose you shall have your liberty with her.

LADY FIDGET: As he behaves himself; and for your sake I'll give him admittance and freedom.

HORNER: All sorts of freedom, Madam?

SIR JASPAR: Ay, ay, ay, all sorts of freedom thou can'st take, and so go to her, begin thy new employment; wheedle her, jest with her, and be better acquainted one with another.

HORNER: I think I know her already, therefore may venter with her, my secret for hers –   [*Aside.*]

[HORNER *and Lady* FIDGET *whisper.*]

SIR JASPAR: Sister *Cuz*,[1] I have provided an innocent Play-fellow for you there.

DAINTY: Who he!

SQUEAMISH: There's a Play-fellow indeed.

SIR JASPAR: Yes sure, what he is good enough to play at Cards, Blind-mans buff, or the fool with sometimes.

SQUEAMISH: Foh, we'l have no such Play-fellows.

DAINTY: No, Sir, you shan't choose Play-fellows for us, we thank you.

SIR JASPAR: Nay, pray hear me.   [*Whispering to them.*]

LADY FIDGET: But, poor Gentleman, cou'd you be so generous? so truly a Man of honour, as for the sakes of us Women of honour, to cause your self to be reported no Man? No Man! and to suffer your self the greatest Shame that cou'd fall upon a Man, that none might fall upon us Women by your conversation; but indeed, Sir, as perfectly, perfectly, the same Man as before your going into *France*, Sir; as perfectly, perfectly, Sir.

HORNER: As perfectly, perfectly, Madam; nay, I scorn you shou'd take my word; I desire to be try'd only, Madam.

LADY FIDGET: Well, that's spoken again like a Man of honour, all Men of honour desire to come to the test: But indeed, generally you Men report such things of your selves, one does not know how, or whom to believe; and it is come to that pass, we dare not take your words, no more than your Taylors, without some staid Servant of yours be bound with you; but I have so strong a faith in your honour, dear, dear, noble Sir, that I'd forfeit mine for yours at any time, dear Sir.

HORNER: No, Madam, you shou'd not need to forfeit it for me, I have given you security already to save you harmless my late reputation being so well known in the World, Madam.

LADY FIDGET: But if upon any future falling out, or upon a suspition of my

1. Cousin. A general term of endearment.

taking the trust out of your hands, to employ some other, you your self shou'd betray your trust, dear Sir; I mean, if you'l give me leave to speak obscenely, you might tell, dear Sir.

HORNER: If I did, no body wou'd believe me; the reputation of impotency is as hardly recover'd again in the World, as that of cowardise, dear Madam.

LADY FIDGET: Nay then, as one may say, you may do your worst, dear, dear, Sir.

SIR JASPAR: Come, is your Ladyship reconciled to him yet? have you agreed on matters? for I must be gone to *Whitehal*.

LADY FIDGET: Why, indeed, Sir *Jaspar*, Master *Horner* is a thousand, thousand times a better Man, than I thought him: Cosen *Squeamish*, Sister *Dainty*, I can name him now, truly not long ago you know, I thought his very name obscenity, and I wou'd as soon have lain with him, as have nam'd him.

SIR JASPAR: Very likely, poor Madam.

DAINTY: I believe it.

SQUEAMISH: No doubt on't.

SIR JASPAR: Well, well – that your Ladyship is as virtuous as any she, – I know, and him all the Town knows – heh, he, he; therefore now you like him, get you gone to your business together; go, go, to your business, I say, pleasure, whilst I go to my pleasure, business.

LADY FIDGET: Come then dear Gallant.

HORNER: Come away, my dearest Mistriss.

SIR JASPAR: So, so, why 'tis as I'd have it.   [*Exit* SR. JASPAR.]

HORNER: And as I'd have it.

LADY FIDGET:
Who for his business, from his Wife will run;
Takes the best care, to have her bus'ness done.

[*Exeunt omnes.*]

Act III, Scene I

[ALITHEA, *and Mrs.* PINCHWIFE.]

ALITHEA: Sister, what ailes you, you are grown melancholy?

MRS. PINCHWIFE: Wou'd it not make any one melancholy, to see you go every day fluttering about abroad whil'st I must stay at home like a poor lonely, sullen Bird in a cage?

ALITHEA: Ay, Sister, but you came young, and just from the nest to your cage, so that I thought you lik'd it; and cou'd be as chearful in't, as others that took their flight themselves early, and are hopping abroad in the open Air.

MRS. PINCHWIFE: Nay, I confess I was quiet enough, till my Husband told me, what pure[1] lives, the *London* Ladies live abroad, with their dancing, meetings, and junketings, and drest every day in their best gowns; and I warrant you, play at nine Pins every day of the week, so they do.

[*Enter Mr.* PINCHWIFE.]

PINCHWIFE: Come, what's here to do? you are putting the Town pleasures in her head, and setting her a longing.

ALITHEA: Yes, after Nine-pins; you suffer none to give her those longings, you mean, but your self.

PINCHWIFE: I tell her of the vanities of the Town like a Confessor.

ALITHEA: A Confessor! just such a Confessor, as he that by forbidding a silly Oastler to grease the Horses teeth, taught him to do't.

PINCHWIFE: Come Mistriss *Flippant*, good Precepts are lost, when bad Examples are still before us; the liberty you take abroad makes her hanker after it; and out of humour at home, poor Wretch! she desired not to come to *London*, I wou'd bring her.

ALITHEA: Very well.

PINCHWIFE: She has been this week in Town, and never desired, till this afternoon, to go abroad.

ALITHEA: Was she not at a Play yesterday?

PINCHWIFE: Yes, but she ne'er ask'd me; I was my self the cause of her going.

ALITHEA: Then if she ask you again, you are the cause of her asking, and not my example.

PINCHWIFE: Well, to morrow night I shall be rid of you; and the next day before 'tis light, she and I'll be rid of the Town, and my dreadful apprehensions: Come, be not melancholly, for thou sha't go into the Country after to morrow, Dearest.

ALITHEA: Great comfort.

MRS. PINCHWIFE: Pish, what d'ye tell me of the Country for?

PINCHWIFE: How's this! what, pish at the Country?

MRS. PINCHWIFE: Let me alone, I am not well.

PINCHWIFE: O, if that be all – what ailes my dearest?

MRS. PINCHWIFE: Truly I don't know; but I have not been well, since you told me there was a Gallant at the Play in love with me.

PINCHWIFE: Ha –

ALITHEA: That's by my example too.

PINCHWIFE: Nay, if you are not well, but are so concern'd, because a lew'd Fellow chanc'd to lye, and say he lik'd you, you'l make me sick too.

MRS. PINCHWIFE: Of what sickness?

PINCHWIFE: O, of that which is worse than the Plague, Jealousy.

1. Fine.

MRS. PINCHWIFE: Pish, you jear, I'm sure there's no such disease in our Receipt-book at home.

PINCHWIFE: No, thou never met'st with it, poor Innocent – well, if thou Cuckold me, 'twill be my own fault – for Cuckolds and Bastards, are generally makers of their own fortune.   [*Aside.*]

MRS. PINCHWIFE: Well, but pray Bud, let's go to a Play to night.

PINCHWIFE: 'Tis just done, she comes from it; but why are you so eager to see a Play?

MRS. PINCHWIFE: Faith Dear, not that I care one pin for their talk there; but I like to look upon the Player-men, and wou'd see, if I cou'd, the Gallant you say loves me; that's all dear Bud.

PINCHWIFE: Is that all dear Bud?

ALITHEA: This proceeds from my example.

MRS. PINCHWIFE: But if the Play be done, let's go abroad however, dear Bud.

PINCHWIFE: Come have a little patience, and thou shalt go into the Country on Friday.

MRS. PINCHWIFE: Therefore I wou'd see first some sights, to tell my Neighbours of. Nay, I will go abroad, that's once.

ALITHEA: I'm the cause of this desire too.

PINCHWIFE: But now I think on't, who was the cause of *Horners* coming to my Lodging to day? that was you.

ALITHEA: No, you, because you wou'd not let him see your handsome Wife out of your Lodging.

MRS. PINCHWIFE: Why, O Lord! did the Gentleman come hither to see me indeed?

PINCHWIFE: No, no; – You are not cause of that damn'd question too, Mistriss *Alithea* ? – (Well she's in the right of it; he is in love with my Wife – and comes after her – 'tis so – but I'll nip his love in the bud; least he should follow us into the Country, and break his Chariot-wheel near our house, on purpose for an excuse to come to't; but I think I know the Town.)
                                                                      [*Aside.*]

MRS. PINCHWIFE: Come, pray Bud, let's go abroad before 'tis late; for I will go, that's flat and plain.

PINCHWIFE: So! the obstinacy already of a Town-wife, and I must, whilst she's here, humour her like one.   [*Aside.*]
    Sister, how shall we do, that she may not be seen, or known?

ALITHEA: Let her put on her Mask.

PINCHWIFE: Pshaw, a Mask makes People but the more inquisitive, and is as ridiculous a disguise, as a stage-beard; her shape, stature, habit will be known: and if we shou'd meet with *Horner*, he wou'd be sure to take acquaintance with us, must wish her joy, kiss her, talk to her, leer upon her, and the Devil and all; no I'll not use her to a Mask, 'tis dangerous; for Masks have made more Cuckolds, than the best faces that ever were known.

ALITHEA: How will you do then?

MRS. PINCHWIFE: Nay, shall we go? the *Exchange* will be shut, and I have a mind to see that.

PINCHWIFE: So – I have it – I'll dress her up in the Suit, we are to carry down to her Brother, little Sir *James*; nay, I understand the Town tricks: Come let's go dress her; a Mask! no – a Woman mask'd, like a cover'd Dish, gives a Man curiosity, and appetite, when, it may be, uncover'd, 'twou'd turn his stomack; no, no.

ALITHEA: Indeed your comparison is something a greasie one: but I had a gentle Gallant, us'd to say, a Beauty mask'd, like the Sun in Eclipse, gathers together more gazers, than if it shin'd out.   [*Exeunt.*]

[Act III, Scene II]

[The Scene changes to the New Exchange: Enter HORNER, HARCOURT, DORILANT.]

DORILANT: Engag'd to Women, and not Sup with us?

HORNER: Ay, a Pox on'em all.

HARCOURT: You were much a more reasonable Man in the morning, and had as noble resolutions against'em, as a Widdower of a weeks liberty.

DORILANT: Did I ever think, to see you keep company with Women in vain.

HORNER: In vain! no – 'tis, since I can't love'em, to be reveng'd on'em.

HARCOURT: Now your Sting is gone, you look'd in the Box amongst all those Women, like a drone in the hive, all upon you; shov'd and ill-us'd by'em all, and thrust from one side to t'other.

DORILANT: Yet he must be buzzing amongst'em still, like other old beetle-headed,[1] lycorish drones; avoid'em, and hate'em as they hate you.

HORNER: Because I do hate'em, and wou'd hate'em yet more, I'll frequent'em; you may see by Marriage, nothing makes a Man hate a Woman more, than her constant conversation: In short, I converse with'em, as you do with rich Fools, to laugh at'em, and use'em ill.

DORILANT: But I wou'd no more Sup with Women, unless I cou'd lye with'em, than Sup with a rich Coxcomb, unless I cou'd cheat him.

HORNER: Yes, I have known thee Sup with a Fool, for his drinking, if he cou'd set out your hand that way only, you were satisfy'd; and if he were a Wine-swallowing mouth 'twas enough.

HARCOURT: Yes, a Man drink's often with a Fool, as he tosses with a Marker, only to keep his hand in Ure;[2] but do the Ladies drink?

HORNER: Yes, Sir, and I shall have the pleasure at least of laying'em flat with a Bottle; and bring as much scandal that way upon'em, as formerly t'other.

---

1. Block-headed.
2. Throws dice with the score-keeper for practice.

HARCOURT: Perhaps you may prove as weak a Brother amongst'em that way, as t'other.

DORILANT: Foh, drinking with Women, is as unnatural, as scolding with'em; but 'tis a pleasure of decay'd Fornicators, and the basest way of quenching Love.

HARCOURT: Nay, 'tis drowning Love, instead of quenching it; but leave us for civil Women too!

DORILANT: Ay, when he can't be the better for'em; we hardly pardon a Man, that leaves his Friend for a Wench, and that's a pretty lawful call.

HORNER: Faith, I wou'd not leave you for'em, if they wou'd not drink.

DORILANT: Who wou'd disappoint his Company at *Lewis's*,[1] for a Gossiping?

HARCOURT: Foh, Wine and Women good apart, together as nauseous as Sack and Sugar: But hark you, Sir, before you go, a little of your advice, an old maim'd General, when unfit for action is fittest for Counsel; I have other designs upon Women, than eating and drinking with them: I am in love with *Sparkish's* Mistriss, whom he is to marry to morrow, now how shall I get her?

[*Enter* SPARKISH, *looking about.*]

HORNER: Why, here comes one will help you to her.

HARCOURT: He! he, I tell you, is my Rival, and will hinder my love.

HORNER: No, a foolish Rival, and a jealous Huband assist their Rivals designs; for they are sure to make their Women hate them, which is the first step to their love, for another Man.

HARCOURT: But I cannot come near his Mistriss, but in his company.

HORNER: Still the better for you, for Fools are most easily cheated, when they themselves are accessaries; and he is to be bubled[2] of his Mistriss, as of his Money, the common Mistriss, by keeping him company.

SPARKISH: Who is that, that is to be bubled? Faith let me snack,[3] I han't met with a buble since Christmas: gad; I think bubles are like their Brother Woodcocks, go out with the cold weather.

HARCOURT: A Pox, he did not hear all I hope.   [*Apart to* HORNER.]

SPARKISH: Come, you bubling Rogues you, where do we sup – Oh, *Harcourt*, my Mistriss tells me, you have been making fierce love to her all the Play long, hah, ha – but I –

HARCOURT: I make love to her?

SPARKISH: Nay, I forgive thee; for I think I know thee, and I know her, but I am sure I know my self.

HARCOURT: Did she tell you so? I see all Women are like these of the *Exchange*, who to enhance the price of their commodities, report to their fond Customers offers which were never made'em.

1. A tavern whose location is unknown.
2. Cheated.
3. Share.

HORNER: Ay, Women are as apt to tell before the intrigue, as Men after it, and so shew themselves the vainer Sex; but hast thou a Mistriss, *Sparkish*? 'tis as hard for me to believe it, as that thou ever hadst a buble, as you brag'd just now.

SPARKISH: O your Servant, Sir; are you at your raillery, Sir? but we were some of us beforehand with you to day at the Play: the Wits were something bold with you, Sir; did you not hear us laugh?

HARCOURT: Yes, But I thought you had gone to Plays, to laugh at the Poets wit, not at your own.

SPARKISH: Your Servant, Sir, no I thank you; gad I go to a Play as to a Country-treat, I carry my own wine to one, and my own wit to t'other, or else I'm sure I shou'd not be merry at either; and the reason why we are so often lowder, than the Players, is, because we think we speak more wit, and so become the Poets Rivals in his audience: for to tell you the truth, we hate the silly Rogues; nay, so much that we find fault even with their Bawdy upon the Stage, whilst we talk nothing else in the Pit as lowd.

HORNER: But, why should'st thou hate the silly Poets, thou hast too much wit to be one, and they like Whores are only hated by each other; and thou dost scorn writing, I'am sure.

SPARKISH: Yes, I'd have you to know, I scorn writing; but Women, Women, that make Men do all foolish things, make'em write Songs too; every body does it: 'tis ev'n as common with Lovers, as playing with fans; and you can no more help Rhyming to your *Phyllis*, than drinking to your *Phyllis*.

HARCOURT: Nay, Poetry in love is no more to be avoided, than jealousy.

DORILANT: But the Poets damn'd your Songs, did they?

SPARKISH: Damn the Poets, they turn'd'em into Burlesque, as they call it; that Burlesque is a *Hocus-Pocus*-trick, they have got, which by the virtue of *Hictius doctius*,[1] *topsey turvey*, they make a wise and witty Man in the World, a Fool upon the Stage you know not how; and 'tis therefore I hate'em too, for I know not but it may be my own case; for they'l put a Man into a Play for looking a Squint: Their Predecessors were contented to make Serving-men only their Stage-Fools, but these Rogues must have Gentlemen, with a Pox to'em, nay Knights: and indeed you shall hardly see a Fool upon the Stage, but he's a Knight; and to tell you the truth, they have kept me these six years from being a Knight in earnest, for fear of being knighted in a Play, and dubb'd a Fool.

DORILANT: Blame'em not, they must follow their Copy, the Age.

HARCOURT: But why should'st thou be afraid of being in a Play, who expose your self every day in the Play-houses, and as publick Places.

HORNER: 'Tis but being on the Stage, instead of standing on a Bench in the Pit.

---

1. A juggling term.

DORILANT: Don't you give money to Painters to draw you like? and are you afraid of your Pictures, at length in a Play-house, where all your Mistresses may see you.

SPARKISH: A Pox, Painters don't draw the Small Pox, or Pimples in ones face; come damn all your silly Authors whatever, all Books and Booksellers, by the World, and all Readers, courteous or uncourteous.

HARCOURT: But, who comes here, *Sparkish*?

[*Enter Mr.* PINCHWIFE, *and his Wife in Man's Cloaths,* ALITHEA, LUCY *her Maid.*]

SPARKISH: Oh hide me, there's my Mistriss too.

                         [SPARKISH *hides himself behind* HARCOURT.]

HARCOURT: She sees you.

SPARKISH: But I will not see her, 'tis time to go to *Whitehal*, and I must not fail the drawing Room.

HARCOURT: Pray, first carry me, and reconcile me to her.

SPARKISH: Another time, faith the King will have sup't.

HARCOURT: Not with the worse stomach for thy absence; thou art one of those Fools, that think their attendance at the King's Meals, as necessary as his Physicians, when you are more troublesom to him, than his Doctors, or his Dogs.

SPARKISH: Pshaw, I know my interest, Sir, prethee hide me.

HORNER: Your Servant, *Pinchwife*, – what he knows us not –

PINCHWIFE: Come along.   [*To his Wife aside.*]

MRS. PINCHWIFE: Pray, have you any Ballads, give me six-penny worth?

CLASP: We have no Ballads.

MRS. PINCHWIFE: Then give me *Covent-garden*-Drollery, and a Play or two – Oh here's *Tarugos* Wiles, and the Slighted Maiden, I'll have them.[1]

PINCHWIFE: No, Playes are not for your reading; come along, will you discover your self?   [*Apart to her.*]

HORNER: Who is that pretty Youth with him, *Sparkish*?

SPARKISH: I believe his Wife's Brother, because he's something like her, but I never saw her but once.

HORNER: Extreamly handsom, I have seen a face like it too; let us follow'em.

[*Exeunt* PINCHWIFE, *Mistriss* PINCHWIFE, ALITHEA, LUCY, HORNER, DORILANT *following them.*]

HARCOURT: Come, *Sparkish*, your Mistriss saw you, and will be angry you go not to her; besides I wou'd fain be reconcil'd to her, which none but you can do, dear Friend.

SPARKISH: Well that's a better reason, dear Friend; I wou'd not go near her

---

1. All titles of contemporary plays or collections of songs, poems and prologues.

now, for her's, or my own sake, but I can deny you nothing; for though I have known thee a great while, never go, if I do not love thee, as well as a new Acquaintance.

HARCOURT: I am oblig'd to you indeed, dear Friend, I wou'd be well with her only, to be well with thee still; for these tyes to Wives usually dissolve all tyes to Friends: I wou'd be contented, she shou'd enjoy you a nights, but I wou'd have you to my self a dayes, as I have had, dear Friend.

SPARKISH: And thou shalt enjoy me a dayes, dear, dear Friend, never stir; and I'll be divorced from her, sooner than from thee; come along –

HARCOURT: So we are hard put to't, when we make our Rival our Procurer; but neither she, nor her Brother, wou'd let me come near her now: when all's done, a Rival is the best cloak to steal to a Mistress under, without suspicion; and when we have once got to her as we desire, we throw him off like other Cloaks. [*Aside.*]

[*Exit* SPARKISH, *and* HARCOURT *following him.*
Re-enter Mr. PINCHWIFE, *Mistress* PINCHWIFE *in Man's Cloaths.*]

PINCHWIFE: Sister, if you will not go, we must leave you – [*To* ALITHEA.] The Fool her Gallant, and she, will muster up all the young santerers of this place, and they will leave their dear Seamstresses to follow us; what a swarm of Cuckolds, and Cuckold-makers are here? [*Aside.*] Come let's be gone Mistriss Margery.

MRS.PINCHWIFE: Don't you believe that, I han't half my belly full of sights yet.

PINCHWIFE: Then walk this way.

MRS. PINCHWIFE: Lord, what a power of brave signs are here! stay – the Bull's-head, the Rams-head, and the Stags-head, Dear –

PINCHWIFE: Nay, if every Husbands proper sign here were visible, they wou'd be all alike.

MRS. PINCHWIFE: What d'ye mean by that, Bud?

PINCHWIFE: 'Tis no matter – no matter, Bud.

MRS. PINCHWIFE: Pray tell me; nay, I will know.

PINCHWIFE: They wou'd be all Bulls, Stags, and Rams heads.

[*Exeunt Mr.* PINCHWIFE, *Mrs.* PINCHWIFE.
Re-enter SPARKISH, HARCOURT, ALITHEA, LUCY, *at t'other door.*]

SPARKISH: Come, dear Madam, for my sake you shall be reconciled to him.

ALITHEA: For your sake I hate him.

HARCOURT: That's something too cruel, Madam, to hate me for his sake.

SPARKISH: Ay indeed, Madam, too, too cruel to me, to hate my Friend for my sake.

ALITHEA: I hate him because he is your Enemy; and you ought to hate him too, for making love to me, if you love me.

SPARKISH: That's a good one, I hate a Man for loving you; if he did love you, 'tis but what he can't help, and 'tis your fault not his, if he admires you: I hate a Man for being of my opinion, I'll ne'er do't, by the World.

ALITHEA: Is it for your honour or mine, to suffer a Man to make love to me, who am to marry you to morrow?

SPARKISH: Is it for your honour or mine, to have me jealous? That he makes love to you, is a sign you are handsome; and that I am not jealous, is a sign you are virtuous, that I think is for your honour.

ALITHEA: But 'tis your honour too, I am concerned for.

HARCOURT: But why, dearest Madam, will you be more concern'd for his honour, than he is himself; let his honour alone for my sake, and his, he, he, has no honour –

SPARKISH: How's that?

HARCOURT: But what, my dear Friend can guard himself.

SPARKISH: O ho – that's right again.

HARCOURT: Your care of his honour argues his neglect of it, which is no honour to my dear Friend here; therefore once more, let his honour go which way it will, dear Madam.

SPARKISH: Ay, ay, were it for my honour to marry a Woman, whose virtue I suspected, and cou'd not trust her in a Friends hands?

ALITHEA: Are you not afraid to loose me?

HARCOURT: He afraid to loose you, Madam! No, no – you may see how the most estimable, and most glorious Creature in the World, is valued by him; will you not see it?

SPARKISH: Right, honest *Franck*, I have that noble value for her, that I cannot be jealous of her.

ALITHEA: You mistake him, he means you care not for me, nor who has me.

SPARKISH: Lord, Madam, I see you are jealous; will you wrest a poor Mans meaning from his words?

ALITHEA: You astonish me, Sir, with your want of jealousie.

SPARKISH: And you make me guiddy, Madam, with your jealousie, and fears, and virtue, and honour; gad, I see virtue makes a Woman as troublesome, as a little reading, or learning.

ALITHEA: Monstrous!

LUCY: (Well to see what easie Husbands these Women of quality can meet with, a poor Chamber-maid can never have such Lady-like luck; besides he's thrown away upon her, she'l make no use of her fortune, her blessing, none to a Gentleman, for a pure Cuckold, for it requires good breeding to be a Cuckold.)   [*Behind.*]

ALITHEA: I tell you then plainly, he pursues me to marry me.

SPARKISH: Pshaw –

HARCOURT: Come, Madam, you see you strive in vain to make him jealous of me; my dear Friend is the kindest Creature in the World to me.

SPARKISH: Poor fellow.

HARCOURT: But his kindness only is not enough for me, without your favour; your good opinion, dear Madam, 'tis that must perfect my happiness:

good Gentleman he believes all I say, wou'd you wou'd do so, jealous of me! I wou'd not wrong him nor you for the World.

SPARKISH: Look you there; hear him, hear him, and do not walk away so.

[ALITHEA *walks carelessly, to and fro.*]

HARCOURT: I love you, Madam, so –

SPARKISH: How's that! Nay – now you begin to go too far indeed.

HARCOURT: So much I confess, I say I love you, that I wou'd not have you miserable, and cast your self away upon so unworthy, and inconsiderable a thing, as what you see here.

[*Clapping his hand on his breast, points at* SPARKISH.]

SPARKISH: No faith, I believe thou woud'st not, now his meaning is plain: but I knew before thou woud'st not wrong me nor her.

HARCOURT: No, no, Heavens forbid, the glory of her Sex shou'd fall so low as into the embraces of such a contemptible Wretch, the last of Mankind – my dear Friend here – I injure him.   [*Embracing* SPARKISH.]

ALITHEA: Very well.

SPARKISH: No, no, dear Friend, I knew it Madam, you see he will rather wrong himself than me, in giving himself such names.

ALITHEA: Do not you understand him yet?

SPARKISH: Yes, how modestly he speaks of himself, poor Fellow.

ALITHEA: Methinks he speaks impudently of your self, since – before your self too, insomuch that I can no longer suffer his scurrilous abusiveness to you, no more than his love to me.   [*Offers to go.*]

SPARKISH: Nay, nay, Madam, pray stay, his love to you: Lord, Madam, has he not spoke yet plain enough?

ALITHEA: Yes indeed, I shou'd think so.

SPARKISH: Well then, by the World, a Man can't speak civilly to a Woman now, but presently she says, he makes love to her: Nay, Madam, you shall stay, with your pardon, since you have not yet understood him, till he has made an eclaircisment of his love to you, that is what kind of love it is; answer to thy Catechisme: Friend, do you love my Mistriss here?

HARCOURT: Yes, I wish she wou'd not doubt it

SPARKISH: But how do you love her?

HARCOURT: With all my Soul.

ALITHEA: I thank him, methinks he speaks plain enough now.

SPARKISH: You are out still.   [*To* ALITHEA.]

But with what kind of love, Harcourt?

HARCOURT: With the best, and truest love in the World.

SPARKISH: Look you there then, that is with no matrimonial love, I'm sure.

ALITHEA: How's that, do you say matrimonial love is not best?

SPARKISH: Gad, I went too far e're I was aware: But speak for thy self *Harcourt*, you said you wou'd not wrong me, nor her.

HARCOURT: No, no, Madam, e'n take him for Heaven's sake.

SPARKISH: Look you there, Madam.

HARCOURT: Who shou'd in all justice be yours, he that loves you most. [*Claps his hand on his breast.*]

ALITHEA: Look you there, Mr. *Sparkish*, who's that?

SPARKISH: Who shou'd it be? go on *Harcourt*.

HARCOURT: Who loves you more than Women, Titles, or fortune Fools. [*Points at* SPARKISH.]

SPARKISH: Look you there, he means me stil, for he points at me.

ALITHEA: Ridiculous!

HARCOURT: Who can only match your Faith, and constancy in love.

SPARKISH: Ay.

HARCOURT: Who knows, if it be possible, how to value so much beauty and virtue.

SPARKISH: Ay.

HARCOURT: Whose love can no more be equall'd in the world, than that Heavenly form of yours.

SPARKISH: No –

HARCOURT: Who cou'd no more suffer a Rival, than your absence, and yet cou'd no more suspect your virtue, than his own constancy in his love to you.

SPARKISH: No –

HARCOURT: Who in fine loves you better than his eyes, that first made him love you.

SPARKISH: Ay – nay, Madam, faith you shan't go, till –

ALITHEA: Have a care, lest you make me stay too long –

SPARKISH: But till he has saluted you; that I may be assur'd you are friends, after his honest advice and declaration: Come pray, Madam, be friends with him.

[*Enter Master* PINCHWIFE, *Mistriss* PINCHWIFE.]

ALITHEA: You must pardon me, Sir, that I am not yet so obedient to you.

PINCHWIFE: What, invite your Wife to kiss Men? Monstrous, are you not asham'd? I will never forgive you.

SPARKISH: Are you not asham'd, that I shou'd have more confidence in the chastity of your Family, than you have; you must not teach me, I am a man of honour, Sir, though I am frank and free; I am frank, Sir –

PINCHWIFE: Very frank, Sir, to share your Wife with your friends.

SPARKISH: He is an humble, menial Friend, such as reconciles the differences of the Marriage-bed; you know Man and Wife do not alwayes agree, I design him for that use, therefore wou'd have him well with my Wife.

PINCHWIFE: A menial Friend – you will get a great many menial Friends, by shewing your Wife as you do.

SPARKISH: What then, it may be I have a pleasure in't, as I have to shew fine
   Clothes, at a Play-house the first day, and count money before poor
   Rogues.

PINCHWIFE: He that shews his wife, or money will be in danger of having
   them borrowed sometimes.

SPARKISH: I love to be envy'd, and wou'd not marry a Wife, that I alone cou'd
   love; loving alone is as dull, as eating alone; is it not a frank age, and I
   am a frank Person? and to tell you the truth, it may be I love to have
   Rivals in a Wife, they make her seem to a Man still, but as a kept
   Mistriss; and so good night, for I must to *Whitehal*. Madam, I hope you
   are now reconcil'd to my Friend; and so I wish you a good night,
   Madam, and sleep if you can, for to morrow you know I must visit you
   early with a Canonical Gentleman. Good night dear *Harcourt*.

                                                    [*Exit* SPARKISH.]

HARCOURT: Madam, I hope you will not refuse my visit to morrow, if it
   shou'd be earlyer, with a Canonical Gentleman, than Mr. *Sparkish's*.

PINCHWIFE: This Gentle-woman is yet under my care, therefore you must yet
   forbear your freedom with her, Sir.

                      [*Coming between* ALITHEA *and* HARCOURT.]

HARCOURT: Must, Sir –

PINCHWIFE: Yes, Sir, she is my Sister.

HARCOURT: 'Tis well she is, Sir – for I must be her Servant, Sir. Madam –

PINCHWIFE: Come away Sister, we had been gone, if it had not been for you,
   and so avoided these lewd Rakehells, who seem to haunt us.

                      [*Enter* HORNER, DORILANT *to them.*]

HORNER: How now *Pinchwife*?

PINCHWIFE: Your Servant.

HORNER: What, I see a little time in the Country makes a Man turn wild and
   unsociable, and only fit to converse with his Horses, Dogs, and his
   Herds.

PINCHWIFE: I have business, Sir, and must mind it; your business is pleasure,
   therefore you and I must go different wayes.

HORNER: Well, you may go on, but this pretty young Gentleman –

                                       [*Takes hold of Mrs.* PINCHWIFE.]

HARCOURT: The Lady –

DORILANT: And the Maid –

HORNER: Shall stay with us, for I suppose their business is the same with
   ours, pleasure.

PINCHWIFE: 'Sdeath he knows her, she carries it so sillily, yet if he does not, I
   shou'd be more silly to discover it first.   [*Aside.*]

ALITHEA: Pray, let us go, Sir.

PINCHWIFE: Come, come –

HORNER: Had you not rather stay with us?   [*To Mrs.* PINCHWIFE.]
   Prethee *Pinchwife*, who is this pretty young Gentleman?

PINCHWIFE: One to whom I'm a guardian. (I wish I cou'd keep her out of
    your hands –)   [*Aside.*]
HORNER: Who is he? I never saw any thing so pretty in all my life.
PINCHWIFE: Pshaw, do not look upon him so much, he's a poor bashful
    youth, you'l put him out of countenance. Come away Brother.
                        [*Offers to take her away.*]

HORNER: O your Brother!
PINCHWIFE: Yes, my Wifes Brother; come, come, she'l stay supper for us.
HORNER: I thought so, for he is very like her I saw you at the Play with,
    whom I told you, I was in love with.
MRS. PINCHWIFE: O Jeminy! is this he that was in love with me, I am glad on't
    I vow, for he's a curious fine Gentleman, and I love him already too.
                                 [*Aside.*]
    Is this he Bud?   [*to Mr.* PINCHWIFE.]
PINCHWIFE: Come away, come away.   [*To his Wife.*]
HORNER: Why, what hast are you in? why wont you let me talk with him?
PINCHWIFE: Because you'l debauch him, he's yet young and innocent, and I
    wou'd not have him debauch'd for any thing in the World.
    How she gazes on him! the Divel –   [*Aside.*]
HORNER: *Harcourt, Dorilant,* look you here, this is the likeness of that
    Dowdey he told us of, his Wife, did you ever see a lovelyer Creature?
    the Rogue has reason to be jealous of his Wife, since she is like him, for
    she wou'd make all that see her, in love with her.
HARCOURT: And as I remember now, she is as like him here as can be.
DORILANT: She is indeed very pretty, if she be like him.
HORNER: Very pretty, a very pretty commendation – she is a glorious
    Creature, beautiful beyond all things I ever beheld.
PINCHWIFE: So, so.
HARCOURT: More beautiful than a Poets first Mistriss of Imagination.
HORNER: Or another Mans last Mistriss of flesh and blood.
MRS. PINCHWIFE: Nay, now you jeer, Sir; pray don't jeer me –
PINCHWIFE: Come, come. (By Heavens she'l discover her self.)   [*Aside.*]
HORNER: I speak of your Sister, Sir.
PINCHWIFE: Ay, but saying she was handsom, if like him, made him blush. (I
    am upon a wrack –)   [*Aside.*]
HORNER: Methinks he is so handsom, he shou'd not be a Man.
PINCHWIFE: O there 'tis out, he has discovered her, I am not able to suffer any
    longer. (Come, come away, I say –)   [*To his Wife.*]
HORNER: Nay, by your leave, Sir, he shall not go yet – *Harcourt, Dorilant,* let
    us torment this jealous Rogue a little.   [*To them.*]
HARCOURT: } How?
DORILANT:
HORNER: I'll shew you.
PINCHWIFE: Come, pray let him go, I cannot stay fooling any longer; I tell you
    his Sister stays supper for us.

HORNER: Do's she, come then we'l all go sup with her and thee.

PINCHWIFE: No, now I think on't, having staid so long for us, I warrant she's gone to bed – (I wish she and I were well out of their hands –) [*Aside.*] Come, I must rise early to morrow, come.

HORNER: Well then, if she be gone to bed, I wish her and you a good night But pray, young Gentleman, present my humble Service to her.

MRS. PINCHWIFE: Thank you heartily, Sir.

PINCHWIFE: S'death, she will discover her self yet in spight of me.   [*Aside.*] He is something more civil to you, for your kindness to his Sister, than I am, it seems.

HORNER: Tell her, dear sweet little Gentleman, for all your Brother there, that you have reviv'd the love, I had for her at first sight in the Play-house.

MRS. PINCHWIFE: But did you love her indeed, and indeed?

PINCHWIFE: So, so.   [*Aside.*]
    Away, I say.

HORNER: Nay stay; yes indeed, and indeed, pray do you tell her so, and give her this kiss from me.   [*Kisses her.*]

PINCHWIFE: O Heavens! what do I suffer; now 'tis too plain he knows her, and yet –   [*Aside.*]

HORNER: And this, and this –   [*Kisses her again.*]

MRS. PINCHWIFE: What do you kiss me for, I am no Woman.

PINCHWIFE: So – there 'tis out.   [*Aside.*]
    Come, I cannot, nor will stay any longer.

HORNER: Nay, they shall send your Lady a kiss too; here *Harcourt, Dorilant,* will you not?   [*They kiss her.*]

PINCHWIFE: How, do I suffer this? was I not accusing another just now, for this rascally patience, in permitting his Wife to be kiss'd before his face? ten thousand ulcers gnaw away their lips.   [*Aside.*]
    Come, come.

HORNER: Good night dear little Gentleman; Madam good-night; farewel *Pinchwife.* (Did not I tell you, I wou'd raise his jealous gall.)

[*Apart to* HARCOURT *and* DORILANT.]

[*Exeunt* HORNER, HARCOURT *and* DORILANT.]

PINCHWIFE: So they are gone at last; stay, let me see first if the Coach be at this door.   [*Exit.*]

HORNER: What not gone yet? will you be sure to do as I desired you, sweet Sir?

[HORNER, HARCOURT, DORILANT *return.*]

MRS. PINCHWIFE: Sweet Sir, but what will you give me then?

HORNER: Any thing, come away into the next walk.

[*Exit* HORNER, *haling away Mrs.* PINCHWIFE.]

ALITHEA: Hold, hold, – what d'ye do?

LUCY: Stay, stay, hold –

HARCOURT: Hold Madam, hold, let him present him, he'l come presently; nay, I will never let you go, till you answer my question.

[ALITHEA, LUCY *strugling with* HARCOURT *and* DORILANT.]

LUCY: For God's sake, Sir, I must follow'em.

DORILANT: No, I have something to present you with too, you shan't follow them.

[PINCHWIFE *returns.*]

PINCHWIFE: Where? – how? – what's become of? gone – whither?

LUCY: He's only gone with the Gentleman, who will give him something, an't please your Worship.

PINCHWIFE: Something – give him something, with a Pox – where are they?

ALITHEA: In the next walk only, Brother.

PINCHWIFE: Only, only; where, where?

[*Exit* PINCHWIFE, *and returns presently, then goes out again.*]

HARCOURT: What's the matter with him? why so much concern'd? but dearest Madam –

ALITHEA: Pray, let me go, Sir, I have said, and suffer'd enough already.

HARCOURT: Then you will not look upon, nor pitty my sufferings?

ALITHEA: To look upon'em, when I cannot help'em, were cruelty, not pitty, therefore I will never see you more.

HARCOURT: Let me then, Madam, have my priviledge of a banished Lover, complaining or railing, and giving you but a farewell reason; why, if you cannot condescend to marry me, you shou'd not take that wretch my Rival.

ALITHEA: He only, not you, since my honour is engag'd so far to him, can give me a reason, why I shou'd not marry him; but if he be true, and what I think him to me, I must be so to him; your Servant, Sir.

HARCOURT: Have Women only constancy when 'tis a vice, and like fortune only true to fools?

DORILANT: Thou sha't not stir thou robust Creature, you see I can deal with you, therefore you shou'd stay the rather, and be kind.

[*To* LUCY, *who struggles to get from him.*]

[*Enter* PINCHWIFE.]

PINCHWIFE: Gone, gone, not to be found; quite gone, ten thousand plagues go with'em; which way went they?

ALITHEA: But into t'other walk, Brother.

LUCY: Their business will be done presently sure, an't please your Worship, it can't be long in doing I'm sure on't.

ALITHEA: Are they not there?
PINCHWIFE: No, you know where they are, you infamous Wretch, Eternal shame of your Family, which you do not dishonour enough your self, you think, but you must help her to do it too, thou legion of Bawds.
ALITHEA: Good Brother.
PINCHWIFE: Damn'd, damn'd Sister.
ALITHEA: Look you here, she's coming.

[*Enter Mistriss* PINCHWIFE *in Mans cloaths, running with her hat under her arm, full of Oranges and dried fruit,* HORNER *following.*]

MRS. PINCHWIFE: O dear Bud, look you here what I have got, see.
PINCHWIFE: And what I have got here too, which you can't see.
                                        [*Aside rubbing his forehead.*]
MRS. PINCHWIFE: The fine Gentleman has given me better things yet
PINCHWIFE: Has he so? (Out of breath and colour'd – I must hold yet.)
                                                              [*Aside.*]
HORNER: I have only given your little Brother an Orange, Sir.
PINCHWIFE: Thank you, Sir.   [*To* HORNER.]
    You have only squeez'd my Orange, I suppose, and given it me again;
    yet I must have a City-patience.[1]   [*Aside.*]
    Come, come away   [*To his Wife.*]
MRS. PINCHWIFE: Stay, till I have put up my fine things, Bud.

[*Enter Sir* JASPAR FIDGET.]

SIR JASPAR: O Master *Horner*, come, come, the Ladies stay for you; your Mistriss, my Wife, wonders you make not more hast to her.
HORNER: I have staid this half hour for you here, and 'tis your fault I am not now with your Wife.
SIR JASPAR: But pray, don't let her know so much, the truth on't is, I was advancing a certain Project to his Majesty, about – I'll tell you.
HORNER: No, let's go, and hear it at your house: Good night sweet little Gentleman; one kiss more, you'l remember me now I hope. [*Kisses her.*]
DORILANT: What, Sir *Jaspar*, will you separate Friends? he promis'd to sup with us; and if you take him to your house, you'l be in danger of our company too.
SIR JASPAR: Alas Gentlemen my house is not fit for you, there are none but civil Women there, which are not for your turn; he you know can bear with the society of civil Women, now, ha, ha, ha; besides he's one of my Family; – he's – heh, heh, heh.
DORILANT: What is he?
SIR JASPAR: Faith my Eunuch, since you'l have it, heh, he, he.
                            [*Exeunt Sir* JASPAR FIDGET, *and* HORNER.]

1. The patience of a city cuckold.

DORILANT: I rather wish thou wert his, or my Cuckold: *Harcourt*, what a good
   Cuckold is lost there, for want of a Man to make him one; thee and I
   cannot have *Horners* privilege, who can make use of it.
HARCOURT: Ay, to poor *Horner* 'tis like coming to an estate at threescore,
   when a Man can't be the better for't.
PINCHWIFE: Come.
MRS. PINCHWIFE: Presently Bud.
DORILANT: Come let us go too: Madam, your Servant   [*To* ALITHEA.]
   Good night Strapper. –   [*To* LUCY.]
HARCOURT: Madam, though you will not let me have a good day, or night, I
   wish you one; but dare not name the other half of my wish.
ALITHEA: Good night, Sir, for ever.
MRS. PINCHWIFE: I don't know where to put this here, dear Bud, you shall eat
   it; nay, you shall have part of the fine Gentlemans good things, or treat
   as you call it, when we come home.
PINCHWIFE: Indeed I deserve it, since I furnish'd the best part of it.
                                              [*Strikes away the Orange.*]

             The Gallant treats, presents, and gives the Ball;
             But 'tis the absent Cuckold, pays for all.

Act IV, Scene I

[*In Pinchwife's house in the morning.*
LUCY, ALITHEA dress'd in new Cloths.]

LUCY: Well – Madam, now have I dress'd you, and set you out with so many
   ornaments, and spent upon you ounces of essence, and pulvilio;[1] and all
   this for no other purpose, but as People adorn, and perfume a Corps, for
   a stinking second-hand-grave, such or as bad I think Master *Sparkish's*
   bed.
ALITHEA: Hold your peace.
LUCY: Nay, Madam, I will ask you the reason, why you wou'd banish poor
   Master *Harcourt* for ever from your sight? how cou'd you be so
   hard-hearted?
ALITHEA: 'Twas because I was not hard-hearted.
LUCY: No, no; 'twas stark love and kindness, I warrant.
ALITHEA: It was so; I wou'd see him no more, because I love him.
LUCY: Hey day, a very pretty reason.
ALITHEA: You do not understand me.
LUCY: I wish you may your self.

1. A perfumed powder.

ALITHEA: I was engag'd to marry, you see, another man, whom my justice will not suffer me to deceive, or injure.

LUCY: Can there be a greater cheat, or wrong done to a Man, than to give him your person, without your heart, I shou'd make a conscience of it.

ALITHEA: I'll retrieve it for him after I am married a while.

LUCY: The Woman that marries to love better, will be as much mistaken, as the Wencher that marries to live better. No, Madam, marrying to encrease love, is like gaming to become rich; alas you only loose, what little stock you had before.

ALITHEA: I find by your Rhetorick you have been brib'd to betray me.

LUCY: Only by his merit, that has brib'd your heart you see against your word, and rigid honour; but what a Divel is this honour? 'tis sure a disease in the head, like the Megrim, or Falling-sickness, that alwayes hurries People away to do themselves mischief; Men loose their lives by it: Women what's dearer to'em, their love, the life of life.

ALITHEA: Come, pray talk you no more of honour, nor Master *Harcourt*; I wish the other wou'd come, to secure my fidelity to him, and his right in me.

LUCY: You will marry him then?

ALITHEA: Certainly, I have given him already my word, and will my hand too, to make it good when he comes.

LUCY: Well, I wish I may never stick pin more, if he be not an errant[1] Natural, to t'other fine Gentleman.

ALITHEA: I own he wants the wit of *Harcourt*, which I will dispense withal, for another want he has, which is want of jealousie, which men of wit seldom want

LUCY: Lord, Madam, what shou'd you do with a fool to your Husband, you intend to be honest don't you? then that husbandly virtue, credulity, is thrown away upon you.

ALITHEA: He only that could suspect my virtue, shou'd have cause to do it; 'tis *Sparkish's* confidence in my truth, that obliges me to be so faithful to him.

LUCY: You are not sure his opinion may last.

ALITHEA: I am satisfied, 'tis impossible for him to be jealous, after the proofs I have had of him: Jealousie in a Husband, Heaven defend me from it, it begets a thousand plagues to a poor Woman, the loss of her honour, her quiet, and her –

LUCY: And her pleasure.

ALITHEA: What d'ye mean, Impertinent?

LUCY: Liberty is a great pleasure, Madam.

ALITHEA: I say loss of her honour, her quiet, nay, her life sometimes; and what's as bad almost, the loss of this Town, that is, she is sent into the Country, which is the last ill usage of a Husband to a Wife, I think.

1. Arrant.

LUCY: O do's the wind lye there?   [*Aside.*]
Then of necessity, Madam, you think a man must carry his Wife into the Country, if he be wise; the Country is as terrible I find to our young English Ladies, as a Monastery to those abroad: and on my Virginity, I think they wou'd rather marry a *London*-Goaler, than a high Sheriff of a County, since neither can stir from his employment: formerly Women of wit married Fools, for a great Estate, a fine seat, or the like; but now 'tis for a pretty seat only in *Lincoln's Inn-fields*, St. *James's-fields*, or the *Pall-mall.*[1]

[*Enter to them* SPARKISH, *and* HARCOURT *dress'd like a Parson.*]

SPARKISH: Madam, your humble Servant, a happy day to you, and to us all.
HARCOURT: Amen. –
ALITHEA: Who have we here?
SPARKISH: My Chaplain faith – O Madam, poor *Harcourt* remembers his humble service to you; and in obedience to your last commands, refrains coming into your sight
ALITHEA: Is not that he?
SPARKISH: No, fye no; but to shew that he ne're intended to hinder our Match has sent his Brother here to joyn our hands: when I get me a Wife, I must get her a Chaplain, according to the Custom; this is his Brother, and my Chaplain.
ALITHEA: His Brother?
LUCY: And your Chaplain, to preach in your Pulpit then –   [*Aside.*]
ALITHEA: His Brother!
SPARKISH: Nay, I knew you wou'd not believe it; I told you, Sir, she wou'd take you for your Brother *Frank*.
ALITHEA: Believe it!
LUCY: His Brother! hah, ha, he, he has a trick left still it seems –   [*Aside.*]
SPARKISH: Come my dearest, pray let us go to Church before the Canonical hour is past.[2]
ALITHEA: For shame you are abus'd still.
SPARKISH: By the World 'tis strange now you are so incredulous.
ALITHEA: 'Tis strange you are so credulous.
SPARKISH: Dearest of my life, hear me, I tell you this is *Ned Harcourt* of *Cambridge*, by the world, you see he has a sneaking Colledg look; 'tis true he's something like his Brother *Frank*, and they differ from each other no more than in their age, for they were Twins.
LUCY: Hah, ha, he.
ALITHEA: Your Servant, Sir, I cannot be so deceiv'd, though you are; but come let's hear, how do you know what you affirm so confidently?

1. All fashionable areas in Restoration London.
2. The hours established for marriage in the Anglican Book of Canons were between 8 a.m. and 12 noon.

SPARKISH: Why, I'll tell you all; *Frank Harcourt* coming to me this morning, to
   wish me joy and present his service to you: I ask'd him, if he cou'd help
   me to a Parson; whereupon he told me, he had a Brother in Town who
   was in Orders, and he went straight away, and sent him, you see there,
   to me.

ALITHEA: Yes, *Frank* goes, and puts on a black-coat, then tell's you, he is *Ned*,
   that's all you have for't.

SPARKISH: Pshaw, pshaw, I tell you by the same token, the Midwife put her
   Garter about *Frank's* neck, to know'em asunder, they were so like.

ALITHEA: Frank tell's you this too.

SPARKISH: Ay, and *Ned* there too; nay, they are both in a Story.

ALITHEA: So, so, very foolish.

SPARKISH: Lord, if you won't believe one, you had best trye him by your
   Chamber-maid there; for Chamber-maids must needs know Chaplains
   from other Men, they are so us'd to'em.

LUCY: Let's see; nay, I'll be sworn he has the Canonical smirk, and the filthy,
   clammy palm of a Chaplain.

ALITHEA: Well, most reverend Doctor, pray let us make an end of this fooling.

HARCOURT: With all my soul, Divine, Heavenly Creature, when you please.

ALITHEA: He speaks like a Chaplain indeed.

SPARKISH: Why, was there not, soul, Divine, Heavenly, in what he said.

ALITHEA: Once more, most impertinent Black-coat, cease your persecution,
   and let us have a Conclusion of this ridiculous love.

HARCOURT: I had forgot, I must sute my Stile to my Coat, or I wear it in vain.
                                                                   [*Aside.*]

ALITHEA: I have no more patience left, let us make once an end of this
   troublesome Love, I say.

HARCOURT: So be it, Seraphick Lady, when your Honour shall think it meet,
   and convenient so to do.

SPARKISH: Gad I'm sure none but a Chaplain cou'd speak so, I think.

ALITHEA: Let me tell you Sir, this dull trick will not serve your turn, though
   you delay our marriage, you shall not hinder it.

HARCOURT: Far be it from me, Munificent Patroness, to delay your Marriage,
   I desire nothing more than to marry you presently, which I might do, if
   you your self wou'd; for my Noble, Good-natur'd and thrice Generous
   Patron here wou'd not hinder it.

SPARKISH: No, poor man, not I faith.

HARCOURT: And now, Madam, let me tell you plainly, no body else shall
   marry you by Heavens, I'll die first, for I'm sure I shou'd die after it.

LUCY: How his Love has made him forget his Function, as I have seen it in
   real Parsons.

ALITHEA: That was spoken like a Chaplain too, now you understand him, I
   hope.

SPARKISH: Poor man, he takes it hainously to be refus'd; I can't blame him, 'tis putting an indignity upon him not to be suffer'd, but you'l pardon me Madam, it shan't be, he shall marry us, come away, pray Madam.

LUCY: Hah, ha, he, more ado! 'tis late.

ALITHEA: Invincible stupidity, I tell you he wou'd marry me, as your Rival, not as your Chaplain.

SPARKISH: Come, come Madam.   [*Pulling her away.*]

LUCY: I pray Madam, do not refuse this Reverend Divine, the honour and satisfaction of marrying you; for I dare say, he has set his heart upon't, good Doctor.

ALITHEA: What can you hope, or design by this?

HARCOURT: I cou'd answer her, a reprieve for a day only, often revokes a hasty doom; at worst, if she will not take mercy on me, and let me marry her, I have at least the Lovers second pleasure, hindring my Rivals enjoyment, though but for a time.

SPARKISH: Come Madam, 'tis e'ne twelve a clock, and my Mother charg'd me never to be married out of the Canonical hours; come, come, Lord here's such a deal of modesty, I warrant the first day.

LUCY: Yes, an't please your Worship, married women shew all their Modesty the first day, because married men shew all their love the first day.

[*Exeunt* SPARKISH, ALITHEA, HARCOURT *and* LUCY.]

[Act IV, Scene II]

[*The Scene changes to a Bed-chamber, where appear:* PINCHWIFE, *Mrs.* PINCHWIFE.]

PINCHWIFE: Come tell me, I say.

MRS. PINCHWIFE: Lord, han't I told it an hundred times over.

PINCHWIFE: I wou'd try, if in the repetition of the ungrateful tale, I cou'd find her altering it in the least circumstance, for if her story be false, she is so too.   [*Aside.*]

Come how was't Baggage?

MRS. PINCHWIFE: Lord, what pleasure you take to hear it sure!

PINCHWIFE: No, you take more in telling it I find, but speak how was't?

MRS. PINCHWIFE: He carried me up into the house, next to the Exchange.

PINCHWIFE: So, and you two were only in the room.

MRS. PINCHWIFE: Yes, for he sent away a youth that was there, for some dryed fruit, and China Oranges.[1]

PINCHWIFE: Did he so? Damn him for it – and for –

MRS. PINCHWIFE: But presently came up the Gentlewoman of the house.

PINCHWIFE: O 'twas well she did, but what did he do whilst the fruit came?

MRS. PINCHWIFE: He kiss'd me an hundred times, and told me he fancied he

---

1. Sweet oranges which were supposed to come originally from China.

kiss'd my fine Sister, meaning me you know, whom he said he lov'd
with all his Soul, and bid me be sure to tell her so, and to desire her to
be at her window, by eleven of the clock this morning, and he wou'd
walk under it at that time.

PINCHWIFE: And he was as good as his word, very punctual, a pox reward
him for't.   [*Aside.*]

MRS. PINCHWIFE: Well, and he said if you were not within, he wou'd come up
to her, meaning me you know, Bud, still.

PINCHWIFE: So – he knew her certainly, but for this confession, I am oblig'd
to her simplicity.   [*Aside.*]
But what you stood very still, when he kiss'd you?

MRS. PINCHWIFE: Yes I warrant you, wou'd you have had me discover'd my
self?

PINCHWIFE: But you told me, he did some beastliness to you, as you call'd it,
what was't?

MRS. PINCHWIFE: Why, he put –

PINCHWIFE: What?

MRS. PINCHWIFE: Why he put the tip of his tongue between my lips, and so
musl'd me – and I said, I'd bite it.

PINCHWIFE: An eternal canker seize it, for a dog.

MRS. PINCHWIFE: Nay, you need not be so angry with him neither, for to say
truth, he has the sweetest breath I ever knew.

PINCHWIFE: The Devil – you were satisfied with it then, and wou'd do it
again.

MRS. PINCHWIFE: Not unless he shou'd force me.

PINCHWIFE: Force you, changeling! I tell you no woman can be forced.

MRS. PINCHWIFE: Yes, but she may sure, by such a one as he, for he's a proper,
goodly strong man, 'tis hard, let me tell you, to resist him.

PINCHWIFE: So, 'tis plain she loves him, yet she has not love enough to make
her conceal it from me, but the sight of him will increase her aversion
for me, and love for him; and that love instruct her how to deceive me,
and satisfie him, all Ideot as she is: Love, 'twas he gave women first
their craft, their art of deluding; out of natures hands, they came plain,
open, silly and fit for slaves, as she and Heaven intended'em; but
damn'd Love – Well – I must strangle that little Monster, whilest I can
deal with him. Go fetch Pen, Ink and Paper out of the next room:

MRS. PINCHWIFE: Yes Bud.   [*Exit Mrs.* PINCHWIFE.]

PINCHWIFE: Why should Women have more invention in love than men? It
can only be, because they have more desires, more solliciting passions,
more lust, and more of the Devil.   [*Aside.*]

[*Mistris* PINCHWIFE *returns.*]

Come, Minks, sit down and write.

MRS. PINCHWIFE: Ay, dear Bud, but I can't do't very well.

PINCHWIFE: I wish you cou'd not at all.

MRS. PINCHWIFE: But what shou'd I write for?

PINCHWIFE: I'll have you write a Letter to your Lover.

MRS. PINCHWIFE: O Lord, to the fine Gentleman a Letter!

PINCHWIFE: Yes, to the fine Gentleman.

MRS. PINCHWIFE: Lord, you do but jeer; sure you jest.

PINCHWIFE: I am not so merry, come write as I bid you.

MRS. PINCHWIFE: What, do you think I am a fool?

PINCHWIFE: She's afraid I would not dictate any love to him, therefore she's unwilling; but you had best begin.

MRS. PINCHWIFE: Indeed, and indeed, but I won't, so I won't.

PINCHWIFE: Why?

MRS. PINCHWIFE: Because he's in Town, you may send for him if you will.

PINCHWIFE: Very well, you wou'd have him brought to you; is it come to this? I say take the pen and write, or you'll provoke me.

MRS. PINCHWIFE: Lord, what d'ye make a fool of me for? Don't I know that Letters are never writ, but from the Countrey to *London*, and from *London* into the Countrey; now he's in Town, and I am in Town too; therefore I can't write to him you know.

PINCHWIFE: So I am glad it is no worse, she is innocent enough yet. [*Aside.*] Yes you may when your Husband bids you write Letters to people that are in Town.

MRS. PINCHWIFE: O may I so! Then I'm satisfied.

PINCHWIFE: Come begin – Sir –   [*Dictates.*]

MRS. PINCHWIFE: Shan't I say, Dear Sir? You know one says always something more than bare Sir.

PINCHWIFE: Write as I bid you, or I will write Whore with this Penknife in your Face.

MRS. PINCHWIFE: Nay good Bud – Sir –   [*She writes.*]

PINCHWIFE: Though I suffer'd last night your nauseous, loath'd Kisses and Embraces – Write.

MRS. PINCHWIFE: Nay, why shou'd I say so, you know I told you, he had a sweet breath.

PINCHWIFE: Write.

MRS. PINCHWIFE: Let me but put out, loath'd.

PINCHWIFE: Write I say.

MRS. PINCHWIFE: Well then.   [*Writes.*]

PINCHWIFE: Let's see what have you writ?   [*Takes the paper, and reads.*] Though I suffer'd last night your kisses and embraces – Thou impudent creature, where is nauseous and loath'd?

MRS. PINCHWIFE: I can't abide to write such filthy words.

PINCHWIFE: Once more write as I'd have you, and question it not, or I will spoil thy writing with this, I will stab out those eyes that cause my mischief.   [*Holds up the penknife.*]

MRS. PINCHWIFE: O Lord, I will.

PINCHWIFE: So – so – Let's see now!   [*Reads.*]

Though I suffer'd last night your nauseous, loath'd kisses, and embraces; Go on – Yet I would not have you presume that you shall ever repeat them – So – *[She writes.]*

MRS. PINCHWIFE: I have writ it.

PINCHWIFE: On then – I then conceal'd my self from your knowledge, to avoid your insolencies – *[She writes.]*

MRS. PINCHWIFE: So –

PINCHWIFE: The same reason now I am out of your hands – *[She writes.]*

MRS. PINCHWIFE: So –

PINCHWIFE: Makes me own to you my unfortunate, though innocent frolick, of being in man's cloths. *[She writes.]*

MRS. PINCHWIFE: So –

PINCHWIFE: That you may for ever more cease to pursue her, who hates and detests you – *[She writes on.]*

MRS. PINCHWIFE: So – h – *[Sighs.]*

PINCHWIFE: What do you sigh? – detests you – as much as she loves her Husband and her Honour –

MRS. PINCHWIFE: I vow Husband he'll ne'er believe, I shou'd write such a Letter.

PINCHWIFE: What he'd expect a kinder from you? come now your name only.

MRS. PINCHWIFE: What, shan't I say your most faithful, humble Servant till death?

PINCHWIFE: No, tormenting Fiend; her stile I find wou'd be very soft. *[Aside.]* Come wrap it up now, whilst I go fetch wax and a candle; and write on the back side, for Mr. *Horner*. *[Exit PINCHWIFE.]*

MRS. PINCHWIFE: For Mr. *Horner* – So, I am glad he has told me his name; Dear Mr. *Horner*, but why should I send thee such a Letter, that will vex thee, and make thee angry with me; – well I will not send it – Ay but then my husband will kill me – for I see plainly, he won't let me love Mr. *Horner* – but what care I for my Husband – I won't so I won't send poor Mr. *Horner* such a Letter – but then my Husband – But oh – what if I writ at bottom, my Husband made me write it – Ay but then my Husband wou'd see't – Can one have no shift, ah, a *London* woman wou'd have had a hundred presently; stay – what if I shou'd write a Letter, and wrap it up like this, and write upon't too; ay but then my Husband wou'd see't – I don't know what to do – But yet y vads[1] I'll try, so I will – for I will not send this Letter to poor Mr. *Horner*, come what will on't.

[She writes, and repeats what she hath writ.]

Dear, Sweet Mr. *Horner* – So – My Husband wou'd have me send you a base, rude, unmannerly Letter – but I won't – *so* – and wou'd have me forbid you loving me – but I won't *so* – and wou'd have me say to you, I hate you poor Mr. *Horner* – but I won't tell a lye for him – *there* – for

1. In faith.

I'm sure if you and I were in the Countrey at cards together, – *so* – I cou'd not help treading on your Toe under the Table – so – or rubbing knees with you, and staring in your face, 'till you saw me – *very well* – and then looking down, and blushing for an hour together – *so* – but I must make haste before my Husband come; and now he has taught me to write Letters: You shall have longer ones from me, who am

Dear, dear, poor dear Mr. *Horner*, your most
Humble Friend, and Servant to command
'till death, *Margery Pinchwife.*

Stay I must give him a hint at bottom – *so* – now wrap it up just like t'other – *so* – now write for Mr. *Horner*, – But oh now what shall I do with it? for here comes my Husband.

[*Enter* PINCHWIFE.]

PINCHWIFE: I have been detained by a Sparkish Coxcomb, who pretended a visit to me; but I fear 'twas to my Wife.   [*Aside.*]
What, have you done?

MRS. PINCHWIFE: Ay, ay Bud, just now.

PINCHWIFE: Let's see't, what d'ye tremble for; what, you wou'd not have it go?

MRS. PINCHWIFE: Here. – No I must not give him that, [*He opens, and reads the first Letter.*] so I had been served if I had given him this.   [*Aside.*]

PINCHWIFE: Come, where's the Wax and Seal?

MRS. PINCHWIFE: Lord, what shall I do now? Nay then I have it –   [*Aside.*]
Pray let me see't, Lord you think me so errand a fool, I cannot seal a Letter, I will do't, so I will.

[*Snatches the Letter from him, changes it for the other, seals it, and delivers it to him.*]

PINCHWIFE: Nay, I believe you will learn that, and other things too, which I wou'd not have you.

MRS. PINCHWIFE: So, han't I done it curiously? I think I have, there's my Letter going to Mr. *Horner*; since he'll needs have me send Letters to Folks.
[*Aside.*]

PINCHWIFE: 'Tis very well, but I warrant, you wou'd not have it go now?

MRS. PINCHWIFE: Yes indeed, but I wou'd, Bud, now.

PINCHWIFE: Well you are a good Girl then, come let me lock you up in your chamber, 'till I come back; and be sure you come not within three strides of the window, when I am gone; for I have a spye in the street.
[*Exit Mrs.* PINCHWIFE.]

[PINCHWIFE *locks the door.*]

At least, 'tis fit she think so, if we do not cheat women, they'll cheat us; and fraud may be justly used with secret enemies, of which a Wife is the most dangerous; and he that has a handsome one to keep, and a Frontier Town, must provide against treachery, rather than open Force – Now I have secur'd all within, I'll deal with the Foe without with false intelligence.   [*Holds up the Letter.*]

[*Exit* PINCHWIFE.]

[Act IV, Scene III]

[*The Scene changes to Horner's Lodging.*
QUACK *and* HORNER.]

QUACK: Well Sir, how fadges[1] the new design; have you not the luck of all your brother Projectors, to deceive only your self at last.

HORNER: No, good *Domine* Doctor, I deceive you it seems, and others too; for the grave Matrons, and old ridgid Husbands think me as unfit for love, as they are; but their Wives, Sisters and Daughters, know some of 'em better things already.

QUACK: Already!

HORNER: Already, I say; last night I was drunk with half a dozen of your civil persons, as you call 'em, and people of Honour, and so was made free of their Society, and dressing rooms for ever hereafter; and am already come to the privileges of sleeping upon their Pallats, warming Smocks, tying Shooes and Garters, and the like Doctor, already, already Doctor.

QUACK: You have made use of your time, Sir.

HORNER: I tell thee, I am now no more interruption to'em, when they sing, or talk bawdy, than a little squab French Page, who speaks no English.

QUACK: But do civil persons, and women of Honour drink, and sing bawdy Songs?

HORNER: O amongst Friends, amongst Friends; for your Bigots in Honour, are just like those in Religion; they fear the eye of the world, more than the eye of Heaven, and think there is no virtue, but railing at vice; and no sin, but giving scandal: They rail at a poor, little, kept Player, and keep themselves some young, modest Pulpit Comedian to be privy to their sins in their Closets, not to tell 'em of them in their Chappels.

QUACK: Nay, the truth on't is, Priests amongst the women now, have quite got the better of us Lay Confessors, Physicians.

HORNER: And they are rather their Patients, but –

[*Enter my Lady* FIDGET, *looking about her.*]

Now we talk of women of Honour, here comes one, step behind the

1. Succeeds or thrives

Screen there, and but observe; if I have not particular privileges, with the women of reputation already, Doctor, already.

LADY FIDGET: Well *Horner*, am not I a woman of Honour? you see I'm as good as my word.

HORNER: And you shall see Madam, I'll not be behind hand with you in honour; and I'll be as good as my word too, if you please but to withdraw into the next room.

LADY FIDGET: But first, my dear Sir, you must promise to have a care of my dear Honour.

HORNER: If you talk a word more of your Honour, you'll make me incapable to wrong it; to talk of Honour in the mysteries of Love, is like talking of Heaven, or the Deity in an operation of Witchcraft, just when you are employing the Devil, it makes the charm impotent.

LADY FIDGET: Nay, fie, let us not be smooty; but you talk of mysteries, and bewitching to me, I don't understand you.

HORNER: I tell you Madam, the word money in a Mistresses mouth, at such a nick of time, is not a more disheartning sound to a younger Brother, than that of Honour to an eager Lover like my self.

LADY FIDGET: But you can't blame a Lady of my reputation to be chary.

HORNER: Chary – I have been chary of it already, by the report I have caus'd of my self.

LADY FIDGET: Ay, but if you shou'd ever let other women know that dear secret, it would come out; nay, you must have a great care of your conduct; for my acquaintance are so censorious, (oh 'tis a wicked censorious world, Mr. *Horner*) I say, are so censorious, and detracting, that perhaps they'll talk to the prejudice of my Honour, though you shou'd not let them know the dear secret.

HORNER: Nay Madam, rather than they shall prejudice your Honour, I'll prejudice theirs; and to serve you, I'll lye with'em all, make the secret their own, and then they'll keep it: I am a *Machiavel* in love Madam.

LADY FIDGET: O, no Sir, not that way.

HORNER: Nay, the Devil take me, if censorious women are to be silenc'd any other way.

LADY FIDGET: A secret is better kept I hope, by a single person, than a multitude; therefore pray do not trust any body else with it, dear, dear Mr. *Horner*.   [*Embracing him.*]

[*Enter Sir* JASPAR FIDGET.]

SIR JASPAR: How now!

LADY FIDGET: O my Husband – prevented – and what's almost as bad, found with my arms about another man – that will appear too much – what shall I say?   [*Aside.*]

Sir *Jaspar* come hither, I am trying if Mr. *Horner* were ticklish, and he's as ticklish as can be, I love to torment the confounded Toad; let you and I tickle him.

SIR JASPAR: No, your Ladyship will tickle him better without me, I suppose, but is this your buying China, I tbought you had been at the China House?

HORNER: China-House, that's my Cue, I must take it.   [*Aside.*]
A Pox, can't you keep your impertinent Wives at home? some men are troubled with the Husbands, but I with the Wives; but I'd have you to know, since I cannot be your Journey-man by night, I will not be your drudge by day, to squire your wife about, and be your man of straw, or scare-crow only to Pyes and Jays; that would be nibling at your forbidden fruit; I shall be shortly the Hackney Gentleman-Usher of the Town.

SIR JASPAR: Heh, heh, he, poor fellow he's in the right on't faith, to squire women about for other folks, is as ungrateful an employment, as to tell money for other folks;   [*Aside.*]
heh, he, he, ben't angry *Horner* –

LADY FIDGET: No, 'tis I have more reason to be angry, who am left by you, to go abroad indecently alone; or, what is more indecent, to pin my self upon such ill bred people of your acquaintance, as this is.

SIR JASPAR: Nay, pr'ythee what has he done?

LADY FIDGET: Nay, he has done nothing.

SIR JASPAR: But what d'ye take ill, if he has done nothing?

LADY FIDGET: Hah, hah, hah, Faith, I can't but laugh however; why d'ye think the unmannerly toad wou'd not come down to me to the Coach, I was fain to come up to fetch him, or go without him, which I was resolved not to do; for he knows China very well, and has himself very good, but will not let me see it, lest I should beg some; but I will find it out, and have what I came for yet.

[*Exit Lady* FIDGET, *and locks the door, followed by* HORNER *to the door.*]

HORNER: Lock the door Madam –   [*Apart to Lady* FIDGET.]
So, she has got into my chamber, and lock'd me out; oh the impertinency of woman-kind! Well Sir *Jaspar*, plain dealing is a Jewel; if ever you suffer your Wife to trouble me again here, she shall carry you home a pair of Horns, by my Lord Major[1] she shall; though I cannot furnish you my self, you are sure, yet I'll find a way.

SIR JASPAR: Hah, ha, he, at my first coming in, and finding her arms about him, tickling him it seems, I was half jealous, but now I see my folly.
                    [*Aside.*]
Heh, he, he, poor *Horner.*

HORNER: Nay, though you laugh now, 'twill be my turn e're long: Oh women, more impertinent, more cunning, and more mischievous than their Monkeys, and to me almost as ugly – now is she throwing my things about, and rifling all I have, but I'll get into her the back way, and so rifle her for it –

1. Lord Mayor.

SIR JASPAR: Hah, ha, ha, poor angry *Horner*.

HORNER: Stay here a little, I'll ferret her out to you presently, I warrant.

[*Exit* HORNER *at t'other door.*]

SIR JASPAR: Wife, my Lady *Fidget*, Wife, he is coming into you the back way.

[*Sir* JASPAR *calls through the door to his Wife, she answers from within.*]

LADY FIDGET: Let him come, and welcome, which way he will.

SIR JASPAR: He'll catch you, and use you roughly, and be too strong for you.

LADY FIDGET: Don't you trouble your self, let him if he can.

QUACK: [*Behind.*] This indeed, I cou'd not have believ'd from him, nor any but my own eyes.

[*Enter Mistris* SQUEAMISH.]

SQUEAMISH: Where's this Woman-hater, this Toad, this ugly, greasie, dirty Sloven?

SIR JASPAR: So the women all will have him ugly, methinks he is a comely person; but his wants make his form contemptible to'em; and 'tis e'en as my Wife said yesterday, talking of him, that a proper handsome Eunuch, was as ridiculous a thing, as a Gigantick Coward.

SQUEAMISH: Sir *Jaspar*, your Servant, where is the odious Beast?

SIR JASPAR: He's within in his chamber, with my Wife; she's playing the wag with him.

SQUEAMISH: Is she so, and he's a clownish beast, he'll give her no quarter, he'll play the wag with her again, let me tell you; come, let's go help her – What, the door's lock't?

SIR JASPAR: Ay, my Wife lock't it –

SQUEAMISH: Did she so, let us break it open then?

SIR JASPAR: No, no, he'll do her no hurt.

SQUEAMISH: No – But is there no other way to get into'em, whither goes this? I will disturb'em   [*Aside.*]

[*Exit* SQUEAMISH *at another door.*
Enter old Lady SQUEAMISH.]

LADY SQUEAMISH: Where is this Harlotry, this Impudent Baggage, this rambling Tomrigg?[1] O Sir *Jaspar*, I'm glad to see you here, did you not see my vil'd[2] Grandchild come in hither just now?

SIR JASPAR: Yes.

LADY SQUEAMISH: Ay, but where is she then? where is she? Lord Sir *Jaspar* I have e'ne ratled my self to pieces in pursuit of her, but can you tell what she makes here, they say below, no woman lodges here.

1. Tomrigg has the double meaning of tomboy and strumpet.
2. Vile.

SIR JASPAR: No.

LADY SQUEAMISH: No – What does she here then? say if it be not a womans lodging, what makes she here? but are you sure no woman lodges here?

SIR JASPAR: No, nor no man neither, this is Mr. *Horners* Lodging.

LADY SQUEAMISH: Is it so are you sure?

SIR JASPAR: Yes, yes.

LADY SQUEAMISH: So then there's no hurt in't I hope, but where is he?

SIR JASPAR: He's in the next room with my Wife.

LADY SQUEAMISH: Nay if you trust him with your wife, I may with my Biddy, they say he's a merry harmless man now, e'ne as harmless a man as ever came out of *Italy* with a good voice,[1] and as pretty harmless company for a Lady, as a Snake without his teeth.

SIR JASPAR: Ay, ay poor man.

[*Enter Mrs.* SQUEAMISH.]

SQUEAMISH: I can't find'em – Oh are you here, Grandmother, I follow'd you must know my Lady *Fidget* hither, 'tis the prettyest lodging, and I have been staring on the prettyest Pictures.

[*Enter Lady* FIDGET *with a piece of China in her hand,*
and HORNER *following.*]

LADY FIDGET: And I have been toyling and moyling, for the pretti'st piece of China, my Dear.

HORNER: Nay she has been too hard for me do what I cou'd.

SQUEAMISH: Oh Lord I'le have some China too, good Mr.*Horner*, don't think to give other people China, and me none, come in with me too.

HORNER: Upon my honour I have none left now.

SQUEAMISH: Nay, nay I have known you deny your China before now, but you shan't put me off so, come –

HORNER: This Lady had the last there.

LADY FIDGET: Yes indeed Madam, to my certain knowledge he has no more left.

SQUEAMISH: O but it may be he may have some you could not find.

LADY FIDGET: What d'y think if he had had any left, I would not have had it too, for we women of quality never think we have China enough.

HORNER: Do not take it ill, I cannot make China for you all, but I will have a Rol-waggon[2] for you too, another time.

SQUEAMISH: Thank you dear Toad.   [*To* HORNER *aside.*]

LADY FIDGET: What do you mean by that promise?

1. A reference to the Italian castrati who often sang in London.
2. A rollwagon is a cylindrical-bodied Chinese vase. Its phallic shape explains Horner's *double-entendre*.

HORNER: Alas she has an innocent, literal understanding.

[*Apart to Lady* FIDGET.]

LADY SQUEAMISH: Poor Mr. *Horner*, he has enough to doe to please you all, I see.

HORNER: Ay Madam, you see how they use me.

LADY SQUEAMISH: Poor Gentleman I pitty you.

HORNER: I thank you Madam, I could never find pitty, but from such reverend Ladies as you are, the young ones will never spare a man.

SQUEAMISH: Come come, Beast, and go dine with us, for we shall want a man at Hombre after dinner.

HORNER: That's all their use of me Madam you see.

SQUEAMISH: Come Sloven, I'le lead you to be sure of you.

[*Pulls him by the Crevat.*]

LADY SQUEAMISH: Alas poor man how she tuggs him, kiss, kiss her, that's the way to make such nice women quiet.

HORNER: No Madam, that Remedy is worse than the Torment, they know I dare suffer any thing rather than do it.

LADY SQUEAMISH: Prythee kiss her, and I'le give you her Picture in little, that you admir'd so last night, prythee do.

HORNER: Well nothing but that could bribe me, I love a woman only in Effigie, and good Painting as much as I hate them – I'le do't, for I cou'd adore the Devil well painted. [*Kisses Mrs.* SQUEAMISH.]

SQUEAMISH: Foh, you filthy Toad, nay now I've done jesting.

LADY SQUEAMISH: Ha, ha, ha, I told you so.

SQUEAMISH: Foh a kiss of his –

SIR JASPAR: Has no more hurt in't, than one of my Spaniels.

SQUEAMISH: Nor no more good neither.

QUACK: I will now believe any thing he tells me. [*Behind.*]

[*Enter Mr.* PINCHWIFE.]

LADY FIDGET: O Lord here's a man, Sir *Jaspar*, my Mask, my Mask, I would not be seen here for the world.

SIR JASPAR: What not when I am with you.

LADY FIDGET: No, no my honour – let's be gone.

SQUEAMISH: Oh Grandmother, let us be gone, make hast, make hast, I know not how he may censure us.

LADY FIDGET: Be found in the lodging of any thing like a man, away.

[*Exeunt Sir* JASPAR, *Lady* FIDGET, *Old Lady* SQUEAMISH,
Mrs. SQUEAMISH.]

QUACK: What's here another Cuckold – he looks like one, and none else sure have any business with him. [*Behind.*]

HORNER: Well what brings my dear friend hither?

PINCHWIFE: Your impertinency.

HORNER: My impertinency – why you Gentlemen that have got handsome

Wives, think you have a privilege of saying any thing to your friends, and are as brutish, as if you were our Creditors.

PINCHWIFE: No Sir, I'le ne're trust you any way.

HORNER: But why not, dear *Jack*, why diffide[1] in me, thou knowst so well.

PINCHWIFE: Because I do know you so well.

HORNER: Han't I been always thy friend honest *Jack*, always ready to serve thee, in love, or battle, before thou wert married, and am so still.

PINCHWIFE: I believe so you wou'd be my second now indeed.

HORNER: Well then dear *Jack*, why so unkind, so grum, so strange to me, come prythee kiss me deare Rogue, gad I was always I say, and am still as much thy Servant as –

PINCHWIFE: As I am yours Sir. What you wou'd send a kiss to my Wife, is that it?

HORNER: So there 'tis – a man can't shew his friendship to a married man, but presently he talks of his wife to you, prythee let thy Wife alone, and let thee and I be all one, as we were wont, what thou art as shye of my kindness, as a Lumbard-street Alderman of a Courtiers civility at Lockets.[2]

PINCHWIFE: But you are over kind to me, as kind, as if I were your Cuckold already, yet I must confess you ought to be kind and civil to me, since I am so kind, so civil to you, as to bring you this, look you there Sir.

[*Delivers him a Letter.*]

HORNER: What is't?

PINCHWIFE: Only a Love Letter Sir.

HORNER: From whom – how, this is from your Wife – hum – and hum –

[*Reads.*]

PINCHWIFE: Even from my Wife Sir, am I not wondrous kind and civil to you, now too?

But you'l not think her so. [*Aside.*]

HORNER: Ha, is this a trick of his or hers. [*Aside.*]

PINCHWIFE: The Gentleman's surpriz'd I find, what you expected a kinder Letter?

HORNER: No faith not I, how cou'd I.

PINCHWIFE: Yes yes, I'm sure you did, a man so well made as you are must needs be disappointed, if the women declare not their passion at first sight or opportunity.

HORNER: But what should this mean? stay the Postscript.

Be sure you love me whatsoever my husband says to the contrary, and let him not see this, lest he should come home, and pinch me, or kill my Squirrel. [*Reads aside.*]

It seems he knows not what the Letter contains. [*Aside.*]

PINCHWIFE: Come ne're wonder at it so much.

1. Distrust.
2. A fashionable restaurant at Charing Cross.

HORNER: Faith I can't help it.

PINCHWIFE: Now I think I have deserv'd your infinite friendship, and kindness, and have shewed my self sufficiently an obliging kind friend and husband, am I not so, to bring a Letter from my Wife to her Gallant?

HORNER: Ay, the Devil take me, art thou, the most obliging, kind friend and husband in the world, ha, ha.

PINCHWIFE: Well you may be merry Sir, but in short I must tell you Sir, my honour will suffer no jesting.

HORNER: What do'st thou mean?

PINCHWIFE: Does the Letter want a Comment? then know Sir, though I have been so civil a husband, as to bring you a Letter from my Wife, to let you kiss and court her to my face, I will not be a Cuckold Sir, I will not.

HORNER: Thou art mad with jealousie, I never saw thy Wife in my life, but at the Play yesterday, and I know not if it were she or no, I court her, kiss her!

PINCHWIFE: I will not be a Cuckold I say, there will be danger in making me a Cuckold.

HORNER: Why, wert thou not well cur'd of thy last clap?

PINCHWIFE: I weare a Sword.

HORNER: It should be taken from thee, lest thou should'st do thy self a mischiefe with it, thou art mad, Man.

PINCHWIFE: As mad as I am, and as merry as you are, I must have more reason from you e're we part, I say again though, you kiss'd, and courted last night my Wife in man's clothes, as she confesses in her Letter.

HORNER: Ha –   [*Aside.*]

PINCHWIFE: Both she and I say you must not design it again, for you have mistaken your woman, as you have done your man.

HORNER: Oh – I understand something now –   [*Aside.*]
Was that thy Wife? why would'st thou not tell me 'twas she? faith my freedome with her was your fault, not mine.

PINCHWIFE: Faith so 'twas –   [*Aside.*]

HORNER: Fye, I'de never do't to a woman before her husbands face, sure.

PINCHWIFE: But I had rather you should do't to my wife before my face, than behind my back, and that you shall never doe.

HORNER: No – you will hinder me.

PINCHWIFE: If I would not hinder you, you see by her Letter, she wou'd.

HORNER: Well, I must e'ne acquiess then, and be contented with what she writes.

PINCHWIFE: I'le assure you 'twas voluntarily writ, I had no hand in't you may believe me.

HORNER: I do believe thee, faith.

PINCHWIFE: And believe her too, for she's an innocent creature, has no dissembling in her, and so fare you well Sir.

HORNER: Pray however present my humble service to her, and tell her I will

obey her Letter to a tittle, and fulfill her desires be what they will, or
with what difficulty soever I do't, and you shall be no more jealous of
me, I warrant her, and you –

PINCHWIFE: Well then fare you well, and play with any mans honour but
mine, kiss any mans wife but mine, and welcome –

[*Exit Mr.* PINCHWIFE.]

HORNER: Ha, ha, ha, Doctor.

QUACK: It seems he has not heard the report of you, or does not believe it.

HORNER: Ha, ha, now Doctor what think you?

QUACK: Pray let's see the Letter – hum – for – deare – love you –

[*Reads the Letter.*]

HORNER: I wonder how she cou'd contrive it! what say'st thou to't, 'tis an
Original.

QUACK: So are your Cuckolds too Originals: for they are like no other
common Cuckolds, and I will henceforth believe it not impossible for
you to Cuckold the Grand Signior[1] amidst his Guards of Eunuchs, that
I say –

HORNER: And I say for the Letter, 'tis the first love Letter that ever was
without Flames, Darts, Fates, Destinies, Lying and Dissembling in't.

[*Enter* SPARKISH *pulling in Mr.* PINCHWIFE.]

SPARKISH: Come back, you are a pretty Brother-in-law, neither go to Church,
nor to dinner with your Sister Bride.

PINCHWIFE: My Sister denies her marriage, and you see is gone away from
you dissatisfy'd.

SPARKISH: Pshaw, upon a foolish scruple, that our Parson was not in lawful
Orders, and did not say all the Common Prayer, but 'tis her modesty
only I believe, but let women be never so modest the first day, they'l be
sure to come to themselves by night, and I shall have enough of her
then; in the mean time, *Harry Horner,* you must dine with me, I keep my
wedding at my Aunts in the Piazza.[2]

HORNER: Thy wedding, what stale Maid has liv'd to despaire of a husband,
or what young one of a Gallant?

SPARKISH: O your Servant Sir – this Gentlemans Sister then – No stale Maid.

HORNER: I'm sorry for't.

PINCHWIFE: How comes he so concern'd for her –   [*Aside.*]

SPARKISH: You sorry for't, why do you know any ill by her?

HORNER: No, I know none but by thee, 'tis for her sake, not yours, and
another mans sake that might have hop'd, I thought –

SPARKISH: Another Man, another man, what is his Name?

HORNER: Nay since 'tis past he shall be nameless.

Poor *Harcourt* I am sorry thou hast mist her –   [*Aside.*]

1. The Sultan of Turkey at Constantinople.
2. The Piazza of Covent Garden.

PINCHWIFE: He seems to be much troubled at the match –   [*Aside.*]

SPARKISH: Prythee tell me – nay you shan't go Brother.

PINCHWIFE: I must of necessity, but I'le come to you to dinner.

[*Exit* PINCHWIFE.]

SPARKISH: But *Harry*, what have I a Rival in my Wife already? but withal my heart, for he may be of use to me hereafter, for though my hunger is now my sawce, and I can fall on heartily without, but the time will come, when a Rival will be as good sawce for a married man to a wife, as an Orange to Veale.

HORNER: O thou damn'd Rogue, thou hast set my teeth on edge with thy Orange.

SPARKISH: Then let's to dinner, there I was with you againe, come.

HORNER: But who dines with thee?

SPARKISH: My Friends and Relations, my Brother *Pinchwife* you see of your acquaintance.

HORNER: And his Wife.

SPARKISH: No gad, he'l nere let her come amongst us good fellows, your stingy country Coxcomb keeps his wife from his friends, as he does his little Firkin of Ale, for his own drinking, and a Gentleman can't get a smack on't, but his servants, when his back is turn'd broach it at their pleasures, and dust it away,[1] ha, ha, ha, gad I am witty, I think, considering I was married to day, by the world, but come –

HORNER: No, I will not dine with you, unless you can fetch her too.

SPARKISH: Pshaw what pleasure can'st thou have with women now, *Harry*?

HORNER: My eyes are not gone, I love a good prospect yet, and will not dine with you, unless she does too, go fetch her therefore, but do not tell her husband, 'tis for my sake.

SPARKISH: Well I'le go try what I can do, in the mean time come away to my Aunts lodging, 'tis in the way to *Pinchwifes*.

HORNER: The poor woman has call'd for aid, and stretch'd forth her hand Doctor, I cannot but help her over the Pale out of the Bryars.

[*Exeunt* SPARKISH, HORNER, QUACK.]

[Act IV, Scene IV]

[*The Scene changes to Pinchwife's house. Mrs.* PINCHWIFE *alone leaning on her elbow. A Table, Pen, Ink, and Paper.*]

MRS. PINCHWIFE: Well 'tis e'ne so, I have got the *London* disease, they call Love, I am sick of my Husband, and for my Gallant; I have heard this distemper, call'd a Feaver, but methinks 'tis liker an Ague, for when I think of my Husband, I tremble and am in a cold sweat, and have

1. Drink it down quickly.

inclinations to vomit, but when I think of my Gallant, dear Mr. *Horner*, my hot fit comes, and I am all in a Feaver, indeed, & as in other Feavers, my own Chamber is tedious to me, and I would fain be remov'd to his, and then methinks I shou'd be well; ah poor Mr. *Horner*, well I cannot, will not stay here, therefore I'le make an end of my Letter to him, which shall be a finer Letter than my last, because I have studied it like any thing; O Sick, Sick!   [*Takes the Pen and writes.*]

[*Enter Mr.* PINCHWIFE *who seeing her writing steales softly behind her, and looking over her shoulder, snatches the paper from her.*]

PINCHWIFE: What writing more Letters?

MRS. PINCHWIFE: O Lord Budd, why d'ye fright me so?

[*She offers to run out: he stops her, and reads.*]

PINCHWIFE: How's this! nay you shall not stir Madam.

Deare, Deare, deare, Mr *Horner* – very well – I have taught you to write Letters to good purpose – but let's see't.

First I am to beg your pardon for my boldness in writing to you, which I'de have you to know, I would not have done, had not you said first you lov'd me so extreamly, which if you doe, you will never suffer me to lye in the arms of another man, whom I loath, nauseate, and detest – (Now you can write these filthy words) but what follows – Therefore I hope you will speedily find some way to free me from this unfortunate match, which was never, I assure you, of my choice, but I'm afraid 'tis already too far gone; however if you love me, as I do you, you will try what you can do, but you must help me away before to morrow, or else alass I shall be for ever out of your reach, for I can defer no longer our – our – [*The Letter concludes.*] what is to follow our – speak what? our Journey into the Country I suppose – Oh Woman, damn'd Woman, and Love, damn'd Love, their old Tempter, for this is one of his miracles, in a moment, he can make those blind that cou'd see, and those see that were blind, those dumb that could speak, and those prattle who were dumb before, nay what is more than all, make these dow-bak'd,[1] sensless, indocile animals, Women, too hard for us their Politick Lords and Rulers in a moment; But make an end of your Letter, and then I'le make an end of you thus, and all my plagues together.

[*Draws his Sword.*]

MRS. PINCHWIFE: O Lord, O Lord you are such a Passionate Man, Budd.

[*Enter* SPARKISH.]

SPARKISH: How now what's here to doe.

PINCHWIFE: This Fool here now!

SPARKISH: What drawn upon your Wife? you shou'd never do that but at night in the dark when you can't hurt her, this is my Sister In Law is it

1. Dough-baked or feeble-minded.

not? [*Pulls aside her Handkercheife.*] ay faith e'ne our Country *Margery,* one may know her, come she and you must go dine with me, dinner's ready, come, but where's my Wife, is she not come home yet, where is she?

PINCHWIFE: Making you a Cuckold, 'tis that they all doe, as soon as they can.

SPARKISH: What the Wedding day? no, a Wife that designs to make a Cully of her Husband, will be sure to let him win the first stake of love, by the world, but come they stay dinner for us, come I'le lead down our *Margery.*

PINCHWIFE: No – Sir go we'l follow you,

SPARKISH: I will not wag without you.

PINCHWIFE: This Coxcomb is a sensible[1] torment to me amidst the greatest in the world.

SPARKISH: Come, come Madam Margery.

PINCHWIFE: No I'le lead her my way, what wou'd you treat your friends with mine, for want of your own Wife?

[Leads her to t'other door, and locks her in and returns.]

I am contented my rage shou'd take breath –   [*Aside.*]

SPARKISH: I told *Horner* this.

PINCHWIFE: Come now.

SPARKISH: Lord, how shye you are of your Wife, but let me tell you Brother, we men of wit have amongst us a saying, that Cuckolding like the small Pox comes with a fear, and you may keep your Wife as much as you will out of danger of infection, but if her constitution incline her to't, she'l have it sooner or later by the world, say they.

PINCHWIFE: What a thing is a Cuckold, that every fool can make him ridiculous –   [*Aside.*]

Well Sir – But let me advise you, now you are come to be concern'd, because you suspect the danger, not to neglect the means to prevent it, especially when the greatest share of the Malady will light upon your own head, for –

How'sere the kind Wife's Belly comes to swell.
The Husband breeds[2] for her, and first is ill.

Act V, Scene I

[*Mr. Pinchwife's House.*
Enter Mr. PINCHWIFE *and Mrs.* PINCHWIFE, *a Table and Candle.*]

PINCHWIFE: Come take the Pen and make an end of the Letter, just as you

---

1. Acutely felt.
2. Breeds in the sense of develops. The husband develops horns, which make him ill.

intended, if you are false in a tittle, I shall soon perceive it, and punish you with this as you deserve, [*Lays his hand on his Sword.*] write what was to follow – let's see – (you must make haste and help me away before to morrow, or else I shall be for ever out of your reach, for I can defer no longer our –) What follows our? –

MRS. PINCHWIFE: Must all out then Budd? – Look you there then.

[*Mrs.* PINCHWIFE *takes the Pen and writes.*]

PINCHWIFE: Let's see – (For I can defer no longer our Wedding – Your slighted *Alithea*) What's the meaning of this, my Sisters name to't, speak, unriddle?

MRS. PINCHWIFE: Yes indeed Budd.

PINCHWIFE: But why her name to't speak – speak I say?

MRS. PINCHWIFE: Ay but you'l tell her then again, if you wou'd not tell her again.

PINCHWIFE: I will not, I am stunn'd, my head turns round, speak.

MRS. PINCHWIFE: Won't you tell her indeed, and indeed.

PINCHWFE: No, speak I say.

MRS. PINCHWIFE: She'l be angry with me, but I had rather she should be angry with me than you Budd; and to tell you the truth, 'twas she made me write the Letter, and taught me what I should write.

PINCHWIFE: Ha – I thought the stile was somewhat better than her own, but how cou'd she come to you to teach you, since I had lock'd you up alone.

MRS. PINCHWIFE: O through the key hole Budd.

PINCHWIFE: But why should she make you write a Letter for her to him, since she can write her self?

MRS. PINCHWIFE: Why she said because – for I was unwilling to do it.

PINCHWIFE: Because what – because.

MRS. PINCHWIFE: Because lest Mr. *Horner* should be cruel, and refuse her, or vaine afterwards, and shew the Letter, she might disown it, the hand not being hers.

PINCHWIFE: How's this? ha – then I think I shall come to my self again – This changeling cou'd not invent this lye, but if she cou'd, why should she? she might think I should soon discover it – stay – now I think on't too, *Horner* said he was sorry she had married *Sparkish*, and her disowning her marriage to me, makes me think she has evaded it, for *Horner's* sake, yet why should she take this course, but men in love are fools, women may well be so. –   [*Aside.*]

But hark you Madam, your Sister went out in the moming, and I have not seen her within since.

MRS. PINCHWIFE: A lack a day she has been crying all day above it seems in a corner.

PINCHWIFE: Where is she, let me speak with her.

MRS. PINCHWIFE: O Lord then he'l discover all –   [*Aside.*]

Pray hold Budd, what d'y mean to discover me, she'l know I have told you then, pray Budd let me talk with her first –

PINCHWIFE: I must speak with her to know whether *Horner* ever made her any promise; and whether she be married to *Sparkish* or no.

MRS. PINCHWIFE: Pray dear Budd don't, till I have spoken with her and told her that I have told you all, for she'll kill me else.

PINCHWIFE: Go then and bid her come out to me.

MRS. PINCHWIFE: Yes, yes Budd –

PINCHWIFE: Let me see –

MRS. PINCHWIFE: I'le go, but she is not within to come to him, I have just got time to know of *Lucy* her Maid, who first set me on work, what lye I shall tell next, for I am e'ne at my wits end –   [*Exit Mrs.* PINCHWIFE.]

PINCHWIFE: Well I resolve it, *Horner* shall have her, I'd rather give him my Sister than lend him my Wife, and such an alliance will prevent his pretensions to my Wife sure, – I'le make him of kinn to her, and then he won't care for her.

[*Mrs.* PINCHWIFE *returns.*]

MRS. PINCHWIFE: O Lord Budd I told you what anger you would make me with my Sister.

PINCHWIFE: Won't she come hither?

MRS. PINCHWIFE: No no, alack a day, she's asham'd to look you in the face, and she says if you go in to her, she'l run away down stairs, and shamefully go her self to Mr. *Horner*, who has promis'd her marriage she says, and she will have no other, so she won't –

PINCHWIFE: Did he so – promise her marriage – then she shall have no other, go tell her so, and if she will come and discourse with me a little concerning the means, I will about it immediately, go –

[*Exit Mrs.* PINCHWIFE.]

His estate is equal to *Sparkish's*, and his extraction as much better than his, as his parts are, but my chief reason is, I'd rather be of kin to him by the name of Brother-in-law, than that of Cuckold

[*Enter Mrs.* PINCHWIFE.]

Well what says she now?

MRS. PINCHWIFE: Why she says she would only have you lead her to *Horners* lodging – with whom she first will discourse the matter before she talk with you, which yet she cannot doe; for alack poor creature, she says she can't so much as look you in the face, therefore she'l come to you in a mask, and you must excuse her if she make you no answer to any question of yours, till you have brought her to Mr. *Horner*, and if you will not chide her, nor question her, she'l come out to you immediately.

PINCHWIFE: Let her come I will not speak a word to her, nor require a word from her.

MRS. PINCHWIFE: Oh I forgot, besides she says, she cannot look you in the face, though through a mask, therefore wou'd desire you to put out the Candle.

PINCHWIFE: I agree to all, let her make haste –

[*Exit Mrs.* PINCHWIFE, *puts out the Candle.*]

there 'tis out – My case is something better, I'd rather fight with *Horner* for not lying with my Sister, than for lying with my Wife, and of the two I had rather find my Sister too forward than my Wife; I expected no other from her free education, as she calls it, and her passion for the Town – well – Wife and Sister are names which make us expect, Love and duty, pleasure and comfort, but we find em plagues and torments, and are equally, though differently troublesome to their keeper; for we have as much a-doe to get people to lye with our Sisters, as to keep'em from lying with our Wives.

[*Enter Mrs.* PINCHWIFE *Masked, and in Hoods and Scarves, and a night Gown*[1] *and Petticoat of* ALITHEA's *in the dark.*]

What are you come Sister? let us go then – but first let me lock up my Wife, Mrs. *Margery* where are you?

MRS. PINCHWIFE: Here Budd.

PINCHWIFE: Come hither, that I may lock you up, get you in. [*Locks the door.*] Come Sister where are you now?

[*Mrs.* PINCHWIFE *gives him her hand, but when he lets her go, she steals softly on t'other side of him, and is lead away by him for his Sister* ALITHEA.]

[Act V, Scene II]

[*The scene changes to Horner's Lodging.* QUACK, HORNER.]

QUACK: What all alone, not so much as one of your Cuckolds here, nor one of their Wives! they use to take their turns with you, as if they were to watch you.

HORNER: Yes it often happens, that a Cuckold is but his Wifes spye, and is more upon family duty, when he is with her gallant abroad hindring his pleasure, than when he is at home with her playing the Gallant, but the hardest duty a married woman imposes upon a lover is, keeping her husband company always.

QUACK: And his fondness wearies you almost as soon as hers.

HORNER: A Pox, keeping a Cuckold company after you have had his Wife, is as tiresome as the company of a Country Squire to a witty fellow of the Town, when he has got all his Mony.

---

1. A loose, informal gown that could be worn out of doors.

QUACK: And as at first a man makes a friend of the Husband to get the Wife, so at last you are faine to fall out with the Wife to be rid of the Husband.

HORNER: Ay, most Cuckold-makers are true Courtiers, when once a poor man has crack'd his credit for 'em, they can't abide to come neer him.

QUACK: But at first to draw him in are so sweet, so kind, so dear, just as you are to *Pinchwife*, but what becomes of that intrigue with his Wife?

HORNER: A Pox he's as surly as an Alderman that has been bit, and since he's so coy, his Wife's kindness is in vain, for she's a silly innocent.

QUACK: Did she not send you a Letter by him?

HORNER: Yes, but that's a riddle I have not yet solv'd – allow the poor creature to be willing, she is silly too, and he keeps her up so close –

QUACK: Yes, so close that he makes her but the more willing, and adds but revenge to her love, which two when met seldome faile of satisfying each other one way or other.

HORNER: What here's the man we are talking of I think.

[*Enter Mr.* PINCHWIFE *leading in his Wife Masqued, Muffled, and in her Sister's Gown.*]

HORNER: Pshaw.

QUACK: Bringing his Wife to you is the next thing to bringing a Love Letter from her.

HORNER: What means this?

PINCHWIFE: The last time you know Sir I brought you a love Letter, now you see a Mistress, I think you'l say I am a civil man to you.

HORNER: Ay the Devil take me will I say thou art the civillest man I ever met with, and I have known some; I fancy, I understand thee now, better than I did the Letter, but hark thee in thy eare –

PINCHWIFE: What?

HORNER: Nothing but the usual question man, is she sound on thy word?

PINCHWIFE: What you take her for a Wench and me for a Pimp?

HORNER: Pshaw, wench and Pimp, paw[1] words, I know thou art an honest fellow, and hast a great acquaintance among the Ladies, and perhaps hast made love for me rather than let me make love to thy Wife –

PINCHWIFE: Come Sir, in short, I am for no fooling.

HORNER: Nor I neither, therefore prythee let's see her face presently, make her show man, art thou sure I don't know her?

PINCHWIFE: I am sure you doe know her.

HORNER: A Pox why dost thou bring her to me then?

PINCHWIFE: Because she's a Relation of mine.

HORNER: Is she faith man, then thou art still more civil and obliging, dear Rogue.

PINCHWIFE: Who desir'd me to bring her to you.

1. Nasty.

HORNER: Then she is obliging, dear Rogue.

PINCHWIFE: You'l make her welcome for my sake I hope.

HORNER: I hope she is handsome enough to make her self wellcome; prythee let her unmask.

PINCHWIFE: Doe you speak to her, she wou'd never be rul'd by me.

HORNER: Madam –   [*Mrs.* PINCHWIFE *whispers to* Horner.]
She says she must speak with me in private, withdraw prythee.

PINCHWIFE: She's unwilling it seems I shou'd know all her undecent conduct in this business –   [*Aside.*]
Well then Ile leave you together, and hope when I am gone you'l agree, if not you and I shan't agree Sir. –

HORNER: What means the Fool? – if she and I agree 'tis no matter what you and I do.
[*Whispers to Mrs.* PINCHWIFE, *who makes signs with her hand for him to be gone.*]

PINCHWIFE: In the mean time I'le fetch a Parson, and find out *Sparkish* and disabuse him. You wou'd have me fetch a Parson, would you not, well then – Now I think I am rid of her, and shall have no more trouble with her – Our Sisters and Daughters like Usurers money, are safest, when put out; but our Wifes, like their writings, never safe, but in our Closets under Lock and Key.   [*Exit Mr.* PINCHWIFE.]

[*Enter* BOY.]

BOY: Sir *Jaspar Fidget* Sir is coming up.

HORNER: Here's the trouble of a Cuckold, now we are talking of, a pox on him, has he not enough to doe to hinder his Wifes sport, but he must other women's too. – Step in here Madam.   [*Exit Mrs.* PINCHWIFE.]

[*Enter Sir* JASPAR.]

SIR JASPAR: My best and dearest Friend.

HORNER: The old stile Doctor –
Well be short, for I am busie, what would your impertinent Wife have now?

SIR JASPAR: Well guess'd y' faith, for I do come from her.

HORNER: To invite me to supper, tell her I can't come, go.

SIR JASPAR: Nay, now you are out faith, for my Lady and the whole knot of the virtuous gang, as they call themselves, are resolv'd upon a frolick of coming to you to night in a Masquerade, and are all drest already.

HORNER: I shan't be at home.

SIR JASPAR: Lord how churlish he is to women – nay prythee don't disappoint 'em, they'l think 'tis my fault, prythee don't, I'le send in the Banquet and the Fiddles, but make no noise on't, for the poor virtuous Rogues would not have it known for the world, that they go a Masquerading, and they would come to no mans Ball, but yours.

HORNER: Well, well – get you gone, and tell em if they come, 'twill be at the peril of their honour and yours.

SIR JASPAR: Heh, he, he – we'l trust you for that, farewell – [*Exit Sir* JASPAR.]

HORNER: Doctor anon you too shall be my guest.

But now I'm going to a private feast.

[Act V, Scene III]

[*The Scene changes to the Piazza of Covent Garden.*
SPARKISH, PINCHWIFE. SPARKISH *with the Letter in his hand.*]

SPARKISH: But who would have thought a woman could have been false to me, by the world, I could not have thought it.

PINCHWIFE: You were for giving and taking liberty, she has taken it only Sir, now you find in that Letter, you are a frank person, and so is she you see there.

SPARKISH: Nay if this be her hand – for I never saw it.

PINCHWIFE: 'Tis no matter whether that be her hand or no, I am sure this hand at her desire lead her to Mr. *Horner*, with whom I left her just now, to go fetch a Parson to'em at their desire too, to deprive you of her for ever, for it seems yours was but a mock marriage.

SPARKISH: Indeed she wou'd needs have it that 'twas *Harcourt* himself in a Parsons habit, that married us, but I'm sure he told me 'twas his Brother *Ned*.

PINCHWIFE: O there 'tis out and you were deceiv'd not she, for you are such a frank person – but I must be gone – you'l find her at Mr. *Horners*, goe and believe your eyes. [*Exit Mr.* PINCHWIFE.]

SPARKISH: Nay I'le to her, and call her as many Crocodiles, Syrens, Harpies, and other heathenish names, as a Poet would do a Mistress, who had refus'd to heare his suit, nay more his Verses on her. But stay, is not that she following a Torch at t'other end of the Piazza, and from *Horners* certainly – 'tis so –

[*Enter* ALITHEA *following a Torch, and* LUCY *behind.*]

You are well met Madam though you don't think so; what you have made a short visit to Mr. *Horner*, but I suppose you'l return to him presently, by that time the Parson can be with him.

ALITHEA: Mr. *Horner*, and the Parson Sir –

SPARKISH: Come Madam no more dissembling, no more jilting for I am no more a frank person.

ALITHEA: How's this.

LUCY: So 'twill work I see – [*Aside.*]

SPARKISH: Cou'd you find out no easie Country Fool to abuse? none but me, a Gentleman of wit and pleasure about the Town, but it was your pride to be too hard for a man of parts, unworthy false woman, false as a

friend that lends a man mony to lose, false as dice, who undoe those
that trust all they have to 'em.

LUCY: He has been a great bubble by his similes as they say –   [*Aside.*]

ALITHEA: You have been too merry Sir at your wedding dinner sure.

SPARKISH: What d'y mock me too?

ALITHEA: Or you have been deluded.

SPARKISH: By you.

ALITHEA: Let me understand you.

SPARKISH: Have you the confidence, I should call it something else, since you
know your guilt, to stand my just reproaches? you did not write an
impudent Letter to Mr. *Horner*, who I find now has club'd with you in
deluding me with his aversion for women, that I might not forsooth
suspect him for my Rival.

LUCY: D'y think the Gentleman can be jealous now Madam –   [*Aside.*]

ALITHEA: I write a Letter to Mr. *Horner*!

SPARKISH: Nay Madam, do not deny it, your Brother shew'd it me just now,
and told me likewise he left you at *Horners* lodging to fetch a Parson to
marry you to him, and I wish you joy Madam, joy, joy, and to him too
much joy, and to my self more joy for not marrying you.

ALITHEA: So I find my Brother would break off the match, and I can consent
to't, since I see this Gentleman can be made jealous.   [*Aside.*]
O *Lucy*, by his rude usage and jealousie, he makes me almost afraid I am
married to him, art thou sure 'twas *Harcourt* himself and no Parson that
married us.

SPARKISH: No Madam I thank you, I suppose that was a contrivance too of
Mr. *Horners* and yours, to make *Harcourt* play the Parson, but I would
as little as you have him one now, no not for the world, for shall I tell
you another truth, I never had any passion for you, 'till now, for now I
hate you, 'tis true I might have married your portion, as other men of
parts of the Town do sometimes, and so your Servant, and to shew my
unconcernedness, I'le come to your wedding, and resign you with as
much joy as I would a stale wench to a new Cully, nay with as much joy
as I would after the first night, if I had been married to you, there's for
you, and so your Servant, Servant.   [*Exit* SPARKISH.]

ALITHEA: How was I deceiv'd in a man!

LUCY: You'l believe then a fool may be made jealous now? for that easiness
in him that suffers him to be led by a Wife, will likewise permit him to
be perswaded against her by others.

ALITHEA: But marry Mr. *Horner*, my brother does not intend it sure; if I
thought he did, I would take thy advice, and Mr. *Harcourt* for my
Husband, and now I wish, that if there be any over-wise woman of the
Town, who like me would marry a fool, for fortune, liberty, or title, first
that her husband may love Play, and be a Cully to all the Town, but her,
and suffer none but fortune to be mistress of his purse, then if for liberty,
that he may send her into the Country under the conduct of some

housewifely, mother-in law; and if for title, may the world give 'em none but that of Cuckold.

LUCY: And for her greater Curse Madam, may he not deserve it.

ALITHEA: Away impertinent – is not this my old Lady *Lanterlus*?[1]

LUCY: Yes Madam.

(and here I hope we shall find Mr. *Harcourt* –)   [*Aside.*]

[*Exeunt* ALITHEA, LUCY.]

[Act V, Scene IV]

[*The Scene changes again to Horner's Lodging.* HORNER, *Lady* FIDGET, *Mrs.* DAYNTY FIDGET, *Mrs.* SQUEAMISH, *a Table, Banquet, and Bottles.*]

HORNER: A Pox they are come too soon – before I have sent back my new – Mistress, all I have now to do, is to lock her in, that they may not see her –   [*Aside.*]

LADY FIDGET: That we may be sure of our wellcome, we have brought our entertainment with us, and are resolv'd to treat thee, dear Toad.

DAINTY: And that we may be merry to purpose, have left Sir *Jaspar* and my old Lady *Squeamish* quarrelling at home at Baggammon.

SQUEAMISH: Therefore let us make use of our time, lest they should chance to interrupt us.

LADY FIDGET: Let us sit then.

HORNER: First that you may be private, let me lock this door, and that, and I'le wait upon you presently.

LADY FIDGET: No Sir, shut 'em only and your lips for ever, for we must trust you as much as our women.

HORNER: You know all vanity's kill'd in me, I have no occasion for talking.

LADY FIDGET: Now Ladies, supposing we had drank each of us our two Bottles, let us speak the truth of our hearts.

DAINTY and SQUEAMISH: Agreed.

LADY FIDGET: By this brimmer, for truth is no where else to be found,

(Not in thy heart false man.)   [*Aside to* HORNER.]

HORNER: You have found me a true man I'm sure.   [*Aside to Lady* FIDGET.]

LADY FIDGET: Not every way –   [*Aside to* HORNER.]

But let us sit and be merry.

Lady FIDGET *Sings.*

1

Why should our damn'd Tyrants oblige us to live.
On the pittance of Pleasure which they only give.

1. Her name is the same as a popular card-game, Lanterloo, often abbreviated to Loo, or Lu.

We must not rejoyce,
With Wine and with noise.
In vaine we must wake in a dull bed alone.
Whilst to our warm Rival the Bottle, they're gone.
Then lay aside charms,
And take up these arms*   *The Glasses.

2

'Tis Wine only gives 'em their Courage and Wit,
Because we live sober to men we submit.
If for Beauties you'd pass.
Take a lick of the Glass.
'Twill mend your complexions, and when they are gone,
The best red we have is the red of the Grape.
Then Sisters lay't on.
And dam a good shape.

DAINTY: Dear Brimmer, well in token of our openness and plain dealing, let us throw our Masques over our heads.

HORNER: So 'twill come to the Glasses anon.

SQUEAMISH: Lovely Brimmer, let me enjoy him first.

LADY FIDGET: No, I never part with a Gallant, till I've try'd him. Dear Brimmer that mak'st our Husbands short sighted.

DAINTY: And our bashful gallants bold.

SQUEAMISH: And for want of a Gallant, the Butler lovely in our eyes, drink Eunuch.

LADY FIDGET: Drink thou representative of a Husband, damn a Husband.

DAINTY: And as it were a Husband, an old keeper.

SQUEAMISH: And an old Grandmother.

HORNER: And an English Bawd, and a French Chirurgion.

LADY FIDGET: Ay we have all reason to curse 'em.

HORNER: For my sake Ladies.

LADY FIDGET: No, for our own, for the first spoils all young gallants industry.

DAINTY: And the others art makes 'em bold only with common women.

SQUEAMISH: And rather run the hazard of the vile distemper amongst them, than of a denial amongst us.

DAINTY: The filthy Toads chuse Mistresses now, as they do Stuffs, for having been fancy'd and worn by others.

SQUEAMISH: For being common and cheap.

LADY FIDGET: Whilst women of quality, like the richest Stuffs, lye untumbled, and unask'd for.

HORNER: Ay neat, and cheap, and new often they think best.

DAINTY: No Sir, the Beasts will be known by a Mistriss longer than by a suit.

SQUEAMISH: And 'tis not for cheapness neither.

LADY FIDGET: No, for the vain fopps will take up Druggets, and embroider 'em, but I wonder at the depraved appetites of witty men, they use to be out of the common road, and hate imitation, pray tell me beast, when you were a man, why you rather chose to club with a multitude in a common house, for an entertainment, than to be the only guest at a good Table.

HORNER: Why faith ceremony and expectation are unsufferable to those that are sharp bent, people always eat with the best stomach at an ordinary, where every man is snatching for the best bit.

LADY FIDGET: Though he get a cut over the fingers – but I have heard people eat most heartily of another man's meat, that is, what they do not pay for.

HORNER: When they are sure of their wellcome and freedome, for ceremony in love and eating, is as ridiculous as in fighting, falling on briskly is all should be done in those occasions.

LADY FIDGET: Well then let me tell you Sir, there is no where more freedome than in our houses, and we take freedom from a young person as a sign of good breeding, and a person may be as free as he pleases with us, as frolick, as gamesome, as wild as he will.

HORNER: Han't I heard you all declaim against wild men.

LADY FIDGET: Yes, but for all that, we think wildness in a man, as desireable a quality, as in a Duck, or Rabbet; a tame man, foh.

HORNER: I know not, but your Reputations frightned me, as much as your Faces invited me.

LADY FIDGET: Our Reputation, Lord! Why should you not think, that we women make use of our Reputation, as you men of yours, only to deceive the world with less suspicion; our virtue is like the State-man's Religion, the Quakers Word, the Gamesters Oath, and the Great Man's Honour, but to cheat those that trust us.

SQUEAMISH: And that Demureness, Coyness, and Modesty, that you see in our Faces in the Boxes at Plays, is as much a sign of a kind woman, as a Vizard-mask in the Pit.

DAINTY: For I assure you, women are least mask'd, when they have the Velvet Vizard on.

LADY FIDGET: You wou'd have found us modest women in our denyals only.

SQUEAMISH: Our bashfulness is only the reflection of the Men's.

DAINTY: We blush, when they are shame-fac'd.

HORNER: I beg your pardon Ladies, I was deceiv'd in you devilisly, but why, that mighty pretence to Honour?

LADY FIDGET: We have told you; but sometimes 'twas for the same reason you men pretend business often, to avoid ill company, to enjoy the better, and more privately those you love.

HORNER: But why, wou'd you ne'er give a Friend a wink then?

LADY FIDGET: Faith, your Reputation frightned us as much, as ours did you, you were so notoriously lewd.

HORNER: And you so seemingly honest

LADY FIDGET: Was that all that deterr'd you?

HORNER: And so expensive – you allow freedom you say.

LADY FIDGET: Ay, ay.

HORNER: That I was afraid of losing my little money, as well as my little time, both which my other pleasures required.

LADY FIDGET: Money, foh – you talk like a little fellow now, do such as we expect money?

HORNER: I beg your pardon, Madam, I must confess, I have heard that great Ladies, like great Merchants, set but the higher prizes[1] upon what they have, because they are not in necessity of taking the first offer.

DAINTY: Such as we, make sale of our hearts?

SQUEAMISH: We brib'd for our Love? Foh.

HORNER: With your pardon, Ladies, I know, like great men in Offices, you seem to exact flattery and attendance only from your Followers, but you have receivers about you, and such fees to pay, a man is afraid to pass your Grants;[2] besides we must let you win at Cards, or we lose your hearts; and if you make an assignation, 'tis at a Goldsmiths, Jewellers, or China house, where for your Honour, you deposit to him, he must pawn his, to the punctual Citt, and so paying for what you take up, pays for what he takes up. [3]

DAINTY: Wou'd you not have us assur'd of our Gallants Love?

SQUEAMISH: For Love is better known by Liberality, than by Jealousie.

LADY FIDGET: For one may be dissembled, the other not – but my Jealousie can be no longer dissembled, and they are telling-ripe: [*Aside.*] Come here's to our Gallants in waiting, whom we must name, and I'll begin, this is my false Rogue.   [*Claps him on the back.*]

SQUEAMISH: How!

HORNER: So all will out now –

SQUEAMISH: Did you not tell me, 'twas for my sake only, you reported your self no man?   [*Aside to* HORNER.]

DAINTY: Oh Wretch! did you not swear to me, 'twas for my Love, and Honour, you pass'd for that thing you do?   [*Aside to* HORNER.]

HORNER: So, so.

LADY FIDGET: Come, speak Ladies, this is my false Villain.

SQUEAMISH, And mine too.

DAINTY: And mine.

HORNER: Well then, you are all three my false Rogues too, and there's an end on't.

LADY FIDGET: Well then, there's no remedy, Sister Sharers, let us not fall out,

1. Prices.
2. Accept what you grant.
3. He pays for what he obtains, with the double meaning of paying for lifting the ladies' skirts.

but have a care of our Honour; though we get no Presents, no Jewels of him, we are savers of our Honour, the Jewel of most value and use, which shines yet to the world unsuspected, though it be counterfeit

HORNER: Nay, and is e'en as good, as if it were true, provided the world think so; for Honour, like Beauty now, only depends on the opinion of others.

LADY FIDGET: Well Harry Common, I hope you can be true to three, swear, but 'tis no purpose, to require your Oath; for you are as often forsworn, as you swear to new women.

HORNER: Come, faith Madam, let us e'en pardon one another, for all the difference I find betwixt we men, and you women, we forswear our selves at the beginning of an Amour, you, as long as it lasts.

[*Enter Sir* JASPAR FIDGET, *and old Lady* SQUEAMISH.]

SIR JASPAR: Oh my Lady *Fidget*, was this your cunning, to come to Mr. *Horner* without me; but you have been no where else I hope.

LADY FIDGET: No, Sir *Jaspar*.

LADY SQUEAMISH: And you came straight hither Biddy.

SQUEAMISH: Yes indeed, Lady Grandmother.

SIR JASPAR: 'Tis well, 'tis well, I knew when once they were throughly acquainted with poor *Horner*, they'd ne'er be from him; you may let her masquerade it with my Wife, and *Horner*, and I warrant her Reputation safe.

[*Enter* BOY.]

BOY: O Sir, here's the Gentleman come, whom you bid me not suffer to come up, without giving you notice, with a Lady too, and other Gentlemen –

HORNER: Do you all go in there, whil'st I send'em away, and Boy, do you desire'em to stay below 'til I come, which shall be immediately.

[*Exeunt Sir* JASPAR, *Lady* SQUEAMISH, *Lady* FIDGET, *Mistris* DAINTY SQUEAMISH.]

BOY, Yes Sir. [*Exit.*]

[*Exit* HORNER *at t'other door, and returns with Mistris* PINCHWIFE.]

HORNER: You wou'd not take my advice to be gone home, before your Husband came back, he'll now discover all, yet pray my Dearest be perswaded to go home, and leave the rest to my management, I'll let you down the back way.

MRS. PINCHWIFE: I don't know the way home, so I don't.

HORNER: My man shall wait upon you.

MRS. PINCHWIFE: No, don't you believe, that I'll go at all; what are you weary of me already?

HORNER: No my life, 'tis that I may love you long, 'tis to secure my love, and
your Reputation with your Husband, he'll never receive you again else.

MRS. PINCHWIFE: What care I, d'ye think to frighten me with that? I don't
intend to go to him again; you shall be my Husband now.

HORNER: I cannot be your Husband, Dearest, since you are married to him.

MRS. PINCHWIFE: O wou'd you make me believe that – don't I see every day
at *London* here, women leave their first Husbands, and go, and live with
other men as their Wives, pish, pshaw, you'd make me angry, but that I
love you so mainly.

HORNER: So, they are coming up – In again, in, I hear'em:

[*Exit Mistris* PINCHWIFE.]

Well, a silly Mistriss, is like a weak place, soon got, soon lost, a man has
scarce time for plunder; she betrays her Husband, first to her Gallant,
and then her Gallant, to her Husband

[*Enter* PINCHWIFE, ALITHEA, HARCOURT, SPARKISH, LUCY, *and a Parson.*]

PINCHWIFE: Come Madam, 'tis not the sudden change of your dress, the
confidence of your asseverations, and your false witness there, shall
perswade me, I did not bring you hither, just now; here's my witness,
who cannot deny it, since you must be confronted – Mr. *Horner*, did not
I bring this Lady to you just now?

HORNER: Now must I wrong one woman for anothers sake, but that's no new
thing with me; for in these cases I am still on the criminal's side, against
the innocent.   [*Aside.*]

ALITHEA: Pray, speak Sir.

HORNER: It must be so – I must be impudent, and try my luck, Impudence
uses to be too hard for truth.   [*Aside.*]

PINCHWIFE: What, you are studying an evasion, or excuse for her, speak Sir.

HORNER: No faith, I am something backward only, to speak in womens
affairs or disputes.

PINCHWIFE: She bids you speak.

ALITHEA: Ay, pray Sir do, pray satisfie him.

HORNER: Then truly, you did bring that Lady to me just now.

PINCHWIFE: O ho –

ALITHEA: How Sir –

HARCOURT: How, *Horner*!

ALITHEA: What mean you Sir, I always took you for a man of Honour?

HORNER: Ay, so much a man of Honour, that I must save my Mistriss, I thank
you, come what will on't.   [*Aside.*]

SPARKISH: So if I had had her, she'd have made me believe, the Moon had
been made of a Christmas pye.

LUCY: Now cou'd I speak, if I durst, and 'solve the Riddle, who am the
Author of it.   [*Aside.*]

ALITHEA: O unfortunate Woman! a combination against my Honour, which most concerns me now, because you share in my disgrace, Sir, and it is your censure which I must now suffer, that troubles me, not theirs.

HARCOURT: Madam, then have no trouble, you shall now see 'tis possible for me to love too, without being jealous, I will not only believe your innocence my self, but make all the world believe it –

Horner I must now be concern'd for this Ladies Honour.

[Apart to HORNER.]

HORNER: And I must be concern'd for a Ladies Honour too.

HARCOURT: This Lady has her Honour, and I will protect it.

HORNER: My Lady has not her Honour, but has given it me to keep, and I will preserve it.

HARCOURT: I understand you not.

HORNER: I wou'd not have you.

MRS. PINCHWIFE: What's the matter with 'em all.

[Mistress PINCHWIFE peeping in behind.]

PINCHWIFE: Come, come, Mr. *Horner*, no more disputing, here's the Parson, I brought him not in vain.

HARCOURT: No Sir, I'll employ him, if this Lady please.

PINCHWIFE: How, what d'ye mean?

SPARKISH: Ay, what does he mean?

HORNER: Why, I have resign'd your Sister to him, he has my consent.

PINCHWIFE: But he has not mine Sir, a womans injur'd Honour, no more than a man's, can be repair'd or satisfied by any, but him that first wrong'd it; and you shall marry her presently, or –   [*Lays his hand on his Sword.*]

[Enter to them Mistress PINCHWIFE.]

MRS. PINCHWIFE: O Lord, they'll kill poor Mr. *Horner*, besides he shan't marry her, whilest I stand by, and look on, I'll not lose my second Husband so.

PINCHWIFE: What do I see?

ALITHEA: My Sister in my cloaths!

SPARKISH: Ha!

MRS. PINCHWIFE: Nay, pray now don't quarrel about finding work for the Parson, he shall marry me to Mr. *Horner*; for now I believe, you have enough of me.   [*To Mr.* PINCHWIFE.]

HORNER: Damn'd, damn'd loving Changeling.

MRS. PINCHWIFE: Pray Sister, pardon me for telling so many lyes of you.

HARCOURT: I suppose the Riddle is plain now.

LUCY: No, that must be my work, good Sir, hear me.

[Kneels to Mr. PINCHWIFE, who stands doggedly, with his hat over his eyes.]

PINCHWIFE: I will never hear woman again, but make 'em all silent, thus –

[Offers to draw upon his Wife.]

HORNER: No, that must not be.

PINCHWIFE: You then shall go first, 'tis all one to me.

[Offers to draw on HORNER, stopt by HARCOURT.]

HARCOURT: Hold

[*Enter Sir* JASPAR FIDGET, *Lady* FIDGET, *Lady* SQUEAMISH,
Mrs. DAINTY FIDGET, *Mrs.* SQUEAMISH.]

SIR JASPAR: What's the matter, what's the matter, pray what's the matter Sir,
I beseech you communicate Sir.

PINCHWIFE: Why my Wife has communicated Sir, as your Wife may have
done too Sir, if she knows him Sir –

SIR JASPAR: Pshaw, with him, ha, ha, he.

PINCHWIFE: D'ye mock me Sir, a Cuckold is a kind of a wild Beast, have a
care Sir –

SIR JASPAR: No sure, you mock me Sir – he cuckold you! it can't be, ha, ha, he,
why, I'll tell you Sir.   [*Offers to whisper.*]

PINCHWIFE: I tell you again, he has whor'd my Wife, and yours too, if he
knows her, and all the women he comes near; 'tis not his dissembling,
his hypocrisie can wheedle me.

SIR JASPAR: How does he dissemble, is he a Hypocrite? nay then – how –
Wife – Sister is he an Hypocrite?

LADY SQUEAMISH: An Hypocrite, a dissembler, speak young Harlotry, speak
how?

SIR JASPAR: Nay then – O my head too – O thou libidinous Lady!

LADY SQUEAMISH: O thou Harloting, Harlotry, hast thou don't then?

SIR JASPAR: Speak good *Horner*, art thou a dissembler, a Rogue? hast thou –

HORNER: Soh –

LUCY: I'll fetch you off, and her too, if she will but hold her tongue.
                                                    [*Apart to* HORNER.]

HORNER: Canst thou? I'll give thee –   [*Apart to* LUCY.]

LUCY [*to Mr.* PINCHWIFE.]: Pray have but patience to hear me Sir, who am the
unfortunate cause of all this confusion, your Wife is innocent, I only
culpable; for I put her upon telling you all these lyes, concerning my
Mistress, in order to the breaking off the match, between Mr. *Sparkish*
and her, to make way for Mr. *Harcourt*.

SPARKISH: Did you so eternal Rotten-tooth, then it seems my Mistress was
not false to me, I was only deceiv'd by you, brother that shou'd have
been, now man of conduct,[1] who is a frank person now, to bring your
Wife to her Lover – ha –

LUCY: I assure you Sir, she came not to Mr. *Horner* out of love, for she loves
him no more –

MRS. PINCHWIFE: Hold, I told lyes for you, but you shall tell none for me, for
I do love Mr *Horner* with all my soul, and no body shall say me nay;
pray don't you go to make poor Mr. *Horner* believe to the contrary, 'tis
spitefully done of you, I'm sure.

---

1. An ironic reference to Pinchwife as a man of exemplary conduct.

HORNER: Peace, Dear Ideot.   [*Aside to Mrs.* PINCHWIFE.]
MRS. PINCHWIFE: Nay, I will not peace.
PINCHWIFE: Not 'til I make you.

[*Enter* DORILANT, QUACK.]

DORILANT: *Horner*, your Servant, I am the Doctors Guest, he must excuse our intrusion.
QUACK: But what's the matter Gentlemen, for Heavens sake, what's the matter?
HORNER: Oh 'tis well you are come – 'tis a censorious world we live in, you may have brought me a reprieve, or else I had died for a crime, I never committed, and these innocent Ladies had suffer'd with me, therefore pray satisfie these worthy, honourable, jealous Gentlemen – that –
                                                      [*Whispers.*]
QUACK: O I understand you, is that all – Sir *Jasper*, by heavens and upon the word of a Physician Sir, –   [*Whispers to Sir* JASPER.]
SIR JASPAR: Nay I do believe you truly – pardon me my virtuous Lady, and dear of honour.
LADY SQUEAMISH: What then all's right again.
SIR JASPAR: Ay, ay, and now let us satisfie him too.
                                    [*They whisper with Mr.* PINCHWIFE.]
PINCHWIFE: An Eunuch! pray no fooling with me.
QUACK: I'le bring half the Chirurgions in Town to swear it.
PINCHWIFE: They – they'l sweare a man that bled to death through his wounds died of an Apoplexy.
QUACK: Pray hear me Sir – why all the Town has heard the report of him.
PINCHWIFE: But does all the Town believe it.
QUACK: Pray inquire a little, and first of all these.
PINCHWIFE: I'm sure when I left the Town he was the lewdest fellow in't.
QUACK: I tell you Sir he has been in *France* since, pray ask but these Ladies and Gentlemen, your friend Mr. *Dorilant*, Gentlemen and Ladies, han't you all heard the late sad report of poor Mr. *Horner*.
LADIES: Ay, ay, ay.
DORILANT: Why thou jealous Fool do'st thou doubt it, he's an errant French Capon.
MRS. PINCHWIFE: 'Tis false Sir, you shall not disparage poor Mr. *Horner*, for to my certain knowledge –
LUCY: O hold –
SQUEAMISH: Stop her mouth –   [*Aside to* LUCY.]
LADY FIDGET: Upon my honour Sir, 'tis as true.   [*To* PINCHWIFE.]
DAINTY: D'y think we would have been seen in his company –
SQUEAMISH: Trust our unspotted reputations with him!
LADY FIDGET: This you get, and we too, by trusting your secret to a fool
                                                      [*Aside to* HORNER.]

HORNER: Peace Madam, – well Doctor is not this a good design that carryes a man on unsuspected, and brings him off safe. –   [*Aside to* QUACK.]

PINCHWIFE: Well, if this were true, but my Wife   [*Aside.*]

[DORILANT *whispers with Mrs.* PINCHWIFE.]

ALITHEA: Come Brother your Wife is yet innocent you see, but have a care of too strong an imagination, least like an overconcern'd timerous Gamester by fancying an unlucky cast it should come, Women and Fortune are truest still to those that trust 'em.

LUCY: And any wild thing grows but the more fierce and hungry for being kept up, and more dangerous to the Keeper.

ALITHEA: There's doctrine for all Husbands Mr. *Harcourt*.

HARCOURT: I edifie Madam so much, that I am impatient till I am one.

DORILANT: And I edifie so much by example I will never be one.

SPARKISH: And because I will not disparage my parts I'le ne're be one.

HORNER: And I alass can't be one.

PINCHWIFE: But I must be one – against my will to a Country-Wife, with a Country-murrain to me.

MRS. PINCHWIFE: And I must be a Country Wife still too I find, for I can't like a City one, be rid of my musty Husband and doe what I list.   [*Aside.*]

HORNER: Now Sir I must pronounce your Wife Innocent, though I blush whilst I do it, and I am the only man by her now expos'd to shame, which I will straight drown in Wine, as you shall your suspition, and the Ladies troubles we'l divert with a Ballet, Doctor where are your Maskers.

LUCY: Indeed she's Innocent Sir, I am her witness, and her end of coming out was but to see her Sisters Wedding, and what she has said to your face of her love to Mr. *Horner* was but the usual innocent revenge on a Husbands jealousie, was it not Madam speak –

MRS. PINCHWIFE: Since you'l have me tell more lyes –

[*Aside to* LUCY *and* HORNER.]

　　Yes indeed Budd.

PINCHWIFE: For my own sake fain I wou'd all believe.
　　Cuckolds like Lovers shou'd themselves deceive.
　　But – [*sighs*] –
　　His honour is least safe, (too late I find)
　　Who trusts it with a foolish Wife or Friend

A Dance of Cuckolds.

HORNER: Vain Fopps, but court, and dress, and keep a puther,[1]
　　To pass for Womens men, with one another.
　　But he who aimes by women to be priz'd,
　　First by the men you see must be despis'd.

―――――――――

1. Pother.

Finis

Epilogue

spoken by Mrs. Knep

Now you the Vigorous, who dayly here
O're Vizard-Mask, in publick domineer,
And what you'd doe to her if in Place where;
Nay have the confidence, to cry come out,
Yet when she says lead on, you are not stout;
But to your well-drest Brother straight turn round
And cry, Pox on her Ned, she can't be sound:
then slink away, a fresh one to ingage,
With so much seeming heat and loving Rage,
You'd frighten listning Actress on the Stage:
Till she at last has seen you huffing come,
And talk of keeping in the Tyreing-Room,
Yet cannot be provok'd to lead her home:
Next you Fallstaffs *of fifty, who beset*
Your Buckram Maidenheads,[1] *which your friends get;*
And whilst to them, you of Atchievements boast,
They share the booty, and laugh at your cost.
In fine, you Essens't Boyes, both Old and Young,
Who wou'd be thought so eager, brisk, and strong,
Yet do the Ladies, not their Husbands, wrong:
Whose Purses for your manhood make excuse,
And keep your Flanders Mares for shew, not use;[2]
Encourag'd by our Womans Man to day,
A Horners *part may vainly think to Play;*
And may Intreagues so bashfully disown
That they may doubted be by few or none,
May kiss the Cards at Picquet, Hombre, – Lu,
And so be thought to kiss the Lady too;
But Gallants, have a care faith, what you do.
The World, which to no man his due will give,
You by experience know you can deceive,
And men may still believe you Vigorous,
But then we Women, – there's no cous'ning us.

1. A reference to *Henry IV*, II.ii.
2. Flanders mares were kept for breeding, in contrast to the women kept for show.

Love for Love

WILLIAM CONGREVE

INTRODUCTION

Dryden and Wycherley were playwrights who had begun their literary careers at the Restoration. During their lives turbulent political upheavals profoundly changed the nature of English society. Both men, albeit for different reasons, found it difficult to adjust to life in London following the Glorious Revolution of 1688. In complete contrast, William Congreve, who was born in Bardsey in Yorkshire in January 1670, was a child of this new age. His father was the second son of a Staffordshire squire, who followed a long family tradition by joining the army. In 1674 his father was given a commission as a lieutenant in the Irish army and travelled with his family, first to Youghal, next to Carrickfergus, and then to Kilkenny, where he joined the Duke of Ormond's regiment. This move enabled Congreve to receive free education at Kilkenny College, which enjoyed an outstanding academic reputation. There he received his grounding in classical languages and literature which he put to good use as a member of Dryden's literary circle in the 1690s.

After Kilkenny College, Congreve continued his education at Trinity College, Dublin. He entered the staunchly Protestant College in 1686 at a time when it was experiencing grave difficulties because of the accession of the Catholic James II. Congreve was not a particularly committed student but used his time in Dublin to extend his knowledge of the classics and to acquaint himself with the pleasures of theatre-going and convivial socialising. In 1689 he moved to London, and in 1691 enrolled (like Wycherley before him) in the Middle Temple. He seems to have paid even less attention to his legal studies than Wycherley and was soon a member of Dryden's circle of wits and writers who met regularly at Will's Coffee House. He contributed a translation of some fragments of Homer for Dryden's *Examen Poeticum* of 1693 and, in the process, earned Dryden's admiration.

They were unlikely friends. Dryden was a Catholic and a committed supporter of the old Stuart dynasty; Congreve was a Protestant, a Whig, and a firm admirer of the new monarchs, William and Mary. Despite their political differences, Dryden and Congreve shared a profound mutual respect. Dryden soon came to see Congreve as his natural successor in London's literary world. When Congreve wrote his first play in 1692, *The Old Batchelour,* Dryden suggested some alterations and amendments to suit the play to 'the fashionable cutt of the town'.[1] Even so he declared it to be the best first play by an author that he had ever seen and he commended it to the manager of Drury Lane. Although it was swiftly accepted, changes in the acting company meant that it was not performed until March, 1693. The play was a huge success; its festive tone pleased the town, and it brought Congreve instant fame. It also brought him the friendship of the players at Drury Lane and, in particular, of the actress Anne Bracegirdle. Congreve was soon in love with this vivacious young member of the company and went on to write a series of complex and challenging roles for her in his future plays.

Congreve's second play, *The Double Dealer,* was performed in December, 1693. The overall tone of the play was far darker than that of his first, more exuberant comedy; though it impressed his friends (including Dryden), it failed to please contemporary audiences. By way of response, Congreve included a stinging attack on his critics in the first edition of the play, which he wisely omitted from later editions. After this reverse, Congreve enjoyed an unqualified success with his third comedy, *Love for Love.* He had written the play for the company at the Theatre Royal, Drury Lane, in 1694. However, that year the leading players in the company rebelled against the unscrupulous tactics of the manager Christopher Rich and were eventually given permission by the Lord Chamberlain to form their own actors' company at the converted tennis court in Lincoln's Inn Fields. In view of Congreve's friendship with the players, it is not at all surprising that he sided with them. He gladly

---

1. Quoted from John C. Hodges, *William Congreve the Man: A Biography from New Sources* (New York: Modern Language Association of America, 1941) p. 40.

agreed that they should open their newly converted theatre with a production of *Love for Love* in April 1695. He had written the play with specific actors in mind and had conceived the role of Angelica for Anne Bracegirdle's lively and playful personality. The production was so successful that Congreve was made a shareholder in the actors' company.

Love for Love

Love for Love is strikingly different from earlier Restoration comedies, such as those of Wycherley and Etherege. This is apparent even from the setting of the play, which no longer makes use of the parks, taverns and shopping arcades of contemporary London, but instead focuses on two simple domestic interiors: the lodgings of the young hero of the play, Valentine, and a room in the house of Mr Foresight. This is a clear visual indication that Congreve, unlike earlier writers of Restoration comedy, is not concerned with the values and behaviour of the town, but rather with the complex politics of family life. This makes his play far closer in spirit to the work of Molière than anything written in the earlier reign of Charles II. For Congreve, like Molière, what matters is the ordered stability of family and social life; any extreme or deviant behaviour which threatens this ordered stability is the object of satire.

    Love for Love has at its centre a main plot, around which a series of subplots are layered. In the main plot young Valentine Legend has run up extensive debts, partly in pursuit of libertine pleasure, and partly in pursuit of a rich young heiress, Angelica. She obviously enjoys his company and his wit but has given him no firm sign of commitment. During the course of the main action, these two young people test each other's responses almost to breaking point. In earlier Restoration comedies, there was no real basis for trust; here there is, but the individuals involved wish to be absolutely certain before committing themselves. Valentine's father, Sir Sampson Legend, is willing to give his son £4000 to settle his debts, but only if he will sign away his right to inherit the family estate in favour of his younger brother, a sailor called Ben. Having obtained the cash, Valentine pretends to be mad. This ruse helps him to avoid signing Sir Sampson's deed; but Valentine also exploits it as a means of testing Angelica's responses. However, she is an expert at reading facial expressions and body language and sees through the ruse. In revenge she pretends to consider marrying Sir Sampson in preference to Valentine. In so doing, she pushes Valentine to an abject public admission of his ruse and to a confession that what he did was out of love for her. Now that all is seemingly lost, he might just as well sign away his fortune. Only at that point does Angelica dismiss Sir Sampson and confess her love for Valentine.

The various subplots involve a delightful gallery of eccentric or libidinous individuals, driven by a wide variety of sexual or material appetites. The most eccentric of all is Angelica's uncle, old Foresight, who is foolishly convinced of the importance of signs, portents and astrological predictions. While his nurse brings him his urinal 'just upon the turning of the Tide', his wanton young wife has merry sport with her lovers. The current one is Valentine's friend, Scandal, who more than meets his match in Mrs Foresight. Before they sleep together, they engage in suggestive and probing verbal exchanges; the day after, however, she denies to his face that anything happened. Scandal is lost for words.

The most foolish of the characters surrounding Angelica and Valentine is Tattle. He has a lively sexual appetite and almost succeeds in seducing Foresight's daughter from his first marriage, Miss Prue. However, his real aim is to marry a rich partner. The same aim is shared by Mrs Frail, who is Mrs Foresight's sister. She is just as promiscuous as her sister, but is prepared to stoop to anything to trap a rich husband. She makes a concerted effort to entrap young Ben, when he seems likely to inherit Sir Sampson's estate. Eventually, however, Tattle and Mrs Frail are tricked by Valentine into marrying each other, disguised in the habits of a nun and a friar. They deserve no better.

The action in the play is both rumbustious and lively; and the plot is full of overt and covert sexuality as these various young characters pursue each other or test each other's responses. Under the laughter, however, serious issues are addressed. In a world that is less than perfect, Congreve nevertheless shows the possibility of achieving order and stability through trust and freely given consent. The old Restoration world of libertine cynicism was only held together by the absolute authority of the ruler. These are the values that Sir Sampson Legend still holds sacred. He is convinced he has the right to wield absolute authority over his son and to reject him utterly if he is crossed. The proposal to marry his son's beloved is another way of asserting his authority. When Angelica pretends to take his proposal seriously, she is merely testing Valentine. In fact, she and Valentine both despise the old order represented by Sir

Sampson and both believe in the new order of contractually based trust and consent. In Molière's play *L'Avare*, Harpagon's desire to marry his son's beloved was shown to be an abuse of his accepted authority as a father. In Congreve's more deliberately political play, that same absolute authority of a father is questioned and even subjected to ridicule. The worlds of micro- and macro-politics begin to merge. At the end of the play, Sir Sampson is rejected with the same derision as William and Mary had rejected the values of James II. Congreve's festive comedy may thus be seen as a deliberate celebration of the new social and personal values ushered in by the Glorious Revolution of 1688.

Congreve's career had now reached a distinct peak. His comedy *Love for Love* had cemented his reputation as the leading dramatist of the age. In 1695 he also wrote several poems on state occasions – the first to mark the death of Queen Mary and another to celebrate one of William III's military victories – which were much admired. During a visit to his parents in Ireland in 1696, he wrote his first tragedy, *The Mourning Bride*, which was performed with great success at Lincoln's Inn Fields in February 1697. Once again there was a clear political subtext to the play, which contributed to its contemporary popularity.[1] It was at this point that Congreve suffered the first major setback in his career. In 1698, a non-juring High Church clergyman called Jeremy Collier published a ferocious attack on the work of contemporary playwrights: it was called *A Short View of the Immorality and Profaneness of the English Stage*. Congreve, along with other playwrights such as Vanbrugh, was unwisely provoked into publishing a response. The public stir caused by this controversy shook him profoundly and particularly when he realised that Collier's coarse and abusive views were widely shared at the time.

Congreve's final play *The Way of the World* was performed in March 1700. It included another exacting and complex role for Anne Bracegirdle as the attractive but mercurial heroine Millamant. With its intricate plot and its multilayered exploration of how personal and social stability can only be achieved on the basis of mature deliberation and freely given consent, it was a play that once again brilliantly bound together the spheres of the personal and the political. Arguably it was a play that was too demanding for the less well-educated, middle-class audiences who were beginning to

---

1. For a detailed analysis of the play and its hidden references to the Glorious Revolution, see D. Thomas, *William Congreve* (London: Macmillan, 1992) pp. 104–11.

frequent London's theatres. Congreve himself commented in his Dedication to Ralph, Earl of Montague that, 'little of it was prepar'd for that general Taste which seems now to be predominant in the Pallats of our Audience'. The lukewarm contemporary response to the play persuaded Congreve to cease writing plays altogether.

Initially this did not mean a complete break with the theatre. He wrote a polished libretto for a masque called *The Judgement of Paris* which formed the basis for an exciting operatic competition in 1700.[1] He wrote a further opera libretto on the theme of *Semele* in 1705. This was to be set to music by his main musical collaborator, John Eccles, and was almost certainly intended to be the first production at the new Queen's Theatre in the Haymarket in 1705. Vanbrugh had designed and built the theatre and had persuaded Congreve to become a joint patentee in the new venture. Not only did Eccles fail to complete his score in time for the opening, but the new theatre had a variety of serious design flaws which were eventually put right only at great expense. Congreve extracted himself from the project as soon as he could, but both he and Vanbrugh lost a great deal of money in the process. This marked his final break with the theatre.[2]

Congreve's personal life mirrored the disarray in his professional life during the early years of the 1700s. His relationship with Anne Bracegirdle slowly foundered. Although he had written a number of roles for her where she agreed to marriage on stage, in her relationship with Congreve she steadfastly refused to 'dwindle into a wife'. A change of administration from Whig to Tory, with the accession of Queen Anne in 1702, meant that a number of financial sinecures which Congreve had enjoyed under the Whigs were lost to him. Even his health was not of the best. It was fortunate that he still had a firm circle of friends at Will's Coffee House and at the more illustrious Kit-Kat Club (a group of distinguished Whig writers and politicians who gathered at the house of the publisher, Jacob Tonson).

A distinct improvement in his life came with the accession of George I to the throne in 1714, ushering in decades of unbroken Whig rule. Congreve's powerful friends in the Whig hierarchy secured a reasonably generous sinecure for him as Secretary to the Island of Jamaica which brought him an annual salary of £700. At around the same period, Congreve became acquainted with

1. For details see ibid., pp. 111–15.
2. For further details see ibid., pp. 7–9, 46–9.

Henrietta Godolphin, wife of Francis (later Earl of) Godolphin and daughter of the Duke of Marlborough; she was given the title of the Duchess of Marlborough by special Act of Parliament in 1722 on the death of her father. Their friendship blossomed into a discreet but enduring love affair which made them inseparable until Congreve's death. After a season they spent together in Bath in 1723, Henrietta gave birth to a daughter, christened Mary, who was almost certainly their child. However, their discretion was such that no one suspected this at the time. Their relationship was tolerated by Henrietta's husband and generally accepted by their contemporaries. Congreve's friends at times complained that they saw too little of him because of the time he spent with Henrietta. She was a loyal and devoted companion who nursed him without complaint during his final years of sickness between 1726 and 1729. At his death in January 1729, she ensured that he was buried in appropriate style in Westminster Abbey and chose to lie close to him in the Abbey after her own death in 1733. Although divorce and remarriage was out of the question for Henrietta, Congreve enjoyed with her the kind of mature and stable relationship, based on mutual consent, about which he had written with such passionate conviction in his plays.

Edwards ad vivdl.   *Walker sculp.*

Mr. Wilson & Mrs. Mattocks, in the Characters of Ben & Miss Prue.

But pray Miss why are you so scornful?

Mr Wilson and Mrs Mattocks in the characters of Ben and Miss Prue in *Love for Love*, reproduced from *The New English Theatre* (London: T. Lowndes & Partners, 1776)

Love for Love

A
Comedy

Acted at the
THEATRE in Little Lincolns-Inn Fields,
BY
His Majesty's Servants,

Written by Mr. CONGREVE.

Nudus agris, nudus nummis paternis,
Insanire parat certa ratione modoque. Hor.[1]

LONDON:
Printed for *Jacob Tonson* at the *Judge's-Head,* near
the *Inner-Temple-Gate* in *Fleetstreet,* 1695.

---

1. 'A madman, stripped of your paternal estate, stripped of your money ... / He will make no more of it, than if he should set about raving by right reason and rule' (Horace, *Satires II*).

TO THE

RIGHT HONOURABLE

CHARLES

Earl of *Dorset* and *Middlesex*,
*Lord Chamberlain of His Majesty's Houshold, and Knight
of the Most Noble Order of the Garter, &c.*[1]

MY LORD,

A young Poet, is liable to the same Vanity and Indiscretion with a Young
Lover; and the Great Man that smiles upon one, and the Fine Woman that
looks kindly upon t'other, are each of 'em in Danger of having the Favour
publish'd with the first Opportunity.

But there may be a different Motive, which will a little distinguish the
Offenders. For tho' one should have a Vanity in ruining another's
Reputation, yet the other may only have an Ambition to advance his own.
And I beg leave, my Lord, that I may plead the latter, both as the Cause and
Excuse of this Dedication.

Whoever is King, is also the Father of his Country; and as no body can
dispute Your Lordship's *Monarchy* in *Poetry*; so all that are concern'd, ought
to acknowledge Your Universal Patronage: And it is only presuming on the
Priviledge of a Loyal Subject, that I have ventur'd to make this my Address
of Thanks, to Your Lordship; which at the same time, includes a Prayer for
Your Protection.

I am not Ignorant of the Common Form of Poetical Dedications, which
are generally made up of Panegyricks, where the Authors endeavour to
distinguish their Patrons, by the shining Characters they give them, above
other Men. But that, my Lord, is not my business at this time, nor is Your
Lordship *now* to be distinguish'd. I am contented with the Honour I do my
self in this Epistle; without the Vanity of attempting to add to, or explain
Your Lordship's Character.

I confess it is not without some strugling, that I behave my self in this
Case, as I ought: For it is very hard to be pleased with a Subject, and yet
forbear it. But I chuse rather to follow Pliny's Precept, than his Example,
when in his Panegyrick to the Emperour Trajan, he says,

> *Nec minus considerabo quid aures ejus pati
> possint, Quam quid virtutibus debeatur.*[2]

I hope I may be excus'd the Pedantry of a Quotation, when it is so justly

1. The dedication of this play to the Earl of Dorset and Middlesex, at the time Lord
   Chamberlain, was a genuine expression of gratitude to the man who had given his
   permission to the rebel actors of Drury Lane to set up their own actors' company
   in the reconverted tennis court at Lincoln's Inn Fields. Congreve's comedy was the
   first play produced by the new actors' company.
2. Nor shall I less consider what will make him blush to hear, than what the merit of
   his virtues might claim to be spoken.

apply'd. Here are some Lines in the Print, (and which your Lordship read before this Play was Acted) that were omitted on the Stage; and particularly one whole Scene in the Third Act, which not only helps the Design forward with less Precipitation, but also heightens the ridiculous Character of *Foresight*, which indeed seems to be maim'd without it. But I found my self in great danger of a long Play, and was glad to help it where I could. Tho' notwithstanding my Care, and the kind Reception it had from the Town; I could heartily wish it yet shorter: But the Number of Different Characters represented in it, would have been too much crowded in less room.

This Reflection on Prolixity, (a Fault, for which scarce any one Beauty will attone) warns me not to be tedious now, and detain Your Lordship any longer with the Trifles of,

MY LORD,
Your Lordship's
Most Obedient
and Most Humble
Servant,
WILL. CONGREVE.

A Prologue

FOR
The opening of the new Play-House,
propos'd to be spoken by
Mrs. Bracegirdle in Man's Cloaths.
Sent from an unknown Hand.

Custom, which everywhere bears mighty Sway,
Brings me to act the Orator to Day:
But Women, you will say, are ill at Speeches,
'Tis true, and therefore I appear in Breeches:
Not for Example to you City-Wives;
That by Prescription's setled for your Lives.
Was it for gain the Husband first consented?
O yes, their Gains are mightily augmented:

Making Horns with her Hands over her Head.

And yet, methinks, it must have cost some Strife:
A Passive Husband, and an Active Wife!
'Tis awkward, very awkward, by my Life.
But to my Speech, Assemblies of all Nations
Still are suppos'd to open with Orations:

Mine shall begin, to shew our Obligations.
To you, our Benefactors, lowly Bowing,
Whose Favours have prevented our undoing;
A long Egyptian *Bondage we endur'd,*
Till Freedom, by your Justice we procur'd:[1]
Our Taskmasters were grown such very Jews,
We must at length have Play'd in Wooden Shooes,
Had not your Bounty taught us to refuse.
Freedom's of English *growth, I think, alone;*
What for lost English *Freedom can attone?*
A Free-born Player loaths to be compell'd;
Our Rulers Tyraniz'd, and We Rebell'd.
Freedom! the Wise Man's Wish, the Poor Man's Wealth;
Which you, and I, and most of us enjoy by Stealth;
The Soul of Pleasure, and the Sweet of Life,
The Woman's Charter, Widdow, Maid or Wife,
This they'd have cancell'd, and thence grew the Strife.
But you perhaps, wou'd have me here confess
How we obtain'd the Favour; – Can't you guess?
Why then I'll tell you, (for I hate a Lye)
By Brib'ry, errant Brib'ry, let me dye:
I was their Agent, but by Jove I swear
No honourable Member had a share
Tho' young and able Members bid me Fair:
I chose a wiser way to make you willing,
Which has not cost the House a single Shilling;
Now you suspect at least I went a Billing.
You see I'm Young, and to that Air of Youth,
Some will add Beauty, and a little Truth;
These Pow'rful Charms, improv'd by Pow'rful Arts,
Prevail'd to captivate your op'ning Hearts.
Thus furnish'd, I prefer'd my poor Petition,
And brib'd ye to commiserate our Condition:
I Laugh'd, and Sigh'd, and Sung, and Leer'd upon ye;
With Roguish Loving Looks, and that way won ye:
The Young Men kiss'd me, and the Old I kiss'd,
And luringly, I led them as I list.
The Ladies in meer Pity took our Parts,
Pity's the darling Passion of their Hearts.
Thus Bribing, or thus Brib'd, fear no Disgraces;
For thus you may take Bribes, and keep your Places.

---

1. A reference to the quarrel of the players with John Rich, the manager of Drury Lane, which led to the formation of the actors' company at Lincoln's Inn Fields.

Prologue

Spoken at the opening of the
New House,
By Mr. Betterton.

The Husbandman in vain renews his Toil,
To cultivate each Year a hungry Soil;
And fondly hopes for rich and generous Fruit,
When what should feed the Tree, devours the Root:
Th'unladen Boughs, he sees, bode certain Dearth,
Unless transplanted to more kindly Earth.
So, the poor Husbands of the Stage, who found
Their Labours lost upon the ungrateful Ground,
This last and only Remedy have prov'd;
And hope new Fruit from ancient Stocks remov'd.[1]
Well may they hope, when you so kindly aid,
And plant a Soil which you so rich have made.
As Nature gave the World to Man's first Age,
So from your Bounty, we receive this Stage;
The Freedom Man was born to, you've restor'd,
And to our World, such Plenty you afford,
It seems like Eden, *fruitful of its own accord.*
But since in Paradise *frail Flesh gave way,*
And when but two were made, both went astray;
Forbear your Wonder, and the Fault forgive,
If in our larger Family we grieve
One falling Adam, *and one tempted* Eve.[2]
We who remain, would gratefully repay
What our Endeavours can, and bring this day,
The First-fruit Offering, of a Virgin Play.
We hope there's something that may please each Taste,
And tho' of Homely Fare we make the Feast,
Yet you will find variety at least.
There's Humour, which for chearful Friends we got,
And for the thinking Party there's a Plot.
We've something too, to gratifie ill Nature,
(If there be any here) and that is Satire.
Tho Satire scarce dares grin, 'tis grown so mild;
Or only shews its Teeth, as if it smil'd.
As Asses Thistles, Poets mumble Wit,
And dare not bite, for fear of being bit.

1. A further reference to the rebellion of the players.
2. A reference to two players who returned to Drury Lane.

They hold their Pens, as Swords are held by Fools,
And are afraid to use their own Edge-Tools.
Since the Plain-Dealers *Scenes of Manly Rage,*[1]
Not one has dar'd to lash this Crying Age.
This time, the Poet owns the bold Essay,
Yet hopes there's no ill-manners in his Play:
And he declares by me, he has design'd
Affront to none, but frankly speaks his mind.
And shou'd th' ensuing Scenes not chance to hit,
He offers but this one Excuse, 'twas writ
Before your late Encouragement of Wit.

Dramatis Personae

MEN

SIR SAMPSON LEGEND, Father to VALENTINE and BEN.	Mr. *Underhill*
VALENTINE, Fallen under his Father's Displeasure by his expensive way of living, in love with ANGELICA.	Mr. *Betterton*
SCANDAL, His Friend, a Free Speaker.	Mr. *Smith*
TATTLE, A half-witted Beau, vain of his Amours, yet valuing himself for Secresie.	Mr. *Bowman*
BEN, SIR SAMPSON'S Younger Son, half home-bred, and half Sea-bred, design'd to marry MISS PRUE.	Mr. *Dogget*
FORESIGHT, An illiterate Old Fellow, peevish and positive, superstitious, and pretending to understand Astrology, Palmistry, Phisiognomy, Omens, Dreams, &c. Uncle to ANGELICA.	Mr. *Sanford*
JEREMY, Servant to VALENTINE.	Mr. *Bowen*
TRAPLAND, A Scrivener.	Mr. *Triffusis*
BUCKRAM, A Lawyer.	Mr. *Freeman*

WOMEN

ANGELICA, Niece to FORESIGHT, of a considerable Fortune in her own Hands.	Mrs. *Bracegirdle*
MRS. FORESIGHT, Second Wife to FORESIGHT.	Mrs. *Bowman*
MRS. FRAIL, Sister to MRS. FORESIGHT, a Woman of the Town.	Mrs. *Barry*
MISS PRUE, Daughter to FORESIGHT by a former Wife, a silly, awkard, Country Girl.	Mrs. *Ayliff*
NURSE to MISS PRUE.	Mrs. *Leigh.*
JENNY, Maid to ANGELICA.	Mrs. *Lawson*
A Steward, Officers, Sailors, and several Servants.	

The SCENE in LONDON.

1. A reference to Wycherley's play of the same title.

Act I, Scene I

*[*VALENTINE *in his Chamber Reading.* JEREMY *waiting, Several Books upon the Table.]*

VALENTINE: *Jeremy.*

JEREMY: Sir.

VALENTINE: Here, take away; I'll walk a turn, and digest what I have read –

JEREMY: You'll grow Devilish fat upon this Paper-Diet.

[Aside and taking away the Books.]

VALENTINE: And d'ye hear, go you to Breakfast – There's a Page doubled down in *Epictetus*,[1] that is a Feast for an Emperour.

JEREMY: Was *Epictetus* a real Cook, or did he only write Receipts?

VALENTINE: Read, read, Sirrah, and refine your Appetite; learn to live upon Instruction; feast your Mind, and mortifie your Flesh; Read, and take your Nourishment in at your Eyes; shut up your Mouth, and chew the Cud of Understanding. So *Epictetus* advises.

JEREMY: O Lord! I have heard much of him, when I waited upon a Gentleman at *Cambridge*: Pray what was that *Epictetus*?

VALENTINE: A very rich Man. – Not worth a Groat.

JEREMY: Humph, and so he has made a very fine Feast, where there is nothing to be eaten.

VALENTINE: Yes.

JEREMY: Sir, you're a Gentleman, and probably understand this fine Feeding: But if you please, I had rather be at Board-Wages. Does your *Epictetus*, or your *Seneca* here, or any of these poor rich Rogues, teach you how to pay your Debts without Money? Will they shut up the Mouths of your Creditors? Will *Plato* be Bail for you? Or *Diogenes*, because he understands Confinement, and liv'd in a Tub, go to Prison for you? 'Slife, Sir, what do you mean, to mew your self up here with Three or Four musty Books, in commendation of Starving and Poverty?

VALENTINE: Why, Sirrah, I have no Money, you know it; and therefore resolve to rail at all that have: And in that I but follow the Examples of the wisest and wittiest Men in all Ages; these Poets and Philosophers whom you naturally hate, for just such another Reason; because they abound in Sense, and you are a Fool.

JEREMY: Aye, Sir, I am a Fool, I know it: And yet, Heav'n help me, I'm poor enough to be a Wit – But I was always a Fool, when I told you what your Expences would bring you to; your Coaches and your Liveries; your Treats and your Balls; your being in Love with a Lady, that did not care a Farthing for you in your Prosperity; and keeping Company with Wits, that car'd for nothing but your Prosperity; and now when you are poor, hate you as much as they do one another.

---

1. A Greek stoic philosopher.

VALENTINE: Well; and now I am poor, I have an opportunity to be reveng'd on 'em all; I'll pursue *Angelica* with more Love then ever, and appear more notoriously her Admirer in this Restraint, than when I openly rival'd the rich Fops, that made Court to her; so shall my Poverty be a Mortification to her Pride, and perhaps, make her compassionate[1] that Love, which has principally reduc'd me to this Lowness of Fortune. And for the Wits, I'm sure I'm in a Condition to be even with them –

JEREMY: Nay, your Condition is pretty even with theirs, that's the truth on't.

VALENTINE: I'll take some of their Trade out of their Hands.

JEREMY: Now Heav'n of Mercy continue the Tax upon Paper; you don't mean to write!

VALENTINE: Yes, I do; I'll write a Play.

JEREMY: Hem! – Sir, if you please to give me a small Certificate of Three Lines – only to certifie those whom it may concern; That the Bearer hereof, *Jeremy Fetch* by Name, has for the space of Sev'n Years truly and faithfully serv'd *Valentine Legend* Esq; and that he is not now turn'd away for any Misdemeanour; but does voluntarily dismiss his Master from any future Authority over him –

VALENTINE: No, Sirrah, you shall live with me still.

JEREMY: Sir, it's impossible – I may die with you, starve with you, or be damn'd with your Works: But to live even Three days, the Life of a Play,[2] I no more expect it, than to be Canoniz'd for a Muse after my Decease.

VALENTINE: You are witty, you Rogue, I shall want your Help; – I'll have you learn to make Couplets, to tag the ends of Acts: d'ye hear, get the Maids to Crambo[3] in an Evening, and learn the knack of Rhiming, you may arrive at the height of a Song, sent by an unknown Hand, or a Chocolate-House Lampoon.

JEREMY: But Sir, Is this the way to recover your Father's Favour? Why Sir *Sampson* will be irreconcilable. If your Younger Brother shou'd come from Sea, he'd never look upon you again. You're undone, Sir; you're ruin'd; you won't have a Friend left in the World, if you turn Poet – Ah Pox confound that *Will's* Coffee-House, it has ruin'd more Young Men than the *Royal Oak* Lottery – Nothing thrives that belongs to't. The Man of the House would have been an Alderman by this time with half the Trade, if he had set up in the City – For my part, I never sit at the Door, that I don't get double the Stomach that I do at a Horse-Race. The Air upon *Banstead-Downs* is nothing to it for a Whetter; yet I never see it, but the Spirit of Famine appears to me; sometimes like a decay'd Porter, worn out with pimping, and carrying *Billet-doux* and Songs; not like other Porters for Hire, but for the Jests sake. Now like a thin Chairman,

1. Take pity on.
2. The third day was the playwright's benefit.
3. To play word games.

melted down to half his Proportion, with carrying a Poet upon Tick, to visit some great Fortune; and his Fare to be paid him like the Wages of Sin, either at the Day of Marriage, or the Day of Death.

VALENTINE: Very well, Sir; can you proceed?

JEREMY: Sometimes like a bilk'd Bookseller, with a meagre terrify'd Countenance, that looks as if he had written for himself, or were resolv'd to turn Author, and bring the rest of his Brethren into the same Condition. And Lastly, In the Form of a worn-out Punk,[1] with Verses in her Hand, which her Vanity had preferr'd to Settlements, without a whole Tatter to her Tail, but as ragged as one of the Muses; or as if she were carrying her Linnen to the Paper-Mill, to be converted into Folio Books, of Warning to all Young Maids, not to prefer Poetry to good Sense; or lying in the Arms of a needy Wit, before the Embraces of a wealthy Fool.

[*Enter* SCANDAL.]

SCANDAL: What, *Jeremy* holding forth?

VALENTINE: The Rogue has (with all the Wit he could muster up) been declaiming against Wit.

SCANDAL: Aye? Why then I'm afraid *Jeremy* has Wit: For where-ever it is, it's always contriving its own Ruine.

JEREMY: Why so I have been telling my Master, Sir: Mr. *Scandal*, for Heaven's sake, Sir, try if you can disswade him from turning Poet.

SCANDAL: Poet! He shall turn Soldier first, and rather depend upon the outside of his Head, than the Lining. Why, what the Devil has not your Poverty made you Enemies enough? Must you needs shew your Wit to get more?

JEREMY: Ay, more indeed; for who cares for any Body that has more Wit than himself?

SCANDAL: *Jeremy* speaks like an Oracle. Don't you see how worthless great Men, and dull rich Rogues, avoid a witty Man of small Fortune? Why, he looks like a Writ of Enquiry into their Titles and Estates; and seems Commission'd by Heav'n to seize the better half.

VALENTINE: Therefore I would rail in my Writings, and be reveng'd.

SCANDAL: Rail: At whom? the whole World? Impotent and vain! Who would die a Martyr to Sense in a Country where the Religion is Folly? You may stand at Bay for a while; but when the full Cry is against you, you won't have fair Play for your Life. If you can't be fairly run down by the Hounds, you will be treacherously shot by the Huntsmen. – No, turn Pimp, Flatterer, Quack, Lawyer, Parson, be Chaplain to an Atheist, or Stallion to an Old Woman, any thing but Poet; a Modern Poet is worse, more servile, timorous, and fawning than any I have nam'd: Without

1. Whore

you could retrieve the Ancient Honours of the Name, recall the Stage of *Athens*, and be allow'd the force of open honest Satire.

VALENTINE: You are as inveterate against our Poets, as if your Character had been lately expos'd upon the Stage. – Nay, I am not violently bent upon the Trade, –   [*One Knocks.*]
Jeremy, see who's there.   [*Exit* JEREMY.]
But tell me what you would have me do? – What do the World say of me, and of my forc'd Confinement?

SCANDAL: The World behaves it self, as it used to do on such Occasions; some pity you, and condemn your Father: Others excuse him, and blame you: only the Ladies are merciful, and wish you well, since Love and Pleasurable Expence, have been your greatest faults.

[*Enter* JEREMY.]

VALENTINE: How now?

JEREMY: Nothing new, Sir; I have dispatch'd some half a Dozen Duns with as much Dexterity, as a hungry Judge do's Causes at Dinner time.

VALENTINE: What answer have you given 'em?

SCANDAL: Patience, I suppose, the old Receipt.

JEREMY: No, faith Sir; I have put 'em off so long with patience and forbearance, and other fair words; that I was forc'd now to tell 'em in plain downright *English* –

VALENTINE: What?

JEREMY: That they should be paid.

VALENTINE: When?

JEREMY: To morrow.

VALENTINE: And how the Devil do you mean to keep your word?

JEREMY: Keep it? Not at all; it has been so very much stretch'd, that I reckon it will break of course by to morrow, and no body be surpriz'd at the Matter – [*Knocking*] – Again! Sir, if you don't like my Negotiation, will you be pleas'd to answer these your self.

VALENTINE: See who they are.   [*Exit* JEREMY.]
By this, *Scandal*, you may see what it is to be great; Secretaries of State, Presidents of the Council, and Generals of an Army lead just such a life as I do; have just such Crowds of Visitants in a morning, all soliciting of past promises; which are but a civiller sort of Duns, that lay claim to voluntary Debts.

SCANDAL: And you, like a true great Man, having engaged their Attendance, and promis'd more than ever you intend to perform; are more perplex'd to find Evasions, than you would be to invent the honest means of keeping your word, and gratifying your Creditors.

VALENTINE: *Scandal*, learn to spare your Friends, and do not provoke your Enemies; this liberty of your Tongue, will one day bring a Confinement on your Body, my Friend.

[*Re-enter* JEREMY.]

JEREMY: O Sir, there's *Trapland* the Scrivener,[1] with two suspicious Fellows like lawful Pads,[2] that wou'd knock a Man down with Pocket-Tipstaves, – And there's your Father's Steward, and the Nurse with one of your Children from *Twitnam*.[3]

VALENTINE: Pox on her, cou'd she find no other time to fling my Sins in my Face: Here, give her this,   [*Gives Money.*]
and bid her trouble me no more; a thoughtless two handed Whore, she knows my Condition well enough, and might have overlaid[4] the Child a Fortnight ago, if she had had any forecast in her.

SCANDAL: What is it Bouncing *Margery*, and my Godson?

JEREMY: Yes, Sir.

SCANDAL: My Blessing to the Boy, with this Token   [*Gives Money.*]
of my Love. And d'ee hear, bid *Margery* put more Flocks in her Bed, shift twice a Week, and not work so hard, that she may not smell so vigorously. – I shall take the Air shortly.

VALENTINE: *Scandal*, don't spoil my Boy's Milk: – Bid *Trapland* come in.
                                      [*Exit* JEREMY.]
If I can give that *Cerberus* a Sop, I shall be at rest for one day.

[*Enter* TRAPLAND *and* JEREMY.]

O Mr, *Trapland*! my old Friend! Welcome. *Jeremy*, a Chair quickly: A Bottle of Sack[5] and a Toast – fly – a Chair first.

TRAPLAND A good Morning to you Mr. *Valentine*, and to you Mr. *Scandal*.

SCANDAL: The Morning's a very good Morning, if you don't spoil it.

VALENTINE: Come sit you down, you know his way.

TRAPLAND: [*sits.*] There is a Debt, Mr. Valentine, of 1500 l. of pretty long standing –

VALENTINE: I cannot talk about Business with a Thirsty Palate. – Sirrah the Sack. –

TRAPLAND: And I desire to know what Course you have taken for the Payment?

VALENTINE: Faith and Troth, I am heartily glad to see you, – fill, fill to honest Mr. *Trapland*, fuller.

TRAPLAND: Hold, Sweet-heart. – This is not to our Business: – my Service to you Mr. *Scandal* – [*Drinks*] – I have forborn as long –

VALENTINE: T'other Glass, and then we'll talk. Fill, *Jeremy*.

TRAPLAND: No more, in truth. I have forborn, I say –

1. Moneylender.
2. Footpads or muggers.
3. Twickenham.
4. Smothered.
5. Sherry.

VALENTINE: Sirrah, fill when I bid you. – And how do's your handsome Daughter – Come a good Husband to her. [*Drinks.*]

TRAPLAND: Thank you – I have been out of this Money –

VALENTINE: Drink first. *Scandal*, why do you not Drink? [*They Drink.*]

TRAPLAND: And in short, I can be put off no longer.

VALENTINE: I was much oblig'd to you for your Supply: It did me Signal Service in my necessity. But you delight in doing good. – *Scandal*, Drink to me, my Friend *Trapland's* Health. An honester Man lives not, nor one more ready to serve his Friend in Distress, tho' I say it to his face. Come, fill each Man his Glass.

SCANDAL: What, I know *Trapland* has been a Whoremaster, and loves a Wench still. You never knew a Whoremaster, that was not an honest Fellow.

TRAPLAND: Fie, Mr. *Scandal*, you never knew –

SCANDAL: What don't I know? – I know the Buxom black Widdow in the *Poultry*[1] – 800 l. a Year Joynture, and 20000 l. in Money. A hah! Old *Trap*.

VALENTINE: Say you so, I'faith: Come, we'll remember the Widow: I know where abouts you are: Come, to the Widow –

TRAPLAND: No more indeed.

VALENTINE: What, the Widows Health; give it him – off with it: [*They Drink.*] A Lovely Girl, I'faith, black sparkling Eyes, soft pouting Ruby-Lips! better sealing there, than a Bond for a Million, hah!

TRAPLAND: No, no, there's no such thing, we'd better mind our business. – You're a Wag.

VALENTINE: No faith, we'll mind the Widow's business, fill again. – Pretty round heaving Breasts, – a *Barbary* shape,[2] and a Jut with her Bum, would stir an *Anchoret*:[3] And the prettiest Foot! Oh if a Man could but fasten his Eyes to her Feet, as they steal in and out, and play at Bo-peep under her Petticoats, ah! Mr. *Trapland* ?

TRAPLAND: Verily, give me a Glass, – you're a Wag, – and here's to the Widow. [*Drinks.*]

SCANDAL: He begins to Chuckle; – ply him close, or he'l relapse into a Dun.

[*Enter Officer.*]

OFFICER: By your leave, Gentlemen, – Mr. *Trapland*, if we must do our office, tell us. – We have half a dozen Gentlemen to Arrest in *Pall-Mall* and *Covent-Garden*; and if we don't make haste, the Chairmen will be abroad, and block up the Chocolate-Houses, and then our labour's lost.

TRAPLAND: 'Udso that's true, Mr. *Valentine* I love Mirth, but business must be done, are you ready to –

1. The road leading from Cheapside to Cornhill.
2. With the shape of a Barbary (North African) steed.
3. Hermit.

JEREMY: Sir, your Father's Steward says he comes to make Proposals concerning your Debts.

VALENTINE: Bid him come in: Mr. *Trapland*, send away your Officer, You shall have an answer presently.

TRAPLAND: Mr. *Snap* stay within Call.   [*Exit Officer.*]

[*Enter* STEWARD *and Whispers* VALENTINE.]

SCANDAL: Here's a Dog now, a Traytor in his Wine, Sirrah refund the Sack: *Jeremy* fetch him some warm water, or I'll rip up his Stomach, and go the shortest way to his Conscience.

TRAPLAND: Mr. *Scandal*, you are Uncivil; I did not value your Sack; but you cannot expect it again, when I have drank it.

SCANDAL: And how do you expect to have your Money again, when a Gentleman has spent it?

VALENTINE: You need say no more, I understand the Conditions; they are very hard, but my Necessity is very pressing: I agree to 'em, take Mr. *Trapland* with you, and let him draw the Writing – Mr. *Trapland*, you know this Man, he shall satisfie you.

TRAPLAND: Sincerely, I am loth to be thus pressing, but my necessity.

VALENTINE: No Apology, good Mr. Scrivener, you shall be paid.

TRAPLAND: I hope you forgive me, my business requires –

[*Exeunt* STEWARD, TRAPLAND *and* JEREMY.]

SCANDAL: He begs Pardon like a Hangman at an Execution.

VALENTINE: But I have got a Reprieve.

SCANDAL: I am surpriz'd; what, do's your Father relent?

VALENTINE: No; He has sent me the hardest Conditions in the World: You have heard of a Booby-Brother of mine, that was sent to Sea three Years ago? This Brother, my Father hears is Landed; whereupon he very affectionately sends me word; If I will make a Deed of Conveyance of my Right to his Estate after his Death, to my younger Brother, he will immediately furnish me with Four thousand Pound to pay my Debts, and make my Fortune. This was once propos'd before, and I refus'd it; but the present impatience of my Creditors for their Money, and my own impatience of Confinement, and absence from *Angelica*, force me to consent.

SCANDAL: A very desperate demonstration of your love to *Angelica*: And I think she has never given you any assurance of hers.

VALENTINE: You know her temper; she never gave me any great reason either for hope or despair.

SCANDAL: Women of her airy temper, as they seldom think before they act, so they rarely give us any light to guess at what they mean: But you have little reason to believe that a Woman of this Age, who has had an indifference for you in your Prosperity, will fall in love with your ill Fortune; besides, *Angelica* has a great Fortune of her own; and great Fortunes either expect another great Fortune, or a Fool.

[*Enter* JEREMY.]

JEREMY: More Misfortunes, Sir.

VALENTINE: What, another Dun?

JEREMY: No Sir, but Mr. *Tattle* is come to wait upon you.

VALENTINE: Well, I can't help it, – you must bring him up; He knows I don't
go abroad. [*Exit* JEREMY.]

SCANDAL: Pox on him, I'll be gone.

VALENTINE: No, prithee stay: *Tattle* and you should never be asunder; you are
light and shadow, and shew one another; he is perfectly thy reverse both
in humour and understanding; and as you set up for Defamation, he is
a mender of Reputations.

SCANDAL: A mender of Reputations! aye, just as he is a keeper of secrets,
another Vertue that he sets up for in the same manner. For the Rogue
will speak aloud in the posture of a Whisper; and deny a Woman's
name, while he gives you the marks of her Person: He will forswear
receiving a Letter from her, and at the same time, shew you her Hand
upon the Superscription: And yet perhaps he has Counterfeited the
Hand too; and sworn to a truth; but he hopes not to be believ'd; and
refuses the reputation of a Ladies favour, as a Doctor says, No, to a
Bishoprick, only that it may be granted him – In short, he is a publick
Professor of Secresie, and makes Proclamation that he holds private
Intelligence. – He's here.

[*Enter* TATTLE.]

TATTLE: *Valentine* good Morrow, *Scandal* I am Yours. – That is, when you
speak well of me.

SCANDAL: That is, when I am yours; for while I am my own, or any body's
else, that will never happen

TATTLE: How Inhumane!

VALENTINE: Why *Tattle*, you need not be much concern'd at any thing that he
says: For to converse with *Scandal*, is to play at *Losing Loadum;*[1] you
must lose a good Name to him, before you can win it for your self.

TATTLE: But how Barbarous that is, and how unfortunate for him, that the
World shall think the better of any Person for his Calumniation! – I
thank Heav'n, it has always been a part of my Character, to handle the
Reputation of others very tenderly.

SCANDAL: Aye, such rotten Reputations as you have to deal with, are to be
handl'd tenderly indeed.

TATTLE: Nay, but why rotten? Why should you say rotten, when you know
not the persons of whom you speak? How cruel that is?

SCANDAL: Not know 'em? Why, thou never hadst to do with any body that
did not stink to all the Town.

1. A card game in which the object is to lose tricks rather than win them.

TATTLE: Ha, ha, ha; nay, now you make a Jest of it indeed. For there is nothing more known, than that no body knows any thing of that nature of me: As I hope to be sav'd, *Valentine*, I never expos'd a Woman, since I knew what Woman was.

VALENTINE: And yet you have convers'd with several.

TATTLE: To be free with you, I have – I don't care if I own that – Nay more (I'm going to say a bold Word now) I never could meddle with a Woman that had to do with any body else.

SCANDAL: How!

VALENTINE: Nay faith, I'm apt to believe him – Except her Husband, *Tattle*.

TATTLE: Oh that –

SCANDAL: What think you of that Noble Commoner, Mrs. *Drab*?

TATTLE: Pooh, I know Madam *Drab* has made her Brags in three or four places, that I said this and that, and writ to her, and did I know not what – But, upon my Reputation, she did me wrong – Well, well, that was Malice – But I know the bottom of it. She was brib'd to that by one that we all know – A Man too. Only to bring me into Disgrace with a certain Woman of Quality –

SCANDAL: Whom we all know.

TATTLE: No matter for that – Yes, yes, every body knows – No doubt on't, every body knows my Secrets – But I soon satisfy'd the Lady of my Innocence; for I told her – Madam, says I, there are some Persons who make it their Business to tell Stories, and say this and that of one and t'other, and every thing in the World; and, says I, if your Grace[1] –

SCANDAL: Grace!

TATTLE: O Lord, what have I said? my Unlucky Tongue!

VALENTINE: Ha, ha, ha.

SCANDAL: Why, *Tattle*, thou hast more Impudence than one can in reason expect: I shall have an esteem for thee, well, and ha, ha, ha, well, go on, and what did you say to her Grace?

VALENTINE: I confess this is something extraordinary.

TATTLE: Not a word as I hope to be sav'd; an errant *Lapsus Linguae* – Come, let's talk of something else.

VALENTINE: Well, but how did you acquit your self?

TATTLE: Pooh, pooh, nothing at all, I only rally'd with you – a Woman of ord'nary Rank was a little jealous of me, and I told her something or other, faith – I know not what – Come, let's talk of something else.

[*Hums a Song.*]

SCANDAL: Hang him, let him alone, he has a mind we should enquire.

TATTLE: *Valentine*, I Supp'd last Night with your Mistress, and her Unkle Old *Foresight*: I think your Father lies at *Foresight's*.

VALENTINE: Yes.

---

1. The form of address for a duchess.

TATTLE: Upon my Soul *Angelica's* a fine Woman – And so is Mrs. *Foresight*, and her Sister Mrs. *Frail*.

SCANDAL: Yes, Mrs. *Frail* is a very fine Woman, we all know her.

TATTLE: Oh that is not fair.

SCANDAL: What?

TATTLE: To tell.

SCANDAL: To tell what? Why, what do you know of Mrs. *Frail*?

TATTLE: Who I? Upon Honour I don't know whether she be Man or Woman; but by the smoothness of her Chin, and roundness of her Lips.

SCANDAL: No!

TATTLE: No.

SCANDAL: She says otherwise.

TATTLE: Impossible!

SCANDAL: Yes Faith. Ask *Valentine* else.

TATTLE: Why then, as I hope to be sav'd, I believe a Woman only obliges a Man to Secresie, that she may have the pleasure of telling her self.

SCANDAL: No doubt on't. Well, but has she done you wrong, or no? You have had her? Ha?

TATTLE: Tho' I have more Honour than to tell first; I have more Manners than to contradict what a Lady has declar'd.

SCANDAL: Well, you own it?

TATTLE: I am strangely surpriz'd! Yes, yes, I can't deny't, if she taxes me with it.

SCANDAL: She'll be here by and by, she sees *Valentine* every Morning.

TATTLE: How!

VALENTINE: She does me the favour – I mean of a Visit sometimes. I did not think she had granted more to any body.

SCANDAL: Nor I faith – But *Tattle* does not use to bely a Lady; it is contrary to his Character – How one may be deceiv'd in a Woman, *Valentine*?

TATTLE: Nay, what do you mean, Gentlemen?

SCANDAL: I'm resolv'd I'll ask her.

TATTLE: O Barbarous! why did you not tell me –

SCANDAL: No, you told us.

TATTLE: And bid me ask *Valentine*.

VALENTINE: What did I say? I hope you won't bring me to confess an Answer, when you never ask'd me the Question.

TATTLE: But, Gentlemen, this is the most inhumane Proceeding –

VALENTINE: Nay, if you have known *Scandal* thus long, and cannot avoid such a palpable Decoy as this was; the Ladies have a fine time, whose Reputations are in your keeping.

[*Enter* JEREMY.]

JEREMY: Sir, Mrs. *Frail* has sent to know if you are stirring.

VALENTINE: Shew her up, when she comes. [*Exit* JEREMY.]

TATTLE: I'll be gone.

VALENTINE: You'll meet her.

TATTLE: Have you not a back way?

VALENTINE: If there were, you have more Discretion, than to give *Scandal* such an Advantage; why, your running away will prove all that he can tell her.

TATTLE: *Scandal*, you will not be so ungenerous – O, I shall lose my Reputation of Secresie for ever – I shall never be receiv'd but upon Publick Days; and my Visits will never be admitted beyond a Drawing-Room: I shall never see a Bed-Chamber again, never be lock't in a Closet, nor run behind a Screen, or under a Table; never be distinguish'd among the Waiting-Women by the Name of Trusty Mr. *Tattle* more – You will not be so cruel.

VALENTINE: *Scandal*, have pity on him; he'll yield to any Conditions.

TATTLE: Any, any Terms.

SCANDAL: Come then, sacrifice half a Dozen Women of good Reputation to me presently – Come, where are you familiar – And see that they are Women of Quality too, the first Quality –

TATTLE: 'Tis very hard – Won't a Baronet's Lady pass?

SCANDAL: No, nothing under a Right Honourable.

TATTLE: O inhumane! You don't expect their Names.

SCANDAL: No, their Titles shall serve.

TATTLE: Alas, that's the same thing: Pray spare me their Titles; I'll describe their Persons.

SCANDAL: Well, begin then: But take notice, if you are so ill a Painter, that I cannot know the Person by your Picture of her, you must be condemned, like other bad Painters, to write the Name at the bottom.

TATTLE: Well, first then –

[*Enter* MRS. FRAIL.]

O unfortunate! she's come already; will you have Patience till another time – I'll double the number.

SCANDAL: Well, on that Condition – Take heed you don't fail me.

MRS. FRAIL: Hey day! I shall get a fine Reputation by coming to see Fellows in a Morning. *Scandal*, you Devil, are you here too? Oh Mr. *Tattle*, every thing is safe with you, we know.

SCANDAL: *Tattle*.

TATTLE: Mum – O Madam, you do me too much Honour.

VALENTINE: Well Lady Galloper, how does *Angelica*?

MRS. FRAIL: *Angelica*? Manners!

VALENTINE: What, you will allow an absent Lover –

MRS. FRAIL: No, I'll allow a Lover present with his Mistress to be particular – But otherwise I think his Passion ought to give place to his Manners.

VALENTINE: But what if he have more Passion than Manners?

MRS. FRAIL: Then let him Marry and reform.

VALENTINE: Marriage indeed may qualifie the Fury of his Passion, but it very rarely mends a Man's Manners.

MRS. FRAIL: You are the most mistaken in the World; there is no Creature perfectly Civil, but a Husband. For in a little time he grows only rude to his Wife, and that is the highest good Breeding, for it begets his Civility to other People. Well, I'll tell you News; but I suppose you hear your Brother *Benjamin* is landed. And my Brother *Foresight's* Daughter is come out of the Country – I assure you, there's a Match talk'd of by the Old People – Well, if he be but as great a Sea-Beast, as she is a Land-Monster, we shall have a most Amphibious Breed – The Progeny will be all Otters: he has been bred at Sea, and she has never been out of the Country.

VALENTINE: Pox take 'em, their Conjunction bodes no good, I'm sure.

MRS. FRAIL: Now you talk of Conjunction, my Brother *Foresight* has cast both their Nativities, and prognosticates an Admiral and an eminent Justice of the Peace to be the Issue-Male of their two Bodies; 'tis the most superstitious Old Fool! He would have perswaded me, that this was an Unlucky Day, and wou'd not let me come abroad: But I invented a Dream, and sent him to *Artimedorus*[1] for Interpretation, and so stole out to see you. Well, and what will you give me now? Come, I must have something.

VALENTINE: Step into the next Room – and I'll give you something.

SCANDAL: Ay, we'll all give you something.

MRS. FRAIL: Well, what will you all give me?

VALENTINE: Mine's a Secret.

MRS. FRAIL: I thought you would give me something, that would be a trouble to you to keep.

VALENTINE: And *Scandal* shall give you a good Name.

MRS. FRAIL: That's more than he has for himself And what will you give me, Mr. *Tattle*?

TATTLE: I? My Soul, Madam.

MRS. FRAIL: Pooh, No I thank you, I have enough to do to take care of my own. Well; but I'll come and see you one of these Mornings: I hear you have a great many Pictures.

TATTLE: I have a pretty good Collection at your Service, some Originals.

SCANDAL: Hang him, he has nothing but the *Seasons* and the *Twelve Caesars*, paultry Copies; and the *Five Senses*,[2] as ill represented as they are in himself: And he himself is the only Original you will see there.

MRS. FRAIL: Ay, but I hear he has a Closet of Beauties.

SCANDAL: Yes, all that have done him Favours, if you will believe him.

MRS. FRAIL: Ay, let me see those, Mr. *Tattle*.

---

1. An ancient Greek writer, famous for interpreting dreams.
2. Prints of paintings by Pierre Brueghel le Jeune.

TATTLE: Oh Madam, those are Sacred to Love and Contemplation. No Man but the Painter and my self was ever blest with the Sight.

MRS. FRAIL: Well, but a Woman –

TATTLE: Nor Woman, till she consented to have her Picture there too – for then she is obliged to keep the Secret.

SCANDAL: No, no; come to me if you wou'd see Pictures.

MRS. FRAIL: You?

SCANDAL: Yes Faith, I can shew you your own Picture, and most of your Acquaintance to the Life, and as like as at *Knellers*.[1]

MRS. FRAIL: O lying Creature – *Valentine*, does not he lye? – I can't believe a word he says.

VALENTINE: No indeed, he speaks truth now: For as *Tattle* has Pictures of all that have granted him favours, he has the Pictures of all that have refus'd him: If Satyrs, Descriptions, Characters and Lampoons are Pictures.

SCANDAL: Yes, mine are most in black and white – And yet there are some set out in their true Colours, both Men and Women. I can shew you Pride, Folly, Affectation, Wantonness, Inconstancy, Covetousness, Dissimulation, Malice, and Ignorance, all in one Piece. Then I can shew you Lying, Foppery, Vanity, Cowardise, Bragging, Lechery, Impotence and Ugliness in another Piece; and yet one of these is a celebrated Beauty, and t'other a profest Beau. I have Paintings too, some pleasant enough.

MRS. FRAIL: Come, let's hear 'em.

SCANDAL: Why, I have a Beau in a Bagnio,[2] Cupping for a Complexion, and Sweating for a Shape.

MRS. FRAIL: So.

SCANDAL: Then I have a Lady burning of Brandy in a Cellar with a Hackney-Coachman.

MRS. FRAIL: O Devil! Well, but that Story is not true.

SCANDAL: I have some Hieroglyphicks too; I have a Lawyer with a hundred Hands, two Heads, and but one Face; a Divine with two Faces, and one Head; and I have a Soldier with his Brains in his Belly, and his Heart where his Head shou'd be.

MRS. FRAIL: And no Head?

SCANDAL: No Head.

MRS. FRAIL: Pooh, this is all Invention. Have you ne're a Poet?

SCANDAL: Yes, I have a Poet weighing Words, and selling Praise for Praise, and a Critick picking his Pocket. I have another large Piece too, representing a School; where there are huge Proportion'd Criticks, with long Wigs, Lac'd Coats, Steinkirk Cravats,[3] and terrible Faces; with

1. Godfrey Kneller was the most distinguished portrait painter of the age.
2. A Turkish bath.
3. Fashionable, loosely tied neckcloths.

Catcalls[1] in their Hands, and Horn-Books about their Necks,[2] I have
many more of this kind, very well Painted, as you shall see.

MRS. FRAIL: Well, I'll come, if it be only to disprove you.

[*Enter* JEREMY.]

JEREMY: Sir, here's the Steward again from your Father.

VALENTINE: I'll come to him – will you give me leave, I'll wait on you again
presently.

MRS. FRAIL: No, I'll be gone. Come, who Squires me to the *Exchange*,[3] I must
call my Sister *Foresight* there.

SCANDAL: I will; I have a mind to your Sister.

MRS. FRAIL: Civil!

TATTLE: I will; because I have a tender for your Ladiship.

MRS. FRAIL: That's somewhat the better reason, to my Opinion.

SCANDAL: Well, if *Tattle* entertains you, I have the better opportunity to
engage your Sister.

VALENTINE: Tell *Angelica*, I am about making hard Conditions to come
abroad, and be at Liberty to see her.

SCANDAL: I'll give an account of you, and your Proceedings. If Indiscretion
be a sign of Love, you are the most a Lover of any Body that I know:
You fancy that parting with your Estate, will help you to your Mistress.
– In my mind he is a thoughtless Adventurer,

> *Who hopes to purchase Wealth, by selling Land;*
> *Or win a Mistress, with a losing hand.*   [*Exeunt.*]

Act II, Scene I

[*A Room in Foresight's House.*
FORESIGHT *and* SERVANT.]

FORESIGHT: Hey day! What are all the Women of my Family abroad? Is not
my Wife come home? Nor my Sister, nor my Daughter?

SERVANT: No, Sir.

FORESIGHT: Mercy on us, what can be the meaning of it? Sure the Moon is in
all her Fortitudes;[4] Is my Neice *Angelica* at home?

1. Pocket whistles used to express shrill disappointment in the theatre.
2. Alphabet books with horn covers.
3. The New Exchange, a fashionable shopping area with covered walkways in the
   Strand.
4. The moon is at the height of its influence.

SERVANT: Yes, Sir.

FORESIGHT: I believe you lie, Sir.

SERVANT: Sir?

FORESIGHT: I say you lie, Sir. It is impossible that any thing should be as I would have it; for I was born, Sir, when the Crab was ascending,[1] and all my Affairs go backward.

SERVANT: I can't tell indeed, Sir.

FORESIGHT: No, I know you can't, Sir: But I can tell, Sir, and foretell, Sir.

[*Enter* NURSE.]

Nurse, Where's your young Mistress?

NURSE: Wee'st heart,[2] I know not, they're none of 'em come home yet: Poor Child, I warrant she's fond o'seeing the Town, – Marry, pray Heav'n they ha' given her any Dinner – good lack-a-day, ha, ha, ha, O strange; I'll vow and swear now, ha, ha, ha, Marry and did you ever see the like!

FORESIGHT: Why how now, what's the matter?

NURSE: Pray Heav'n send your Worship good Luck, Marry and Amen with all my heart, for you have put on one Stocking with the wrong side outward.

FORESIGHT: Ha, How? Faith and troth I'm glad of it, and so I have, that may be good Luck in troth, in troth it may, very good Luck: Nay, I have had some Omens; I got out of Bed backwards too this morning, without Premeditation; pretty good that too; but then I stumbl'd coming down Stairs, and met a Weasel;[3] bad Omens those: some bad, some good, our lives are checquer'd, Mirth and Sorrow, Want and Plenty, Night and Day, make up our time, – But in troth I am pleas'd at my Stocking, very well pleas'd at my Stocking – oh here's my Neice! –

[*Enter* ANGELICA.]

Sirrah, go tell Sir *Sampson Legend* I'll wait on him if he's at leisure – 'tis now Three a Clock, a very good hour for Business, Mercury governs this hour. [*Exit* SERVANT.]

ANGELICA: Is not it a good hour for Pleasure too? Uncle, pray lend me your Coach, mine's out of Order.

FORESIGHT: What, wou'd you be gadding too? Sure all Females are mad to day – It is of evil portent, and bodes Mischief to the Master of a Family – I remember an old Prophesie written by *Messehalah* the *Arabian*,[4] and thus translated by a Reverend *Buckinghamshire* Bard.[5]

---

1. The sign of Cancer.
2. Woe's my heart.
3. The weasel was considered unlucky as it was associated with witchcraft.
4. A ninth-century Jewish astrologer.
5. John Mason, a hymn writer and visionary priest.

> *When Housewives all the House forsake,*
> *And leave good Man to Brew and Bake,*
> *Withouten Guile, then be it said,*
> *That House doth stond upon its Head;*
> *And when the Head is set in Grond,*
> *Ne marl, if it be fruitful fond.*

Fruitful, the Head fruitful, that bodes Horns; the Fruit of the Head is Horns – Dear Neice, stay at home – For by the Head of the House is meant the Husband; the Prophecy needs no Explanation.

ANGELICA: Well, but I can neither make you a Cuckold, Uncle, by going abroad; nor secure you from being one, by staying at home.

FORESIGHT: Yes, yes; while there's one Woman left, the Prophesie is not in full Force.

ANGELICA: But my Inclinations are in force, I have a mind to go abroad; and if you won't lend me your Coach, I'll take a Hackney, or a Chair, and leave you to erect a Scheme, and find who's in Conjunction with your Wife. Why don't you keep her at Home, if you're Jealous when she's abroad? You know my Aunt is a little Retrograde (as you call it) in her Nature, Uncle, I'm afraid you are not Lord of the Ascendant, ha, ha, ha.

FORESIGHT: Well, Jill-flirt, you are very pert – and always ridiculing that Celestial Science.

ANGELICA: Nay Uncle, don't be angry – If you are, I'll reap up all your false Prophesies, ridiculous Dreams, and idle Divinations. I'll swear you are a Nusance to the Neighbourhood – What a Bustle did you keep against the last Invisible Eclipse, laying in Provision as 'twere for a Siege? What a World of Fire and Candle, Matches and Tinderboxes did you purchase! One would have thought we were ever after to live under Ground, or at least making a Voyage to *Greenland*, to inhabit there all the dark Season.

FORESIGHT: Why, you malapert Slut –

ANGELICA: Will you lend me your Coach, or I'll go on – Nay, I'll declare how you prophecy'd Popery was coming, only because the Butler had mislaid some of the Apostle's Spoons, and thought they were lost. Away went Religion and Spoon-meat[1] together – Indeed, Uncle, I'll indite you for a Wizard.

FORESIGHT: How Hussie! was there ever such a provoking Minx?

NURSE: O merciful Father, how she talks!

ANGELICA: Yes, I can make Oath of your unlawful Midnight Practices; you and the old Nurse there –

NURSE: Marry Heav'n defend – I at Midnight Practices – Lord, what's here to do? – I in unlawful Doings with my Masters Worship – Why, did you ever hear the like now – Sir, did ever I do anything of your Midnight

1. Broth.

Concerns – but warm your Bed, and tuck you up, and set the Candle, and your Tobacco-Box, and your Urinal by you, and now and then rub the Soles of your Feet? – O Lord, I!

ANGELICA: Yes, I saw you together, through the Key-hole of the Closet, one Night, like *Saul* and the Witch of *Endor*,[1] turning the Sieve and Sheers,[2] and pricking your Thumbs, to write poor innocent Servants Names in Blood, about a little Nutmeg-Grater, which she had forgot in the Caudle[3] Cup – Nay, I know something worse, if I would speak of it –

FORESIGHT: I defie you, Hussie; but I'll remember this, I'll be reveng'd on you, Cockatrice; I'll hamper you – You have your Fortune in your own Hands – But I'll find a way to make your Lover, your Prodigal Spend-thrift Gallant, *Valentine*, pay for all, I will.

ANGELICA: Will you? I care not, but all shall out then – Look to it, Nurse; I can bring Witness that you have a great unnatural Teat under your Left Arm, and he another; and that you Suckle a Young Devil in the Shape of a Tabby-Cat, by turns, I can.

NURSE: A Teat, a Teat, I an unnatural Teat! O the false slanderous thing; feel, feel here, if I have any thing but like another Christian, [*crying*] or any Teats, but two that han't given Suck this Thirty Years.

FORESIGHT: I will have Patience, since it is the Will of the Stars I should be thus tormented – This is the effect of the malicious Conjunctions and Oppositions in the Third House of my Nativity; there the Curse of Kindred was foretold But I will have my Doors lock'd up – I'll punish you, not a Man shall enter my House.

ANGELICA: Do Uncle, lock 'em up quickly before my Aunt come home – You'll have a Letter for Alimony to morrow morning – But let me be gone first, and then let no Mankind come near the House, but Converse with Spirits and the Celestial Signs, the Bull, and the Ram, and the Goat. Bless me! there are a great many Horn'd Beasts among the Twelve Signs, Uncle. But Cuckolds go to Heav'n.

FORESIGHT: But there's but one Virgin among the Twelve Signs, Spitfire, but one Virgin.

ANGELICA: Nor there had not been that one, if she had had to do with any thing but Astrologers, Uncle. That makes my Aunt go abroad.

FORESIGHT: How? how? is that the reason? Come, you know something; tell me, and I'll forgive you; do, good Neice – Come, you shall have my Coach and Horses – Faith and Troth you shall – Does my Wife complain? Come, I know Women tell one another – She is so young and sanguine, has a wanton Hazle Eye, and was born under *Gemini*, which

1. A reference to the passage in I Samuel 28 where the witch of Endor conjures up the spirit of Samuel for Saul.
2. A method of divination, holding a sieve between the open points of a pair of shears.
3. Spiced gruel and wine.

may incline her to Society; she has a Mole upon her Lip, with a moist Palm, and an open Liberality on the Mount of *Venus*.

ANGELICA: Ha, ha, ha.

FORESIGHT: Do you laugh? – Well Gentlewoman, I'll – But come, be a good Girl, don't perplex your poor Uncle, tell me – won't you speak? Odd I'll –

[*Enter* SERVANT.]

SERVANT: Sir *Sampson* is coming down to wait upon you –

ANGELICA: Good bu'y Uncle – Call me a Chair – I'll find out my Aunt, and tell her, she must not come home.   [*Exit* ANGELICA *and Servant.*]

FORESIGHT: I'm so perplex'd and vex'd, I am not fit to receive him; I shall scarce recover my self before the Hour be past: Go Nurse, tell Sir *Sampson* I'm ready to wait on him.

NURSE: Yes, Sir.   [*Exit.*]

FORESIGHT: Well – Why, if I was born to be a Cuckold, there's no more to be said –

[*Enter* SIR SAMPSON LEGEND *with a Paper.*]

SIR SAMPSON: Nor no more to be done, Old Boy; that's plain – here 'tis, I have it in my Hand, Old *Ptolomee*;[1] I'll make the ungracious Prodigal know who begat him; I will, old *Nostrodamus*.[2] What, I warrant my Son thought nothing belong'd to a Father, but Forgiveness and Affection; no Authority, no Correction, no Arbitrary Power; nothing to be done, but for him to offend, and me to pardon. I warrant you, if he danc'd till Doomsday, he thought I was to pay the Piper. Well, but here it is under Black and White, *Signatum, Sigillatum*, and *Deliberatum*; that as soon as my Son *Benjamin* is arriv'd, he is to make over to him his Right of Inheritance. Where's my Daughter that is to be – hah! old Merlin![3] body o' me, I'm so glad I'm reveng'd on this undutiful Rogue.

FORESIGHT: Odso, let me see; Let me see the Paper – Ay, faith and troth, here 'tis, if it will but hold – I wish things were done, and the Conveyance made – When was this Sign'd, what Hour? Odso, you should have consulted me for the time. Well, but we'll make haste –

SIR SAMPSON: Haste, ay, ay; haste enough, my Son *Ben* will be in Town to night – I have order'd my Lawyer to draw up Writings of Settlement and Joynture – All shall be done to Night – No matter for the time; prithee, Brother *Foresight*, leave Superstition – Pox o'th time; there's no time but the time present, there's no more to be said of what's past, and all that is to come will happen. If the Sun shine by Day, and the Stars by

1. An eminent astrologer of the second century.
2. A famous French astrologer, physician to Henri II.
3. The Arthurian magician.

Night, why, we shall know one another's Faces without the help of a
Candle, and that's all the Stars are good for.

FORESIGHT: How, how? Sir *Sampson*, that all? Give me leave to contradict
you, and tell you, you are ignorant.

SIR SAMPSON: I tell you I am wise; and *sapiens dominabitur astris;*[1] there's Latin
for you to prove it, and an Argument to confound your *Ephemeris*[2] –
Ignorant! – I tell you, I have travel'd old *Fircu*, and know the Globe. I
have seen the *Antipodes*, where the Sun rises at Midnight, and sets at
Noon-day.

FORESIGHT: But I tell you, I have travell'd, and travell'd in the Cœlestial
Spheres, know the *Signs* and the *Planets*, and their Houses. Can judge of
Motions Direct and Retrograde, of *Sextiles, Quadrates, Trines* and *Oppositions,* Fiery *Trigons* and Aquatical *Trigons.*[3] Know whether Life shall be
long or short, Happy or Unhappy; whether Diseases are Cureable or
Incureable. If Journeys shall be prosperous, Undertakings successful;
or Goods stoll'n recover'd, I know –

SIR SAMPSON: I know the length of the Emperour of *China's* Foot; have kiss'd
the Great *Mogul's* Slipper, and rid a Hunting upon an Elephant with the
Cham of *Tartary* – Body o' me, I have made a Cuckold of a King, and the
present Majesty of *Bantam* is the Issue of these Loyns.

FORESIGHT: I know when Travellers lie or speak Truth, when they don't
know it themselves.

SIR SAMPSON: I have known an Astrologer made a Cuckold in the twinckling
of a Star; and seen a Conjurer, that cou'd not keep the Devil out of his
Wives Circle.

FORESIGHT: What does he twit me with my Wife too, I must be better
inform'd of this – [*Aside*] – Do you mean my Wife, Sir *Sampson*? Tho'
you made a Cuckold of the King of *Bantam*, yet by the Body of the Sun –

SIR SAMPSON: By the Horns of the Moon, you wou'd say, Brother *Capricorn*.

FORESIGHT: *Capricorn* in your Teeth, thou Modern *Mandevil*; Ferdinand Mendez
Pinto[4] was but a Type of thee, thou Lyar of the first Magnitude. Take
back your Paper of Inheritance; send your Son to Sea again. I'll wed my
Daughter to an *Egyptian* Mummy, e're she shall Incorporate with a
Contemner of Sciences, and a defamer of Vertue.

SIR SAMPSON: Body o' me, I have gone too far; – I must not provoke honest
Albumazar[5] – an *Egyptian* Mummy is an Illustrious Creature, my trusty
Hieroglyphick; and may have significations of futurity about him;
Odsbuds, I wou'd my Son were an *Egyptian* Mummy for thy sake. What,
thou art not angry for a Jest, my good *Haly*[6] – I Reverence the Sun,

---

1. A well-known tag: 'A wise man will be ruled by the stars'.
2. A popular monthly almanac.
3. Positions of the planets as they move through the signs of the Zodiac.
4. Both authors wrote colourful accounts of their travels.
5. A Persian astrologer.
6. Another famous Persian astrologer.

Moon and Stars with all my heart. – What, I'll make thee a Present of a Mummy: Now I think on't, Body o' me, I have a Shoulder of an *Egyptian* King, that I purloyn'd from one of the Pyramids, powder'd with Hieroglyphicks, thou shalt have it sent home to thy House, and make an Entertainment for all the *Philomaths*,[1] and Students in Physick and Astrology in and about London.

FORESIGHT: But what do you know of my Wife, Sir Sampson?

SIR SAMPSON: Thy Wife is a Constellation of Vertues; she's the Moon, and thou art the Man in the Moon: Nay, she is more Illustrious than the Moon; for she has her Chastity without her Inconstancy. 'S'bud I was but in Jest.

[*Enter* JEREMY.]

How now, who sent for you? Ha! what wou'd you have?

FORESIGHT: Nay, if you were but in Jest. – Who's that Fellow? I don't like his Physiognomy.

SIR SAMPSON: My Son, Sir; what Son, Sir? My Son *Benjamin*, hoh?

JEREMY: No, Sir, Mr. *Valentine*, my master, – 'tis the first time he has been abroad since his Confinement, and he comes to pay his Duty to you.

SIR SAMPSON: Well, Sir.

[*Enter* VALENTINE.]

JEREMY: He is here, Sir.

VALENTINE: Your Blessing, Sir.

SIR SAMPSON: You've had it already, Sir, I think I sent it you to day in a Bill of Four thousand Pound: A great deal of Money, Brother *Foresight*.

FORESIGHT: Aye indeed, Sir *Sampson*, a great deal of Money for a young Man, I wonder what he can do with it!

SIR SAMPSON: Body o' me, so do I. – Heark ye, *Valentine*, if there is too much, refund the Superfluity; Do'st hear Boy?

VALENTINE: Superfluity, Sir, it will scarce pay my Debts, – I hope you will have more Indulgence, than to oblige me to those hard Conditions, which my necessity Sign'd to.

SIR SAMPSON: Sir, how I beseech you, what were you pleas'd to intimate, concerning Indulgence?

VALENTINE: Why, Sir, that you wou'd not go to the extremity of the Conditions, but release me at least from some part. –

SIR SAMPSON: Oh Sir, I understand you – that's all, ha?

VALENTINE: Yes, Sir, all that I presume to ask. – But what you, out of Fatherly fondness, will be pleas'd to add, shall be doubly welcome.

SIR SAMPSON: No doubt of it, sweet Sir, but your filial Piety, and my Fatherly fondness wou'd fit like two Tallies – Here's a Rogue, Brother *Foresight*, makes a Bargain under Hand and Seal in the Morning, and would be

1. Scholars.

releas'd from it in the Afternoon; here's a Rogue, Dog, here's Conscience and Honesty; this is your Wit now, this is the Morality of your Wits! You are a Wit, and have been a Beau, and may be a – Why, Sirrah, is it not here under Hand and Seal – Can you deny it?

VALENTINE: Sir, I don't deny it. –

SIR SAMPSON: Sirrah, you'l be hang'd; I shall live to see you go up *Holborn-hill*,[1] – Has he not a Rogues face? – Speak, Brother, you understand Physiognomy, a hanging look to me; – of all my Boys the most unlike me; a has a damn'd *Tyburn* face, without the benefit o' the Clergy.

FORESIGHT: Hum – truly I don't care to discourage a young Man, – he has a violent death in his face; but I hope no danger of Hanging.

VALENTINE: Sir, is this Usage for your Son? – for that old, Weather-headed fool, I know how to laugh at him; but you, Sir –

SIR SAMPSON: You Sir; and you Sir: – Why, who are you Sir?

VALENTINE: Your Son, Sir.

SIR SAMPSON: That's more than I know, Sir, and I believe not.

VALENTINE: Faith, I hope not.

SIR SAMPSON: What, wou'd you have your Mother a Whore! Did you ever hear the like! Did you ever hear the like! Body o' me –

VALENTINE: I would have an excuse for your Barbarity and Unnatural Usage.

SIR SAMPSON: Excuse! Impudence! why Sirrah, mayn't I do what I please? Are not you my Slave? Did not I beget you? And might not I have chosen whether I would have begot you or no? Ouns who are you? Whence came you? What brought you into the World? How came you here, Sir? Here, to stand here, upon those two Leggs, and look erect with that audacious face, hah? Answer me that? Did you come a Voluntier into the World? Or did I beat up for you with the lawful Authority of a Parent, and press you to the service?

VALENTINE: I know no more why I came, than you do why you call'd me. But here I am, and if you don't mean to provide for me, I desire you wou'd leave me as you found me.

SIR SAMPSON: With all my heart: Come, Uncase, Strip, and go naked out of the World as you came into't.

VALENTINE: My Cloaths are soon put off: – But you must also deprive me of Reason, Thought, Passions, Inclinations, Affections, Appetites, Senses, and the huge Train of Attendants that you begot along with me.

SIR SAMPSON: Body o' me, what a many headed Monster have I propagated?

VALENTINE I am of myself, a plain easie simple Creature; and to be kept at small expence; but the Retinue that you gave me are craving and invincible; they are so many Devils that you have rais'd, and will have employment.

SIR SAMPSON: 'Oons, what had I to do to get Children, – can't a private man be born without all these followers: – Why nothing under an Emperour

---

1. The route to the gallows at Tyburn.

should be born with Appetites, – Why at this rate a fellow that has but a Groat in his Pocket, may have a Stomach capable of a Ten Shilling Ordinary.

JEREMY: Nay, that's as clear as the Sun; I'll make Oath of it before any Justice in *Middlesex*.

SIR SAMPSON: Here's a Cormorant too, – 'S'heart this Fellow was not born with you? – I did not beget him, did I? –

JEREMY: By the Provision that's made for me, you might have begot me too: – Nay, and to tell your Worship another truth, I believe you did, for I find I was born with those same Whoreson Appetites too; that my Master speaks of.

SIR SAMPSON: Why look you there now, – I'll maintain it, that by the rule of right Reason, this fellow ought to have been born without a Palate. – 'S'heart, what shou'd he do with a distinguishing taste? – I warrant now he'd rather eat a Pheasant, than a piece of poor *John*;[1] and smell, now, why I warrant he can smell, and loves Perfumes above a stink. – Why there's it; and Musick, don't you love Musick, Scoundrell?

JEREMY: Yes, I have a reasonable good Ear, Sir, as to Jiggs and Country Dances; and the like; I don't much matter[2] your *Sola's* or *Sonata's*, they give me the Spleen.

SIR SAMPSON: The Spleen, ha, ha, ha, a Pox confound you – *Sola's* and *Sonata's*? 'Oons whose Son are you? how were you engendred, Muck-worm?

JEREMY: I am by my Father, the Son of a Chair-man, my Mother sold Oysters in Winter, and Cucumbers in Summer; and I came up Stairs into the World; for I was born in a Cellar.

FORESIGHT: By your Looks, you shou'd go up Stairs out of the World too, Friend.

SIR SAMPSON: And if this Rogue were Anatomiz'd now, and dissected, he has his Vessels of Digestion and Concoction, and so forth, large enough for the inside of a Cardinal, this Son of a Cucumber. – These things are unaccountable and unreasonable, – Body o' me, why was not I a Bear? that my Cubs might have liv'd upon sucking their Paws; Nature has been provident only to Bears and Spiders; the one has its Nutriment in his own hands; and t'other spins his Habitation out of his Entrails.

VALENTINE: Fortune was provident enough to supply all the Necessities of my Nature; if I had my right of Inheritance,

SIR SAMPSON: Again! 'Ouns han't you four thousand Pound – If I had it again, I wou'd not give thee a Groat, – What, would'st thou have me turn Pelican, and feed thee out of my own vitals? – 'S'heart, live by your Wits, – You were always fond of the Wits, – Now let's see, if you have Wit enough to keep your self? – Your Brother will be in Town to Night,

1. Dried, salted hake.
2. Like.

or to morrow morning, and then look you perform Covenants, and so
your Friend and Servant – Come Brother *Foresight*.

[*Exeunt* SIR SAMPSON *and* FORESIGHT.]

JEREMY: I told you what your visit wou'd come to.

VALENTINE: 'Tis as much as I expected – I did not come to see him: I came to
Angelica; but since she was gone abroad, it was easily turn'd another
way; and at least look'd well on my side: What's here? Mrs. *Foresight*
and Mrs. *Frail*, they are earnest, – I'll avoid 'em, – Come this way, and
go and enquire when *Angelica* will return. [*Exeunt.*]

[*Enter* MRS. FORESIGHT *and* MRS. FRAIL.]

MRS. FRAIL: What have you to do to watch me? – 'S'life I'll do what I please.

MRS. FORESIGHT: You will?

MRS. FRAIL: Yes marry will I – A great piece of business to go to *Covent-Garden
Square* in a Hackney-Coach, and take a turn with one's Friend.

MRS. FORESIGHT: Nay, two or three Turns, I'll take my Oath.

MRS. FRAIL: Well, what if I took twenty – I warrant if you had been there, it
had been only innocent Recreation – Lord, where's the comfort of this
Life, if we can't have the happiness of conversing where we like.

MRS. FORESIGHT: But can't you converse at home? – I own it, I think there's
no happiness like conversing with an agreeable man; I don't quarrel at
that, nor I don't think but your Conversation was very innocent; but the
place is publick, and to be seen with a man in a Hackney-Coach is
scandalous: What if any Body else shou'd have seen you alight as I
did? – How can any Body be happy, while they're in perpetual fear of
being seen and censur'd? – Besides, it wou'd not only reflect upon you,
Sister, but me.

MRS. FRAIL: Pooh, here's a Clutter – why should it reflect upon you? – I don't
doubt but you have thought your self happy in a Hackney-Coach before
now. – If I had gone to *Knights-bridge*, or to *Chelsey*, or to *Spring-Garden*,
or *Barn-Elms*[1] with a man alone – something might have been said.

MRS. FORESIGHT: Why, was I ever in any of these places? What do you mean
Sister?

MRS. FRAIL: Was I? what do you mean?

MRS. FORESIGHT: You have been at a worse place.

MRS. FRAIL: I at a worse place, and with a man!

MRS. FORESIGHT: I suppose you would not go alone to the *World's-End*.[2]

MRS. FRAIL: The World's end! What, do you mean to banter me?

MRS. FORESIGHT: Poor innocent! you don't know that there's a place call'd the
World's-End? I'll swear you can keep your Countenance purely, you'd
make an Admirable Player.

1. All of these locations, away from the centre of London, were used for assignations.
2. In Chelsea.

MRS. FRAIL: I'll swear you have a great deal of Impudence, and in my mind too much for the Stage.

MRS. FORESIGHT: Very well, that will appear who has most, You never were at the *World's End*?

MRS. FRAIL: No.

MRS. FORESIGHT: You deny it positively to my Face.

MRS. FRAIL: Your Face, what's Your Face?

MRS. FORESIGHT: No matter for that, it's as good a Face as yours.

MRS. FRAIL: Not by a Dozen Years wearing. – But I do deny it positively to Your Face then.

MRS. FORESIGHT: I'll allow you now to find fault with my Face; – for I'll swear your impudence has put me out of Countenance: – But look you here now, – where did you lose this Gold Bodkin?[1] – Oh Sister, Sister!

MRS. FRAIL: My Bodkin!

MRS. FORESIGHT: Nay, 'tis Yours, look at it.

MRS. FRAIL: Well, if you go to that, where did you find this Bodkin? – Oh Sister, Sister! – Sister every way.

MRS. FORESIGHT: [*aside.*] O Devil on't, that I cou'd not discover her, without betraying my self.

MRS. FRAIL: I have heard Gentlemen say, Sister; that one should take great care when one makes a thrust in Fencing, not to lye open ones self.

MRS. FORESIGHT: It's very true, Sister: Well since all's out, and as you say, since we are both Wounded, let us do that is often done in Duels, take care of one another, and grow better Friends than before.

MRS. FRAIL: With all my heart, ours are but slight Flesh-wounds, and if we keep 'em from Air, not at all dangerous: Well, give me your Hand in token of sisterly secresie and affection.

MRS. FORESIGHT: Here 'tis with all my heart.

MRS. FRAIL: Well, as an earnest of Friendship and Confidence; I'll acquaint you with a design that I have: To tell Truth, and speak openly one to another; I'm afraid the World have observ'd us more than we have observ'd one another. You have a Rich Husband, and are provided for, I am at a loss, and have no great Stock either of Fortune or Reputation; and therefore must look sharply about me. Sir *Sampson* has a Son that is expected to Night; and by the Account I have heard of his Education can be no Conjurer: The Estate You know is to be made over to him: – Now if I cou'd wheedle him, Sister, ha? You understand me?

MRS. FORESIGHT: I do; and will help you to the utmost of my power – And I can tell you one thing that falls out luckily enough; my awkard Daughter-in-Law,[2] who you know is design'd for his Wife, is grown fond of Mr. *Tattle*; now if we can improve that, and make her have an Aversion for the Booby, it may go a great way towards his liking of you.

1. An ornamental hairpin.
2. Stepdaughter.

Here they come together; and let us contrive some way or other to leave
'em together.

[*Enter* TATTLE, *and* MISS PRUE.]

MISS PRUE: Mother, Mother, Mother, look you here.

MRS. FORESIGHT: Fie, fie, Miss, how you bawl – besides, I have told you, you
must not call me Mother.

MISS PRUE: What must I call you then, are not you my Father's Wife?

MRS. FORESIGHT: Madam; you must say Madam – By my Soul, I shall fancy
my self Old indeed, to have this great Girl call me Mother – Well, but
Miss, what are you so overjoy'd at?

MISS PRUE: Look you here, Madam then, what Mr. *Tattle* has giv'n me – Look
you here Cousin, here's a Snuff-box; nay, there's Snuff in't; – here, will
you have any – Oh good! how sweet it is – Mr. *Tattle* is all over sweet,
his Perruke is sweet, and his Gloves are sweet, – and his Handkerchief
is sweet, pure sweet, sweeter than Roses – Smell him Mother, Madam, I
mean – He gave me this Ring for a kiss.

TATTLE: O fie Miss, you must not kiss and tell.

MISS PRUE: Yes; I may tell my Mother – And he says he'll give me something
to make me smell so – Oh pray lend me your Handkerchief – Smell
Cousin; he says, he'll give me something that will make my Smocks
smell this way – Is not it pure? – It's better than Lavender mun[1] – I'm
resolv'd I won't let Nurse put any more Lavender among my Smocks –
ha, Cousin?

MRS. FRAIL: Fie, Miss; amongst your Linnen, you must say – You must never
say Smock.

MISS PRUE: Why, It is not bawdy, is it Cousin?

TATTLE: Oh Madam; you are too severe upon Miss; you must not find fault
with her pretty simplicity, it becomes her strangely – pretty Miss, don't
let 'em perswade you out of your Innocency.

MRS. FORESIGHT: Oh, Demm you Toad – I wish you don't perswade her out
of her Innocency.

TATTLE: Who I, Madam? – Oh Lord, how can your Ladyship have such a
thought – sure you don't know me?

MRS. FRAIL: Ah Devil, sly Devil – He's as close, Sister, as a Confessor – He
thinks we don't observe him.

MRS. FORESIGHT: A cunning Cur; how soon he cou'd find out a fresh harmless
Creature; and left us, Sister, presently.

TATTLE: Upon Reputation. –

MRS. FORESIGHT: They're all so, Sister, these Men – they love to have the
spoiling of a Young Thing, they are as fond of it, as of being first in the
Fashion, or of seeing a new Play the first day, – I warrant it wou'd break

1. An interesting parallel to the modern interjection 'man'.

Love for Love

Mr. *Tattle's* Heart, to think that any body else shou'd be before-hand with him.

TATTLE: Oh Lord, I swear I wou'd not for the World –

MRS. FRAIL: O hang you; who'll believe you? – You'd be hang'd before you'd confess – we know you – she's very pretty! – Lord, what pure red and white! – she looks so wholsome; – ne're stir, I don't know, but I fancy, if I were a Man –

MISS PRUE: How you love to jear one, Cousin.

MRS. FORESIGHT: Heark'ee, Sister – by my Soul the Girl is spoil'd already – d'ee think shee'll ever endure a great lubberly Tarpawlin – Gad I warrant you, she won't let him come near her, after Mr. *Tattle*.

MRS. FRAIL: O' my Soul, I'm afraid not – eh! – filthy Creature, that smells all of Pitch and Tarr – Devil take you, you confounded Toad – why did you see her, before she was Married?

MRS. FORESIGHT: Nay, why did we let him – my Husband will hang us – He'll think we brought 'em acquainted.

MRS. FRAIL: Come, Faith let us be gone – If my Brother *Foresight* shou'd find us with them; – He'd think so, sure enough.

MRS. FORESIGHT: So he wou'd – but then leaving 'em together is as bad – And he's such a sly Devil, he'll never miss an opportunity.

MRS. FRAIL: I don't care; I won't be seen in't.

MRS. FORESIGHT: Well, if you should, Mr. *Tattle*, you'll have a world to answer for, remember I wash my Hands of it, I'm thoroughly Innocent.

[*Exeunt* MRS. FORESIGHT *and* MRS. FRAIL.]

MISS PRUE: What makes 'em go away, Mr. *Tattle*? What do they mean, do you know?

TATTLE: Yes, my Dear – I think I can guess – But hang me if I know the reason of it.

MISS PRUE: Come, must not we go too?

TATTLE: No, no, they don't mean that.

MISS PRUE: No! what then? what shall you and I do together?

TATTLE: I must make Love to you, pretty Miss; will you let me make Love to you?

MISS PRUE: Yes, if you please.

TATTLE: [*aside*.] Frank, I Gad at least. What a Pox do's Mrs. *Foresight* mean by this Civility? Is it to make a Fool of me? Or do's she leave us together out of good Morality, and do as she would be done by – Gad I'll understand it so.

MISS PRUE: Well, and how will you make Love to me – Come, I long to have you begin; – must I make Love too? You must tell me how.

TATTLE: You must let me speak Miss, you must not speak first; I must ask you Questions, and you must answer.

MISS PRUE: What, is it like the Catechisme? – Come then ask me.

TATTLE: De'e you think you can Love me?

MISS PRUE: Yes.

TATTLE: Pooh, Pox, you must not say yes already; I shan't care a Farthing for
  you then in a twinckling.

MISS PRUE: What must I say then?

TATTLE: Why you must say no, or you believe not, or you can't tell –

MISS PRUE: Why, must I tell a Lie then?

TATTLE: Yes, if you would be well-bred. All well-bred Persons Lie – Besides,
  you are a Woman, you must never speak what you think: Your words
  must contradict your thoughts; but your Actions may contradict your
  words. So, when I ask you, if you can Love me, you must say no, but
  you must Love me too – If I tell you you are Handsome, you must deny
  it, and say I flatter you – But you must think your self more Charming
  than I speak you: – And like me, for the Beauty which I say you have,
  as much as if I had it my self – If I ask you to Kiss me, you must be
  angry, but you must not refuse me. If I ask you for more, you must be
  more angry, – but more complying; and as soon as ever I make you say
  you'l cry out, you must be sure to hold your Tongue.

MISS PRUE: O Lord, I swear this is pure, – I like it better than our old fashion'd
  Country way of speaking ones mind; – and must not you lie too?

TATTLE: Hum – Yes – But you must believe I speak Truth.

MISS PRUE: O *Gemini*! well, I always had a great mind to tell Lies – but they
  frighted me, and said it was a sin.

TATTLE: Well, my pretty Creature; will you make me happy by giving me a
  Kiss?

MISS PRUE: No, indeed; I'm angry at you. –   [*Runs and Kisses him.*]

TATTLE: Hold, hold, that's pretty well, – but you should not have given it me,
  but have suffer'd me to take it.

MISS PRUE: Well, we'll do it again.

TATTLE: With all my heart, – Now then my little Angel.   [*Kisses her.*]

MISS PRUE: Pish.

TATTLE: That's right, – again my Charmer.   [*Kisses again.*]

MISS PRUE: O fie, now I can't abide you.

TATTLE: Admirable! That was as well as if you had been born and bred in
  Covent-Garden, all the days of your Life; – And won't you shew me,
  pretty Miss, where your Bed-Chamber is?

MISS PRUE: No, indeed won't I: But I'll run there, and hide my self from you
  behind the Curtains.

TATTLE: I'll follow you.

MISS PRUE: Ah, but I'll hold the Door with both Hands, and be angry; – and
  you shall push me down before you come in.

TATTLE: No, I'll come in first, and push you down afterwards.

MISS PRUE: Will you? then I'll be more angry, and more complying.

TATTLE: Then I'll make you cry out.

MISS PRUE: Oh but you sha'nt, for I'll hold my Tongue. –

TATTLE: Oh my Dear, apt Scholar.

MISS PRUE: Well, now I'll run and make more haste than you. [*Exit* MISS PRUE.]

TATTLE, You shall not fly so fast, as I'll pursue.   [*Exit after her.*]

Act III, Scene I

[*Enter* NURSE.]

NURSE: Miss, Miss, Miss *Prue* – Mercy on me, marry and Amen: Why, what's become of the Child? – Why Miss, Miss *Foresight* – Sure she has not lock'd her self up in her Chamber, and gone to sleep, or to Prayers; Miss, Miss, I hear her – Come to your Father, Child: Open the Door – Open the Door Miss – I hear you cry husht – O Lord, who's there? [*peeps*] What's here to do? – O the Father! a Man with her! – Why, Miss I say, God's my Life, here's fine doings towards – O Lord, We're all undone – O you young Harlotry [*knocks*] Ods my Life, won't you open the Door? I'll come in the back way.   [*Exit.*]

[TATTLE *and* MISS PRUE *at the Door.*]

MISS PRUE: O Lord, she's coming – and she'll tell my Father, what shall I do now?

TATTLE: Pox take her; if she had staid two Minutes longer, I shou'd have wish'd for her coming.

MISS PRUE: O Dear, what shall I say? Tell me, Mr. *Tattle*, tell me a Lie.

TATTLE: There's no occasion for a Lie; I cou'd never tell a Lie to no purpose – But since we have done nothing; we must say nothing, I think. I hear her – I'll leave you together, and come off as you can.

[*Thrusts her in, and shuts the Door.*]

[*Enter* VALENTINE, SCANDAL, *and* ANGELICA.]

ANGELICA: You can't accuse me of Inconstancy; I never told you, that I lov'd you.

VALENTINE: But I can accuse you of Uncertainty, for not telling me whether you did or no.

ANGELICA: You mistake Indifference for Uncertainty; I never had Concern enough to ask my self the Question.

SCANDAL: Nor good Nature enough to answer him that did ask you: I'll say that for you, Madam.

ANGELICA: What, are you setting up for good Nature?

SCANDAL: Only for the affectation of it, as the Women do for ill Nature.

ANGELICA: Perswade your Friend, that it is all Affectation.

VALENTINE: I shall receive no Benefit from the Opinion: For I know no effectual Difference between continued Affectation and Reality.

TATTLE [*coming up.*] *Scandal*, are you in private Discourse, any thing of
Secresie?   [*Aside to* SCANDAL.]

SCANDAL: Yes, but I dare trust you; We were talking of *Angelica's* Love for
Valentine; you won't speak of it.

TATTLE: No, no, not a Syllable – I know that's a Secret, for it's whisper'd
every where.

SCANDAL: Ha, ha, ha.

ANGELICA: What is, Mr. *Tattle*? I heard you say something was whisper'd
every where.

SCANDAL: Your Love of *Valentine*.

ANGELICA: How!

TATTLE: No, Madam, his Love for your Ladyship – Gad take me, I beg your
Pardon – for I never beard a Word of your Ladyships Passion, till this
instant.

ANGELICA: My Passion! And who told you of my Passion, pray Sir?

SCANDAL: Why, is the Devil in you? Did not I tell it you for a Secret?

TATTLE: Gadso; but I thought she might have been trusted with her own
Affairs.

SCANDAL: Is that your Discretion? trust a Woman with her self?

TATTLE: You say true, I beg your Pardon; – I'll bring all off – It was impossible, Madam, for me to imagine, that a Person of your Ladyship's Wit
and Gallantry, could have so long receiv'd the passionate Addresses of
the accomplisht *Valentine* and yet remain insensible; therefore you will
pardon me, if from a just weight of his Merit, with your Ladyship's
good Judgment, I form'd the Ballance of a reciprocal Affection.

VALENTINE: O the Devil, what damn'd Costive[1] Poet has given thee this
Lesson of Fustian to get by Rote?

ANGELICA: I dare swear you wrong him, it is his own – And Mr. *Tattle* only
judges of the Success of others, from the Effects of his own Merit. For
certainly Mr. *Tattle* was never deny'd any thing in his Life.

TATTLE: O Lord! yes indeed, Madam, several times.

ANGELICA: I swear I don't think 'tis possible.

TATTLE: Yes, I vow and swear I have: Lord, Madam, I'm the most unfortunate
Man in the World, and the most cruelly us'd by the Ladies.

ANGELICA: Nay, now you're ungrateful.

TATTLE: No, I hope not – 'tis as much Ingratitude to own some Favours, as
to conceal others.

VALENTINE: There, now it's out.

ANGELICA: I don't understand you now. I thought you had never ask'd any
thing, but what a Lady might modestly grant, and you confess.

SCANDAL: So faith, your Business is done here; now you may go brag
somewhere else.

TATTLE: Brag! O Heav'ns! Why, did I name any body?

1. Constipated.

ANGELICA: No; I suppose that is not in your Power; but you wou'd if you cou'd, no doubt on't.

TATTLE: Not in my Power, Madam! What does your Ladyship mean, that I have no Womans Reputation in my Power?

SCANDAL: [*aside.*] Ouns, why you won't own it, will you?

TATTLE: Faith, Madam, you're in the right; no more I have, as I hope to be sav'd; I never had it in my Power to say any thing to a Lady's Prejudice in my Life – For as I was telling you Madam, I have been the most unsuccessful Creature living, in things of that nature; and never had the good Fortune to be trusted once with a Lady's Secret, not once.

ANGELICA: No.

VALENTINE: Not once, I dare answer for him.

SCANDAL: And I'll answer for him; for I'm sure if he had, he wou'd have told me; I find, Madam, you don't know Mr. *Tattle*.

TATTLE: No indeed, Madam, you don't know me at all, I find: For sure my intimate Friends wou'd have known –

ANGELICA: Then it seems you would have told, if you had been trusted.

TATTLE: O pox, *Scandal*, that was too far put – Never have told Particulars, Madam. Perhaps I might have talk'd as of a Third Person – or have introduc'd an Amour of my own, in Conversation, by way of Novel: but never have explain'd Particulars.

ANGELICA: But whence comes the Reputation of Mr. *Tattle's* Secresie, if he was never trusted?

SCANDAL: Why thence it arises – The thing is proverbially spoken; but may be apply'd to him – As if we shou'd say in general Terms, He only is Secret who never was trusted; a Satyrical Proverb upon our Sex – There's another upon yours – As she is chaste, who was never ask'd the Question.[1] That's all.

VALENTINE: A couple of very civil Proverbs, truly: 'Tis hard to tell whether the Lady or Mr. *Tattle* be the more oblig'd to you. For you found her vertue, upon the Backwardness of the Men; and his Secresie, upon the mistrust of the Women.

TATTLE: Gad, it's very true, Madam, I think we are oblig'd to acquit our selves – And for my part – But your Ladyship is to speak first –

ANGELICA: Am I? Well, I freely confess I have resisted a great deal of Temptation.

TATTLE: And I Gad, I have given some Temptation that has not been resisted.

VALENTINE: Good.

ANGELICA: I cite *Valentine* here, to declare to the Court, how fruitless he has found his Endeavours, and to confess all his Solicitations and my Denials.

VALENTINE: I am ready to plead, Not guilty for you; and Guilty, for my self.

SCANDAL: So, why this is fair, here's Demonstration with a Witness.

---

1. A quotation from Ovid's *Amores I.*

TATTLE: Well, my Witnesses are not present – But I confess I have had Favours from Persons – But as the Favours are numberless, so the Persons are nameless.

SCANDAL: Pooh, pox, this proves nothing.

TATTLE: No? I can shew Letters, Locketts, Pictures, and Rings; and if there be occasion for Witnesses, I can summon the Maids at the Chocolate-Houses, all the Porters of *Pall-Mall* and *Covent-Garden*, the Door-keepers at the Play-House, the Drawers at *Locket's*, *Pontack's*, the *Rummer, Spring Garden*;[1] my own Landlady and *Valet de Chambre*; all who shall make Oath, that I receive more Letters than the Secretary's Office; and that I have more Vizor-Masks to enquire for me, than ever went to see the Hermaphrodite, or the Naked Prince.[2] And it is notorious, that in a Country Church, once, an Enquiry being made, who I was, it was answer'd, I was the famous *Tattle*, who had ruin'd so many Women.

VALENTINE: It was there, I suppose, you got the Nick-Name of the *Great Turk*.

TATTLE: True; I was call'd *Turk-Tattle* all over the Parish – The next Sunday all the Old Women kept their Daughters at home, and the Parson had not half his Congregation. He wou'd have brought me in to the Spiritual Court, but I was reveng'd upon him, for he had a handsom Daughter whom I initiated into the Science. But I repented it afterwards, for it was talk'd of in Town – And a Lady of Quality that shall be nameless, in a raging Fit of Jealousie, came down in her Coach and Six Horses, and expos'd her self upon my Account; Gad, I was sorry for it with all my Heart – You know whom I mean – You know where we raffl'd –

SCANDAL: Mum, *Tattle*.

VALENTINE: 'Sdeath, are not you asham'd?

ANGELICA: O barbarous! I never heard so insolent a piece of Vanity – Fie, Mr. *Tattle* – I'll swear I could not have believ'd it – Is this your Secresie?

TATTLE: Gad so, the Heat of my Story carry'd me beyond my Discretion, as the Heat of the Lady's Passion hurry'd her beyond her Reputation – But I hope you don't know whom I mean; for there were a great many Ladies raffled – Pox on't, now could I bite off my Tongue.

SCANDAL: No don't; for then you'l tell us no more – Come, I'll recommend a Song to you upon the Hint of my two Proverbs, and I see one in the next Room that will sing it.   [*Goes to the Door.*]

TATTLE: For Heaven's sake, if you do guess, say nothing; Gad, I'm very unfortunate.

[*Re-enter SCANDAL, with one to Sing.*]

SCANDAL: Pray sing the first Song in the last new Play.

1. Popular taverns and eating places.
2. Popular attractions for visitors to London.

SONG
Set by Mr. *John Eccles.*

A Nymph and a Swain to Apollo *once pray'd,*
The Swain had been Jilted, the Nymph been Betray'd;
Their Intent was to try if his Oracle knew
E're a Nymph that was Chaste, or a Swain that was True.

Apollo *was mute, and had like t' have been pos'd,*[1]
But sagely at length he this Secret disclos'd:
He alone won't Betray in whom none will Confide,
And the Nymph may be Chaste that has never been Try'd.

[*Enter* SIR SAMPSON, MRS. FRAIL, MISS PRUE, *and* SERVANT.]

SIR SAMPSON: Is *Ben* come? Odso, my Son *Ben* come? Odd, I'm glad on't:
Where is he? I long to see him. Now, Mrs. *Frail*, you shall see my Son
Ben – Body o'me, he's the Hopes of my Family – I han't seen him these
Three Years – I warrant he's grown – Call him in, bid him make haste –
I'm ready to cry for Joy.   [*Exit* SERVANT.]

MRS. FRAIL: Now Miss, you shall see your Husband.

MISS PRUE: [*aside to* MRS. FRAIL.] Pish, he shall be none of my Husband.

MRS. FRAIL: Hush: Well he shan't, leave that to me – I'll beckon Mr. *Tattle* to
us.

ANGELICA: Won't you stay and see your Brother?

VALENTINE: We are the Twin-Stars, and cannot shine in one Sphere: when he
Rises I must set – Besides, if I shou'd stay, I don't know but my Father
in good Nature may press me to the immediate Signing the Deed of
Conveyance of my Estate, and I'll defer it as long as I can – Well, you'll
come to a Resolution.

ANGELICA: I can't. Resolution must come to me, or I shall never have one.

SCANDAL: Come, *Valentine*, I'll go with you; I've something in my Head to
communicate to you.   [*Exit* VALENTINE *and* SCANDAL.]

SIR SAMPSON: What, is my Son *Valentine* gone? What, is he sneak'd off, and
would not see his Brother? There's an Unnatural Whelp! There's an
ill-natur'd Dog! What, were you here too, Madam, and could not keep
him! Cou'd neither Love, nor Duty, nor Natural Affection oblige him.
Odsbud, Madam, have no more to say to him; he is not worth your
Consideration. The Rogue has not a Drachm of Generous Love about
him: All Interest, all Interest; he's an undone Scoundrel, and courts your
Estate: Body o' me, he does not care a Doit[2] for your Person.

ANGELICA: I'm pretty even with him, Sir *Sampson*; for if ever I cou'd have

1. Baffled.
2. A Dutch coin of no value.

lik'd any thing in him, it shou'd have been his Estate too: But since that's gone, the Bait's off; and the naked Hook appears.

SIR SAMPSON: Odsbud, well spoken; and you are a Wiser Woman than I thought you were: For most young Women now-a-days are to be tempted with a naked Hook.

ANGELICA: If I marry, Sir *Sampson*, I'm for a good Estate with any Man, and for any Man with a good Estate: Therefore if I were obliged to make a Choice, I declare I'd rather have you than your Son.

SIR SAMPSON: Faith and Troth you're a wise Woman, and I'm glad to hear you say so; I was afraid you were in Love with the Reprobate; Odd, I was sorry for you with all my Heart: Hang him, Mungrel; cast him off; you shall see the Rogue shew himself and make Love to some desponding *Cadua*[1] of Fourscore for Sustenance. Odd, I love to see a young Spendthrift forc'd to cling to an Old Woman for Support, like Ivy round a dead Oak: Faith I do; I love to see 'em hug and cotten together, like Down upon a Thistle.

[*Enter* BEN. LEGEND *and* SERVANT.]

BEN: Where's Father?

SERVANT: There, Sir, his back's toward you.

SIR SAMPSON: My Son *Ben*! bless thee my dear Boy; body o' me, thou art heartily welcome.

BEN: Thank you Father, and I'm glad to see you.

SIR SAMPSON: Odsbud, and I'm glad to see thee, kiss me Boy, kiss me again and again, dear *Ben*.   [*Kisses him*.]

BEN: So, so, enough Father – Mess, I'de rather kiss these Gentlewomen.

SIR SAMPSON: And so thou shalt, – Mrs. *Angelica*, my Son *Ben*.

BEN: Forsooth an you please – [*Salutes her*.] Nay Mistress, I'm not for dropping Anchor here; About Ship I' faith –   [*Kisses* MRS. FRAIL.]
Nay, and you too, my little Cock-boat – so –   [*Kisses* MISS PRUE.]

TATTLE: Sir, you're welcome a-shore.

BEN: Thank you, thank you Friend.

SIR SAMPSON: Thou hast been many a weary League *Ben*, since I saw thee.

BEN: Ey, ey, been! Been far enough, an that be all – well Father, and how do all at home? How do's Brother *Dick*, and Brother *Val*?

SIR SAMPSON: *Dick*, body o' me, *Dick* has been dead these two Years; I writ you word, when you were at *Legorne*.[2]

BEN: Mess, and that's true: marry I had forgot. *Dick's* dead as you say – well, and how? I have a many Questions to ask you; well, you be'nt Marry'd again, Father, be you?

1. An off-putting, lecherous old woman.
2. Livorno, on the north-west coast of Italy.

SIR SAMPSON: No, I intend you shall Marry, *Ben*; I would not Marry for thy sake.

BEN: Nay, what do's that signifie ? – an you Marry again – Why then, I'll go to Sea again, so there's one for t'other, an that be all – Pray don't let me be your hindrance; e'en Marry a God's Name an the wind sit that way. As for my part, may-hap I have no mind to Marry.

MRS. FRAIL: That wou'd be pity, such a Handsome Young Gentleman.

BEN: Handsome! he, he, he, nay forsooth, an you be for Joking, I'll Joke with you, for I love my jest, an the Ship were sinking, as we sayn at Sea. But I'll tell you why I don't much stand towards Matrimonie. I love to roam about from Port to Port, and from Land to Land: I could never abide to be Portbound as we call it: Now a man that is marry'd, has as it were, d'ee see, his feet in the Bilboes,[1] and may hap may'nt get 'em out again when he wou'd.

SIR SAMPSON: *Ben's* a Wagg.

BEN: A man that is marri'd, d'ee see, is no more like another man, than a Galley-slave is like one of us free Sailors, he is chain'd to an Oar all his life; and may-hap forc'd to tug a leaky Vessel into the Bargain.

SIR SAMPSON: A very Wag, *Ben's* a very Wag; only a little rough, he wants a little Polishing.

MRS. FRAIL: Not at all; I like his humour mightily, it's plain and honest, I shou'd like such a humour in a Husband extreamly.

BEN: Say'n you so forsooth? Marry and I shou'd like such a handsome Gentlewoman for a Bed-fellow hugely, how say you Mistress, wou'd you like going to Sea? Mess you're a tight vessel, and well rigg'd, an you were but as well Mann'd.

MRS. FRAIL: I shou'd not doubt that, if you were Master of me.

BEN: But I'll tell you one thing, an you come to Sea in a high Wind, or that Lady. – You mayn't carry so much Sail o' your head[2] – Top and Top-gallant by the Mess.[3]

MRS. FRAIL: No, why so?

BEN: Why an you do, You may run the risk to be overset, and then you'll carry your Keels above Water, he, he, he.

ANGELICA: I swear, Mr. *Benjamin* is the verriest Wag in nature; an absolute Sea-wit.

SIR SAMPSON: Nay, *Ben* has Parts, but as I told you before, they want a little Polishing: You must not take any thing ill Madam.

BEN: No, I hope the Gentlewoman is not angry; I mean all in good part: For

1. Ship's irons.
2. A reference to the *fontange* head-dress fashionable at the time: a structure of stiff frills of linen and lace, wired up to a considerable height, and in the shape of a half-closed fan.
3. Short for topsail and topgallant sail, i.e. under full sail.

if I give a Jest, I'll take a Jest: And so forsooth you may be as free with me.

ANGELICA: I thank you, Sir, I am not at all offended; – but methinks Sir *Sampson*, You shou'd leave him alone with his Mistress. Mr. *Tattle*, we must not hinder Lovers.

TATTLE: Well *Miss*, I have your promise.   [*Aside to* MISS PRUE.]

SIR SAMPSON: Body o' me, Madam, you say true: – Look you *Ben*; this is your Mistress, – Come *Miss*, you must not be shame-fac'd, we'll leave you together.

MISS PRUE: I can't abide to be left alone, mayn't my Cousin stay with me?

SIR SAMPSON: No, no. Come, let's away.

BEN: Look you Father, may-hap the young Woman mayn't take a liking to me. –

SIR SAMPSON: I warrant thee Boy, Come, come, we'll be gone; I'll venture that.
                [*Exeunt all but* BEN *and* MISS PRUE.]

BEN: Come Mistress, will you please to sit down, for an you stand a stern a that'n,[1] we shall never grapple together, – Come, I'll haule a Chair; there, an you please to sit, I'll sit by you.

MISS PRUE: You need not sit so near one, if you have any thing to say, I can hear you farther off; I an't deaf.

BEN: Why that's true as you say, nor I an't dumb, I can be heard as far as another, I'll heave off to please you.   [*Sits further off.*]
An we were a League asunder, I'de undertake to hold Discourse with you, an 'twere not a main high Wind indeed, and full in my Teeth. Look you forsooth, I am as it were, bound for the Land of Matrimony; 'tis a Voyage d'ee see that was none of my seeking, I was commanded by Father, and if you like of it, may-hap I may steer into your Harbour. How say you Mistress? the short of the thing is this, that if you like me, and I like you, we may chance to swing in a Hammock together.

MISS PRUE: I don't know what to say to you, nor I don't care to speak with you at all.

BEN: No, I'm sorry for that. – But pray why are you so scornful?

MISS PRUE: As long as one must not speak one's mind, one had better not speak at all, I think, and truly I won't tell a lie for the matter.

BEN: Nay, You say true in that, it's but a folly to lie: For to speak one thing, and to think just the contrary way; is as it were, to look one way, and to row another. Now, for my part d'ee see, I'm for carrying things above Board, I'm not for keeping any thing under Hatches, – so that if you ben't as willing as I, say so a God's name, there's no harm done; may-hap you may be shame-fac'd, some Maidens tho'f they love a man well enough, yet they don't care to tell'n so to's face: If that's the Case, why silence gives consent.

MISS PRUE: But I'm sure it is not so, for I'll speak sooner than you should

---

1. With your back turned.

believe that; and I'll speak truth, tho' one should always tell a lie to a man; and I don't care, let my Father do what he will; I'm too big to be whipt, so I'll tell you plainly, I don't like you, nor love you at all, nor never will, that's more: So, there's your answer for you; and don't trouble me no more, you ugly thing.

BEN: Look you Young Woman, You may learn to give good words however. I spoke you fair d'ee see, and civil. – As for your Love or your liking, I don't value it of a Rope's end; – And may-hap I like you as little as you do me: – What I said was in Obedience to Father; Gad I fear a Whipping no more than you do, But I tell you one thing, if you shou'd give such Language at Sea, you'd have a Cat o' Nine-tails laid cross your Shoulders. Flesh! who are you? You heard t'other handsome Young Woman speak civilly to me, of her own accord: Whatever you think of your self, Gad I don't think you are any more to compare to her, than a Cann of Small-beer to a Bowl of Punch.

MISS PRUE: Well, and there's a handsome Gentleman, and a fine Gentleman, and a sweet Gentleman, that was here that loves me, and I love him; and if he sees you speak to me any more, he'l thrash your Jacket for you, he will, you great Sea-calf.

BEN: What, do you mean that fair-Weather Spark that was here just now? Will he thrash my Jacket ? – Let'n, – let'n, – But an he comes near me, may-hap I may giv'n a Salt Eel for's Supper, for all that. What do's Father mean to leave me alone as soon as I come home, with such a dirty dowdy. – Sea-calf? I an't Calf enough to lick your Chalk'd face, You Cheese-curd you. – Marry thee! Oons I'll Marry a Lapland-Witch as soon, and live upon selling of contrary Winds, and Wrack'd vessels.

MISS PRUE: I won't be call'd Names, nor I won't be abus'd thus, so I won't. – If I were a man, – [*Crys.*] – You durst not talk at this rate – No you durst not, you stinking Tar-barrel.

[*Enter* MRS. FORESIGHT, *and* MRS. FRAIL.]

MRS. FORESIGHT: They have quarrel'd just as we cou'd wish.

BEN: Tar-barrel? Let your Sweet-heart there call me so, if he'll take your part, Your *Tom Essence*,[1] and I'll say something to him; Gad I'll lace his Musk-Doublet for him, I'll make him stink; he shall smell more like a Weasel than a Civet-Cat, afore I ha' done with 'en.

MRS. FORESIGHT: Bless me, what's the matter? *Miss*, what do's she cry ? – Mr. *Benjamin*, what have you done to her?

BEN: Let her cry: The more she cries, the less she'll – she has been gathering foul weather in her Mouth, and now it rains out at her Eyes.

MRS. FORESIGHT: Come, *Miss*, come along with me, and tell me, poor Child.

MRS. FRAIL: Lord, what shall we do, there's my Brother *Foresight*, and Sir *Sampson* coming. Sister, do you take *Miss* down into the Parlour, and I'll

1. A comedy by Tom Rawlins, based on Molière.

carry Mr. *Benjamin* into my Chamber, for they must not know that they are fall'n out – Come, Sir, will you venture your self with me?

[*Looks kindly on Him.*]

BEN: Venture, *Mess*, and that I will, tho' 'twere to Sea in a Storm. [*Exeunt.*]

[*Enter* SIR SAMPSON *and* FORESIGHT.]

SIR SAMPSON: I left 'em together here; What are they gone? *Ben's* a brisk Boy: He has got her into a Corner, Father's own Son, faith, he'll touzle her, and mouzle her: The Rogue's sharp set, coming from Sea, if he should not stay for saying Grace, old *Foresight*, but fall too without the help of a Parson, ha? Odd if he should I cou'd not be angry with him; twould be but like me, *A Chip of the Old Block*. Ha! thou'rt melancholly old Prognostication; As melancholly as if thou hadst spilt the Salt, or par'd thy Nails of a Sunday: – Come, Cheer up, look about thee: Look up old Star-Gazer. Now is he poring upon the Ground for a crooked Pin, or an old Horse-nail, with the head towards him.

FORESIGHT: Sir *Sampson*, we'll have the Wedding to morrow morning.

SIR SAMPSON: With all my Heart.

FORESIGHT: At Ten a Clock, punctually at Ten.

SIR SAMPSON: To a Minute, to a Second; thou shall set thy Watch, and the Bridegroom shall observe its Motions; they shall be married to a Minute, go to Bed to a Minute; and when the Alarm strikes, they shall keep time like the Figures of St. *Dunstan's* Clock,[1] and *Consummatum est* shall ring all over the Parish. [*Enter* SCANDAL.]

SCANDAL: Sir *Sampson*, sad News.

FORESIGHT: Bless us!

SIR SAMPSON: Why, what's the matter?

SCANDAL: Can't you guess at what ought to afflict you and him, and all of us, more than any thing else?

SIR SAMPSON: Body o' me, I don't know any universal Grievance, but a new Tax, and the loss of the Canary Fleet.[2] Without Popery shou'd be landed in the *West*,[3] or the *French* Fleet were at Anchor at *Blackwall*.

SCANDAL: No. Undoubtedly Mr. *Foresight* knew all this, and might have prevented it.

FORESIGHT: 'Tis no Earthquake!

SCANDAL: No, not yet; nor Whirlwind. But we don't know what it may come to – But it has had a Consequence already that touches us all.

SIR SAMPSON: Why, body o' me, out with't.

SCANDAL: Something has appear'd to your Son *Valentine* – He's gone to Bed upon't, and very ill – He speaks little, yet says he has a World to say.

1. The quarter-jacks.
2. A reference to the British fleet patrolling the coasts of Spain and Africa.
3. King James II.

Asks for his Father and the Wise *Foresight*; talks of *Raymond Lully*,[1] and the Ghost of *Lilly*.[2] He has Secrets to impart I suppose to you two. I can get nothing out of him but Sighs. He desires he may see you in the Morning, but would not be disturb'd to Night, because he has some Business to do in a Dream.

SIR SAMPSON: Hoity toity, What have I to do with his Dreams or his Divination – Body o' me, this is a Trick to defer Signing the Conveyance. I warrant the Devil will tell him in a Dream, that he must not part with his Estate: But I'll bring him a Parson to tell him, that the Devil's a Liar – Or if that won't do, I'll bring a Lawyer that shall out-lie the Devil. And so I'll try whether my Black-Guard or his shall get the better of the Day.   [*Exit.*]

SCANDAL: Alas, Mr. *Foresight*, I'm afraid all is not right – You are a Wise Man, and a Conscientious Man; a Searcher into Obscurity and Futurity; and if you commit an Error, it is with a great deal of Consideration, and Discretion, and Caution.

FORESIGHT: Ah, good Mr. *Scandal* –

SCANDAL: Nay, nay, 'tis manifest; I do not flatter you – But Sir *Sampson* is hasty, very hasty; – I'm afraid he is not scrupulous enough, Mr. *Foresight* – He has been wicked, and Heav'n grant he may mean well in his Affair with you – But my Mind gives me, these things cannot be wholly insignificant. You are wise, and shou'd not be over-reach'd, methinks you shou'd not –

FORESIGHT: Alas Mr. *Scandal* – *Humanum est errare*.

SCANDAL: You say true, Man will err; meer Man will err – but you are something more – There have been wise Men; but they were such as you – Men who consulted the Stars, and were Observers of Omens – *Solomon* was wise, but how? – by his Judgment in Astrology – So says *Pineda*[3] in his Third Book and Eighth Chapter –

FORESIGHT: You are learn'd, Mr. *Scandal* –

SCANDAL: A Trifler – but a Lover of Art – And the Wise Men of the East ow'd their Instruction to a Star, which is rightly observ'd by *Gregory* the Great[4] in favour of Astrology! And *Albertus Magnus*[5] makes it the most valuable Science, Because, says he, it teaches us to consider the Causation of Causes, in the Causes of things.

FORESIGHT: I protest I honour you, Mr. *Scandal* – I did not think you had been read in these matters – Few Young Men are inclin'd –

SCANDAL: I thank my Stars that have inclin'd me – But I fear this Marriage and making over this Estate, this transferring of a rightful Inheritance,

---

1. A Franciscan philosopher of the thirteenth century.
2. A well-known English astrologer.
3. A Spanish Jesuit.
4. A sixth-century pope.
5. A philosopher who taught Aquinas but who also valued astrology

will bring Judgments upon us. I prophesie it, and I wou'd not have the Fate of *Cassandra*, not to be believ'd. *Valentine* is disturb'd, what can be the Cause of that? And Sir *Sampson* is hurry'd on by an unusual Violence – I fear he does not act wholly from himself; methinks he does not look as he used to do.

FORESIGHT: He was always of an impetuous Nature – But as to this marriage I have consulted the Stars; and all Appearances are prosperous –

SCANDAL: Come, come, Mr. *Foresight*, let not the Prospect of Worldly Lucre carry you beyond your Judgment, nor against your Conscience – You are not satisfy'd that you act justly.

FORESIGHT: How!

SCANDAL: You are not satisfy'd, I say – I am loath to discourage you – But it is palpable that you are not satisfy'd.

FORESIGHT: How does it appear, Mr. *Scandal*? I think I am very well satisfy'd.

SCANDAL: Either you suffer your self to deceive your self; or you do not know your self.

FORESIGHT: Pray explain your self.

SCANDAL: Do you sleep well o'nights?

FORESIGHT: Very well.

SCANDAL: Are you certain? You do not look so.

FORESIGHT: I am in Health, I think.

SCANDAL: So was *Valentine* this Morning; and look'd just so.

FORESIGHT: How! Am I alter'd any way? I don't perceive it.

SCANDAL: That may be, but your Beard is longer than it was two Hours ago.

FORESIGHT: Indeed! bless me.

[*Enter* MRS. FORESIGHT.]

MRS. FORESIGHT: Husband, will you go to Bed? It's Ten a Clock. Mr. *Scandal*, your Servant –

SCANDAL: Pox on her, she has interrupted my Design – But I must work her into the Project. You keep early Hours, Madam.

MRS. FORESIGHT: Mr. *Foresight* is punctual, we sit up after him.

FORESIGHT: My Dear, pray lend me your Glass, your little Looking-glass.

SCANDAL: Pray lend it him, Madam – I'll tell you the reason. [*She gives him the Glass:* SCANDAL *and she whisper*.] My Passion for you is grown so violent – that I am no longer Master of my self – I was interrupted in the morning, when you had Charity enough to give me your Attention, and I had Hopes of finding another opportunity of explaining my self to you – but was disappointed all this day; and the Uneasiness that has attended me ever since, brings me now hither at this unseasonable hour –

MRS. FORESIGHT: Was there ever such Impudence, to make Love to me before my Husband's Face? I'll Swear I'll tell him.

SCANDAL: Do, I'll dye a Martyr, rather than disclaim my Passion. But come a little farther this way, and I'll tell you what Project I had to get him out of the way; that I might have an opportunity of waiting upon you.

[*Whisper.*]

FORESIGHT: [*looking in the Glass.*] I do not see any Revolution here; – Methinks I look with a serene and benign aspect – pale, a little pale – but the Roses of these Cheeks have been gather'd many Years ; – ha! I do not like that suddain flushing – gone already! – hem, hem, hem! faintish. My Heart is pretty good; yet it beats; and my Pulses ha! – I have none – Mercy on me – hum – Yes, here they are – Gallop, gallop, gallop, gallop, gallop, gallop, hey! Whither will they hurry me ? – Now they're gone again – And now I'm faint again; and pale again, and hem! and my hem! – breath, hem! – grows short; hem! hem! he, he, hem!

SCANDAL: It takes, pursue it in the name of Love and Pleasure.

MRS. FORESIGHT: How do you do, Mr. *Foresight*?

FORESIGHT: Hum, not so well as I thought I was. Lend me your Hand.

SCANDAL: Look you there now – Your Lady says your Sleep has been unquiet of late.

FORESIGHT: Very likely.

MRS. FORESIGHT: O, mighty restless, but I was afraid to tell him so – He has been subject to Talking and Starting.

SCANDAL: And did not use to be so.

MRS. FORESIGHT: Never, never; till within these three Nights; I cannot say that he has once broken my Rest, since we have been Marry'd.

FORESIGHT: I will go to Bed.

SCANDAL: Do so, Mr. *Foresight*, and say your Pray'rs; – He looks better than he did.

MRS. FORESIGHT: Nurse, Nurse!   [*Calls.*]

FORESIGHT: Do you think so, Mr. *Scandal*?

SCANDAL: Yes, yes, I hope this will be gone by Morning, taking it in time –

FORESIGHT: I hope so.

[*Enter* NURSE.]

MRS. FORESIGHT: Nurse; your Master is not well; put him to Bed.

SCANDAL: I hope you will be able to see *Valentine* in the Morning, – you had best take a little Diacodion[1] and Cowslip water,[2] and lye upon your back, may be you may dream.

FORESIGHT: I thank you Mr. *Scandal*, I will – Nurse, let me have a Watch-light, and lay the Crums of Comfort[3] by me. –

NURSE: Yes, Sir.

FORESIGHT: And – hem, hem! I am very faint. –

SCANDAL: No, no, you look much better.

1. A narcotic syrup distilled from poppy-heads.
2. A sleeping cordial made from cowslips.
3. A popular devotional manual.

FORESIGHT: Do I? And d'ye hear – bring me, let me see – within a quarter of Twelve – hem – he, hem! – just upon the turning of the Tide, bring me the Urinal; – And I hope, neither the Lord of my Ascendant, nor the Moon will be combust; and then I may do well.

SCANDAL: I hope so – Leave that to me; I will erect a Scheme; and I hope I shall find both *Sol* and *Venus* in the sixth House.

FORESIGHT: I thank you, Mr. *Scandal*, indeed that wou'd be a great Comfort to me. Hem, hem! good Night.   [*Exit.*]

SCANDAL: Good Night, good Mr. *Foresight*; – and I hope *Mars* and *Venus* will be in Conjunction; – while your Wife and I are together.

MRS. FORESIGHT: Well; and what use do you hope to make of this Project? You don't think, that you are ever like to succeed in your design upon me?

SCANDAL: Yes, Faith I do; I have a better Opinion both of you and my self than to despair.

MRS. FORESIGHT: Did you ever hear such a Toad – heark'ee Devil; do you think any Woman Honest?

SCANDAL: Yes, several, very honest; – they'll cheat a little at Cards, sometimes, but that's nothing.

MRS. FORESIGHT: Pshaw! but Vertuous, I mean.

SCANDAL: Yes, Faith, I believe some Women are Vertuous too; but 'tis as I believe some Men are Valiant, thro' fear – For why shou'd a Man court Danger, or a Woman shun Pleasure?

MRS. FORESIGHT: O Monstrous! What are Conscience and Honour?

SCANDAL: Why, Honour is a publick Enemy; and Conscience a Domestick Thief; and he that wou'd secure his Pleasure, must pay a Tribute to one, and go halves with the t'other. As for Honour, that you have secur'd, for you have purchas'd a perpetual opportunity for Pleasure.

MRS. FORESIGHT: An Opportunity for Pleasure!

SCANDAL: Aye, your Husband, a Husband is an opportunity for Pleasure, so you have taken care of Honour, and 'tis the least I can do to take care of Conscience.

MRS. FORESIGHT: And so you think we are free for one another?

SCANDAL: Yes Faith, I think so; I love to speak my mind.

MRS. FORESIGHT: Why then I'll speak my mind. Now as to this Affair between you and me. Here you make love to me; why, I'll confess it does not displease me. Your Person is well enough, and your Understanding is not a-miss.

SCANDAL: I have no great Opinion of my self; yet I think, I'm neither Deform'd, nor a Fool.

MRS. FORESIGHT: But you have a Villanous Character; you are a Libertine in Speech, as well as Practice.

SCANDAL: Come, I know what you wou'd say, – you think it more dangerous to be seen in Conversation with me, than to allow some other Men the last Favour; you mistake, the liberty I take in Talking, is purely affected, for the Service of your Sex. He that first cries out stop Thief, is often he

that has stolen the Treasure. I am a Jugler, that act by Confederacy; and
if you please, we'll put a Trick upon the world.

MRS. FORESIGHT: Aye; but you are such an universal Jugler, – that I'm afraid
you have a great many Confederates.

SCANDAL: Faith, I'm sound.

MRS. FORESIGHT: O, fie – I'll Swear you're Impudent.

SCANDAL: I'll Swear you're Handsome.

MRS. FORESIGHT: Pish, you'd tell me so, tho' you did not think so.

SCANDAL: And you'd think so, tho' I should not tell you so: And now I think
we know one another pretty well.

MRS. FORESIGHT: O Lord, who's here?

[*Enter* MRS. FRAIL, *and* BEN.]

BEN: Mess, I love to speak my mind – Father has nothing to do with me –
Nay, I can't say that neither; he has something to do with me. But what
do's that signifie? If so be, that I ben't minded to be steer'd by him; 'tis
as tho'f he should strive against Wind and Tyde.

MRS. FRAIL: Aye, but my Dear, we must keep it secret, till the Estate be setled;
for you know, Marrying without an Estate, is like Sailing in a Ship
without Ballast.

BEN: He, he, he; why that's true; just so for all the World it is indeed, as like
as two Cable Ropes.

MRS. FRAIL: And tho' I have a good Portion;[1] you know one wou'd not
venture all in one bottom.

BEN: Why that's true again; for may-hap one bottom may spring a Leak. You
have hit it indeed, Mess you've nick'd the Channel.

MRS. FRAIL: Well, but if you shou'd forsake me after all, you'd break my
Heart.

BEN: Break your Heart? I'de rather the *Mary-gold* shou'd break her Cable in
a storm, as well as I love her. Flesh, you don't think I'm false-hearted,
like a Land-man. A Sailer will be honest, tho'f may-hap he has never a
Penny of Mony in his Pocket – May-hap I may not have so fair a Face,
as a Citizen or a Courtier; but for all that, I've as good Blood in my
Veins, and a Heart as sound as a Bisket.

MRS. FRAIL: And will you love me always?

BEN: Nay, an I love once, I'll stick like pitch; I'll tell you that. Come, I'll sing
you a Song of a Sailor.

MRS. FRAIL: Hold, there's my Sister, I'll call her to hear it.

MRS. FORESIGHT: Well; I won't go to Bed to my Husband to Night; because I'll
retire to my own Chamber, and think of what you have said.

SCANDAL: Well; You'll give me leave to wait upon you to your Chamber-
door; and leave you my last Instructions?

1. Dowry.

MRS. FORESIGHT: Hold, here's my Sister coming toward us.

MRS. FRAIL: If it won't interrupt you, I'll entertain you with a Song.

BEN: The Song was made upon one of our Ships-Crew's Wife; our Boat-swain made the Song, may-hap you may know her, Sir. Before she was Marry'd, she was call'd buxom *Joan* of *Deptford*.

SCANDAL: I have heard of her.   [BEN *Sings.*]

BALLAD
Set by Mr. John Eccles

A Souldier and a Sailor,
A Tinker, and a Tailor,
Had once a doubtful strife, Sir,
To make a Maid a Wife, Sir,
Whose Name was Buxom Joan.
For now the time was ended,
When she no more intended,
To lick her Lips at Men, Sir,
And gnaw the Sheets in vain, Sir,
And lie o' Nights alone.

The Souldier Swore like Thunder,
He lov'd her more than Plunder;
And shew'd her many a Scar, Sir,
That he had brought from far, Sir.
With Fighting for her sake.
The Tailor thought to please her,
With off'ring her his Measure.
The Tinker too with Mettle,
Said he could mend her Kettle,
And stop up ev'ry leak.

But while these three were prating,
The Sailor slily waiting,
Thought if it came about, Sir,
That they should all fall out, Sir:
He then might play his part.
And just e'en as he meant, Sir,
To Loggerheads they went, Sir,
And then he let fly at her,
A shot 'twixt wind and water,
That won this Fair Maids Heart.

BEN: If some of our Crew that came to see me, are not gone; you shall see, that we Sailors can Dance sometimes, as well as other Folks. [*Whistles.*]

I warrant that brings 'em, an' they be within hearing.

[*Enter* SEAMEN.]

Oh here they be – And Fiddles along with 'em; come, my Lads, let's have a round, and I'll make one. [*Dance.*]
We're merry Folk, we Sailors, we han't much to care for. Thus we live at Sea; eat Bisket, and drink Flip;[1] put on a clean Shirt once a Quarter – Come home and lie with our Landladies once a Year, get rid of a little Mony; and then put off with the next fair wind. How de'e like us?
MRS. FRAIL: O' you are the happiest, merriest Men alive.
MRS. FORESIGHT: We're beholding to Mr. *Benjamin* for this Entertainment. I believe it's late.
BEN: Why, forsooth, an you think so, you had best go to Bed. For my part, I mean to toss a Can, and remember my Sweet-Heart, a-fore I turn in; may-hap I may dream of her.
MRS. FORESIGHT: Mr. *Scandal*, you had best go to Bed and Dream too.
SCANDAL: Why Faith, I have a good lively Imagination; and can Dream as much to the purpose as another, if I set about it: But Dreaming is the poor retreat of a lazy, hopeless, and imperfect Lover; 'tis the last glimpse of Love to worn-out Sinners, and the faint dawning of a Bliss to wishing Girls, and growing Boys.

> There's nought but willing, waking Love, that can
> Make Blest the Ripen'd Maid, and Finish'd Man. [*Exeunt.*]

Act IV, Scene I

[*Valentine's Lodging.*
Enter SCANDAL, *and* JEREMY.]

SCANDAL: Well, Is your Master ready; do's he look madly, and talk madly?
JEREMY: Yes, Sir; you need make no great doubt of that; he that was so near turning Poet yesterday morning, can't be much to seek in playing the Madman to day.
SCANDAL: Would he have *Angelica* acquainted with the Reason of his design?
JEREMY: No, Sir, not yet; – He has a mind to try, whether his playing the Madman, won't make her play the Fool, and fall in Love with him; or at least own that she has lov'd him all this while, and conceal'd it.
SCANDAL: I saw her take Coach just now with her Maid; and think I heard her bid the Coach-man drive hither.

1. A mixture of weak beer and sweetened brandy.

JEREMY: Like enough, Sir, for I told her Maid this morning, my Master was run stark mad only for Love of her Mistress; I hear a Coach stop; if it should be she, Sir, I believe he would not see her, till he hears how she takes it.

SCANDAL: Well, I'll try her – 'tis she, here she comes.

[*Enter* ANGELICA *with* JENNY.]

ANGELICA: Mr. *Scandal*, I suppose you don't think it a Novelty, to see a Woman visit a Man at his own Lodgings in a morning.

SCANDAL: Not upon a kind occasion, Madam. But when a Lady comes Tyrannically to insult a ruin'd Lover, and make manifest the cruel Triumphs of her Beauty; the barbarity of it, something surprizes me.

ANGELICA: I don't like Raillery from a serious Face – pray tell me what is the matter.

JEREMY: No strange matter, Madam; my Master's mad, that's all: I suppose your Ladyship has thought him so a great while.

ANGELICA: How d'ye mean, mad?

JEREMY: Why faith, Madam, he's mad for want of his Wits, just as he was poor for want of Money; his Head is e'en as light as his Pockets; and any body that has a mind to a bad Bargain, can't do better than to beg him for his Estate.

ANGELICA: If you speak Truth, your endeavouring at Wit is very unseasonable –

SCANDAL: She's concern'd, and loves him. [*Aside.*]

ANGELICA: Mr. *Scandal*, you can't think me guilty of so much Inhumanity, as not to be concern'd for a Man I must own my self oblig'd to – pray tell me truth.

SCANDAL: Faith, Madam, I wish telling a Lie would mend the matter. But this is no new effect of an unsuccessful Passion.

ANGELICA: [*aside.*] I know not what to think – Yet I shou'd be vext to have a trick put upon me – May I not see him?

SCANDAL: I'm afraid the Physician is not willing you shou'd see him yet – *Jeremy*, go in and enquire. [*Exit* JEREMY.]

ANGELICA: Ha! I saw him wink and smile – I fancy 'tis a trick – I'll try – I would disguise to all the World a Failing, which I must own to you – I fear my Happiness depends upon the recovery of *Valentine*. Therefore I conjure you, as you are his Friend, and as you have Compassion upon one fearful of Affliction, to tell me what I am to hope for – I cannot speak – But you may tell me, tell me, for you know what I wou'd ask?

SCANDAL: So, this is pretty plain – Be not too much concern'd, Madam; I hope his Condition is not desperate: An Acknowledgment of Love from you, perhaps, may work a Cure; as the fear of your Aversion occasion'd his Distemper.

ANGELICA: [*aside.*] Say you so; nay, then I'm convinc'd: And if I don't play

Trick for Trick, may I never taste the Pleasure of Revenge – Acknowledgment of Love! I find you have mistaken my Compassion, and think
me guilty of a Weakness I am a Stranger to. But I have too much Sincerity to deceive you, and too much Charity to suffer him to be deluded
with vain Hopes. Good Nature and Humanity oblige me to be
concern'd for him; but to Love is neither in my Power nor Inclination;
and if he can't be cur'd without I suck the Poyson from his Wounds, I'm
afraid he won't recover his Senses till I lose mine.

SCANDAL: Hey, brave Woman, I' faith – Won't you see him then, if he desire
it?

ANGELICA: What signifie a Madman's Desires? Besides, 'twou'd make me
uneasie – If I don't see him, perhaps my Concern for him may lessen –
If I forget him, 'tis no more than he has done by himself: and now the
Surprize is over, methinks I am not half so sorry for him as I was –

SCANDAL: So, faith good Nature works a-pace; you were confessing just now
an Obligation to his Love.

ANGELICA: But I have consider'd that Passions are unreasonable and
involuntary; if he loves, he can't help it; and if I don't love, I can't help
it; no more than he can help his being a Man, or I my being a Woman;
or no more than I can help my want of Inclination to stay longer here –
Come, *Jenny*.   [*Exit* ANGELICA *and* JENNY.]

SCANDAL: Humh! – An admirable Composition, faith, this same Womankind.

[*Enter* JEREMY.]

JEREMY: What, is she gone, Sir?

SCANDAL: Gone; why she was never here, nor any where else; nor I don't
know her if I see her; nor you neither.

JEREMY: Good lack! What's the matter now? Are any more of us to be mad?
Why, Sir, my Master longs to see her; and is almost mad in good earnest,
with the Joyful News of her being here.

SCANDAL: We are all under a mistake – Ask no Questions, for I can't resolve
you; but I'll inform your Master. In the mean time, if our Project succeed
no better with his Father, than it does with his Mistress, he may descend
from his Exaltation of madness into the road of common Sense, and be
content only to be made a Fool with other reasonable People. I hear Sir
Sampson, you know your Cue; I'll to your Master. | [*Exit.*]

[*Enter* SIR SAMPSON LEGEND *with a Lawyer.*]

SIR SAMPSON: D'ye see, Mr. *Buckram*, here's the Paper sign'd with his own
Hand.

BUCKRAM: Good, Sir. And the Conveyance is ready drawn in this Box, if he
be ready to sign and seal.

SIR SAMPSON: Ready, body o' me, he must be ready; his Sham-sickness shan't excuse him – O, here's his Scoundrel. Sirrah, where's your Master?

JEREMY: Ah, Sir, he's quite gone.

SIR SAMPSON: Gone! What, he is not dead?

JEREMY: No, Sir, not dead.

SIR SAMPSON: What, is he gone out of Town, run away, ha! has he trick't me? speak, Varlet.

JEREMY: No, no, Sir; he's safe enough, Sir, an he were but as sound, poor Gentleman. He is indeed here, Sir, and not here, Sir.

SIR SAMPSON: Hey day, Rascal, do you banter me? Sirrah, d'ye banter me – Speak Sirrah, where is he, for I will find him.

JEREMY: Would you could, Sir; for he has lost himself. Indeed, Sir, I have almost broke my Heart about him – I can't refrain Tears when I think of him, Sir; I'm as melancholy for him as a Passing-Bell, Sir; or a Horse in a Pound.

SIR SAMPSON: A Pox confound your Similitudes, Sir – Speak to be understood, and tell me in plain Terms what the matter is with him, or I'll crack your Fools Skull.

JEREMY: Ah, you've hit it, Sir; that's the matter with him, Sir; his Skull's crack'd, poor Gentleman; he's stark mad, Sir.

SIR SAMPSON: Mad!

BUCKRAM: What, is he *Non Compos*?

JEREMY: Quite *Non Compos*, Sir.

BUCKRAM: Why then all's obliterated, Sir *Sampson*, if he be *Non Compos mentis*, his Act and Deed will be of no effect, it is not good in Law.

SIR SAMPSON: Oo'ns, I won't believe it; let me see him, Sir – Mad, I'll make him find his Senses.

JEREMY: Mr. *Scandal* is with him, Sir; I'll knock at the Door.

[*Goes to the Scene, which opens and discovers* VALENTINE *upon a Couch disorderly dress'd,* SCANDAL *by him.*][1]

SIR SAMPSON: How now, what's here to do? –

VALENTINE: [*starting.*] Ha! who's that?

SCANDAL: For Heav'ns sake softly, Sir, and gently; don't provoke him.

VALENTINE: Answer me; Who is that? and that?

SIR SAMPSON: Gads bobs, does he not know me? Is he mischievous? I'll speak gently – *Val, Val,* do'st thou not know me, Boy? Not know thy own Father, *Val*! I am thy own Father, and this is honest *Brief Buckram* the Lawyer.

VALENTINE: It may be so – I did not know you – the World is full – There are People that we do know, and People that we do not know; and yet the Sun shines upon all alike – There are Fathers that have many Children;

1. A painted shutter opens to reveal Valentine on a couch.

and there are Children that have many Fathers – 'tis strange! But I am
Truth, and come to give the World the Lie.

SIR SAMPSON: Body o' me, I know not what to say to him.

VALENTINE: Why does that Lawyer wear black? – Does he carry his
Conscience withoutside? – Lawyer, what art thou? Dost thou know me?

BUCKRAM: O Lord, what must I say? – Yes, Sir.

VALENTINE: Thou liest, for I am Truth. 'Tis hard I cannot get a Livelyhood
amongst you. I have been sworn out of *Westminster-Hall* [1] the first Day
of every Term – Let me see – No matter how long – But I'll tell you one
thing; it's a Question that would puzzle an Arithmetician, if you should
ask him, whether the Bible saves more Souls in *Westminster-Abby*, or
damns more in *Westminster Hall*: For my part, I am Truth, and can't tell;
I have very few Acquaintance.

SIR SAMPSON: Body o' me, he talks sensibly in his madness – Has he no
Intervals?

JEREMY: Very short, Sir.

BUCKRAM: Sir, I can do you no Service while he's in this Condition: Here's
your Paper, Sir – he may do me a mischief if I stay – The Conveyance is
ready, Sir. If he recover his Senses.   [*Exit*.]

SIR SAMPSON: Hold, hold, don't you go yet.

SCANDAL: You'd better let him go, Sir; and send for him if there be occasion;
for I fancy his Presence provokes him more.

VALENTINE: Is the Lawyer gone? 'tis well, then we may drink about without
going together by the Ears:[2] – heigh ho! What a Clock is't? My Father
here! Your Blessing, Sir?

SIR SAMPSON: He recovers – bless thee, *Val* – How do'st thou do, Boy?

VALENTINE: Thank you, Sir, pretty well – I have been a little out of Order;
won't you please to sit, Sir?

SIR SAMPSON: Ay boy – Come, thou shalt sit down by me.

VALENTINE: Sir, 'tis my Duty to wait.

SIR SAMPSON: No, no, come, come, sit you down, honest *Val*: How do'st thou
do? let me feel thy Pulse – Oh, pretty well now, *Val*: Body o' me, I was
sorry to see thee indisposed: But I'm glad thou'rt better, honest *Val*.

VALENTINE: I thank you, Sir.

SCANDAL: [*aside*.] Miracle! the Monster grows loving.

SIR SAMPSON: Let me feel thy Hand again, *Val*: it does not shake – I believe
thou can'st write, *Val*: Ha, boy? Thou can'st write thy Name, *Val*? –
Jeremy, step and overtake Mr. *Buckram*, bid him make haste back with
the Conveyance – quick – quick   [*In Whisper to* JEREMY.]
                                                        [*Exit* JEREMY.]

SCANDAL: [*aside*.] That ever I shou'd suspect such a Heathen of any Remorse!

1. The principal law-courts.
2. Quarrelling.

SIR SAMPSON: Do'st thou know this Paper, *Val*: I know thou'rt honest, and wilt perform Articles.   [*Shews him the Paper, but holds it out of his reach.*]

VALENTINE: Pray let me see it, Sir. You hold it so far off; that I can't tell whether I know it or no.

SIR SAMPSON: See it, boy? Aye, aye, why thou do'st see it – 'tis thy own Hand, *Val*. Why, let me see, I can read it as plain as can be: Look you here [*reads*] *The Condition of this Obligation* – Look you, as plain as can be, so it begins – And then at the bottom – *As witness my Hand*, VALENTINE LEGEND, in great Letters. Why, 'tis as plain as the Nose in one's Face: What, are my Eyes better than thine? I believe I can read it farther off yet – let me see.   [*Stretches his Arm as far as he can.*]

VALENTINE: Will you please to let me hold it, Sir?

SIR SAMPSON: Let thee hold it, say'st thou – Aye, with all my Heart – What matter is it who holds it? What need any body hold it? – I'll put it up in my Pocket, *Val*: And then no body need hold it [*puts the Paper in his Pocket*]. There *Val*: it's safe enough, Boy – But thou shalt have it as soon as thou hast set thy Hand to another Paper, little *Val*.

[*Re-enter* JEREMY *with* BUCKRAM.]

VALENTINE: What, is my bad Genius here again! Oh no, 'tis the Lawyer with an itching Palm; and he's come to be scratch'd – My Nails are not long enough – Let me have a Pair of Red hot Tongues quickly, quickly, and you shall see me act St. *Dunstan*, and lead the Devil by the Nose.

BUCKRAM: O Lord, let me be gone; I'll not venture my self with a Madman.
[*Exit* BUCKRAM.]

VALENTINE: Ha, ha, ha; you need not run so fast, Honesty will not overtake you – Ha, ha, ha, the Rogue found me out to be in *Forma Pauperis* presently.[1]

SIR SAMPSON: Oo'ns! What a vexation is here! I know not what to do, or say, nor which way to go.

VALENTINE: Who's that, that's out of his Way ? – I am Truth, and can set him right – Hearkee, Friend, the straight Road is the worst way you can go – He that follows his Nose always, will very often be led into a Stink. *Probatum est*. But what are you for? Religion or Politicks? There's a couple of Topicks for you, no more like one another than Oyl and Vinegar; and yet those two beaten together by a State-Cook, make Sauce for the whole Nation.

SIR SAMPSON: What the Devil had I to do, ever to beget Sons? Why did I ever marry?

VALENTINE: Because thou wer't a Monster; old Boy: – The two greatest Monsters in the World are a Man and a Woman; what's thy Opinion?

---

1. Exempt from legal costs because of poverty.

SIR SAMPSON: Why, my Opinion is, that those two Monsters join'd together, make yet a greater, that's a Man and his Wife.

VALENTINE: A ha! Old Truepenny, say'st thou so? thou hast nick'd it – But its wonderful strange, *Jeremy*!

JEREMY: What is, Sir?

VALENTINE: That Gray Hairs shou'd cover a Green Head – and I make a Fool of my Father.

[*Enter* FORESIGHT, MRS. FORESIGHT, *and* MRS. FRAIL.]

VALENTINE: What's here! *Erra Pater*?[1] or a bearded Sybil? If Prophecy comes, Truth must give place.   [*Exit with* JEREMY.]

FORESIGHT: What says he? What, did he prophesie? Ha, Sir *Sampson*, bless us! How are we?

SIR SAMPSON: Are we? A Pox o' your Prognostication – Why, we are Fools as we use to be – Oo'ns that you cou'd not foresee that the Moon wou'd predominate, and my Son be mad – Where's your Oppositions, your Trines, and your Quadrates? – What did your *Cardan* and your *Ptolomee* tell you? Your *Messahalah* and your *Longomontanus*,[2] your Harmony of Chiromancy with Astrology. Ah! pox on't, that I that know the World, and Men and Manners, that don't believe a Syllable in the Sky and Stars, and Sun and Almanacks, and Trash, should be directed by a Dreamer, an Omen-hunter, and defer Business in Expectation of a lucky Hour. When, body o' me, there never was a lucky Hour after the first opportunity.
                              [*Exit* SIR SAMPSON.]

FORESIGHT: Ah, Sir *Sampson*, Heav'n help your Head – This is none of your lucky Hour; *Nemo omnibus horis sapit*.[3] What, is he gone, and in contempt of Science! Ill Stars and unconvertible Ignorance attend him.

SCANDAL: You must excuse his Passion, Mr. *Foresight*; for he has been heartily vex'd – His Son is *Non compos mentis*, and thereby incapable of making any Conveyance in Law; so that all his measures are disappointed.

FORESIGHT: Ha! say you so?

MRS. FRAIL: What, has my Sea-Lover lost his Anchor of Hope then?
                              [*Aside to* MRS. FORESIGHT.]

MRS. FORESIGHT: Oh Sister, what will you do with him?

MRS. FRAIL: Do with him, send him to Sea again in the next foul Weather – He's us'd to an inconstant Element, and won't be surpriz'd to see the Tide turn'd.

FORESIGHT: Wherein was I mistaken, not to foresee this?   [*Considers.*]

SCANDAL: Madam, you and I can tell him something else, that he did not foresee, and more particularly relating to his own Fortune.
                              [*Aside to* MRS. FORESIGHT.]

1. An astrologer.
2. Cardan was an Italian, Longomontanus a Danish astrologer.
3. No man is at all times wise and in his perfect wits.

MRS. FORESIGHT: What do you mean? I don't understand you.

SCANDAL: Hush, softly – the Pleasures of last Night, my Dear, too considerable to be forgot so soon.

MRS. FORESIGHT: Last Night! and what wou'd your Impudence infer from last night? last Night was like the Night before, I think.

SCANDAL: 'S'death do you make no difference between me and your Husband?

MRS. FORESIGHT: Not much, – he's superstitious; and you are mad in my opinion.

SCANDAL: You make me mad – You are not serious – Pray recollect your self.

MRS. FORESIGHT: O yes, now I remember, you were very impertinent and impudent, – and would have come to Bed to me.

SCANDAL: And did not?

MRS. FORESIGHT: Did not! with that face can you ask the Question?

SCANDAL: This I have heard of before, but never believ'd. I have been told she had that admirable quality of forgetting to a man's face in the morning, that she had layn with him all night, and denying favours with more impudence, than she cou'd grant 'em. – Madam, I'm your humble Servant, and honour you. – You look pretty well, Mr. *Foresight*; – How did you rest last night?

FORESIGHT: Truly Mr. *Scandal*, I was so taken up with broken Dreams and distracted Visions, that I remember little.

SCANDAL: 'Twas a very forgetting Night. – But would you not talk with *Valentine*, perhaps you may understand him; I'm apt to believe there is something mysterious in his Discourses, and sometimes rather think him inspir'd than mad.

FORESIGHT: You speak with singular good Judgment, Mr. *Scandal*, truly, – I am inclining to your *Turkish* opinion in this matter, and do reverence a man whom the vulgar think mad. Let us go in to him.

MRS. FRAIL: Sister, do you stay with them; I'll find out my Lover, and give him his discharge, and come to you. O' my Conscience, here he comes.

[*Exeunt* FORESIGHT, MRS. FORESIGHT *and* SCANDAL.]

[*Enter* BEN.]

BEN: All mad, I think – Flesh, I believe all the *Calentures*[1] of the Sea are come ashore, for my part.

MRS. FRAIL: Mr. *Benjamin* in Choler!

BEN: No, I'm pleas'd well enough, now I have found you, – Mess, I've had such a Hurricane upon your account yonder. –

MRS. FRAIL: My account, pray what's the matter?

BEN: Why, Father came and found me squabling with yon chitty fac'd thing, as he would have me marry, – so he ask'd what was the matter. – He ask'd in a surly sort of a way – (It seems Brother *Val* is gone mad, and

1. A tropical fever.

so that put'n into a passion; but what did I know that, what's that to me?) – So he ask'd in a surly sort of manner, – and Gad I answer'd 'n as surlily, – What tho'f he be my Father, I an't bound Prentice to 'en: – so faith I told 'n in plain terms, if I were minded to marry, I'de marry to please my self not him; and for the Young Woman that he provided for me, I thought it more fitting for her to learn her Sampler, and make Dirt-pies, than to look after a Husband; for my part I was none of her man. – I had another Voyage to make, let him take it as he will.

MRS. FRAIL: So then you intend to go to Sea again?

BEN: Nay, nay, my mind run upon you, – but I wou'd not tell him so much. – So he said he'd make my heart ake; and if so be that he cou'd get a Woman to his mind, he'd marry himself. Gad, says I, an you play the fool and marry at these years, there's more danger of your head's aking than my heart. – He was woundy angry when I gav'n that wipe. – He had'nt a word to say, and so I left 'n, and the Green Girl together; – May hap the Bee may bite, and he'l marry her himself; with all my heart.

MRS. FRAIL: And were you this undutiful and graceless Wretch to your Father?

BEN: Then why was he graceless first, – if I am undutiful and Graceless, why did he beget me so? I did not get my self.

MRS. FRAIL: O Impiety! how have I been mistaken! what an inhumane merciless Creature have I set my heart upon? O I am happy to have discover'd the Shelves and Quicksands that lurk beneath that faithless smiling face.

BEN: Hey toss! what's the matter now? why you ben't angry, be you?

MRS. FRAIL: O see me no more, – for thou wert born amongst Rocks, suckl'd by Whales, Cradled in a Tempest, and whistled to by Winds; and thou art come forth with Finns and Scales, and three rows of Teeth, a most outragious Fish of prey.

BEN: Lord, Lord, she's mad, poor Young Woman, Love has turn'd her senses, her Brain is quite overset. Well-a-day, how shall I do to set her to rights.

MRS. FRAIL: No, no, I am not mad, Monster, I am wise enough to find you out. – Had'st thou the Impudence to aspire at being a Husband with that stubborn and disobedient temper? – You that know not how to submit to a Father, presume to have a sufficient stock of Duty to undergo a Wife? I should have been finely fobb'd indeed, very finely fobb'd.

BEN: Hearkee forsooth; If so be that you are in your right senses, d'ee see; for ought as I perceive I'm like to be finely fobb'd, – if I have got anger here upon your account, and you are tack'd about already. – What d'ee mean, after all your fair speeches, and stroaking my Cheeks, and Kissing and Hugging, what wou'd you sheer off so? wou'd you, and leave me aground?

MRS. FRAIL: No, I'll leave you a-drift, and go which way you will.

BEN: What, are you false hearted then?

MRS. FRAIL: Only the Wind's chang'd.

BEN: More shame for you, – the Wind's chang'd? – it's an ill Wind blows no body good, – may-hap I have good riddance on you, if these be your Tricks, – What d'ee mean all this while, to make a fool of me?

MRS. FRAIL: Any fool, but a Husband.

BEN: Husband! Gad I wou'd not be your Husband, if you wou'd have me; now I know your mind, tho'f you had your weight in Gold and Jewels, and tho'f I lov'd you never so well.

MRS. FRAIL: Why canst thou love, Porpoise?

BEN: No matter what I can do? don't call Names, – I don't love You so well as to bear that, whatever I did, – I'm glad you shew your self, Mistress: – Let them marry you, as don't know you: Gad I know you too well, by sad experience; – I believe he that marries you will go to Sea in a Hen-peck'd Frigat. – I believe that, Young Woman – and may-hap may come to an Anchor at *Cuckolds-point;*[1] so there's a dash for you, take it as you will, may-hap you may holla after me when I won't come too.

[Exit.]

MRS. FRAIL: Ha, ha, ha, no doubt on't. –   [*Sings.*]
My true Love is gone to Sea. –

[Enter MRS. FORESIGHT.]

O Sister, had you come a minute sooner, you would have seen the Resolution of a Lover, – Honest *Tarr* and I are parted; – and with the same indifference that we met. – O' my life I am half vex'd at the insensibility of a Brute that I despis'd.

MRS. FORESIGHT: What then, he bore it most Heroically?

MRS. FRAIL: Most Tyranically, – for you see he has got the start of me; and I the poor forsaken Maid am left complaining on the Shore. But I'll tell you a hint that he has given me; Sir *Sampson* is enrag'd, and talks desperately of committing Matrimony himself. – If he has a mind to throw himself away, he can't do it more effectually than upon me, if we could bring it about.

MRS. FORESIGHT: Oh hang him old Fox, he's too cunning, besides he hates both you and me. – But I have a project in my head for you, and I have gone a good way towards it. I have almost made a Bargain with *Jeremy*, *Valentine's* man, to sell his Master to us.

MRS. FRAIL: Sell him, how?

MRS. FORESIGHT: *Valentine* raves upon *Angelica*, and took me for her, and *Jeremy* says will take any body for her that he imposes on him. – Now I have promis'd him Mountains; if in one of his mad fits he will bring you to him in her stead, and get you married together, and put to Bed together; and after Consummation, Girl, there's no revoking. And if he should recover his Senses, he'll be glad at least to make you a good

---

1. A spit on the Surrey side of the Thames.

Settlement. – Here they come, stand aside a little, and tell me how you like the design.

[*Enter* VALENTINE, SCANDAL, FORESIGHT, *and* JEREMY.]

SCANDAL: And have you given your Master a hint of their Plot upon him?
[*To* JEREMY.]

JEREMY: Yes, Sir; he says he'll favour it, and mistake her for *Angelica*.

SCANDAL: It may make sport.

FORESIGHT: Mercy on us!

VALENTINE: Husht – Interrupt me not – I'll whisper Prediction to thee, and thou shalt Prophesie; – I am Truth, and can teach thy Tongue a new Trick, – I have told thee what's past, – Now I tell what's to come; – Dost thou know what will happen to morrow? – Answer me not – for I will tell thee. Tomorrow, Knaves will thrive thro' craft, and Fools thro' Fortune; and Honesty will go as it did, Frost-nip't in a Summer suit. Ask me Questions concerning to morrow?

SCANDAL: Ask him, Mr. *Foresight*.

FORESIGHT: Pray what will be done at Court?

VALENTINE: *Scandal* will tell you; – I am Truth, I never come there.

FORESIGHT: In the City?

VALENTINE: Oh, Prayers will be said in empty Churches, at the usual Hours. Yet you will see such Zealous Faces behind Counters, as if Religion were to be sold in every Shop. Oh things will go methodically in the City, the Clocks will strike Twelve at Noon, and the Horn'd Herd Buz in the Exchange at Two. Wives and Husbands will drive distinct Trades, and Care and Pleasure separately Occupy the Family. Coffee-Houses will be full of Smoak and Stratagem. And the cropt Prentice that sweeps his Master's Shop in the morning, may ten to one, dirty his Sheets before Night. But there are two things that you will see very strange; which are Wanton Wives, with their Legs at liberty, and Tame Cuckolds, with Chains about their Necks. But hold, I must examine you before I go further; You look suspiciously. Are you a Husband?

FORESIGHT: I am Married.

VALENTINE: Poor Creature! Is your Wife of *Covent-Garden* Parish?

FORESIGHT: No; St. *Martins* in the Fields.

VALENTINE: Alas, poor Man; his Eyes are sunk, and his Hands shrivell'd; his Legs dwindl'd, and his back bow'd, Pray, pray, for a Metamorphosis – Change thy Shape, and shake off Age; get thee *Medea's* Kettle,[1] and be boil'd a-new, come forth with lab'ring *Callous* Hands, a Chine of Steel, and *Atlas'* Shoulders. Let *Taliacotius*[2] trim the Calves of Twenty Chair-men, and make thee Pedestals to stand erect upon, and look Matrimony

1. To restore youth.
2. A famous Italian surgeon.

in the face. Ha, ha, ha! That a Man shou'd have a Stomach to a Wedding Supper, when the Pidgeons ought rather to be laid to his feet,[1] ha, ha, ha.

FORESIGHT: His Frenzy is very high now, Mr. *Scandal*.

SCANDAL: I believe it is a Spring Tide.

FORESIGHT: Very likely truly; You understand these Matters – Mr. *Scandal*, I shall be very glad to confer with you about these things which he has utter'd. – His Sayings are very Mysterious and Hieroglyphical.

VALENTINE: Oh, why would *Angelica* be absent from my Eyes so long?

JEREMY: She's here, Sir.

MRS. FORESIGHT: Now, Sister.

MRS. FRAIL: O Lord, what must I say?

SCANDAL: Humour him, Madam, by all means.

VALENTINE: Where is she? Oh I see her – she comes, like Riches, Health, and Liberty at once, to a despairing, starving, and abandon'd Wretch. Oh welcome, welcome.

MRS. FRAIL: How de'e you, Sir? Can I serve you?

VALENTINE: Heark'ee; – I have a Secret to tell you – *Endymion* and the Moon shall meet us upon Mount *Latmos*,[2] and we'll be Marry'd in the dead of Night. – But say not a word. *Hymen* shall put his Torch into a dark Lanthorn, that it may be secret; and *Juno* shall give her *Peacock*[3] Poppy-water,[4] that he may fold his Ogling Tail, and *Argos's* hundred Eyes be shut, ha? No body shall know, but *Jeremy*.

MRS. FRAIL: No, no, we'll keep it secret, it shall be done presently.

VALENTINE: The sooner the better – *Jeremy*, come hither – closer – that none may overhear us; – *Jeremy*, I can tell you News; – *Angelica* is turn'd Nun; and I am turning Fryar, and yet we'll Marry one another in spite of the Pope – Get me a Coul and Beads, that I may play my part, – For she'll meet me Two Hours hence in black and white, and a long veil to cover the Project, and we won't see one anothers Faces, till we have done something to be asham'd of; and then we'll blush once for all.

[*Enter* TATTLE, *and* ANGELICA.]

JEREMY: I'll take care, and –

VALENTINE: Whisper.

ANGELICA: Nay, Mr. *Tattle*, If you make Love to me, you spoil my design, for I intended to make you my Confident.

TATTLE: But, Madam, to throw away your Person, such a Person! and such a Fortune, on a Madman!

ANGELICA: I never lov'd him till he was Mad; but don't tell any body so.

1. Supposedly a cure for the plague.
2. Spenser's Latmian shepherd.
3. Referred to in Ovid's *Metamorphoses I*.
4. A dormitive.

SCANDAL: How's this! *Tattle* making Love to *Angelica*

TATTLE: Tell, Madam! alas you don't know me – I have much ado to tell your Ladyship, how long I have been in Love with you – but encourag'd by the impossibility of *Valentine's* making any more Addresses to you, I have ventur'd to declare the very inmost Passion of my Heart. Oh, Madam, look upon us both. There you see the ruins of a poor decay'd Creature – Here, a compleat and lively Figure, with Youth and Health, and all his five Senses in perfection, Madam, and to all this, the most passionate Lover –

ANGELICA: O fie for shame, hold your Tongue, A passionate Lover, and five Senses in perfection! When you are as Mad as *Valentine*, I'll believe you love me, and the maddest shall take me.

VALENTINE: It is enough. Ha! Who's here?

MRS. FRAIL: [*to* JEREMY.] O Lord, her coming will spoil all.

JEREMY: No, no, Madam, he won't know her, if he shou'd, I can perswade him.

VALENTINE: [*whispers.*] *Scandal*, who are all these? Foreigners? If they are, I'll tell you what I think – get away all the Company but *Angelica*, that I may discover my design to her.

SCANDAL: I will, – I have discover'd something of *Tattle*, that is of a piece with Mrs. *Frail*. He Courts *Angelica*, if we cou'd contrive to couple 'em together – Heark'ee – [*Whisper.*]

MRS. FORESIGHT: He won't know you, Cousin, he knows no body.

FORESIGHT: But he knows more than any body, – Oh Neice, he knows things past and to come, and all the profound Secrets of Time.

TATTLE: Look you, Mr. *Foresight*, It is not my way to make many words of Matters, and so I shan't say much, – But in short, de'e see, I will hold you a Hundred Pound now, that I know more Secrets than he.

FORESIGHT: How! I cannot Read that knowledge in your Face, Mr. *Tattle* – Pray, what do you know?

TATTLE: Why de'e think I'll tell you, Sir! Read it in my Face? No, Sir, 'tis written in my Heart. And safer there, Sir, than Letters writ in Juice of Lemon, for no Fire can fetch it out. I am no blab, Sir.

VALENTINE: Acquaint *Jeremy* with it, he may easily bring it about, – They are welcome, and I'll tell 'em so my self. [*To* SCANDAL.] What, do you look strange upon me? – Then I must be plain. [*Coming up to them.*] I am Truth, and hate an Old Acquaintance with a new Face.

[SCANDAL *goes aside with* JEREMY.]

TATTLE: Do you know me, *Valentine*?

VALENTINE: You? Who are you? No, I hope not.

TATTLE: I am *Jack Tattle*, your Friend.

VALENTINE: My Friend, what to do? I am no Married Man, and thou can'st not lie with my Wife? I am very poor, and thou can'st not borrow Money of me; Then what Employment have I for a Friend.

TATTLE: Hah! A good open Speaker, and not to be trusted with a Secret.

ANGELICA: Do you know me, *Valentine*?

VALENTINE: Oh very well.

ANGELICA: Who am I?

VALENTINE: You're a Woman, – One to whom Heav'n gave Beauty, when it grafted Roses on a Briar. You are the reflection of Heav'n in a Pond, and he that leaps at you is sunk. You are all white, a sheet of lovely spotless Paper, when you first are Born; but you are to be scrawl'd and blotted by every Goose's Quill. I know you; for I lov'd a Woman, and lov'd her so long, that I found out a strange thing: I found out what a Woman was good for.

TATTLE: Aye, prithee, what's that?

VALENTINE: Why to keep a Secret.

TATTLE: O Lord!

VALENTINE: O exceeding good to keep a Secret: For tho' she should tell, yet she is not to be believ'd.

TATTLE: Hah! good again, faith.

VALENTINE: I would have Musick – Sing me the Song that I like –

SONG
Set by Mr. Finger

> *I tell thee,* Charmion, *could I Time retrieve,*
> *And could again begin to Love and Live,*
> *To you I should my earliest Off'ring give;*
>   *I know my Eyes would lead my Heart to you.*
>   *And I should all my Vows and Oaths renew,*
>   *But to be plain, I never would be true.*
>
> *For by our weak and weary Truth, I find,*
> *Love hates to center in a Point assign'd,*
> *But runs with Joy the Circle of the Mind.*
>   *Then never let us chain what should be free,*
>   *But for relief of either Sex agree,*
>   *Since Women love to change, and so do we.*

No more, for I am melancholly.   [*Walks musing.*]

JEREMY: [*to* SCANDAL.] I'll do't, Sir.

SCANDAL: Mr. *Foresight*, we had best leave him. He may grow outragious, and do mischief.

FORESIGHT: I will be directed by you.

JEREMY: [*to* MRS. FRAIL.] You'll meet, Madam; – I'll take care every thing shall be ready.

MRS. FRAIL: Thou shalt do what thou wilt, have what thou wilt, in short, I will deny thee nothing.

TATTLE: [*to* ANGELICA.] Madam, shall I wait upon you?

ANGELICA: No, I'll stay with him – Mr. *Scandal* will protect me. Aunt, Mr. *Tattle* desires you would give him leave to wait on you.

TATTLE: Pox on't, there's no coming off; now she has said that – Madam, will you do me the Honour?

MRS. FORESIGHT: Mr. *Tattle* might have us'd less Ceremony.

SCANDAL: *Jeremy*, follow *Tattle*.

[*Exeunt* FORESIGHT, MRS. FORESIGHT, TATTLE, MRS. FRAIL, *and* JEREMY.]

ANGELICA: Mr. *Scandal*, I only stay till my Maid comes, and because I had a Mind to be rid of Mr. *Tattle*.

SCANDAL: Madam, I am very glad that I overheard a better Reason,which you gave to Mr. *Tattle*; for his impertinence forc'd you to acknowledge a Kindness for *Valentine*, which you deny'd to all his Sufferings and my Sollicitations. So I'll leave him to make use of the Discovery; and your Ladyship to the free Confession of your Inclinations.

ANGELICA: Oh Heavens! You wont leave me alone with a Madman?

SCANDAL: No, Madam; I only leave a Madman to his Remedy.

[*Exit* SCANDAL.]

VALENTINE: Madam, you need not be very much afraid, for I fancy I begin to come to my self.

ANGELICA: [*aside.*] Aye, but if I don't fit you, I'll be hang'd.

VALENTINE: You see what disguises Love makes us put on; Gods have been in counterfeited Shapes for the same Reason; and the Divine Part of me, my Mind, has worn this Masque of Madness, and this motly Livery, only as the Slave of Love, and Menial Creature of your Beauty.

ANGELICA: Mercy on me, how he talks! poor *Valentine*!

VALENTINE: Nay faith, now let us understand one another, Hypocrisie apart, – The Comedy draws toward an end, and let us think of leaving acting, and be our selves; and since you have lov'd me, you must own I have at length deserv'd you shou'd confess it.

ANGELICA: [*Sighs.*] I would I had lov'd you – for Heaven knows I pitie you; and could I have foreseen the sad Effects, I wou'd have striven; but that's too late. [*Sighs.*]

VALENTINE: What sad Effects ? – What's too late? my seeming Madness has deceiv'd my Father, and procur'd me time to think of means to reconcile me to him; and preserve the right of my Inheritance to his Estate; which otherwise by Articles, I must this Morning have resign'd: And this I had inform'd you of to Day, but you were gone, before I knew you had been here.

ANGELICA: How! I thought your love of me had caus'd this Transport in your Soul; which, it seems, you only counterfeited, for mercenary Ends and sordid Interest.

VALENTINE: Nay, now you do me Wrong; for if any Interest was considered, it was yours; since I thought I wanted more than Love, to make me worthy of you.

ANGELICA: Then you thought me mercenary – But how am I deluded by this Interval of Sense, to reason with a Madman?

VALENTINE: Oh, 'tis barbarous to misunderstand me longer.

[*Enter* JEREMY.]

ANGELICA: Oh here's a reasonable Creature – sure he will not have the Impudence to persevere – Come, *Jeremy*, acknowledge your Trick, and confess your Master's Madness counterfeit.

JEREMY: Counterfeit, Madam! I'll maintain him to be as absolutely and substantially Mad, as any Freeholder in *Bethlehem*;[1] Nay, he's as Mad as any Projector,[2] Fanatick, Chymist, Lover, or Poet in *Europe*.

VALENTINE: Sirrah, you lie; I am not Mad.

ANGELICA: Ha, ha, ha, you see he denies it.

JEREMY: O Lord, Madam, did you ever know any Madman Mad enough to own it?

VALENTINE: Sot, can't you apprehend?

ANGELICA: Why he talk'd very sensibly just now.

JEREMY: Yes, Madam; He has Intervals: But you see he begins to look wild again now.

VALENTINE: Why you Thick-Skull'd Rascal, I tell you the Farce is done, and I will be Mad no longer.   [*Beats him.*]

ANGELICA: Ha, ha, ha, is he mad, or no, *Jeremy*?

JEREMY: Partly I think – for he does not know his Mind Two Hours – I'm sure I left him just now, in a Humour to be mad: And I think I have not found him very quiet at this present.   [*One Knocks.*] Who's there?

VALENTINE: Go see, you Sot. I'm very glad that I can move your Mirth, tho' not your Compassion.   [*Exit* JEREMY.]

ANGELICA: I did not think you had Apprehension enough to be exceptious: But Madmen shew themselves most, by over pretending to a sound Understanding; as Drunken men do by over acting Sobriety; I was half inclining to believe you, till I accidentally touch'd upon your tender Part: But now you have restor'd me to my former Opinion and Compassion.

[*Enter* JEREMY.]

JEREMY: Sir, your Father has sent to know if you are any better yet – Will you please to be Mad, Sir, or how?

VALENTINE: Stupidity! You know the Penalty of all I'm worth must pay for

1. Madman in Bedlam.
2. Speculator.

the Confession of my Senses; I'm Mad, and will be Mad to every Body but this Lady.

JEREMY: So – Just the very backside of Truth, – But lying is a Figure in Speech, that interlards the greatest part of my Conversation – Madam, your Ladyships Woman.   [*Goes to the Door.*]

[*Enter* JENNY.]

ANGELICA: Well, have you been there? – Come hither.

JENNY: [*aside to* ANGELICA.] Yes, Madam, Sir *Sampson* will wait upon you presently.

VALENTINE: You are not leaving me in this Uncertainty?

ANGELICA: Wou'd any thing, but a Madman complain of Uncertainty? Uncertainty and Expectation are the Joys of Life. Security is an insipid thing, and the overtaking and possessing of a Wish, discovers the Folly of the Chase. Never let us know one another better; for the Pleasure of a Masquerade is done, when we come to shew Faces; But I'll tell you two things before I leave you; I am not the Fool you take me for; and you are Mad and don't know it.   [*Exeunt* ANGELICA *and* JENNY.]

VALENTINE: From a Riddle, you can expect nothing but a Riddle. There's my Instruction, and the Moral of my Lesson.

[*Re-enter* JEREMY.]

JEREMY: What, is the Lady gone again, Sir? I hope you understood one another before she went.

VALENTINE: Understood! She is harder to be understood than a Piece of *Ægyptian* Antiquity, or an *Irish* Manuscript; you may pore till you spoil your Eyes, and not improve your Knowledge.

JEREMY: I have heard 'em say, Sir, they read hard *Hebrew* Books backwards; may be you begin to read at the wrong End.

VALENTINE: They say so of a Witches Pray'r, and Dreams and *Dutch* Almanacks are to be understood by contraries. But there's Regularity and Method in that; she is a Medal without a Reverse or Inscription; for Indifference has both sides alike. Yet while she does not seem to hate me, I will pursue her, and know her if it be possible, in spight of the Opinion of my Satirical Friend, *Scandal*, who says,

> *That Women are like Tricks by slight of Hand,*
> *Which, to admire, we should not understand.*   [*Exeunt.*]

Act V, Scene I

*[A Room in Foresight's House.
Enter* ANGELICA *and* JENNY.]

ANGELICA: Where is Sir *Sampson*? Did you not tell me, he would be here before me?

JENNY: He's at the great Glass in the Dining-Room, Madam, setting his Cravat and Wig.

ANGELICA: How! I'm glad on't – If he has a mind I should like him, it's a sign he likes me; and that's more than half my Design.

JENNY: I hear him, Madam.

ANGELICA: Leave me, and d'ye hear, if *Valentine* shou'd come, or send, I am not to be spoken with.   [*Exit* JENNY.]

[Enter SIR SAMPSON.]

SIR SAMPSON: I have not been honour'd with the Commands of a fair Lady, a great while – Odd, Madam, you have reviv'd me – Not since I was Five and Thirty.

ANGELICA: Why you have no great reason to complain, Sir *Sampson*, that is not long ago.

SIR SAMPSON: Zooks, but it is, Madam, a very great while; to a Man that admires a fine Woman, as much as I do.

ANGELICA: You're an absolute Courtier, Sir *Sampson*.

SIR SAMPSON: Not at all, Madam: Odsbud you wrong me; I am not so old neither, to be a bare Courtier, only a Man of Words. Odd, I have warm Blood about me yet, I can Serve a Lady any way – Come, come, let me tell you, you Women think a Man old too soon, faith and troth you do – Come, don't despise Fifty; odd Fifty, in a hale Constitution, is no such contemptible Age.

ANGELICA: Fifty a contemptible Age! Not at all, a very fashionable Age I think – I assure you I know very considerable Beaus, that set a good Face upon Fifty, Fifty! I have seen Fifty in a side Box by Candle-light, out-blossom Five and Twenty.

SIR SAMPSON: O Pox, outsides, outsides; a pize[1] take 'em, meer outsides. Hang your side-Box Beaus; no, I'm none of those, none of your forc'd Trees, that pretend to Blossom in the Fall; and Bud when they should bring forth Fruit. I am of a long liv'd Race, and inherit Vigour, none of my Family married till Fifty; yet they begot Sons and Daughters till Four-score. I am of your Patriarchs, I, a Branch of one of your *Antideluvian* Families, Fellows, that the Flood could not wash away.

1. Pox.

Well, Madam, what are your Commands? Has any young Rogue
affronted you, and shall I cut his Throat? or –

ANGELICA: No, Sir *Sampson*, I have no Quarrel upon my Hands – I have more
Occasion for your Conduct than your Courage at this time. To tell you
the Truth, I'm weary of living single, and want a Husband.

SIR SAMPSON: Odsbud, and 'tis pity you should – [*Aside.*] Odd, wou'd she
wou'd like me, then I shou'd hamper my young Rogues: Odd, wou'd
she wou'd; faith and troth she's devilish Handsom. – Madam, you
deserve a good Husband, and 'twere pity you shou'd be thrown away
upon any of these young idle Rogues about the Town. Odd, there's ne're
a young Fellow worth hanging – that's a very young Fellow – Pize on
'em, they never think beforehand of any thing; – And if they commit
Matrimony, 'tis as they commit Murder; out of a Frolick: And are ready
to hang themselves, or to be hang'd by the Law, the next Morning. –
Odso, have a care, Madam.

ANGELICA: Therefore I ask your Advice, Sir *Sampson*: I have Fortune enough
to make any Man easie that I can like; If there were such a thing as a
young agreeable Man, with a reasonable Stock of good Nature and
Sense – For I would neither have an absolute Wit, nor a Fool.

SIR SAMPSON: Odd, you are hard to please, Madam; to find a young Fellow
that is neither a Wit in his own Eye, nor a Fool in the Eye of the World,
is a very hard Task. But, faith and troth you speak very discreetly; For I
hate both a Wit and a Fool.

ANGELICA: She that marries a Fool, Sir *Sampson*, commits the Reputation of
her Honesty or Understanding to the Censure of the World: And she
that marries a very Witty Man, submits both to the Severity and insolent
Conduct of her Husband. I should like a Man of Wit for a Lover, because
I would have such an one in my Power; but I would no more be his
Wife, than his Enemy. For his Malice is not a more terrible Consequence
of his Aversion, than his Jealousie is of his Love.

SIR SAMPSON: None of old *Foresight's Sybills* ever utter'd such a Truth.
Odsbud, you have won my Heart: I hate a Wit; I had a Son that was
spoil'd among 'em; a good hopeful Lad, till he learn'd to be a Wit – And
might have risen in the State – But, a pox on't, his Wit run him out of
his Money, and now his Poverty has run him out of his Wits.

ANGELICA: Sir *Sampson*, as your Friend, I must tell you, you are very much
abus'd in that Matter; He's no more Mad than you are.

SIR SAMPSON: How, Madam! Wou'd I cou'd prove it.

ANGELICA: I can tell you how that may be done – But it is a thing that wou'd
make me appear to be too much concern'd in your Affairs.

SIR SAMPSON: [*aside.*] Odsbud I believe she likes me – Ah, Madam, all my
Affairs are scarce worthy to be laid at your Feet; And I wish, Madam,
they stood in a better Posture, that I might make a more becoming Offer
to a Lady of your incomparable Beauty and Merit. – If I had *Peru* in one
Hand, and *Mexico* in t'other, and the *Eastern* Empire under my Feet; it

would make me only a more glorious Victim to be offer'd at the Shrine
of your Beauty.

ANGELICA: Bless me, Sir *Sampson*, what's the matter?

SIR SAMPSON: Odd, Madam, I love you – And if you wou'd take my Advice
in a Husband –

ANGELICA: Hold, hold, Sir *Sampson*. I ask'd your Advice for a Husband, and
you are giving me your Consent – I was indeed thinking to propose
something like it in a Jest, to satisfie you about *Valentine*: For if a Match
were seemingly carried on, between you and me, it would oblige him to
throw off his Disguise of Madness, in Apprehension of losing me: For
you know he has long pretended a Passion for me.

SIR SAMPSON: Gadzooks, a most ingenious Contrivance – If we were to go
through with it. But why must the Match only be seemingly carried
on? – Odd, let it be a real Contract.

ANGELICA: O fie, Sir *Sampson*, what would the World say?

SIR SAMPSON: Say, they would say, you were a wise Woman, and I a happy
Man. Odd, Madam, I'll love you as long as I live; and leave you a good
Jointure when I die.

ANGELICA: Aye; But that is not in your Power, Sir *Sampson*; for when *Valentine*
confesses himself in his Senses; he must make over his Inheritance to his
younger Brother.

SIR SAMPSON: Odd, you're cunning, a wary Baggage! Faith and Troth I like
you the better – But, I warrant you, I have a Proviso in the Obligation
in favour of my self – Body o'me, I have a Trick to turn the Settlement
upon the Issue Male of our Two Bodies begotten. Odsbud, let us find
Children, and I'll find an Estate.

ANGELICA: Will you? well, do you find the Estate, and leave the t'other to
me –

SIR SAMPSON: O Rogue! But I'll trust you. And will you consent? Is it a Match
then?

ANGELICA: Let me consult my Lawyer concerning this Obligation; and if I
find what you propose practicable; I'll give you my Answer.

SIR SAMPSON: With all my Heart; – Come in with me, and I'll lend you the
Bond, – You shall consult your Lawyer, and I'll consult a Parson;
Odzooks I'm a Young Man: Odzooks I'm a young Man, and I'll make it
appear – Odd, you're devilish Handsom; Faith and Troth, you're very
Handsom, and I'm very Young, and very Lusty – Odsbud, Hussy, you
know how to chuse, and so do I; – Odd, I think we are very well met; –
Give me your Hand, Odd let me kiss it; 'tis as warm and as soft – as
what? – Odd, as t'other Hand – give me t'other Hand, and I'll mumble
'em, and kiss 'em till they melt in my Mouth.

ANGELICA: Hold, Sir – You're profuse of your Vigour before your time: You'll
spend your Estate before you come to it.

SIR SAMPSON: No, no, only give you a Rent-roll of my Possessions – Ah!
Baggage – I warrant you for little *Sampson*: Odd, *Sampson's* a very good

Name for an able Fellow: Your *Sampsons* were strong Dogs from the Beginning.

ANGELICA: Have a care, and don't over-act your Part – If you remember, the strongest *Sampson* of your Name, pull'd an old House over his Head at last.

SIR SAMPSON: Say you so, Hussy? – Come lets go then; Odd, I long to be pulling down too, come away – Odso, here's some body coming.

[*Exeunt.*]

[*Enter* TATTLE *and* JEREMY.]

TATTLE: Is not that she, gone out just now?

JEREMY: Aye, Sir, she's just going to the Place of appointment. Ah Sir, if you are not very faithful and close in this Business, you'll certainly be the Death of a Person that has a most extraordinary Passion for your Honour's Service.

TATTLE: Aye, who's that?

JEREMY: Even my unworthy self, Sir – Sir, I have had an Appetite to be fed with your Commands a great while; – And now, Sir, my former Master, having much troubled the Fountain of his Understanding; it is a very plausible Occasion for me to quench my Thirst at the Spring of your Bounty – I thought I could not recommend my self better to you, Sir, than by the delivery of a great Beauty and Fortune into your Arms, whom I have heard you Sigh for.

TATTLE: I'll make thy Fortune; say no more – Thou art a pretty Fellow, and can'st carry a Message to a Lady, in a pretty soft kind of Phrase, and with a good perswading Accent.

JEREMY: Sir, I have the Seeds of Rhetorick and Oratory in my Head – I have been at *Cambridge*.

TATTLE: Ay; 'tis well enough for a Servant to be bred at an University: But the Education is a little too pedantick for a Gentleman. I hope you are secret in your Nature, private, close, ha?

JEREMY: O Sir, for that Sir, 'tis my chief Talent; I'm as secret as the Head of *Nilus*.[1]

TATTLE: Aye? Who's he, tho? A Privy Counsellor?

JEREMY: O Ignorance! [*aside.*] A cunning *Ægyptian*, Sir, that with his Arms would over-run the Country, yet no body could ever find out his Head-Quarters.

TATTLE: Close Dog! A good Whoremaster, I warrant him – the time draws nigh, *Jeremy. Angelica* will be veil'd like a Nun; and I must be hooded like a Friar; ha, *Jeremy*?

JEREMY: Aye, Sir, hooded like a Hawk, to seize at first sight upon the Quarry. It is the Whim of my Master's Madness to be so dress'd; and she is so in Love with him, she'll comply with any thing to please him. Poor Lady,

1. The source of the Nile.

I'm sure she'll have reason to pray for me, when she finds what a happy Exchange she has made, between a Madman and so Accomplish'd a Gentleman.

TATTLE: Ay faith, so she will, *Jeremy*: You're a good Friend to her, poor Creature – I swear I do it hardly so much in consideration of my self; as Compassion to her.

JEREMY: 'Tis an Act of Charity, Sir, to save a fine Woman with Thirty Thousand Pound, from throwing her self away.

TATTLE: So 'tis, faith – I might have sav'd several others in my time; but I'Gad I could never find in my Heart to Marry any body before.

JEREMY: Well, Sir, I'll go and tell her my Master's coming; and meet you in half a quarter of an hour, with your Disguise, at your own Lodgings. You must talk· a little madly, she won't distinguish the Tone of your Voice.

TATTLE: No, no, let me alone for a Counterfeit; – I'll be ready for you.

[*Enter* MISS PRUE.]

MISS PRUE: O Mr. *Tattle*, are you here! I'm glad I have found you; I have been looking up and down for you like any thing, till I'm as tired as any thing in the World.

TATTLE: [*aside.*] O Pox, how shall I get rid of this foolish Girl?

MISS PRUE: O I have pure News, I can tell you pure News – I must not marry the Seaman now – my Father says so. Why won't you be my Husband? You say you love me, and you won't be my Husband. And I know you may be my Husband now if you please.

TATTLE: O fie, Miss: Who told you so, Child?

MISS PRUE: Why, my Father – I told him that you lov'd me.

TATTLE: O fie, Miss, why did you do so? and who told you so, Child?

MISS PRUE: Who? Why you did; did not you?

TATTLE: O Pox, that was Yesterday, Miss, that was a great while ago, Child. I have been asleep since; slept a whole Night, and did not so much as dream of the matter.

MISS PRUE: Pshaw, O but I dream't that it was so tho.

TATTLE: Ay, but your Father will tell you that Dreams come by Contraries, Child – O fie; what, we must not love one another now – Pshaw, that would be a foolish thing indeed – Fie, fie, you're a Woman now, and must think of a new Man every Morning, and forget him every Night – No, no, to marry, is to be a Child again, and play with the same Rattle always: O fie, marrying is a paw[1] thing.

MISS PRUE: Well, but don't you love me as well as you did last Night then?

TATTLE: No, no, Child, you would not have me.

MISS PRUE: No? Yes but I would tho.

1. Foolish or beneath contempt.

TATTLE: Pshaw, but I tell you, you would not – You forget you're a Woman, and don't know your own mind.

MISS PRUE: But here's my Father, and he knows my Mind.

[*Enter* FORESIGHT.]

FORESIGHT: O, Mr. *Tattle*, your Servant, you are a close Man; but methinks your Love to my Daughter was a Secret I might have been trusted with, – Or had you a mind to try if I could discover it by my Art – hum, ha! I think there is something in your Physiognomy, that has a resemblance of her; and the Girl is like me.

TATTLE: And so you wou'd infer, that you and I are alike – [*aside*] what do's the Old Prig mean? I'll banter him, and laugh at him, and leave him.

I fancy you have a wrong Notion of Faces.

FORESIGHT: How? What? A wrong Notion! How so?

TATTLE: In the way of Art: I have some taking Features, not obvious to Vulgar Eyes; that are Indications of a sudden turn of good Fortune, in the Lottery of Wives; and promise a great Beauty and great Fortune reserved alone for me, by a private Intriegue of Destiny, kept secret from the piercing Eye of Perspicuity; from all Astrologers, and the Stars themselves.

FORESIGHT: How! I will make it appear that what you say is impossible.

TATTLE: Sir, I beg your Pardon, I'm in haste –

FORESIGHT: For what?

TATTLE: To be married, Sir, married.

FORESIGHT: Aye, but pray take me along with you, Sir –

TATTLE: No, Sir; 'tis to be done Privately – I never make Confidents.

FORESIGHT: Well; but my Consent I mean – You won't marry my Daughter without my Consent?

TATTLE: Who I, Sir? I'm an absolute Stranger to you and your Daughter, Sir.

FORESIGHT: Hey day! What time of the Moon is this?

TATTLE: Very true, Sir, and desire to continue so. I have no more love for your Daughter, than I have likeness of you; and I have a Secret in my Heart, which you wou'd be glad to know, and shan't know; and yet you shall know it too, and be sorry for't afterwards. I'd have you to know, Sir, that I am as knowing as the Stars, and as secret as the Night. – And I'm going to be Married just now, yet did not know of it half an Hour ago; and the Lady stays for me, and does not know of it yet – There's a Mystery for you, – I know you love to untie Difficulties – Or if you can't solve this; stay here a Quarter of an Hour, and I'll come and explain it to you.

[*Exit.*]

MISS PRUE: O Father, why will you let him go? Won't you make him be my Husband?

FORESIGHT: Mercy on us, what do these Lunacies portend? Alas! he's Mad, Child, stark Wild.

MISS PRUE: What, and must not I have e're a Husband then? What, must I go to Bed to Nurse again, and be a Child as long as she's an Old Woman? Indeed but I won't: For now my Mind is set upon a Man, I will have a Man some way or other. Oh! methinks I'm sick when I think of a Man; and if I can't have one, I wou'd go to sleep all my Life: For when I'm awake, it makes me wish and long, and I don't know for what – And I'd rather be always a sleeping, than sick with thinking.

FORESIGHT: O fearful! I think the Girl's influenc'd too, – Hussy you shall have a Rod.

MISS PRUE: A Fiddle of a Rod, I'll have a Husband; and if you won't get me one, I'll get one for my self: I'll marry our *Robbin* the Butler, he says he loves me, and he's a Handsome Man, and shall be my Husband: I warrant he'll be my Husband and thank me too, for he told me so.

[*Enter* SCANDAL, MRS. FORESIGHT *and* NURSE.]

FORESIGHT: Did he so – I'll dispatch him for't presently; Rogue! Oh, Nurse, come hither.

NURSE: What is your Worship's Pleasure?

FORESIGHT: Here, take your young Mistress, and lock her up presently, till farther Orders from me – not a Word Hussy – Do what I bid you, no Reply, away. And bid *Robin* make ready to give an Account of his Plate and Linnen, d'ee hear, begone when I bid you.

[*Exeunt* NURSE *and* MISS PRUE.]

MRS. FORESIGHT: What's the Matter, Husband?

FORESIGHT: 'Tis not convenient to tell you now – Mr. *Scandal*, Heav'n keep us all in our Senses – I fear there is a contagious Frenzy abroad. How does *Valentine*?

SCANDAL: O I hope he will do well again – I have a Message from him to your Niece *Angelica*.

FORESIGHT: I think she has not return'd, since she went abroad with Sir *Sampson*.

[*Enter* BEN.]

MRS. FORESIGHT: Here's Mr. *Benjamin*, he can tell us if his Father be come Home.

BEN: Who, Father? ay, he's come home with a Vengeance.

MRS. FORESIGHT: Why, What's the Matter?

BEN: Matter! Why he's Mad.

FORESIGHT: Mercy on us, I was afraid of this.

BEN: And there's the handsome young Woman, she, as they say, Brother *Val* went mad for, she's mad too, I think.

FORESIGHT: O my poor Niece, my poor Niece, is she gone too? Well, I shall run mad next.

MRS. FORESIGHT: Well, but how mad? how d'ee mean?

BEN: Nay, I'll give you leave to guess – I'll undertake to make a voyage to

Love for Love

Antegoa – No, hold, I maynt say so neither – But I'll sail as far as *Ligorn*,[1] and back again, before you shall guess at the matter, and do nothing else; Mess you may take in all the Points of the Compass, and not hit Right.

MRS. FORESIGHT: Your Experiment will take up a little too much time.

BEN: Why then I'll tell you, There's a new wedding upon the Stocks; and they two are a going to be married to rights.

SCANDAL: Who?

BEN: Why Father and – the Young Woman. I can't hit of her Name.

SCANDAL: *Angelica*?

BEN: Aye, the same.

MRS. FORESIGHT: Sir *Sampson* and *Angelica*, impossible!

BEN: That may be – but I'm sure it is as I tell you.

SCANDAL: 'S'death it's a Jest. I can't believe it.

BEN: Look you, Friend, it's nothing to me, whether you believe it or no. What I say is true; d'ee see, they are married, or just going to be married, I know not which.

FORESIGHT: Well, but they are not Mad, that is, not Lunatick?

BEN: I don't know what you may call Madness – But she's mad for a Husband, and he's Horn-mad, I think, or they'd ne're make a Match together – Here they come.

[*Enter* SIR SAMPSON, ANGELICA, *with* BUCKRAM.]

SIR SAMPSON: Where is this old Soothsayer? This Uncle of mine elect? a ha, Old *Foresight*, Uncle *Foresight*, wish me Joy Uncle *Foresight*, double Joy, both as Uncle and Astrologer; here's a Conjunction that was not foretold in all your *Ephemeris*[2] – The brightest Star in the blew Firmament – is shot from above, in a Jelly of Love,[3] and so forth; and I'm Lord of the Ascendant. Odd, you're an old Fellow, *Foresight*; Uncle I mean, a very old Fellow, Uncle *Foresight*; and yet you shall live to dance at my Wedding; faith and troth you shall. Odd we'll have the Musick of the Spheres for thee, old *Lilly*, that we will, and thou shalt lead up a Dance in *via Lactea*.[4]

FORESIGHT: I'm Thunder-strook! You are not married to my Niece?

SIR SAMPSON: Not absolutely married, Uncle; but very near it, within a Kiss of the matter, as you see. [*Kisses* ANGELICA.]

ANGELICA: 'Tis very true indeed, Uncle; I hope you'll be my Father, and give me.

SIR SAMPSON: That he shall, or I'll burn his Globes – Body o'me, he shall be thy Father, I'll make him thy Father, and thou shalt make me a Father,

---

1. Probably Antigua in the West Indies and Livorno in Italy.
2. Astronomical almanac.
3. A quotation from Dryden's play *Tyrannick Love*.
4. The Milky Way.

and I'll make thee a Mother, and we'll beget Sons and Daughters enough to put the Weekly Bills out of Countenance.

SCANDAL: Death and Hell! Where's *Valentine*?   [*Exit* SCANDAL.]

MRS. FORESIGHT: This is so surprising –

SIR SAMPSON: How! What does my Aunt say? Surprizing, Aunt? Not at all, for a young Couple to make a Match in Winter? Not at all – It's a Plot to undermine Cold Weather; and destroy that Usurper of a Bed call'd a Warming-Pan.

MRS. FORESIGHT: I'm glad to hear you have so much Fire in you, Sir *Sampson*.

BEN: Mess, I fear his Fire's little better than Tinder; may hap it will only serve to light up a Match for some body else. The Young Woman's a Handsom Young Woman, I can't deny it: But, Father, if I might be your Pilot in this Case, you should not marry her. It's just the same thing, as if so be you should sail so far as the *Streights* without Provision.[1]

SIR SAMPSON: Who gave you Authority to speak, Sirrah? To your Element, Fish, be mute, Fish, and to Sea, rule your Helm, Sirrah, don't direct me.

BEN: Well, well, take you care of your own Helm, or you mayn't keep your own Vessel steddy.

SIR SAMPSON: Why you impudent Tarpaulin! Sirrah, do you bring your Fore-castle Jests upon your Father? But I shall be even with you, I wont give you a Groat. Mr. *Buckram* is the Conveyance so worded, that nothing can possibly descend to this Scoundrel? I would not so much as have him have the Prospect of an Estate; tho' there were no way to come to it, but by the *North-East* Passage.[2]

BUCKRAM: Sir, it is drawn according to your Directions; there is not the least Cranny of the Law unstopt.

BEN: Lawyer, I believe there's many a Cranny and Leak unstopt in your Conscience – If so be that one had a Pump to your Bosom, I believe we shou'd discover a foul Hold. They say a Witch will sail in a Sieve – But I believe the Devil wou'd not venture aboard o' your Conscience. And that's for you.

SIR SAMPSON: Hold your Tongue, Sirrah. How now, who's there?

[*Enter* TATTLE *and* MRS. FRAIL.]

MRS. FRAIL: O, Sister, the most unlucky Accident!

MRS. FORESIGHT: What's the Matter?

TATTLE: O, the Two most unfortunate poor Creatures in the World we are.

FORESIGHT: Bless us! How so?

MRS. FRAIL: Ah Mr. *Tattle* and I, poor Mr. *Tattle* and I are – I can't speak it out.

TATTLE: Nor I – But poor Mrs. *Frail* and I are –

MRS. FRAIL: Married.

MRS. FORESIGHT: Married! How?

1. The Straits of Gibraltar.
2. An impossibly difficult sea route to the east, past the north of Norway and Siberia.

TATTLE: Suddainly – before we knew where we were – that Villain *Jeremy*, by the help of Disguises, trickt us into one another.

FORESIGHT: Why, you told me just now, you went hence in haste to be married.

ANGELICA: But I believe Mr. *Tattle* meant the Favour to me, I thank him.

TATTLE: I did, as I hope to be sav'd, Madam, my Intentions were good – But this is the most cruel thing, to marry one does not know how, nor why, nor wherefore – The Devil take me if ever I was so much concern'd at any thing in my Life.

ANGELICA: 'Tis very unhappy, if you don't care for one another.

TATTLE: The least in the World – That is for my Part, I speak for my self. Gad, I never had the least thought of serious Kindness – I never lik'd any body less in my Life. Poor Woman! Gad I'm sorry for her too; for I have no reason to hate her neither; but I believe I shall lead her a damn'd sort of a Life.

MRS. FORESIGHT: [*aside to* MRS. FRAIL.] He's better than no Husband at all – tho he's a Coxcomb.

MRS. FRAIL: [*to her.*] Aye, aye, it's well it's no worse – Nay, for my part I always despised Mr. *Tattle* of all things; nothing but his being my Husband could have made me like him less.

TATTLE: Look you there, I thought as much – pox on't, I wish we could keep it secret, why I don't believe any of this Company wou'd speak of it.

MRS. FRAIL: But, my Dear, that's impossible; the Parson and that Rogue *Jeremy* will publish it.

TATTLE: Aye, my Dear, so they will as you say.

ANGELICA: O you'll agree very well in a little time; Custom will make it easie to you.

TATTLE: Easie! Pox on't, I don't believe I shall sleep to Night.

SIR SAMPSON: Sleep Quotha! No, why you would not sleep o' your Wedding Night? I'm an older Fellow than you, and don't mean to sleep.

BEN: Why there's another Match now, as tho'f a couple of Privateers were looking for a Prize, and should fall foul of one another. I'm sorry for the Young Man with all my Heart. Look you, Friend, if I may advise you, when she's going, for that you must expect, I have Experience of her, when she's going, let her go. For no *Matrimony* is tough enough to hold her, and if she can't drag her Anchor along with her, she'll break her Cable, I can tell you that. Who's here? the Madman?

[*Enter* VALENTINE *dress'd,* SCANDAL, *and* JEREMY.]

VALENTINE: No; here's the Fool; and if occasion be, I'll give it under my hand.

SIR SAMPSON: How now?

VALENTINE: Sir, I'm come to acknowledge my Errors, and ask your Pardon.

SIR SAMPSON: What, have you found your Senses at last then? In good time, Sir.

VALENTINE: You were abus'd, Sir, I never was Distracted.

FORESIGHT: How! Not Mad! Mr. *Scandal*.

SCANDAL: No really, Sir; I'm his Witness, it was all Counterfeit.

VALENTINE: I thought I had Reasons – But it was a poor Contrivance, the Effect has shewn it such.

SIR SAMPSON: Contrivance, what to cheat me? to cheat your Father! Sirrah, could you hope to prosper?

VALENTINE: Indeed, I thought, Sir, when the Father endeavoured to undo the Son, it was a reasonable return of Nature.

SIR SAMPSON: Very good, Sir – Mr. *Buckram*, are you ready? – Come, Sir, will you sign and seal?

VALENTINE: If you please, Sir; but first I would ask this Lady one Question

SIR SAMPSON: Sir, you must ask my leave first; that Lady, No, Sir; you shall ask that Lady no Questions, till you have ask'd her Blessing, Sir; that Lady is to be my Wife.

VALENTINE: I have heard as much, Sir; but I wou'd have it from her own Mouth.

SIR SAMPSON: That's as much as to say, I lie, Sir, and you don't believe what I say.

VALENTINE: Pardon me, Sir. But I reflect that I very lately counterfeited Madness; I don't know but the Frolick may go round.

SIR SAMPSON: Come, Chuck, satisfie him, answer him; – Come, come, Mr. *Buckram*, the Pen and Ink.

BUCKRAM: Here it is, Sir, with the Deed, all is ready.

[VALENTINE *goes to* ANGELICA.]

ANGELICA: 'Tis true, you have a great while pretended Love to me; nay, what if you were sincere? still you must pardon me, if I think my own Inclinations have a better Right to dispose of my Person, than yours.

SIR SAMPSON: Are you answer'd now, Sir?

VALENTINE: Yes, Sir.

SIR SAMPSON: Where's your Plot, Sir? and your Contrivance now, Sir? Will you sign, Sir? Come, will you sign and seal?

VALENTINE: With all my Heart, Sir,

SCANDAL: 'S'death, you are not mad indeed, to ruine your self?

VALENTINE: I have been disappointed of my only Hope; and he that loses hope may part with any thing. I never valu'd Fortune, but as it was subservient to my Pleasure; and my only Pleasure was to please this Lady: I have made many vain Attempts, and find at last, that nothing but my Ruine can effect it: Which, for that Reason, I will sign to – Give me the Paper.

ANGELICA: [*aside.*] Generous *Valentine*!

BUCKRAM: Here is the Deed, Sir.

VALENTINE: But where is the Bond, by which I am oblig'd to sign this?

BUCKRAM: Sir *Sampson* you have it.

ANGELICA: No, I have it; and I'll use it, as I would every thing that is an Enemy to *Valentine*.   [*Tears the Paper.*]

SIR SAMPSON: How now!

VALENTINE: Ha!

ANGELICA: [*to* VALENTINE.] Had I the World to give you, it cou'd not make me worthy of so generous and faithful a Passion: Here's my Hand, my Heart was always yours, and struggl'd very hard to make this utmost Tryal of your Virtue.

VALENTINE: Between Pleasure and Amazement, I am lost – But on my Knees I take the Blessing.

SIR SAMPSON: Oons, what is the meaning of this?

BEN: Mess, here's the Wind chang'd again. Father, you and I may make a Voyage together now.

ANGELICA: Well, Sir *Sampson*, since I have plaid you a Trick, I'll advise you, how you may avoid such another. Learn to be a good Father, or you'll never get a second Wife. I always lov'd your Son, and hated your unforgiving Nature. I was resolv'd to try him to the utmost; I have try'd you too, and know you both. You have not more Faults than he has Virtues; and 'tis hardly more Pleasure to me, that I can make him and my self happy, than that I can punish you.

VALENTINE: If my happiness cou'd receive Addition, this Kind surprize would make it double.

SIR SAMPSON: Oons you're a *Crocodile.*

FORESIGHT: Really, Sir *Sampson*, this is a sudden Eclipse –

SIR SAMPSON: You're an illiterate Fool, and I'm another, and the Stars are Lyars; and if I had Breath enough, I'd curse them and you, my self and every Body – Oons, Cully'd, Bubbl'd, Jilted, Woman-bobb'd at last – I have not Patience.   [*Exit* SIR SAMPSON.]

TATTLE: If the Gentleman is in this disorder for want of a Wife, I can spare him mine. [*To* JEREMY.] Oh are you there, Sir? I'm indebted to you for my Happiness.

JEREMY: Sir, I ask you Ten Thousand Pardons, 'twas an errant mistake – You see, Sir, my Master was never mad, nor any thing like it – Then how could it be otherwise?

VALENTINE: *Tattle*, I thank you, you would have interposed between me and Heav'n; but Providence laid Purgatory in your way – You have but Justice.

SCANDAL: I hear the Fiddles that Sir *Sampson* provided for his own Wedding; methinks 'tis pity they should not be employ'd when the Match is so much mended. *Valentine*, tho it be Morning, we may have a Dance.

VALENTINE: Any thing, my Friend, every thing that looks like Joy and Transport.

SCANDAL: Call 'em, *Jeremy.*

ANGELICA: I have done dissembling now, *Valentine*; and if that Coldness which I have always worn before you, should turn to an extream Fondness, you must not suspect it.

VALENTINE: I'll prevent that suspicion – For I intend to doat on at that immoderate rate, that your Fondness shall never distinguish it self enough, to be taken notice of. If ever you seem to love too much, it must be only when I can't love enough.

ANGELICA: Have a care of large Promises; You know you are apt to run more in Debt than you are able to pay.

VALENTINE: Therefore I yield my Body as your Prisoner, and make your best on't.

SCANDAL: The Musick stays for you. [*Dance.*]

SCANDAL: Well, Madam, You have done Exemplary Justice, in punishing an inhumane Father, and rewarding a Faithful Lover: But there is a Third good Work, which I, in particular, must thank you for; I was an Infidel to your Sex; and you have converted me – For now I am convinc'd that all Women are not like Fortune, blind in bestowing Favours, either on those who do not merit, or who do not want 'em.

ANGELICA: 'Tis an unreasonable Accusation, that you lay upon our Sex: You tax us with Injustice, only to cover your own want of Merit. You would all have the Reward of Love; but few have the Constancy to stay till it becomes your due. Men are generally Hypocrites and Infidels, they pretend to Worship, but have neither Zeal nor Faith: How few, like *Valentine*, would persevere even unto Martyrdom, and sacrifice their Interest to their Constancy! In admiring me, you misplace the Novelty.

The Miracle to Day is, that we find
A Lover true: Not that a Woman's Kind. [*Exeunt Omnes.*]

Finis

Epilogue

Spoken at the opening of the New House,
By Mrs. Bracegirdle

Sure Providence at first, design'd this Place[1]
To be the Player's Refuge in distress;
For still in every Storm, they all run hither,
As to a Shed, that shields 'em from the Weather.
But thinking of this change which last befel us,
It's like what I have heard our Poets tell us:
For when behind our Scenes their Suits are pleading,
To help their Love, sometimes they show their Reading;

1. Lisle's Tennis Court.

And wanting ready Cash to pay for Hearts,
They top their Learning on us, and their Parts.
Once of Philosophers they told us Stories,
Whom, as I think they call'd-Py-Pythagories,
I'm sure 'tis some such Latin *Name they give 'em,*
And we, who know no better, must believe 'em.
Now to these Men (say they) such Souls were given,
That after Death, ne're went to Hell, nor Heaven,
But liv'd, I know not how, in Beasts; and then
When many Years were past, in Men again.
Methinks, we Players *resemble such a Soul,*
That, does from Bodies, we from Houses strole.
Thus Aristotle's *Soul, of old that was,*
May now be damn'd to animate an Ass;
Or in this very House, for ought we know,
is doing painful Penance in some Beau,
And this our Audience, which did once resort
To shining Theatres to see our Sport,
Now find us toss'd into a Tennis-Court.
These Walls but t'other Day were fill'd with Noise
of Roaring Gamesters, and your Damme Boys.
Then bounding Balls and Rackets they encompass'd,
And now they're fill'd with Jests, and Flights, and Bombast!
I vow, I don't much like this Transmigration,
Stroling from Place to Place, by Circulation.
Grant Heaven, we don't return to our first Station.
I know not what these think, but for my Part,
I can't reflect without an aking Heart,
How we shou'd end in our Original, a Cart.
But we can't fear, since you're so good to save us.
That you have only set us up, to leave us.
Thus from the past, we hope for future Grace,
I beg it –
And some here know I have a begging Face.
Then pray continue this your kind behaviour,
For a clear Stage won't do, without your Favour.

Bibliography

Seventeenth-century French Theatre

Arnott, Peter, *An Introduction to the French Theatre* (London: Macmillan, 1977).

Lawrenson, T. E., *The French Stage and Playhouse in the Seventeenth Century* (New York: AMS Press, 1986).

Lough, J., *Seventeenth-century French Drama: The Background* (Oxford: Clarendon Press, 1979).

Mongrédien, G., *Daily Life in the French Theatre at the Time of Molière* (London: Allen & Unwin, 1969).

Wiley, W. L., *The Early Public Theatres in France* (Cambridge, Mass.: Harvard University Press, 1960).

Racine and Molière

Forman, Edward, *Racine: Appraisal and Re-appraisal* (Bristol: Bristol University Press, 1991).

Guicharnaud, J., *Molière: A Collection of Critical Essays* (Englewood Cliffs, NJ: Prentice Hall, 1964).

Hall, Gaston, *Comedy in Context: Essays on Molière* (Jackson: University of Mississippi Press, 1984).

Hawcroft, Michael, *Word as Action: Racine, Rhetoric, and Theatrical Language* (Oxford: Clarendon Press, 1992).

Howarth, W. D., *Molière: Stage and Study* (Oxford: Clarendon Press, 1973).

Howarth, W. D., *Molière: A Playwright and his Audience* (Cambridge: Cambridge University Press, 1982).

Knight, R. C. (ed.), *Racine: Modern Judgements* (London: Macmillan, 1969).

Maskell, David, *Racine: A Theatrical Reading* (Oxford: Clarendon Press, 1991).

Moore, W. G., *Molière: A New Criticism* (Oxford: Clarendon Press, 1949).

de Mourgues, Odette, *Racine, or the Triumph of Relevance* (Cambridge: Cambridge University Press, 1967).

Pocock, G., *Corneille and Racine: Problems of Tragic Form* (Cambridge: Cambridge University Press, 1973).

Wheatley, K. E., *Racine and English Classicism* (Austin: University of Texas Press, 1956).

Wilcox, J., *The Relation of Molière to Restoration Comedy* [1938] (New York: Benjamin Blom, 1964).

Yarrow, P. J., *Racine* (Oxford: Blackwell, 1978).

Seventeenth-century English Theatre

Avery, E. and Scouten, A. (eds), *The London Stage*, Part I (Carbondale: University of Illinois Press, 1959).

Craik, T. W. (ed.), *The Revels History of Drama in English, 1660–1750*, vol. 5 (London: Methuen, 1976).

Holland, Peter, *The Ornament of Action: Text and Performance in Restoration Comedy* (Cambridge: Cambridge University Press, 1979).

Leacroft, Richard, *The Development of the English Playhouse* (London: Eyre Methuen, 1973).

Leacroft, Richard and Leacroft, Helen, *Theatre and Playhouse* (London: Methuen, 1984).

Mullin, Donald C., *The Development of the Playhouse* (Berkeley: University of California Press, 1970).

Nicoll, A., *The Garrick Stage* (Manchester: Manchester University Press, 1980).

Powell, Jocelyn, *Restoration Theatre Production* (London: Routledge & Kegan Paul, 1984).

Summers, M., *The Restoration Theatre* (London: Kegan Paul, 1934).

Summers, M., *The Playhouse of Pepys* [1935] (New York: Humanities Press, 1964).

Thomas, David (ed.), *Theatre in Europe: A Documentary History. Restoration and Georgian England, 1660–1788* (Cambridge: Cambridge University Press, 1989).

Thomas, David, *The Restoration Stage: From Tennis Court to Playhouse*, video (Coventry: University of Warwick School of Theatre Studies and Princeton, NJ: Films for the Humanities, 1996).

Dryden, Wycherley, Congreve

Connely, Willard, *Brawny Wycherley: First Master in English Modern Comedy* [1930] (Port Washington: Kennikat Press, 1969).

Dobree, B., *Restoration Comedy* (London: Oxford University Press, 1924).

Fujimura, T. H., *The Restoration Comedy of Wit* (Princeton, NJ: Princeton University Press, 1952).

Holland, N., *The First Modern Comedies* (Cambridge, Mass.: Harvard University Press, 1959).

Hopkins, David, *John Dryden* (Cambridge: Cambridge University Press, 1989).

Hughes, Derek, *English Drama, 1660–1700* (Oxford: Clarendon Press, 1996).

Hume, R. D., *The Development of English Drama in the Late 17th Century* (Oxford: Clarendon Press, 1976).

Loftis, J. C. (ed.), *Restoration Drama: Modern Essays* (London: Oxford University Press, 1966).

Lynch, K. M., *The Social Mode of Restoration Comedy* (New York, 1926).

Nicoll, A., *A History of Restoration Drama* (Cambridge: Cambridge University Press, 1952).

Thomas, David, *William Congreve* (London: Macmillan, 1992).

van Voris, W. H., *The Cultivated Stance: The Design of Congreve's Plays* (Dublin: Dolmen Press, 1965).

Zimbardo, R., *Wycherley's Drama: A Link in the Development of English Satire* (New Haven, CT: Yale University Press, 1965).